Dictionary of Literary Biography

78 *American Short-Story Writers, 1880-1910,* edited by Bobby Ellen Kimbel, with the assistance of William E. Grant (1988)

79 *American Magazine Journalists, 1850-1900,* edited by Sam G. Riley (1988)

80 *Restoration and Eighteenth-Century Dramatists, First Series,* edited by Paula R. Backscheider (1989)

81 *Austrian Fiction Writers, 1875-1913,* edited by James Hardin and Donald G. Daviau (1989)

82 *Chicano Writers, First Series,* edited by Francisco A. Lomelí and Carl R. Shirley (1989)

83 *French Novelists Since 1960,* edited by Catharine Savage Brosman (1989)

84 *Restoration and Eighteenth-Century Dramatists, Second Series,* edited by Paula R. Backscheider (1989)

85 *Austrian Fiction Writers After 1914,* edited by James Hardin and Donald G. Daviau (1989)

86 *American Short-Story Writers, 1910-1945, First Series,* edited by Bobby Ellen Kimbel (1989)

87 *British Mystery and Thriller Writers Since 1940, First Series,* edited by Bernard Benstock and Thomas F. Staley (1989)

88 *Canadian Writers, 1920-1959, Second Series,* edited by W. H. New (1989)

89 *Restoration and Eighteenth-Century Dramatists, Third Series,* edited by Paula R. Backscheider (1989)

90 *German Writers in the Age of Goethe, 1789-1832,* edited by James Hardin and Christoph E. Schweitzer (1989)

91 *American Magazine Journalists, 1900-1960, First Series,* edited by Sam G. Riley (1990)

92 *Canadian Writers, 1890-1920,* edited by W. H. New (1990)

93 *British Romantic Poets, 1789-1832, First Series,* edited by John R. Greenfield (1990)

94 *German Writers in the Age of Goethe: Sturm und Drang to Classicism,* edited by James Hardin and Christoph E. Schweitzer (1990)

95 *Eighteenth-Century British Poets, First Series,* edited by John Sitter (1990)

96 *British Romantic Poets, 1789-1832, Second Series,* edited by John R. Greenfield (1990)

97 *German Writers from the Enlightenment to Sturm und Drang, 1720-1764,* edited by James Hardin and Christoph E. Schweitzer (1990)

98 *Modern British Essayists, First Series,* edited by Robert Beum (1990)

99 *Canadian Writers Before 1890,* edited by W. H. New (1990)

100 *Modern British Essayists, Second Series,* edited by Robert Beum (1990)

101 *British Prose Writers, 1660-1800, First Series,* edited by Donald T. Siebert (1991)

102 *American Short-Story Writers, 1910-1945, Second Series,* edited by Bobby Ellen Kimbel (1991)

103 *American Literary Biographers, First Series,* edited by Steven Serafin (1991)

104 *British Prose Writers, 1660-1800, Second Series,* edited by Donald T. Siebert (1991)

105 *American Poets Since World War II, Second Series,* edited by R. S. Gwynn (1991)

106 *British Literary Publishing Houses, 1820-1880,* edited by Patricia J. Anderson and Jonathan Rose (1991)

107 *British Romantic Prose Writers, 1789-1832, First Series,* edited by John R. Greenfield (1991)

108 *Twentieth-Century Spanish Poets, First Series,* edited by Michael L. Perna (1991)

109 *Eighteenth-Century British Poets, Second Series,* edited by John Sitter (1991)

110 *British Romantic Prose Writers, 1789-1832, Second Series,* edited by John R. Greenfield (1991)

111 *American Literary Biographers, Second Series,* edited by Steven Serafin (1991)

112 *British Literary Publishing Houses, 1881-1965,* edited by Jonathan Rose and Patricia J. Anderson (1991)

113 *Modern Latin-American Fiction Writers, First Series,* edited by William Luis (1992)

114 *Twentieth-Century Italian Poets, First Series,* edited by Giovanna Wedel De Stasio, Glauco Cambon, and Antonio Illiano (1992)

115 *Medieval Philosophers,* edited by Jeremiah Hackett (1992)

116 *British Romantic Novelists, 1789-1832,* edited by Bradford K. Mudge (1992)

117 *Twentieth-Century Caribbean and Black African Writers, First Series,* edited by Bernth Lindfors and Reinhard Sander (1992)

118 *Twentieth-Century German Dramatists, 1889-1918,* edited by Wolfgang D. Elfe and James Hardin (1992)

119 *Nineteenth-Century French Fiction Writers: Romanticism and Realism, 1800-1860,* edited by Catharine Savage Brosman (1992)

120 *American Poets Since World War II, Third Series,* edited by R. S. Gwynn (1992)

121 *Seventeenth-Century British Nondramatic Poets, First Series,* edited by M. Thomas Hester (1992)

122 *Chicano Writers, Second Series,* edited by Francisco A. Lomelí and Carl R. Shirley (1992)

123 *Nineteenth-Century French Fiction Writers: Naturalism and Beyond, 1860-1900,* edited by Catharine Savage Brosman (1992)

124 *Twentieth-Century German Dramatists, 1919-1992,* edited by Wolfgang D. Elfe and James Hardin (1992)

125 *Twentieth-Century Caribbean and Black African Writers, Second Series,* edited by Bernth Lindfors and Reinhard Sander (1993)

126 *Seventeenth-Century British Nondramatic Poets, Second Series,* edited by M. Thomas Hester (1993)

127 *American Newspaper Publishers, 1950-1990,* edited by Perry J. Ashley (1993)

128 *Twentieth-Century Italian Poets, Second Series,* edited by Giovanna Wedel De Stasio, Glauco Cambon, and Antonio Illiano (1993)

129 *Nineteenth-Century German Writers, 1841-1900,* edited by James Hardin and Siegfried Mews (1993)

130 *American Short-Story Writers Since World War II,* edited by Patrick Meanor (1993)

131 *Seventeenth-Century British Nondramatic Poets, Third Series,* edited by M. Thomas Hester (1993)

132 *Sixteenth-Century British Nondramatic Writers, First Series,* edited by David A. Richardson (1993)

133 *Nineteenth-Century German Writers to 1840,* edited by James Hardin and Siegfried Mews (1993)

134 *Twentieth-Century Spanish Poets, Second Series,* edited by Jerry Phillips Winfield (1994)

135 *British Short-Fiction Writers, 1880-1914: The Realist Tradition,* edited by William B. Thesing (1994)

136 *Sixteenth-Century British Nondramatic Writers, Second Series,* edited by David A. Richardson (1994)

137 *American Magazine Journalists, 1900-1960, Second Series,* edited by Sam G. Riley (1994)

138 *German Writers and Works of the High Middle Ages: 1170-1280,* edited by James Hardin and Will Hasty (1994)

139 *British Short-Fiction Writers, 1945-1980,* edited by Dean Baldwin (1994)

140 *American Book-Collectors and Bibliographers, First Series,* edited by Joseph Rosenblum (1994)

141 *British Children's Writers, 1880-1914,* edited by Laura M. Zaidman (1994)

142 *Eighteenth-Century British Literary Biographers,* edited by Steven Serafin (1994)

143 *American Novelists Since World War II, Third Series,* edited by James R. Giles and Wanda H. Giles (1994)

144 *Nineteenth-Century British Literary Biographers,* edited by Steven Serafin (1994)

145 *Modern Latin-American Fiction Writers, Second Series,* edited by William Luis and Ann González (1994)

146 *Old and Middle English Literature,* edited by Jeffrey Helterman and Jerome Mitchell (1994)

147 *South Slavic Writers Before World War II,* edited by Vasa D. Mihailovich (1994)

148 *German Writers and Works of the Early Middle Ages: 800-1170,* edited by Will Hasty and James Hardin (1994)

149 *Late Nineteenth- and Early Twentieth-Century British Literary Biographers,* edited by Steven Serafin (1995)

150 *Early Modern Russian Writers, Late Seventeenth and Eighteenth Centuries,* edited by Marcus C. Levitt (1995)

151 *British Prose Writers of the Early Seventeenth Century,* edited by Clayton D. Lein (1995)

152 *American Novelists Since World War II, Fourth Series,* edited by James R. Giles and Wanda H. Giles (1995)

153 *Late-Victorian and Edwardian British Novelists, First Series,* edited by George M. Johnson (1995)

154 *The British Literary Book Trade, 1700-1820,* edited by James K. Bracken and Joel Silver (1995)

155 *Twentieth-Century British Literary Biographers,* edited by Steven Serafin (1995)

156 *British Short-Fiction Writers, 1880-1914: The Romantic Tradition,* edited by William F. Naufftus (1995)

157 *Twentieth-Century Caribbean and Black African Writers, Third Series,* edited by Bernth Lindfors and Reinhard Sander (1995)

158 *British Reform Writers, 1789-1832,* edited by Gary Kelly and Edd Applegate (1995)

159 *British Short-Fiction Writers, 1800-1880,* edited by John R. Greenfield (1996)

160 *British Children's Writers, 1914-1960,* edited by Donald R. Hettinga and Gary D. Schmidt (1996)

161 *British Children's Writers Since 1960, First Series,* edited by Caroline Hunt (1996)

162 *British Short-Fiction Writers, 1915-1945,* edited by John H. Rogers (1996)

163 *British Children's Writers, 1800-1880,* edited by Meena Khorana (1996)

164 *German Baroque Writers, 1580-1660,* edited by James Hardin (1996)

165 *American Poets Since World War II, Fourth Series,* edited by Joseph Conte (1996)

166 *British Travel Writers, 1837-1875,* edited by Barbara Brothers and Julia Gergits (1996)

167 *Sixteenth-Century British Nondramatic Writers, Third Series,* edited by David A. Richardson (1996)

168 *German Baroque Writers, 1661-1730,* edited by James Hardin (1996)

169 *American Poets Since World War II, Fifth Series,* edited by Joseph Conte (1996)

170 *The British Literary Book Trade, 1475-1700,* edited by James K. Bracken and Joel Silver (1996)

171 *Twentieth-Century American Sportswriters,* edited by Richard Orodenker (1996)

172 *Sixteenth-Century British Nondramatic Writers, Fourth Series,* edited by David A. Richardson (1996)

173 *American Novelists Since World War II, Fifth Series,* edited by James R. Giles and Wanda H. Giles (1996)

174 *British Travel Writers, 1876-1909,* edited by Barbara Brothers and Julia Gergits (1997)

175 *Native American Writers of the United States,* edited by Kenneth M. Roemer (1997)

176 *Ancient Greek Authors,* edited by Ward W. Briggs (1997)

177 *Italian Novelists Since World War II, 1945-1965,* edited by Augustus Pallotta (1997)

178 *British Fantasy and Science-Fiction Writers Before World War I,* edited by Darren Harris-Fain (1997)

179 *German Writers of the Renaissance and Reformation, 1280-1580,* edited by James Hardin and Max Reinhart (1997)

180 *Japanese Fiction Writers, 1868-1945,* edited by Van C. Gessel (1997)

181 *South Slavic Writers Since World War II,* edited by Vasa D. Mihailovich (1997)

182 *Japanese Fiction Writers Since World War II,* edited by Van C. Gessel (1997)

183 *American Travel Writers, 1776-1864,* edited by James J. Schramer and Donald Ross (1997)

184 *Nineteenth-Century British Book-Collectors and Bibliographers,* edited by William Baker and Kenneth Womack (1997)

185 *American Literary Journalists, 1945-1995, First Series,* edited by Arthur J. Kaul (1998)

186 *Nineteenth-Century American Western Writers,* edited by Robert L. Gale (1998)

187 *American Book Collectors and Bibliographers, Second Series,* edited by Joseph Rosenblum (1998)

188 *American Book and Magazine Illustrators to 1920,* edited by Steven E. Smith, Catherine A. Hastedt, and Donald H. Dyal (1998)

189 *American Travel Writers, 1850-1915,* edited by Donald Ross and James J. Schramer (1998)

190 *British Reform Writers, 1832-1914,* edited by Gary Kelly and Edd Applegate (1998)

191 *British Novelists Between the Wars,* edited by George M. Johnson (1998)

192 *French Dramatists, 1789-1914,* edited by Barbara T. Cooper (1998)

193 *American Poets Since World War II, Sixth Series,* edited by Joseph Conte (1998)

194 *British Novelists Since 1960, Second Series,* edited by Merritt Moseley (1998)

195 *British Travel Writers, 1910-1939,* edited by Barbara Brothers and Julia Gergits (1998)

196 *Italian Novelists Since World War II, 1965-1995,* edited by Augustus Pallotta (1999)

197 *Late-Victorian and Edwardian British Novelists, Second Series,* edited by George M. Johnson (1999)

198 *Russian Literature in the Age of Pushkin and Gogol: Prose,* edited by Christine A. Rydel (1999)

199 *Victorian Women Poets,* edited by William B. Thesing (1999)

200 *American Women Prose Writers to 1820,* edited by Carla J. Mulford, with Angela Vietto and Amy E. Winans (1999)

201 *Twentieth-Century British Book Collectors and Bibliographers,* edited by William Baker and Kenneth Womack (1999)

202 *Nineteenth-Century American Fiction Writers,* edited by Kent P. Ljungquist (1999)

203 *Medieval Japanese Writers,* edited by Steven D. Carter (1999)

204 *British Travel Writers, 1940–1997,* edited by Barbara Brothers and Julia M. Gergits (1999)

205 *Russian Literature in the Age of Pushkin and Gogol: Poetry and Drama,* edited by Christine A. Rydel (1999)

206 *Twentieth-Century American Western Writers, First Series,* edited by Richard H. Cracroft (1999)

207 *British Novelists Since 1960, Third Series,* edited by Merritt Moseley (1999)

208 *Literature of the French and Occitan Middle Ages: Eleventh to Fifteenth Centuries,* edited by Deborah Sinnreich-Levi and Ian S. Laurie (1999)

209 *Chicano Writers, Third Series,* edited by Francisco A. Lomelí and Carl R. Shirley (1999)

210 *Ernest Hemingway: A Documentary Volume,* edited by Robert W. Trogdon (1999)

211 *Ancient Roman Writers,* edited by Ward W. Briggs (1999)

212 *Twentieth-Century American Western Writers, Second Series,* edited by Richard H. Cracroft (1999)

213 *Pre-Nineteenth-Century British Book Collectors and Bibliographers,* edited by William Baker and Kenneth Womack (1999)

214 *Twentieth-Century Danish Writers,* edited by Marianne Stecher-Hansen (1999)

215 *Twentieth-Century Eastern European Writers, First Series,* edited by Steven Serafin (1999)

216 *British Poets of the Great War: Brooke, Rosenberg, Thomas. A Documentary Volume,* edited by Patrick Quinn (2000)

217 *Nineteenth-Century French Poets,* edited by Robert Beum (2000)

218 *American Short-Story Writers Since World War II, Second Series,* edited by Patrick Meanor and Gwen Crane (2000)

Documentary Series

1 *Sherwood Anderson, Willa Cather, John Dos Passos, Theodore Dreiser, F. Scott Fitzgerald, Ernest Hemingway, Sinclair Lewis,* edited by Margaret A. Van Antwerp (1982)

2 *James Gould Cozzens, James T. Farrell, William Faulkner, John O'Hara, John Steinbeck, Thomas Wolfe, Richard Wright,* edited by Margaret A. Van Antwerp (1982)

3 *Saul Bellow, Jack Kerouac, Norman Mailer, Vladimir Nabokov, John Updike, Kurt Vonnegut,* edited by Mary Bruccoli (1983)

4 *Tennessee Williams,* edited by Margaret A. Van Antwerp and Sally Johns (1984)

5 *American Transcendentalists,* edited by Joel Myerson (1988)

6 *Hardboiled Mystery Writers: Raymond Chandler, Dashiell Hammett, Ross Macdonald,* edited by Matthew J. Bruccoli and Richard Layman (1989)

7 *Modern American Poets: James Dickey, Robert Frost, Marianne Moore,* edited by Karen L. Rood (1989)

8 *The Black Aesthetic Movement,* edited by Jeffrey Louis Decker (1991)

9 *American Writers of the Vietnam War: W. D. Ehrhart, Larry Heinemann, Tim O'Brien, Walter McDonald, John M. Del Vecchio,* edited by Ronald Baughman (1991)

10 *The Bloomsbury Group,* edited by Edward L. Bishop (1992)

11 *American Proletarian Culture: The Twenties and The Thirties,* edited by Jon Christian Suggs (1993)

12 *Southern Women Writers: Flannery O'Connor, Katherine Anne Porter, Eudora Welty,* edited by Mary Ann Wimsatt and Karen L. Rood (1994)

13 *The House of Scribner, 1846-1904,* edited by John Delaney (1996)

14 *Four Women Writers for Children, 1868-1918,* edited by Caroline C. Hunt (1996)

15 *American Expatriate Writers: Paris in the Twenties,* edited by Matthew J. Bruccoli and Robert W. Trogdon (1997)

16 *The House of Scribner, 1905-1930,* edited by John Delaney (1997)

17 *The House of Scribner, 1931-1984,* edited by John Delaney (1998)

18 *British Poets of The Great War: Sassoon, Graves, Owen,* edited by Patrick Quinn (1999)

19 *James Dickey,* edited by Judith S. Baughman (1999)

See also DLB 210, 216

Yearbooks

1980 edited by Karen L. Rood, Jean W. Ross, and Richard Ziegfeld (1981)

1981 edited by Karen L. Rood, Jean W. Ross, and Richard Ziegfeld (1982)

1982 edited by Richard Ziegfeld; associate editors: Jean W. Ross and Lynne C. Zeigler (1983)

1983 edited by Mary Bruccoli and Jean W. Ross, associate editor Richard Ziegfeld (1984)

1984 edited by Jean W. Ross (1985)

1985 edited by Jean W. Ross (1986)

1986 edited by J. M. Brook (1987)

1987 edited by J. M. Brook (1988)

1988 edited by J. M. Brook (1989)

1989 edited by J. M. Brook (1990)

1990 edited by James W. Hipp (1991)

1991 edited by James W. Hipp (1992)

1992 edited by James W. Hipp (1993)

1993 edited by James W. Hipp, contributing editor George Garrett (1994)

1994 edited by James W. Hipp, contributing editor George Garrett (1995)

1995 edited by James W. Hipp, contributing editor George Garrett (1996)

1996 edited by Samuel W. Bruce and L. Kay Webster, contributing editor George Garrett (1997)

1997 edited by Matthew J. Bruccoli and George Garrett, with the assistance of L. Kay Webster (1998)

1998 edited by Matthew J. Bruccoli, contributing editor George Garrett, with the assistance of D. W. Thomas (1999)

Concise Series

Concise Dictionary of American Literary Biography, 7 volumes (1988-1999): *The New Consciousness, 1941-1968; Colonization to the American Renaissance, 1640-1865; Realism, Naturalism, and Local Color, 1865-1917; The Twenties, 1917-1929; The Age of Maturity, 1929-1941; Broadening Views, 1968-1988; Supplement: Modern Writers, 1900–1998.*

Concise Dictionary of British Literary Biography, 8 volumes (1991-1992): *Writers of the Middle Ages and Renaissance Before 1660; Writers of the Restoration and Eighteenth Century, 1660-1789; Writers of the Romantic Period, 1789-1832; Victorian Writers, 1832-1890; Late-Victorian and Edwardian Writers, 1890-1914; Modern Writers, 1914-1945; Writers After World War II, 1945-1960; Contemporary Writers, 1960 to Present.*

Concise Dictionary of World Literary Biography, 20 volumes projected (1999-): *Ancient Greek and Roman Writers; German Writers.*

Dictionary of Literary Biography® • Volume Two Hundred Eighteen

American Short-Story Writers Since World War II

Second Series

Dictionary of Literary Biography® • Volume Two Hundred Eighteen

American Short-Story Writers Since World War II
Second Series

Edited by
Patrick Meanor
State University of New York at Oneonta

and

Gwen Crane
State University of New York at Oneonta

A Bruccoli Clark Layman Book
The Gale Group
Detroit • San Francisco • London • Boston • Woodbridge, Conn.

Matthew J. Bruccoli and Richard Layman, Editorial Directors
C. E. Frazer Clark Jr., Managing Editor
Karen L. Rood, Senior Editor

Printed in the United States of America

The paper used in this publication meets the minimum requirements
of American National Standard for Information Sciences–Permanence
Paper for Printed Library Materials, ANSI Z39.48-1984. ∞™

Library of Congress Cataloging-in-Publication Data

American short-story writers since World War II. Second series / edited by Patrick Meanor and Gwen Crane.
p. cm.–(Dictionary of literary biography: v. 218)
"A Bruccoli Clark Layman book."
Includes bibliographical references and index.
ISBN 0-7876-3127-2 (alk. paper)
1. Short stories, American–Dictionaries. 2. American fiction–20th century–Bio-bibliography–Dictionaries. 3. Authors, American–20th century–Biography–Dictionaries. 4. Short stories, American–Bio-bibliography–Dictionaries. 5. American fiction–20th century–Dictionaries. I. Meanor, Patrick. II. Crane, Gwen. III. Series.
PS374.S5 A3964 1999
813'.0109'03–dc21 99–048543
[B] CIP

10 9 8 7 6 5 4 3 2 1

Dictionary of Literary Biography® • Volume Two Hundred Eighteen

American Short-Story Writers Since World War II

Second Series

Contents

Plan of the Series

... Almost the most prodigious asset of a country, and perhaps its most precious possession, is its native literary product—when that product is fine and noble and enduring.

Mark Twain*

The advisory board, the editors, and the publisher of the *Dictionary of Literary Biography* are joined in endorsing Mark Twain's declaration. The literature of a nation provides an inexhaustible resource of permanent worth. We intend to make literature and its creators better understood and more accessible to students and the reading public, while satisfying the standards of teachers and scholars.

To meet these requirements, *literary biography* has been construed in terms of the author's achievement. The most important thing about a writer is his writing. Accordingly, the entries in *DLB* are career biographies, tracing the development of the author's canon and the evolution of his reputation.

The purpose of *DLB* is not only to provide reliable information in a convenient format but also to place the figures in the larger perspective of literary history and to offer appraisals of their accomplishments by qualified scholars.

The publication plan for *DLB* resulted from two years of preparation. The project was proposed to Bruccoli Clark by Frederick G. Ruffner, president of the Gale Research Company, in November 1975. After specimen entries were prepared and typeset, an advisory board was formed to refine the entry format and develop the series rationale. In meetings held during 1976, the publisher, series editors, and advisory board approved the scheme for a comprehensive biographical dictionary of persons who contributed to North American literature. Editorial work on the first volume began in January 1977, and it was published in 1978. In order to make *DLB* more than a reference tool and to compile volumes that individually have claim to status as literary history, it was decided to organize volumes by topic, period, or genre. Each of these freestanding volumes provides a biographical-bibliographical guide and overview for a particular area of literature. We are convinced that this organization—as opposed to a single alphabet method—constitutes a valuable innovation in the presentation of reference material. The volume plan necessarily requires many decisions for the placement and treatment of authors who might properly be included in two or three volumes. In some instances a major figure will be included in separate volumes, but with different entries emphasizing the aspect of his career appropriate to each volume. Ernest Hemingway, for example, is represented in *American Writers in Paris, 1920–1939* by an entry focusing on his expatriate apprenticeship; he is also in *American Novelists, 1910–1945* with an entry surveying his entire career, as well as in *American Short-Story Writers, 1910–1945, Second Series* with an entry concentrating on his short stories. Each volume includes a cumulative index of the subject authors and articles. Comprehensive indexes to the entire series are planned.

Since 1981 the series has been further augmented by the *DLB Yearbooks,* which update published entries and add new entries to keep the *DLB* current with contemporary activity. There have also been *DLB Documentary Series* volumes which provide biographical and critical source materials for figures whose work is judged to have particular interest for students. One of these companion volumes is devoted entirely to Tennessee Williams.

We define literature as the *intellectual commerce of a nation:* not merely as belles lettres but as that ample and complex process by which ideas are generated, shaped, and transmitted. *DLB* entries are not limited to "creative writers" but extend to other figures who in their time and in their way influenced the mind of a people. Thus the series encompasses historians, journalists, publishers, book collectors, and screenwriters. By this means readers of *DLB* may be aided to perceive literature not as cult scripture in the keeping of intellectual high priests but firmly positioned at the center of a nation's life.

DLB includes the major writers appropriate to each volume and those standing in the ranks behind

**From an unpublished section of Mark Twain's autobiography, copyright by the Mark Twain Company*

them. Scholarly and critical counsel has been sought in deciding which minor figures to include and how full their entries should be. Wherever possible, useful references are made to figures who do not warrant separate entries.

Each *DLB* volume has an expert volume editor responsible for planning the volume, selecting the figures for inclusion, and assigning the entries. Volume editors are also responsible for preparing, where appropriate, appendices surveying the major periodicals and literary and intellectual movements for their volumes, as well as lists of further readings. Work on the series as a whole is coordinated at the Bruccoli Clark Layman editorial center in Columbia, South Carolina, where the editorial staff is responsible for accuracy and utility of the published volumes.

One feature that distinguishes *DLB* is the illustration policy–its concern with the iconography of literature. Just as an author is influenced by his surroundings, so is the reader's understanding of the author enhanced by a knowledge of his environment. Therefore *DLB* volumes include not only drawings, paintings, and photographs of authors, often depicting them at various stages in their careers, but also illustrations of their families and places where they lived. Title pages are regularly reproduced in facsimile along with dust jackets for modern authors. The dust jackets are a special feature of *DLB* because they often document better than anything else the way in which an author's work was perceived in its own time. Specimens of the writers' manuscripts and letters are included when feasible.

Samuel Johnson rightly decreed that "The chief glory of every people arises from its authors." The purpose of the *Dictionary of Literary Biography* is to compile literary history in the surest way available to us–by accurate and comprehensive treatment of the lives and work of those who contributed to it.

The *DLB* Advisory Board

Introduction

This volume of the *Dictionary of Literary Biography* continues the series begun with *DLB 130: American Short-Story Writers Since World War II.* After that war the pace of cultural change in the United States was accelerated. As the United States became an international superpower, fear of the Soviet Union sparked Senator Joseph McCarthy's investigations into communist infiltration of the federal government, giving rise to a new generation of voices questioning the principles that temporarily lofted McCarthy to power. Women who had worked in war-related industries during the war lost their jobs to returning veterans and spent the 1950s in their kitchens, experimenting with new labor-saving devices and instant cake mixes, only to re-enter the public sphere in the women's liberation movement of the 1960s. In that decade the civil rights and antiwar movements coalesced to produce a general re-examination of authority. All these radical upheavals are reflected in the developments in the short story during these decades. This volume, as well as *DLB 130,* charts the representative voices in the debates and revolutions of the second half of the twentieth century.

During the 1920s, 1930s, and 1940s an author could make a living by writing short stories for the large-circulation magazines. After World War II, however, weekly magazines such as *The Saturday Evening Post* and *Collier's* declined and eventually ceased publication. Starting in the 1950s, the massive presence of television began to undermine the reading habits of the American public. Widespread television viewing ushered in what George Garrett has called "the new illiteracy." Because the popular market for short stories has shrunk, most American short fiction is published by literary journals and university presses. There are recent signs that the short-story form is gaining ground with readers and publishers, but no more than a dozen magazines pay four-figure prices for a story.

Collections of stories did not sell well during the 1950s, 1960s, and early 1970s. At the same time the market-driven publishing business also made it difficult for experimental writers to get their novels published. Many of the remaining magazines began to feature memoirs, frequently in place of short stories. One of the effects of Truman Capote's nonfiction novel *In Cold Blood* (1965) was to blur distinctions between fiction and nonfiction, and writers such as Edward Abbey, Joan Didion, Annie Dillard, John McPhee, and Gay Talese began to publish personal essays that could be mistaken for first-person short stories.

During these same years the experimental techniques of avant-garde European writers such as Samuel Beckett, Franz Kafka, and André Breton became new models replacing, in some instances, the earlier influences of Ernest Hemingway, William Faulkner, F. Scott Fitzgerald, and Sherwood Anderson. Experimental techniques were appearing in the work of American authors such as Donald Barthelme, John Barth, and Thomas Pynchon–writers also influenced by South Americans such as Jorge Luis Borges and so-called literary outlaws such as Charles Bukowski and William S. Burroughs. Professors in the creative-writing programs that began to emerge at universities stressed originality of method rather than content, thus encouraging a variety of new forms. By the late 1940s, the Writers' Workshop at the University of Iowa, the oldest creative-writing program in the United States, was sending out graduates to initiate new creative-writing programs nationwide.

Another factor influenced the gradual migration of writers to college campuses. Because of the dwindling commercial market for short stories, fiction writers could no longer make a living in New York, and they began accepting jobs at colleges and universities. Tenured positions in English departments enabled them to support their families and continue writing or to stop writing altogether.

While the universities became protective environments for many fiction writers, certain risks arose in their sometimes-insular atmospheres. Hortense Calisher, one of the most respected American fiction writers, suggests that "the university has willy-nilly become the café." Writers, who often need a variety of experiences to spark their imaginations, spend a large portion of their time enclosed within the walls of graduate schools. In her introduction to *Best American Short Stories 1981,* Calisher warns that writers must be careful in talking too much about their craft: "If one teaches and writes there as well, the effect of immersion in talk about 'techniques' may also enter in. Subtlest of all influences or hazards for the silent persona of a writer may be the constant verbalization of energies and meditations better saved for the page." She points out that during the 1970s and 1980s a growing number of stories were set in academia. Concurring with Calisher on the possible negative repercussions of the creative-writing industry, John Updike wrote in his introduction to *Best American Short Stories 1984,*

> Now, for the bright young graduates that pour out of the Iowa Writers' Workshop and its sister institutions, publishing short stories is a kind of accreditation, a certificate of worthiness to teach the so-called art of fiction. The Popular market for fiction has shriveled while the academic importance of "creative writing" has swelled; academic quarterlies, operating under one form of subsidy or another, absorb some of the excess. The suspicion persists that short fiction, like poetry since Kipling and Bridges, has gone from being a popular to a fine art, an art preserved in a kind of floating museum made up of many little superfluous magazines.

Though Calisher and Updike warn against some of the hazards of creative-writing schools, the fact remains that whatever their long-term effects, creative-writing programs have played important roles in the lives of the writers covered in this *DLB* volume, nearly all of whom have either graduated from or taught in creative-writing programs. Furthermore, since the 1950s, academic quarterlies have become a major venue for the publication of short fiction in America.

The few national magazines that still publish short stories have established much higher literary standards than many of the magazines that folded in the 1950s and 1960s. *Esquire* has always been one of the most desirable places to publish because it pays well and its readership is literate and sophisticated. Particularly during the late 1960s and early 1970s, *Esquire* published many younger writers who eventually attained major careers. Since its inception in the late 1950s, *Playboy* has published stories by established writers and paid them handsomely, but it has published less and less fiction over time. The only weekly mainstream magazine to publish short fiction is *The New Yorker,* which launched and sustained the careers of Hortense Calisher and Ann Beattie. The literary editor at *The New Yorker* is now Bill Buford, formerly an editor at *Granta,* an influential British literary magazine. *Harper's,* edited by Lewis H. Lapham, and *The Atlantic Monthly,* whose fiction editor is Michael Curtis, continue to publish one story a month. *Redbook* continues to publish short stories monthly. Her frequent appearances in the pages of that magazine, however, have caused Merrill Joan Gerber to be dismissed in some quarters as a "writer for women's magazines," a label she has been trying to shed for some years. Almost half the writers in this volume have published fiction in one or more of these high-paying but increasingly selective magazines.

Many other writers in this volume, however, established their literary reputations without selling fiction to national magazines. Powerful editors of academic journals have fostered and promoted writers whose work seemed to express their aesthetic and political tastes. For many years, Frederick Turner directed and edited the conservative *Kenyon Review,* later edited by David Lynn. The *North American Review,* at the University of Northern Iowa, edited by Robley Wilson, has been particularly sympathetic to experimental fiction writers, as has *Chicago Review* under the editorship of Andrew Rathmann. Another respected literary journal, *Witness,* based at Oakland Community College and edited by Peter Stine, devotes each issue to a specific topic, such as "Writings from Prison," "The Holocaust," and "Evangelism and American Politics." Certainly *The Iowa Review,* edited by David Hamilton, has maintained its influence as the journal connected to the Iowa Writers' Workshop. Academic journals based in the South that have traditionally published excellent fiction are *Carolina Review,* edited by Robert West; *The Southern Review,* edited by James Olney; *The Sewanee Review,* edited by George Core; and *The Virginia Quarterly Review,* edited by Staige Blackford. Other academic journals that publish short stories are *TriQuarterly,* edited by the influential Reginald Gibbons until 1997; *The Georgia Review,* edited by Stanley W. Lindberg; *Southwest Review,* edited by Willard Spiegelman; *The Missouri Review,* edited by Speer Morgan and Greg Michalson; *Ploughshares,* founded by Dewitt Henry and Peter O'Malley; and *Cimarron Review,* whose fiction editor in 1975–1981 was Gordon Weaver.

There are other highly influential journals that are not connected to any particular university. Their literary reputation is usually built around the tastes of an editor who publishes only those writers whom he or she holds in high esteem. Bradford Morrow's journal *Conjunctions,* which only recently became affiliated with Bard College, has been publishing fiction with a heavily international-multicultural emphasis and a postmodernist perspective. Certainly founding editor Frederick Morgan's conservative tastes helped determine the kinds of stories that *The Hudson Review* would be most likely to accept during the late 1940s and the 1950s, just as the liberal political sympathies of William Phillips, a founding editor of *Partisan Review,* surely influenced the kind of work that appeared there from the late 1930s until 1978. Other powerful editors include George Plimpton of *The Paris Review* and Theodore Solotaroff, who as editor of *New American Review* during the 1960s and 1970s was responsible for the promotion of major writers such as Philip Roth and Stanley Elkin.

Journals devoted exclusively to publishing short fiction include *Short Story,* edited by Mary Rohrberger; *Story,* edited by Lois Rosenthal; and Francis Ford Coppola's *Zoetrope: All Story.* Two critical journals devoted to the study of short fiction are *Journal of the Short Story in English,* published at the University of Angers in France, and *Studies in Short Fiction,* edited by Michael O'Shea at Newberry College in Newberry, South Carolina.

Until recently many trade publishing houses–with the notable exceptions of Knopf, Norton, Holt, Putnam, Scribner, and Little, Brown, among a few others–have not published or promoted short-story collections. As a result, university presses have also become the most important vehicles for the publication of short fiction. In his introduction to *The Iowa Award: The Best Stories From Twenty Years* (1991), Frank Conroy, head of the Iowa Writers' Workshop, claims that the success of the university presses in promoting short fiction has "contributed significantly to the forces responsible for the current resurgence of interest of the big houses in serious short fiction."

In addition to sparking the flight of writers to universities and the emergence of academic literary quarterlies, the lack of major publishers' interest in short fiction gave rise to independent associations of writers who established their own little magazines. Several of the writers in this volume have rarely, or never, taught in university writing programs, published their works with university presses, or appeared in university-related scholarly journals. They sought no direct connections with either the commercial New York literary scene or the academic world. The little magazines created independent centers where writers were free to establish their own aesthetic communities. Many of the editors of and contributors to these magazines strongly objected to the homogenized eclecticism coming out of the more-conservative writing programs and academic journals. The more-radical founders of maverick publications have claimed that the emphasis on craft and technique in university workshops has inadvertently replaced viable aesthetic and cultural traditions that had previously activated innovative fiction writing. Little magazines, many of them short-lived, in which now-influential fiction writers found places for their work include *The Falcon* (1970–1980); *Chelsea,* founded by Robert Kelly and others in 1958; and *Evergreen Review* (1957–1973), edited by Barney Rosset and Donald Allen. Other little magazines that included short fiction are Irving Rosenthal and Paul Carroll's *Big Table* (1959–1960); *Lillabulero* (1967–1974), founded by Russell Banks and William Mathews; *Kulchur* (1960–1966), edited by Gilbert Sorrentino, Joel Oppenheimer, LeRoi Jones, and others; and *Neon* (1956–1960), edited by Sorrentino and Hubert Selby.

The so-called small presses have had about the same life expectancy as the little magazines, but several of the survivors have maintained the integrity of their single-minded vision in the face of overwhelming pressures. John Martin's Black Sparrow Press in Santa Rosa, California, is responsible to a great extent for the literary careers of some highly influential short-story writers, such as Charles Bukowski, Paul Goodman, Fielding Dawson, and Paul Bowles. William D. Turnbull's North Point Press of San Francisco–whose books are now distributed by Farrar, Straus and Giroux–publishes several respected writers, including Lydia Davis and Deborah Eisenberg.

Other important factors that substantially promote writers' careers are the annual prizes that include publication of a writer's story in an anthology of prize-winners. Shannon Ravenel, whom Updike called "that St. Louis saint of scrutiny" in his introduction to *Best American Short Stories 1984,* is probably the most influential editor of short stories in the United States today. As a senior editor of Algonquin Books of Chapel Hill, she has served as the co-editor of *Best American Short Stories* anthologies for the past twenty years, sifting through between 1,500 and 2,000 short stories yearly and sending her choice of the best 100 to a co-editor for the final awarding of the prizes. Her co-editors have included the most respected short-story writers in America. Not only are the prizewinners given national recognition, but they also receive a substantial sum of money. Most of the writers in this *DLB* volume have had one or more stories published in this distinguished series. Many have also had short fiction published in the O. Henry Awards and Pushcart Prize anthologies. Publishers often look to such anthologies when scouting around for fresh talent.

Several university presses play an active role in promoting short fiction by awarding annual prizes that include the publication of a collection of an individual author's short stories and by publishing short-fiction series. In 1980 the University of Pittsburgh Press, under director Frederick Hetzel, created the Drue Heinz Literature Prize specifically to recognize and encourage the writing of short fiction and to address the neglect of short fiction by the national publishing community. The University of Pittsburgh Press awards $5,000 annually to an outstanding young short-fiction writer and publishes his or her first collection. The press also began to publish short-story collections in what has come to be known as the University of Pittsburgh Short-Story Series. The University of Missouri Press, under editor Clair Wilcox, also initiated a short-fiction series known as The University of Missouri

Press Breakthrough Series. The University of Georgia Press has sponsored the Flannery O'Connor Award for Short Fiction for many years. The University of Iowa Press gives two publication prizes to short-story writers, the Iowa Short Fiction Award and the John Simmons Short Fiction Award. The University of Illinois has published more than sixty volumes in its Illinois Short Fiction Series.

The writers included in this volume may be divided into three general, sometimes overlapping, categories based primarily on their approach to their subject matter and thematic concerns and the geographic location or social class of their characters: realists or neorealists (including minimalists), postmodernists or metafictionists, and other writers whose work is more difficult to categorize.

The largest number of writers in this volume belong to the realist or neorealist category of short-fiction writers. In 1973 Tom Wolfe seemed to think that the pervasive influences of Kafka and Beckett had pretty much replaced realistic writing. But there is little question that, with the appearance of the powerful voice of Raymond Carver, realism was back. Richard Stern calls himself a realist even though he employs some modernist techniques. American writing has always had a strong attachment to geography. Specific landscapes–named or not–are integral parts of the work of most of the writers considered in this volume. Although he often includes allusions to myth, fantasy, and allegory in his stories, Madison Smartt Bell has been categorized with Carver, Russell Banks, and Andre Dubus, as "Dirty Realists," a term that suggests the working-class victims who are the principal characters of their fiction. Another epithet used to characterize their work is "Trailer-Park Fiction," because many of their protagonists' lives are rootless, poverty-ridden, and empty. Early marriages end in divorce and are riddled with alcoholism, adultery, abuse, and other self-destructive behaviors. The men drink, and the women and children suffer. The alienation and brutality that these writers portray are sometimes more disturbing than the generalized cosmic dread and nihilism of Kafka and Beckett–because their downtrodden characters live in affluent America. Though Peter Taylor's characters are generally middle class, they inhabit Gothic emotional shadows that place some of his stories in this category.

The terms *postmodernist* and *metafictionist* are difficult to define. They refer to the kind of fiction that shows a consciousness of itself as an artificial creation. Though suggesting that all works of fiction are ultimately about themselves, critic Raymond Federman claims that this self-reflexive fiction "continually turns back on itself and draws the reader into itself as a text, as an ongoing narration, and before the reader knows what is happening, the text is telling him about itself" (*Columbia Literary History of the United States,* 1988). Donald Barthelme's fiction stands as a stellar example of postmodernist experimentation, and other writers acknowledge his groundbreaking influence. Among the writers in this volume who have experimented in metafictional modes are Ann Beattie, T. Coraghessan Boyle, Rick DeMarinis, Barry Hannah, Amy Hempel, Janet Kauffman, Michael Martone, William Maxwell, and Grace Paley. Elizabeth Spencer, who wrote traditionally structured stories until 1960, experimented with shifting, unstable narrative strategies throughout the following decade and abandoned chronological coherence and narrative omniscience in the stories she wrote during the 1970s, allowing her characters to become authors in their own right and producing tales that stand as studies of the tale-teller's art.

Other writers in this volume do not participate markedly in either of these literary traditions. They are generally not experimental enough to be considered postmodernists or metafictionists, but some, such as Fielding Dawson and Alfred Chester, are both nonaligned and experimental. Paul Bowles, James Purdy, and Reynolds Price may be viewed as outsiders because they write about outsiders–lost souls, alcoholics, drug addicts, homosexuals before gay liberation, and other tormented victims involved in habitual self-destructive behaviors. Toni Cade Bambara and Bharati Mukherjee write primarily about the cultural clashes and immigrant experiences that have in the past two centuries produced a racially defined set of outsiders. Most of the female authors discussed in this volume devote at least some of their stories to female characters in search of a new niche in the reformulated families and social structures of the 1970s, 1980s, and 1990s. Although Calisher rejects the label of feminist or women's writer, she consciously chooses to write about those "outside the fold," and many of her characters are displaced females who can maintain their freedom only by avoiding any stable identity. R. V. Cassill specializes in character studies of those who have been isolated by psychic disturbances, trapped not so much by society as within their own nightmares. Paul Theroux's characters suffer similar difficulties: his perennial tourists travel the globe as sightseers and ambassadors, imprisoned within the blinders of prejudice and seeing only projections of their racist and elitist expectations. In their oblivion to their psychological isolation, they are a peculiarly tragic class of outsiders.

Though the world of short fiction is relatively peaceful compared to the endless bickering that goes on among contemporary American poets, there are a few ongoing skirmishes between some of the more conservative critics and certain writers, particularly regarding the relationship of style and content. In 1986 Madison Smartt Bell mounted a stinging attack in "Less is Less: The Dwindling American Short Story," in the April issue of *Harper's*. The object of his barbs was a group of young, highly successful writers that includes David Leavitt, Amy Hempel, and Bobbie Ann Mason. Bell took issue with their philosophical stance toward life, which he characterized as "nihilistic" and "deterministic" and criticized the movement of their stories as "reductive rather than expansive." Blaming the minimalist style of Raymond Carver, Ann Beattie, and Mary Robison for these younger writers' "facelessly uniform" stories, "impoverished language," and "starved eloquence," Bell charged the young writers with the inability to transform the "trivial into something other than 'trivial'" and questioned their ability to reconstitute "dreariness into an epiphany."

Cultural critics Sven Birkerts and Bruce Bawer decry the state of the contemporary American short story for the same reasons. (See "The School of Gordon Lish" in Birkerts's *An Artificial Wilderness* [1987] and "The Literary Brat Pack" in Bawer's *Diminishing Fictions* [1988].) They direct their criticism at Gordon Lish, the influential fiction editor at *Esquire* (1969–1977) and later an editor at Alfred A. Knopf, blaming him for influencing younger writers to adopt Carver's minimalist style. Lish was responsible for promoting Carver's early career and, according to D. T. Max, he actually formulated Carver's early and highly distinctive style. Beneath their attacks lies a revulsion for the effect of the media, especially television, on the language of contemporary fiction writers. Birkerts sees these writers as belonging to "Lish's squadron" and the "Knopf corral" and criticizes Lish for championing writers such as Amy Hempel, Robison, Michael Martone, Barry Hannah, Janet Kauffman, Noy Holland, and Leon Rooke. Birkerts unfairly compares the accomplishments of these writers to those of an earlier generation of European authors such as Virginia Woolf, Franz Kafka, James Joyce, and Hermann Broch and finds the younger generation wanting.

Defining the short-story form has been an abiding concern of the scholars participating in the ongoing battles between the "ancients" and the "moderns." In his *Form and Meaning in Fiction* (1975), short-story theorist Norman Friedman calls for a critical consensus on rigorously, logically articulated criteria for distinguishing the short story from other kinds of writing. A leading short-story critic, Mary Rohrberger, has offered a different approach in her studies of the form, suggesting that literary developments do not lend themselves to the kind of logical rigor Friedman seeks and that critics and scholars can hope only to approximate a definition of the short story in the form of metaphor. Structuralists, poststructuralists, narratologists, and cognitive psychologists have all produced definitions, many of them interesting, yet none sufficiently inclusive. It is difficult to find even two critics arriving at the kind of critical consensus Friedman demands. In the decades following World War II, the short stories produced by American writers have defied generalization. Calisher, however, has provided a useful metaphorical definition of the short story as it has evolved since World War II: the short story today, she wrote in the introduction to her *Collected Stories* (1975), "is an apocalypse, served in a very small cup." A survey of the stories discussed in this *DLB* volume reveals a fertile field of vibrantly individualistic writers, many passionately involved in expanding the boundaries of their art. Paradoxically, while critics worry about the stifling effects of the academic writing programs where increasing numbers of our younger writers sojourn, the work these younger authors produce continues to evolve in unexpectedly exuberant ways. The short story has flourished since World War II, continually redefining the paradigms that shape it and serving as a richly varied chronicle of a tumultuous age. The writers of the late twentieth century are using new tools to explore new territory–a historical and intellectual landscape marred by unprecedented violence, illuminated by new knowledge, and shadowed with profound philosophical and religious doubts.

When the authors discussed in this volume look on the world as God's text, they find his authorial intentions inscrutable. Their frequently experimental accounts of their travels through this uncharted text arrive like reconnaissance dispatches sent to their readers. One of Grace Paley's narrators holds God accountable for a faulty creation, but when she looks on her own authorial work, she finds it good: God's historical narrative is flawed, but the narrator feels at the end of her tale that she has been "right to invent for my friends and for my children a report on these private deaths and the condition of our lifelong attachments." More and more often in the work of the younger writers in this volume, God becomes more of an absence than a guiding presence behind a world careening out of control, and humans become increasingly undesirable or ineffective substitute stewards. "Accident rules the world," one of T. Coraghessan Boyle's characters intones, "accident and depravity." Cassill believes that "disaffection" forms the "heart of human nature"; Theroux believes that hubris is the identifying feature of the species, and narcissism the hallmark of the artist. Frank O'Connor's important study *The Lonely Voice* (1963) argues that this generalized disaffection and alienation makes the short story an increasingly suitable medium for postwar artistic expression. Early writers of the short story noted this suitability long before O'Connor, however. Edgar Allan Poe and Nathaniel Hawthorne both filled their stories with lonely, guilt-ridden characters struggling in isolation to keep their sanity, locked in a condition G. K. Chesterton described as "the morbid life of the lonely mind."

Twentieth-century writers are dealing with unprecedented visions of morbidity. As the postwar worldview has darkened, the short story has of necessity developed a new formal and semiotic vocabulary to describe scenes and emotional states that seem as familiar as our own skins and as alien as a lunar landscape. Many of these authors at least allude to older formal structures, only to revise them in unexpected ways, as when Janet Kauffman begins a fablelike animal story with an echo of Belgian Surrealist painter René Magritte, announcing "This is not a fable." Elsewhere, she evokes Aristotelian patterns of plot but only to dismiss Aristotle's prescriptions, describing her stories as essentially "a lot of middle" and refusing to apologize for her omission of beginnings and endings. Her stories thus begin to resemble the photographs that figure prominently in the stories themselves, forming snapshots of moments rather than linear plots. Many of the other writers in this volume share Kauffman's preoccupation with the vocabulary and techniques of photography. Beattie uses photographs to propel her plots and as models for her narrative style; Wright Morris combines images and words in his idiosyncratic "photo-texts." Barthelme pioneered the combination of text and image in his much-commented-on montages of old engravings and new, surrealistic commentaries. Kauffman has brought this textual strategy into the computer age by embracing the potential of cyberspace for combining image and text in ways not available to Barthelme. Many of their predecessors and contemporaries have also employed the language of the visual arts in discussing their work, supporting Nadine Gordimer's comparison of the short-story plot to "the flash of fireflies, in and out, now here, now there, in darkness." Recent attempts to analyze the short story from the cognitive psychologist's view also focus on the "fireflie's flash" quality of these brief pieces, distinguishing the reader's experience of short fiction from that of the developed chronologies of the novella and the novel.

Yet, the stories discussed in this volume resist the cognitive psychologists' definitions as emphatically as they do Aristotle's. Many short-story writers continue to develop older forms of "diachronic" structure in their work with depicting change over time in the short-story cycle. Following Sherwood Anderson's example in *Winesburg, Ohio* (1919), these authors–including Lynne Sharon Schwartz, Theroux, and Bell–link their stories through shared characters and locations into longer studies of individuals and their communities. Many others create a more subtle sense of cohesion in their story collections by writing repeatedly of a single region: Doris Betts makes the Southern Christian community her chosen landscape; Peter Taylor focuses on the disintegrating middle-class families and communities of Tennessee and Missouri as his own staked territory; and Calisher and Faust lay claim to Manhattan. Bell, another Manhattanite, goes so far as to call New York City a "tragic monster" that acts as more of a character than a backdrop in his stories. William Goyen imports classical myth into a Texas landscape to create his distinctive view of Southern culture; Rick DeMarinis returns repeatedly to the open vistas of the West, where his recurring interest in the subterranean missile silos beneath the North Dakota plains makes his Western landscapes into allegorical representations of the apocalypticism pervading the American urban scene as well as the Western Arcadia his characters populate.

While the contemporary short story defies most critical attempts at definition, the stories discussed in this volume do function as windows into their authors' personal experiences of a variously disastrous age, often exemplifying quite exactly Calisher's metaphor of "an apocalypse in a very small cup." Many of the stories directly address the effects of the wars that have reshaped American culture since 1940. Irvin Faust's stories demonstrate the unbearable experience of Jewish survivor guilt in "Jake Bluffstein and Hitler" and, the final abstraction and commodification of World War II, when Hitler himself is repackaged for a new generation of television viewers in Faust's story "The Benedict Arnold Show." Faust's masterful ventriloquism captures such historical moments in a few lines of specific dialect, encapsulating complex epiphanies within the straitened confines of the short story and tracking the mood of the country through prewar innocence to grievous experience to calloused cynicism. Michael Martone examines the fundamental role of the war in shaping American identity in "The Teakwood Desk of the U.S.S. *Indiana*" and makes the domestic experience of World War II a unifying theme in his collection *Seeing Eye* (1995). Shirley Ann Grau also focuses on the domestic effects of the war in several short portraits of grieving war widows. Reynolds Price depicts a young boy observing the war from a distance and trying to determine "what it is to be a man" in wartime. In one of his later stories, "Waiting at Dachau," Price sends a shakily married couple to visit a concentration-camp memorial, where they find a mirror of their own fracturing union in the history of Jewish prisoners betraying one another. As in many of Price's stories, a genius for betrayal and cruelty lies at the heart of his definition of "what it is to be human" in the twentieth century.

Later writers depict later wars, to different ends. Military posturings and maneuverings frequently stand as glosses on nonmilitary abuses of power: Robert Bausch, a Vietnam War veteran, demonstrates how ultimately unauthorized, unqualified military authorities are models for mismanagement in the domestic arena, where pathetically inept father figures fail to marshal their wives and children into any traditional order. Mukherjee writes of Vietnam veterans who quite literally bring the war home with them, continuing U.S. military policies in their living rooms with their Vietnamese wives and children and launching individual campaigns against Asian immigrant neighbors. After the atomic bombing of Hiroshima and the gas chambers of Auschwitz, all traditions of doctrinal order–political, philosophical, religious, and familial–begin to fail, revealing a void where reliable authority was assumed to reside. One of Grau's war widows rejects the passive role imposed on her by distant military stage managers and local family members. Grau conveys both the glory and the futility of that rebellion in the space of a few pages.

Anticipating later scholars, literary theorist George Lukács observed in 1920 the natural suitability of the short story for depicting "the strangeness and ambiguity" of modern life, a "strangeness" short-story scholar Charles May has elaborated as "the arbitrary nature of experiences whose workings are always without cause or reason." The author's shaping power is more obviously foregrounded in the short story than it is in the novel. The reader of the short story is compelled to consider the decision making involved in beginning and ending such brief pieces, to question the author's choices, and, in an extension of Lukács's theory, to go on to question all arbitrary authority–aesthetic, political, or cosmological. For Lukács's more-orthodox Marxist students, this invitation to question the role of the author, and by extension to question the role of all authority figures, makes the short story a valuable political tool. Several of the authors included in this volume do in fact use the short-story form with specifically political intent. Bambara, for instance, considered her writing just one facet of her lifelong political and social activism. Bambara's brief vignettes highlight the need for revolution and the frequently disastrous consequences of radical change; the urgency of her message is amplified by the brevity of those pieces, which leave the reader shocked by the silence following the final lines, a silence that demands some response from the reader.

Since 1978, when the Pulitzer Prize–winning *Stories of John Cheever* became the first short-story collection in a long time to find a place on the best-seller lists, interest in the short story as a marketable commodity and a fit subject for academic research has mushroomed, though the market for individual stories lags behind that for book-length collections. In a 1999 interview Frederick Busch observed that "the most excellent short story, the most wonderful soul-stretching short story as a work of gorgeous language and breathtaking event is alive and plentiful, but not *well,* because . . . the selection process, for whatever reason, is not very good." Busch hopes that the situation will improve if magazine editors can be kept in their jobs long enough to become more experienced. Other writers have had better luck with their editors, as Bambara did in meeting Toni Morrison while Morrison was an editor at Random House. Bambara and Morrison became close and mutually supportive colleagues and friends. Cynthia Ozick has been important in promoting the writing of Merrill Joan Gerber. Gordon Lish and George Plimpton have been generous in promoting the careers of new writers. The hostility many critics expressed toward the short story during the furor over minimalism has abated somewhat in recent years. Writing for *The New York Times Book Review* (18 April 1999), critic Gary Krist recently commented on the current importance of the short story: "In the last two decades, it's been the short story that has given us the more nuanced picture of the way we live now–the ironic rhythms of our speech, the casual heartbreak of our small domestic failures, the twisted warp and woof of our daily moral compromises. Future historians trying to determine what it was like to be alive in *fin de millennium* America should read the last two decades of *O. Henry* and *Best American* short-story collections."

–Patrick Meanor and Gwen Crane

Acknowledgments

This book was produced by Bruccoli Clark Layman, Inc. Karen L. Rood is senior editor for the *Dictionary of Literary Biography* series. Traci S. Britoni was the in-house editor. She was assisted by Philip B. Dematteis, Penelope M. Hope, and Charles Brower.

Production manager is Philip B. Dematteis.

Administrative support was provided by Ann M. Cheschi, Tenesha S. Lee, and Joann Whittaker.

Accountant is Kathy Weston. Accounting assistant is Angi Pleasant.

Copyediting supervisor is Phyllis A. Avant. Senior copyeditor is Thom Harman. The copyediting staff includes Brenda Carol Blanton, James Denton, Worthy B. Evans, Melissa D. Hinton, William Tobias Mathes, and Jennifer S. Reid. Freelance copyeditors were Ronald D. Aiken II and Rebecca Mayo.

Editorial assistant is Margo Dowling.

Editorial trainee is Carol A. Fairman.

Indexing specialist is Alex Snead.

Layout and graphics supervisor is Janet E. Hill. Graphics staff includes Karla Corley Brown and Zoe R. Cook.

Office manager is Kathy Lawler Merlette.

Photography editors are Charles Mims, Scott Nemzek, Alison Smith, and Paul Talbot. Digital photographic copy work was performed by Joseph M. Bruccoli.

SGML supervisor is Cory McNair. The SGML staff includes Tim Bedford, Linda Drake, Frank Graham, and Alex Snead.

Systems manager is Marie L. Parker.

Kimberly Kelly performed data entry.

Typesetting supervisor is Kathleen M. Flanagan. The typesetting staff includes Mark J. McEwan, Kimberly Kelley, and Patricia Flanagan Salisbury. Freelance typesetter is Delores Plastow.

Walter W. Ross and Steven Gross did library research. They were assisted by the following librarians at the Thomas Cooper Library of the University of South Carolina: Linda Holderfield and the interlibrary-loan staff; reference-department head Virginia Stefanie Buck, Stefanie DuBose, Rebecca Feind, Karen Joseph, Donna Lehman, Charlene Loope, Anthony McKissick, Jean Rhyne, and Kwamine Simpson; circulation-department head Caroline Taylor; and acquisitions-searching supervisor David Haggard.

Dictionary of Literary Biography® • Volume Two Hundred Eighteen

American Short-Story Writers Since World War II
Second Series

Dictionary of Literary Biography

Toni Cade Bambara

(25 March 1939 - 9 December 1995)

Teri Ann Doerksen
Hartwick College

See also the Bambara entry in *DLB 38: Afro-American Writers After 1955: Dramatists and Prose Writers.*

BOOKS: *Gorilla, My Love* (New York: Random House, 1972; London: Women's Press, 1984);

The Sea Birds Are Still Alive: Collected Stories (New York: Random House, 1977; London: Women's Press, 1984);

The Salt Eaters (New York: Random House, 1980; London: Women's Press, 1982);

Deep Sightings and Rescue Missions: Fiction, Essays, and Conversations, edited by Toni Morrison (New York: Pantheon, 1996; London: Women's Press, 1997);

Those Bones Are Not My Child (New York: Pantheon, 1999).

PRODUCED SCRIPTS: *Zora,* television, WGBH, 1971;

"The Johnson Girls," television, adapted by Bambara from her short story, *Soul Show,* National Educational Television, 1972;

Transactions, video, School of Social Work, Atlanta University, 1979;

The Long Night, television, ABC, 1981;

Epitaph for Willie, television, K. Heran Productions, 1982;

Tar Baby, television, adapted by Bambara from Toni Morrison's novel, Sanger/Brooks Film Productions, 1984;

Raymond's Run, television, adapted by Bambara from her short story, Public Broadcasting Service, 1985;

The Bombing of Osage Avenue, television, WHYY, 1986;

Cecil B. Moore: Master Tactician of Direct Action, television, WHYY, 1987;

Toni Cade Bambara (photograph by Nikky Finney; from the dust jacket for Gorilla, My Love, *1972)*

W. E. B. Du Bois, A Biography In Four Voices, video, script by Bambara, Thulani Davis, Amiri Baraka, and Wesley Brown, Scribe Video Center/California Newsreel, 1995.

RECORDING: *Toni Cade Bambara Reads "The Organizer's Wife,"* read by Bambara, Columbia, Mo.: American Audio Prose Library, II0282-R, 1982.

OTHER: *The Black Woman: An Anthology,* edited, with contributions, by Bambara, as Toni Cade (New York: New American Library, 1970);

"Raymond's Run," in *Tales and Stories for Black Folks,* edited by Bambara (Garden City, N.Y.: Zenith, 1971);

Southern Black Utterances Today, edited by Bambara and Leah Wise (Chapel Hill, N.C.: Institute for Southern Studies, 1975);

Southern Exposure, 3 (Spring/Summer 1976), edited by Bambara;

Cecelia Smith, *Cracks,* preface by Bambara (Atlanta: Select Press, 1979);

Cherríe Moraga and Gloria Anzaldúa, eds., *This Bridge Called My Back: Radical Women of Color,* foreword by Bambara (Watertown, Mass.: Persephone Press, 1981);

Zora Neale Hurston, *The Sanctified Church: Collected Essays by Zora Neale Hurston,* foreword by Bambara (Berkeley: Turtle Island, 1982);

Gloria Wade-Gayles, *No Crystal Stair: Visions of Race and Sex in Black Women's Fiction,* includes contributions by Bambara (New York: Pilgrim Press, 1984);

"Salvation Is the Issue," in *Black Women Writers (Nineteen Fifty to Nineteen Eighty): A Critical Evaluation,* edited by Mari Evans (Garden City, N.Y.: Doubleday/Anchor, 1984), pp. 41–71;

Julie Dash, *Daughters of the Dust: The Making of an African American Woman's Film,* preface by Bambara (New York: New Press, 1992).

During the twenty-five years of her career as an artist and civil-rights activist, Toni Cade Bambara became known for her enormously diverse talents and her adherence to the egalitarian principles that consistently guided her work in all areas. She first appeared on the literary scene as a writer of short stories, and she established her reputation with two short-story collections, but she never allowed herself to be limited by a single genre. Bambara edited anthologies of essays, short stories, and black folklore. She wrote short stories, a novel, and television scripts. Throughout all her writings her vision remained remarkably consistent. Her work shows an unwavering commitment to exploring and improving African American social, political, and cultural conditions. In a 1983 interview with Claudia Tate, Bambara compared her work to a test of contemporary cultural presuppositions: "What I strive to do in writing, and in general . . . is to examine philosophical, historical, political, metaphysical truths, or rather assumptions. I try to trace them through various contexts to see if they work. They may be traps. They may inhibit growth." In particular, Bambara's fiction tests preconceived ideas about race and gender by representing situations in which assumptions about what it means to be female and African American are called into question.

Bambara began writing and publishing during the 1960s, and she was one of the first of a rapidly growing number of African American women who effectively combined writing and political activism to produce social change. Her early career was a heady mix of hands-on work in politics and education and growing professional relationships with other key writers and activists, including Toni Morrison, Barbara Christian, Audre Lorde, and Alice Childress. With these colleagues and friends, Bambara explored ways of improving conditions for African Americans, and particularly for African American women; her writing was only one facet of an activism that encompassed her life. In her introduction to Bambara's posthumous collection, *Deep Sightings and Rescue Missions: Fiction, Essays, and Conversations* (1996), Morrison wrote of Bambara that

> There was no division in her mind between optimism and ruthless vigilance; between aesthetic obligation and the aesthetics of obligation. There was no doubt whatsoever that the work she did had work to do. She always knew what her work was for. Any hint that art was over there and politics was over here would break her up into tears of laughter, or elicit a look so withering it made silence the only intelligent response. More often she met the art/politics fake debate with a slight wave-away of the fingers on her beautiful hand, like the dismissal of a mindless, desperate fly who had maybe two little hours of life left.

Bambara's short stories, written primarily during the 1960s and 1970s, illustrate the changing nature of her activism during these decades. Her first book, *Gorilla, My Love* (1972), celebrates urban African American life, black English, and a spirit of hopefulness inspired by the Civil Rights movement. In contrast, her second book, *The Sea Birds Are Still Alive: Collected Stories* (1977) reveals the tensions born of the late 1970s; the stories reflect both an international perspective and an awareness of the difficulty of initiating beneficial change. Bambara's third volume that includes short stories, *Deep Sightings and Rescue Missions,* is substantially different from the first two. A posthumous mixed-genre collection from the last fifteen years of her life, it includes stories with a depth and complexity beyond that of Bambara's earlier years and grapples with death, cancer, abortion, and incipient revolution.

Bambara's vision and desire to invoke change were strongly influenced by her personal history; in particular, she saw the process of naming and renaming as a kind of personal revision that could act as a catalyst for other types of change. She was born Miltona Mirkin Cade on 25 March 1939 in New York City's Harlem, to Helen Brent Henderson Cade and Walter Cade II. Her father had wanted all his children to be named for him.

Although Bambara's only brother was given the name Walter, Bambara told Louis Massiah, in a 1994 interview published in *Deep Sightings and Rescue Missions* as "How She Came By Her Name," that "when it came to Walter Mae or Walterina, my mother put her foot down. So my father then named me after his employer in that great plantation tradition." By kindergarten she was asking to be called Toni, and by the time she reached college she was known as Toni Cade even to her professors. She changed her name legally to Toni Cade Bambara in 1970; there are several conflicting versions of how she chose the name "Bambara." Early accounts suggest that she adopted the name when she found it written in a sketchbook discovered in a trunk full of her grandmother's possessions; however, in her last interview, she told Massiah that while she was pregnant with her daughter in 1970, she was "toting around an African artbook," trying to find a name for her child:

> I have always been fond of the Chiwaras. The Chiwaras are made by the Dogon and the Bambaras. I tried out Dogon first: Karma Bene Dogon. Well, that sounds like "Karma Bene, well doggone!" That didn't work, and Toni Cade Dogon definitely did not work! Then it became Bambara. Karma Bene Bambara. That worked. Toni Cade Bambara–the minute I said it I immediately inhabited it, felt very at home in the world. This was my name.

Her daughter, Karma, is her only child.

Bambara had a richly varied life and education, which contributed to her ability to create works with a multifaceted, global outlook. Her early childhood was spent in Harlem in the 1940s, where she developed a strong attachment to her urban environment. Early visits to the Apollo Theatre with her father and exposure to the musical culture of post–World War II Harlem honed her delight in the arts; afternoons at the Speaker's Corner with her mother, listening to political arguments, sparked her lifelong interest in politics. As she remarked to Massiah, she saw Speaker's Corner as the educational center of the black community: "I knew that Speaker's Corner was valuable, because when we left Harlem most people seemed to be kind of airheads. They were not raising critical questions. There was no street culture." Her informal education in politics was succeeded by a formal degree from Queens College, where she received her bachelor of arts degree in theater arts and English literature in 1959. That same year marked the beginning of her writing career: her first short story, "Sweet Town," appeared in *Vendome Magazine,* and she won the John Golden Award for Fiction from Queen's College and the Peter Pauper Press Award in Journalism from the *Long Island Star.*

After she received her degree Bambara went abroad, spending time at the University of Florence studying Commedia dell'Arte, and at the Ecole de Mime Etienne Decroux in Paris, both in 1961. Later, she broadened her education with courses in linguistics, dance, and cinema at several distinguished New York colleges, studios, and institutes. During the 1960s she engaged with new ideas and with her community; she served as a social worker and a theater manager, directed neighborhood programs, and wrote stories and essays; her jobs during this period included a position as a family and youth caseworker for the New York Department of Welfare and director of recreation in the psychiatric division of the Metropolitan Hospital of New York City. Her life during this decade exemplifies the claim Bambara made to Massiah: "I never thought of myself as a writer. I always thought of myself as a community person who writes and does a few other things."

During the second half of the 1960s Bambara's dedication to education and to writing became more evident, while her public work continued. Bambara earned a master of arts degree in American literature from the City College of New York in 1965, and soon afterward she became a teacher there. She developed an effective dynamic between learning and teaching, using what she learned in her work with families and organizations to help build the City College SEEK program (Search for Education, Elevation, Knowledge), a program she told Massiah was designed by the school to "get these colored people in here, let them fail and flunk out so we don't have to be bothered with them again," but which, with her help, became a tremendous success. She wrote several short-fiction pieces while she was working for the SEEK program, during a period in which she met other black women writers who influenced and shaped her writing and her activism in indelible ways. Despite pessimistic administrative expectations, the SEEK program attracted a wide range of serious scholars, and Bambara's colleagues there included such highly respected figures as Barbara Christian, Audre Lorde, and June Jordan. Through her work editing her first compilation, *The Black Woman: An Anthology* (1970), Bambara came to know Alice Childress and Nikki Giovanni, who contributed a story and a poem, respectively, to the collection. From this time on, she was a part of a network of noted writers, feminists, and race theorists, whose work helped to catalyze change nationwide. From 1969 to 1974 Bambara was an assistant professor at Livingston College of Rutgers University, publishing articles, essays, and short stories regularly in many varied and respected publications, including *Essence, The New York Times, Ms., Black World,* and *Prairie Schooner.*

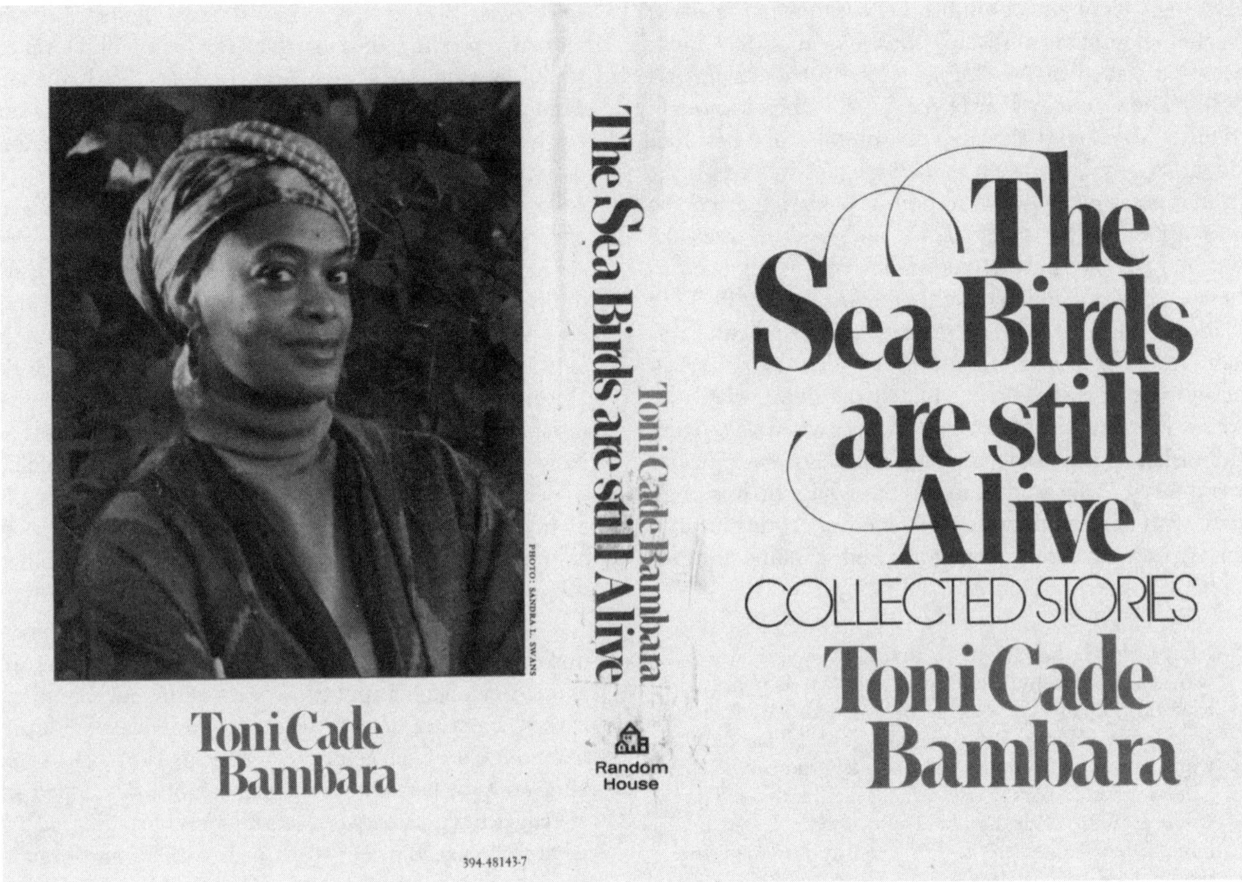

Dust jacket for Bambara's 1977 book, in which the title story depicts strained relations between Vietnamese and Western passengers on a boat off the coast of South Vietnam

Bambara's first two book-length publications were anthologies designed for classroom use. *The Black Woman,* published in 1970, is a collection of essays, poems, and short stories by both well-known authors and students from the SEEK program; the collection was intended to illuminate the connections between the women's movement and the Civil Rights movement. During the next year she published *Tales and Stories for Black Folks* (1971), designed to introduce young black readers to African American folklore, and to a storytelling tradition that has its roots in Africa. Although it had been published for the high-school and college classroom, the collection had larger appeal and developed a wide readership. On the heels of these two successful publications, Bambara's friend Hattie Gossett suggested that she put together a collection of her own work rather than the work of others and indicated that Toni Morrison, an editor at Random House, was interested in helping Bambara publish a book of her short stories. Bambara told Massiah in 1994 that she was excited at this possibility: "So I pulled out a bunch of stuff from under the mattress, from the bottom drawer, the trunks, and I spread this stuff around, and I thought, Ooh, a collection."

Gorilla, My Love, published in 1972, includes fifteen stories, mostly written between 1959 and 1970. It was the best known and most widely acclaimed book that Bambara ever published. The stories are preceded by a humorous disclaimer titled "A Sort of Preface" that denies any use of actual events or characters, because

> it's no use using bits and snatches even of real events and real people, even if you do cover, guise, switch-around and change-up cause next thing you know your best friend's laundry cart is squeaking past but your bell ain't ringing so you trot down the block after her and there's this drafty cold pressure front the weatherman surely did not predict and your friend says in this chilly way that it's really something when your own friend stabs you in the back with a pen. . . .

Nevertheless, the book was praised for the very quality the preface most vehemently denies: capturing the essence of "real events and real people." In particular, critics noted the language in which the pieces were written. Both narrative voices and character voices are rendered in an exuberant dialect that captures the spirit of excitement in urban African American communities in the 1960s. As Anne Tyler said about Bambara's fiction in a review of *The Salt Eaters* (1980) (*The Washington Post Book World,* 30 March 1980), "what pulls us along is the language of its characters, which is startlingly beautiful without once striking a false note. Everything these people say, you feel, ordinary, real-life people are saying right now on any street corner. It's only that the rest of us didn't realize it was sheer poetry they were speaking."

The stories in *Gorilla, My Love* feel more vital and ebullient than those in Bambara's later collections, in part because the younger and more naively insightful narrators of many of these pieces are able to articulate from a child's perspective a theme that was to persist through all of Bambara's writings: that life is the place where heritage and contemporaneity meet. These stories are loci where youth intersects with age, tradition with technology. Many of the stories are written from the perspective of ten- to twelve-year-old girls like Hazel Elizabeth Deborah Parker, a girl much smaller than the name she inhabits but clearly ready to grow into it when the time comes. In "Gorilla, My Love," Hazel struggles with the duplicity of the adult world, seeing a deep divide between herself and the adults around her. When she discovers that her "Hunca Bubba" is in love, and now wants to be called Jefferson Winston Vale, she thinks back to the spring before, when a movie titled *Gorilla, My Love* had been perceived as a betrayal by its youthful audience, who understandably expected gorillas, not religious themes; Hazel had become a leader in the near riot that had followed. Later the connection is made clear; when Hazel was much younger, her Hunca Bubba had said she was cute and that he would wait to marry her when she grew up. Now, on the eve of his marriage to another woman, she rebels, letting him know how deeply he has disappointed her. At the end of the story, she turns for comfort to her little brother, "Cause he is my blood brother and understands that we must stick together or be forever lost, what with grown-ups playin change-up and turnin you round every which way so bad. And don't even say they sorry."

Other stories emphasize the importance of steadfast and reliable adults in stabilizing the world of childhood. In "Blues Ain't No Mockin Bird," one of the rare stories set in a small town instead of the city, the young narrator and her cousin watch the confrontation between her grandparents and the movie crew that has come to film their farm for the food-stamp campaign. While the narrator may not understand the implications of the documentary crew's choice–the implicit assumption on the crew's part that this family is poor enough, downtrodden enough, picturesque enough, and black enough to make good publicity for a government program for the poor–her grandparents understand enough to want these men off their property. Instead of operating at the level of rudeness exhibited by the cameraman and interviewer, however, the grandparents exemplify a quiet dignity and politeness, matched when necessary by force, that deeply impresses the narrator. When Granny insists that the crewmen mind their manners and will not address them until they address her properly, when she insists that they stop calling her "aunty" because "Your mama and I are not related," she establishes herself as anything but the weak and dependent woman they seem to expect. When Grandaddy Cain returns, carrying the dead and bleeding body of a chicken hawk, the interaction becomes even more dramatic. Before the startled eyes of the camera crew, he does what he has to do to protect his flock of chickens: he kills the hawk's mate at close range with a thrown hammer. His strength appears to frighten them; as Cathy, the cousin, says, the white crew "can't stand Grandaddy so tall and silent and like a king." The crewmen understand the lesson, though, and do not protest when Grandaddy does what he has to do to protect his family, taking their camera in his huge hand, wet with hawk's blood, and exposing the film to the light. The children understand as well: they come from strong people and have the means to protect themselves and to change peoples' assumptions. This understanding is exemplified in Cathy's comment at the end of the story that when she grows up she is going to write a story "about the proper use of the hammer."

Although many of the narrators in this collection are young, *Gorilla, My Love* should by no means be dismissed as a children's book. There are older voices here as well; for example, Miss Hazel of "My Man Bovanne," who finds herself in a topsy-turvy struggle with her children over what constitutes proper behavior when they find her dancing in the street with a blind man "like one of them sex-starved ladies gettin on in years and not too discriminating." Violet, the narrator of "Playin With Punjab," matter-of-factly elaborates on the dangers of naively accepting favors from a loan shark. The sisters in "The Johnson Girls" discuss the ins and outs of men and relationships. The ages and interests of the narrators, however, are not the defining qualities of these stories; instead, this is a collection about individuals discovering their connections to other generations, to other people, to their communities. It is, in a sense, a group of stories that celebrates coming-of-age, while dramatically extending the reader's ideas about what that term means. These are stories of beginnings and of upbeat revelations experienced at all stages of life.

The freshness of voice and perspective that characterizes *Gorilla, My Love* is still present in Bambara's second collection, *The Sea Birds Are Still Alive,* but Bambara's experiences between the publication of *Gorilla, My Love* in 1972 and the appearance of *The Sea Birds Are Still Alive* in 1977 significantly changed the thematics that define the second collection. Bambara made two influential trips during this period, one to Cuba in 1973 and one to Vietnam in 1975. During her travels she met with several groups dedicated to improving the position of women, including the Federation of Cuban Women and the Women's Union in Vietnam. Bambara was deeply affected by the ability of the Cuban women to transcend color and class issues in their dealings with one another and was perhaps even more impressed that, despite the turmoil of Vietnamese politics, women there were fighting to re-imagine traditional gender roles in their culture. Bambara's reassessment of the potential for social activism during this period was also spurred by experiences within the United States. Seeking a new perspective, Bambara left New York City, where she had lived most of her life, and moved to the South in 1974, relocating to Atlanta, where she helped to found the Southern Collective of African-American Writers.

Given Bambara's experiences in the 1970s, it is not surprising that *The Sea Birds Are Still Alive* focuses more on community and less on the individual, or that its stories are set around the world from one another, instead of around the block. While settings and motives change, however, reviewers noted that characters stay essentially the same; as Margo Jefferson remarked in a review in *Newsweek* (2 May 1977): "As in her previous volume . . . Her people are edgy adolescents, fast-talking the adult world into manageable proportions; grandparents determined to wield the power and shun the pathos of old age; young women and men who formed their political convictions in the fury of the '60s and find themselves grasping for air in the torpor of the '70s; manicurists, singers and students struggling to trim the rhetoric of their wishes to the smaller, tighter fit of reality." Nevertheless, this collection received mixed reviews, in part because the unrestrained optimism of *Gorilla, My Love* is replaced here by a sensibility of limitations and an understanding of the difficulty of effecting real change. The language, too, shifts in this volume, from the rich dialect of *Gorilla, My Love* to a more measured diction.

The first two stories, set in the United States, illustrate this multilevel shift in tone. In "The Organizer's Wife," Virginia, who has always felt trapped in her small, rural southern town, has married an activist and political organizer in hopes of leaving with him. Instead, she finds herself alone when he is imprisoned for "disturbing the peace." The plot of the story centers around her encounter with the minister who has allowed the church board to sell the land on which the local co-op, her husband's greatest hope, is situated. Torn between exhilaration that the loss of the co-op will leave them free to go and anger that the minister was willing to sell out the town's only hope in order to maintain "order," she finds herself attacking the minister verbally and physically. In the last scene, Virginia is making plans to stay in the town and to take up the work her husband left off. The garden she had resented all her life becomes a symbol of possibility and independence for her: "She sure as hell was going to keep up the garden. How else to feed the people?" As with many stories in *Gorilla, My Love,* this one ends on a note of optimism, but it is an optimism tempered by violence, upheaval, and the loss of treasured dreams; at the same time, it demonstrates the need for political action in the face of ceaseless tyranny.

"The Apprentice" relies on many of the same themes. The story opens with the narrator and a friend, Naomi, stopping their car when they see a police officer frisking a black man. As Naomi asks briskly and professionally whether she can contact anyone on the black man's behalf, the narrator sits in their car, noting that if the officer were really looking for a stolen car, it made no sense that he had left the registration papers for the man's car on the hood, instead of checking on them by police radio. Naomi's insistence on getting involved stands in contrast with the narrator's mild reluctance; as the narrator notes, "Naomi assumes everybody wakes up each morning plotting out exactly what to do to hasten the revolution. If you mention to her, for example, that you are working on a project or thinking about going somewhere or buying something, she'll listen enthusiastically waiting for you to get to the point, certain that it will soon all be revealed if she is patient. Then you finish saying what you had to say, and she shrugs–'But how does that free the people?'" Once again, this is a story told from the point of view of someone who is already tired, who is already somewhat disheartened, who knows that the revolution has not yet begun, and who knows that she will need all her strength when it does begin.

The title story of the collection, "The Sea Birds Are Still Alive," illustrates the need for political action, but rather than depicting revolutionary work in progress in the United States, the story is instead set in southeast Asia, on a boat loaded with Vietnamese natives and Western foreigners, with the characters eyeing one another with suspicion and making their own plans for the future of Vietnam. A collage of vignettes, "The Sea

Birds Are Still Alive" addresses not the revolution itself, but its aftermath and the dilemmas it produces for those affected by it. Like the larger collection, this story works through a juxtaposition of images, letting the reader see from the perspective of the old woman spitting betel juice at the shoes of the wealthy American businessman; of the businessman admiring a little girl feeding the gulls; of a woman whose life had been training children for the front; of a woman who has been tortured, and who, when she was released from the prison camp and given food, fed the food to the gulls in the expectation that they would die of poison.

After the publication of *The Sea Birds Are Still Alive,* Bambara turned to work in other genres. In 1980 she published her first novel, *The Salt Eaters,* which won the American Book Award and the Langston Hughes Society Award in 1981. Later that same year, Bambara was given a National Endowment for the Arts Literature Grant. Much of her time during the 1980s was dedicated to moviemaking, a genre she had favored since her theater work two decades before, and she produced almost-yearly movies for video and television until 1988. Her work on the television documentary *The Bombing of Osage Avenue* (1986), for which she wrote the script and narrated, earned her the Best Documentary Award from the Pennsylvania Association of Broadcasters and a Documentary Award from the National Black Programming Consortium, both in 1986. She participated in writing a book with Julie Dash and Bell Hooks about the making of the motion picture *Daughters of the Dust,* which Dash directed; both the motion picture and the book appeared in 1992.

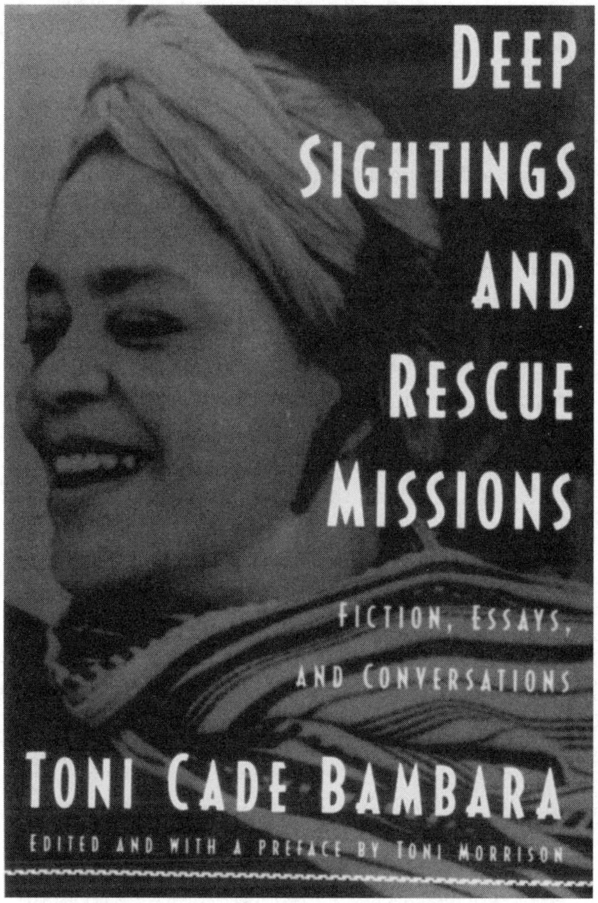

Dust jacket for Bambara's 1996 book, a posthumously published collection that includes stories in which characters deal with death

Early in 1993 Toni Cade Bambara was diagnosed with colon cancer. During a brief remission in 1994 she told Massiah that her diagnosis did not surprise her: "For several years I had been stuck–spiritually, financially, psychically, physically. Finally my intestines were blocked. I knew I had been blocked because I couldn't feel my spirit guides around me. . . . I knew that I had cancer. So when the doctor told me I had cancer, I already knew." Soon after the interview, the cancer recurred, and Toni Cade Bambara died 9 December 1995. After her death several of her remaining unpublished works were gathered by her daughter, Karma, and her lifelong friend and editor Toni Morrison, in the collection *Deep Sightings and Rescue Missions,* which comprises six short stories, the 1994 Massiah interview, and essays about movies and literature. Morrison also edited *Those Bones Are Not My Child* (1999), an unfinished novel.

The stories from *Deep Sightings and Rescue Missions* are distinct from Bambara's earlier work, as one would expect given the long hiatus between publications. Overall these are powerful pieces, dealing straightforwardly with cancer and death, chaos and disruption. Although these stories were probably written over the entire eighteen-year period between the publication of *The Sea Birds Are Still Alive* and Bambara's death, they address issues raised by her final years and her illness, while also including the themes of community, intergenerational connections, and communication that characterize the earlier short-story collections. "Going Critical" is the lead story in this volume and most directly deals with Bambara's situation before her death. In the piece, a mother, Clara, is dying of cancer because she had been exposed to radiation by the United States government during nuclear-bomb tests. Now, on the verge of winning a suit against the government, she is also near death, and, more important to her, she sees her adult daughter, Honey, headed toward personal disaster. As she walks on the beach with Honey, Clara tries to articulate what she wants to say: "And she still did not altogether know what it was. When my time comes, Honey, release me 'cause I've got work to do yet? Watch yourself and try not to be pulled off of the path by your in-laws? Develop the gifts, girl, and try to push at least one life in the direction of resurrection?"

A second story, "Ice," picks up similar themes of intergenerational connections being renewed by the threat of death. In the story a group of children in a poor neighborhood watches over a litter of puppies during a winter so cold that their parents are burning books and dollhouses to warm their families. When the children save the puppies from a mean watchdog, only to find them frozen to death in a puddle after they return home from school, they blame their parents for not stepping forward to do something: "None of the grown-ups can look us kids in the face because of the puppies. They must have been squealing in the cold . . ." As the children bury the puppies in the frozen woods, they see Mrs. Blue, "the crazy old lady" of the neighborhood, watching them from her porch. Some of the children ridicule her; some are pitying. The narrator of the story is thoughtful. After considering the winter, her own pain when her dollhouse was burning, and the deep-down hurt of seeing the dead puppies, she thinks about what she will tell her children about this winter when she is old. The answer leads her to compassion:

> But what if my kids notice there's a hole in the story, I ask myself, a hole I will fall right through in the telling. Suppose they ask, "But Mommy, didn't you go see about the old lady?" So then I'll tell them how I put my boots back on and put them silly pot-holder mittens on too to carry one of Aunt Myrtle's casseroles down to Mrs. Blue. And with the moon pushing at my back, I'm thinking that maybe I'll sit with Mrs. Blue a while even though she is a spooky sort of person.

This kind of connection between old age and youth, between heritage and the future, and between members of the black community was one of the goals that Bambara strived for throughout her life and career. Although she moved away from short stories after the 1970s, her early collections provide some of the clearest examples of the way her writing intersected with her desire to improve and support the African American community. Bambara's works reflect both the power of her voice and the insistence of her activism. Her stories are both a revelation about the period during which she wrote and a call to action that is still as valid as it was when these works were first published.

Interviews:

Claudia Tate, "Toni Cade Bambara," in *Black Women Writers at Work,* edited by Tate (New York: Continuum, 1983), pp. 12–38;

Justine Tally, "Not About to Play It Safe: An Interview With Toni Cade Bambara," *Revista Canaria de Estudios Ingleses,* 11 (November 1985): 141–153;

Louis Massiah, "How She Came by Her Name," in Bambara's *Deep Sightings and Rescue Missions: Fiction, Essays, and Conversations* (New York: Pantheon, 1996).

References:

Elliott Butler-Evans, *Race, Gender, and Desire: Narrative Strategies in the Fiction of Toni Cade Bambara, Toni Morrison, and Alice Walker* (Philadelphia: Temple University Press, 1989);

Nancy D. Hargrove, "The Comic Sense in the Short Stories of Toni Cade Bambara," *Revista Canaria de Estudios Ingleses,* 11 (November 1985): 133–140;

Lois F. Lyles, "Time, Motion, Sound and Fury in *The Sea Birds Are Still Alive,*" *College Language Association Journal,* 36 (December 1992): 134–144;

Martha M. Vertreace, "Toni Cade Bambara: The Dance of Character and Community," in *American Women Writing Fiction: Memory, Identity, Family, Space,* edited by Mickey Pearlman (Lexington: University Press of Kentucky, 1989), pp. 155–166.

Robert Bausch

(18 April 1945 –)

Richard E. Lee
State University of New York College at Oneonta

BOOKS: *On the Way Home* (New York: St. Martin's Press, 1982);
The Lives of Riley Chance (New York: St. Martin's Press, 1984);
Almighty Me (Boston: Houghton Mifflin, 1991);
How to Write with a Savage Pen (New York: American Heritage Publishers, 1994);
The White Rooster and Other Stories (Layton, Utah: Gibbs Smith, 1995).

OTHER: "George Garrett's Military / Army Stories," in *To Come Up Grinning: A Tribute to George Garrett,* edited by Paul Ruffin and Stuart White (Huntsville: Texas Review Press, 1989), pp. 8–11.

SELECTED PERIODICAL PUBLICATION–UNCOLLECTED: "ESSAY: Happy Endings." *Folio: A Literary Journal* (Winter 1987–1988): 58–62.

Robert Bausch (photograph by JoAnn Macri; from the dust jacket for The Lives of Riley Chance, *1984)*

The author of three novels and one collection of short fiction, Robert Bausch writes deft narratives that invite examination, refuse easy answers, and embrace a universalist vision of the human condition. All of his fiction interrogates the ways in which individuals, especially men, struggle with their inability to sustain the only fine thing in their lives: their authentic connections to family as an anchor. His ambivalence about the paradox of order powers his work: human beings live under the thumbs of systems and institutions that crush their spirits; yet, they require order and ritual lest they fragment into solipsism. Bausch's short fiction is especially luminous; in it he tends to avoid direct thematic statement in favor of suggestion and implication. In the stylistic tradition of Ernest Hemingway, Sherwood Anderson, and John Cheever, Bausch presents deceptively simple narratives in which little of major moment occurs. In the narrative tradition of Henry James, and perhaps Raymond Carver, he tends to focus on character development more than plot. He establishes a matrix within which his characters must exist–usually a tacit, mainstream one that the reader supplies.

In the aesthetic tradition of the modernists, Bausch tends toward stories that lead up to, but do not detail, the crossroads that his protagonists approach. Each story throws a spotlight upon a seminal moment of potential epiphany, though seldom are the characters aware of the threshold they are about to cross. His stories, each direct and clean as a chilling wind, examine pettiness, pretension, the smugness of contemporary middle-class existence in America, the inconsequentiality of individuals, and human beings' insistent will to ignore the grim futility of their lives. Irony and juxtaposition are the keys to his narrative style, as fragmentation–with a subtle weave of the possibility of completeness through faith–is the stylistic touchstone. Bausch celebrates being human at the same instant that he sketches the emotionally fractured characters who point up the human capacity to delude onself about even the most important things and people in one's life.

Robert Charles Bausch was born 18 April 1945 in Fort Benning, Georgia, to businessman Robert Carl and Helen Simmons Bausch. His identical twin, Richard Bauscher, is also a writer, and they have four other siblings. The family moved to Washington, D.C., in 1947 and then to Silver Spring, Maryland, when he was five. The family moved to Virginia shortly after the twins graduated from high school. Robert and his brother Richard enlisted in the Air Force in August 1965; he was discharged in 1969, and he married Gerri Marrese on 21 March of the following year. Bausch left the service a sergeant, having been, among other things, an instructor of survival tactics–practical experience that found its way into his first novel, *On the Way Home* (1982). Bausch now lives in Virginia with his second wife, Denny, whom in a January 1998 conversation with Richard E. Lee he called "the spiritual source of most of the work I have done since *On the Way Home*." Of his four children, Suzanne, Sara Hadley, Julie Ann, and David, his son from his second marriage, Bausch said,

> I loved every year of my children–I have a thirteen-year-old son, the last child, that I still go fishing almost every day with, and hunting whenever we can–but between 1 and 7 is so powerfully exquisite, so fulfilling and absolutely wondrous, no wonder some people can't stop at four, like I did. I wish I had eight now. I've been a daddy all my life, and I really don't know what I'll do when my son leaves for college. It will be the strangest feeling in the world. No one becoming in my house; no one learning the world. . . .

It is the issue of "becoming," of "learning the world," which is often at the core of his short fiction. Many, if not all, of his protagonists are at a liminal crux, an experiential doorway, which will redefine their awareness of themselves as acting agents in their dealings with the world.

Bausch's formal education has included time at the University of Illinois (1967–1968), Northern Virginia College (1970–1972), and George Mason University, where he received his bachelor of arts degree in 1974 and his master of arts degree in English the following year. He has been an instructor of creative writing at the Woodbridge Campus of Northern Virginia Community College since 1975. Additionally, he has lectured and taught at George Mason University, the University of Virginia, and Johns Hopkins University. He teaches as many as sixteen courses a year, six each semester and four during the summer. His commitment to teaching–to the "learnings of the world" of which students partake–is quite obviously the engine that drives his life and is just as obviously of a piece with his love of his children. On teaching and writing, Bausch remarked in a *Contemporary Authors* (volume 109, 1983) interview that

> I began writing when I was in the eighth grade, wrote steadily (and loved it best–I've not felt since as excited about writing as I did then) until my high school English teachers (who meant well, I'm sure) convinced me (by correcting my writing rather than responding to it) that I had nothing of any importance to say. . . . I started writing again in the service–when I went to funerals three to five times a month (and more frequently as the Vietnam War unraveled)–and have continued to write ever since. . . . I am more a teacher than a writer, since I derive as much satisfaction out of a good job there, and since I devote more of my time to teaching than writing.

Although Bausch refuses to make a connection between his life and his writing, saying in the *Contemporary Authors* interview that "Writing is totally separate and by itself and doesn't seem to be influenced by things–crises, horrors, games, shows, or picnics–in my life," he is perhaps being a bit disingenuous. The themes, tropes, and motifs that concern him, though divorced from the mundane concerns of his life, are woven throughout by his conception of himself as a teacher, a husband, a father, and a Roman Catholic. Indeed, the seemingly innocuous comment about his funeral attendance during the Vietnam War era is a Bausch trademark: misdirection in the service of insulation. The best of his characters wrap themselves in humble ritual and seek to mitigate their egos. As Bausch relates in his 1989 essay, "George Garrett's Military / Army Stories,"

> When I was in the military, circumstances I would rather not divulge led a very "thoughtful" commanding officer to consider me a "prime recipient" of the squadron's appointment as designated "volunteer" for the funeral squad. . . . this fellow believed it would do me good to be a first hand witness to the "great cost" of the "abatoir" of Vietnam. I spent two and a half years going to funerals. The honor squads from our base were responsible for every military funeral within a thousand mile radius of Chicago . . . One of the ways I insulated myself from this daily ritual of practiced respect and counterfeit grief was to read.

This issue of "insulation" from the occasional confrontations with reality is a cornerstone of his fiction. Each of his characters superimposes a world of ritualized order as a template over the seeming chaos of actuality. Further, his characters historicize their lives to create structure and controllable memory where before there had been ungainly reality. As the prodigal daughter

Nicky remarks about her father in the short story "Family Lore": "It is as though seeing him as he actually is destroys something essential and gentle in my memory." Yet, faith in the shields they wield will carry some of his more self-aware protagonists to a place where faith is rewarded and a more legitimate memory is secure. It is not that ignorance is bliss, but rather that those who attempt to see essential truths, through the Christian eyes of forbearance, will be rewarded with a sense of balance, if not a final sense of comfort.

Commenting on the tendency of critics to dismissively categorize his writing as "depressing," Bausch has written in his "ESSAY: Happy Endings," published in *Folio: A Literary Journal* (Winter 1987–1988), "And now when people ask me why I write depressing books, I can answer that I don't. I write books that confront life as realistically and honestly as I can. I write about the same things writers have always written about . . . Things which mean something more than simply what happens in the end." His work on his novels has informed his short fiction with a density that often confounds a reading that seeks out stories as disposable commodities, to be read once and then discarded. Indeed, his novels often overtly treat themes that the short fiction addresses more obliquely and suggestively.

His published novels treat issues of authoritarianism, forgiveness, faith, and other concerns that are inextricable from the weave of his short fiction. The novels also squarely deal with cultural and societal structures, norms, and expectations, especially the impact of institutions and movements (such as patriotism, feminism, capitalism, and the role of Catholic faith in everyday life). His novels tend toward macrocosmic and historical structures, while the short fiction presents lives lived in interstitial spaces. In other words, the short fiction presents "spots in time" while the novels paint panoramically.

His first published novel, *On the Way Home,* concerns the return of Michael Sumner to his family after being reported dead in Vietnam. His parents have left their Chicago home and relocated to Florida after getting the news of his supposed death in an attempt to leave behind the memories of Michael's presence. Ironically, when he escapes from imprisonment in a POW camp and returns to his family, the absence of a familiar geography serves to increase the disoriented Michael's difficult readjustment to civilian life. The father figure–an important leitmotif in all of Bausch's work–is a retired police officer unable to cope with a son who does not react predictably and to whom seemingly nothing physical has happened. The father's inability to control the patterns of life around him as easily as he schedules his fishing trips eventually undermines his relationships with son, wife, and self; the recognition that order is merely an imposition on the randomness of reality is a terrifying counterpoint to the disordered perceptions and fragmented narrative the reader glimpses in Michael's mind. Since the violence foreshadowed throughout the novel does not come to pass, the reader is thrown back on analyzing the themes of self-deception, the family romance, and the uncomfortable unwillingness of "real" life to simulate narrative structure.

Bausch's second novel, *The Lives of Riley Chance* (1984), underscores another motif prevalent in his short fiction: the futility of attempts at bridging the gap between cause and effect, of predicting the consequences of one's actions. The novel opens with a quotation from a play by August Strindberg: "Life is not so mathematically idiotic as only to permit the big to eat the small." In other words, the clean connection cherished in modern, sound-bite driven culture between (simple) cause and (explained) event is rarely an authentic interpretation of any structure of reality. As the novel begins, Riley Chance is being interviewed regarding the strangulation of a woman in a cab, during this, his third reincarnation. He has, in fact, seen a movie of his "first death," when he fell from a dirigible, and this movie sparks a remembrance of past lives and begins the trouble that leads to his interrogation. His previous lives are emblematic of the law of unintended consequences, as his first attempt at redressing a wrong–murdering a man who was tormenting his sister–ends in his father's arrest for the crime. Significantly, his father is a heroic factory worker and union organizer during the late nineteenth century and Riley is, in this life, a ten-year-old boy–irony requires that innocent motives result in dire consequences.

His memory of his second life concerns the theft of alms from a Catholic church poor box during the Great Depression and the philosophical question of the greater good; again a young boy, Riley steals money from the church to comfort a poor neighbor, then discovers that the pauper has already been stealing regularly from the alms box. "Maybe you can't get living right," Riley opines; "maybe it's only a little love you need to keep you from fever and fret." But Riley's "feel-good pop-psychology," which Carol Verderese in her review of the novel for *The New York Times* (13 May 1984) called "one of the few false . . . notes" in the novel, is misdirection. The narrative thrust is more grim and gnostic, revealed in the quotations that open the second and third parts: "Earth is the place for expiation of old and forgotten sins," a Hindu saying, and "This world, this theatre of pride and wrong / Swarms with sick fools who talk of happiness . . . ," a quotation from Voltaire.

Dust jacket for Bausch's 1995 book, a collection of ten stories written over a period of twenty-two years

Riley's third incarnation involves the poignant recognition that life is often a sum of unchosen options; Riley's depression over a friend's lack of faith and subsequent suicide examines the thesis of faith and Blaise Pascal's notion that a good gambler's belief in an afterlife is logical and theologically relevant. As Verderese observed in her review, referring to the frame-narrative interrogation about the death of the woman in the taxicab, "That he was actually trying to fulfill her [the woman's] last dying wish is one of the many ironies in Riley's lives." The cab driver incorrectly suspects Riley of killing the woman, spurring the interrogation in the frame narrative. Episodes detailing the ironic outcomes of well-intentioned–often feeble, rarely altruistic–actions are also to be found in the shorter fiction.

Almighty Me (1991), Bausch's third novel, concerns the cosmically ironic actions of a car salesman who is given the powers of God for one year. The novel points to the possibility that Catholic doctrine twines and weaves its way, subtly, throughout the short fiction, but openly in the novels. Bausch's treatment of the rituals and trappings of Roman Catholicism in *The Lives of Riley Chance* is additionally relevant to a study of the short fiction because of the many asides and glancing allusions he makes throughout his short-story collection, *The White Rooster and Other Stories* (1995). For example, in "The Perfect Prayer" a little girl unsuccessfully prays to the Holy Ghost to save her dying father; the obnoxious Uncle Phil in "Family Lore" learned to argue the law from the Jesuits at Loyola University. The wayward son of "The White Rooster" declares himself "no longer a Catholic" after the suicide of his first wife. Given Bausch's loose way with geographical settings and detail (many stories are set, like "Vigilance" and "Wakefulness," in some ubiquitous suburban tract), perhaps the mention of Maryland as the site of one of the other remembrances in "Family Lore" is not innocuous. In fact, a soft allusion to the Virgin Mary surfaces in almost half of the ten stories, with character names such as Mary (the wife in "Wakefulness), Marie (Nicky's dead mother in "Family Lore"), Maury (the uncle in "The Perfect Prayer"), and two major, if supporting, characters named only Mother (in "Stag Party" and "The Perfect Prayer"). The Catholic ideas of confession and catharsis are at the center of several stories, notably "Wakefulness" and "The Cougar." Indeed, the first and last tales of the collection, "The Cougar" and "The White Rooster," provide a frame for the parable of the Prodigal Son–a tale central to Catholicism and woven into most of the stories by way of the organizing principle of forgiveness for all, and forbearance especially for the weakest.

The short fiction collected in *The White Rooster and Other Stories* represents writing done over a period of some twenty-two years, and the presentation of character at its most vulnerable unites the stories in the collection. The five men, four women, and a young girl who are at the centers of the ten stories in *The White Rooster and Other Stories* are presented at moments that will force them to wrestle with the reality of the necessary deceptions by which their fragile lives proceed. The crucial moment that will strip bare the protagonist, although announced in each story, is sometimes outside the actual narrative structure of the piece, which is consistent with the modernist aesthetic that the actual crisis point be exterior to the unraveling of the plot. Bausch also varies the degree of awareness he allows his characters in the first-person narratives of "Family Lore," "Stag Party," and "The Perfect Prayer," as well as in the third-person narrations that dominate the book.

The major characters of the stories are like the segments of an orange: each protagonist is depicted in terms of his or her relationship to a familial structure (or attempts to re-create a familial structure); the solidity of the family connection is tested; the segmented individual is presented as a solitary piece. But the orange/family is still there to refer to as a totalizing possibility, completing the individual. All the protagonists share a lumpen, white, middle-class suburban background with stereotypical goals and expectations. The class status of each of the actors in the stories is relevant to the alienation each will experience. For example, characters who are successful economically (such as the uncles in "Family Lore") are alienated from the potential for personal fulfillment. In the same way that the characters seek order, so the ordering of the stories in the collection matters–the first and last tales create a frame, and the rest ironize core concepts by juxtaposition and repetition.

In the opening story of the collection, "Cougar," a stockbroker named Tom Mays verges on mental collapse as he travels alone from his American hometown to the lake where he has spent so many family vacations. His blurted lie to the avuncular camp owner–that he and his wife are going to be divorced–exposes the fragility of all the webs of relationships that had sustained him. A significant detail, related to the issue of what work one does and who one is, is that the father here, Tom Mays, fancies himself a poet. "Family Lore," the next story, concerns a distanced but loving daughter's recognition of her father's fragile sense of self in relation to his overbearing older brothers. Here again a lie, the father's self-serving use of a family anecdote about an "encore fish" and the daughter's uncomfortable awareness of her father's deception, is at the center. The narrator's father, younger brother to an overbearing lawyer, has appropriated a story in which he tricks his older brother by placing the same fish on a hook several times. This appropriation gives the narrator's father a sense of status within his family. Yet, the narrator recognizes that her father was the butt of the practical joke, not the initiator. The theme of authoritarianism, manifested by individuals' attempts to reconstruct the past on their own terms as they attempt to control the world around them, is one of the three great themes that resound throughout these stories.

The next story is "The Stag Party," which Bausch began writing in 1975, rewriting it into its final form only in 1987. A first-person narrative, "The Stag Party" follows a lonely young man–four years after his doting mother's death–as he attends an American Legion striptease show with an acquaintance, a vaguely disreputable former co-worker of his late mother. The narrator's interpretation of the salacious event is juxtaposed with those of the frenzied, drooling drunks (including the acquaintance) as he causes a near riot by trying to rescue one of the strippers. The second of Bausch's organizing tropes surfaces here. As his chivalric attempts to rescue a stripper who is being pawed by the crowd are rejected (she calls him a "sad little freak"), and as he sits under arrest in the back of a squad car after being pummeled by the angry crowd, the narrator muses, "I cannot say, even now, what I was afraid of. I looked for the stripper in the crowd, and discovered in my simmering terror that I felt inconsolably sad for all of them: the strippers, Bennet, and the veterans of the Great War. I loved and forgave them all." This acceptance of human frailty, and the beneficence of forgiveness, is an organizing principle throughout Bausch's fiction. A practicing Hindu might refer to this principle as the interconnectedness of all living things; a good Catholic would point out that it recalls the recognition of Christ within every person.

"Vigilance" features the cliché of the policeman who is a criminal; as the first suspect in all arsons should be the first firefighter on the scene, so should the first suspects of burglaries that benefit the paranoid establishment of neighborhood watches be the leaders of the watch group. The twin motifs of the shallowness of self-perception and the unreliability of human beings' visions of themselves are insinuated here. This narrative is one in which the protagonist is blithely unaware of the shining epiphany that he will experience but not register–reading it is a bit like watching a car crash in which the passengers are asleep. The focus of the narrative, a retired cop, is exposed to the reader in all his alienated glory in the first paragraph.

> Cochran was bored, approaching forty. He lived alone in a neighborhood called Nottingham Estates. That was how his life had turned out. Until recently, he would have said he was a confirmed bachelor, living the high life of a single man with means. But lately he had begun to wonder if it was worth it, having nothing to lose and no one to depend on him. . . . He felt useful trying to establish a neighborhood watch.

His fury at the lack of attendance at his first meeting, which he had obsessively organized, leads him to send out a questionnaire with confrontational and insulting questions such as, "Do you care at all about the safety of your loved ones? Yes___No___" and, "Do you want your child to be kidnapped? Yes___No___." The plot develops around the burglary and the loose family group Cochran co-opts to generate community fervor for his project.

"The One Thing in Life" details the tensions between a married couple as they pirouette around one another, replacing communication with assumption. Told from the point of view of a woman determined to become pregnant (artificially) before her biological clock ticks down, this story revisits the control theme begun in "Family Lore." It also introduces, obliquely, the third major organizing theme: the "duties of love" and the importance of magic or faith, dreams, and goals in the otherwise chartless wastes of human lives. The protagonist, Joan, wrestles with herself in dreams during the fruitless period of her attempts at natural conception, envisioning herself as a Russian doll, with smaller versions revealed within. "And then she would struggle against a wild, blue wind, and the powerful resistance of the dream's logic, trying to sink down into herself and get to the doll inside, while the doll, mirroring every move of her outer body, tried to do the same, and the dream disintegrated; collapsed like elaborate, intricately formed ash." Here, too, is an attempt to place a template over chaos. Intriguingly, this passage continues by investigating Joan's reflection on the dream itself:

> She would wake from these dreams without fear. They were not nightmares until she was fully awake and discovered herself lying in bed, listening to Biggs breathing next to her, and then she was overtaken by a cold, senseless apprehension that everything in her whole life and memory was as hollow and fragile as the dream . . . and there was nothing in front of her; nothing in her future except an older, more limited, and less comfortable version of herself.

The primary stylistic and syntactic structures Bausch uses are evident in this passage. When Bausch allows the reader access to the interior monologues of his characters, these often come in long strings of almost stream-of-consciousness sentences, as in the long second sentence of the quotation. Bausch's syntactic signature is a dependent clause after a semicolon; his consistent use of this structure, and of the sentence fragment, serves both to replicate the rhythms of speech–he is deft in his treatment of dialogue throughout–and to highlight the fragmented nature of the perceptions and connections of the characters about whom he writes.

That irony and juxtaposition are the keys to the ordering of the stories in the collection is nowhere more evident than in the cascade of fractured families and dreams unfulfilled that tumble through "Perfection," "Wakefulness," "The Perfect Prayer," and "The Hairpiece." After the aching would-be mother of Joan in "The One Thing in Life" comes the gloating self-satisfaction of the perfect homemaker Judy Flynn, in "Perfection," "who dreamed of being Judy Flynn for most of her teen years and therefore saw her marriage as a kind of achievement." She "was sometimes troubled by the perfection in her life," the brand-new home, the two ideal children, the focused and loving husband of eight happy years: "Sometimes she longed for just one minor, insoluble problem so that her life might be slightly complicated." Unbeknownst to Judy, as she regularly and vocally hugs herself in contentment–abrading the nerves of all in earshot as she sings the praise song of her life–her electrician husband is dead. The story takes place in the gap between his electrocution at work and her notification of his death. As a counterpoint to the unanswered request in "The Perfect Prayer," Judy gets her "insoluble problem." The reader is set up to anticipate her reaction, but that expectation is deflated halfway through the story with clinical detachment: "if Marv had been electrocuted earlier in the marriage, before they had achieved perfection, before they had purchased the new house, and before Randy had been born, Judy might have found the strength she needed to endure the loss." As in the case of Joan in "The One Thing in Life," it is not merely the spouse who matters for security–indeed, sanity–but the idea of the spouse mythologized. Marriage is never celebrated: what is suggested is that solitariness is not the answer to human growth. Life requires that one seeks to avoid solipsism.

Judy Flynn's fate, and the throwaway manner in which it is related, proves again the facility of Bausch's use of misdirection and of the danger of building narrative expectations. Judy is like the reader who comes to expect something specific from a text and is disturbed by its refusal to stick to a desired script. Anticipated outcomes rarely emerge; the law of unintended consequences, so eloquently developed in the novels, is here introduced obliquely: "As it was, she sank into the sort of grief and depression that evolves into a way of life. In the years that followed, nothing very good happened to Judy. . . . she never got over the beauty of her house in Lee's Crossing Estates and the wonderful, exquisite life she had lived there."

Judy's halcyon memories of her life in the protection of Lee's Crossing Estates, falsely remembered or not, are not the point of the story. Nor is the point the cliché that pride goes before a fall. Rather, the confuting of standard narrative expectation (as in *On the Way Home*) refocuses the reader on the life of quiet desperation Judy pursues, evidenced by the pathological intensity Judy betrays, with no one now watching and no knowledge, yet, of the fate of her husband, as she struggles to recover a spoon that has fallen out of reach between counter and stove in her dream home. Furthermore, the story itself occurs within one of those interstices–between the plates of "real" history–that perhaps define short fiction as a genre in opposition to the novel. Perhaps the spoon between the counter and stove may be seen as a stand-in for short fiction itelf, as Judy unwittingly waits for history to catch up with her with the news of her husband's death.

The next story, "Wakefulness," exposes the black heart at the core of suburban co-existence, as the smug civility of neighborly nods gives way to voyeurism and emotional torture. Jameson, an appliance-store manager nearing sixty, intrudes upon the mind and memories of

Lang, an elderly neighbor who owns dogs that bark incessantly. As Jameson, increasingly aware of his avoidance of the fact of his growing senescence, regresses to adolescent torture of his solitary neighbor (making "silent" phone calls late at night, eliciting hints of Lang's troubled relationship with his alienated son, Bobby), he comes unpleasantly close to an awareness of the epiphany:

> Something far down in his memory began to weep. And then he was warm again, in the light of his own house, being admired by his mother and father as he had always been. . . . He awoke to what he realized was silence. . . . The new snow saddened him. It came down like memory, softly and in silence under the streetlights. He would not have been able to put into words what he was feeling. The night seemed the very start of the end of something.

At this moment, at the close of the story that summons also the close of his life, Jameson comes as near as any of Bausch's characters will to a full recognition of the gnawing poignancy that is self-awareness. The leitmotif of memory construction (first observed in "Family Lore"), and of the human tendency to narratize past events so that they serve the innocent needs of self-deception, resurfaces here:

> And yet, in the midst of his profound sadness–a sadness very much like grief–he felt both cruel and divine. The sights and sounds, the feelings and impressions of all his days came back to him now as though only a vague memory of a lost dream. He remembered his own absent children, who were other people now and rarely called. . . . And time. The strange passage of time.

The eighth story in the collection, "The Perfect Prayer," concerning the little girl who prays to the Holy Ghost for her father to get off the couch in the parlor where he is too ill to play with her, presents another juxtaposition. The narrative tension in this story, in contrast to the epiphanic moment of introspection/retrospection that Jameson experiences in "Wakefulness," stems from a deferred moment. The eight-year-old narrator of "The Perfect Prayer" dreams of her father's death but asks for the intercession of the Holy Ghost–often symbolized as a white dove: "I place my hands just right again. I picture the Holy Ghost, and whisper in my soul, 'Please, if you wouldn't mind, let Daddy get well in the morning. Amen.' I say it three times. . . . I just know, in all my life, I will never again be so happy." Of course she is right; the father's death, her crashed dreams of an intercessory supernatural agent, her belief in herself as an actor in the events of her life, all these things will happen–but after the story ends. Again, as in "Perfection," history picks up again after the interlude that the focus of short fiction affords.

In the penultimate story, "The Hairpiece," a wife estranged from her step-sons deals with the death of her husband, their father. Attempting closure, and seeing the sons for who they are, she deals with each of them according to his needs. She comforts the younger, manipulative son at the funeral, although neither he nor his brother had visited his sick father: "only then did she realize how truly selfish and useless George's sons were. . . . She had been married to George for twenty-one years, and in that time she never truly escaped the feeling that they were being terrorized by his sons." Jane thinks upon reflection, " . . . she tolerated them–even hoped they might grow to like her, if only for her forbearance and patience." She forces a confrontation with the older boy to give him a toupee his father realized was too much of an affectation to wear. It is a telling totem: people seek to mold their images, yet are often blind to the real impressions they make upon others. Jane gives a glimpse of a man, the son now grown, who has allowed any sense of completeness to recede as he isolated himself from his father. As he leaves with the ridiculous hairpiece, he has "the sad, broken look of a man leaving home for the last time, carrying, in a little white box, all his earthly goods."

Bausch often uses an omniscient third-person narrative technique, but he also often refuses to explicate the consequences of his characters' confrontations. He is adept at presenting the requisite slice-of-life and insists that readers engage his stories actively. This "difficulty" provides a certain disorientation, as each seemingly simple tale requires more than the usual passivity of a reader being addressed over the heads of the characters. This presentation led Linda Rodgers in a *New York Times* review (24 December 1995) to remark that "the problem with these stories isn't their grim outlook. Instead it's their execution: endings that seem to dwindle off, without much resolution or insight; language that fails to engage." Rodgers's unsurprising inability to identify an absence (what is "language that fails to engage"?), after her acknowledgment of the fragmentary nature of the existences of the people in the collection, is summarily dismissive. The troubling lack of connectedness among the characters is an obvious thematic linkage among the stories; what is perhaps not so obvious is that the narratives themselves create a similar lack of consonance with the reader. Rodgers, astute as she is in her recognition of the essentially alienated quality of the middle-class lives of the characters throughout *The White Rooster and Other Stories,* misses a much more interesting point completely: the use of language to connect with others is doomed because of the imprecision of language itself. This metanarrative does not easily lend itself to the activities of book reviewers: Bausch likes to tell the story of the book reviewer analyzing his novel *Almighty Me* who kept referring to the author as Bausch's twin brother, Richard. Robert Bausch appreciates the irony implicit in the imprecise use of language that attempts to refer transparently but instead calls attention to itself.

However, Bausch knows, and insists that the reader also recognize, the difficulties inherent in translating experience into words; he consistently calls the reader's attention to the impossibility of true connective conversation–at the same time that he insists that even efforts doomed to failure are worth the effort as exercises in one's essential humanity. As Bausch has Jameson say in "Wakefulness": "He would not have been able to put into words what he was feeling." Lies take on the force of truth, as in "Family Lore" or, perhaps more directly, in "Cougar": "There was an awkward silence. Then Tom said, 'It's just one of those things. We're trying to work it out.' The words seemed to rush out of his mouth before he could recognize them. Each one shocked him–as though he heard himself speaking a language he had never heard . . . And just like that, Tom believed himself."

The many family rifts and unhealed scars that populate *The White Rooster and Other Stories,* the sense of memory, and of history, as re-creatable and malleable things, raise this collection into the realm of metanarrative. These are stories about what it means to make stories–the stories that power one's life are always and inevitably open to rewriting. It is appropriate that Tom in "Cougar" fancies himself a poet, a maker. The other metanarrative possibility, also suggested in "Perfection" and "The Perfect Prayer," is to view the work as an examination of short fiction as a genre. Both of these ideas are part of a larger philosophical vantage: that there are spaces, times, and ways for any individual to effect change. Whatever the doubts one may harbor as to the nature of God, life, destiny, and the other big questions, one has the possibility of (Christian) grace in the immediate choices one makes regarding interactions with others.

This sense of possibility is what slides out from underneath the facile reading of Bausch's writing that sees only "grim outlooks." The last story in the collection, the title story, functions as a capstone for the collection and also revisits the themes of the first story, "Cougar," thus providing a frame for the collection. Appropriately, the New Testament parable of the Prodigal Son, with all its sense of hope for the estranged, powers both stories, as well as at least three others; however, while Tom Mays, the successful stockbroker of "Cougar," leaves the reader with a sense that his return to his family will not settle anything between himself and his wife, the fragile rapprochement that seems possible between Morgan Huff and his son in "The White Rooster" allows the reader to hope for reconnection.

Bausch relates that he wrote the original version of "The White Rooster" in 1973, while "a sophomore in college. . . . The couple in the earlier story were young, newly married. The central problem was the rooster and what to do with it." Although the "problem" of the rooster remains, the story–like so much of his fiction–deals with complex character interactions that often refuse the simplistic satisfactions of plot resolution. The plot of "The White Rooster" is the story of the prodigal, though Morgan must be prodded into a semblance of delight at his son's return (and there is no patient brother put out by the reconciliation). A rooster crawls under the Huff's suburban house, "which was kept nearly as clean," by wife Sarah, "as Morgan kept the yard." In a displaced act of fury and disgust at the return of his son, Ernie, and his third wife, Junee ("it rhymed with *toupee,*" says the narrator, perhaps alluding to "The Hairpiece"), Morgan manages to get the bird out, puts it in a plastic bag, attaches the bag to his car's exhaust pipe, and asphyxiates it. As Morgan and Ernie circle each other emotionally, trying to determine if a reconciliation is worth the effort, the story ends with a sad, knowing nod towards a father's worst fears. They are going to dispose of the rooster's carcass together–an upbeat note–but as Morgan watches his son cross the yard to get a shovel, "Ernie moved through the blue shade like an apparition, and when he had disappeared around the house, Morgan said to himself, 'It just doesn't matter.' He knew that when he went to bed that night, when all the colors died, he would try to escape once again, in brief black sleep, the memory, the certainty, that he had never saved his son from anything." Here, again, is the mix of memory and desire so poignantly reminiscent of T. S. Eliot's *The Waste Land* (1922). But Bausch concludes with a reiteration of the necessity of wrapping randomness in ritual, of attempting to salvage dignity in the face of the maelstrom: "And for some reason he did not understand, he discovered that he was humming an idle, lost song, while still in tears, he wrapped the white rooster in the torn plastic."

The "apparition" that is Ernie is reminiscent of the ghostly specter of the cougar that haunts, but is not definitively present, in the first story in the collection and reminds the reader that the first and last tales frame all the rest. They also sum up and recapitulate the three primary organizing principles of Bausch's work, which might be termed–in recognition of the strong influence of Catholicism in Bausch's work–Father (figures of authoritarianism and illusory control), Son (patience with the weak, forbearance, and forgiveness), and Holy Ghost (the necessity of acts of faith, of a belief in the magical possibilities of life). More importantly, the resounding paradox of human reliance upon structure and ritual–though these are traps and snares–peeks through in the last line of the collection. The absurd image of a man humming a tune while wrapping a dead rooster in plastic disturbs the reader long enough to recognize that Morgan is insulating himself from the anarchy of events by encapsulating himself within a ritualized action. He is the father figure writ large, one whose attempts at control, though doomed to fail (he cannot protect his son, or any one else), are acts of will railing against a clockwork universe. Morgan keeps a "perfect yard," thereby warding off incursions from the outside world–including his son, who has broken his heart by staying away for nine years.

"The rooster could not have come from any place Morgan knew of. He and his wife Sarah lived alone in what most people would call a suburb." Magic enters their rutted lives, where Sarah cares for the hearth, while Morgan manicures Mother Nature. In "Cougar," Tom Mays leaves his family in an attempted act of re-creation, bypasses his usual refueling stop on the long drive, writes poetry instead of selling stocks, and reinforces his alienation from all rituals at the same time as he reenacts them. The Father principle in this fiction exercises authority by controlling the flow of memories, of stories, which are the stock of family structure. When Uncle Phil gets to tell the story of the "encore fish" in "Family Lore" with himself as the star (although his younger brother, Nicky's dad, had used it to show himself in a stronger light), the power and the authority of memory and narrative are made clear.

Morgan blames his son for the suicide of his first wife, but the reader knows from Bausch's novels to beware of simplistic cause-and-effect relationships. The principle of the Son requires forbearance: since one cannot know all of the subtleties of any situation, one should recognize godliness in everyone and refuse rushes to judgment. Further, one must forgive. The Huffs seek solace from a priest after the death of their beloved daughter-in-law:

> "There's two ways to look at it," Father Burns, the parish priest, said. He was nearly as old as Morgan. He was a kind, sad man who always looked as if he'd been left out of something–as if someone had thrown a party and no one had told him about it. "We each have free will, and this girl chose to die."
>
> "Yes, but why?" Morgan said.
>
> "The other way . . . the other way is not so pleasant to contemplate."
>
> "If Ernie hadn't left her, she'd still be alive."
>
> "Yes" . . . "My son killed her."
>
> The priest shook his head, but he didn't say anything. He clearly believed it too.

The priest serves several roles in this exchange: he is guilty of not being Christlike, but he is depicted as one of the self-aware. He resembles Judy Flynn, in "Perfection," whose rituals fail to satisfy, although she has achieved her dreams. He serves as a transitional thematic marker–from Father, to Son, to Holy Ghost–occupying the middle space in the story, after the narrative alert that Ernie had talked "skeptically of a 'personal God,' of the impossibility of such a thing. 'There is no God,' he said. He did not believe in anything after death, and so felt 'compelled to make this life what I want it to be.'" The transition to Father Burns immediately after this reminiscence is jarring, unless the reader considers the thematic structures of all the stories in the volume. Ernie here resembles a grown-up version of the little girl in "The Perfect Prayer," who has lost her faith after being "refused" her request. He is also reminiscent of Nicky from "Family Lore," Jameson and Lang's absent children in "Wakefulness," and the lost children–now grown–in "The Hairpiece." Father Burns comes to represent the otherwise absent spiritual center of the whole collection.

Bausch has no pious regard for priests, however. The administrators of institutions are to be avoided, if possible, though one must have faith in the potential for magic in one's life. In his 1989 essay on Garrett's military fiction, Bausch writes that the "wisdom in living . . . is learning to know the difference between things that are good and wonderful . . . and those various laws, customs, syndications and temples we have erected to honor and preserve them. Along the way, we might watch out for the guardians, the priests and enforcers, who impose the system and its order on all the willing and unwilling victims of civilization." Recognizing the conundrum presented in his fiction, he states firmly that " . . . the order is one we need; one we *must* preserve. And therein lies the most profound irony of all."

Bausch inevitably writes as a man, a father, and a Roman Catholic. He recognizes the incongruity and impossibility of human attempts at attachments to others at the precise moment he insists that one must have faith in the possibility of a complete life well lived. His writing is ironic, mordantly humorous, and refreshing.

Reference:

Elizabeth Kastor, "The Author, Giving Rise to 'Violence,'" *Washington Post,* 2 March 1992, pp. B1, B4.

Ann Beattie

(8 September 1947 –   )

Gwen Crane
State University of New York College at Oneonta

See also the Beattie entry in *DLB Yearbook: 1982.*

BOOKS: *Chilly Scenes of Winter* (Garden City, N.Y.: Doubleday, 1976);
Distortions (Garden City, N.Y.: Doubleday, 1976);
Secrets and Surprises: Short Stories (New York: Random House, 1978; London: Hamilton, 1979);
Falling in Place: A Novel (New York: Random House, 1980; London: Secker & Warburg, 1981);
Jacklighting (Worcester, Mass.: Metacom Press, 1981);
The Burning House: Short Stories (New York: Random House, 1982; London: Secker & Warburg, 1983);
Love Always: A Novel (New York: Random House, 1985; London: Joseph, 1990);
Spectacles, illustrated by Winslow Pels (New York: Ariel/Workman, 1985);
Where You'll Find Me, and Other Stories (New York: Linden Press/Simon & Schuster, 1986; London: Macmillan, 1987);
Alex Katz (New York: Abrams, 1987);
Picturing Will (New York: Random House, 1989; London: Cape, 1990);
What Was Mine: Stories (New York: Random House, 1991);
Another You (New York: Knopf, 1995);
My Life, Starring Dara Falcon (New York: Knopf, 1997);
Park City: New and Selected Stories (New York: Knopf, 1998).

PRODUCED SCRIPT: "Weekend," television, *American Playhouse,* PBS, 10 April 1982.

RECORDINGS: *Spectacles,* read by Beattie, Caedmon Audio, Cpl 1786, 1986;
Where You'll Find Me, and Other Stories, read by Beattie, Simon & Schuster, 1987;
Ann Beattie Reads: "Desire," "Learning to Fall," "Snow," "Skeletons," read by Beattie, American Audio Prose Library, 1987.

Ann Beattie (photograph by Jimm Roberts; from the dust jacket for Park City, *1998)*

OTHER: "A Biting Dog," illustrated by David Gates, in *Wonders, Writings and Drawings for the Child in Us All,* edited by Jonathan Cott and Mary Gimbel (New York: Rolling Stone, 1980), pp. 86–90;

The Best American Short Stories, 1987, edited by Beattie and Shannon Ravenel; introduction by Beattie (Boston: Houghton Mifflin, 1987);

Sally Mann, *At Twelve: Portraits of Young Women,* introduction by Beattie (New York: Aperture, 1988);

Alice Rose George, Abigail Heyman, and Ethan Hoffman, eds., *Flesh and Blood: Photographers' Images of Their Own Families,* introduction by Beattie (New York: Picture Project, 1992; Manchester: Cornerhouse, 1992);

The American Story: Short Stories from the Rea Award, edited by Beattie, Michael Rea, and others (New York: Ecco Press, 1994);

"Peter Taylor's 'The Old Forest,'" in *The Craft of Peter Taylor,* edited by C. Ralph Stephens and Lynda B. Salamon (Tuscaloosa: University of Alabama Press, 1995), pp. 105–110;

Ploughshares, special fiction issue, edited by Beattie, 21 (Fall 1995);

Mary Motley Kalergis, *With this Ring: A Portrait of Marriage,* introduction by Beattie (Norfolk, Va.: Chrysler Museum of Art, 1997).

SELECTED PERIODICAL PUBLICATIONS–UNCOLLECTED:

FICTION

"A Rose for Judy Garland's Casket," *Western Humanities Review,* 26 (Spring 1972): 147–152;

"Aunt Violet," *Washington Post Magazine,* 12 March 1978, pp. 37–42;

"Late Summer: Driving North," *Story Quarterly,* 7/8 (1978): 69–82;

"Warmer," *Washington Post Magazine,* 3 August 1980, pp. 20–29;

"Mr. B. and the Miraculous Christmas Tree," *House and Garden,* 153 (December 1981): 78, 157, 185;

"Blue," *Vogue,* 172 (April 1982): 376–377;

"Dancing," *New England Review,* 5 (Autumn-Winter 1982): 176–181;

"Moving Water," *New Yorker,* 58 (8 November 1982): 38–42;

"One Day," *New Yorker,* 59 (29 August 1983): 28–31;

"A Shaggy Love Story," *Ladies Home Journal,* 101 (June 1984): 88, 146, 148;

"On the Radio," *Harper's Magazine,* 270 (June 1985): 29–31;

"Name Day," *Antaeus,* 64–65 (Spring–Autumn 1990): 181–188;

"Such Occasions," *New England Review,* 13 (Fall 1990): 101–107;

"It's Not That I'm Lying," *Esquire,* 120 (July 1993): 77–79;

"Fireback," *Virginia Quarterly Review,* 70 (Summer 1994): 421–429;

"Coydog," *Yale Review,* 83 (April 1995): 41–55;

"Buried Treasure," *Ploughshares,* 22 (Fall 1996): 9–37.

NONFICTION

"What I'm Writing, What I'm Reading," *New York Times Book Review,* 31 May 1981, p. 3;

"Journals," *Film Comment,* 17 (September–October 1981): 2, 4;

"Grant Wood Country: A Return to the Iowa of the Famed Painter as a Dazzling Retrospective Tours the U.S.," *Life,* 6 (September 1983): 56–63;

"The Sirens' Call: Joel Meyerowitz's Photographs," *Architectural Digest,* 45 (June 1988): 40–42;

"Painterly Porcelains: Ceramicist Scott McDowell Impresses Images from Art and Nature into Clay," *House and Garden,* 162 (March 1990): 76–80;

"The Point of It All," *McCalls,* 119 (November 1991): 72–76;

"Show of Hands," *Mademoiselle,* (July 1992): 119–120;

"Where Characters Come From," *Mississippi Review,* 21 (Spring 1993): 45–50;

"The Infamous Fall of Howell the Clown," *Antaeus,* no. 75–76 (Autumn 1994): 31–48;

"Hiding Out in Mañanaland," *Preservation,* 49 (January/February 1997): 28–33;

"Stirring the Pot," *Allure,* (August 1998): 82–83;

"An Inspirational Hotel," *Attaché,* (September 1997): 23.

Ann Beattie's powerful contrast in her writing of tellingly detailed descriptions and stark silence has caused her work to be placed in the contemporary canon of literary minimalism, a movement identified by critics–not by the so-called minimalists themselves–in the 1970s. This controversial term has been applied to the different fictions of Raymond Carver, Amy Hemple, Frederick Barthelme, Bobbie Ann Mason, Tobias Wolff, and others. While some of these authors–especially Carver–remain inspirations whom Beattie admiringly acknowledges, her prolific and continually evolving work in the following decades defies categorization within any stylistic school.

Charlotte Ann Beattie was born 8 September 1947 in Washington, D.C., where she enjoyed a stable, suburban family life with her mother, Charlotte, a housewife, and her father, James, an administrator for the Department of Health, Education, and Welfare. She was an artistic child, writing stories, drawing, and reading widely with the encouragement of her parents. Utterly uninspired by the "mediocre academic programs and teachers" at Woodrow Wilson High School, she fell into an undiagnosed depression, graduating with barely passing grades in 1965. She frequently writes of children who feel and observe more acutely than their parents realize. Her autodidactic studies

DISTORTIONS
ANN BEATTIE
DISTORTIONS
ANN BEATTIE
PHOTO BY TRISHA ORR
Ann Beattie is a frequent contributor to The New Yorker and has had short stories published in such magazines as The Atlantic and Transatlantic Review. Her first novel, Chilly Scenes of Winter, is being published simultaneously with DISTORTIONS. Ms. Beattie teaches at the University of Virginia and lives with her husband in Cobham, Virginia.
DOUBLEDAY

Dust jacket for Beattie's 1976 collection of short stories, unified by their focus on disintegrating marriages

included an intense engagement with Ernest Hemingway's work, and she learned early and independently to appreciate both his darker insights and his austere code of authorial self-editing. He remains a lasting influence, as she wryly acknowledged when, after her accountant urged her to incorporate in the 1980s, she named her corporation "Irony and Pity, Inc.," drawing on a line from Jake Barnes, the protagonist of Hemingway's *The Sun Also Rises* (1926).

After earning a bachelor of arts degree at American University in 1969, Beattie began graduate work in English at the University of Connecticut. As Jaye Berman Montresor notes in the introduction to *The Critical Response to Ann Beattie* (1993), Beattie began writing stories during this period because she was "so goddamn bored" with graduate school. She received her master of arts degree in 1970, but she left the Ph.D. program in 1972 without completing her degree. Her first published story, "A Rose for Judy Garland's Casket," appeared in the *Western Humanities Review* before the year was out. Although she had to endure twenty-two rejections from *The New Yorker* magazine before her short story "A Platonic Relationship" was accepted in 1974, she soon became a regular contributor to *The New Yorker* and her work was so enthusiastically received that she swiftly became an important figure on the American literary scene. She accepted a series of prominent teaching positions: she was a visiting writer and lecturer at the University of Virginia during 1975–1977 and was the Briggs Copeland Lecturer in English at Harvard University in 1977–1978. In 1977 she was awarded a Guggenheim Fellowship. Hollywood also took notice of her work, and her novel *Chilly Scenes of Winter* (1976) was made into a motion picture by Joan Micklin Silver, retitled *Head over Heels* when it was released in 1979. Beattie had a minor role as a waitress in the movie, which failed at the box office; it was more successful after being re-edited–with a new ending–and re-released under the original title in 1982, the same year that her television-play adaptation of her short story "Weekend" aired on the Public Broadcasting System series *American Playhouse*.

In 1980 Beattie returned to the University of Virginia as a visiting writer, and she received the Award in

Literature from the American Academy and Institute of Arts and Letters; that same year she was named one of the Distinguished Alumnae of American University. Her alma mater celebrated her achievements again in 1983 by awarding her an honorary doctorate.

Her early fame would prove beneficial in eventually freeing her for full-time writing without the distractions of a salaried academic position; her notoriety would also prove irksome, however, as she attracted devotees, critics, and imitators whose admiration, envy, and occasional rancor threatened her autonomous artistic development. She would eventually make the blandishments and perils of fame central subjects in two of her novels, *Love Always* (1985), and *My Life, Starring Dara Falcon* (1997). In the 1970s Beattie drew the attention of reviewers who quickly labeled her the embodiment of the Woodstock generation, the spokesperson for the disillusioned survivors of the turbulent, idealistic 1960s. Her characters were pigeonholed as postlapsarian hippies privileged with enough education and leisure time to worry about their lost causes and new consumerism. Once labeled as the literary voice and chronicler of her disaffected, guiltily affluent contemporaries, Beattie has found the title unshakable. For example, in reviewing Beattie's short-story collection *Park City: New and Selected Stories* (1998), Lorrie Moore in *The New York Times Book Review* (28 June 1998) characterized Beattie's literary landscape as "white, educated, upper-middle-class and pharmaceutically calm–no one ever struggles convincingly at a job; inheritances are referred to in many of the stories."

While this description may apply to some of Beattie's characters, Moore ignored many of Beattie's most interesting creations: the impecunious drifters and dropouts, the overweight lingerie salesclerk, the Puerto Rican rock fan, the suicidal juvenile pyromaniac, the retarded hitchhiker, and, in "It's Just Another Day in Big Bear City, California," the extraterrestrial Scrabble-players. These vividly rendered characters all appear in Beattie's first short-story collection, *Distortions* (1976), which was published simultaneously with *Chilly Scenes of Winter*. Reviewing Beattie's body of work as a whole, Moore goes on to identify the primary subject of Beattie's work as divorce: "the precipitating event" for Beattie's stories is "the prospect and actuality of uncoupling." Certainly divorce is a prominent topic in *Distortions,* which begins and ends with portraits of marriages that will survive only by defying all odds. The collection opens with "Dwarf House," which opens in the middle of a conversation, as MacDonald visits his older brother James (who is four feet, six and three-quarter inches tall) in James' new home, a house he shares with several other dwarves and a giant. MacDonald's mother has sent him to ask James if he is happy. James responds ambiguously, denying MacDonald any easy answers, but announcing his engagement to a woman even shorter than himself. His only request is that MacDonald bring him an artificially dyed parakeet–a fittingly freakish pet for his bizarre new residence. MacDonald's guilt over his normal height is exacerbated by his lifelong resentment of his needy and hostile brother. He reports back to his mother's home, where she spends her days ruing her marriage and watching her maid struggling with an unhappy marriage of her own. The maid's husband is an alcoholic; MacDonald and his own wife seem to be drifting into alcoholism as well, anesthetizing themselves against disappointment. MacDonald flirts with the idea of adultery with his secretary as they sit in a dark bar where the jukebox plays Tammy Wynette's "D-I-V-O-R-C-E." But divorce will not help MacDonald; Betty the secretary can offer him neither redemption nor joy–only a temporary anodyne:

> "Isn't this place awful?" he says. "But the spiced shrimp are great."
> Betty smiles.
> "If you don't feel like smiling, don't smile," he says.
> "Then all the pills would be for nothing."
> "Everything is for nothing," he says.
> "If you weren't drinking, you could take one of the pills," Betty says. "Then you wouldn't feel that way."

Despite the clear evidence that none of the characters in this story have found in marriage either answers to life's questions or happiness, James and his fiancée proceed with their outdoor wedding, where a long-haired hippie minister releases James's new parakeet, dyed a brilliant green, as a symbol of "the new freedom of marriage, and of the ascension of the spirit." This wildly unlikely scene resembles one of Diane Arbus's disturbingly stark black-and-white photographic portraits of freaks–those startling portraits of grotesquely deformed, crippled, and rejected figures that were published as coffee-table books in the 1970s, and which in fact appear on a coffee table in "The Lifeguard," the final story in *Distortions,* forming a referential frame for the collection as a whole. But Beattie alleviates Arbus's grim, grainy vision with splashes of unexpected color and light. As MacDonald's wife notes, the freakish, cage-reared parakeet will probably die in its new freedom, and the marriage thus seems symbolically doomed; however, in the last lines of the story, MacDonald sees that "the bride is smiling beautifully–a smile no pills could produce–and that the sun is shining on her hair so that it sparkles. She looks small, and bright, and so lovely that MacDonald, on his knees to kiss her, doesn't want to get up." In this luminous moment, future disasters seem irrelevant. James and his bride seem to have tran-

Dust jacket for Beattie's 1978 book, which reveals the influence of Irish novelist-playwright Samuel Beckett

scended fate, to have taken responsibility for their own future happiness, even if it lasts no longer than the life of the parakeet.

The equation of transcendent flight with imaginative self-determination is a theme throughout Beattie's novels as well as her stories, as can be seen in the eponymous protagonist of Beattie's 1997 novel *My Life, Starring Dara Falcon,* which traces the tireless Dara Falcon's almost entirely imaginary career as a self-styled star of stage and screen. (Ms. Falcon's talents, it turns out, are best suited to soaring flights of off-stage fantasy.) Beattie has also used avian metaphors to describe her own experience as a writer, telling James Plath in an interview published in *Michigan Quarterly Review* in 1993 that once she knows the first sentence of a story–"then I can fly."

Beattie's refusal to adumbrate her characters' futures or to offer more details than are absolutely necessary to the stories she wants to tell, meets all the criteria critics established for literary minimalism in the 1970s, a style marked by understatement and taut prose; however, as Christina Murphy observed in her 1986 monograph on Beattie, this literary application of the term followed a much earlier usage in the plastic arts, where the focus was "upon the use of space itself as a counterpoint to line, or artistic intent. Space was perceived as a 'free' medium (one not affected by intent) and the desired effect in minimalist art was to combine intentional design with nonintentional space so that the nonintentional or 'free' medium could give greater shape, and thus more import, to the intentional aspects of a work." Beattie's lifelong involvement with the visual arts has enhanced her dramatic employment of such spacial contrasts between her stringently edited text and her equally important ellipses: "Those unstated things that happen off the page are so often what contemporary fiction is about," she observes, "They're not empty spaces–they're referential spaces." But in leaving interpretation of those "referential spaces" to her reader, Beattie has risked being seriously misread. Responses to her work vary phenomenally: in a 1985 essay republished in *The Critical Response to Ann Beattie,* critic Carolyn Porter finds her spare characterizations "passive, passionless . . . understated, drab . . .

hopeless." Reviewing *Distortions* for *The Hudson Review* (1977), Peter Glassman reads the same material and hears "a soft and subtle sensibility of sympathy, participation and hopefulness."

In "Less is Less," his influential 1983 *New Criterion* essay, Joshua Gilder criticized indeterminacy in literature as both ethically and aesthetically irresponsible. Gilder perceived the open-ended quality of Beattie's work as claustrophobically static, rather than an opportunity for readers to imagine further scenes, or a valid expression of twentieth-century epistemological insecurities: "Things like plot and character development have no place here," Gilder claimed, "They imply movement, and the only movement allowed in these stories is a steady constriction of vision, a tighter and tighter hold on reality until finally all life is squeezed out and the pulse stops."

J. D. O'Hara, the University of Connecticut professor whom Beattie credits with having taught her both to read responsibly and to edit surgically, countered minimalism's critics in a review of *Chilly Scenes of Winter* and *Distortions* for *The New York Times Book Review* (15 August 1976), remarking: "Traditionally, the novel has relied on action spun out and woven into a plot, complete with beginning and end. Little in our own lives corresponds to this orderliness." Denied the pyramidal template of expository beginning, central climax, and concluding denouement, and apparently impervious to the humor that other readers find so fundamental to Beattie's worldview, Gilder saw only anomie in Beattie's work: "One thing that her fiction says loud and clear is that there is no redemption from despair and hopelessness, especially not in art." Beattie told Montresor in a 1991 interview: "I don't think I can legislate taste." Just as she declines the role of moral or aesthetic proctor, she ignores the advice of those who would take that office upon themselves. When asked by Neila C. Seshachari in a 1990 interview for *Weber Studies,* later republished in *The Critical Response to Ann Beattie,* to respond to Tom Wolfe's condemnation–he called minimalists who write about "very tiny domestic" situations "K-Mart realists"–Beattie observed that "He's entitled to call them anything he likes. But . . . trying to legislate form and toss writers out of the field, or the K-Mart parking lot, is simply folly." Readers waiting for some moment of didactic, moralizing closure in Beattie's work are disappointed; her characters do not march along any teleological path toward universal truth. As she remarked in an interview with Larry McCaffery and Sinda Gregory, published in *Literary Review* (Winter 1984) and reprinted in *The Critical Response to Ann Beattie,* "I certainly don't feel it's the obligation of *any artist* to supply answers." She makes a similar point in her introduction to *The Best American Short Stories, 1987:* "Of course the intelligent reader, however impressed, does not care to believe that there is one truth. That is why the perceiver turned to art to begin with."

Beattie's writing is marked by precipitous beginnings and abrupt endings. "I'm interested in making stories as visual as possible and kind of freeze-framing the stories that I write," she told Montresor in their 1991 interview. Some readers are bothered by Beattie's reticence at crucial points within her narratives; however, her omissions are not the ethical abdications Gilder called them, as Beattie told Plath in 1993: "I'm certainly trying to do a lot of things by delivering the detail or information between the lines. I hope you will realize that I might have given you the same set of facts, but in a different order. I'm trying to elicit particular emotional reactions."

Within their frames, her tales are divided into multiple scenes, like a mullioned window. Her recycling of images, situations, and allusions refer the reader back to the beginning of each narrative; she intends each scene to be re-read in the light of following passages. She remarked to Plath that she hopes her stories "come clear" in retrospect, after the reader arrives at the end of a story: "The last image gets superimposed on the first image, if you will." The flight of the liberated green parakeet in "Dwarf House," for example, should send the reader back to reconsider the Puerto Rican maid ejected from her house by her abusive husband earlier in the story. She has only one outfit to wear throughout the tale: a green, jungle-patterned dress that visually echoes the flash of green when the minister releases the parakeet. The bird and the maid are the only points of color anywhere in "Dwarf House." The maid's ejection from her home seems an unmitigated disaster, on first reading; reconsidering her situation in the light of the parakeet's release from his cage, however, the reader must wonder whether to view the maid as pitiably exiled or enviably liberated to create a new future for herself. Divorce, which seems a dead end for MacDonald in the bar scene with Betty, seems for the maid both as likely and as unlikely an avenue to happiness as the dwarves' marriage. The reader is left to decide.

While divorce does figure largely in Beattie's work, Beattie herself still believes in the possibilities of marriage. In 1973 she married David Gates, a musician and writer who had been a fellow graduate student at the University of Connecticut. They separated in 1980 and divorced in 1982, but Beattie married again in 1988; she and her second husband, Lincoln Perry, a nationally renowned painter, divide their time between Maine and Key West, Florida. When asked about her first marriage, she listed her former husband among the people she has most trusted to assess her work, noting

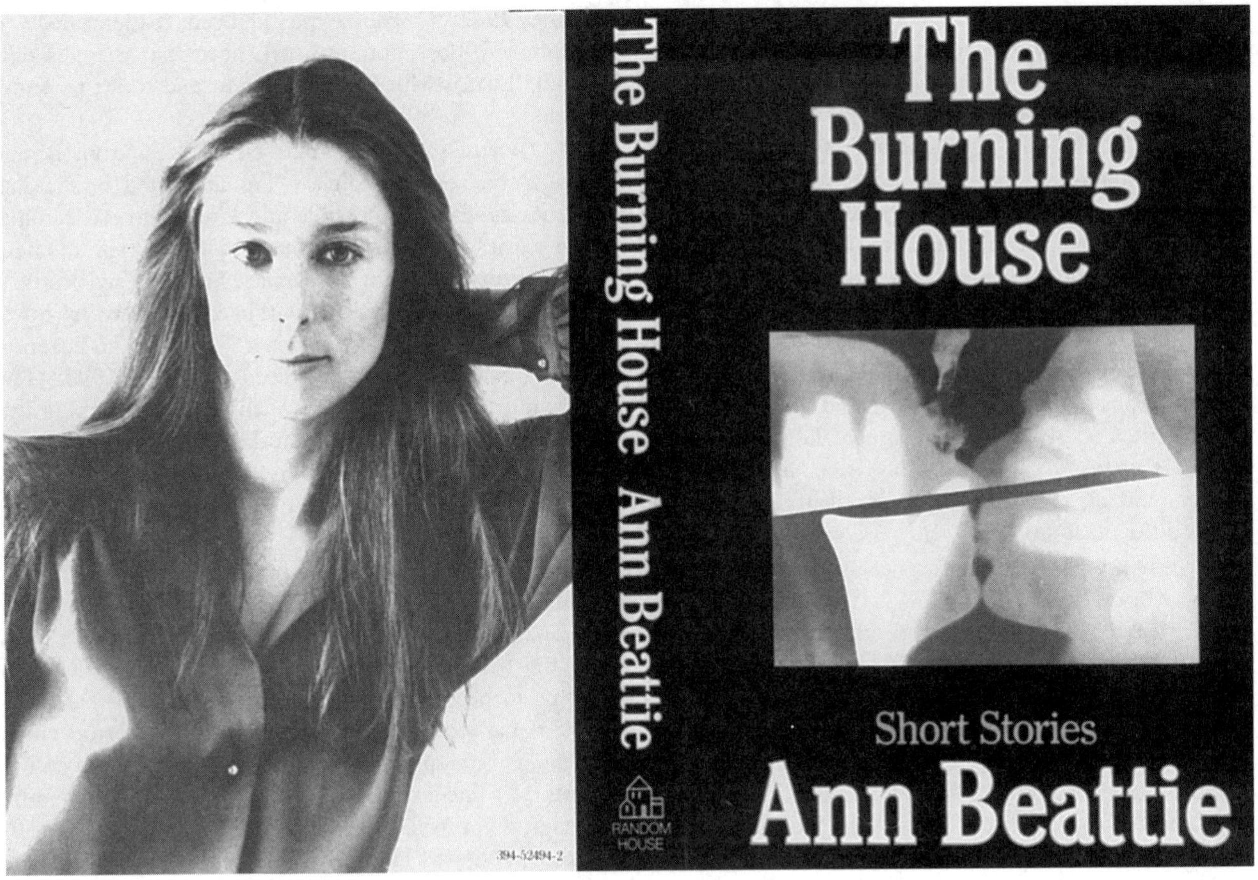

Dust jacket for Beattie's 1982 book, a collection of stories written during the break-up of her first marriage

that she continued to call on him for "help and advice" even after they were divorced. "Sometimes I don't have a clear perspective on my work," she has remarked, and in a 1978 interview with G. E. Murray, she offered an example of Gates's editorial acuity: "I didn't think [the story] 'Snakes' Shoes' amounted to much, so I ripped it up and tossed it in the pantry, where the garbage piled up. Later my husband asked what happened to the story about the two people who sit on a rock at Hall's Pond. He dug it out, patched it together, and got it off to *The New Yorker,* where it eventually appeared." In detailing the homely rituals of the writing process, she again described in her interview with McCaffery and Gregory in 1984 a relationship that lived on, however transformed, after divorce: "I used to always work in my husband's clothes. He's not my husband any longer, but I still occasionally put on the essential plaid shirt."

"Snakes' Shoes," the story rescued from the pantry, follows "Dwarf House" in *Distortions* and shows how the ties that bind a marriage tend in Beattie's universe to linger long after they have been legally sundered. This story, which many critics consider one of Beattie's finest, begins with a conversation among a young child, her divorced parents, Richard and Alice, and her uncle, Sam. Sam is a compulsive and charming fabulist. When the child is frightened by a small snake, he calms her with an elaborate and highly entertaining lie about how snakes shed their feet in the summer, leaving tiny shoes littering the forest floor. He also claims to have written Lewis Carroll's *Alice's Adventures in Wonderland* (1865). Sam does not just tell stories, however; he sometimes tries to reify his fictions.

For instance, in arranging this group's country vacation together, Sam is attempting to realize an imagined happy ending he has composed for Alice, Richard, and their daughter. He feels their divorce is not going well, and he imagines that if he can give them a new perspective–how them the happy ending he is imaging for them–then that ending will become reality. He asks them to step through the distorted looking-glass of his view of their circumstances into a future he is designing for them. At the end of the story the daughter has been borrowing a fellow vacationers' binoculars. The reader can see Sam seizing on the idea of new perspectives and points of view in this final scene with his niece and her parents:

> "I wish I could look through that man's glasses again," the little girl said.
>
> "Here," Sam said, making two circles with the thumb and first finger of each hand. "Look through these."
>
> She leaned over and looked up at the trees through Sam's fingers.
>
> "Much clearer, huh?" Sam said.
>
> "Yes," she said. She liked this game.
>
> "Let me see," Richard said, leaning to look through his brother's fingers.
>
> "Don't forget me," Alice said, and she leaned across Richard to peer through the circles. As she leaned across him, Richard kissed the back of her neck.

Beattie ends the story with this kiss, which promises at least continued affection between Richard and Alice, if not remarriage.

Even the most unpromising marriages in *Distortions* tend to provide a modicum of at least creature comfort. As Glassman has remarked, Beattie's characters' "humane and courageous hunger for the sensation of at least fellowship leads the stories' people to contrive strained and desperate terms of association with one another." In "Eric Clapton's Lover" Beattie depicts a couple that resembles skinny Jack Sprat and his fat-gobbling wife. They both find their marriage inadequately nourishing and warming: he dreams of eating flan on a tropical island, while she imagines that bulking up on spicy, hot food will make her a more definite, assertive feminist. The story concludes with the couple snowed in together: "'It's hard to imagine that somewhere in the world it's warm today,' Beth said, forehead against the foggy window. She was chewing celery, heavily sprinkled with chili powder." Even as they have drifted apart, the husband has recognized the permanence of family: "Nothing ever came entirely apart." Framed within the window in the last scene they look less mismatched than they did in the opening lines of the story: chilled to have discovered that they have not married their soulmates, they are nonetheless similar in their desires, and there remains the possibility–however slight–that they will notice their similarities, if snowed in together long enough. On the other hand, this may be a New England redaction of Jean-Paul Sartre's play *Huis Clos* (1945; translated as *No Exit,* 1946), in which hell is defined as being locked up without any mirrors except those to be found in the faces of one's fellow prisoners. Again, the reader is left to decide.

Some of the other marriages in *Distortions,* however, are quite unambiguously hellish. "Downhill" opens with the narrator worrying that her dog will abandon her. She wonders whether her common-law husband, Jon, tempted by "the beauty of all the women with neatly arranged hair," will leave her as well; the reader gradually realizes that the narrator has, prior to the opening scene, suffered a nervous breakdown. Plath has called Beattie's stories "'fictions of aftermath,' where most of the conflict or turning points have already occurred, leaving the characters to cope with or work through resultant problems." In her 1993 interview with Plath, Beattie admitted to "lopping off beginnings," saying "I write many pages before I feel my way into the material. . . . Finally, if you've got it right in your head and you are clear on who they are and you can animate them, you don't need an introduction." As the reader is drawn into the narrator's distorted perceptions in "Downhill," the long-suffering husband seems imminently poised to flee the burdens of caretaker. The final lines thus again surprise the reader in their unsettling suggestion that the husband does not want his wife to recover. His need to control her and keep her confined in their home may actually be the cause of her illness. He threatens her with abandonment not because he wants to escape her illness, but because he takes a martyred martinet's satisfaction in mastering her. The minor crisis depicted in the opening pages has been only one of a series of separations designed to end in reunion: "Jon leaves so he can come back. Certain of this, I call and they both come–Jon and the dog–to settle down with me. We have come to the end, yet we are safe." Earlier in the story she has likened herself to a mutinous naval crew. When her minor, ritual revolution has been quelled, "he smiles, approvingly, and as he sits down his hand slides across the sheet like a rudder through still waters." His oddly sinister, satisfied smile reassures the narrator, but not the reader, who must now return to the beginning of the story to reconsider the definition of "safety" for the narrator. She seems "safely" confined by a masterful manipulator.

The final piece in *Distortions,* "The Lifeguard," paradoxically confirms both the menace of those who must be the captains of their relationships, and the comforts, however bleak and attenuated, of families successfully weathering appalling storms. Like Sam in "Snake's Shoes," David Warner is a fabulist, vacationing at the beach with his family and hallucinating happy story endings: "He has been feeling lately that something good is going to happen. There is a visual distortion that accompanies the feeling; he sees, imagines he sees, sunsets when there could not possibly be sunsets. He sees them at midnight, when the moon shines over the water, then burns sun-bright, and the birds sing. Even the seagulls are quiet at midnight, so he is not just imagining that one thing is another. He is just plain inventing." But he is not the only fabulist on the beach: his wife, Toby, fantasizes about having an affair with the lifeguard, and their children's playmates in the surf include a disturbed child who is dreaming of death. The callow young lifeguard should have noticed the

Dust jacket for Beattie's 1986 book, which includes admiring allusions to works by Ernest Hemingway and Ezra Pound

child, having been a psychology major at one time, but "everything in psychology can have a million answers. He switched majors." The troubled child takes charge of a boat, enlists David's daughter, Penelope, and her twin brother, Andrew, as his crew, steers them out beyond easy reach of the lifeguard, and sets fire to the boat, killing both the twins and himself. The Arbus-influenced pictures of dwarves and giants that open this collection are recalled in this final tale when Toby peruses a volume of Arbus's photographs; this allusive symmetry, combined with the children's grotesquely unnatural deaths, should lend a claustrophobic sense of closure to the collection. However, Beattie again elides the easy answer, the finality of the traditional denouement. In his grief, David's surviving son, Randy, finds solace in his Captain Magic Slate: "He liked to write on it and draw pictures, then zip up the top part and watch it all disappear." With a Captain Magic Slate, stories and images too terrible to absorb can simply be erased. While the lifeguard finds multiple meanings, answers, and endings intolerable, David's son now finds them necessary, and in the last line he is presented as learning, like the other storytellers in *Distortions,* to reinscribe the palimpsest of his past in ways the reader can only guess at. While Gilder may find that Beattie offers her characters and readers "no redemption from despair and hopelessness, especially not in art," there are ways to read Beattie's writing in which art is, in fact, the surest (and perhaps the sole) source of the redemption Gilder looks for in the well-crafted narrative.

Most of the characters in Beattie's second collection, *Secrets and Surprises* (1978), turn out to be storytellers of some sort. "I'm conscious that people tell stories. It's not just writers who tell stories," Beattie observed in an interview with Steven R. Centola, published in *Contemporary Literature* (1990). She sees ordinary people composing artful narratives every day: "I'm absolutely amazed at how perfectly lucid the elevator operator is." Compulsive storytelling can also be a symptom of insanity: in "It's Not That I'm Lying," one of Beattie's uncollected stories, published in *Esquire* (July 1993), a mental patient finds she cannot avoid fictionalizing her medical history: "You realize, doctor, that because I am constantly asked to tell the same story, naturally I get bored and omit parts of it or give special emphasis to some things some days, and others another day. It's not that I'm lying . . . I do try to be consistent in pointing out that I suffered delusions. . . . How do my chances seem for being discharged for the weekend?"

While most of Beattie's storytellers in *Secrets and Surprises* escape institutionalization, many, particularly the most gifted, are unhealthily convinced by their own fictions. The narrator of "A Clever-Kids Story" reminisces about her brother, Joseph, who died in Vietnam. They shared a bed as children, and he would tell stories in the dark, tales of two children who magically vanquish robbers and fly unaided along the seashore. His stories calmed their vague anxieties as they both intuited domestic disaster on the horizon: their parents argued, and their mother, pregnant a third time, had an abortion. In his fanciful flights, however, Joseph lost touch with reality altogether. When he grew up, he refused to dodge the draft, not on principle, but because "he thought he wouldn't die; he thought he was indestructible. He really thought that he would always be in control, that he would always be the storyteller." Long after Joseph's death, the narrator happens to be sharing Joseph's bed with a friend who has a crush on her; she tries to warn him about life's dangers, adopting Joseph's storytelling techniques: "'There's a demon in the corner,'" she begins. "'A demon'" she repeats. Her drowsy friend misunderstands, thinking she must want to make love: "He smoothed my hair from my face and, kindly, kissed my neck, moved his hand up my ribs. It was not what I wanted at all, but I closed my eyes, not knowing now what to say." Her story is aborted, like the fetus her mother had aborted while she and Joseph were children.

Most of the other storytellers in *Secrets and Surprises* fare no better than this. Even the best-intentioned, kindliest audiences misunderstand, straining and failing to hear tales told across vast chasms of gender, age, and existential isolation. They tell each other tales to fend off the external influences shaping their lives–cold and insensible forces like the blizzards that trap so many Beattie characters in their homes. In part they are simply trying to communicate, and they find stories the only way to express their feelings. Those who do not tell stories write letters, dubious dispatches in which they revise the past and distort the present. Dan, an art teacher in the story "Colorado," is one of the more sincere letter-writers in *Secrets and Surprises,* but he is woefully ineffective: "Penelope was living with a man named Dan. Robert could not understand this, because Dan and Penelope did not communicate even well enough for her to ask him to fix her boots. She hobbled over to Robert's apartment instead." After Penelope moves in with Robert, Robert finds a letter from Dan at their apartment: "It was Penelope's name, written over and over, and a lot of profanity. He showed it to her. Neither of them said anything. He put it back on the table, next to an old letter from his mother that begged him to go back to graduate school." Penelope and Robert then drive to the Rocky Mountains, for no real reason. Dan's heartfelt letter elicits no response at all, except to drive Penelope halfway across the country in a flight from intimacy.

When communication does take place, it is often non-verbal. In "Weekend," a husband can speak to his wife only through photographs. The reader spends much of the story trying to understand what holds Lenore to George, a pompous, vain, condescending English professor who has, since being denied tenure, been living on an inheritance: "He has always kept a journal, and he is a great letter writer. An aunt left him most of her estate, ten thousand dollars, and said in her will that he was the only one who really cared, who took the time, again and again, to write." Despite his aunt's accolades, George's attempts at communication consist of little but professorial posturings. In the absence of an academic post, George's great work is his idea of himself, the cultured, magisterial aesthete and raconteur. When guests visit, he directs their attention to "tiny oil paintings of fruit, prints with small details from the unicorn tapestries. He pretends to like small, elegant things. Actually, when they visit museums in New York, he goes first to El Grecos and big Mark Rothko canvases. She could never get him to admit that what he said or did was sometimes false." His conversations with Lenore are only slightly less dishonest than his performances for his guests: "Once, long ago, when he asked if he was still the man of her dreams, she said, 'We don't get along well anymore.' 'Don't talk about it,' he said–no denial, no protest. At best, she could say things and get away with them; she could never get him to continue such a conversation." Early in the story, Lenore explains that she stays with him, despite his barely concealed affairs with a series of former students, because she "has a comfortable house. She cooks. She keeps busy and she loves her two children." Later, in one of the many surprising passages Beattie has built into this collection, Lenore has been left alone with one of George's guests while George is off having sex with a worshipful coed. The guest, Julie, an embarrassed friend of the student, wonders why Lenore puts up with George's humiliations. "'I'll show you something,' Lenore says," and retrieves some photographs she had found in George's darkroom: "They were left out by mistake, no doubt . . . They are high-contrast photographs of George's face. In all of them he looks very serious and very sad; in some of them his eyes seem to be narrowed in pain. In one, his mouth is open. It is an excellent photograph of a man in agony, a man about to scream. 'What are they?' Julie whispers. 'Pictures he took of himself,' Lenore says. She shrugs. 'So I stay,' she says."

Men are better storytellers than women in *Secrets and Surprises.* In her first two story collections, Beattie's women spend less time composing fictions and more time gardening, creating things out of the earth instead of airy imagination. Lenore stays not for George's public persona but for what she sees as the real George, even if the real George can only communicate with her through the photos he leaves around the house. After their guests have departed, she and George "sit in silence, listening to the rain. She slides over closer to him, puts her hand on his shoulder and leans her head there, as if he could protect her from the awful things he has wished into being."

Many of Beattie's female characters resist domineering males more vigorously than Lenore does, but never too effectively. In "Deer Season," Elena is an art historian pursuing grant-supported research on Jean-Jacques Rousseau and living with her sister in the Adirondacks. She dates a local painter briefly, until their tenuous relationship erupts in a strangely vacuous argument revealing nothing but both Elena's and the painter's baseless insecurities. Before he has even tried to seduce her, he accuses her of not wanting to have sex and offers to take her home: "'You're trying to make me a puppet,' she said. 'You're making a mockery of me before I even speak.' . . . She was humiliated to be sent home, like a child being sent from the room after it has

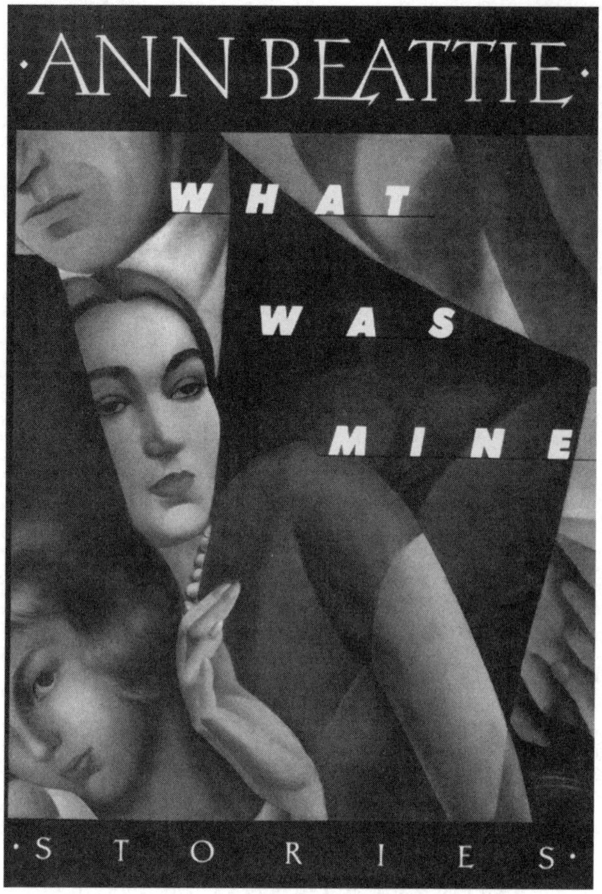

Dust jacket for Beattie's 1991 book, which includes some of her most experimental stories

cutely performed for all the guests." After this breakup, she avoids men until a year later, when a former lover arrives for a visit. He urges her to go away with him, and she finds herself mindlessly agreeing. In the intervening year, she has somehow learned to enjoy being a puppet-child. She remembers her father "throwing her in the air, hollering 'onetwothree, onetwothree.' She could remember how light, how buoyant she had felt being tossed high in the air, and thought that perhaps being powerless was nice, in a way. She stared at the guide lights without counting, as the car moved slowly along the highway." The story ends here, with Elena being hauled down out of the mountains as if she were a deer across the hood of a hunter's truck. In her stories published in the late 1970s and early 1980s, Beattie's women characters often seem to be claimed as trophies, bagged and collected by men who proceed either to infantilize them or to dehumanize them altogether. In the story "Shifting," however, there is one exception: Natalie, married to Larry, a graduate student who treats her like one of the household furnishings covered by his homeowner's insurance, learns to operate a stick shift so that she can drive herself to the election polls. She is obsessed with her friend Andy's Vietnam War injury: she repeatedly imagines the moment of his physical dismemberment, when he stepped on a land mine and his body was suddenly revealed to be merely an assemblage of discrete limbs arcing through the air. In taking charge of her life, she proves that she is herself more than the sum of her parts, that she is a willful director of her own life. While learning to drive, she takes ownership of her body, as well as her car, when she has sex with her teenaged driving instructor. Her revolutionary shift is not entirely successful, however. Examining her body in a mirror, she finds it whole and not displeasing, but imperfect. Projecting a goal for her evolution as a feminist, she arrives at an oxymoronic impossibility–she would like to become a sentient stone, sensitive only to itself: "If she were the piece of sculpture and if she could feel, she would like her sense of isolation."

This dismal view of solipsism as the end of female autonomy can be read as a feminist's despair at ever achieving both freedom and meaningful relationships, as several of Beattie's works have been interpreted. But Beattie generally eschews overtly political commentaries in her work. One of her more-recent characters laments that she is not a better activist, but also wishes "so many feminists hadn't become shrill. Or clownish, like Camille Paglia." Beattie supports the feminist movement, but when asked by Montresor to define her form of feminism, she responded only that "It has to do with thinking about my position in society." When asked to reconcile her feminist sympathies with the antifeminist threads in her work–Beattie's women, especially the pretty ones, tend to betray each other–Beattie replied that she writes about what she sees around her: "I'll just put it there because it is a given. If Skylab is falling, then Skylab is falling. If a lot of women are competitive, I'll put it there. A lot of women are competitive."

Beattie's images of isolated psyches are as existentialist as they are feminist, growing out of her profound admiration for the works of Samuel Beckett, one of the precursors of literary minimalism, and an important figure in Beattie's early graduate studies. In "The Hum Inside the Skull: A Symposium," published in *The New York Times Book Review* (13 May 1984), Beatie remarks "In those days, the only modern writer I recall thinking a lot about was Samuel Beckett." Beattie's insane characters, her victims of nervous breakdowns, tend to think in circular, looping patterns not unlike those of Beckett's narrators' as they spiral into self-absorbed oblivion. Elena, transfixed by the passing road markers as she gratefully sinks into powerlessness in "Deer Season," resembles Beckett's title character in *Murphy* (1938), who wills himself into catatonia, relieved to be powerlessly bound to his rocking chair, as does the insane narrator of "Downhill," finally happy and safe only when confined to her bed. Beattie has remarked that she envies Beckett's ability to convey the tedium of daily life without becoming tedious himself; like Beckett, Beattie frequently explores the potential meanings inherent in lists of quotidian activities and domestic detritus. In 1977 Glassman approvingly noted Beckett's influence in Beattie's early work, calling her "as brave, and for that matter, as funny, as Beckett." Joseph Epstein, on the other hand, acidly disapproved of Beattie's philosophical position, dismissing her in an article, originally published in *Commentary* (March 1983) and reprinted in *The Critical Response to Ann Beattie,* as "the L. L. Bean of what passes for 60's existentialism." Beattie continued to cite Beckett as an inspiration, telling McCaffery and Gregory in 1984: "There are so many people who are together because of all the obvious reasons: they don't want to be lonely or they are in the habit of being together, or this whole Beckettian thing–I can't stay and I can't go. This tug interests me more than the fact that they're not communicating–I want to find out why they're staying and not going."

Divorce would seem to be one of the focal issues informing *The Burning House* (1982). Although Beattie did not realize it at the time, her first marriage was disintegrating as she wrote the dark stories in her third collection; as she told Montresor in 1991, "*The Burning House* was written in '79, and I left in '80. And if you had asked me in 1979, I would have answered you quite honestly that I was a perfectly happy married woman. But then you look back and you think, 'Hmm, look what I knew in 1979.' It's harrowing, in a way." In writing the powerful final scene of the title story in *The Burning House,* Beattie was inspired by a comment made by a male friend during the late 1970s: "It was one of those remarks that come so much from left field that it has a kind of resounding clarity. . . . When I typed that line– 'Are you staying or going?'–I knew then exactly what the husband would say, and it just had to be a much more intensified version of what my friend had said to me." The husband tells his wife he is leaving, saying it in a way that changes her view of their marriage. She has not understood her husband at all.

Another Beckett allusion occurs in "The Cinderella Waltz." A precocious nine-year-old, Louise, is carrying around a copy of Beckett's play *Happy Days* (1961). Like Winnie in *Happy Days,* Louise is much occupied with packing and unpacking her bag, as she shuttles between her divorced parents' homes; her father, Milo, teasingly calls her an "old bag lady." Milo now lives with his lover Bradley. Louise and her mother are both fond of Bradley, who seems much more likeable than the petulant Milo; however, the reader is left to wonder why Milo stays with Bradley, whom he finds increasingly irritating. The answer suggested by Louise's reading is that offered by Beckett's Winnie, who needs her husband as an audience: "I used to think that I would learn to talk alone . . . but no. . . . Ergo you are there." Winnie's revised Cartesian formulation could explain much about Milo. He needs other people only as audiences: he wants applause, not communication. On announcing, with champagne, that he will be relocating, a decision which will generally wreck his loved ones' lives, he crows, "This is a toast to me because I am going to be going to San Francisco." Narcissistically, he values Louise only for the opportunities she provides him for roleplaying: he is the fairy prince to his fairy princess daughter, when the mood strikes him to play that role.

Most of the men in *The Burning House* imagine themselves playing similarly fantastic, romantic roles. References to the heroes of popular culture abound, lending the entire collection a thematic coherence. Beattie's critics complain that such topical references merely play to *The New Yorker* readership's expectations of a slick, entertaining, urbane style. Other readers find more interesting reverberations in these repeated allusions. In the opening story, "Learning to Fall," the narrator is babysitting for Andrew, the young son of her friend Ruth, while Ruth attends a dance class where she is this week "learning to fall" artfully. The narrator is afraid of falling: afraid of physically falling down the center space in the Guggenheim Museum she takes Andrew to visit and afraid of emotionally falling into a serious relationship with her lover, Raymond. Andrew, on the other hand, is fearless. He wears a Superman patch on the knee of his jeans and clearly believes he could fly to the bottom floor of the museum if he needed to. Her lover, Raymond, is similarly intrepid in his entreaties. In the end, the overpowered narrator surrenders: "What will happen can't be stopped. Aim for grace."

References to Superman and other heroic pop icons are sprinkled throughout this collection. In "Winter, 1978," a Beverly Hills art collector imagines himself as Superman and also refers to Krypto the Superdog. When he returns to Connecticut for a funeral, he wears cowboy garb inappropriate to the occasion and the season; his deceased uncle has decorated his home, equally inappropriately, with a wall poster of the Lone Ranger and Tonto and with a paperweight that, when shaken, showers snow on a Texas cowboy. B.B., the divorced father in "Desire," notes that his second wife's doctor looks like Tonto and amuses himself by reading Batman comics. In "Sunshine and Shadow" the demoralized Jake imagines that his lover's green eyes will have on him the same power that "Kryptonite had on Superman."

Allusions to fairy tales return at the end of the book in the title story, "The Burning House," in which the significance of all the earlier references becomes clear. The characters in "The Burning House" are more self-conscious and more astute than those in the preceding pieces. Like Milo in "The Cinderella Waltz," J.D., a former English professor who left academia after losing his wife and son in a car crash, believes in fairy tales, but with a difference: "'You probably shouldn't listen to me. All I can do myself is run away, hide out. I'm not the learned professor. You know what I believe. I believe all that wicked fairy-tale crap: your heart will break, your house will burn.'" J.D. is refusing to advise the narrator, Amy, what she should do about the disintegration of her marriage to his former student, Frank, who is drifting away from her: "One night a week or so ago," the narrator recalls, "I thought we were really attuned to each other, communicating by telepathic waves, and as I lay in bed about to speak I realized that the vibrations really existed: they were him snoring." Unlike J.D., Frank still believes that he can effect rescues and deeds of derring-do as a latter-day knight; he cannot do these things while married to the narrator, however. He generalizes on the arrested development of the American male: "'Your whole life,'" he tells his wife, "'you've made one mistake–you've surrounded yourself with men. Let me tell you something . . . Men think they're Spider-Man and Buck Rogers and Superman. You know what we all feel inside that you don't feel? That we're going to the stars.'" He takes her hand and announces his own departure: "'I'm looking down on all of this from space,' he whispers. 'I'm already gone.'" Frank's compelling and articulate self-assessment is unusual. Most of Beattie's characters first misapprehend themselves and then misread others' responses.

Instances of complete miscommunication also punctuate the stories comprising the collection *Where You'll Find Me* (1986). After learning of her husband's adultery in "Times," the main character, Cammy, suddenly understands "how ironic it was that all during the past summer, when she was falling more deeply in love with Peter, he was having a flirtation and then an affair with someone else. Cammy had begun to be comfortable with how subtly attuned to each other they were, and she had been deluded."

Even more alarming is "Coney Island," the story of high-school friends Drew and Chester, who are waiting to hear the results of fertility tests being performed on Chester's wife, Holly. Chester and Holly seem to have established the kind of closeness only imagined by Frank's wife in "The Burning House." Chester can hear himself adopting Holly's thought patterns in his own speech, and when she was wheeled out of exploratory surgery, he reached over to warm her feet with his hands even before she groggily complained of the cold. As the story opens, Chester, although distracted with concern for his wife, rouses himself to listen to his friend Drew's plans to reclaim, briefly, a recently married former girlfriend. Fifteen years of friendship entails a kind of loyalty, even if Chester does not approve of Drew's self-serving scheme. But in the final lines of the story, Drew manages to invalidate those fifteen years with a single insensitive and obtuse question, revealing not just a comic moment of misapprehension, but fifteen years of completely blind self-involvement. Drew, like Milo in Beattie's "Cinderella Waltz," uses people only as foils, as though those around him were empty ciphers or "referential spaces," serving only to reflect back upon himself. Drew seems to justify Pearl Bell's observation that "there is as much drinking, malice, and domestic cruelty in Beattie's world as in Cheever's, but her burned-out relics of the '60's, unlike Cheever's guilty suburbanites, have lost whatever promptings of moral intelligence or constancy they may have once possessed." Other readers of *Where You'll Find Me* focus on the characters' continuing efforts to find a new ethical footing, as Chester seems to be seeking in his marriage to Holly, a marriage in which he is gradually outgrowing his emotionally stunted friend Drew.

Holly's concern with her biological clock in "Coney Island" is shared by other female characters in this collection. Thirty-four-year-old Jo in "Summer People" seems to be attempting an end-run around her husband's refusal to have children, seducing him, with increasingly impersonal fervor, every night; he suspects she has stopped taking the pill. In "The Big Outside World," thirty-five-year-old Renee has suffered a miscarriage; her husband no longer cares whether or not they have children, but she does, and her maternal instincts take the form of attempting to adopt a forlorn cat that reminds Renee of her lost child. In "Janus," which David Wyatt called Beattie's "most accomplished short story" in a *Southern Review* article in 1991, Andrea, a real estate agent, develops an obsessive attachment to a decorative bowl that she places as a kind of talisman in houses she is trying to sell. Pets become surrogate children for many of Beattie's characters. Similarly, the bowl becomes the central focus of Andrea's life: "All the way home, Andrea wondered how she could have left the bowl behind. It was like leaving a friend at an outing–just walking off. Sometimes there were stories in the paper about families forgetting a child somewhere and driving to the next city. Andrea had only gone a mile down the road before she remembered." The bowl comes to stand for all the people Andrea has not been able to love, and in its inviolate, pristine still-

Dust jacket for Beattie's 1998 book, in which the title story continues Beattie's gradual abandonment of the minimalist style of her early fiction

ness it simultaneously comes to mirror her own solitary, barren predicament.

While the women are interested in procreation, the men are interested in sex as a defense against middle age. In "Spiritus" Beattie depicts a comfortably married businessman doing his best to resist the rejuvenating prospects of an affair; Drew in "Coney Island" similarly seems drawn to his newlywed former girlfriend purely at an instinctive level, although he decides that the adrenaline rush he feels must be love at last. These men are drawn to unions not with other people, but with half-formed ideas of themselves.

Other characters find their redemption not in biological coupling and reproduction, but in artistic creation, in the stories they tell. Asked to recount her experiences in the emergency room following an embarrassingly clumsy mishap, Kate in "Where You'll Find Me" responds with a less painful fiction instead: "'I had a dream last night about the ballerinas at Victoria Pool,' I say. 'It was like Victoria Pool was a stage set instead of a real place, and tall, thin ballerinas kept parading in and twirling and pirouetting.' . . . 'You just told a little story,' Howard said. 'You didn't answer the question.'" *Where You'll Find Me* has been called Beattie's best, most carefully crafted short-story collection; it is also one of her most self-conscious in its many discussions of the writer's craft. Tom recalls his wife's preoccupation with eighteenth-century novels in the story "Summer People," and "for a second, he wanted them all to be transformed into characters in one of those novels . . . Henry Fielding would simply step in and predict the future. The author could tell him what it would be like, what would happen, if he had to try, another time, to love somebody."

Beattie dismisses Fielding's authorial strategies even as Tom wistfully recalls them; but, she also alludes to authors she genuinely admires in these stories. She incorporated latter-day versions of Hemingway's big-game hunters in several earlier stories; in *Where You'll Find Me,* she told one interviewer, she has modeled an entire story as a variation on one of Hemingway's, rewriting his story "Cat in the Rain"(1925) into her own "The Big Outside World." In the story "When Can I See You Again," she seems to be offering a similar homage to Ezra Pound's much-anthologized poem "In a Station of the Metro" (1913): in an airport, a slightly cracked young man uses his art not to reflect reality, but to defend himself against it. Wearing a hat decorated with bananas, apples, and other fruits sewn out of cloth, he accosts people, peddling watercolors accompanied by calligraphy defining what he calls "the language of fruit": "'Currants,' the boy said, flipping the page. 'Currants mean "Remember me."' He began to sidestep when Martha quickened her pace. . . . 'The orange is faithfulness,' he said, talking faster. 'Gooseberries are probably the most popular. I don't know why. I think because people love something exotic. Gooseberries mean "I want to see you again."'" After escaping to the baggage claim area, Martha ruminates on whether she wants to see an old lover again. When she looks up, she sees the fruit artist forced onto the moving baggage conveyer belt by an irate traveler. He steadies himself, "portfolio clutched to his chest like a shield. . . . By now, of course, the faces around him would have begun to blur; not puzzled individual faces at all: gooseberries on a branch."

Revising one of Pound's most severely framed images–his "The apparition of these faces in the crowd / Petals on a wet, black bough"–aptly continues one of the themes of this volume as Beattie repeatedly reminds the reader, with references to other authors and a foregrounding of her own narrative machinations, that modern art is no longer mimetic, but allusive–no longer a mirror of reality, but an artist's filtered, cropped revision of reality. She continued exploring this idea in her next collection, *What Was Mine* (1991), where her narrators step out from behind their omniscient wizard's curtains to declare themselves and their artifice to their audience. "Installation #6" is presented as a transcription of an art-gallery docent's taped commentary; while directing the visitor to the disappointing single exhibit–a vastly uncommunicative manhole cover under a spotlight–the docent disclaims all qualifications as an art critic, calling himself nothing more than a conscientious handyman. "The Working Girl," which Beattie has likened to such experimental works as John Barth's *Lost in the Funhouse* (1968), is told by an intrusive narrator who repeatedly undermines her own textual authority. "The Working Girl" is Beattie's clearest expression of what Wyatt called her "distrust of story." This aesthetically heterodox collection yokes Beattie's most experimental works with her most conventional, as Beattie dramatically abandons her "distrust of story" in the concluding tale, "Windy Day at the Reservoir," her most fully rounded, traditionally structured short story to date. Even in that tale, however, her characters prefer artistically crafted fiction to the unpredictably dysfunctional world in which they actually live.

Although experimenting with self-conscious artificiality in *What Was Mine,* Beattie continued to develop traditional characterization, introducing some of her most recognizable and appealing narrative voices. Half of these twelve stories are written from the male point of view, and this male perspective is both less alien and less alienated than in Beattie's earlier writing. Her male narrators are either retired or working out of their homes; their concerns are more centered in the domestic realm and less scattered in the big outside world of game-hunting and philandering. When they do hoard trophies, they are collecting leaves or seashells, rather than souvenirs of sexual conquests; when they list their accomplishments, they count their children, rather than their seductions.

Most of the characters in *What Was Mine* are too alarmed by life to be calmed by leaves and lists, however. In "The Longest Day of the Year," the narrator explains why she had to divorce her second husband: "He went to Vietnam and came back loony. He thought trucks on the highway would blow up if we passed them. He was given three tickets for driving too slow on an interstate. He lied, telling them that he had rheumatism in his foot and that sometimes he just couldn't push too hard on the accelerator. Actually, he thought everything was going to blow up."

Birds have figured in almost all of Beattie's stories throughout her career, usually associated with artistic expression. In the story "When Can I See You Again," in *Where You'll Find Me,* a refractive crystal swan, glued to a dashboard, prismatically illuminates the car's interior, making sitting in the front seat "like reclining in a Jackson Pollock." Whether the birds seem to be competent fliers, like those in the last lines of "In Amalfi," or seem to be struggling ineptly, like the penguin-shaped salt-shaker fallen over to rest on its beak in "Coney Island," the images appear so regularly that the reader begins to watch for them, as the viewer watches for Alfred Hitchcock to appear in each of his movies.

In *What Was Mine,* Beattie's avian metaphors suggest the threat of Icarean disaster, and the characters' best-laid plans frequently fail. Accidents, and acts of violence so senseless that they seem like accidents, have marked much of Beattie's work: her novel *Falling in Place* (1980) unfolds around a boy's accidental shooting of his sister, and young victims of violence or disease leave bereft parents in many of her stories. The somewhat older characters in *What Was Mine* seem to be coping better with their misfortunes than those in *The Burning House;* none of these older characters has arrived at middle age unscathed, however. Once traumatized by the unexpected–muggings, suddenly swarming bees, falling cans of paint, and, most often, car accidents–the characters spend the rest of their lives waiting for the next unforeseeable disaster. The older they become, the more reasons they have to fear flying, driving, or even walking on the street. Like Tom in "Summer People," they want life to follow the kind of predictable path one might find in a conventionally plotted story or movie, but experience has taught them to expect only the unexpected. Some fall into morbid paralysis, like the mother in "Horatio's Trick." When her son Nicholas had crashed his bicycle and broken his thumb the year before, she overreacted and has been frightened ever since. Her son chastises her: "'If I had told you that the car was driving funny before I got it fixed, you would have bitten your nails some more and refused to ride in it. I wish you'd stop being scared. I wish you'd just stop.' . . . Nicholas had scored his point. She was just sitting there, scared to death."

No matter how cautious Beattie's characters are, however, in Beattie's stories accidents are inevitable. Attending to auto maintenance helps not at all in the story "Television," where a car falls into a hole in the car wash. In the uncollected story "Coydog," published in *The Yale Review* (April 1995), a family routinely schedules its Fourth of July reunion for June 28 to avoid holiday traffic accidents, but the story of one such weekend catalogues other kinds of accidental collisions and spills that ultimately splinter the family. In *Where You'll Find Me* many of the aging characters are older than forty, and many of them experience health problems that surprise and traumatize them as memorably as any other unavoidable yet apparently random disaster. The many physicians appearing in these stories provide neither prevention nor solace, appearing more alien than the extraterrestrials Beattie wrote of in *Distortions.*

Most of the characters continue to create. In "Where You'll Find Me," the title story, Beattie depicts a rare example of an adult relating well enough to a child to pass on some hard-earned skills: what the narrator remembers most clearly about his stepfather is his unconditional affection and his "practical advice about how to assemble a world." In "Windy Day at the Reservoir" Mrs. Brikel, recovering from the drowning death of her retarded son Royce, also creates worlds as she shapes a new life for herself. In this uncharacteristically informative story, Beattie offers both a postscript and some predictions about the bereaved mother's future, a future that the mother approaches with an apparently indomitable "buoyance" of heart.

Creativity on the part of characters produces more uneven results in the eight new stories Beattie included along with twenty-eight previously collected tales in her 1998 collection, *Park City,* which won the *Dictionary of Literary Biography Yearbook* Award for a Distinguished Volume of Short Stories Published in 1998. In "Cosmos," a teacher begins to "mythologize" her own life to make a point in the classroom; when one of her foreign students fails to understand the creative license the teacher is taking, nightmarish chaos results. In "Second Question," the imaginative fictions of gay men–the stories they tell each other while playing a game called "What-If" and stories they tell themselves about magical luck–seem flimsy defense against the implacability of AIDS. The narrator of "Going Home With Uccello" watches her lover–who is not a gifted storyteller–failing to believe his own fictional version of their relationship. He manages only to convince his lover that he loves her not at all.

In both *What Was Mine* and the new stories in *Park City,* Beattie seems to be developing a more expansive short-story form. In her earlier works, reticence was her most powerful tool. In "Photographs and Fantasies in the Stories of Ann Beattie" Stacey Olster offered a quotation from Diane Arbus as a gloss on Beattie's refusal to explicate her own early works: "'Maybe the comment has to be implicit in the pictures,' she wrote. ' . . . If these are shattering enough, anything like comment or judgment on the subjects would betray both them and us.'" In her works in the 1990s, Beattie expanded upon the elliptical, "freeze-framed" moments of her earlier stories to include more information on the larger context of her characters' lives, so that individual scenes are commented on by the preceding and following events. Rather than analyzing lives into discrete images, she is combining those images into a more linear narrative. In "The Siamese Twins Go Snorkeling," one of the most interesting pieces in *Park City,* Alice, an artist, is depicted moving through a similar aesthetic transition, as Harry, a long-time subject for Alice's drawings, looks at pictures of himself on Alice's wall:

> The way Alice had hung the drawings evoked a sort of Humpty-Dumpty in reverse, so that first you saw the breakage, and then you moved into the present, which was highly detailed, and very realistic. No more indecipherable shapes falling down. For years she had seen him as a shape, turning, and then something happened and she had begun to draw him as he was, drawn him full figure, in precise detail, and clearly with great feeling. After all that time of being interested in how he might come apart, she had started to be interested in the way he was put together.

As Alice is beginning to explore unmapped areas in her art, she and her new husband, Ames, approach their future with modest optimism. They invite her muse, Henry, to join them in a glass of champagne: "'So then,' Ames said, raising his glass, 'here's to possibility.'" Alice ultimately embraces this new direction in her life and in her work; the tale ends with Alice, Ames, and Henry forming a new kind of familial trinity.

In the title story of *Park City,* Beattie continues to move away from the brevity and the painfully spare prose style of her earlier minimalist texts, eliding less of her characters' histories, detailing more of their motivations, and simply allowing the reader to spend more time with them before anything dramatic occurs. The effect is more naturalistic and less self-referential, although Beattie's characters do seem articulate about sharing Beattie's new aversion to the obviously effortful and the preciously miniaturized. In "Park City" the narrator is accompanying her sister Janet; Janet's unworthy new fiancé, Damon; Damon's daughter, Lyric; and Janet's daughter, Nell, on a trip to Utah, where they expect to commune with nature but find themselves isolated in an appallingly graceless luxury condominium at a commercialized resort: "'I'd actually say there's something deenergizing about this place,'" Janet's teenaged daughter remarks, "'But that's true of any place that seems artificial, I guess.'" "'Maybe at the very least we should go up by the miniature golf course and get on one of the rides before we leave,'" the narrator suggests. "'You scared me,'" the teenager replies. "'I thought for a minute you were suggesting miniature golf.'" "Deenergizing" was one of the more common criticisms brought to bear by reviewers hostile to the "miniaturized" stories Beattie produced in the 1970s and 1980s; as she investigates the possibilities of the longer short-story form in *Park City,* Beattie would seem here to be laughing both at herself and at her early critics.

A recurring theme in this story is the advisability of the "slow start" and the danger of rash actions–whether that takes the form of impulsively committing to a new relationship or leaping aboard a speeding ski lift. Again, there seems a sly joke lurking here, as Beattie is conspicuously moving away from her own trademark pattern of precipitous "starts" to her stories. Critics, however, have noted similar sea changes and stylistic innovations in Beattie's work at various points in her career. As early as 1977, William Pritchard found in "Weekend" evidence that Beattie was no longer "a prisoner of her clever mannerisms, but is working through them to something more interesting, more human."

Beattie has always chafed against assessments of her work that would confine her to the critics' expectations. She may have abandoned her minimalist's "distrust of story," but it seems unlikely that she will abandon her distrust of neat academic categorization as she strikes out in unpredictable directions in her future work. She writes, she told Montresor in 1991, not to demonstrate or prescribe poetic principles, but, rather, "to find things out on a personal level." She also wants her work to produce an emotional response in her readers: "If . . . six people that I care about are moved by it and say, in effect, that I did it right, that means more than hundreds of people applauding." What does seem safely predictable about Ann Beattie's career is that she will continue to explore surprising ways to please herself and those six friends and to illuminate the times in which she lives for the rest of her readers.

Interviews:

Bob Miner, "Ann Beattie: 'I Write Best When I Am Sick,'" *Village Voice,* 21 (9 August 1976): 33–34;

G. E. Murray, "A Conversation with Ann Beattie," *Story Quarterly,* 7/8 (1978): 62–68;

Maggie Lewis, "The Sixties: Where Are They Now? Novelist Ann Beattie Knows," *Christian Science Monitor,* 23 October 1979, pp. B6–B10;

Joyce Maynard, "Visiting Ann Beattie," *New York Times Book Review,* 11 May 1980, pp. 1, 39–41;

Annie Leibovitz, "Ann Beattie," *Vogue,* 170 (July 1980): 148–151, 193–194;

Nancy Connors, "Interview with Ann Beattie," *Cleveland Plain Dealer,* 23 June 1985, pp. P1–P2;

"Media's Advice Blitz Makes 'Everybody Feel Inadequate': A Conversation with Ann Beattie," *U.S. News and World Report,* 99 (29 July 1985): 62;

W. Goldstein, "PW Interviews," *Publisher's Weekly,* 230 (19 September 1986): 120–121;

Steven R. Centola, "An Interview with Ann Beattie," *Contemporary Literature,* 31 (1990): 405–422;

Josh Getlin, "Novelist Focuses on Childhood Isolation," *Los Angeles Times,* 18 January 1990, pp. E1, 14–15;

P. H. Samway, "An Interview With Ann Beattie," *America,* 162 (12 May 1990): 469–471;

Nancy Sharkey, "'Do I Have a Collection?': Interview with Ann Beattie," *New York Times Book Review,* 26 May 1991, p. 3;

Carlin Romano, "Author Ann Beattie, Demystifying Herself," *Philadelphia Inquirer,* 29 July 1991, pp. 1C, 8C;

Larry McCaffery and Sinda Gregory, "A Conversation with Ann Beattie," in *The Critical Response to Ann Beattie,* edited by Jaye Berman Montresor (Westport, Conn.: Greenwood Press, 1993), 97–109;

Jaye Berman Montresor, "This Was in 1991, in Iowa City: Talking with Ann Beattie," in *The Critical Response to Ann Beattie,* pp. 218–254;

James Plath, "Counternarrative: An Interview with Ann Beattie," *Michigan Quarterly Review,* 32 (1993): 359–379;

Neila C. Seshachari, "Picturing Ann Beattie: A Dialogue," in *The Critical Response to Ann Beattie,* edited by Montresor (Westport, Conn.: Greenwood Press, 1993), pp. 187–204.

Bibliographies:

Carolyn Porter, "A Bibliography of Writings by Ann Beattie," in *Contemporary American Women Writers: Narrative Strategies,* edited by Catherine Rainwater and William J. Scheick (Lexington: University Press of Kentucky, 1985), pp. 26–28;

Harry Opperman, "Ann Beattie: A Checklist," *Bulletin of Bibliography,* 44 (June 1987): 111–118.

References:

John W. Aldridge, "Less Is a Lot Less," in his *Talents and Technicians: Literary Chic and the New Assembly-Line Fiction* (New York: Scribners / Toronto: Maxwell Macmillan Canada / New York: Maxwell Macmillan International, 1992), pp. 45–78;

Georgia Brown, "Chilly Views of Beattie," *Canto,* 3 (August 1980): 165–173;

Steven R. Centola, "Redefining the American Dream: Ann Beattie and the Pursuit of Happiness," *CLA Journal,* 34 (December 1990): 161–173;

Miriam Healy Clark, "Postmodernism and Its Children: The Case of Ann Beattie's 'A Windy Day at the Reservoir,'" *South Atlantic Review,* 61 (Winter, 1996): 77–87;

Deborah DeZure, "Images of Void in Beattie's 'Shifting,'" *Studies in Short Fiction,* 26 (Winter 1989): 11–15;

Joseph Epstein, "Ann Beattie and the Hippoisie," in *The Critical Response to Ann Beattie,* edited by Jaye Berman Montresor (Westport, Conn.: Greenwood Press, 1993), pp. 57–64;

Joshua Gilder, "Down and Out: The Stories of Ann Beattie," *New Criterion,* 1 (1982): 51–56;

Gilder, "Less is Less," *New Criterion,* 2 (1983): 78–82;

Thomas Griffith, "Rejoice if You Can," *Atlantic Monthly,* 246 (September 1980): 28–29;

Doris Grumbach, "Ann Beattie," *Washington Magazine,* 11 (August 1976): 225–231;

Jane Bowers Hill, "Ann Beattie's Children as Redeemers," *Critique: Studies in Modern Fiction,* 27 (Summer 1986): 197–212;

Don Lee, "About Ann Beattie," *Ploughshares,* 21 (Fall 1995): 231–236;

Jaye Berman Montresor, ed., *The Critical Response to Ann Beattie,* Critical Responses in Arts and Letters, no. 4 (Westport, Conn.: Greenwood Press, 1993);

Christina Murphy, *Ann Beattie* (Boston: Twayne, 1986);

Stacey Olster, "Photographs and Fantasies in the Stories of Ann Beattie," in *The Critical Response to Ann Beattie,* pp. 117–128;

James Plath, "My Lover the Car: Ann Beattie's 'A Vintage Thunderbird' and Other Vehicles," *Kansas Quarterly,* 21, no. 4 (1989): 113–119;

Carolyn Porter, "Ann Beattie: The Art of the Missing," in *The Critical Response to Ann Beattie,* pp. 75–89;

Barbara Schapiro, "Ann Beattie and the Culture of Narcissism," *Webster Review,* 10 (Fall 1985): 86–101;

Leo Schneiderman, "Ann Beattie: Emotional Loss and Strategies of Reparation," *American Journal of Psychoanalysis,* 53 (December 1993): 317–334;

Kenneth E. Story, "Throwing a Spotlight on the Past: Narrative Method in Ann Beattie's 'Jacklighting,'" *Studies in Short Fiction,* 27 (Winter 1990): 106–110;

P. Wilner, "Ann Beattie Between the Lines," *Harper's Bazaar,* 119 (November 1985): 90–97;

David Wyatt, "Ann Beattie," *Southern Review,* 28 (1991): 145–159.

Madison Smartt Bell

(1 August 1957 -)

Muriel A. Charpentier
Université de la Sorbonne-Nouvelle, Paris

BOOKS: *The Washington Square Ensemble* (New York: Viking, 1983);
History of the Owen Graduate School of Management (Knoxville, Tenn.: Vanderbilt University, 1985);
Waiting for the End of the World (New York: Ticknor & Fields, 1985);
Straight Cut (New York: Ticknor & Fields, 1986);
Zero db and Other Stories (New York: Ticknor & Fields, 1987);
The Year of Silence (New York: Ticknor & Fields, 1987);
Soldier's Joy (New York: Ticknor & Fields, 1989);
Barking Man and Other Stories (New York: Ticknor & Fields, 1990);
Doctor Sleep (New York: Harcourt Brace Jovanovich, 1991);
Save Me, Joe Louis (New York: Harcourt Brace, 1993);
All Souls' Rising (New York: Pantheon, 1995);
Ten Indians (New York: Pantheon, 1996);
Narrative Design: A Writer's Guide to Structure (New York: Norton, 1997).

Madison Smartt Bell (courtesy of Bell)

Effusive critical acclaim can be as debilitating as it is gratifying for young writers. Madison Smartt Bell, named by critics very early in his career as one of the best writers of his generation, has been singularly unaffected by the enthusiastic critical reception of his first novel, *The Washington Square Ensemble* (1983). Apparently oblivious to the eager expectations of readers scrutinizing his subsequent publications, he has avoided the paralysis common to writers of highly lauded first novels, going on in the following fifteen years to publish nine novels, two collections of short stories, a nonfiction history of the Owen Graduate School of Management, and a primer for creative writing (a subject he currently teaches at Goucher College in Maryland). While he resists being labeled, Bell has nonetheless been categorized with writers from what Bill Buford, former editor of *Granta,* has called the "dirty realism" movement. Bell's work was included in *Granta's* special summer 1996 issue focusing on "the best of young American novelists." He has received several other literary honors, including the Lillian Smith Award (1989) for his novel *Soldier's Joy.* His first historical novel, *All Souls' Rising,* was named a finalist for the 1995 National Book Award and the PEN/Faulkner Award. This novel, which plunges into the violent nineteenth-century slave rebellions in Haiti, marked not only a new level of critical recognition but also a turning point in Bell's career, as he moved from earlier depictions of disenfranchised individuals in modern urban America to a more sweeping portrayal of a whole people struggling for acceptance as human beings. Despite his occasionally grim subject matter, Bell's short fiction is leavened by the same buoyant and exuberant style that has characterized his longer works.

Bell was born in Nashville, Tennessee, the son of Henry Denmark Bell and Allen (Wigginton) Bell. His father practiced law and his mother simultaneously managed a riding school and worked the farm that Bell grew up on in Williamson County. After graduating from Princeton University in 1979, Bell went on to receive a master's degree from Hollins College in 1981. He developed an intense interest in the authors involved in the regional literary movement of the 1930s known as the Southern Renascence or Agrarian Movement and wrote his master's thesis on Madison Jones. After completing his graduate work, Bell lived in New York and London. He held various odd jobs during this period, working as a security guard, production assistant, soundman, and picture-research assistant. Employing his skills as a writer, he also worked as a manuscript reader and copywriter and authored a number of readers' guides between 1980 and 1983 before accepting an assistant professorship at Goucher College. In 1984 and 1986 Bell also taught at the Poetry Center of the 92nd Street Y in New York City; he continued teaching creative writing at the Iowa Writers' Workshop in 1987 and 1988 and at the Johns Hopkins Writing Seminars in 1989 before returning to Goucher College. Bell married poet Elizabeth Spires in 1985; with their daughter, Celia, they currently live in Maryland, where Bell and Spires are both Writers in Residence at Goucher.

When his first collection of short stories, *Zero db and Other Stories,* was published in 1987, Bell had already published three well-received novels. This first short-story volume, however, includes Bell's earliest fiction. In his autobiographical essay "One Art," Bell recalls that the story "Triptych II" was written "out of desperation" during a difficult period in his life. Bell developed severe chronic asthma at the age of two; in the following years he suffered frequent bouts of bronchitis. During long periods when his health kept him from school he indulged in reading, which became his favorite activity. Bell's unusual childhood was also shaped by his parents' heterodox social position: they were educated professionals who also happened to run a productive farm. Bell's attorney father worked out of a law firm in Nashville and later in Franklin, the Williamson County seat. When the senior Bell married Wigginton in the mid 1950s, they bought a farm near Franklin. Bell's atypical experience of both cultured education and agrarian pastoral life isolated him from other children: his mother had taught him to read well before he began attending school, where his classmates had had no such advantage. Bell recalls, interestingly, that at this time he developed his lifelong habit of talking to himself, *sotto voce* but audibly, telling himself little stories, transforming his classmates' overheard conversations into dialogues by adding "he said" or "she said" under his breath. This early evidence of his predisposition to write was confirmed in his senior year of high school, when he was again confined to bed for an extended period with a collapsed lung. During this "odd imprisonment" he composed the story later titled "Triptych II," which he originally wrote "in pencil and hid in a drawer." After dropping out of Princeton for one term to work on the Ingram Book Company's receiving docks in Nashville, Bell submitted a revised version of "Triptych" ("Triptych I") to George Garrett, his creative-writing teacher at Princeton. Because he knew and admired Garrett's work, Bell was encouraged when Garrett offered to include the short story in the journal *Intro,* which Garrett edited. Bell accepted the offer, and his story was published in 1978. Bell recalls other Princeton faculty members as "good masters and good examples," listing among those to whom he is most greatly indebted William Goyen, Stephen Koch, Rosanne Coggeshall, and Richard Dillard.

Anne Bernays, reviewing *Zero db* for *The New York Times Book Review* (15 February 1987), compares Bell's range of voice to that of the Peruvian singer Yma Sumac; Bernays's evocation of the semantic field of music generates an illuminating metaphor to characterize Bell's writing. "Triptych I," as its title suggests, unfolds into a tripartite structure, a structure mirrored in the arrangement of the stories in the collection as a whole. The first and third parts of the story describe the annual hog killing that takes place on the Denmark family's farm, where the Denmarks are assisted by the Tylers, a black family employed on the farm. Readers view the hog killing primarily through the eyes of Lisa, the Denmarks' five-year-old daughter. Lisa witnesses a grisly but banal demonstration of domestic violence: "Robert and Jack Lee were blocking out a hog that had already been gutted. Jack cut off the head with a chopping ax, and then used the ax to separate the backbone out from the ribs. The spine came out in one piece, with the stiff little tail still at the end of it." Lisa is both disturbed and thrilled by this gory ritual: "The hog-killing animated her and she couldn't sit still for long." But she does not fully grasp what is taking place, even when, after falling into a scalding trough, she only narrowly escapes the hogs' fate before being rescued by Ben Tyler. The same thoughtless disregard for life and the implicit correlation between humans and animals informs the second part of the story. After unblinkingly detailing the hog killing, Bell offers an indoor scene unflinchingly depicting the death of Amelia Tyler, who dies while her husband Ben is outside taking care of the hogs. The character Ben Tyler shares a number of similarities with the Benjamin Taylor who worked as a long-time employee on the Bell family farm, a black man Bell recalls affectionately in "One Art."

Bell's mastery in building an atmosphere that draws the character and reader, both unaware, into a

Dust jacket for Bell's first collection of short stories, which includes fiction written before his early novels

poignantly epiphanic experience is well displayed in "Triptych II," particularly in the beautifully conveyed image of the drunk old man, Mr. Eliot, rapturously playing the violin:

> he played things he had never known, moving in a heavy, certain suspension full of sound, a shadowy fluid. In the end the fluid would enter every room of the house, washing the dimness away. Mr. Eliot moved freely then, not from light to dark boundaries but in the common absorbing night of the world. An electric power animated him and he felt little bonding to the body he carried with him. It was a pitiful stranger, but he was compassionate toward it.

Fluidity, an arresting metaphor in this passage, is also the quality that constitutes the core of the writing and the reading process, according to what Bell wrote in *Narrative Design: A Writer's Guide to Structure* (1997): "The experience of imagining and composing any story is . . . fluid. . . . So too is the experience of *reading* a good story. The reader is carried fluidly along the currents of the narrative, is moved and influenced without quite knowing how it happened."

Like "Triptych I," "Triptych II" engages the reader with an opening scene of agrarian violence and proceeds to unfold in a flowing, three-part movement. Part one graphically parallels the hog-killing in "Triptych I" with another outdoor scene of carnage in which a peacock is killed by other peacocks; the peacock "was caught with a lucky spike that pierced through his little eye to his brain." The second part of the story describes the lonely and mechanical life of old Mr. Eliot; the third part consists of a single short scene of a bull being transported to a slaughterhouse, a scene presented through the eyes of the bull itself.

"Triptych I" and "Triptych II" address the theme of death by joining together scenes of the brutal slaughter or natural deaths of animals with the deaths of human beings. These parallels are underscored by the suggested personification of the animals, as in the startling image of the heads of seven slaughtered hogs: "In the vague December light each face seemed to possess some secret." Just as the animals' deaths are sudden, so are those of the human figures: Amelia Tyler is seized suddenly, dying before her husband returns from the hog killing; Mr. Eliot's veins rupture unexpectedly, just as Amelia's brain malignancy does. The hog slaughter in "Triptych I" is reiterated in the peacock and bull slaughters in "Triptych II." "Triptych I" describes vivid images, as Bell strives to convey what his "inner eye has *seen.*" Bell sustains this effort by using Lisa as a narrator: she communicates the world as she "sees" it, and her perspective illustrates not only the world she views but also the state of a mind still incompletely formed. The second portion of *Zero db* (including the stories "Irene," "The Lie Detector," "I ♥ New York," and "The Forgotten Bridge") primarily tracks the peregrinations of a narrator drifting through the suburbs of New York City, tracing a path through Williamsburg, Newark, and Hoboken. This unmoored narrator shares Bell's experiences and his fascination for New York City. Bell has acknowledged an autobiographical element in these stories:

> I think I have always seen New York as a sort of beautiful tragic monster. The idea of the smashing together of so many different cultures and so many people in such a small area appealed to me. Then too, in the first years I lived in New York I had no regular employment so I saw a great deal of the street life and to some extent in the early books I was reporting on my ways of getting along at street level.

Fred Chappell, in a review of *Zero db* for the *Washington Post* (1 February 1987), notes that seven of the eleven stories in the collection reveal Bell's "characteristic theme"–"the helplessness of compassion in a casually cruel world." Chappell finds that "feelings of brotherhood arise and persist" especially in the stories "The Naked Lady," "The Lie Detector," "The Forgotten Bridge," and "The Structure and Meaning of Dormitory and Food Services."

In the latter story, Bell interweaves first-person passages narrated by a Princeton graduate with second-person discourses based on imperative forms and a variety of topographical descriptions portraying the buildings and landscapes of the Princeton campus. Both narrative techniques conflate in the final paragraph where the reader, addressed as "you," is enjoined by a narrative "I" to "grope" his "way through it"–the dark? the story?–if he "wants to know." Bell emphasizes the striking inconclusiveness of the story by the paradoxically assertive yet self-negating authorial voice taunting the reader: "Look at the tables right near where you're standing. You haven't got a chance of picking me out." This voice leads the reader through Princeton's meandering corridors with frequent, condescending admonitions such as "Take a deep breath," "so you've got to be careful," and "read on." Readers eventually arrive at what may be an accidental "portrait of the artist as a young man": "I looked sad and desperate. My hair was long and greasy, and there were black rings around my eyes. My shirt-tail was out and I had food spills on my shirt."

"Irene" is the most beautiful and obliquely poetic story of the collection. The idle narrator justifies his living in a squalid Newark neighborhood with an intertextual reference, quoting from Farid ud-din Attar's *The Conference of Birds* (ca. thirteenth century): "He who wishes to live in peace must go to the ruins, as the madmen do." The perversely "house-proud" narrator develops a sort of religious reverence for one area in his new flat, delimited by two columns topped with Corinthian capitals. He venerates "the sacred vacancy of the space behind the columns." Projecting his fantasies into this space transforms it into an objective correlative for his vision of artistic creation:

> I thought that one day soon I would cross over into the space behind the columns and write a book that would amaze the world, compose music that would make the world weep, invent a complete and perfect philosophy that would make the world comprehensible to itself.

But he immediately adds that "delusions of grandeur prevented" him from "settling down to do anything." So the space beyond the columns comes to symbolize his "joblessness and general inertia" or even "the vacant space" in his mind. The significance of this very personal, subjective space comes further into question with the intrusion of another subjectivity into that space. The young Hispanic girl with whom the narrator has fallen hopelessly in love visits his apartment, arriving in a state of emotional distress, and he is unable to communicate any consolation to her: "Irene cried on and I sat on the trunk with my back to the window, feeling enormous, clumsy and stupid." After the narrator has left this neighborhood, he reflects on his feelings for Irene. She becomes a ghostly figure in his private universe, "stuck" in his head "at the intersection between the imagined and the real."

Bell continues his examination of the impossibility of love in "Monkey Park." Perry, a fisherman, visits Carolee while her husband, Alphonse, is working. Perry and Carolee share a peculiarly intense relationship that defies articulation, leaving them in awkward silence. They dine together before joining Alphonse in a bar and finally going to a park. Alphonse falls asleep in the park, leaving Perry and Carolee alone, watching monkeys in a cage. The monkeys return their gaze, as if Perry and Carolee were the main park attraction. This inversion points up the prison-like impasse their relationship has reached. The story ends with a nostalgic prolepsis as Perry announces his departure.

The futility of attempting to love in "Monkey Park" figures largely in "The Lie Detector" and "The Forgotten Bridge"; the latter two stories are also linked by a reappearing character, the Puerto Rican apartment superintendent Eugenio Benson. In "The Lie Detector," the isolated narrator, "recuperating from a bad love affair" and in search of a new apartment, knows he is being tricked but cannot decide by whom–Benson the super or Lubin, the Hasidic landlord. When the narrator finds himself lying during a polygraph test for a job interview, he abandons his lie: "I had lost track of the lie now, and I might never find it again. Out beyond the window I could see the bright ribbon of train tracks curling away over the bridge. . . . So maybe the lie was out there, too, I thought, even if I could not see it. It was just there, floating around with the other particles of the atmosphere." Ultimately he is hired.

The suspicious super makes his next appearance in "The Forgotten Bridge" as the narrator becomes acquainted with some Hispanic gang members and is forced to recognize "the inverse square law of sectarianism and racial animosity." The narrator of "I ♥ New York" similarly confronts urban tensions and violence, and, like the narrator of "Irene," he fails to help people: "I wish I had something to say to you," he tells a desperate man whose wife was beaten to death six months earlier in a Brooklyn subway station. This narrator finally distances himself by going up on a bridge where the people seem "no bigger than cockroaches." On the bridge he achieves a state of healing solitude: "When I put my hand out over the railing my hand covered all the people up and I couldn't see any of them anymore."

The narrator of the title story works as a cinema soundman, just as Bell himself had. Throughout "Zero db," Bell cultivates a metaphorical parallel between the ephemeral nature of sound and the transience of love. Recovering from a break-up, as do other narrators in this collection, this narrator finds himself in a bar addressing a tape recorder instead of his ex-girlfriend. The story offers a slim possibility of redemption in relationships, however, when the narrator records a grimly amusing conversation going on behind him in the bar. The conversation concerns an Asian hit man who goes crazy because, during an assignment, he found it impossible to kill his target without injuring the man's Doberman at the same time. The hit man eventually adopts the dog, cooking him homemade soup, and retires from his lethal profession.

The relationships and parallels between injured animals and isolated humans remain themes in "Today Is a Good Day to Die," Bell's first foray into historical fiction. The story is narrated in the present tense by a young lieutenant on detached duty with the Seventh Cavalry, which is spending the winter of 1875–1876 at Fort Robinson. Feeling useless, the lieutenant takes long, aimless rides. When his horse breaks a leg on New Year's Eve, the young officer must kill the animal. Lost in the snowy wilderness, the lieutenant meets two Indians; although he cannot communicate with them, they rescue him. The second part of the story takes place in June of that year, when the lieutenant participates in "his first engagement with any enemy" at the disastrous Battle of Little Bighorn. He witnesses the violence of war and its consequences:

> Most of the two hundred and fifty corpses are scattered near the top. They have all been stripped to the skin and scarcely a scrap of leather or cloth remains to them. All that is left is paper money, blowing fitfully over the dead like leaves.

In a hallucinatory flight from the dreadful scene, the lieutenant is on a "long trajectory to nowhere." During the following three days he slowly reviews and takes leave of the remnants of his life before finally departing with a Christ-like calm, greeting vultures with the biblical admonishment: *"Take and eat what God hath given thee."*

"The Naked Lady" reconsiders the hope of redemption through artistic creation, a theme repeated throughout the collection. The art form in question is sculpture, and Bell seems to have sculpted his prose deliberately, achieving powerful effects through brevity and authenticity of voice. The narrator, expressing himself in broken English, tells about his friend Monroe, a sculptor who is struggling to put a failed relationship behind him. The narrator tries to help Monroe by taking him to bars to get drunk. This excursion apparently works, triggering a creative outburst as Monroe begins sculpting a critical self-portrait: "It looked like it was thinkin about all the foolish things Monroe had got up to in his life so far." In *Narrative Design,* Bell uses the metaphor of sculpting when discussing the transformation of raw material into crafted narrative:

> The writer models a unitary mass of information in the same way that a sculptor models a blob of clay or carves a block of stone. Perhaps there is something in the mass to begin with that suggests the form the artist will give it. In that case, form is indwelling, inherent in experience, in the block.

The parallels between Bell's biography and those of his characters demonstrate Bell's belief that fiction springs from the raw material of the author's experiences.

Prominent among the many animals Bell includes in his first collection are the dogs romping through several of the stories; it is not surprising that his second collection is titled *Barking Man and Other Stories* (1990). Like William Faulkner in *Sanctuary* (1931), Bell creates his own version of a canine world in these tales. He introduces the reader to a catholic range of breeds, from the Doberman (an epitome of strength in "Black and Tan") to the diminutive poodle (a featured character in "Petit Cachou"). In the title story, the main character himself takes on the role of a dog. This collection received more mixed and qualified reviews than *Zero db,* but critics concurred in praising the quality of the writing in most of the stories.

In "Black and Tan," set in the rural South, Peter Jackson, a tobacco farmer who has lost his wife and his two grown children over a two-year span, becomes a breeder of Dobermans. In a childhood memory, Jackson recalls being cared for by a Doberman: his parents' fears for their child were soon allayed when they saw that the Doberman had come to love the infant Peter, and they entrusted their child to this canine babysitter. This recollection is actually one of Bell's own, as he reveals in "One Art":

> My parents had a big red Doberman named Wotan, who was attached to my mother as a child might have been. How this dog would respond to my appearance was a subject of some concern. . . . As it happened, Wotan easily transferred much of his love and loyalty to me. When I was a little older my mother discovered that she could leave me in my playpen out in the yard . . . under the dog's supervision.

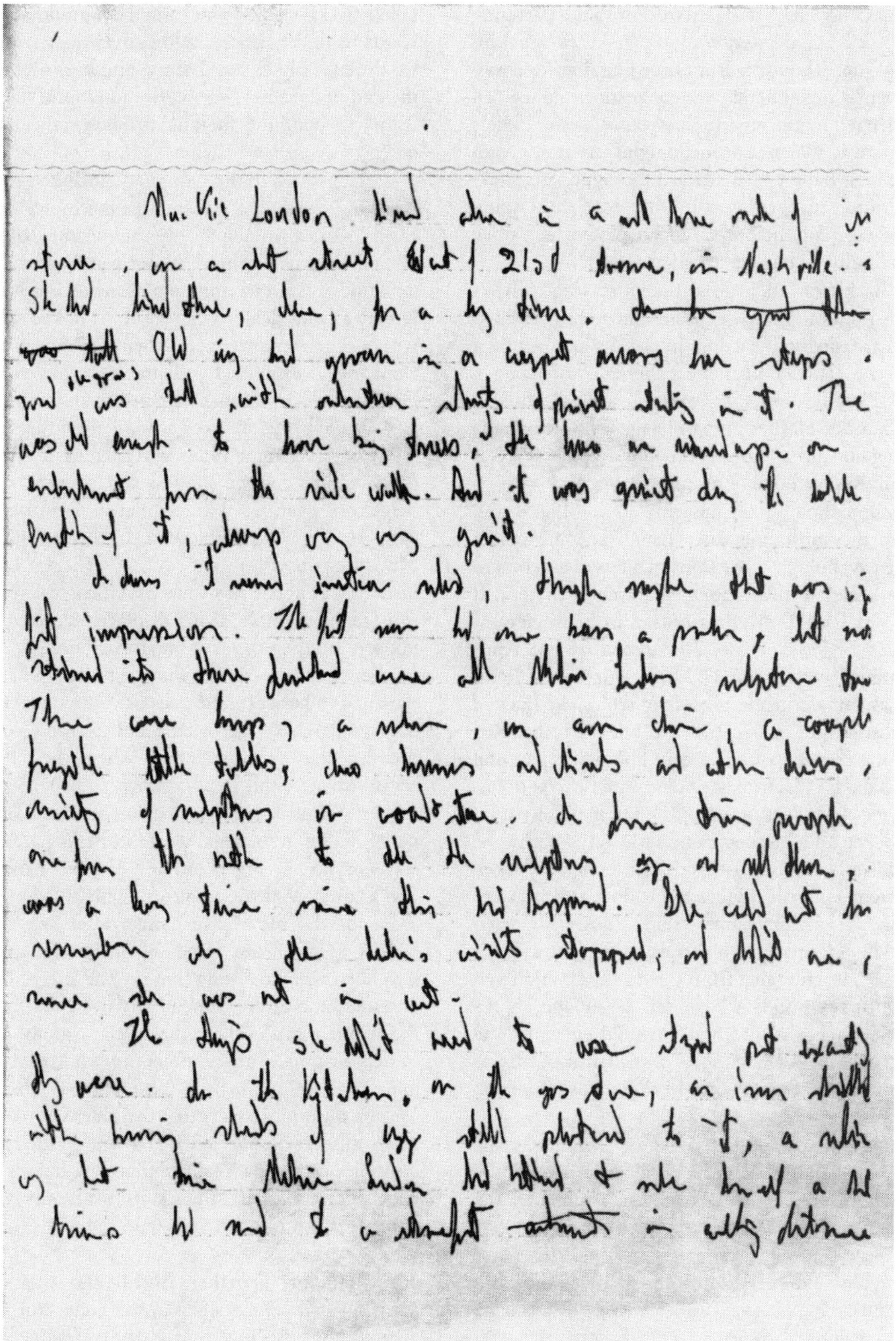

Page from the first draft for "Dragon Seed," collected in Bell's 1990 book, Barking Man and Other Stories *(Collection of Madison Smartt Bell)*

"Black and Tan," narrated by Trimble, a part-time deputy, unveils the mysterious and pain-stricken evolution of Jackson, who turns from breeding dogs to counseling juvenile delinquents, which he does quite well until challenged by the incorrigible young Bantry. Their confrontation is violent but meaningful. After succeeding in pointing Bantry back toward the right path, Jackson decides to retire, relieved by the prospect of aging and finally escaping the burden of survival, which since losing his family he has perceived as a curse.

In "Barking Man," Alf, a student staying with his brother in London and descending into schizophrenia, behaves increasingly like a dog. In trances induced by a hypnotist, he actually lives the experience of being a dog. Alf's identification with canines escalates until he viciously attacks another human being. The story ends with Alf again undergoing therapeutic hypnotism, but without any visible hope of his improvement.

Psychopathology thematically joins "Black and Tan" with the substantial tale "Petit Cachou," which details the psychological reactions of a few characters to what should be an ideal setting, the French Riviera. It is, in fact, as Rick DeMarinis puts it in his review of *Barking Man* for the *New York Times Book Review* (8 April 1990) "grained with hurt." DeMarinis describes "Petit Cachou" as "an astringent novella in which the lives of utterly dissimilar characters are cleverly braided together in a comedy of adolescent libido and parental dismay." Ton-Ton Detroit, an exiled American peddler, is, like other characters in this story, fascinated by a little pickpocket and his dog. The little boy roams the streets endlessly in search of possible booty, hypnotically crooning childish rhymes to his dog, as if he were always in an hallucinatory state (possibly drug-induced). In a central night scene, Ton-Ton Detroit watches the pair emerging from the darkness, and even as he rebuffs the child, he wonders about the child's special abilities. He is sure that the child controls "the dog's every step with his mind." But then it occurs to him that "perhaps it was really the dog whose thoughts controlled the boy."

As the little pickpocket wanders, so do the male characters in "Finding Natasha" and "Move on Up," both of whom are in search of a lost woman in the streets of New York City. Both "Finding Natasha" (which appeared in *Best American Short Stories 1990*) and "Move on Up" explore the themes of mutability and loss. In "Finding Natasha," Stuart's loss of Natasha grows into a general concern with all disappearances: "Every time he heard about someone else missing he wondered how many just vanished without being missed." When he finally finds Natasha, she is devastated by drug abuse. Hal, the searching character in "Move on Up," knows that Judith is probably dead, killed by crack or some other drug addiction, but he wants to find her body and provide her with a funeral for the sake of her son, Benny. Hal lives on the street; at the end of the story, he still has not found Judith, but he wants to continue looking for her rather than being taken to a homeless shelter.

"Customs of the Country" (included in *Best American Short Stories 1989*) reshuffles the topics and roles of earlier stories, showing how the narrator tries by leading a faultless life to retrieve her son, Davey, from a foster family. She recounts her life with Patrick, Davey's father, a drug dealer who got her hooked on Dilaudid without her knowledge. When he was arrested, she went into withdrawal, still unaware of her addiction. Davey made a nuisance of himself, and before she realized that she was ill, she responded with rage and seriously injured him. Now working as a waitress, she comes home to her spotless flat to hear one of her neighbors beat his wife regularly. Reviewing *Barking Man* for *The Washington Post* (15 April 1990), Patrick McGrath observes that Bell's "splicing of the two instances of abuse has solid psychological resonance: it is a telling example of the displacement of guilt, and it imposes on the story a strong formal design." When the mother finally realizes that her son will never be returned to her care, she goes next door and knocks her abusive neighbor out with a skillet. She recognizes the pointlessness of this action when the abused wife refuses to seize this opportunity to escape.

"Witness" records another instance of domestic violence. Set in the legal world in Bell's native Williamson County, it draws on the judicial experiences of Bell's father. Wilson, an attorney involved in the case of a friend who may be in danger after her former husband's release from a mental institution, tries to help her, even while realizing that no one shares his concern and that little can be done in any event. He goes to visit the woman and finds the entire family murdered. When Trimble (the same deputy who narrated "Black and Tan") tells him that the killer has been arrested, Wilson bitterly answers that the killer will "plead insanity." Wilson's already-fractured faith in the legal system crumbles when he realizes that the killer's "freedom was better protected" than Wilson's family. In the final scene, Wilson is left literally and morally groping in the dark.

"Holding Together" may be the strangest and yet the most compelling story in the collection. It is a fantasy combined with a bleak and realistic narrative of torture. The narrator endures a variety of ordeals that evoke a sense of kinship in the reader, except that the narrator is in fact another of Bell's animals–in this case, a mouse (an articulate and clever Oriental mouse that masters the divinatory science of the I Ching). Bell's handling of this complex of the fantastic and the realistic demonstrates his own mastery of the science of the short-story genre, a mastery noted by Rick DeMarinis: "In hands as skilled as Mr. Bell's, the short story is the most dynamic and flexible of literary forms."

Bell combines the fantastic with the allegorical in "Dragon's Seed." The narrator, an old and apparently mad woman, Mackie, who holds "colloquy with demons," lives in dismal seclusion. She sculpts heads of Greek mythological characters; her latest subject is Medusa, who represents, in psychoanalytic terms, castration. She befriends Preston, a boy who is being exploited by one of her neighbors, a pornographer. Bell's sexual symbolism in this story points up Preston's ordeal and climaxes when Mackie takes action against the child abuser, transforming herself into a Gorgon and turning the abuser to stone. She completes her physical catharsis by setting his house on fire. Mackie's efforts to help the boy forget his sufferings are particularly poignant: she tells him the stories of the *Iliad* and the *Odyssey* and calls him Jason.

"Mr. Potatohead in Love," the final story in this collection, is a highly surreal narrative. Mr. Potatohead, a street performer, gives an impressionistic account of a day in his life, offering strong visual scenes and vivid oral impressions. The theme of magic is wonderfully echoed by the joyous and rhythmical style employed by Bell in this piece; as Mr. Potatohead observes, "everybody has to know a little rough magic nowadays."

While *The Year of Silence* (1987) is generally considered a novel, it is nonetheless structured as a short-story cycle, following the example of great American works such as Sherwood Anderson's *Winesburg, Ohio* (1919), William Faulkner's *Go Down, Moses and Other Stories* (1942), or, more recently, Russell Banks's *Trailerpark* (1981). Bell's book revolves around the central character, Marian, a young drug addict who commits suicide. The central chapter is devoted to her; all the other chapters focus on people who knew her, some quite well, others only by sight. As Roberta Silman said in her review of *The Year of Silence* for *The New York Times Book Review* (15 November 1987), Bell "has an uncanny understanding of the way many people must struggle to live." Undoubtedly, this insight has contributed to the warm critical reception of Bell's work and to his readers' anticipation of his continuing publications.

References:

Justin Cronin, "A Conversation with Madison Smartt Bell," *Four Quarters* (Philadelphia: LaSalle University, 1995);

Eve Shelnutt, ed., *My Poor Elephant: 27 Male Writers at Work* (Atlanta: Longstreet Press, 1992).

Doris Betts

(4 June 1932 –)

Deborah E. Barker
University of Mississippi

See also the Betts entry in *DLB Yearbook 1982.*

BOOKS: *The Gentle Insurrection and Other Stories* (New York: Putnam, 1954; London: Gollancz, 1955);
Tall Houses in Winter (New York: Putnam, 1957; London: Cassell, 1958);
The Scarlet Thread (New York: Harper & Row, 1964);
The Astronomer and Other Stories (New York: Harper & Row, 1965);
The River to Pickle Beach (New York: Harper & Row, 1972);
Beasts of the Southern Wild and Other Stories (New York: Harper & Row, 1973);
Heading West (New York: Knopf, 1981);
Souls Raised from the Dead (New York: Knopf, 1994);
The Sharp Teeth of Love (New York: Knopf, 1997).

The appeal of Doris Betts's short stories derives from her ability to give dignity and significance to her ordinary and often unassuming characters. More comfortable living with and writing about the people at the feed store than the academics she works with at the University of North Carolina at Chapel Hill, Betts creates stories that reflect the quiet despair and moments of hope and doubt of everyday people. Using her imagination in combination with voracious reading and a strong sense of place acquired from growing up in a quiet mill town, Betts produces a fictional world that delineates all the subtle complexities of "simple" rural life.

Because of her persistent interest in the dynamic processes of faith and doubt, and because her settings are rooted in the South, critics often label Betts's works as Christian and/or Southern. The critical objections to these categories, however, are equally strong. As one critic for *The New York Times Book Review* (28 October 1973) explained, "Although liberally laced with elements of the southern gothic, the grotesque, black humor, surrealism and fantasy, the writing escapes categorization and remains very much an index of one woman's intriguing mind." The distinctiveness of

Doris Betts (Staff photograph, Communications Division, Georgia Institute of Technology)

Betts's voice and vision was confirmed by the American Academy and Institute of Arts and Letters, which gave her the Award of Merit for the Short Story in 1989. The academy asserted that Betts's "idiosyncratic work, the subtlest modernist practice deeply colored by an intimate knowledge of and joy in her region, astonishes with its wit, passion, and sharp particularity."

Betts herself rejects categorizations, being distrustful of "Christian" as a term that "spoils to a rancid adjective," and she objects to stereotypical images of both Southern and women writers. She does not, however, diminish the significance of religious themes in her work, nor the importance of her religious Southern background. She was born Doris June Waugh on 4 June 1932 in Statesville, North Carolina, the only child of mill worker William Elmore Waugh and his wife, Mary Ellen (née Freeze), a devoted member of the Associate Reformed Presbyterian (ARP) Church. Betts cites her early religious training, especially the study and memorization of the Bible, as a crucial influence on her work as a writer. Describing herself as a "recovering Calvinist," Betts told interviewer Susan Ketchin in 1994 that the ARP members (whom her mother called "ALL Right People") "remain everything that I both loathed and benefitted from simultaneously, because I did benefit from it. I wouldn't trade anything for the knowledge of the Bible or for their love of the Psalms, a predilection which is a total contradiction to their standard Calvinist bent."

Because of her unflinching portrayal of rural and small-town Southern characters, Betts's work is often compared to that of Eudora Welty and William Faulkner; because of her interest in religious themes, her name is also linked to Flannery O'Connor's. Betts, however, questions certain aspects of these comparisons, especially regarding O'Connor's portrayal of faith. Describing herself as belonging to the "tribe of the Apostle Thomas–a natural doubter," Betts always demands the right to question faith and accept doubt as a natural part of life, even of a religious life. For Betts, the struggle for faith defines her characters. This approach, she says, distinguishes her work from O'Connor's static moments of revelation and redemption. As Betts explained in an interview with W. Dale Brown (1996):

> "Life in all its abundance"–that's a biblical quotation I love. That may be one of the differences between my attitude toward fiction and, say, Flannery O'Connor's way. She literally wanted at some moment in her story to have the eternal break through. There is a moment in which the veil goes thin and you see the pines and the sun break through as a wound. I guess I am not as confident as she is. I also don't see that it breaks through very often. If it does break through for me, it's apt to be in something that some person does. I concentrate very much on redeeming the time; *this time* is what we have.

Betts finds that her closest affinity is with writers such as Anton Chekhov, Walker Percy, and Graham Greene.

The importance of redeeming time, not necessarily finding ultimate truth or revelation, is evident in Betts's early short story "Mr. Shawn and Father Scott," which won the *Mademoiselle* College Fiction Contest and was included in *Best Short Stories of 1953.* Father Scott is a typical Betts character. On the surface he is a respectable member of the community, a Catholic priest in a small Southern parish where he is a rather silent member of the (mostly Methodist) Association of City Churchmen. Father Scott's secret sin, however, is the sin of complacency, which Betts sees as a much more corrupting force than doubt. Father Scott is "saved" by the sudden appearance of Mr. Shawn, an enigmatic character who arrives via freight car and sports a long, grey pigtailed wig and a mayonnaise jar full of pennies. To Father Scott's horror, Mr. Shawn, who knows shorthand, writes down every one of Father Scott's speeches and sermons and questions him about what he really means by the standard phrases and platitudes that have come to replace the passion he once felt. It becomes painfully obvious to Father Scott that he has no idea what "the Church stands for" or what "vital answers" we can give to the "new and challenging questions" with which the Church is confronted. When Mr. Shawn suddenly disappears after leaving the priest with a poem that ends with "Let us believe / in / something / now," Father Scott finds himself taking on the role of questioner in his own life and making life difficult for the complacent Methodists in the association. By the end of the story, Father Scott, as he needles one of his fellow clergymen, can feel the grey pigtail hanging down his back, and the aspirin bottle that he always has handy begins to sound like a jar full of pennies. As is true of many of her stories, in "Mr. Shawn and Father Scott" Betts never directly states the influence of mystical or supernatural forces. She leaves it to the reader to decide whether Mr. Shawn was just an eccentric drifter or Father Scott's guardian angel.

Betts began her writing career as a journalist working part-time for the *Statesville Daily Record* while still in high school. When she graduated from high school, she continued working for various newspapers and as a stringer for UPI. Although Betts won a scholarship to Duke University, the total cost of attending the university was still out of reach. While Betts was working for the *Greensboro News,* a friend suggested that she might be able to get a job at the news bureau of the Women's College (now the University of North Carolina, Greensboro) to help pay tuition. As a result, Betts attended the Women's College from 1950 to 1953. Discovering that there was no journalism school at that institution, Betts turned to creative writing and began writing the stories (including "Mr. Shawn and Father Scott") that make up her first collection, *The Gentle Insurrection and Other Stories* (1954), which won the University of North Carolina-Putnam Booklength Manuscript Prize and was praised by the judges of the awards and the national book reviewers.

"Serpents and Doves," another story from this collection, reinforces the notion of complacency as the ultimate sin and introduces another topic that recurs in Betts's fiction: the nature of heaven and hell. In a reaction against her Calvinist upbringing, Betts negates the image of eternal punishment. Hell is a lack of faith in one's own worth, and the afterlife is a place of "hard work," no "golden city, just working and learning and going back again." The Devil, unlike John Milton's fallen angel, is not an immortal or grandiose figure. The Devil, who appears to Jonathan Sykes (the Old Man) as he lies on his deathbed, explains that he has no existence apart from men: "You might say human lives are like stepping stones. I go from one to the other, but there is never a moment when I am off and outside the plane of life and can look down on it from something not temporal." The Old Man assumes that the Devil is there to punish him for the sin that he has run from all his life: his unjust shooting of an inmate during his time as a guard on a chain gang. Although the shooting was in part accidental–the Old Man did not hear the inmate call as he walked to the underbrush to relieve himself–he feels just as responsible for the death as if it were an intentional murder, and, to flee from his guilt, he has moved away from the South that he loves and taken up an anonymous existence in a boardinghouse among strangers. The Devil assures the Old Man that he is not there to pass judgment or sentence him to hell and that the Old Man has wasted a lot of time worrying about nothing. There is no hell, the Devil tells him; there is nothing at all. The Old Man triumphs in the end, however, by discovering the Devil's secret, which is not to strike fear into the hearts of men or tempt them with earthly delights but to make them believe that nothing they do really matters. The Old Man asserts that although he did not mean to kill the inmate, it was never unimportant, and it should not have prevented him from "atonement or accomplishment," the keys to redeeming time.

"Serpents and Doves" is also characteristic of Betts's work because of the importance of death as a moment of reflection, not just for the dying but also for the ones who must carry on. One critic for the *Saturday Review* (10 July 1954) indicates the powerful, yet quiet, nature of the circumstances Betts depicts in this first collection: "the charged atmosphere, subtle tensions, and unexpressed anxieties between well-meaning people who would like to understand one another, but are hopelessly divided by our human isolation." This kind of anxiety and isolation is evident in two of the stories that deal with death. In "The Sword," which was reprinted in 1957 in *A New Southern Harvest* (edited by Robert Penn Warren and Albert Erskine), Bert comes to visit his father, Lester, at his deathbed, only to discover that his father, from whom he always felt distant, was really proud of him. Bert regrets that on returning from World War II he gave his father the impersonal gift of money rather than a war memento, a Japanese sword. Bert has to acknowledge that he never really knew his father–that even the maid, to whom Bert did bring home a gift, had a closer relationship with his father–and that now he never will. Likewise, in "The End of Henry Fribble" Henry is a man who realizes his fate only after it is too late. Henry dominated his submissive wife, Lena, all her life, and after her death he continues to do the same to their daughter, Sarah, even to the point of getting rid of her suitors. As he is dying, Henry calls to Lena, who appears to him and then turns her back and vanishes. Henry sadly realizes at that moment that she will not come to him now and that he is completely alone for eternity.

In "The Very Old Are Beautiful" Betts gives an uplifting view of Mama Bower, who has lived well and dies without regrets. Although she is a difficult old woman who is set in her ways and who drives her daughter-in-law to tears by cleaning the house whenever she visits (no matter how diligently the daughter cleans in anticipation of the visit), she is mourned by those left behind, and the unseasonable blossoming of her favorite apple tree at her death is a symbol of both her hope and her strong will.

Perhaps an even more chilling form of isolation than death is found in those characters who are trapped in their own lives. In "Miss Parker Possessed" a stereotypical spinster librarian feels that she is possessed by the devil, but when she attempts to sexually lure Mr. Harvey, a member of the library board, she finds that her "seductions" (her provocative walk and her sudden outbursts) are taken for signs of old age and the need to retire. This humiliating revelation exorcises the devil; Miss Parker is no longer possessed, but her return to normalcy is also a resignation of her desire for love and passion. In the title story, "The Gentle Insurrection," Lettie, a young girl, gives up her one chance to escape the poverty of a life of sharecropping with her mother and older brother. In this story, originally titled "Yesterday Was the Last Time," the girl has comforted herself all day with the realization that everything she does is for the last time. However, that night, when she hears her boyfriend signal to her, she cannot bring herself to abandon her mother and brother as her father has; she turns over and cries, "for the last time." Lettie's loyalty to her mother is admirable, yet Betts paints such a devastating picture of the family's inability to change their bleak existence that Lettie's decision, like Miss Parker's "exorcism," is an emotional death sentence.

While readers can sympathize with Lettie and Miss Parker, Betts's least sympathetic character is Miss Ward in the ironically titled story "The Sympathetic Visitor." Miss Ward, a store manager, is one of Betts's complacent characters who prides herself on her willingness to pay a condolence call to Nettie Sue, her African American employee, just as she visits all her white workers when they have a death in the family. Miss Ward's deep-seated racism is manifest in her description of Rabbittown, the African American part of town where the streets have no names and where "Chinaberry trees grew in some of the bare yards, and the kinky heads that stuck out from between some of the branches were like brown burrs; it was as if all the trees had some common disease and were full of darkly parasitic growths." After arriving at Nettie Sue's home, Miss Ward discovers that her visit is prompted by more than a sense of duty. She is both thrilled and repulsed by her need to hear all the details of the tragic events that led Nettie Sue's brother, a World War II veteran, to kill his mother with a shotgun and then kill himself: "The strength of the compulsion left her weak; it was hideous, the way some quivering delighted part of her *wanted* to know how it was, *wanted* to smell blood and flesh just the way they had been; the desire rose from something in her that was older than the chanting native women and she shivered, deliciously and with revulsion."

Betts also discovered the limitations of good intentions after writing this story. Although she meant the story to be an indictment of the white shop manager's attitudes about race, she was threatened with a lawsuit by Thurgood Marshall because she based the story on a real-life incident and used the name of one of the people involved. After Betts visited with the woman, apologized, and explained her purpose in writing the story, the suit was dropped. Betts has said that the incident taught her about her responsibility as a writer and the need to protect people's privacy.

Dust jacket for Betts's 1965 book, stories in which characters often find themselves trapped by their egotism and pride

Betts's college years and early twenties were a productive time not only professionally but also personally. In 1952, the summer after her sophomore year, she married Lowry Matthew Betts, a University of South Carolina student whom she met through her association with the ARP Church. After the first semester of her junior year, she moved with her husband to South Carolina, where he finished his degree, and in July 1953 their first child, Doris LewEllyn, was born. The couple moved again, this time to Chapel Hill, where Lowry Betts entered law school and where their second child, David Lowry, was born in 1954. As a young mother of two, Betts continued both her journalism and fiction writing, working outside the home in a variety of jobs as a typing teacher, an office manager, a feature writer and daily columnist for the *Sanford Daily Herald* (1957–1958), a member of the editorial board of the *N.C. Democrat* (1958–1960), and a full-time editor of the *Sanford News Leader* (1960).

During this busy period she published her first novel, *Tall Houses in Winter* (1957), for which she won the Sir Walter Raleigh Award. In this novel, told in retrospect, Ryan Godwin, a man who has rejected his past, his religion, his family's expectations, and the South, returns home after learning he has cancer. He has to face his past and decide whether he wants to go on living. Through his attachment to his orphaned nephew Fen, who may be his own son, Ryan finds the strength to live. Betts recalls writing the novel during her lunch hours, because that was the only time that she had in her busy schedule to work on it. In the same year her family moved to Sanford, North Carolina, where her husband joined the law firm of Pittman and Staton. In 1960 Betts gave birth to her third child, Erskine Moore.

A Guggenheim Fellowship in creative writing for 1958–1959 gave Betts time to work on a second novel, *The Scarlet Thread,* which was published in 1964 and for which she won a second Sir Walter Raleigh Award in 1965. This novel is set in the past and chronicles the Allen family's "material rise and spiritual decline" (as one critic for *The Saturday Review,* 1 February 1965, described it) as well as the history of their community. During this time Betts also began a novella, originally titled "The Learned Astronomer," which, when revised, served as the title piece for her second collection, *The Astronomer and Other Stories* (1965).

In *The Astronomer and Other Stories* Betts continues many of the themes begun in her first collection. In "Careful, Sharp Eggs Underfoot" Wink Thomas, who refuses to leave his economically dying town and his invalid father, finds that, much like Lettie in "The Gentle Insurrection," he is trapped in a hopeless situation. In an effort to make his town rival Roxton, a nearby town with a factory, a hospital, good schools, and a future, Wink single-handedly founds the annual Parsonville Egg Festival with the hope of relieving the "poverty of the area and the monotony of the summers." Betts portrays a grotesquely funny scene in which that year's festival, held under the banner "Ain't Nobody Here But Us Chickens," ends in a town brawl complete with a rotten-egg fight. A clap of thunder, "like the roar of Jehovah's rage over the recalcitrant Israelites," and a huge downpour scatter the motley crowd. Wink, who threw the most eggs, runs all the way home, but his laughter over the ridiculous situation turns to tears of hopelessness, made even more poignant when his confused father begs him not to cry and calls him Orlando, the name of his brother who died young and who had been his father's favorite.

Characters in this collection also find themselves trapped through their own egotism and pride, as in "The Mandarin" and "The Proud and Virtuous." In "The Mandarin" Mrs. Applewhite, a wealthy widow, comes to understand the vastness of her loneliness. Mrs. Applewhite likes to test her neighbors' honesty by leaving a twenty-dollar bill inside a library book to see if the money is turned in. She views this as her version of the ancient dilemma of the Chinese mandarin: presented with the opportunity to push a button that would kill a Chinese mandarin whose death "would make you rich beyond your wildest dreams; and no one–including the Mandarin himself–would ever know you did it, would you push the button?" In the end Mrs. Applewhite realizes that more devastating than her neighbors' lack of honesty is the fact that, because of her inability to love anyone (including her own husband), she herself is like the mandarin: others will profit from her death, but no one will mourn it. In "The Proud and Virtuous" Mildred Stuart, a bored and unappreciated housewife, in what she considers a heroic act of compassion, offers cold water to a chain gang working on the road near her home. She imagines that her presence will be both morally and sexually inspirational to the men and that she will be "a symbol of mercy and decency." Instead, she is humiliated to discover that as she waits breathlessly, the men and the truck have left without stopping at her house. She realizes that the leering guard had only been humoring her, perhaps even laughing at her, and that the men's visit would have been more important and exciting to her than it would ever have been to them.

Two of her most delightful stories are Betts's autobiographical reminiscences of childhood. In "The Spies in the Herb House," set during World War II, she explains that "it was hard to impress the rich of this world," referring to her friend Betty Sue, "who owned almost everything I valued." Betty Sue's list of "valuables" includes her long blonde hair, which (unlike Doris's "bobbed and jealous hair") "fell forth in ripples" when taken out of its twin plaits; the "*True Love* magazine so casually dropped in the living room"; and three older sisters who "had breasts and wore stockings and high-heeled shoes" and went out to drink beer with paratroopers. "Spies in the Herb House," critic Michael McFee asserts, tells "the oldest, most profound story there is: the story of a fall from innocence to experience, of a passage from a small safe world into a large dangerous one." Doris and Betty Sue discover graffiti written on an abandoned herb house, which they interpret as a secret message–"Fight Until Children Killed"–written by Nazi spies. Assuming the message is about them, they decide that their lives are in danger but that they are the only ones who can save the town. Although the girls are drawn into the larger world, it is still a world of right and wrong in which the enemy can be recognized and fought: "There was so much I understood that day–valor, and patriotism, and the nature of the enemy. . . . The German High Command across the sea had taken an interest in my life and in its termination. Oh, do you see that in the days when the spies were in the Herb House the world was still comprehensible to Betty Sue and me?"

In "All That Glisters Isn't Gold," another childhood reminiscence, Betts again subtly presents the nuances of a child's logic. As a special surprise for Doris, her friends Miss Carrie, who takes care of her when her parents go out, and Miss Carrie's nephew Granville clean up the small pond in the backyard that the girl is fond of, and they put in a goldfish. Although the girl is enthralled with the goldfish and spends all afternoon "trying to catch in my fingers that flying piece of light beneath the surface," she cannot bring herself to mention the surprise or thank them for it. The goldfish represents an impossible moment of unity between Miss Carrie's religious beliefs, which mirror the girl's mother's, and Granville's atheism and doubt, which reflect the girl's own questioning of religion. If the girl does not mention the goldfish, she will not have to find out whose idea it was, because she fears it was either Miss Carrie's or Granville's, but not both. She wants to imagine the two coming together in their love for her. Even more crucially, she fears that her own questioning of religious beliefs and her attraction to Granville's atheism threatens to separate her from her mother's love and approval: "Each of his words was like a splinter and each slid invisibly inside me. There was a sore spot wherever one had penetrated; soon there were bruises all over my religion it was not safe to touch. I preferred the soreness from those splinters to the painful operation of having them removed." The narrator never mentions the fish, and the next time she visits Miss Carrie it is gone and the pond is overgrown.

The Astronomer and Other Stories ends with the title novella. As in "Serpents and Doves," in "The Astronomer" true damnation is not based on the enormity of one's sin but on the inability to believe truly in anything. Horton Beam, a widower who has outlived his children as well as his wife, merely tries to pass the time rather than attempting to redeem it. After his retirement from Cory Knitting Mills, he cherishes "his free time lying there, raw and unattached, and he did not plan to use it for any purpose at all." Beam decides to study the stars after reading Walt Whitman's poem "When I Heard the Learn'd Astronomer" and having a dream about riding among the stars "going nowhere special coming from no place remembered." In the Whitman poem the speaker leaves the astronomy lecture hall with its charts and diagrams to gaze silently at the wonder of the stars. Beam, however, prefers the charts that give him a sense of order without purpose–a way to map out what is left of his life. His ordered life is disrupted when Fred Ridge shows up on Beam's porch looking for a room to rent and returns later with his "wife," Eva Leeds. Against his better judgment, Beam allows the couple to stay, and he is drawn into the drama of their lives.

Pregnant Eva, who has left her husband and children to run away with Fred, ends up prostituting herself to get money for an abortion after she finds that Fred does not want children. Although Eva keeps everything from Fred, including the pregnancy, she confides in Beam, whose sympathy turns to love. Engulfed in guilt and depression after the abortion, Eva starts reading everything she can find about religion. After Fred learns of the abortion, Eva begs him and Beam for forgiveness, but as Beam understands, she cannot forgive herself. Eva finally accepts responsibility for what she has done and decides to return home to her husband and children, confess all, and accept the consequences. Like the Devil in "Serpents and Doves," Beam tells Eva that nothing really matters, that she will get over her guilt and that going back to her husband is pointless: he will only divorce her and take the children. But forgetting and growing complacent are what Eva fears: "*This* is what scares me–I'll recover, and there I'll be, not believing again. And everything going smooth. And then what will He do to prove Himself? What terrible thing will He show me next? Something worse than this? Can He take me down someplace more terrible than this? That's what scares me." In the end Beam envies Eva's "iron doubt" that could send her back to a living hell, and he finally looks outward for meaning: "Listen! The Astronomer sent his thought desperately beyond those stars. Listen! *Say* something to me!"

After the publication of *The Astronomer and Other Stories,* Betts began her long and distinguished association with the University of North Carolina at Chapel Hill, starting as a lecturer in the English department in 1966. She was also a visiting lecturer in creative writing at Duke University in 1971. Betts continued to write award-winning fiction, beginning with her third novel, *The River to Pickle Beach* (1972). Set during the political turbulence of the summer of 1968, the novel depicts the violence that spills over into the lives of ordinary people. Betts also published her third collection, *Beasts of the Southern Wild and Other Stories* (1973), which won the Sir Walter Raleigh Award, was selected by *The New York Times* as one of the best books of 1973, and was nominated for the National Book Award in 1974.

Betts's most experimental and best-received collection, *Beasts of the Southern Wild and Other Stories* shows a versatile range of characters, tones, settings, and narrative structures while still exploring important and persistent themes in Betts's writing. The most provocative story in the collection, and one that Betts herself liked, is the title story, which depicts the interracial fantasy of a young white wife and mother married to a domineering racist. In the midst of the daily events in her life as a teacher and housewife, Carol Walsh escapes through daydreams that allow her to indulge her own erotic thoughts and to get back at her husband, in her imagination at least. In her fantasy, it is after the Revolution and blacks have taken over the country. Carol has been chosen as a concubine by Sam Porter, the provost of New African University. Unlike Rob, Carol's real-life husband, Sam is an educated, sensitive man who selects her because of her education and her interest in literature; he never forces himself on her, but she chooses to come to him. In her real life, after Rob unceremoniously wakes her to have sex and then promptly falls asleep, Carol continues her fantasy and imagines that Sam comes to her rescue after she has been raped by a white man. When Sam asks for the name of the man so that he can have him killed, she hesitates and then says "Rob Walsh." Because of its controversial subject matter, Betts was warned by friends not to publish the story under her own name for fear of readers' reactions. Carol's inner life is so vividly and frankly presented that Betts's husband questioned her about the story–

not about whether or not she should publish it but whether or not she was happy.

Another of Betts's favorites from this collection is "The Ugliest Pilgrim," which first appeared in *Red Clay Reader* (1969). A motion-picture adaptation of this popular short story produced by the American Film Institute won the 1981 Academy Award for the best short feature, and a musical version of the story was named the best musical of 1997 by the New York Drama Critics' Circle. "The Ugliest Pilgrim" anticipates the importance of the journey of self-discovery, a theme that recurs in Betts's later novels. Like many of Betts's characters, Violet Karl is isolated, in this case by her ugliness–a huge scar cuts across her face from her nose to her ear–and by years of living alone in a mountain cabin after the death of her father. Violet, however, does not accept her isolation. She saves her money and goes on a pilgrimage to Tulsa to have her affliction of ugliness healed by a television evangelist. The encounter with the evangelist's assistant (the evangelist is elsewhere taping his show) is predictably disappointing: he warns her against vanity and offers to pray with her for inner beauty. Yet, the journey still heals her. Violet finds love when she is befriended by two soldiers, Monty and Flick, who are impressed by her ability to play poker (her father taught her in the lonely nights in the cabin) and feel bad about the inevitable disappointment they fear she will encounter in Tulsa. Though it seems that the soldiers are taking advantage of her–Monty persuades Violet not to stay with relatives, and then has sex with her during an overnight stop in Memphis–they come to care about her and promise to wait in a Fort Smith bus station for her return trip. When the Tulsa preacher fails her, Violet prays to Jesus for beauty. She will know that her prayers have been answered if Monty does not recognize her in the bus station; if she is still ugly, she vows to get back on the bus and never see him again. Monty does recognize her, and as he runs after her, the story, which is told in first person, ends with Violet's words, "Praise God! He's catching me!"

In "The Glory of His Nostrils" another isolated woman is rescued by love. Wanda Quincey, a widow whose bizarre behavior has been an accepted and predictable part of small-town life, becomes an object of scorn after she takes up with Dr. Benjamin, a traveling abortionist. The town was willing to accept Wanda's insanity and unhappiness but not her stepping out of her role as bereaved widow. As two of the townspeople come to the train station to warn her not to leave with Dr. Benjamin, she explains to the doctor, "Pay no attention, honey. Everybody in this whole damn town is crazy."

If *Beasts of the Southern Wild and Other Stories* includes some of Betts's happiest endings, it also includes some of her darkest. In "The Spider Gardens of Madagascar" Coker, a young boy who is left with his paranoid, neurotic mother after his father dies, contemplates the harrowing decision of whether to turn loose his black-widow spider in his room or his mother's. In "Still Life with Fruit" Betts gives a devastatingly frank depiction of a young woman's fears and doubts about motherhood during her delivery. After the delivery, as she looks at her baby, "Gwen touched her throat to make sure no other hand had grabbed it. Something crawled under her skin, like the spider who webbed her eyelids tightening all lines. In both her eyes, the spider spilled her hot, wet eggs–those on the right for bitterness, and those on the left for joy." In "Burning the Bed" a young woman returns home to watch her father, who is the only one left of her family, die. Like Bert in "The Sword," Isabel feels alienated from her father (a preacher), her hometown, and everything about her old life; yet, unlike Bert, she cannot wait until her father dies so that she can return to her new home in Baltimore. Isabel gets herself through the ordeal by writing letters to her lover, Brenda. In a moment of release and defiance she imagines how she and Brenda together (it will take two people to move it) will burn the bed her father lies in, the one she was conceived and born in. It will be like a pagan ritual, "like putting a Viking to sea on his flaming barge." However, when Isabel calls home in the middle of the night, she discovers that Brenda is not alone; with the click of the telephone Isabel realizes that she is now completely alone in the world, without friends, family, or faith.

Two of the most enigmatic stories deal in a realistic yet understated way with the afterlife. In "The Hitchhiker" Rose Marie Duffy, a bored secretary working in a sterile environment, is on her way to work one Monday and passes a series of hitchhikers wearing red. Inexplicably, she turns off the road and into the river. After falling asleep and waking up grounded on a sandbar, she crawls out of her car, takes off her clothes, and waits for help. A fisherman, seemingly a kind of Charon figure, comes to her aid, explaining that he will slow down so that she can try to attract attention from someone onshore, but that is all he can do. He gives her a dress to wear, and as she puts it on she sees that it is red. She has become one of the hitchhikers she herself ignored, and she seems destined for the same fate. She stands up waving her arms "as the towns and cities of the earth drove by." In "Benson Watts Is Dead and in Virginia," readers follow Benson Watts as he crosses over into the next world. If this story is read in light of the Devil's description of heaven in "Serpents and Doves" as a place of working and learning and going

DORIS BETTS is one of the most respected and prolific of the many talented writers originating from and writing about the South. A contributor to many literary magazines and quarterlies, she is the author of three novels and two previous collections of short stories. Her most recent novel, The River to Pickle Beach, was praised in the New York Times Book Review as "tough, wise, compassionate."
Born and brought up in North Carolina's Piedmont country, she is a graduate of the University of North Carolina and became a member of the English Department at the Chapel Hill campus in 1966. While an undergraduate in college she won the Mademoiselle prize for fiction. Her first collection of short stories, The Gentle Insurrection, was published in 1954. She is also the author of Tall Houses in Winter, The Scarlet Thread, and River to Pickle Beach, all novels, and The Astronomer and Other Stories.
Mrs. Betts lives with her husband and three children in Sanford, North Carolina.
Beasts of the Southern Wild & other stories
Doris Betts
Harper & Row
Beasts of the Southern Wild & other stories
by Doris Betts
Author of The River to Pickle Beach

Dust jacket for Betts's 1973 book, in which the title story depicts the interracial fantasy of a white woman married to a white racist

back again, then Watts is not ready for heaven. Watts wakes up in what he takes to be Virginia, with a bracelet that says "TO AVOID G. B.–1. Dwell, then travel 2. Join forces 3. Disremember." Watts joins with two others who mysteriously appear as he did: Olena, a pregnant beautician, and Melvin Drum, who studies religion but does not believe in it. Together they do as the bracelet instructs in order to avoid "G.B." (going back). Although the group can remember many things from their past lives, it seems that whenever they remember anything that has true meaning for them, it causes a headache. Watts, like Horton Beam, is a man who lived his life obtaining knowledge without purpose. He is content to travel aimlessly, simply to exist. Watts begins a possessive affair with Olena that drives Drum away and eventually also alienates Olena, who is drawn to life, her unborn child, and going back. Watts, who felt he needed no one, creates his own hell when he finds himself, as did Mr. Fribble, alone for eternity.

In "The Mother-in-Law," which Anne Tyler called in the *National Observer* (5 January 1974) "the most moving story in the book," Betts employs a creative use of time. A young woman imagines herself a ghost in the past watching her mother-in-law die while her "other self is skipping rope in another state." She assures her mother-in-law that in the future she, the daughter-in-law, will take care of the family–not only her husband, the middle son, but also Ross, the youngest son, who is handicapped. But though the two women, who have never met, share a family, there is also an element of competition. As the daughter returns to the present and to her own life, she imagines the mother-in-law outside trying to get in and "for one icy moment, the ghost of her envy stares at the ghost of mine."

Since the publication of *Beasts of the Southern Wild and Other Stories* Betts's involvement in the university has greatly increased. From 1972 to 1978 she served as director of Freshman-Sophomore English; in 1978 she was the first woman to become a full professor in the English Department; and in 1980 she became Alumni Distinguished Professor. Betts's dedication as an educator is evident by her students' praise of her enthusiasm and tough-mindedness and by the many teaching awards she has won since she began her association with Chapel Hill. In 1973 she won the Tanner Award for distinguished undergraduate teaching; in 1980 she won the Katherine Carmichael Award for teaching; and in 1986 she was named a Celebrated Teacher by the Association of Departments of English, Modern Language Association. In a special tribute the English department at the University of North Carolina established the Doris Betts Teaching Award, which is given to graduate students teaching in the freshman writing program. In 1991 Betts won the UNC Alumni Award for distinguished teaching.

In addition to her service to the English department, Betts has also been active in university affairs. She was director of the North Carolina Fellows Program from 1975 to 1976; she served on the Board of Governors from 1981 to 1984; and she was chair of the faculty from 1982 to 1985. In 1987 she was nominated as candidate for chancellor of the university, and she has even been chair of the Committee on Athletics and the University. Betts's reputation as an academic extends beyond the university as well: in 1978 she served on the literature panel for the National Endowment for the Arts, which she chaired in 1979 and 1980, and she was named to the National Humanities Faculty. In 1984 she was a judge for the PEN/Faulkner Award, and in 1992 she was named to the board of trustees for the National Humanities Center and was elected to the Fellowship of Southern Writers.

Her emphasis on academic affairs has not meant a corresponding decrease in her literary productivity. Since the 1970s Betts has focused on the novel, writing three best-selling and critically well-received novels: *Heading West* (1981), which was chosen as a Book-of-the-Month Club selection; *Souls Raised from the Dead* (1994); and *The Sharp Teeth of Love* (1997). Critical interest in Betts's career can be roughly divided between her early short stories and her later novels. In fact, her early acclaim as a short-story writer seemed almost to hinder critical appreciation of her novels: critic Jonathan Yardley, reviewing her "breakthrough" book, *Heading West,* for *The Washington Post* (29 November 1981), stated that Betts is not suited to the longer novel form, that she "reveals herself to be a short-story writer who is uncomfortable going long distance." Yardley's evaluation was not shared by other critics, nor was it borne out by *Souls Raised from the Dead* and *The Sharp Teeth of Love,* which have both received critical praise. Betts herself, however, acknowledges her shift in genres. Whereas earlier in her career she saw herself primarily as a short-story writer who wrote novels only under pressure from her publishers, in a 17 February 1982 interview with Jean W. Ross, Betts stated:

> I have, I think, reached that age when the short story is no longer as aesthetically pleasing to me. The short story, like the lyric poem, may be the form of youth, when you still believe in the revelation and the isolated moment, and you do believe that people can change in twenty-four-hour periods. Well, you get older; you can't help seeing that the more things change, the more they stay the same, just the way your grandmother told you. And you do become interested then in longer structures and also in the things that abide. And so I have wanted to learn to be a novelist, a better novelist.

While Betts is still focusing on issues of faith and doubt, the nature of sin, and people's propensity to entrap themselves, in the later novels it is as though the isolated and dissatisfied characters of the short stories are increasingly allowed to escape and take a journey of self-discovery. The characters in the novels are able to grow, heal, and make the most of their lives. They are able, in other words, to live up to Betts's desire to redeem time. In *Heading West* Nancy Finch, a thirty-five-year-old librarian, relinquishes full responsibility for her family and takes charge of her own life only after being kidnapped and taken across the country. When she returns home after the ordeal is over and she has outwitted her kidnapper, she finds that in her absence her family has gotten along without her.

Likewise, in *The Sharp Teeth of Love,* a journey into the unknown allows Luna Stone to discover what she wants. Luna leaves her fiancé in Reno to head out on her own adventure. While camping out she meets a young boy, and, with the help of a hard-of-hearing minister with whom she begins to fall in love, she rescues the boy from child prostitution and creates a new family for herself. In both novels the heroines not only find love but also, through the men they meet, find alternative families with strong mothers, the kind that are often missing from Betts's earlier fiction. Both novels also weave multilayered and allusive subtexts within a compelling journey narrative, drawing on Betts's prodigious knowledge of mythology, religion, literature, history, geography, and many other subjects and incorporating several subtly drawn supporting characters whose lives intersect with her heroines'.

In *Souls Raised from the Dead* Betts returns to the themes of death and loss of faith with the story of a single father, Frank Thompson, and his thirteen-year-old daughter, Mary Grace, who is dying of kidney disease. Although Betts has created some devastating portrayals of mothers, Christine, Frank's former wife, is perhaps the most negative. In a painful yet sometimes grotesquely satirical portrait of shallowness and self-absorption, Betts depicts Christine's obsession with her own beauty, which she considers her only asset, and her refusal to accept her responsibilities as a mother. Afraid to donate a kidney for her daughter because of the pain she might experience, Christine must face the guilt she feels after her daughter's death. The real focus of the novel, however, is Frank's struggle to come to terms with his daughter's illness and to learn how to face death, his own emotions, and his desire to believe in someone and something. Frank's mother, Tracey, is a kind of antidote to his former wife. He counts on her faith, love, and constant help to see him through this tragedy. The irony is that his mother is going through her own crisis of faith, which she sees as a kind of religious flu that she will recover from eventually.

With her reputation as a novelist firmly established, Betts has planned a new short-story collection in addition to two new novels. One novel is a major project on which she has been working for several years, tentatively called "Wings of Morning," a family saga set in North Carolina and spanning the period from 1890 to the 1970s. The other new novel is "Who is Sylvia?," the story of a small-town, middle-aged female bank embezzler. While Betts is generous with her time, giving many talks and readings as well as spending time with students and faculty, she is more guarded with her free time at home on Araby Farm in Pittsboro, North Carolina, where she and her husband raise Arabian horses. As she explained to Ross, her time at home is "important to my life, because I really did want to have it all–a home, a family, a marriage that was satisfying, and work, and writing. The way I've done it . . . is to keep those things in pretty much air-tight compartments. When I'm coming here to the university I close the door behind home, and when I go home I close it behind teaching and administration, and just do everything a hundred percent while I'm doing it."

Interviews:

George Wolfe, "The Unique Voice: Doris Betts," in *Kite-Flying and Other Irrational Acts. Conversations with Twelve Southern Writers,* edited by John Carr (Baton Rouge: Louisiana State University Press, 1972), pp. 149–173;

Jean W. Ross, "Interview: Doris Betts," in *Contemporary Authors,* New Revision Series, volume 9, edited by Ann Evory and Linda Metzger (Detroit: Gale, 1983), pp. 51–55;

Susan Ketchin, "Doris Betts: Resting on the Bedrock of Original Sin," in *The Christ-Haunted Landscape: Faith and Doubt in Southern Literature* (Jackson: University Press of Mississippi, 1994), pp. 230–259;

Dannye Romine Powell, *Parting the Curtains: Interviews with Southern Writers* (Winston-Salem, N.C.: John F. Blair, 1994), pp. 15–31;

W. Dale Brown, "Interview with Doris Betts," *Southern Quarterly,* 34, no. 2 (1996): 91–104;

Elizabeth Evans, "Conversations with Doris Betts," *South Carolina Review,* 28, no. 2 (1996): 4–8.

References:

Elizabeth Evans, *Doris Betts* (New York: Twayne, 1997);

David Marion Holman, "Faith and the Unanswerable Questions: The Fiction of Doris Betts," *Southern Literary Journal,* 15, no. 1 (1982): 15–23;

Michael McFee, "Reading a Small History in a Universal Light: Doris Betts, Clyde Edgerton, and the Triumph of True Regionalism," *Pembroke Magazine,* 23 (1991): 59–67;

Dorothy M. Scura, "Doris Betts at Mid-Career: Her Voice and Her Art," in *Southern Women Writers: The New Generation,* edited by Tonette Bond Inge (Tuscaloosa: University of Alabama Press, 1990), pp. 161–179.

Papers:

Doris Betts's papers and correspondence are in the Doris Betts Collection, Mugar Memorial Library, Boston University.

Paul Bowles

(30 December 1910 -   )

Allen Hibbard
Middle Tennessee State University

BOOKS: *The Sheltering Sky* (London: John Lehmann, 1949; New York: New Directions, 1949);
The Delicate Prey and Other Stories (New York: Random House, 1950);
A Little Stone (London: John Lehmann, 1950);
Let It Come Down (London: John Lehmann, 1952; New York: Random House, 1952);
The Spider's House (New York: Random House, 1955; London: Macdonald, 1957);
Yallah (Zurich: Manesse, 1956; New York: McDowell, Obolensky, 1957);
The Hours After Noon (London: Heinemann, 1959);
A Hundred Camels in the Courtyard (San Francisco: City Lights Books, 1962);
Their Heads Are Green (London: Owen, 1963); republished as *Their Heads Are Green and Their Hands Are Blue* (New York: Random House, 1963);
Up Above the World (New York: Simon & Schuster, 1966; London: Owen, 1967);
The Time of Friendship (New York: Holt, Rinehart & Winston, 1967);
Scenes (Los Angeles: Black Sparrow, 1968);
Pages from Cold Point and Other Stories (London: Owen, 1968);
Without Stopping (New York: Putnam, 1972; London: Owen, 1972);
Three Tales (New York: Hallman, 1975);
Things Gone and Things Still Here (Santa Barbara, Cal.: Black Sparrow, 1977);
Collected Stories 1939–1976 (Santa Barbara, Cal.: Black Sparrow, 1979);
Midnight Mass (Santa Barbara, Cal.: Black Sparrow, 1981; London: Owen, 1985);
Next to Nothing: Collected Poems 1926–1977 (Santa Barbara, Cal.: Black Sparrow, 1981);
Points in Time (London: Owen, 1982; New York: Ecco, 1984);
Call at Corazón and Other Stories (London: Owen, 1988);
Unwelcome Words (Bolinas, Cal.: Tombouctou, 1988);
A Distant Episode: The Selected Stories of Paul Bowles (New York: Ecco, 1988);
A Thousand Days for Mokhtar (London: Owen, 1989);
Tangier Journal: 1987–1989 (London: Owen, 1989); reprinted as *Days: Tangier Journal: 1987–1989* (New York: Ecco, 1991);
Too Far from Home: Selected Writings of Paul Bowles, edited by Daniel Halpern, introduction by Joyce Carol Oates (New York: Ecco, 1993; London: Owen, 1994);
The Portable Paul and Jane Bowles, edited by Millicent Dillon (New York: Penguin, 1994).

TRANSLATIONS: F. Frison-Roche, *The Lost Trail of the Sahara* (New York: Prentice-Hall, 1951);
Jean-Paul Sartre, *No Exit* (New York: S. French, 1958);
Larbi Layachi (Driss ben Hamed Charhadi), *A Life Full of Holes* (New York: Grove, 1964; London: Weidenfeld & Nicolson, 1964);
Mohammed Mrabet, *Love with a Few Hairs* (London: Owen, 1967; New York: George Braziller, 1967);
Mrabet, *The Lemon* (London: Owen, 1969; New York: McGraw-Hill, 1972);
Mrabet, *M'Hashish* (San Francisco: City Lights Books, 1969; London: Owen, 1988);
Mohamed Choukri, *For Bread Alone* (London: Owen, 1974; San Francisco: City Lights Books, 1987);
Mrabet, *The Boy Who Set the Fire & Other Stories* (Los Angeles, Cal.: Black Sparrow, 1974);
Choukri, *Jean Genet in Tangier* (New York: Ecco, 1974);
Mrabet, *Hadidan Aharam* (Santa Barbara, Cal.: Black Sparrow, 1975);
Isabelle Eberhardt, *The Oblivion Seekers* (San Francisco: City Lights Books, 1975; London: Owen, 1987);
Mrabet, *Look & Move On* (Santa Barbara, Cal.: Black Sparrow, 1976);
Mrabet, *Harmless Poisons, Blameless Sins* (Santa Barbara, Cal.: Black Sparrow, 1976);
Mrabet, *The Big Mirror* (Santa Barbara, Cal.: Black Sparrow, 1977);
Choukri, *Tennessee Williams in Tangier* (Santa Barbara, Cal.: Cadmus, 1979);

Paul Bowles

Mrabet, *The Beach Cafe & The Voice* (Santa Barbara, Cal.: Black Sparrow, 1979);

Abdeslam Boulaich and others, *Five Eyes* (Santa Barbara, Cal.: Black Sparrow, 1979);

Rodrigo Rey Rosa, *The Path Doubles Back* (New York: Red Ozier, 1982);

Mrabet, *The Chest* (Bolinas, Cal.: Tombouctou, 1983);

Rey Rosa, *The Beggar's Knife* (San Francisco: City Lights Books, 1985);

Jean Ferry and others, *She Woke Me Up So I Killed Her* (San Francisco: Cadmus, 1985);

Mrabet, *Marriage with Papers* (Bolinas, Cal.: Tombouctou, 1986);

Mrabet, *Chocolate Creams and Dollars* (New York: Inanout, 1992);

Rey Rosa, *Dust on Her Tongue* (London: Owen, 1989; San Francisco: City Lights Books, 1992);

Rey Rosa, *The Pelcari Project* (London: Owen, 1991; Tiburon, Cal.: Cadmus Editions, 1997).

Paul Bowles is one of the best American short-story writers of the twentieth century. The most salient aspect of all Bowles's fiction, the four novels as well as the short fiction, is the use of foreign settings. Only a handful of his more than sixty published stories are set in the United States. The bulk take place in various parts of North Africa, where he has lived most of his life. Still others are set in Latin America, Sri Lanka, and Thailand, places Bowles came to know through his travels. Bowles's best-known stories–such as "The Delicate Prey" and "A Distant Episode"–send chills down the spine. The grotesque and horrifying acts in these and some other Bowles stories are connected to fears and misunderstandings accompanying contact between contrasting cultures with contrasting values or, more basically, between the self and the unknown other. In all his stories Bowles masterfully manipulates narrative distance and timing, creating an unnerving kind of suspense. He tells only what he needs to tell just when he needs to tell it.

Paul Frederic Bowles was born in Jamaica, Long Island, New York, on 30 December 1910 to Rena and Claude Bowles. Growing up with no siblings, Paul began at an early age to create his own imaginative world–sketching pictures, dreaming up operas, and hatching fictions. His unusual psychic disposition no doubt developed partly in response to his parents' personalities. From his mother, whom he remembers reading Edgar Allan Poe and Nathaniel Hawthorne stories aloud to him when he was a child, he probably derived his artistic nature. His father, a dentist, was strict and cold. In his autobiography, *Without Stopping* (1972), Bowles recalls how his father enforced "Fletcherization," an eating regimen popular in the first decades of

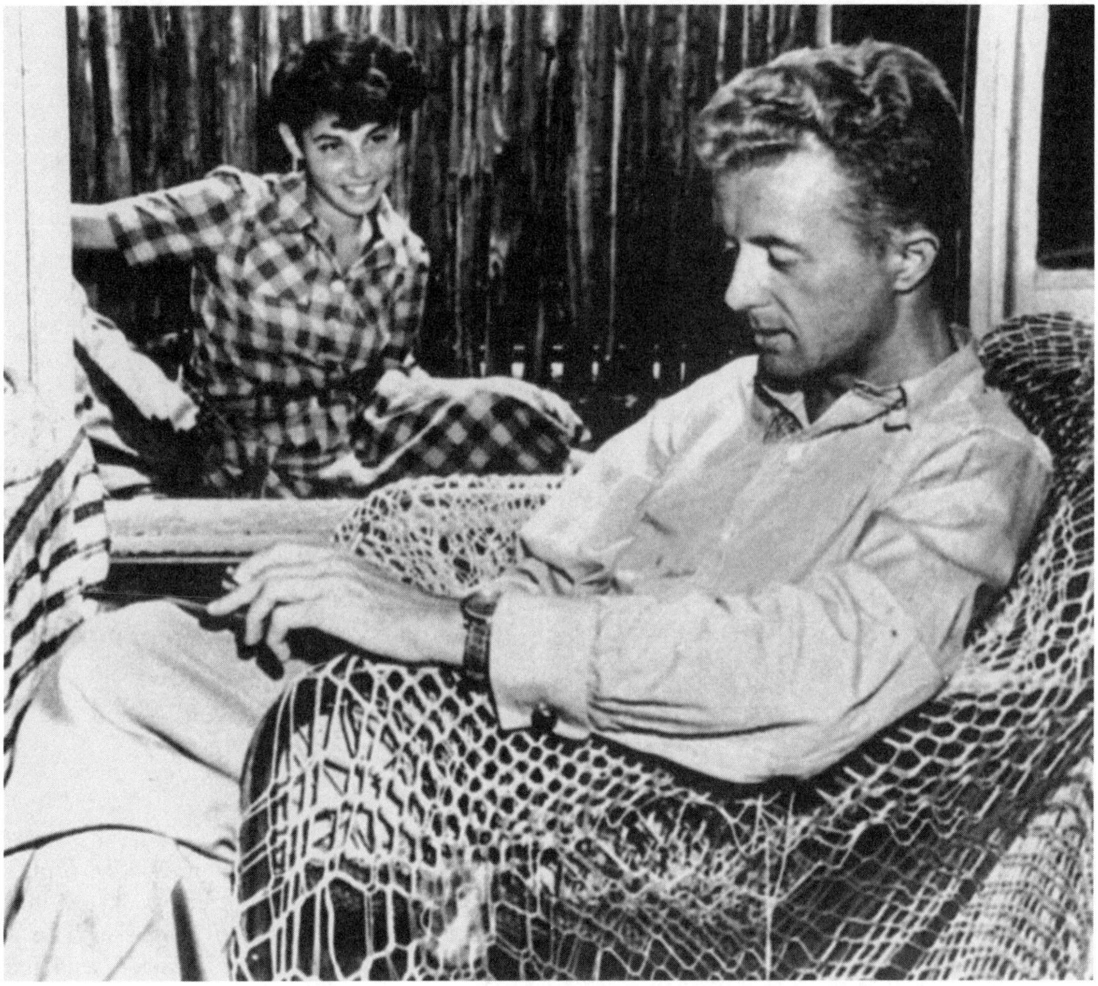

Jane and Paul Bowles in New York, 1944 (photograph by Graphic House)

the century whereby each bite of food must be chewed forty times before swallowing. Bowles hated the routine, which was thought to promote good health, solid work habits, and moral rectitude.

Bowles also submits the story of his father placing his cradle beside an open window in the dead of winter, which Bowles reads as an attempt to extinguish him in infancy. The anecdote, made legendary through retelling, registers a theme Bowles was to return to again and again in his fiction: human vulnerability, particularly the vulnerability of the child in the face of more powerful adults. Thus, Bowles fought against his father, in a variation of the classic Oedipal battle, to establish his own identity.

Bowles displayed his literary bent at an early age. When he was just seventeen, his poem "Spire Song" was published by *transition,* a reputable literary journal of the day that published such writers as James Joyce, Paul Eluard, André Breton, Allen Tate, and Gertrude Stein. When it was time for Bowles to consider colleges, he chose to attend the University of Virginia, no doubt aware that Poe had attended the school nearly a century earlier. Bowles soon left school in favor of a more vibrant, cosmopolitan education promised by life abroad. In setting off for Paris for the first time in 1929, he was following patterns established by other American literary expatriates such as Henry James, Edith Wharton, Gertrude Stein, and Ernest Hemingway. On his return Bowles met composer Henry Dixon Cowell in New York, who in turn gave him an introduction to Aaron Copland, with whom he began studies in musical composition. Having had a taste of life abroad, Bowles began to scheme a way of getting back to Europe. By the spring of 1931 he was back in Paris.

Bowles had a knack for meeting and endearing himself to people with social capital. In Berlin he met Christopher Isherwood, whose Sally Bowles of his Berlin stories, by some accounts, takes her name from the young American traveler Bowles. In Holland he looked up Jiddu Krishnamurti. In Paris he met Ezra Pound,

André Gide, and Virgil Thomson. But Bowles's acquaintance with Stein and Alice B. Toklas, by his own reckoning, took on the most significance. Having corresponded with Stein, the American grand dame of modernism, when he was in America, Bowles had an entrée to her and sought her out on the rue de Fleurus in Paris. His visit to Stein, Toklas, and their dog, Basket, at their country home in Bilignin left a lasting impression on Bowles. Stein, whose literary project involved destabilizing conventional relationships between word and object, began to call Bowles "Freddy" (drawing upon his middle name) because she did not think he looked like a Paul. Bowles later set a letter from Stein to music, calling it "Letter to Freddy." When Bowles read his poetry to Stein, she subjected it to rigorous critique, suggesting he was no poet. It was Stein who first suggested that Bowles go to Morocco, which he did, accompanied by Copland, in 1931. As thoroughly enchanted as he was by Morocco, Bowles could hardly have imagined how integrally tied he would become to the place.

In the 1930s and 1940s Bowles was known primarily as a composer. His music, ranging from concert pieces and operas to musical scores for the theater and motion pictures, has been recognized, admired, and championed by such fellow composers as Virgil Thomson, Ned Rorem, and Phillip Ramey. In 1995 the Eos Ensemble, under the direction of Jonathan Sheffer, presented a festival devoted to Bowles's music, which Bowles himself attended, returning to New York after a twenty-six-year absence.

Bowles is one of the rare people to develop successful careers both as a writer and as a composer. In *Setting the Tone* (1984) Ned Rorem contrasts the mood of Bowles's music with that of his fiction, noting that the music is "nostalgic and witty" while the fiction is "dark and cruel, clearly meant to horrify in an impersonal sort of way." His mastery of the short form, however, is what marks both his fiction and his music.

Though Bowles's writing career did not begin to overtake his career as composer until the late 1940s, by the late 1930s his childhood habit of creating fictions was being rekindled. One pivotal event during this time that likely affected the form of his creative expression was meeting Jane Auer in 1937. The two immediately were intrigued and charmed by one another. The following year, when Paul was twenty-seven and Jane was twenty, the two married. During the early years of their marriage Jane was working on her only completed novel, *Two Serious Ladies* (1943). Paul played an active role as reader and editor of the novel. Crawling in and inhabiting Jane's novel made Paul see that he could perhaps have one of his own.

Dust jacket for Bowles's first collection of short stories, which prompted Leslie Fiedler to label Bowles "the pornographer of terror"

The Bowleses' marriage was anything but conventional. The two lived lives together and separately. Both Jane and Paul Bowles used their marriage as a model for fiction. Her *Two Serious Ladies* features two characters, Mr. and Mrs. Copperfield, who look much like the Bowleses. In their travels through Panama, Mr. Copperfield wanders off into a jungle alone while Mrs. Copperfield becomes involved with a young Panamanian girl named Pacifica. The Copperfields must negotiate their conflicting needs and desires. Paul Bowles's first novel, *The Sheltering Sky* (1949), also features a couple, Kit and Port Moresby, who are obviously modeled on the Bowleses, as is the couple in Jane Bowles's fragment titled "The Iron Table." The Slades in Paul Bowles's fourth novel, *Up Above the World* (1966), also bear some resemblance to the Bowleses.

During the late 1930s and early 1940s the Bowleses made New York their base, sojourning at times in Mexico, where they met Tennessee Williams. At one point in the early 1940s the Bowleses lived in a Brooklyn Heights apartment house also occupied by

Oliver Smith, W. H. Auden, Benjamin Britten, Peter Pears, and Thomas Mann's younger son, Golo. At the time Paul was busy composing music, and somewhat later he reviewed music for the *New York Herald Tribune,* activities that no doubt sharpened his skills to turn the auditory into language and get ideas down quickly and succinctly–skills he later employed and refined in writing fiction.

In his autobiography, *Without Stopping,* Bowles describes how he began to open himself to worlds of fiction. In 1945 he had been reading ethnographic books, including stories from primitive cultures such as the Arapesh and Tarahumara. He decided to try to create his own myths, "adopting the point of view of the primitive mind." In so doing, he adopted a method used by Surrealists, "abandoning conscious control and writing whatever words came from the pen":

> One rainy Sunday I awoke late, put a thermos of coffee by my bedside, and began to write another of these myths. No one disturbed me, and I wrote until I had finished it. I read it over, called it "The Scorpion," and decided that it could be shown to others. . . . It was through this unexpected little gate that I crept back into the land of fiction writing.

Stories that followed shortly thereafter–such as "How Many Midnights," "A Distant Episode," and "At Paso Rojo"–are among his finest.

Bowles's move back to North Africa in 1947, after the devastation of World War II, was crucial and defining. The move away from Western civilization was in the same vein as similar moves taken by other antimodern moderns such as Arthur Rimbaud, Paul Gauguin, D. H. Lawrence, and even Claude Lévi-Strauss. It is unlikely, however, that he thought he would live in the Maghrib, off and on, for the next half century. "I never make plans," Bowles says in a movie documentary titled *Paul Bowles: The Complete Outsider* (1994), made by Regina Weinreich and Catherine Warnow. The comment registers a fundamentally existentialist worldview that runs through *The Sheltering Sky,* the novel Bowles went to North Africa to work on in the late 1940s.

The Delicate Prey and Other Stories was published by Random House in 1950, a year after *The Sheltering Sky.* Reviewing the book for *Saturday Review of Literature* (20 December 1950), Tennessee Williams wrote, "Nowhere in any writing that I can think of has the separateness of the one human psyche been depicted more vividly and shockingly." Among the seventeen stories in the collection are the widely anthologized title story and "A Distant Episode." These grisly tales prompted Leslie A. Fiedler in an essay for the *Kenyon Review* to dub Bowles "the pornographer of terror." "The Delicate Prey" ends with the castration/rape of a young boy, Driss, by a member of another hostile tribe. The story leaves a startling imprint on the reader's mind. Similarly, the American professor of linguistics in "A Distant Episode" fails to understand local codes and falls into the hands of Reguibat tribesmen (the same tribe Driss was a member of), who cut off his tongue and drive him to an imbecilic state, tying tin cans to his body to make him an object of entertainment. In the end the professor runs off into the desert where, stripped completely of social sustenance, he will certainly die.

Most of the other stories in the collection are tame by comparison, yet deserve to be better known. Though Bowles's best-known fiction is set in North Africa, many fine stories, including "At Paso Rojo," "Call at Corazón," "Pastor Dowe at Tacaté," "Señor Ong and Mr. Ha," and "The Echo," are set in Latin America. Recurrent Bowlesean themes surface in "Señor Ong and Mr. Ha." The central character is a young boy named Dionisio, Nicho for short, who lives in an unspecified small town in Latin America. The young boy watches as his aunt, with whom he lives, conducts drug transactions with Señor Ong and Mr. Ha. While it is unclear just how much the child understands about what goes on between these adults (rather like Maisie in Henry James's 1897 novel *What Maisie Knew*), he learns the operation well enough to turn it to his advantage and make enough money to treat his girlfriend Luz to "a lipstick and a pair of dark glasses with red and green jewels all round the rims."

If there is one consistent preoccupation in Bowles's fiction, it is an intense interest in transgressive acts. Though more subtle than "The Delicate Prey" and "A Distant Episode," both "The Echo" and "Pages from Cold Point" deal with crossing boundaries of moral propriety. In "The Echo" a young American coed named Aileen flies to visit her mother in Colombia only to find her involved with a woman named Prue. The tension in the story, accentuated by the precipitous gorge over which the house hangs, revolves around the barely submerged rivalry between Aileen and Prue. Psychic and natural landscapes reinforce one another; balance is barely maintained; and the plot suggests that things could tip one way or another at any point, and at times they do.

"Pages from Cold Point," which Bowles wrote in 1947 aboard the MS *Ferncape* en route from New York to Casablanca, is yet bolder. Like Gore Vidal's novel *The City and the Pillar* (1948), the story depicts homosexuality in a manner uncommon for the times. When his wife Hope dies, Norton, an American university professor, flees with his son Racky to a Caribbean island to escape the scourge of modernity. Norton chronicles his experiences on the island. Gradually the reader learns,

Bowles, Allen Ginsberg, William S. Burroughs, Gregory Corso, and Michael Portman during the Beat writers' 1961 visit to Tangier (photograph by William Targ)

even while Norton tries to turn a blind eye to realities, that Racky is becoming notorious for his sexual exploits with other males on the island. In an attempt to blackmail him, Racky seduces his father. Upon returning from a walk one evening Norton finds his son in his own bedroom: "The top sheet of my bed had been stripped back to the foot. There on the far side of the bed, dark against the whiteness of the lower sheet, lay Racky asleep on his side, and naked."

Between the publication of *The Delicate Prey and Other Stories* and his next small volume of stories, *A Hundred Camels in the Courtyard* (1962), Bowles had published two more novels, *Let It Come Down* (1952) and *The Spider's House* (1955). During the 1950s Bowles continued to travel. One destination was Taprobane, an island off the coast of Sri Lanka that Bowles owned for a short time. During this time Bowles had also developed a close friendship with the young Moroccan painter Ahmed Yacoubi.

A Hundred Camels seems in some way to speak to the Beat experience in Tangier. As Norman Mailer proclaimed in *Advertisements for Myself* (1959), "Paul Bowles opened the world of Hip." Tangier, with its liberal attitude toward drugs and sex, was a magnet for American Beats and hippies. William Seward Burroughs had come to Tangier (or "Interzone," as he calls it in his fiction) in the mid 1950s and looked up Bowles. In his turn, Allen Ginsberg showed up to help Burroughs edit *Naked Lunch* (1959). Others–including Brion Gysin, Gregory Corso, Ira Cohen, and Alfred Chester–were drawn to Tangier in the early 1960s. Ginsberg suggested to Bowles that Lawrence Ferlinghetti at City Lights Books might be interested in doing a volume of his stories. What resulted was the "Kif Quartet": four stories all of which in some way turn on the use of kif. What is more, all four stories are purely Moroccan; no European expatriates are found in them.

Bowles's next volume, *The Time of Friendship* (1967), includes nine stories in addition to the stories of the "Kif Quartet." The title story is one of the strongest, most ambitious stories in the volume. It features a Swiss woman, a schoolteacher named Fräulein Windling, whose romantic yearnings draw her to the North African desert. "Her first sight of the desert and its people had been a transfiguring experience; indeed, it seemed to her now that before coming here she had never been in touch with life at all. She believed firmly that each day she spent here increased the aggregate of her resistance. She coveted the rugged health of the natives, when her own was equally strong, but because she was white and educated, she was convinced that her body was intrinsically inferior." Fräulein Windling retreats from the decadence of the West, seeking sustenance in the more traditional, rooted culture of the Arabs.

In a way calling to mind Gide's Marcel in *L'Immoraliste* (1902), Fräulein Windling becomes enamored of a certain young Arab boy name Slimane. The story traces the development of the "friendship" over the course of three consecutive summers. It also reveals the workings of the woman's desires and the barriers imposed by different cultural frameworks, age, religion, and gender. As Fräulein Windling seeks to establish a relationship with Slimane, she sometimes acts in a patronizing fashion–offering him sweets, sympathizing with his poverty, and teaching him the Christian story of Jesus and the nativity. Slimane's strong Islamic faith, however, makes him difficult to convert. Slimane holds firmly to the Islamic view of Jesus as prophet over the Christian view of Jesus as son of God and savior. "I shall never understand him," the Swiss woman thinks at one point. Indeed, the story is about the difficulty, perhaps even the impossibility, of communication across such wide spaces between self and other. It is a powerful narrative inscribing the dynamics at work in a long history of interaction and conflict between the Islamic East and the Christian West.

A few of the stories–notably "The Hours After Noon" and "Doña Faustina"–embody elements of violence and terror for which Bowles is famous. The former story ends tragically with the death of a Frenchman, M. Royer, who has evidently crossed the threshold of the permissible, chasing young Moroccan girls. As is often the case in Bowles's short fiction, the exact nature of events is ambiguous. The latter story, "Doña Faustina," set in Latin America, unravels like a mystery, with the precise and tight logic of a Poe tale. Two women who run an inn become prime suspects in a case involving the disappearance of children. The two, as it turns out, are mass murderers who have kidnapped and killed children, eating their hearts in order to gain certain powers and throwing the remains to nearby crocodiles. The women escape just before police arrive and discover what has been going on.

The collection also includes several fablelike stories, all set in North Africa. "The Hyena," like Aesop's fables, tells of relations between different kinds of animals, in this case a hyena and a stork. At the heart of the story is the issue of trust. The hyena, known for its deception, gains the trust of the naive stork only to tear open the bird's neck. "The Successor" tells the story of how, by an odd and unpredictable twist of fate, justice is achieved in the relations between two brothers. "The Garden," though only three brief pages, is a powerful statement on the tension between individual talent and social restraint, particularly the restraint imposed by Islam. The central character in the story, an unnamed man, devotes a considerable amount of time to tending a garden of pomegranates and barley at the edge of an oasis in southern Morocco. His wife becomes suspicious when her husband returns happy and satisfied; she thinks he may be hiding some kind of treasure in the garden. The wife, hoping to get him to reveal his secret, thus begins to poison her husband. Fearing she has taken things too far, she flees. Meanwhile the husband recuperates only to find his fellow townsfolk focusing their suspicions on him because of his wife's disappearance. In the end an imam (holy man) comes to visit the man in the garden and strikes him in the face when he will not attribute to God all the bounties of nature.

All three of these fables display the tension between natural and moral law. In the struggle between various forces at work in the world, Bowles continually resists strict, moralistic interpretations. His vision is more or less Manichaean. He believes that forces for ill and good are loose upon the world without any divinity guiding their course. Things are simply what they are.

One final story in the collection deserves mention–"The Frozen Fields." In writing this story, Bowles returned to childhood memories of times spent on his grandparents' farm in New England. The young boy in the story, Donald, is shown in the opening scenes traveling with his father on a train to spend Christmas with his grandparents. When Donald begins to etch pictures on the frosted window, his father tells him to stop. Thus begins a battle between son and father that lies at the heart of the story. Once at the grandparents' house, Donald's father seems to fear that his son will be influenced or corrupted by his Uncle Ivor's special friend, Mr. Gordon. In an attempt to make a man out of his son, the father rubs snow in his face when the two are outdoors together. Donald then dreams of escape. In the final scenes of the story he lies in the dark, listening to the sound of snow hitting the window pane. He imagines a wolf that approaches and places his head on Donald's lap. The story ends with Donald and the wolf running off together across the frozen landscape. The story, although written in the third person, is filtered through the consciousness of young

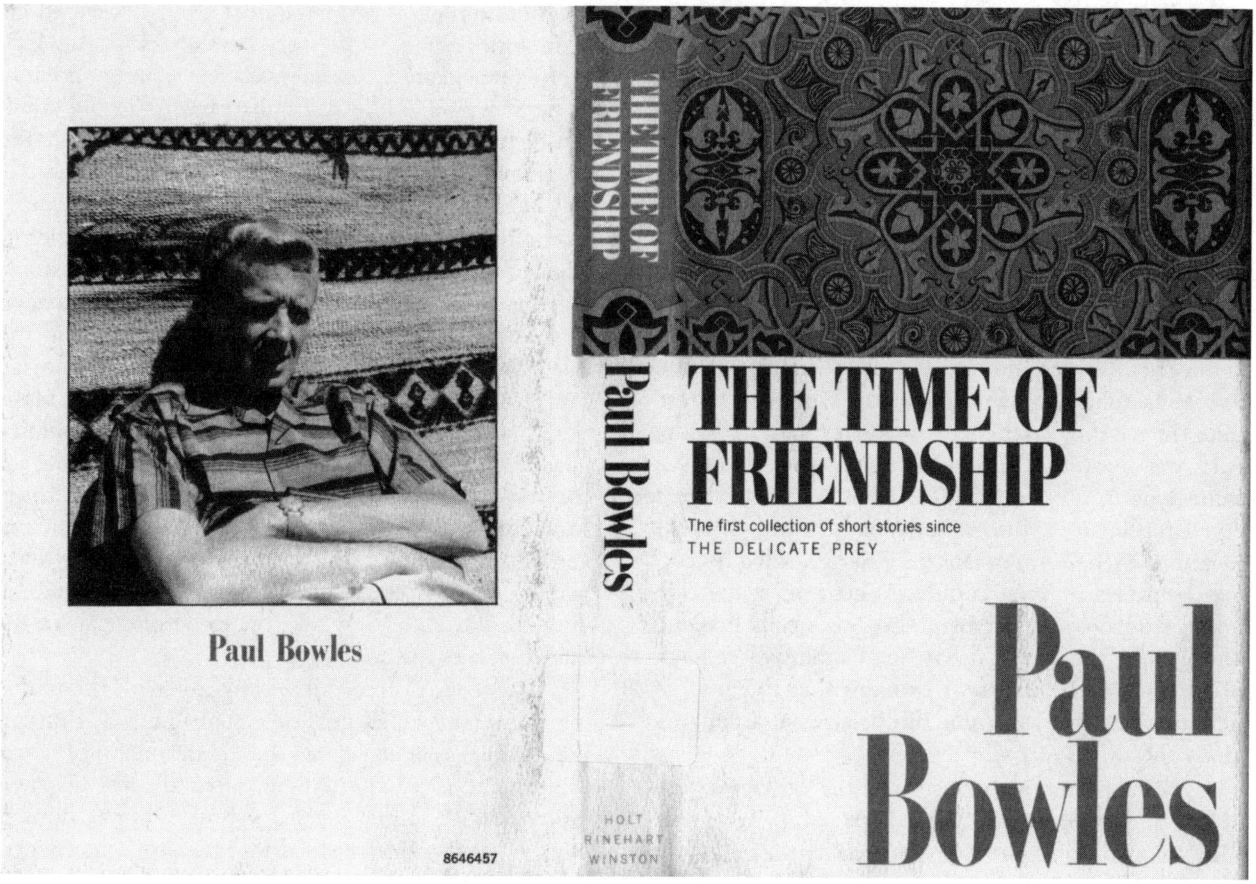

Dust jacket for Bowles's 1967 book, in which the title story offers Bowles's observations on the interaction between the Islamic and Christian worlds

Donald, thus creating sympathy for the child's vulnerability and struggle against the world of adults.

The decade between the publication of *The Time of Friendship* and *Things Gone and Things Still Here* (1977) was a difficult one for Bowles. His wife, Jane, who had not been well since suffering a stroke in 1957, died at a sanatorium in Málaga, Spain, in 1973. In the years before her death, Bowles sought to balance his own needs to write and travel with the needs imposed by his wife's deteriorating condition. When he did travel–for instance, to Thailand in 1966 and to San Fernando State in 1968 to take a position as visiting writer–he always worried about Jane's condition back in Tangier.

Bowles's production tapered off significantly during this period. Between the publication of his fourth and final novel, *Up Above the World,* in 1966 and the collection of nine stories in *Things Gone and Things Still Here* in 1977, however, he did write his autobiography, *Without Stopping,* an undertaking he found painful, not only because it demanded a dredging up of the past but also because the present was so filled with uncertainty and anxiety. The book, published a year before Jane's death, is marked by its dispassionate tone and lack of emotive quality. Events simply pass and are noted in their stark factualness. His friends have often dubbed the book "Without Telling."

The writing of the autobiography was a diversionary chore. Similarly, the great deal of translating Bowles did during this period provided him with a way of "writing," continuing his engagement with language at a time when his own imagination lay fallow. With Larbi Layachi in the early 1960s, Bowles first developed a technique of recording stories told to him by local, illiterate Moroccan storytellers. By far his most productive collaborative translation project was with Mohammed Mrabet. Altogether Bowles "translated" at least a dozen books by Mrabet from 1967 to 1992. The effect of translating can be detected in his own short fiction during this period. His style becomes sparer, less complex. The stories take on more of an oral quality.

While critics generally judged *Things Gone and Things Still Here* to be weaker than Bowles's previous collections, the volume does include many memorable stories. In writing "You Have Left Your Lotus Pods on the Bus," Bowles relied on memories of his experiences in Thailand in 1966. Like so many other stories, this one hinges on cultural misunderstandings, though the results are not as tragic in this story as they are in some others. In one scene three gold-clad Thai monks visit two Americans at their luxurious hotel room. Among the many new things they contemplate are the possible meanings in Western societies of wearing the necktie. One of the Thais comments, "I have noticed that some men wear the two ends equal, and some wear the wide end longer than the narrow, or the narrow longer than the wide. And the neckties themselves, they are not all the same length, are they? Some even with both ends equal reach below the waist. What are the different meanings?" The Americans are just as baffled by certain practices in Thai culture. When, on a bus ride home from visiting temples, the Americans become annoyed by the erratic behavior of a man at the back of the bus, their Thai host explains that this man is helping the driver, warning of obstacles and dangers along the way.

"Allal," one of three stories (the other two are "Call at Corazón" and "The Story of Lahcen and Idir") constituting Frieder Schlaich and Irene von Alberti's movie triptych *Half Moon,* is one of several Bowles stories that involve a transformation from human to animal form. Allal, a young Moroccan boy who is the product of an illegitimate union, is abandoned by his young mother and becomes attached to a snake merchant who has been tormented by townsfolk. Both are outcasts, and Allal takes in the merchant temporarily. Allal finds himself peculiarly drawn to one special snake: "One reddish-gold serpent, which coiled itself lazily in the middle of the floor, he found particularly beautiful. As he stared at it, he felt a great desire to own it and have it always with him."

Allal devises a plan to keep the snake when the merchant leaves. He feeds the snake a concoction of kif and milk, then hides it. The merchant leaves, angry he has lost a prized possession. Allal develops a special rapport with the snake with the aid of the kif paste. At one point he undresses and invites the snake to crawl alongside his naked body. The story becomes at once sexually charged and surrealistic. Allal sheds his human form and slips into the body of the snake, apparently trading places with the snake. The end of the story is especially successful. Snake-as-Allal, behaving madly, runs off. Allal-as-snake is cornered and attacked by three townsmen. He enacts his revenge, "pushing his fangs" into two of the men before a third "severed his head with an axe." The story harks back to Bowles's early surrealistic experiments with writing, notably "The Scorpion." The story also returns to the familiar theme of the child or outcast who must battle the judgment and constraining moral order of society.

One of the strongest stories in the collection is "Reminders of Bouselham," one of the few stories in which Bowles uses a first-person narrator. The storyteller is a young Moroccan-born English expatriate who is trying to discover the truth concerning the relationship between his mother and a young Moroccan gardener named Bouselham. The piece displays how stories circulate within a community (particularly among the English-speaking expatriate community of Tangier) and shows how difficult it is sometimes, when one gets differing and conflicting versions of the story, to determine what actually happened. The stories themselves become more interesting than the truth; they take on an ontological weight that displaces truth.

In order to find out what happened, the narrator eventually looks up Bouselham himself. But can the reader depend upon the truthfulness of what Bouselham says? Bouselham, after all, has his own motives when telling the story. Stories about Bouselham, it seems, are what led the narrator's mother to break off with him and go to Italy. So, at least, the reader is led to believe.

In 1979 Black Sparrow Press brought out *Collected Stories 1939–1976.* The book was widely reviewed and roundly praised. Joyce Carol Oates, for instance, in a review for *The New York Times Book Review* (30 September 1979), later reprinted in *The Profane Art* (1983), writes, "Austere, remorseless, always beautifully crafted, the best of these stories are bleakly unconsoling as the immense deserts about which Bowles writes with such power."

Because they are not a part of *Collected Stories* and because they have not been published by mainstream trade publishers, Bowles's two more recent collections of stories are not nearly as well known as his earlier work. Many of these later stories, however, taken together, represent certain stylistic and thematic shifts. The blatant brutality of "The Delicate Prey" and "A Distant Episode" gives way to a more subtle, devious kind of perversity. These later stories, too, depend more on the movement of memory than actual physical movement.

Many of the stories in *Midnight Mass* (1981)–such as "Madame and Ahmed," "Midnight Mass," "The Dismissal," "Rumor and a Ladder," and "The Eye" (chosen by Joyce Carol Oates for *The Best American Stories of 1979*)–center on the lives of Tangier

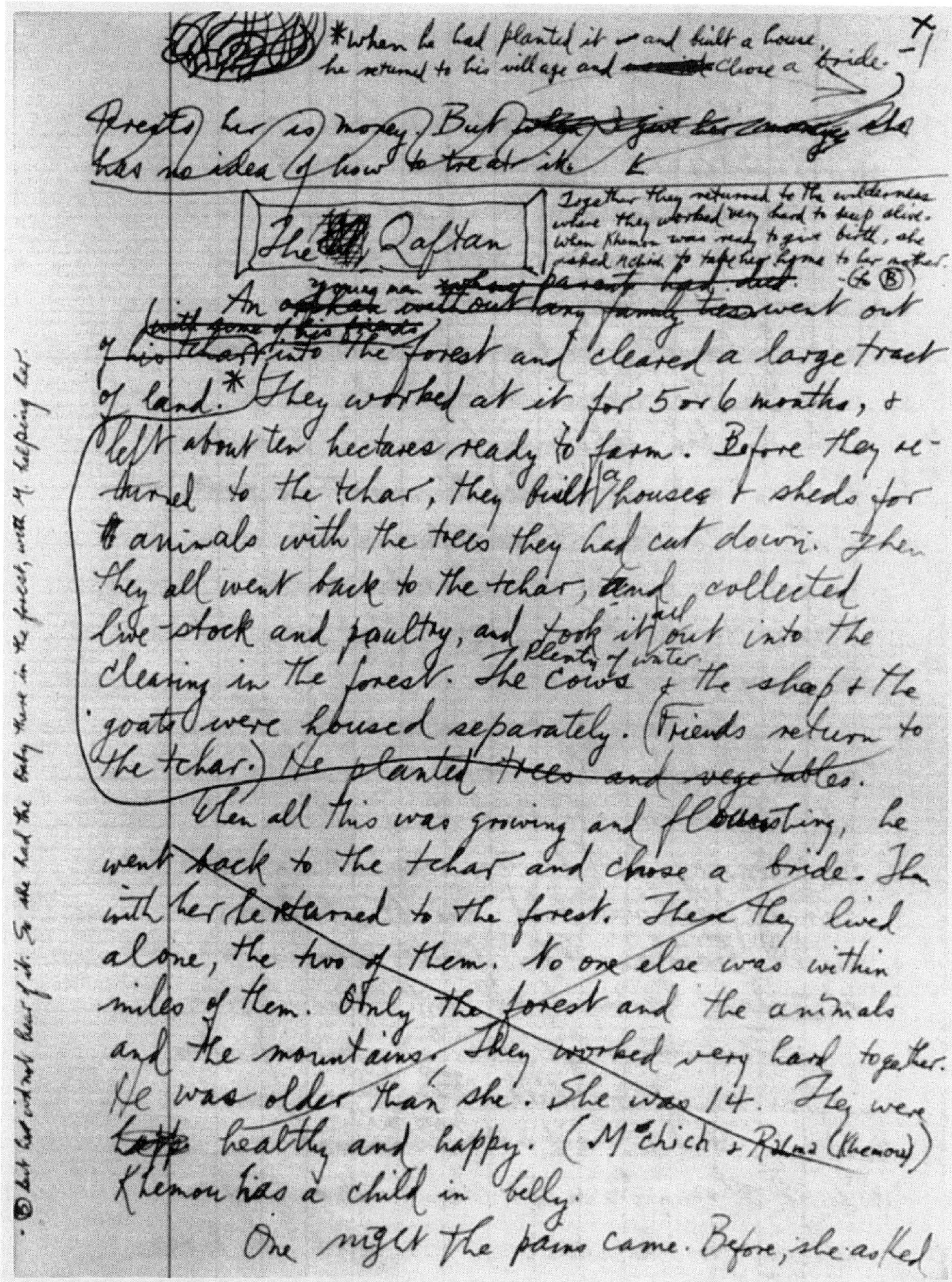

*When he had planted it and built a house, he returned to his village and chose a bride.

Treats her as money. But ~~when I give her money~~ she has no idea of how to treat it. E.

The Qaftan

Together they returned to the wilderness where they worked very hard to keep alive. When Khemou was ready to give birth, she asked Mchich to take her home to her mother. -Go (B)

An ~~orphan without any family ties~~ young man went out ~~with some of his friends~~ ~~of his tchar~~ into the forest and cleared a large tract of land.* They worked at it for 5 or 6 months, & left about ten hectares ready to farm. Before they returned to the tchar, they built a houses & sheds for animals with the trees they had cut down. Then they all went back to the tchar, and collected live-stock and poultry, and took it all out into the clearing in the forest. Plenty of water. The cows & the sheep & the goats were housed separately. (Friends return to the tchar.) ~~He planted trees and vegetables.~~

When all this was growing and flourishing, he went ~~back~~ to the tchar and chose a bride. Then with her he returned to the forest. There they lived alone, the two of them. No one else was within miles of them. Only the forest and the animals and the mountains. They worked very hard together. He was older than she. She was 14. They were ~~happy~~ healthy and happy. (Mchich & Rilma (Khemou)) Khemou has a child in belly.

One night the pains came. Before, she asked

(B) but her did not hear of it. So she had the baby there in the forest, with M. helping her.

Page from the manuscript for Bowles's translation of Mohammed Mrabet's short story "The Qaftan," published in the 1983 collection The Chest *(University of Delaware Library)*

Cover for Bowles's 1988 collection of short stories, including "Unwelcome Words," which was based on Bowles's experiences in Tangier during the 1980s

expatriates and the nature of their relationships with Moroccans. The narrator of "The Eye" perceptively notes how that expatriate community tends to operate: "These people often have reactions similar to those of certain primitive groups: when misfortune overtakes one of their number, the others by mutual consent refrain from offering him aid, and merely sit back to watch, certain that he has called his suffering down upon himself. He has become taboo, and is incapable of receiving help." This analysis is given as background for understanding the particular case of one Canadian expatriate named Marsh who, many thought, fell victim to "slow poisoning by native employees." Rather like the narrator in "Reminders of Bouselham," the narrator in "The Eye" plays the role of detective and tries to put the pieces of the story together. The narrator, who himself had no acquaintance with Marsh, comes upon the Marshes' night watchman, Larbi (who himself is a prime suspect in the minds of fellow expatriates), and gets to the heart of the mystery.

Other stories in the collection, such as "The Husband" and "The Empty Amulet," dwell wholly on the affairs of Moroccan characters as they seek to negotiate conflicts between traditional values, often based on superstition, and encroaching modern cosmologies. The longest and most ambitious story in the volume, "Here to Learn," literalizes the move from provincial Moroccan life to the modern West. As a result of a series of accidental encounters, Malika is taken (by a series of Western men) from her home in a small Moroccan village first to Tangier, then to Spain, then to Switzerland, then to Paris, and finally to Los Angeles. The narrative is filtered through Malika's consciousness, so the reader sees the West, in all its amazing strangeness, through her eyes. In pace, style, and the way fate operates, the story calls to mind Voltaire's *Candide* (1759), though Malika meets with more pleasant experiences than does the naive Candide. The American man named Tex, who took her to Los Angeles, dies unexpectedly, leaving her with a considerable fortune. She then finds herself independent and begins to learn, for the first time really, how to make her own decisions and control her own life. She decides, in the end, to visit her home in Morocco, where she finds her mother dead and the town radically altered.

Midnight Mass includes another award-winning story–"In the Red Room," selected by John Updike for *The Best American Short Stories, 1984*. In his introduction to the volume, Updike writes: "Paul Bowles describes, with an eerie indirection and softness of tone, a blood-soaked private shrine." The shrine Updike refers to is "the red room" of the title. As in "The Eye," the story is successful in large measure because of the narrative strategies employed by Bowles. The first-person narrator probes an experience he had while traveling with his parents in Sri Lanka. In the retelling of the story the three travelers meet a native Singhalese man named Gonzag who invites them back to his home, where he shows them, reverentially, his red room. Later the narrator learns why the room is so special. The day after his wedding, Gonzag had found his wife in bed with a friend who had been his best man: "he shot them both in the face, and later chopped their bodies into pieces." The room commemorates this drama of ill-fated love.

Bowles's last collection of stories, *Unwelcome Words,* was brought out in 1988 by the little-known Tombouctou Press. While these stories are generally leaner and more sedate than earlier ones, they still bear the familiar Bowles impress. He is still attracted to subjects involving moral transgression and violence; he continues to draw material from his expatriate experiences in Tangier. "Julian Vreden" tells a "uniquely American tale of revenge" in which the twenty-year-old Julian and "his friend Mark" murder Julian's parents. Suspicions are aroused when they try to cash in insurance policies. "Hugh Harper" and "Dinner at Sir Nigel's" depict other bizarre and perverse forms of behavior among certain legendary members of the Tangier expatriate community. Harper has a taste for drinking Muslim blood, while Sir Nigel likes to dress in leather and jodhpurs, enacting scenes with black women as dominatrices.

Interspersed between these tales of perversion are three dramatic monologues, a new stylistic development for Bowles. All three stories–"Massachusetts 1932," "New York 1965," and "Tangier 1975"–are set in places important for Bowles. In each, in a manner rather like Robert Browning's in his dramatic monologues, Bowles adopts the voice of the speaker–a lonely New England farmer, an American woman jealous of her roommate's literary success, and an expatriate woman living in Tangier. These later stories show that Bowles has continued to develop and experiment.

A Distant Episode: The Selected Stories of Paul Bowles, published by Ecco Press in 1988, brings together many of Bowles's earlier stories as well as some from *Midnight Mass* and *Unwelcome Words.* This volume in addition includes an important late story not in any other collection–"In Absentia." Like "Unwelcome Words," the story takes an epistolary form and draws on Bowles's own experiences while living in Tangier in the 1980s. The writer of the letters in "Unwelcome Words," in fact, refers to himself as "Paul Bowles" and tells his unnamed correspondent about the deteriorating living conditions in Tangier. Both stories display the attempts of a letter-writer (Bowles himself has always been a prodigious letter-writer) to manipulate and control events from a distance. Such an attempt is especially notable in "In Absentia." The story consists of a series of letters written to two correspondents–Pamela Loeffer, who has just received a divorce settlement and moved to Hawaii, and Susan Choate, a seventeen-year-old Mount Holyoke coed, a relative toward whom the writer apparently has obligations. In his letters the writer tells of his life and tries to imagine the lives of his correspondents. He engineers a meeting between his two correspondents through his artful, calculated use of rhetoric. He accomplishes the meeting, which he desires, by suggesting it would be in their interests, thus veiling his own self-interested motives. To Susan, for instance, he writes: "Staying with Pamela out there" in Hawaii, "you would be in a position, if you were clever enough, to receive financial assistance for the coming year. That wouldn't have occurred to you in your youthful innocence. But it occurred to me, and I see it as a distinct possibility." Once Susan and Pamela meet, however, the narrator finds himself out of touch–unaware of what is going on and unable to influence the course of action. Nonetheless, in the end, the writer seems to have gotten what he wanted out of his epistolary scheme.

"In Absentia" may well be thought of as dramatically displaying the expatriate condition Bowles has long inhabited–removed, writing home, trying to have some kind of impact, and always aware of the power of language. Except for intermittent trips to Paris to publicize his books and to the U.S. to attend to medical needs or to attend concerts devoted to his music, Paul Bowles has remained in Tangier, living in the same apartment he has rented since the 1950s. What was once the edge of town has now been engulfed by ever-expanding suburbs. When asked why he remains there, Bowles responds with a shrug. "Where else would I go, at this point? This is home. I'm a pragmatist."

With his truly distinctive literary and musical works and the novel shape of his life, Paul Bowles will certainly be remembered as one of the most interesting and most talented Americans of the twentieth century.

Letters:

Jeffrey Miller, ed., *In Touch: The Letters of Paul Bowles* (New York: Farrar, Straus & Giroux, 1994);

Dear Paul, Dear Ned: The Correspondence of Paul Bowles and Ned Rorem; introduction by Gavin Lambert (North Pomfret, Vt.: Elysium Press, 1997).

Interviews:

Harvey Breit, "Talk with Paul Bowles," *New York Times Book Review* (9 March 1952): 19;

Oliver Evans, "An Interview with Paul Bowles," *Mediterranean Review,* 1 (Winter 1971): 3–15;

Michael Rogers, "Conversation in Morocco," *Rolling Stone* (23 May 1974): 48–54;

Daniel Halpern, Interview with Paul Bowles, *TriQuarterly,* 33 (Spring 1975): 159–177;

Jeffrey Bailey, Interview with Paul Bowles, *Paris Review,* 81 (1981): 62–98;

"Stories of Violence," *Newsweek International* (4 August 1986): 48;

Gerardo Pina-Rosales, "En Tanger con Paul Bowles: Entrevista," *Nuez: Revista de Arte y Literatura,* 2 (1990): 5–6, 8–9;

Gena Dagel Caponi, ed., *Conversations with Paul Bowles* (Jackson: University Press of Mississippi, 1993);

Abdelhak Elghandor, "Atavism and Civilization: An Interview with Paul Bowles," *Ariel,* 25 (April 1994): 7–30.

Bibliographies:

Cecil R. McLeod, *Paul Bowles: A Checklist: 1929–1969* (Flint, Mich.: Apple Tree Press, 1970);

Jeffrey Miller, *Paul Bowles: A Descriptive Bibliography* (Santa Barbara, Cal.: Black Sparrow, 1986).

Biographies:

Robert Briatte, *Paul Bowles, 2117 Tanger Socco* (Paris: Plon, 1989);

Christopher Sawyer-Lauçanno, *An Invisible Spectator: A Biography of Paul Bowles* (New York: Weidenfeld & Nicolson, 1989);

Michelle Green, *The Dream at the End of the World: Paul Bowles and the Literary Renegades in Tangier* (New York: HarperCollins, 1991);

Gary Pulsifer, ed., *Paul Bowles by His Friends* (London: Owen, 1992);

Gena Dagel Caponi, *Paul Bowles: Romantic Savage* (Carbondale: Southern Illinois University Press, 1994);

Millicent Dillon, *You Are Not I: A Portrait of Paul Bowles* (Berkeley: University of California Press, 1998).

References:

Johannes Willem Bertens, *The Fiction of Paul Bowles: The Soul Is the Weariest Part of the Body* (Amsterdam: Rodopi, 1979);

Robert Craft, "Pipe Dreams," *New York Review of Books,* 23 November 1989, pp. 6, 8–12;

Gena Dagel, "A Nomad in New York: Paul Bowles, 1933–48," *American Music,* 7 (Fall 1989): 278–314;

John Ditsky, "*The Time of Friendship:* The Short Fiction of Paul Bowles," *Twentieth Century Literature,* 32 (Fall/Winter 1986): 373–387;

Chester E. Eisinger, "Paul Bowles and the Passionate Pursuit of Disengagement," in his *Fiction of the Forties* (Chicago: University of Chicago Press, 1963), pp. 283–288;

Oliver Evans, "Paul Bowles and The 'Natural' Man," *Critique,* 1, no. 3 (1959): 43–59;

Leslie A. Fiedler, "Style and Anti-Style in the Short Story," *Kenyon Review,* 13 (Winter 1951): 155–172;

Edward Field, "Tea at Paul Bowles's," *Raritan,* 12, no. 3 (Winter 1993): 92–111;

Ellen G. Friedman, "Variations on Mystery-Thriller: Paul Bowles' *Up Above the World,*" *Armchair Detective,* 19 (Summer 1986): 279–284;

Asad Al Ghalith, "Paul Bowles's Portrayal of Islam in His Moroccan Short Stories," *International Fiction Review,* 19, no. 2 (1992): 103–108;

Mitzi Berger Hamovitch, "Release from Torment: The Fragmented Double in Bowles's *Let It Come Down,*" *Twentieth Century Literature,* 32 (Fall/Winter 1986): 440–450;

Ihab Hassan, "The Pilgrim as Prey: A Note on Paul Bowles," *Western Review,* 19 (1954): 23–36;

Allen Hibbard, "Expatriation and Narration in Two Works by Paul Bowles," *West Virginia Philological Papers,* 32 (1986): 61–71;

Hibbard, *Paul Bowles: A Study of the Short Fiction* (New York: Twayne, 1993);

Richard Lehan, "Existentialism in Recent American Fiction: The Demonic Quest," *Texas Studies in Literature and Language,* 1 (Summer 1959): 181–202;

Bennett Lerner, "Paul Bowles: Lost and Found," in *Perspectives on Music: Essays on Collections at the HRC,* edited by Dave Oliphant and Thomas Zigal (Austin, Tex.: Humanities Research Center, 1985), p. 149;

John Maier, "Morocco in the Fiction of Paul Bowles," in *The Atlantic Connection: 200 Years of Moroccan-American Relations, 1786–1986,* edited by Mohammed El Mansour (Rabat: Edino, 1990), pp. 245–258;

Maier, "Two Moroccan Storytellers in Paul Bowles's *Five Eyes,*" *Postmodern Culture,* 1, no. 3 (1991);

Irving Malin, "Drastic Points," *Review of Contemporary Fiction,* 2, no. 3 (1982): 30–32;

Malin, "*The Time of Friendship,* by Paul Bowles," *Studies in Short Fiction,* 4, no. 3 (1968): 311–313;

Jody McAuliffe, "The Church of the Desert: Reflections on *The Sheltering Sky,*" *South Atlantic Quarterly,* 91, no. 2 (Spring 1992): 419–426;

Jay McInerney, "Paul Bowles in Exile," *Vanity Fair,* 48 (September 1985): 68–76, 131;

Marilyn Moss, "The Child in the Text: Autobiography, Fiction, and the Aesthetics of Deception in *Without Stopping,*" *Twentieth Century Literature,* 32 (Fall/Winter 1986): 314–333;

Eric Mottram, "Paul Bowles: Staticity and Terror," *Review of Contemporary Fiction,* 3, no. 2 (1982): 6–30;

Joyce Carol Oates, "Before God Was Love," *The Profane Art* (New York: Dutton, 1983), pp. 128–131;

Steven E. Olson, "Alien Terrain: Paul Bowles's Filial Landscapes," *Twentieth Century Literature,* 32 (Fall/Winter 1986): 334–349;

Richard F. Patteson, "Paul Bowles/Mohammed Mrabet: Translation, Transformation, and Transcultural Discourse," *Journal of Narrative Technique,* 22 (Fall 1992): 180–190;

Patteson, "Paul Bowles: Two Unfinished Projects," *Library Chronicle of the University of Texas at Austin,* new series, 30 (1985): 57–65;

Patteson, *A World Outside: The Fiction of Paul Bowles* (Austin: University of Texas Press, 1987);

Wayne Pounds, "Paul Bowles and *The Delicate Prey:* The Psychology of Predation," *Revue Belge de Philologie et d'Histoire,* 59, no. 3 (1981): 620–633;

Pounds, *Paul Bowles: The Inner Geography* (New York: Peter Lang, 1985);

Catherine Rainwater, "'Sinister Overtones,' 'Terrible Phrases': Poe's Influence on the Writings of Paul Bowles," *Essays in Literature,* 2 (Fall 1984): 253–266;

Joyce Hamilton Rochat, "The Naturalistic-Existential Rapprochement in Albert Camus' *L'Etranger* and Paul Bowles' *Let It Come Down:* A Comparative Study in Absurdism," dissertation, Michigan State University, 1971;

Ned Rorem, "Paul Bowles," in his *Setting the Tone* (New York: Limelight, 1984), p. 355;

Mary Martin Rountree, "Paul Bowles: Translations from the Moghrebi," *Twentieth Century Literature,* 32 (Fall/Winter 1986): 388–401;

Ralph St. Louis, "The Affirming Silence: Paul Bowles's "Pastor Dowe at Tacaté," *Studies in Short Fiction,* 24 (Fall 1987): 381–386;

Lawrence D. Stewart, *Paul Bowles: The Illumination of North Africa* (Carbondale & Edwardsville: Southern Illinois University Press, 1974);

Stewart, "Paul Bowles and 'The Frozen Fields' of Vision," *Review of Contemporary Fiction,* 2, no. 3 (1982): 64–71;

Marcellette G. Williams, "'Tea in the Sahara': The Function of Time in the Work of Paul Bowles," *Twentieth Century Literature,* 32 (Fall/Winter 1986): 408–423.

Papers:

The two largest collections of Paul Bowles's papers are housed in the Harry Ransom Humanities Research Center at the University of Texas, Austin, and in Special Collections, University of Delaware Library, Newark. Other small collections are at the Rare Book and Manuscript Library, Butler Library, Columbia University, New York, and the Alderman Library, University of Virginia, Charlottesville.

T. Coraghessan Boyle

(2 December 1948 –)

Denis Hennessy
State University of New York College at Oneonta

See also the entry on Boyle in *DLB Yearbook: 1986.*

BOOKS: *Descent of Man: Stories* (Boston: Little, Brown / Atlantic Monthly Press, 1979; London: Gollancz, 1979);

Water Music (Boston: Little, Brown, 1982; London: Gollancz, 1982);

Budding Prospects: A Pastoral (New York: Viking, 1984; London: Gollancz, 1984);

Greasy Lake and Other Stories (New York: Viking, 1985);

World's End (New York: Viking, 1987; London: Macmillan, 1988);

If the River Was Whiskey (New York: Viking, 1989);

East Is East (New York: Viking, 1990; London: Cape, 1991);

The Collected Stories (London: Granta, 1993);

The Road to Wellville (New York: Viking, 1993; London: Granta, 1993);

Without a Hero and Other Stories (New York: Viking, 1994; London: Granta/Penguin, 1995);

The Tortilla Curtain (New York: Viking, 1995; London: Bloomsbury, 1995);

T. C. Boyle Stories (New York: Viking, 1998);

Riven Rock (New York: Viking, 1998; London: Bloomsbury, 1998).

T. Coraghessan Boyle (photograph by Pablo Campos; from the dust jacket for If the River Was Whiskey, *1989)*

Since 1979 T. Coraghessan Boyle has wondered, sometimes with a strong hint of the irony that pervades most of his fiction, why he has not become as popular a writer as John Irving, John Updike, or even Stephen King. Critics and readers have praised his short-story collections and novels, and his short fiction appears regularly in prestigious magazines. Yet, he has never become a household name. Boyle was quoted in *DLB Yearbook: 1986* as saying, "I'm still a wise guy from New York. . . . I've always felt that I would never compromise. I'd do exactly what I wanted and still get my audience." This defiant side of Boyle might explain why his short fiction is not widely admired by the general public while it continues to delight his faithful readers by pushing further and further the power of the short story to lampoon American pretensions and obsessions.

Boyle was born Thomas John Boyle to a second-generation Irish American father and a mother of Dutch-Irish descent, in Peekskill, New York, on 2 December 1948. At seventeen Boyle, who was named after his father, changed his name to T. Coraghessan Boyle, largely as an attempt to distance himself from his alcoholic father and emerge from the lackluster background of a lower-middle-class upbringing. The pronunciation of Coraghessan (kuh-RAGG-issun), a name from the family of his mother, Rosemary Post McDonald Boyle, has been a source of confusion for readers, even providing the idea for a *New Yorker* cartoon in which a character asks for "a book by T. What's-His-Face Boyle." After a barely mediocre academic career at the State University of New York College at Potsdam, where he attempted to study music, Boyle graduated in 1968. Inspired by a creative-writing course he had taken at Potsdam, Boyle continued to write short stories while he taught English to tough adolescents in a Hudson Valley public high school. One of his early stories, "The OD and Hepatitis Railroad or Bust," was published in the *North American Review* (Fall 1972), easing the way to Boyle's acceptance in the Writers' Workshop at the University of Iowa.

Boyle readily admits that drugs and alcohol were preoccupations before he attended Iowa. He had also begun to read widely and to be influenced by John Barth, Thomas Pynchon, Gabriel García Márquez, Eugène Ionesco, and Jean Genet. Other influences assert themselves humorously in stories that parody the styles of Edgar Allan Poe, Arthur Conan Doyle, and Ernest Hemingway, progenitors of the protean flexibility that characterizes the modern short story.

Boyle has built his career as a short-story writer on stylistic innovations and inventive subject matter, always displaying his respect for the power of short fiction to entertain. In a brief autobiography written for Amazon.com he described his literary heroes as Evelyn Waugh, especially in *A Handful of Dust* (1937); Gabriel García Márquez, especially in *One Hundred Years of Solitude* (1967) and his short story "A Very Old Man with Enormous Wings"; and Flannery O'Connor. Her "A Good Man is Hard to Find" (1955) is his favorite story, beating out short fiction by John Cheever, Raymond Carver, and Robert Coover by a narrow margin. "Accident rules the World," Boyle says, "accident and depravity, and I don't have O'Connor's faith to save me from all that."

In 1977 Boyle earned a Ph.D. at Iowa, using as his dissertation a collection of short stories later published as *Descent of Man* (1979). Since earning his doctorate he has taught at the University of Southern California.

Boyle has created a zany image for himself by accentuating his frizzy hair and wearing punk clothing while affecting a semiserious scowl. He also indulges his penchant for the rebellious music of the 1970s by singing lead in a rockabilly band. His flamboyant public persona contrasts with his personal lifestyle: he has been married to Karen Kvashay since 1974, and they have three children, Kerrie, Milo, and Spencer.

Descent of Man, which won the St. Lawrence Award for short fiction in 1980, displays Boyle's overriding theme: the unavoidable reversion of humankind to a prelapsarian animality, a state of being characterized by physical coarseness and the absence of conscience. The reader rarely hears Boyle's voice of judgment in these stories; rather he seems to be snickering behind a first-person narrator or alongside an ostensibly omniscient teller, not with the Joycean indifference of a creator paring his nails but with something approaching a blissful complicity.

The first-person narrator of the title story laments his sagging romance with Jane Good, a scientist whose study of chimpanzees has centered on the super-intelligent ape Konrad. The beast seems to be winning Jane's affections, but not through his intellect. Jane is regressing into coarse habits of hygiene and nutrition and is discovered having sex with Konrad. Boyle leaves the reader debating if the narrator is inferior to Konrad, too different from the Tarzan Jane wants. The irony of the story is intensified as the reader feels inclined to agree with her choice.

In "The Champ" the similarity of man's inclinations to the worst instincts of animals is exemplified by a champion eater with an ulcer who outeats his opponent in a crucial contest as his mother sits ringside encouraging him: "Eat, Angelo, eat . . . clean your plate." In "We are Norseman," narrated in an epic-sounding first person, Norsemen are killing and pillaging, gleefully burning the books right out of Celtic monks' hands as they try to preserve their brand of civilization. Both stories tend to diminish the reader's assessment of man's place on the food chain.

Boyle's voice and tone are more Joycean in these stories than in his later fiction. Yet, if he is the absent modernist creator defined by James Joyce, he is not objective, as Joyce wished to be. As in most of Boyle's stories, his virtuosic language gives the reader a sense of the author laughing behind the scenes. This language play is a major part of the Boyle style.

In this first collection Boyle cannot always achieve the same level of virtuosity. His themes get blurry when he begins taking potshots at man's foibles. In "Heart of a Champion" the language alone cannot sustain the weight of a Lassie-movie parody in which the dog is sidetracked from rescuing his master, Timmy, by a romantic attraction to a coyote. Nor can language sustain "Bloodfall," a story about hippies who cannot postpone their solipsistic lifestyle of drugs, alcohol, and sex just because the skies are sending down torrents of blood in place of rain. The variety of Boyle's themes in the collection, however, demonstrates a potential prowess for short-story writing.

One of the final stories in this first book returns clearly to Boyle's major theme, leaving the reader to question the right of science to meddle in the secrets of nature and ask if man must re-examine his hegemony

Dust jacket for Boyle's first book, in which the title story features a female scientist who has an affair with a chimpanzee

in the food chain. "De Rerum Natura" offers segments of a biography of The Inventor, from his days as a prodigy in the scientific world to his violent, fiery death at the hands of an angry mob. The Inventor has toyed with nature, changing it in bizarre ways: he has developed a cat that does not eat, but just purrs and comforts its owner; he has turned rusted cars into food to feed India. Finally, he has solved the "big mystery"; he has killed God and has slides to prove it. His neighbors, representing mankind, riot in indignation, burning The Inventor's house with him inside.

Like the stories that end Boyle's later collections, "Drowning," the final story in *Descent of Man,* seems to have been chosen to summarize and emphasize his major theme. The story presents man as predatory, without free will, and totally deserving of the harsh destiny that awaits him in a cruel universe. Two people at the beach are presented almost as though they are displayed on slides under a microscope. One is a woman, naturally beautiful and healthy, an artists' model in her spare time; the other is a man, weak looking but a naturally good swimmer. The two are on the same lonely stretch of sand but catch only distant glimpses of one another. As the man swims, the woman sleeps in the sun. She is raped by a casual stroller and then by some passersby who have watched the first attacker's violent assault. Seemingly oblivious to the action on the beach, the swimmer is surprised by a larger-than-usual wave and drowns. Boyle leaves his readers with moral and metaphysical questions about man's inevitable struggle with fate. Because of his ill-preparedness and his weakness of will, he will lose in a struggle with natural disaster or with his own rapacious self-interests.

Boyle's second collection, *Greasy Lake and Other Stories* (1985), published when he was thirty-seven, seems to be his commentary on life from the late 1960s, when he was one of the rebellious baby boomers, until the mid 1980s. The first story, "Greasy Lake," which takes its title from Bruce Springsteen's "Spirits in the Night"–a song on his first album, *Greetings from Asbury Park N.J.* (1973)–also has a line from the song as an epigraph: "It's about a mile down on the dark side of Route 88." Greasy Lake is the setting for a darkly comic tale of self-inflicted trouble. The first-person narrator and his friends are drinking and looking for sex and violence by the shores of a polluted lake. They attack a man and attempt to rape his girlfriend, inviting reprisals that they cannot handle. Demonstrating the failures of youth in the era of the Vietnam War and unfettered sexual exploitation, "Greasy Lake" is one of Boyle's best and most chilling stories.

The stories that follow explore other issues of the 1960s and 1970s, following a pattern of hopes dashed by treachery and disillusionment, with Boyle's never-ending supply of surprises and ironies lightening the mood of the stories. In "Caviar" a young couple, Marie and Nathaniel Trimpie, try unsuccessfully to conceive a baby and then contact a Dr. Ziss to help them with finding a surrogate mother for their child. After artificial insemination, the surrogate, Wendy, has clandestine sex with Nathaniel. After the child is born, Nathaniel, driven by a passionate desire for Wendy, visits her and discovers that she is living with Dr. Ziss. In a rage he beats the doctor and is arrested. Out on bail and locked out of his house by Marie, he takes his boat onto the river, where he feels more natural, in his "element." He finds a sturgeon caught in one of his nets and in the process of cleaning it, "millions" of gelatinous eggs stream from its gut, reminding the reader of the seemingly generous outpouring of nature, which is denied to some, and causing the reader to think about the circuitous and devious means that humans use in attempts to right the inequities of nature.

"Ike and Nina," narrated in the awed and breathless voice of an aide to President Dwight D. Eisenhower, tells a story of a fictional affair Ike had with Nina, the wife of Soviet premier Nikita Khrushchev, consummated during delicate negotiations between the two leaders of 1955. According to the aide, the premier's turn to bellicose behavior can be traced to jealousy triggered by the discovery of the affair. Boyle's imaginative use of narration saves a clever story from being just clever. It reminds the reader of how the course of events can be changed and disrupted by high-level weakness and scandal.

The theme of dreams shattered by reality and perfidy provides unity in *Greasy Lake and Other Stories.* "Whales Weep" deals with the fanaticism of some ecologists. In "The New Moon Party" a candidate who seems similar to George H. W. Bush promises the moon, a new one, during his campaign. After taking office, he has it constructed, losing face and credibility when the large reflecting orb, made of mirrors, almost melts his constituency. "Not a Leg to Stand On" and "Stones in My Pathway, Hellhound On My Trail" give frightening pictures of Americans' callous treatment of the aging and of the horrors of being old in an uncaring world. In "All Shook Up" Boyle returns to Upstate New York to depict Joey, a pathetically hopeful young Elvis Presley imitator, just at the end of the singer's postmortem popularity. The poignant story is narrated by a next-door neighbor, Carl, a high-school guidance counselor who coolly observes the boy's failure and dejection and then slickly seduces Joey's young wife, Cindy. Carl's dispassionate description of Joey's youthful rage at his failure, cuckolding, and disillusionment is one of Boyle's most skillful uses of a deceptively disinterested participant-narrator.

"Rara Avis" seems to be Boyle's attempt to imitate the minimalist style of *New Yorker* short-story writers such as Raymond Carver and Richard Ford. It is one of Boyle's most effective descriptions of repressed life in a small town like Peekskill. The wounded rare bird perched on the roof of a furniture shop in a small rural New York State village draws a crowd of onlookers who are first curious, then cynically reviling, and finally angry enough to want to stone the creature. Even the twelve-year-old boy who is the narrator is drawn into the murderous urge to destroy this anomaly that has ceased to be interesting. The symbolism of the story is contrived, but the last line–"I threw the first stone"–is wrenching. The outcast rara avis represents a young artist who fails to recognize his talent.

The final story in *Greasy Lake and Other Stories,* "The Overcoat II," is an obvious takeoff on Nikolay Gogol's 1842 story "The Overcoat," about the frustrations of Akaky, a Russian office worker. Brought up to date by Boyle, Akaky is a file clerk in Soviet Leningrad during the 1960s, just as helpless, reviled, and suffering–and, as in Gogol's story, his new, warm overcoat is still stolen from him. The only difference with the modern victim is that he is a loyal communist who fully believes that the system will protect him. His enemies are coworkers who are cynical about communism, the sly thief of the tailor who sells Akaky his new coat, and the apparatchik who ends up with the coat. Akaky dies of pneumonia. As in other Boyle stories, cynical self-interest triumphs over innocence.

Reviewing *If the River Was Whiskey* (1989) for *The New York Times* (14 May 1989), Elizabeth Benedict wrote that Boyle succeeded in touching the reader with real emotion only in the title story. She praised Boyle's skillful and clever writing but wished he would be more forthcoming in uncovering the inner hurts that drive his restless energy. Benedict seems to have overlooked stories such as "Rara Avis," "All Shook Up," and "Greasy Lake" in Boyle's first two collections. Even for the casual reader these stories have obvious connections to Boyle's inner life. The same connection is apparent in "Sorry Fugu," the opening story in *If the River Was Whiskey.* While the story is hardly autobiographical, it gives the reader a glimpse at the lower-middle-class view of

Dust jacket for Boyle's 1989 collection of short stories, which includes parodies of Franz Kafka's "A Hunger Artist" and Ernest Hemingway's For Whom the Bell Tolls

upper-class lifestyles that Boyle must have experienced during the years before he became a successful writer. The story is constructed much like a well-told joke. To save his restaurant from failure, Albert needs a good review from the powerful food critic Willa Frank and prepares extra-special meals for her. After two disastrous visits, he is desperate, realizing that her third visit must be good. Luckily, Albert has discerned that Jock, the hulking man Willa brings with her on each visit, is testing and tasting the food with her, perhaps for her. Willa Frank, Albert realizes, needs the primitive oaf to help her form her opinions. On the important night Albert pleases Jock with a coarse but satisfying meal while he plies Willa with carefully chosen delicacies, winning a favorable review and seducing her in the bargain. Albert seems to have found the formula for pleasing critics and the public, a formula that has eluded Boyle as an author.

"Modern Love," which was first published in *Playboy* (March 1988), seems to have been tailored to readers of that magazine. It is a silly story about a girlfriend so fastidious about disease-causing threats in food and the atmosphere that she finally demands a full-body condom. First published in *Harper's,* "Hard Sell" also seems to have been written for a particular audience, in this case politically current and sophisticated readers.

A contrived, obvious tale, "Peace of Mind" is redeemed only by slick style and recognizable characters. It is followed, however, by the masterful "Sinking House," as originally conceived and deftly structured as a Nathaniel Hawthorne romance. Boyle sets up two contrasting suburban American homes to show innocence and experience. Meg, a young wife, lives next door to Muriel, a much older woman whose husband, Monty, dies at the beginning of the story. Monty has abused and dominated Muriel, and after he dies Muriel turns on all the water taps in the house, flooding it so badly that the water seeps outside. She is cleansing the house of Monty. Meg at first is annoyed and then frightened by the flooding. Yet, in the end, after she and the reader have recognized a dark similarity between Monty and Meg's own husband, Sonny, she turns on her own faucets. The modern lifestyles Boyle has depicted in this story and elsewhere in his fiction seem to confirm a creeping loss of soul in the American middle class.

The epigraph to "The Human Fly," from Franz Kafka's "A Hunger Artist" (1922), emphasizes the connection between Kafka's story and Boyle's. Boyle's updating of Kafka's tale emphasizes the plight of the artist in the unsympathetic world that Boyle depicts in many of his stories. His Zoltan sacrifices his life for fame in the eyes of an audience indifferent to his personal well-being. "Me Cago En La Leche" is a less satisfying, more puzzling updating of a work by a well-known author. Subtitled "Robert Jordan in Nicaragua," Boyle's story imitates Ernest Hemingway's style in *For Whom the Bell Tolls* (1940) only superficially as it places a modern version of Hemingway's Robert Jordan among revolutionary guerrillas in Central America, presumably to demonstrate the loss of idealism in late-twentieth-century fights for freedom around the world. In "The Little Chill," Boyle's retelling of the successful movie *The Big Chill* (1983), he adds his owns stiletto-sharp wit to lampooning his generation's hypocrisy and clownish failures.

"King Bee," the story of Ken and Pat, who adopt a monster child named Anthony, is one of the tales in which Boyle writes of the brutish side of humanity, which can horrify if not treated with love and compassion. Anthony is nine when Ken and Pat adopt him, toughened by the brutality of an adoption system that has made him unremorsefully violent, totally intractable, and obsessed with bees, his only interest. The efforts of Ken and Pat and the resources on which they call for help are laughably inadequate, scandalously so. Finally the increasingly suicidal boy causes his own death from the stings of killer bees.

The next story offers a kind of antidote to this senseless battle of man against his unrestrained animality and has an almost romantic resolution. Told by a third-person narrator, "Thawing Out" involves the half-hearted courting of Naina by Marty, a schoolteacher in Upstate New York. Marty declines the first invitation to join Naina's Lithuanian family on their swim in the Hudson River to celebrate the winter solstice, but after frittering away his chances of a warm and loving relationship with her, he presumably wins her by jumping into the ice-cold water with her and her family the following December. The inhumanely cold waves bathe him in warmth as he joins his smiling Naina and her hardy family. The love and acceptance Marty seems to gain in this story are significant among the rejections, disappointments, and frustrations of the other stories.

"The Ape Lady in Retirement" is another installment on ape-human relationships and a bewildering summary of man's ties to his Darwinian predecessor. Beatrice Umbo, a well-known scientist who has studied apes all her life, has returned to Connecticut to retire. Pestered by a local admirer of her work, a young stocky boy named Howard, she allows him to pilot her over Connecticut and Long Island in a small Cessna airplane. With her she takes Konrad, a cigar-smoking ape raised in captivity. After a comic contretemps, Konrad easily kills Howard, and the plane crashes as Konrad and Beatrice carry out their suicide pact. While the story might be read as a horrifyingly comic look at the inevitable victory of man's brutal nature, it seems more likely to be a parody of science and humans' misgivings about themselves.

The title story, which comes last in the book, is arguably the best in the collection, different from the others in tone and style. At times the third-person point of view is that of the son, Tiller, while at other times it is that of his mother, Caroline, or his half-drunk father. There is also an authorial voice arguing in the father's defense, especially at the conclusion. The story depicts the growing awareness of the young boy, whose emotions range from hope to disappointment mirrored in his attempt to have his father believe that the worthless carp he has landed is really a much-desired pike.

The stories in *If the River Was Whiskey* are not perfectly satisfying; there are too many repetitions of past themes. Still the force of Boyle's intelligent commentaries about modern life makes the collection another step in his progress toward a truly significant contribution to the American short story.

Without A Hero (1994) fails to show much broadening of themes. Rather it seems to put Boyle's purpose in a different light, to give his description of the disintegration of pre-baby-boom America a different rationale. Most of the stories in this collection describe the vacuum left by the disappearance of the hero, not only in fiction but in real lives. The first story, "Big Game," is entertaining and clever but ultimately disappointing. It seems too much like the stories in *Descent of Man.* Again Boyle is parodying Hemingway, this time "The Short Happy Life of Francis Macomber" (1936). The setting is a game farm in California that caters to wealthy egomaniacs who crave killing for the bogus trophy of a good hunt. This theme is hackneyed for Boyle and obvious for the reader of his previous collections. The animals suffer ill treatment and an undignified death at the hands of Bernard Puff, the owner of the farm. Boyle's story closely parallels Hemingway's, updating it by making Mike Bender, the Macomber character, a real-estate tycoon and giving the wife a video camera in place of a gun. Again Boyle's subject is the greedy, self-serving dominance of man over God's other creatures. In this story, however, the characterization is weak, and the point is belabored.

Throughout the collection, Boyle depicts an America bereft of her heroes. In "Big Game" the reader notices that even Wilson, Hemingway's formidable guide, is transformed into Puff, an ineffectual bungler killed by a flea-bitten, enraged elephant. Not even the wife escapes with her life. Bender's estate will go in its entirety to their spoiled, cynical daughter.

In "Hopes Rise" Peter and Adrian are in the last stages of a decaying relationship. A flaccid friendliness has replaced all passion as they fret about the extinction of species after species, developments they follow from the comfort of their frumpy urban digs. Then they venture out into a quasi-wilderness to look for the disappearing frogs and discover these seemingly undoomed creatures in a bog, where hundreds of the little creatures are having an orgy of sensual play. Inspired, Peter and Adrian make love with unaccustomed abandon. The reader senses that love returns because of their caring for the humbler creatures but wonders whether Boyle is teetering on absurdity or laughing at his character.

In "Filthy With Things" John and Marsha are overwhelmed by the clutter of all their possessions and call in Suzanne Certaine, Professional Organizer. This hilarious story, in which Boyle takes potshots at an insanely materialistic world, is followed by the title story, in which Boyle offers a stark look at the hero-less world he laments. Irina, a Russian adventuress visiting the United States, is pampered by Casey, a Los Angeles bachelor, who tries to substitute material possessions for genuine emotion. No number of gifts or luxurious

Dust jacket for Boyle's 1994 book, stories in which Boyle depicts Americans of the late twentieth century as cowardly and self-serving

accommodations can make up for his indifference, his attentiveness to work and career, and his inability to love. He cannot be the man Irina wants, "a hero" who is willing to "die for love." Instead he shows the reader just how unheroic the American male can be.

"Acts of God" gives further sad news about the wimpishness of the American male, while Jim, the narrator and protagonist of "Carnal Knowledge," tries to rise to be heroic and fails. To win Alena Jorgensen, Jim converts to vegetarianism and even agrees to help her in her quests to eliminate the dastardly treatment of animals by meat merchants, furriers, and laboratories. Alena dumps Jim for Rolfe, an even more virulent animal-rights activist, whom Alena seems to consider more virile. When Jim realizes he has lost her to Rolfe, he returns to eating hamburgers with a vengeance.

"Little America" focuses on Richard Evelyn Byrd III, a pathetic descendant of the great Antarctic explorer, one of the most heroic Americans. Old and somewhat senile, Richard is lured to a warehouse by a vagrant named Roger. As Roger is relieving Richard of his belongings, they share a drink and end up having a drunken spree. Despite Richard's vulnerability, he survives the ordeal, making a warming shelter out of boxes strewn around the warehouse, showing the same sort of ingenuity that kept his grandfather alive in Little America, his base camp in Antarctica. Ironically, of course, his "Little America" is a diminished version of his grandfather's, and he lives in a diminished nation where men are able to perform only dwarfish feats.

People who look for heroes in this bleak world are doomed to disillusionment, Boyle says again in "Beat," a touching story of a young man much like Boyle himself, who looks for Beat writers Jack Kerouac, Neal Cassady, Allen Ginsberg, and William S. Burroughs–and ends up at the house Kerouac shares with his mother, where he meets them all. Chased out by Kerouac's mother, the young man returns to his own mother, chastened and faced with the reality of a bourgeois life without even the illusion of a hero.

The last two stories in *Without a Hero and Other Stories* combine wit and brilliantly deft wordplay in a haunting call to recognize the diminished glory of American civilization. "The Fog Man" starts out as the narrator's nostalgic memory of youth in a small town in Upstate New York. The fog man of the title is the driver of the truck that goes through the streets near dark during the summer releasing a spray that, according the boy's parents, is meant to kill mosquitoes. The neighborhood children delight in riding through the clouds of insecticide on their bicycles. At the same time, an atomic-power plant opens near the little town. The boy's best friend, Casper, a brilliant but disturbed child, begins taunting the only minority student in the school, a Japanese-African-American girl. Although the narrator at first feels no enmity toward the girl and even accepts her invitation to a junior-high school dance, he finally turns against her after becoming the object of other children's abuse. Adults join in taunting the girl and her family, and finally Casper and the narrator pelt the girl's house with eggs, driving her and her family from the neighborhood. In a subplot the boy describes his grandfather's drinking and his violent attack on his wife. At the end of the story, the following summer, the fog man returns wearing a mask, suggesting a new awareness of the toxic effects of the spray; yet, the narrator once again rides his bicycle through it. This fog and the atomic-power plant are visible representations of the toxic hatred that afflicts the community and has been transmitted to the young narrator and his schoolmates. As Boyle told Tad Friend, "The most valuable thing about the whole human experience is innocence, and you get disabused of it in childhood."

"Sitting on Top of the World" is a suspense story with a twist. Lainie, a fire watcher, is alone on a tower in the Sierras when a suspicious visitor arrives at her perch. Feeling threatened by the man, who has been there before, she nonetheless does not seem to care if he rapes or murders her. She feels lonely and unloved. She and her husband have separated, and their son seems to favor his father. The interloper is strange but friendly, and he confesses his deep attraction to her in their brief communications. At the end of the story she puts away the knife she keeps for protection and waits for him in her bed. The reader is left wondering if he is her "hero" or a criminal.

There are no true heroes in Boyle's short fiction. The reader may ask as well if there are any real, memorable characters in his stories or if the cynicism of his stories has obliterated the humanity of the characters.

T. C. Boyle Stories (1998) brings together the contents of Boyle's first four collections with seven stories previously unpublished in book form. Four of these stories were written in the 1970s and offer little that is thematically or stylistically new. In "I Dated Jane Austen," written in 1977 and first published in a 1980 issue of *Georgia Review,* Boyle enters the story as the narrator and protagonist, Mr. Boyle, who takes the nineteenth-century novelist and her sister to a steamy Italian movie and a disco. Jane seems less interested in Mr. Boyle than in Henry Crawford, one of the characters in her novel *Mansfield Park* (1814).

"Mexico," written in 1997, is different in style and tone from any of Boyle's earlier short stories. In his review of *T. C. Boyle Stories* for *The New York Times Book Review* (8 November 1998), Jim Shepard commented that the recent stories in the book "suggest an increasing willingness to stay committed to the human beings under examination." He added that "Mexico," for example, seems to show Boyle as more humane and compassionate, and less contemptuous, than in his earlier stories. The main character of "Mexico," Lester, seems to be another of Boyle's losers, and the premise of his winning the trip to Mexico by buying a five-dollar chance to benefit a Battered Women's Shelter seems a typically cynical Boyle plot device. Yet, the tone is softer, the mood more like that of Malcolm Lowry's *Under the Volcano* (1947), a novel he mentions in the first paragraph. The third-person narration is limited to Lester's consciousness as his weaknesses and naive choices doom him to humiliation. Gina, the beautiful woman he meets in Mexico, is sympathetic to Lester in the end, but she is not willing to sacrifice anything to be with him.

Boyle's career is probably at its halfway mark, and using any American standard of assessment, it has been successful. Yet, Boyle wants more, and the reader senses this desire in the intensity and fervor of his short stories.

Reference:

Tad Friend, "Rolling Boyle," *New York Times Magazine,* 9 December 1990, pp. 50–68.

Frederick Busch

(1 August 1941 -   )

Charlotte Zoë Walker
State University of New York College at Oneonta

photograph by John Hubbard; from the dust jacket for The Children in the Woods *(1994)*

See also the Busch entry in *DLB 6: American Novelists Since World War II, Second Series.*

BOOKS: *I Wanted a Year Without Fall* (London: Calder & Boyars, 1971);
Hawkes: A Guide to His Fictions (Syracuse: Syracuse University Press, 1973);
Breathing Trouble and Other Stories (London: Calder & Boyars, 1973);
Manual Labor (New York: New Directions, 1974);
Domestic Particulars: A Family Chronicle (New York: New Directions, 1976);
The Mutual Friend (New York: Harper & Row, 1978; London: Harvester, 1978);
Hardwater Country (New York: Knopf, 1979);
Rounds (New York: Farrar, Straus & Giroux, 1979; London: Hamilton, 1980);
Take This Man (New York: Farrar, Straus & Giroux, 1981);
Invisible Mending (Boston: Godine, 1984);
Too Late American Boyhood Blues: Ten Stories (Boston: Godine, 1984);
Sometimes I Live in the Country (Boston: Godine, 1986);
When People Publish: Essays on Writers and Writing (Iowa City: University of Iowa Press, 1986);
War Babies (New York: New Directions, 1989);
Absent Friends (New York: Knopf, 1989);
Harry and Catherine (New York: Knopf, 1990);
Closing Arguments (New York: Ticknor & Fields, 1991);
Long Way from Home (New York: Ticknor & Fields, 1993);
The Children in the Woods: New and Selected Stories (New York: Ticknor & Fields, 1994);
Girls: A Novel (New York: Harmony, 1997);
A Dangerous Profession: A Book about the Writing Life (New York: St. Martin's Press, 1998);
The Night Inspector (New York: Harmony, 1999).

OTHER: *Letters to a Fiction Writer,* edited by Busch (New York: Norton, 1999).

SELECTED PERIODICAL PUBLICATIONS–UNCOLLECTED:

FICTION

"Machias," *Threepenny Review,* 15 (Spring 1994): 1, 26–28;
"Heads," *Harper's,* 293 (October 1996): 79–85;
"Bob's Your Uncle," *Gettysburg Review,* 10 (Spring 1997): 127–141;
"The Ninth, in E Minor," *Georgia Review,* 51 (Spring 1997): 59–69;
"Vespers," *Agni,* no. 49 (1999): 118–131.

NONFICTION

"'Living Writers' Show Students How Literary Art Is Made," *Chronicle of Higher Education,* 23 May 1997, pp. B6–B7;

"Where We Do Our Work," *Zoetrope All-Story,* 2, no. 2 (Summer 1998): 37–39.

Frederick Busch is a distinguished master of the short story in late-twentieth-century America, adding to the vitality of that literary form with his powerful, morally penetrating stories. Of Busch's twenty-three published books, four are nonfiction, thirteen are novels, and six are story collections. Although his novels are as successful and well-crafted as his stories, and perhaps better known, his command of the short-story form is many-faceted. Busch's stories, like his novels, explore the "domestic particulars" of family life with realism but with an often mythic dimensionality and a sense of the interplay between personal life and the larger world. He takes as one of his major motifs children lost in the woods, from the "Hansel and Gretel" fairy tale, and his fiction can often be seen as a literary advocacy for understanding the vulnerability of children.

The elder of two sons, Frederick Busch was born on 1 August 1941 in Brooklyn, New York, to Benjamin Busch, a lawyer (joint author of *Foreign Law: A Guide to Pleading and Proof,* 1959), and Phyllis (Schnell) Busch, a teacher, naturalist, and author. His early life was much influenced by World War II (his father served in the Tenth Mountain Division in Italy and won a Bronze Star), and Busch refers to himself as a "War Baby," a concept that interested him and led to a 1989 novel called *War Babies.* He notes in an essay for *Contemporary Authors Autobiography Series* (1984): "That term has come to mean the generation born when husbands returned from World War II in the mid-1940's, or those, like me, born during the war; it stands for kids who grew up with names like Roosevelt falling about their unperceiving ears, and who can vaguely remember such things–or adult conversation about the fact of such things–as food rationing coupons, blackouts, air-raid drills."

Busch became interested in writing at an early age, even scripting his games with neighbor children. He read constantly as a boy, making use of the public library that was several blocks from his home, and he has written of the mingling of sounds, sights, and smells of his neighborhood on that walk to the library. He attended Muhlenberg College in Allentown, Pennsylvania, a Lutheran-affiliated school, where he received his B.A. in 1962. He has noted that he learned about anti-Semitism while in college, where he was beaten up for being Jewish. He was taught by two particularly inspiring teachers while at Muhlenberg, where he says he "achieved–was actively taught how to achieve–a first-rate education." There he also met Judith Ann Burroughs, whom he married in 1963, a year after his graduation. They have two sons. After attending Columbia University and New York University, Busch began teaching at Colgate University in Hamilton, New York, in 1966. He received his M.A. from Columbia University in 1967. Busch has continued to teach at Colgate, where he is Fairchild Professor of Literature and directs the Living Writers program, which he founded and which brings to Colgate some of the best writers in the country.

Busch has published six short-story collections: *Breathing Trouble and Other Stories* (1973); *Domestic Particulars: A Family Chronicle* (1976), a linked series of stories that is generally treated as a novel; *Hardwater Country* (1979); *Too Late American Boyhood Blues: Ten Stories* (1984); *Absent Friends* (1989); and *The Children in the Woods: New and Selected Stories* (1994), which reprints fifteen stories selected by Busch from the earlier collections along with eight new ones. Another short-story collection, with the working title "Don't Tell Anyone," is expected in 2001. Although it is interesting to see which stories from the earlier collections he chose to include in *The Children in the Woods,* it must be remembered that Busch was culling with a particular thematic arrangement in mind and that many important stories remain available only in his earlier collections. His stories have also been published in some of the most distinguished literary journals and included in *The O. Henry Awards* (1974) and twice in *The Best American Short Stories* (1977 and 1989). "The Ninth, in E Minor," appears in the 1999 *Pushcart Prize* collection. His many awards include a Woodrow Wilson Fellowship (1962–1963), a National Endowment for the Arts grant (1976–1977), a Guggenheim Fellowship (1981–1982), the Ingram Merrill Foundation Fellowship (1981–1982), the National Jewish Book Award for Fiction (1985), the American Academy of Arts and Letters Fiction Award (1986), and the PEN/Malamud Award for achievement in short fiction (1991). In 1995 *The Children in the Woods* was a finalist for the PEN/Faulkner Award.

The relationship between Busch's novels and his short stories is an interesting one. In a review of *Too Late American Boyhood Blues* for the *Washington Post* (11 November 1984), one critic noted Busch's particular sensitivity to both genres: "It is cheering, in view of many instances to the contrary, to find an experienced novelist as alert as is Frederick Busch to the deep differences between the needs of the novel and those of the short story." As one might expect, both the novels and the stories explore similar themes, and Busch has stated that he loves both forms. Of particular interest, however, is the way some of his short stories have led him to novels. In an interview published in *Five Points* (Spring/Summer1999) Busch stated:

> Often when I have written a short story it stays under my saddle and irritates me, and I come back to the characters that I know I want to continue in a different form, which is the novel. I've done that with *Manual Labor,* I've done it with the novel *Harry and Catherine,* which grew out of two early stories–one called "The Trouble With Being Food," which is in *Domestic Particulars;* the other is called "The News," which is in *Too Late American Boyhood Blues.* And those characters of Harry and Catherine were then picked up in the novel. I just kept being fascinated by them. It happens often enough with me to notice it.

Busch's novel *Girls* (1997) also grew out of a short story, "Ralph the Duck," which appeared in *Absent Friends* and again in *The Children in the Woods.*

Busch's first collection of short fiction, *Breathing Trouble,* revealed an artist already confident and skilled in the short-story form and already working with the themes that he continued to develop in his later works. "Bring Your Friends to the Zoo," one of the stories in this first collection, experiments with a second-person narration which, in the guise of giving directions to a visitor to the London Zoo, serves to depict the sadness of a relationship that is ending. The story guides the visitor and his estranged lover through the zoo, ending with an exhibit called the "Moonlight World": "The tiny animal eyes are open, of course, as you shuffle, jangling, for the eyes have grown used to the dark. This nighttime is their day. . . . Come again and bring your friends to the Zoo. Beware pickpockets. Flee. Climb the stairs slowly and try to find her waiting for you at the top. When the visitors leave it is raw golden daylight. Come up blinking, blind."

"Is Anyone Left This Time of Year?," also from *Breathing Trouble,* is about a divorced man returning, reluctantly, to a hotel in Ireland that he used to visit with his wife; all the others are closed at "this time of year." The owners, a mother and daughter, remember him and are curious at his solitary return–the daughter, in fact, expresses a new interest in him. The story makes use of the Irish countryside and the bittersweet, shabby hotel to convey a man's sadness and loneliness.

Busch has referred to *Domestic Particulars* as a novel, and critics have treated it as such, although the author has also called it a collection of short stories. In a 1981 interview with Michael Cunningham, Busch stated that "*Domestic Particulars,* in general, is a series of short stories, all about the same family, arranged chronologically. . . . I thought of the book in sculptural terms." In 1987 he told Donald J. Greiner: "I used to think of it as a seamless chronicle. I thought then that it would be more honest to call it a book of stories. They are finally neither. They are episodes in the life of a family." Busch's remarks do show an imposition of a larger structure–yet, the continuing presence of the short-story form is clear, and any serious reader of Busch's short-story canon will want to read *Domestic Particulars* as a unified collection. Indeed, one of the stories in this volume, "The Trouble with Being Food," was included in *The Best American Short Stories 1977.* This story depicts an overweight man's love for a divorced woman, the mother of two children; the tenderness of the relationship is conveyed richly and yet with restraint. In one of the protagonist's meditations, Busch also introduces the theme of labor and craftsmanship that enriches much of his work: "I think of men in the crotches of all the trees on the town's main street, repairing shoes, restringing guitars, mitering wood, filing down ignition points. All of them are loved by fine women, everyone is smiling, and chamber music makes the shape of a room above the road and fills it."

"Widow Water," a story in Busch's third collection, *Hardwater Country,* is emblematic of many of Busch's fictional concerns. Told in the first person by a middle-aged plumber, the story takes the reader along on jobs for two needy customers–an elderly widow and a young college-professor father whose sump pump is not working. The plumber takes pride in his craftsmanship, which is described to the reader in detail, while he worries about the fragility of the elderly woman and about the poor fathering skills of the young professor, who is diffident toward the plumber but harsh with his little boy in a way that appalls the plumber. When the bright and earnest child discovers that a mouse is what has been clogging the sump pump, his father slaps him for touching it. Though the plumber is saddened by this action and clearly judges the father, he says nothing; but at the end of the story, as he leaves the house with its sump pump restored to use, he offers a tiny nugget of fellowship to the little boy: "What shall we do with your Daddy?"

In the final paragraph, the plumber relates, "I thought to get home to Bella and say how sorry I was for the sorrow I'd made and couldn't take back," then flings the dead mouse into a field: "It rose and sank from the air and was gone. I had primed the earth. It didn't need the prime." An interesting emotional complexity is conveyed: despite present and remembered sadnesses, despite the burden of his own regrets and his consciousness of other people's pain, the plumber finds himself fortunate in his life, skilled at his job and taking a craftsman's pleasure and comfort in it. He is grateful to have a wife to go home to, compassionate toward the old and the young–and also regretting past errors of his own, of which the young father's harshness and foolish-

Busch leading a fiction seminar at the Iowa Writers' Workshop, May 1977; Jayne Anne Phillips is on his left (photograph by Dennis Mathis).

ness seem to remind him. Thus, this story includes several of the elements that continue to appear in Busch's fiction: the concern for children and the ways in which adults fail children; the love of labor and craftsmanship; an unsentimental yet loving exploration of the intricacies of conscience, regret, and consciousness; and the almost mythic presence of the rural landscape.

When asked in an interview published in *Poets & Writers Magazine* (1999) about the depictions of labor in his work, Busch commented:

> I really believe in it. I believe in myself as a worker when I write. . . . my grandfather was a worker, he was a carpenter. My other grandfather was a baker. And I have great respect for work and how it's done by work people, with skills and craft and sweat. I find that I cannot write a story or a novel unless I know what job my character has. . . . When I know their job I've got the character, because that's where they meet the world. . . . I don't know how to do *anything*. I could barely tie my children's shoes when they were little. So I'm full of reverence for people who know stuff. I'm a writer because I don't know anything.

Busch also spoke of the home-renovation details in his novel *Manual Labor* (1974), stating that he took that title "from something Reynolds Price said many years ago, about how writing was the hardest form of manual labor he knows. That novel was not about writing but it was about work and working, and it was meant as a salute to him and to the notion of writing."

Busch has become known and admired for his descriptions of the upstate New York landscape, both cultural and natural. Particular awareness of this dimension of Busch's work seemed to emerge after the publication of his novel *Girls,* in which the rural New York countryside figures powerfully. This same characteristic is also apparent in many of his short stories. For instance, one of the stories in *Breathing Trouble* is about an upstate New York town dump. In *Hardwater Country,* "What You Might as Well Call Love" and "Company" are both concerned with the landscape and its effects on the characters. In response to an interview question on the influence of his childhood experience of nature outings, Busch remarked,

> I rebelled against what I thought of as a compulsion into the appreciation and the study of nature. My mother was a kid from the slums on the lower East Side, and her yen was to get up and out and into the midst of what was beautiful. . . . My brother and I were more urban in our aims, we wanted to play stick ball on the streets–you know, kid stuff–and felt that we were being dragged out into the woods. There it is, the woods again. And I exaggerated how much I have resisted. . . . I was hardly victimized all that much.

He believes that his wife's influence has played the greatest part in his awareness of landscape in his writing: "It really is, I think, through Judy's appreciation of the rhythms of the seasons, and her love of gardening and putting her fingers into the earth, her love of the earth itself, that I became educated to the natural world."

Beyond the biographical influences on his sense of place, Busch's awareness of landscape has strong mythic and literary connections. "I think the conjunction of the elements," he said in the *Five Points* interview, "was my appreciation of the mythic and the sense that in writing one is writing this mythic moment. I saw my characters on a stark landscape encountering their fate in very literary terms." Busch added that he later learned to render those same "important mythic interior moments" in urban settings as well as rural. But, he said:

> I started out very literally in what I thought of as the site of myth itself, which was the dark forest, the darkling plain, the side of a mountain–the place where pretense is stripped away, where to paraphrase Robert Penn Warren, you are alone with It, and it is Its move. That's where I started. Then I began to respond to the landscape in a less programmatic way, I think, and also began to enjoy owning some of it, and moving on aspects of it in my own terms. . . . Finally, you must write about people in their context. And you don't just name the context; you make the context happen, so that the reader feels the context in sensual terms.

Another story from *Hardwater Country,* "The Lesson of the Hôtel Lotti," demonstrates two additional characteristics of Busch's writing: his ability to write sympathetically and convincingly in female as well as male voices and his interest in manipulating texts. In "The Lesson of the Hôtel Lotti" a young woman finds a piece of notepaper in a book that belonged to her mother's lover. She eagerly searches it for a deeper message: "I laughed, because only in stories and in the most arcane probate cases will a letter from the dead fall from among the pages of a book. But I was sure that I had found such a letter, and I did not laugh anymore." But the "text" is in fact blank, a piece of hotel stationery with only the name of the Hôtel Lotti inscribed on it and "No message I could read, no reminder, no clue." However, the blank paper ultimately yields the message she needs, for it leads her to imagine, sympathetically and intensely, her mother's lover, who was more father to her than the man whose name she bears. The theme of language, written or spoken, of texts that speak from blank or wrinkled pages or from old fairy tales, recurs throughout Busch's work.

Busch's fourth collection of short fiction is *Too Late American Boyhood Blues,* about which the reviewer for the *Washington Post* (11 November 1984) noted, "Busch knows just what he is about. Without the slightest sense of constriction, the stories have both beautiful form and that pace, whether disguised or overt, so vital to the short story." She observed that Busch's themes of emotional scars and painful relationships might make for depressing reading matter, but "The fact is that this is simply not so. Busch's great gift is that he can make the reader care, not just about what happens to these people, but about the people themselves."

"The Settlement of Mars," one of the stories in *Too Late American Boyhood Blues,* reveals a progression in Busch's mastery of the form and in his subtle explorations of emotional situations. The narrator remembers the sense of adventure and the sensory details of a vacation visiting old family friends with his father while his mother had gone to a "conference about birds" where "she would stare through heavy binoculars at what was distant and nameable." The boy, nine years old, is by contrast struggling to "see" and to understand what is happening in his life. He is unable to see a hawk in the sky from his vantage point on the grass next to Paula, the fourteen-year-old daughter of the family they are visiting. "I guess I saw enough birds in my life," he tells her, and she replies "That's right, isn't it? Your mother's a bird-watcher. In Colorado, too. I guess there's trouble *there.*" The boy, however, is as unwilling or unable to see what she attempts to spell out about estrangement between his parents as he is to see the bird of prey that has just circled above them.

The story is more complex than this moment, however, and like many of Busch's stories, it includes significant hidden texts. The boy, intrigued as he is by the mysteries of the fourteen-year-old Paula, reads with fascination the comic books and science fiction she offers him from her secret closet library: "And next day . . . I sat in the closet doorway, reading of Martian prisons, and heroes who hacked and slew, unaware that I had neither sniffed nor stared at her, and worried only that I might not finish the book and start another before my father and Bill returned." While other actions go on in the household, he continues reading and "attended to rescues performed by the Warlord of Mars." The story moves finally to a scene in which the narrator, already aware of some betrayal by his absent and often angry mother, sees his father's joyfulness in the shared time with old friends. He is overcome by panic, a sudden overwhelming fear that he might go blind, which leads to his father's gentle reassurance that he only needs glasses, as his mother does.

"Greetings from a Far-Flung Place," a story in Busch's next short fiction collection, *Absent Friends,* takes up again Busch's interest in the interrelatedness of texts. In the first few paragraphs, Busch speaks of "voice" and of a written-and-rewritten letter, with attention to the paper it is written on and the way it is written: "There were three sheets of motel stationery. She had filled one side of one sheet, in her smallest and neatest hand, with beginnings aimed at helping her to locate a voice in which to address her sister." The story is about the struggle to communicate across distance in family relationships.

"In Foreign Tongues," also published in *Absent Friends,* is another work in which Busch manipulates various "texts." The story is about both spoken and scripted language and the interplay between them; the setting is an after-session restaurant gathering of four members of a therapy group. The most frequently referred-to text in the story is one character's "Fat Book," in which he writes down everything he eats as part of an unsuccessful weight-loss plan. In another embedded text, the narrator, who is a script writer, detects echoes of his written dialogue in an exchange reported by another member of the group. Another character has a son who ran away to the navy and works in a submarine, but who remains silent whenever he returns: "He comes home, after listening for all those weeks to blips and bloops, not talking to anyone, just listening. He hears whales and scampi, for all we know, and masses of cold water. Am I right? Cold water gives an echo? And he *hears* all this." The embedded story-within-the-story, of the silent son who listens to sonar and to echoes from the undersea world, enriches and deepens "In Foreign Tongues" as Busch simultaneously explores human beings' difficulties in communication and plays with texts and textuality.

"Folk Tales" in *The Children in the Woods* is another instance in which texts and spoken tales become a crucial part of the story: "Stories hiss and gurgle through the hearts of peasants, I would tell my son if I thought he could bear the news. Most are fragments now, unfastened from the moments of my hearing them." The narrator, Howie, recalls the tales his grandfather told his mother and uncle–tales of pogroms and persecution in Russia and of villagers abandoned to the Cossacks by their rabbi. The story revolves around a visit to the narrator in middle age by his fragile, elderly Uncle Bernie. Howie is reminded that even "Bosco," his uncle's childhood nickname for him, is based on a story: "He'd named me for the chocolate syrup other children, but not I, had been allowed to stir into their milk. . . . It only occurred to me as I spoke with Bernie, that being named for a childhood lament is a comment as bitter as Bosco was said to be sweet."

Bernie complains that Howie has not reached out to him much in adulthood, and Howie attempts to make amends by telling him that he remembers those stories and would like to hear them again. The uncle demurs, complaining about the narrator's neglect of him in recent years: "You wanted stories, you could have called me up, yes?" What Bernie, who feels he is going to die soon, has come to give Howie is not stories, but the key to a safety deposit box, something Howie's mother had asked the uncle to save for him until it is needed. As in a fairy tale, Howie follows the trail to the bank, where the key yields a soft brown paper bag that reminds him of the Jewish neighborhood of his youth. Inside this unlikely container is the "legacy"–a letter from Albert Einstein, answering one Howie as a boy had sent to Einstein, outlining his idea for an atomic bomb. The boy's naive text is presented in its misspelled entirety, followed by Einstein's stern, wise, and compassionate reply. The grown-up Howie, now a divorced, middle-aged counselor, struggles to find meaning for his adult life in this recovered text, but "all I had, at last, was one more story." He considers calling his grown son, perhaps passing the story on to him–but he realizes the son is at present too distant from him. In a brief statement, Howie obliquely conveys one of the genuine and often sorrowful messages of Busch's fiction: "It's what so many of us have come to specialize in: wounded kids."

Dust jacket for Busch's 1994 book, stories that draw their themes from the tale of Hansel and Gretel

"Folk Tales" has an added interest for Busch's readers because the author has provided an autobiographical connection: the boyish letter to Einstein and the scientist's reply are exact replicas of a young Busch's own "brief correspondence" with Einstein. He discusses these letters, the composition of the story, and why for him the story failed, in a piece called "A Relative Lie," an essay particularly revealing of the roots and branches of the creative process, published in *A Dangerous Profession: A Book About the Writing Life* (1998). In discussing the gap between the finished story and what he had intended to write, Busch expresses as a goal "the amalgam of lived or observed or otherwise-historical events and facts that prod the writer, providing him with a need to find narrative and metaphors by which the essence of that amalgam feels (to the writer) honestly served and the reader intelligently entertained."

What Busch had set out to write, he explains, is a story that reveals and explores his mother's myth-making–how the letter from Einstein she always said he, as a child, had crumpled and thrown on the floor, and that she had rescued by carefully ironing, is revealed never to have been crumpled at all. Busch concludes this generous and perceptive essay:

> So I have been–I am–a character in a lie. I live in some body's fiction, you might want to say. And I am trying to tell you, and trying to tell myself, the truth, or some of it, about how a man examines a page of the text that his life, in one of its versions, seems to have become. He seizes it, he pulls it close, he breathes his breath upon it, and he reads it again and again. It has been, surely, violated. It also seems to be whole. He thinks it is both at once.

The Children in the Woods, though it is made up of fifteen stories from earlier collections and eight previously uncollected stories, is remarkable in its faithfulness to the Hansel and Gretel theme reflected in its title, and it is most useful to discuss this book in terms of what Busch has called "maybe the basic myth." As far back as 1986, Charles Baxter, himself a formidable writer of short fiction, noted in *The New York Times Book Review* (1 June 1986) that "The American boy–insufferable, insightful, ubiquitous, pathetic–has been much in Mr. Busch's mind lately, and lost, stolen or strayed children have appeared with increasing frequency in his recent work." Responding to a question in the *Five Points* interview, Busch explained the importance of the Hansel and Gretel theme:

> As one of my characters in "My Father, Cont.," says, [Hansel and Gretel is] the story in which appetite comes first. And it's the parents' appetite. The father says, "Oh but I shall regret the poor children"–when his wife has said "Let's take them into the forest and lose them so that they get eaten by creatures in the forest, and we'll have enough to eat here." It's all about appetite. . . . It seems to me just a remarkable, exciting, salient and in some ways true myth–more than myth–paradigm if you want.

Busch explained that he had especially intended several of the stories in *The Children in the Woods* to fit that motif: "One is 'The Wicked Stepmother,' one is the first part of 'Berceuse' . . . there were a number of new ones. . . . 'Bread' comes first in the book. I was asked to nominate a story of mine to include in the *Norton Anthology of Short Fiction,* and I picked 'Bread' . . . a statement of sorts of the motif I think is so important." Busch added that during the time he was putting together *The Children in the Woods,* he was also teaching *Bleak House* (1852–1853) in his Charles Dickens seminar: "I had read *Bleak House* hard half a dozen times, and for the first time I realized that Dickens called them the Children in the Wood–not woods–but that he meant the same thing. . . . That solidified for me that I would have to call the book that."

"Bread," the lead story in the collection and one that had not appeared in any of his previous books, states the fairy tale motif as Busch intended. The parallels are strong and clear, yet made complex by differences: the children are now adults; the parents, no longer worried about their appetites, are dead; the mother has left sustenance in the freezer, in the form of a lump of bread dough. The protagonists are an adult brother and sister, closing up their parents' house after the parents have died in an accident. The entire story is a metaphorical following of bread crumbs through the woods, as brother and sister attempt to find their way back "home" to an understanding of themselves, their family, their losses, and their love. The bread crumbs are represented in an actual loaf of bread that the brother, who is the narrator, attempts to bake from the dough that his mother left in the freezer. Although the bread is inadvertently burned (in the oven that the witch would have put Hansel in), in the end the brother leads his sister to the safety of the simple love for the two of them–treasured snapshots, bits of their childhood preserved–that he found in the contents of his father's drawer, where he had feared finding some dark secret: "So we climbed toward their room. In the story, you remember, in the dark forest, when something has inevitably eaten all the crumbs, he leads her home by the hand."

This story seems to redeem the fairy tale from the myth of the harsh mother, for this mother, although deceased, has left living yeast in the bread dough in the freezer, which the son wishes to honor, as he wishes to recapture her life, through the baking of the bread. Both mother and father have left hidden gifts for the children in this household, this family.

Another story in *The Children in the Woods,* "One More Wave of Fear," explores a childhood experience of parentally imposed "nature appreciation." Though the story is clearly fiction, it is also closely related to experiences Busch has recalled from his own childhood. The story begins: "I did not grow up despising nature on Argyle Road, at the far southern edge of Prospect Park, in Brooklyn in the 1950s. But I did come to hate the upper-case initial with which my parents said the word. . . . My parents also called it Natural History, or The Out of Doors." Complaining at first of "wearying walks with the Audubon Society or the Brooklyn Bird Club," the narrator pursues this simple friction into areas of considerable complexity. While the family is pursuing Nature, the father is attempting to elude the House Un-American Activities Committee during the McCarthy era. The narrator says of his father, "He forgave America, I forgave my mother, and she forgave the need to have to make me understand her. And we walked the hundreds of acres of Prospect Park."

The parents are shown arguing over a birdcall on one of these outings, but in the end, their concept of "Nature" is undone not only by their own bickering but by squirrels in their attic; and the boy discovers a sort of alliance with the wild creatures under his own roof: "I did cheer them on, though silently." The story concludes on a note that is both disturbing and funny, as the mother bravely and fearfully releases the captured squirrels into "Nature." In another of Busch's many twists on the Hansel and Gretel theme, the mother in this story seems to move from the "stepmother" role to that of the entrapping witch and finally to herself becoming a lost child in the woods as she watches the active squirrels: "She diminished, staring up at them, like the pretty girl in the horror film who at last understands what has come for her."

"Berceuse," the final story in *The Children in the Woods,* further defines the Hansel and Gretel theme while also taking on even more complex issues. The epigraph to the story is the dictionary definition of the title: "Berceuse: n.f. Woman who rocks an infant; rocking chair; cradle that rocks; lullaby." The story is divided into two distinct parts, separated by many years. In the first section the narrator is Kim, the young Lebanese-English wife of Sonny, a Jewish writer. As the story opens, she is recovering from a miscarriage and diverting herself by reading narratives of girls captured by Indians. When the couple is visited by the husband's bitter cousin Miriam, who is in love with him and also obsessed with the Holocaust, Kim seems fearful of being a child in the woods, a captive in this culture that seems to regard her as an enemy. The Hansel and Gretel theme is brought in through Miriam's insistence that the witch's oven in the fairy tale must now be associated with the ovens in Nazi death camps. When Kim and Sonny are alone late at night, they argue about Miriam, her obsession with the Holocaust, and her hostility to Kim for being Sonny's wife and not being Jewish. Sonny says, "She's Miriam, Kim. That's all. Miriam. She takes these things seriously." His wife responds, "Everyone in any area code you can pick takes these things seriously. She takes them *personally.*" In this dialogue, as in the entire story, Busch explores a painful and problematic dimension of the Jewish experience. The story carries a critique of obsessions like Miriam's but conveys also the pain that is embedded in that critique and in the knowledge of persecution.

Nonetheless, the story forces Sonny to a moment of choice between his cousin and his wife when Miriam's general cultural attack on Kim becomes cruelly personal as well, actually suggesting that her baby's death was a punishment for the deaths of Jewish babies. In the middle of Miriam's attack on Kim, Sonny enters the room and asks his cousin to leave their house. As this first section of "Berceuse" ends, Kim and Sonny seem more like brother and sister than husband and wife, and the vanquished Miriam seems to have combined both witch and wicked stepmother roles.

The second part of the story takes place more than twenty years later, with Kim still the narrator, now the personal assistant of a film producer and long-divorced from Sonny. Learning that Sonny has died, she attends his funeral, where she discovers that his second wife is African American. The epiphanic scene of the story takes place when Kim receives a visit from Sonny's grown son from that later marriage. Bringing with him an old, unhappy letter she had written to his father, he wants her to give him more information about what his father was like in his youth. A warm relationship develops between them. Kim, who never had a child of her own and who could not stay married to Sonny, cherishes the opportunity to give something to his son. She is a stepmother of sorts, but one who helps a lost Hansel find his way out of the woods (and is led from the woods herself by the same act). As she kisses his son goodbye, she feels she is kissing Sonny goodbye as well, and her last words to the eighteen-year-old are a salute to his mother: "Sweetheart, tell your mother–I don't know. Tell her I saluted her. Go home." In the final two paragraphs, she burns the old letter to Sonny, and the ashes of the letter become reminiscent of the ashes and the ovens that Miriam lamented in the first half of the story.

This story brings together issues of cultural and racial prejudice, the dehumanizing effects of both war

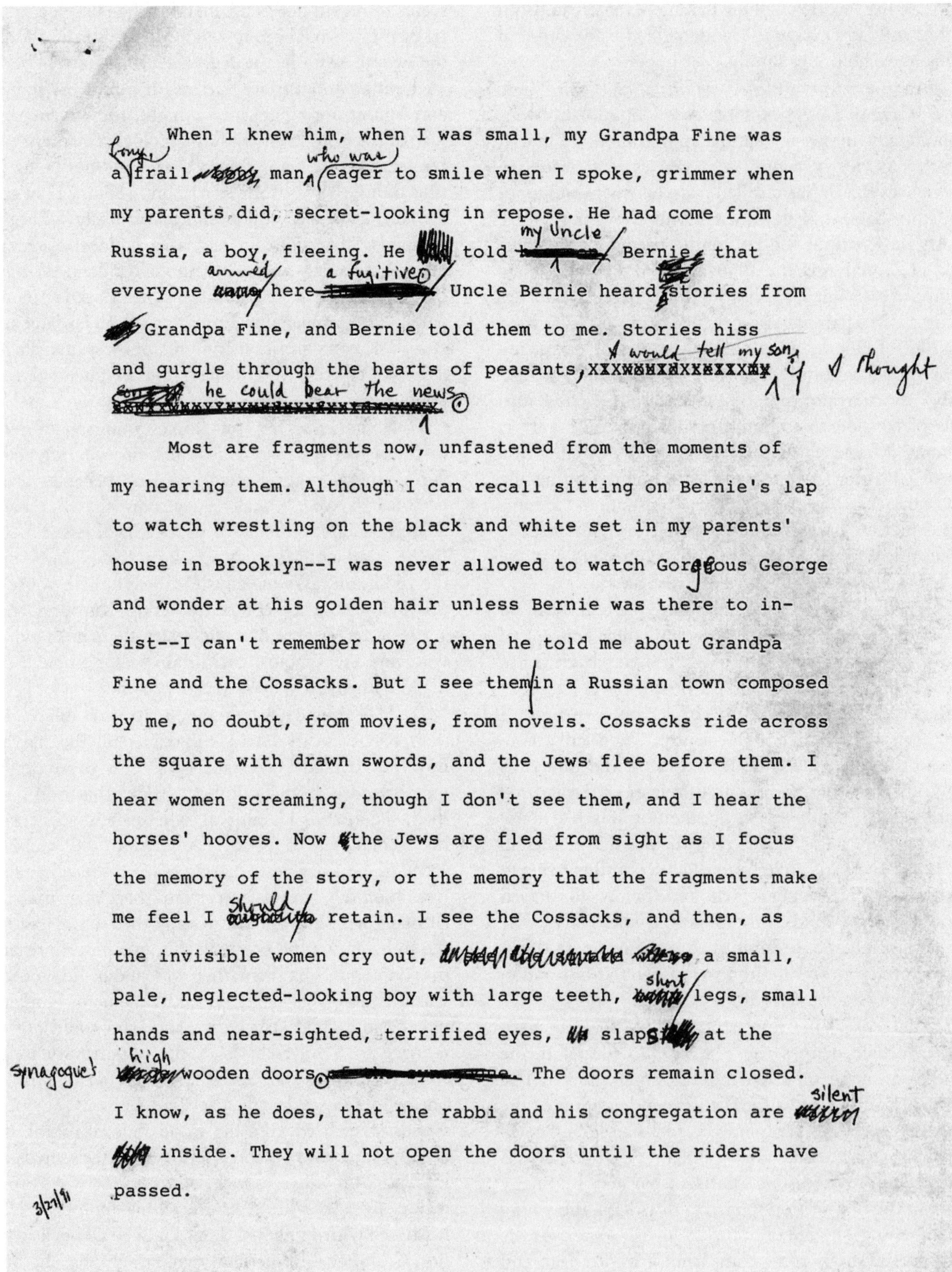
When I knew him, when I was small, my Grandpa Fine was a long, frail man who was eager to smile when I spoke, grimmer when my parents did, secret-looking in repose. He had come from Russia, a boy, fleeing. He told my Uncle Bernie that everyone arrived here a fugitive. Uncle Bernie heard stories from Grandpa Fine, and Bernie told them to me. Stories hiss and gurgle through the hearts of peasants, I would tell my son, if I thought he could bear the news.

Most are fragments now, unfastened from the moments of my hearing them. Although I can recall sitting on Bernie's lap to watch wrestling on the black and white set in my parents' house in Brooklyn--I was never allowed to watch Gorgeous George and wonder at his golden hair unless Bernie was there to insist--I can't remember how or when he told me about Grandpa Fine and the Cossacks. But I see them in a Russian town composed by me, no doubt, from movies, from novels. Cossacks ride across the square with drawn swords, and the Jews flee before them. I hear women screaming, though I don't see them, and I hear the horses' hooves. Now the Jews are fled from sight as I focus the memory of the story, or the memory that the fragments make me feel I should retain. I see the Cossacks, and then, as the invisible women cry out, a small, pale, neglected-looking boy with large teeth, short legs, small hands and near-sighted, terrified eyes, slaps at the high wooden doors synagogue's. The doors remain closed. I know, as he does, that the rabbi and his congregation are silent inside. They will not open the doors until the riders have passed.

3/27/91

First page of the third draft for "Folk Tales," a story collected in Children in the Woods *(Collection of Frederick Busch)* and victimhood, and the ways these great issues are interwoven with personal and familial loss, death, love, and renewal. It seems fitting that this book, inspired by the fairy tale of the children in the woods, should, in its concluding story, explore these major themes with convincing archetypal resonance: Gretel, witch, stepmother, and mother blend in Kim's story; Sonny is both Hansel and father; his son, yet another Hansel. Both "Berceuse" and *The Children in the Woods* conclude with transformation.

For a fuller discussion of the "Hansel and Gretel" motif and of the power of fairy tales in literature, Busch's essay "The Children in the Woods" in *A Dangerous Profession* is extremely valuable. Not only does he discuss the presence of the motif in the stories in *The Children in the Woods,* but he also describes the importance of fairy tales in his own childhood and laments the fact that his students are no longer exposed to these tales. Busch concludes his essay about the dark woods by redefining them as a metaphor for writing itself:

> Serious writing is about the trail of lifesaving bread crumbs that are eaten by the forest birds. It is about being disposable. It is about what you say to yourself even if you have defeated the terrible darkness of night-time in the forest, or the witch and her oven, or the dangerous, unmapped distance that separates you from home. It is about living with a truth you've discerned but don't want to know. It is about hunger, how hunger comes first.

In a review of *The Children in The Woods* for *Studies in Short Fiction* (Spring 1995), one critic summed up his evaluation of Busch's work in this way:

> Since his first novel, *I Wanted a Year Without Fall* (1971), Frederick Busch has been considered a master craftsman of prose; and the stories here are filled with scenes that can only be called gorgeous. . . . In this age when more attention is often paid to what authors wear than the words they write, "master craftsman" is the highest possible praise; and with these new and selected stories, Frederick Busch continues to demonstrate why he deserves this title.

Busch is indeed a master craftsman, both of the sentence and of the story or novel as a whole. His love of the craft of writing is evident in *A Dangerous Profession* and in a collection he edited, *Letters to a Fiction Writer* (1999), as well as in the Living Writers program of readings and lectures that he has organized at Colgate University for more than fifteen years. Busch is also a major literary artist. The strength of his moral vision engenders the spiritual dimension of his work–though Busch himself claims no religious faith or allegiance. Although he is identified as a Jewish writer and explores Jewish themes in his work, his is a mainly cultural Jewishness. When asked in the *Five Points* interview "What's the closest thing to a church or a temple for you?," he replied, "I have none. I have none. That's one of the concerns of *Girls.* Jack keeps asking about prayer. He can't pray. And I've always thought that it would be lovely to be able to pray and to believe, and I cannot and don't. . . . The closest thing I get to religion is my work." His own sense of the religious, however, he defined in a 1987 interview for *Literature and Belief* in terms of "a reaching out in an attempt to embrace or ward off the cosmos, to define the cosmos: What's the nature of the world? What's the nature of reality? What's the nature of me in it? How then do I behave in it? Toward it? Toward myself? Towards my fellow beings? That to me is religious."

Asked in the *Poets & Writers* interview about the treatment of ethical, social, and political realities in his work, Busch commented:

> I think I feel responsibilities, ethical and social responsibilities, as everybody does–and I'm lucky enough to have a way of wedging it into a tiny division of the public consciousness, sometimes, in a story or a novel. I think in my novels I always try, and sometimes in my stories, to have simultaneously a public context and a domestic context going on, the one reflecting the other, in the hope that the domestic matters will reach out and impinge on public matters, and the public matters will reach down and touch domestic matters.

One of the ways in which Busch's art rises above much of the literature and entertainment of his time is the persistent struggle of his characters to find solutions other than death. Though Busch often explores the tragic dimensions of life, death is never the obvious or trite solution in his work that it is in some fiction. His characters, as Greiner puts it, "resist the lure of death that he defines as an unfortunate commonplace in modern literature." Busch commented on this attitude in a personal letter in 1998:

> As to not (usually) killing off my characters: I scold my students for irresponsibility when they conveniently murder the people in their stories. The great chore of living, I try to tell them, is that we're stuck with and in it, and we have to find a way to do it *without* the living death of so many sorrowful people. We're stuck in it not only because, apparently, we want it; we have to be in it for the sake of the people we're reluctant to abandon–lovers, children, even our dogs and cats; living is, maybe, our obligation to those who offer us their love; maybe it's our sentence.

This comment conveys some of the courageous and humane philosophy that characterizes his fiction.

Early in Busch's career a reviewer of *Domestic Particulars* for *The Nation* (6 November 1976) referred to him as "one of our finest short story writers," saying also that "of novelists under 40 in this country, he is one of the very few active practitioners who can combine an astonishing use of language with a really first-rate memory; he is brilliant, imaginative, and more often than not, just." And in 1978 John Romano ended his *New York Arts Journal* essay on Busch with the remark that "his importance, which is already considerable . . . can be expected to grow. He is one of a small party who are resuscitating an ancient use of words, to connect us to our feeling, to refresh our vulnerabilities, to waken in the mind the prospect of an edifying pain." Certainly in the years since those remarks were made, Busch's reputation has continued to grow. Surprisingly few serious critical studies have been devoted to his work, however; Greiner's 1988 study of Busch's novels is the only book of criticism on Busch's fiction. Yet, reviews of each newly published work continue to express a nearly universal appreciation of his place in American letters.

Interviews:

Moira Crone, "Frederick Busch," *City Paper Literary Supplement,* 28 March 1980, p. 5;

Michael Cunningham, "An Interview with Frederick Busch," *Iowa Journal of Literary Studies,* 3 (1981): 67–74;

Bruce W. Jorgensen, "'A Grammar of Events': A Conversation with Frederick Busch," *Literature and Belief,* 7 (1987): 26–40;

Charlotte Zoë Walker, "Practitioner of a Dangerous Profession: A Conversation with Frederick Busch," *Poets & Writers Magazine,* 27 (May/June 1999): 33–37;

Walker, "Frederick Busch: An Interview by Charlotte Zoë Walker," *Five Points,* 3 (Spring/Summer 1999): 41–78.

References:

Sven Birkerts, *American Energies: Essays on Fiction* (New York: Morrow, 1992), pp. 304–308;

Maria S. Bonn, "New Battles: Cultural Signification in Contemporary American Narrative: Papers from an Interdisciplinary Conference on Reconciliation," in *The United States and Viet Nam from War to Peace,* edited by Richard M. Slabey (Jefferson, N.C.: McFarland, 1996), pp. 208–213;

Donald J. Greiner, "The Absent Friends of Frederick Busch," *Gettysburg Review,* 3 (Autumn 1990): 746–754;

Greiner, *Domestic Particulars: The Novels of Frederick Busch* (Columbia: University of South Carolina Press, 1988);

John Romano, "Frederick Busch: Mimesis and Intensity," *New York Arts Journal* (February–March 1978): 23–24.

Papers:

A collection of Frederick Busch's papers and manuscripts through 1990 is housed in the Special Collections Department of the Ohio State University Library.

Hortense Calisher

(20 December 1911 –)

Kathleen Snodgrass

See also the Calisher entry in *DLB 2: American Novelists Since World War II: First Series.*

BOOKS: *In the Absence of Angels: Stories* (Boston: Little, Brown, 1951; London: Heinemann, 1953);

False Entry (Boston: Little, Brown, 1961; London: Secker & Warburg, 1962);

Tale for the Mirror: A Novella and Other Stories (Boston: Little, Brown, 1962; London: Secker & Warburg, 1963);

Textures of Life (Boston: Little, Brown, 1963; London: Secker & Warburg, 1963);

Extreme Magic: A Novella and Other Stories (Boston: Little, Brown, 1964; London: Secker & Warburg, 1964);

Journal from Ellipsia (Boston: Little, Brown, 1965; London: Secker & Warburg, 1966);

The Railway Police and The Last Trolley Ride (Boston: Little, Brown, 1966);

The New Yorkers (Boston: Little, Brown, 1969; London: Cape, 1970);

Queenie (New York: Arbor House, 1971; London: W. H. Allen, 1973);

Standard Dreaming (New York: Arbor House, 1972);

Herself (New York: Arbor House, 1972);

Eagle Eye (New York: Arbor House, 1973);

The Collected Stories of Hortense Calisher (New York: Arbor House, 1975);

On Keeping Women (New York: Arbor House, 1977);

Mysteries of Motion (Garden City, N.Y.: Doubleday, 1983);

Saratoga, Hot (Garden City, N.Y.: Doubleday, 1985);

The Bobby-Soxer (Garden City, N.Y.: Doubleday, 1986);

Age (New York: Weidenfeld & Nicolson, 1987);

Kissing Cousins: A Memory (New York: Weidenfeld & Nicolson, 1988);

The Small Bang, as Jack Fenno (New York: Random House, 1992);

In the Palace of the Movie King (New York: Random House, 1993);

In the Slammer with Carol Smith (New York & London: Marion Boyars, 1996);

The Novellas of Hortense Calisher (New York: Modern Library, 1997).

Hortense Calisher (photograph © Jerry Bauer; from the dust jacket for In the Palace of the Movie King, *1993)*

OTHER: *Best American Short Stories, 1981,* edited by Calisher and Shannon Ravenel (Boston: Houghton Mifflin, 1981);

"1988–1997: Decade of Reunion," in *A Century of Arts & Letters: The History of the National Institutue of Arts & Letters and the American Academy of Arts & Letters as Told, Decade by Decade, by Eleven Members* (New York: Columbia University Press, 1998), pp. 264–291.

SELECTED PERIODICAL PUBLICATIONS–UNCOLLECTED: "Enclosures: Barbara Pym," *New Criterion,* 1 (September 1982): 53–56;

"William Gerhardie: A Resurrection," *New Criterion,* 1 (November 1982): 46–54;

"A Family's Effects: The Eternal Room That Is Always Us," *New York Times,* 1 March 1984, p. 19;

"The Reticence of the American Writer," *New York Times Book Review,* 20 May 1984, pp. 1, 34–35;

"Early Lessons," *New York Times Magazine,* part 2, 28 April 1985, pp. 34, 36, 38;

"The Pevershams' Willie," *Southwest Review,* 72 (Summer 1987): 298–335;

"In Praise of Wang Meng," *Nation,* 249 (30 October 1989): 500–502;

"Nature of the Madhouse," *Story,* 38 (Spring 1990): 106–121;

"The Iron Butterflies," *Southwest Review,* 77 (Winter 1992): 48–56;

"Blind Eye, Wrong Foot," *American Short Fiction,* no. 10 (Summer 1995).

In a career of nearly six decades, novelist and short-story writer Hortense Calisher has produced an impressive body of work–six books of stories and novellas, fourteen novels, and two memoirs–and has received many awards and honors, including a National Endowment for the Arts Lifetime Achievement Award in 1989. Her frequently anthologized stories have earned her several O. Henry Awards and have appeared in several volumes of *Best American Short Stories.* She has not, however, enjoyed the popular acclaim that one might expect to attend such original and well-crafted work. Since the publication of her first novel in 1961, ten years after her first book of stories, Calisher has frequently been called a "writer's writer"; her distinctive style–often labeled "Jamesian," "convoluted," "rococo," and even, by Anthony Burgess, "too Calisherianly articulate" (*The New York Times Book Review,* 7 November 1965)–has remained a critical focal point. For the most part more conventional and stylistically more accessible than her novels, her short stories have also earned her more praise than her full-length fiction.

Calisher was born in New York City on 20 December 1911 to Joseph and Hedwig Lichtstern Calisher. Her father was born in Richmond, Virginia, where his father, Henry Jacob Calisher, was an elder of the synagogue in 1832. Joseph Calisher moved to New York City as a young man and became a manufacturer of fine soaps and perfumes. He met his future wife, a German émigré twenty-two years his junior, at the Saratoga races. As Calisher has commented, the mix of generations, backgrounds, and powerful personalities in her household were "bound to produce someone interested in character, society and time." She has written a dozen autobiographical stories about growing up in that household. Even as they conjure up a bygone era, these stories are never mere period pieces. Eugenie Bolger compares Calisher's achievement to James Joyce's, writing that her stories "are to New York what Joyce's *Dubliners* is to Dublin, the subtlest social observation wrapped in rue" (*New Leader,* 19 January 1976).

In a July 1978 *Mademoiselle* article, which Calisher titled "My Life as a Female Sex Object," she describes not only the sensual atmosphere created by an abundance of nineteenth-century "genteel porn," but also and more important, the emotional and intellectual nurturing she and her younger brother received. (The magazine substituted a tamer, more saccharine title: "The Pride and Joy of Growing Up a Woman.") In his mid fifties when his children were born, Joseph Calisher "made it plain. . . . that we children, as latecomers and intensely craved ones, are glamorously special. . . ." Not only that, she learned early that "women were assumed to have the same brainpower as men." In a book-filled apartment Calisher read voraciously, from Giovanni Boccaccio to the great eighteenth- and nineteenth-century English and French novelists, to the Bible, the book that Calisher credits as the greatest influence on her own work.

Growing up in New York City, Calisher learned not "art," but "an attitude, that art is necessary. . . . that the arts are at the same time holy and plebeian. . . . [and] that art interest . . . is ordinary gospel here" (*The New York Times Magazine,* 28 April 1985). In 1932, in the depths of the Great Depression, she earned an A.B. from Barnard College, with a major in English and minor in philosophy. For a time she worked as an investigator for the Department of Public Welfare. As she told interviewer Roy Newquist, the job exposed her to a world "you would never have seen from the confines of a proper home and the proper schools." On 27 September 1935 Calisher married Heaton Bennet Heffelfinger, a young engineer, by whom she subsequently had two children. As she wrote in her 1972 autobiography, *Herself,* she spent the next decade living in a series of small towns, wanting to write but feeling "paralyzed, not only by the house-and-child life–which is a total-flesh-draining, a catatonia of rest for the beaverish brain, that in a way is craved–but by this immersion in a society where I feel . . . ultimately lunatic-wrong."

Calisher's writing career began quietly: while walking her son to school she began mentally composing her first story, "A Box of Ginger." By the time this story appeared in the 16 October 1948 issue of *The New Yorker,* the magazine had published two other stories by Calisher: "The Middle Drawer" (10 July 1948) and "The Pool of Narcissus" (25 September 1948). Of the thirteen stories in her first collection, *In the Absence of Angels* (1951), seven had appeared in *The New Yorker* within a three-year period, establishing her reputation as a formidable short-story writer.

During the 1950s Calisher and Heffelfinger were divorced. On 27 March 1959 she married Curtis Harnack, a writer who later became president of the Yaddo artists' colony and president and chief executive officer of the School of American Ballet. After receiving two Guggenheim fellowships (1951–1953 and 1953–1954), Calisher was given a Department of State American Specialist's Grant to visit Southeast Asia, where she traveled extensively in 1958, giving readings and lectures. Since then, Calisher has held many visiting professorships and received several honorary doctorates. She has also been active in the world of letters. She was president of American PEN in 1986–1987 and of the American Academy of Arts and Letters in 1987–1990.

"In the Absence of Angels," the title story in Calisher's first collection, is a declaration of intent and orientation. Arrested and awaiting judgment from unidentified totalitarian forces that have taken over the United States, the narrator is clear-eyed about her fate: "They will tell us, finally, that there is no place for people like us, that the middle ground is for angels, not men. But there is a place. For in the absence of angels and arbiters from a world of light, men and women must take their place." Calisher has foresworn creeds and certainties, prescriptions and proscriptions, opting instead for that uneven middle ground where humans struggle to make sense–and, in her case, to make art–from life's muddle. The reader is always aware of a distinctive and questioning mind, a keen sensibility alive to the absurdities and conundrums of the world. Since Calisher writes without a political, cultural, or personal agenda, she resists being pigeonholed as a New York writer, a Jewish writer, or a woman writer. In *Herself* Calisher emphasizes her instinctive tendency to avoid any pat categorizations: "My mind–as far as I can disinter it from the rest of me–seems to have no particular sex. I hold no special brief for 'the family.' I am greedy for experience, but more greedy for some than for others. What pulls me deepest, moves me darkly and lightly, is what I can think of as ordinary experience."

There is nothing ordinary about Calisher's transformation of experience into art. Critics recognized her eloquence and perceptiveness from the outset. In her review of *In the Absence of Angels* for *The New York Times Book Review* (18 November 1951), Gertrude Buckman was one of the first of many reviewers to admire the mixture of mind and heart, of formal brilliance and emotional depth, in Calisher's stories: "She regards the human situation, the relation of one to one, of one to the destroying 'everybody,' with exactitude, compassion and restraint." Other reviewers would echo Shirley Barker's appraisal of Calisher as a "fine storyteller and a perceptive psychologist" (*Library Journal,* 1 November 1951).

Five of the thirteen stories in *In the Absence of Angels* are autobiographical stories about the Elkin family. The center of consciousness is Hester, the elder of the two children. She is caught between her parents: a turn-of-the-century Southern gentleman and his beautiful wife, a perfectionist who lives in a state of permanent exasperation brought on by her husband's easygoing nature and their daughter's awkward and bookish tendencies.

Of the autobiographical stories in Calisher's first book, her first published story, "The Middle Drawer," focuses most intently on the often tumultuous love-hate relationship between mother and daughter. Shortly after her mother's death from cancer, the adult narrator remembers their stormy history–a recurring subject in Calisher's autobiographical stories. As in many of her stories, action and plot are superseded by reflection and character analysis; or, as poet and critic Robert Phillips succinctly puts it, "incident is subordinate to insight" (*Commonweal,* 7 May 1976).

The telling opening sentence–"The drawer was always kept locked"–reverberates throughout all Calisher's autobiographical stories as she unlocks the past, having–like the daughter in "The Middle Drawer"–overcome her initial "reluctance to perform the blasphemy that the living must inevitably perpetuate on the possessions of the dead." In narrative terms "The Middle Drawer" serves as a preamble to the stories that follow. The reader is introduced to the doting, uncritical father but the mother, wounded by a bleak, loveless childhood, looms larger than her spouse. Beautiful, self-possessed, and impossible to please, she has showered her ungainly, ugly duckling of a daughter with casual cruelties. The narrator, a grown woman with a family of her own, has been called home to tend to her dying mother. When her mother asks if she would like to see the mastectomy scar, she has her chance, at last, to deliver "the final barb, the homing shaft, that would maim her mother once and for all, as she felt herself to be maimed." Instead, she responds with exquisite tact and gentleness: "'Why . . . it's a beautiful job, Mother,' she said, distilling the carefully natural tone of her voice. 'Neat as can be. I had no idea. . . . I thought it would be ugly.' . . . she drew her fingertips along the length of the scar in a light, affirmative caress, and they stood eye to eye for an immeasurable second, on equal ground at last." From the perspective of the autobiographical stories that follow, this scene is an especially poignant moment of intimacy and understanding between mother and daughter.

Such moments are hard-won in Calisher's fiction. Many of the nonautobiographical stories in particular examine bleak, urban lives. "Point of Departure," written the same year as "The Middle Drawer," is the first

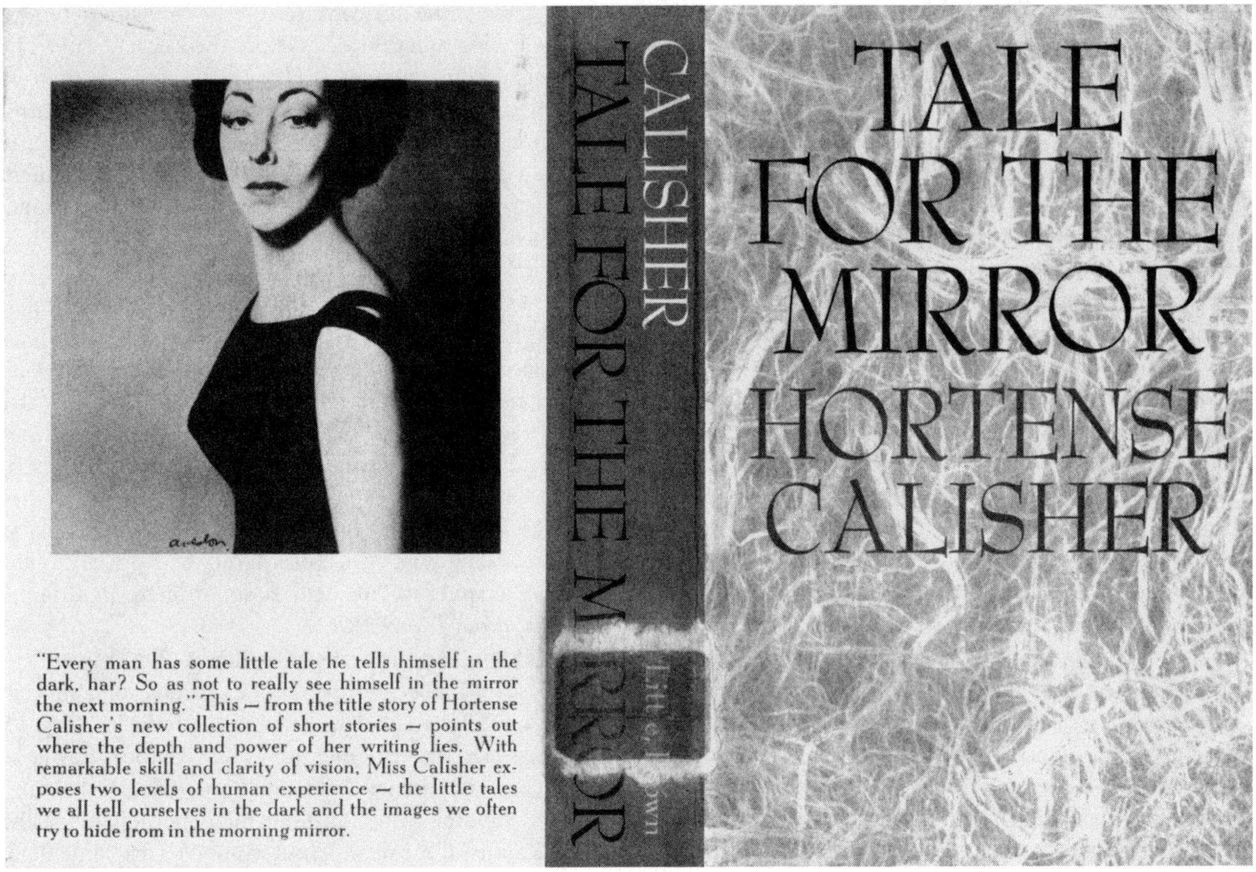

"Every man has some little tale he tells himself in the dark, har? So as not to really see himself in the mirror the next morning." This — from the title story of Hortense Calisher's new collection of short stories — points out where the depth and power of her writing lies. With remarkable skill and clarity of vision, Miss Calisher exposes two levels of human experience — the little tales we all tell ourselves in the dark and the images we often try to hide from in the morning mirror.
CALISHER
TALE FOR THE MIRROR
TALE FOR THE MIRROR
HORTENSE CALISHER

Dust jacket for Calisher's 1962 book, which includes "The Scream on Fifty-Seventh Street," her most frequently anthologized story

of several stories about blighted love affairs, harsh but muted compromises. In this brief sketch of the end of an affair, nuance is everything. The single line of dialogue is spoken by the woman, who has just realized her lover will not be returning: "It's pathetic, isn't it. . . . the spectacle of people trying to reach one another? By any means. Everywhere." It is a spectacle to which Calisher returns repeatedly in her fiction, though not necessarily drawing the same despairing conclusion as the unnamed woman in "Point of Departure."

Between Calisher's first book of short stories and her second, *Tale for the Mirror* (1962), she published her first novel, *False Entry* (1961), a long, ambitious work that took many of her readers by surprise. The narrative consists of a man's memoir of a life spent eluding real intimacy. As is true for many of Calisher's protagonists, he looks back and writes down his life in order to break free of the past. The "false entry" mentioned in the title is his practice of becoming part of other people's lives by means of fictions and misrepresentations, disguising his real self not for any malicious purpose but for the intellectual pleasure he gains from "the protean gap between what is and what might be." It is essentially the same gap the writer straddles.

Many readers considered the novel an aberration, a puzzling departure for a writer who had so clearly demonstrated her mastery of the well-crafted short story. With *Tale for the Mirror* some reviewers were relieved to find themselves back on familiar terrain. Robert Gorham Davis's appraisal of the collection for *The New York Times Book Review* (28 October 1962) is representative: "The comparative brevity of the thirteen stories . . . keeps their author from becoming involved in the too giant complications of character and perception which some critics thought to be the fault of her otherwise brilliant recent novel, 'False Entry.'"

Though continuing to write stories about urban isolation and bitter compromises, Calisher breaks new thematic ground in her second book of stories, often with surprising twists and resolutions. Calisher's most-anthologized story, "The Scream on Fifty-Seventh Street," illustrates a new synthesis in her writing. The newly widowed Mrs. Hazlitt has sublet a New York City apartment. The story deftly alludes to the depths of her loneliness but never underlines them. Through seemingly mundane details, Calisher creates a touching portrait of a woman alone who is determined to stave off despair through rituals, routines, and self-exhortation. Checking the mail–even on a Sunday–she thinks: "One has to tidy one's hair, spruce a bit for the possible regard of someone in the hall, and when she did see someone, although of course they never spoke, she always returned feeling refreshed, reaffirmed."

A radical shift in perspective begins in the middle of the night, when Mrs. Hazlitt hears a piercing and recurring scream. Her detective work eventually turns inward: "What had summoned her last night would have been . . . audible only to those tuned in by necessity–the thin, soaring decibel of those who are no longer in the fold. Alone-oh. Alone-oh." With the revelation comes a "savage pride at having heard it, at belonging to a race some of whom could never adapt to any range less than that. *Some of us,* she thought, *are still responsible.*" At the close of the story she waits for the scream to come again: "She was waiting for a second chance–to answer it." In subsequent stories, novellas, and novels, Calisher reveals an ongoing fascination with those who, by choice or necessity, "are no longer in the fold."

This collection is also notable for a new, whimsical turn in Calisher's writing. Artistry defeats loneliness in "Mrs. Fay Dines on Zebra," a wry and graceful story about a still-lovely but impecunious widow who lives by charm, social adeptness, and her formidable skills as a raconteuse. With only $126.35 in the bank and a nine-year-old son to raise, Arietta Minot Fay works her magic on a lonely, wealthy man, who is captivated by her ability "to peel some secondary skin from the ordinary, making wherever one was–if one was with her–loom like an object under a magnifying glass–large, majestic and there. She made one live in the now. . . ."

In that same collection are two of Calisher's finest autobiographical stories–also about living in the now–in which she skillfully presents social, familial, and psychic changes from a child's intent perspective. "The Coreopsis Kid" takes place as World War I is ending. Hester Elkin is a sallow-skinned, self-conscious nine-year-old, apprehensive about a future that will soon include a baby brother. Just when she is feeling most unlovable and expendable, she finds new evidence of her father's love. At her birth, she discovers, her father, whose toiletry products include "Coreopsis of Japan," sent out hundreds of telegrams announcing the birth of "The Coreopsis Kid." Nevertheless, as in other Calisher stories, there is no unconditionally happy ending; but, rather, there is always the realization that nothing stays the same. Among the Armistice Day parade crowd, which is throwing gifts of oranges to returning soldiers, Hester is reluctant to part with hers: "it was round, perfect, like the world at this moment. . . . She held onto it for as long as she could. Then, closing her eyes tight, she threw it."

In "Time, Gentlemen!" the adult narrator recalls the daily struggles between her parents: her father, with his "Victorian sense of time," luxuriating in the present; her mother, a twentieth-century dynamo, determined to herd her family into the next century. The sensibility of the narrator keeps Calisher's stories from being sepia-toned period pieces. The past is alive because it can never be resolved: years later the narrator still feels torn between the opposing forces of her parents: "Contra, contra I hear their dividing voices, as, with an Eurasian aching, I hear them yet." In these early stories the reader discovers the origins of Calisher's lifelong fascination with being in between: staying in motion as opposed to desiring a fixed role and identity.

Calisher's next book, *Textures of Life* (1963), is her most conventional novel. It charts the course of young newlyweds who slowly shed their pretensions to superiority and become part of everyday life.

A year later Calisher produced *Extreme Magic: A Novella and Other Stories* (1964), a collection of stories that are primarily about middle-aged accommodations and re-alignments. One of the most riveting is "A Christmas Carillon," a merciless character study of a successful writer with the Dickensian name of Grorley. As a young man he was "a gourmet of loneliness." Later, married and a father, he adroitly manages a weekend married life in the suburbs and a weekday bachelor life in the city. When his marriage unravels, he becomes a full-time and eventually dissatisfied bachelor, having "lost the background from which to rebel." With Christmas approaching, he is desperate to find some warm haven. At the end of the story he makes the requisite offerings of contrition and self-abasement and is re-admitted to the family home. In its bittersweet self-awareness the ending is typically Calisherian: "This is middle age, he thought. Stand still and hear the sound of it, banging like carillons, the gathering sound of all the platitudes, sternly coming true."

The middle-aged protagonist of *Extreme Magic,* the novella in this collection, comes to another, more hopeful conclusion. Having lost his family in a house fire, he is determined to remain alone, secure in his tree-lined enclosure and its "safe visual goodness." In the space of a week, however, he cannot help but come to the aid of a neighbor whose alcoholic husband is playing increasingly dangerous games. As a result of his growing concern for someone more needy than himself, he leaves physical and psychic enclosures. The closing paragraph could well appear in other Calisher stories because it touches on so many keynotes of her fiction. The protagonist and the woman he has rescued "stared into the blind current of the river, and beyond it, into a current wider than it or any harbor, into that vast multiplicity where there might be no sure order of good or evil, but surely a movement. . . . which, like some god of unbelievers . . . both took away, took away–and gave."

In 1965 Calisher published *Journal from Ellipsia,* a fabulistic novel of an extraterrestrial bent on becoming human. By turns comic and serious, the novel explores what it is to be human. Stylistically worlds apart from her previous novels, it is nonetheless thematically related. Here, as in much of her fiction, Calisher reveals her fascination with doubleness, discovering new metaphors, new contexts, in which to couch it. At the close of *Journal from Ellipsia* Eli celebrates his being neither otherworldly nor worldly, vowing "Until it dies in One-ness, the I will remember the I. . . . And will record it." For Calisher, the writer straddles worlds and selves, energetically recording a double perspective on reality.

The two novellas in *The Railway Police and The Last Trolley Ride* (1966) are also about life in motion. Part fable and part how-to manual, *The Railway Police* is the story of a professional woman's metamorphosis into a street person. Like the majority of Calisher's protagonists, she chooses an improvised life over one that is safely predictable. Bald since adolescence, the unnamed protagonist has successfully hidden "the felony of [her] private difference," but as she watches the railway police arrest a young vagrant who is "just a hairsbreadth too unshaven" she has a kind of epiphany: "It takes keeping up, any posture of what you are not, takes a sense of fitness to the point of fashion, and the vagrant won't bother with that sort of thing. . . . maybe it's his very function in life to wander about thus exposed so that others may find their signals in him." In time she becomes just such a signal on the move, discarding wigs and possessions. Still, she keeps an elegant Abercrombie bag with one treasure from her past life, a small Picasso, tucked inside it.

The centerpiece of *The Last Trolley Ride* is the last trolley run in a small Upstate New York town. By the time two elderly men describe it to their grandchild years later, that last ride has become a near-mythic, archetypal journey. Even the children on board realize "they were on the voyage they had all along known they were, the original voyage, out." Decades after the trolley ride, the two grandfathers, "Old men, old men. And young," act on impulse and set out on a trip around the world. They bequeath to their grandchildren not only stories of a distant past but also the example of living in the present: "See my dust. *Even from the air,* said my grandfather, faded and gone now. *Even from the air*–you won't learn more."

Calisher's fourth novel, *The New Yorkers* (1969), also dramatizes a movement away from enclosures and safety toward the unpredictable, vital world beyond. A companion novel to *False Entry,* it brings to the forefront an upper-middle-class Jewish family introduced in the earlier work. Calisher's most social novel, the book is a sprawling narrative in which she looks affectionately at the milieu in which she grew up. The novel spans a twelve-year period that begins with a tragic death and ends with a marriage that marks the end of a judge's self-imposed exile from the world. "What was 'public' life?" the judge wonders. "The access of each organism into the current, and its submission to it, held all the drama of life. . . ." This drama continues to enthrall Calisher as well.

Between 1971 and 1977 Calisher published four novels, a memoir, and her *Collected Stories* (1975). *Queenie* (1971) and *Eagle Eye* (1973) are decidedly novels of the 1970s. The former is a lighthearted, satiric romp through the excesses of the era, and the latter is a somber psychological profile of a young man who stayed home from the conflict in Vietnam. In the two other novels of the period, *Standard Dreaming* (1972) and *On Keeping Women* (1977), Calisher goes well beyond the clichés of middle-age identity crises to dramatize harrowing re-evaluations. Published in 1972, Calisher's wonderfully atypical memoir, *Herself,* is part journal, part essay, part book and theater reviews, and part old-fashioned autobiography.

With the publication of *The Collected Stories of Hortense Calisher* in 1975, Calisher's reputation was firmly established as a major short-story writer. Faced with the formal brilliance and imaginative scope of thirty-six stories written over a nearly thirty-year period, reviewers were hard-pressed to "place" Calisher. Writing for *The New York Times Book Review* (19 October 1975), Doris Grumbach compared Calisher's language to John Updike's, her sense of place to James Joyce's and Graham Greene's, her emotional intensity to Flannery O'Connor's, but concluded that Calisher "has her own quality. It is hard to relate her to others in the New York school, because her New York, after all, is an interior landscape, seen very individually." Robert Phillips wrote, "It is impossible to overpraise the psychological acumen which the author brings to each story," and went on to praise "the beauty of Ms. Calisher's language" as well as her range of subject matter (*Commonweal,* 7 May 1976).

It is a tribute to Calisher's power as a short-story writer that critics differed so widely in their preferences. Some singled out the autobiographical stories as the best of the lot; others preferred her stories of urban angst. They also differed about more fundamental matters. Phillips asserted that "story lines are often fragile, if not nonexistent. . . . The landscape is more often than

Dust jacket for Calisher's 1985 book, which includes "Gargantua," a story that continues the consideration of the mother-daughter relationship that Calisher began with one of her earliest stories, "The Middle Drawer" (1948)

not a psychescape of the protagonists." Eugenie Bolger, however, wrote that Calisher "believes in firm structures and plots. Her stories are filled with the detail that establishes mood and place" (*New Leader,* 19 January 1976).

Whatever their differences, reviewers were nearly unanimous in declaring Calisher a master of the short-story form. Novelist Anne Tyler's assessment is representative: "The details are so precise, and the voice so perceptive and intelligent, that we're willing to flow with the story; we begin to trust Hortense Calisher knows exactly where she's leading us. And she does. She draws to the end of her gracious tale, pauses, and then stabs. We never guessed that she would do us in so thoroughly" (*The Washington Post,* 18 September 1977). Given Calisher's description of the short story as "an apocalypse, served in a very small cup," it is clear that such surprises are exactly what she intends.

In her introduction to *The Collected Stories,* Calisher goes on to emphasize the human dimensions of the short story and offers an eloquent defense of the form:

> I do see . . . a certain temperament in the story form. Its very duration, too brief to make a new mode in, verges it always toward that classical corner where sits the human figure. And perhaps the genre flourishes best during those periods of life . . . when the human drama is easier accepted as the main one going. . . .
>
> I go to the short-story world most perhaps for the multiplicity of its voices, which crowd in, endearingly intimate, approachable, from across terra firma whose scale one can almost see. For the writer, that world is as fell–in the sense of a knockdown blow–as any other. It's the world where once I learned, and learn again laboriously, that a writer's own voice may clap in many tongues. . . .

That multiplicity of voices is as evident in Calisher's novels as in her stories, as her books since the publication of *The Collected Stories* amply demonstrate. At age seventy-one Calisher published *Mysteries of Motion* (1983), a novel notable for its formal and thematic complexities. Set in the not-too-distant future, this five-hundred-page novel, an account of the first all-civilian space shuttle, spans years and cultures. Densely textured and richly imagined, the novel is further evidence of Calisher's impressive powers of invention and craft. Two years later, she published *Saratoga, Hot,* a collection of "little novels" that push the limits of the short-story form. Some are, in fact, long short stories but others succeed in breaching the gap between story and novel. They are remarkable for their range of characters and situations.

In "The Passenger" the reader meets a woman whose life bears an uncanny resemblance to Calisher's. Part essay, part reminiscence, and part dramatized incident, this story is held together by repeated references to the motion of the train on which the woman is riding and by the arresting sensibility of the narrator. Anyone interested in learning about the writer behind the stories would do well to read "The Passenger" in conjunction with *Herself.* In "The Passenger" the narrator looks back at her young self and remembers, "I didn't want to be anything there was a prescription for. Then I found out there wasn't any for what I wanted to do–and started being it." It was the beginning of a life spent on the move: "Once, I thought I wanted that. The one house in the one street, forever and alackaday. When all the time it was change that was the devil-wine in my veins. . . ."

First published twenty years after "The Middle Drawer," "Gargantua" also centers on the mother-daughter relationship, but it differs from that first story, which concluded on a somber note, emphasizing "the innumerable small cicatrices imposed on us from our beginnings; we carry them with us always, and from these, from this agony, we are not absolved." "Gargantua" offers a richer, more hopeful legacy: "The people one lives with and loves can be like cornucopias in the mind; even after they are dead, we can abstract their riches, one by one."

In many ways the story is once again about being in between, beginning with the uncertainty about "Gargantua, the mammoth sea lion or gorilla," whose roar from nearby Madison Square Garden can be heard in a New York City hospital room. Is it a land animal or a sea creature? An unresolved indeterminacy permeates the long story, which is centered on sixteen-year-old Hester, waiting impatiently for college to start in the fall but also waiting for her mother's recognition and approval: "to see me both for what I was and what I wasn't yet: a ragged creature but ready to be magnificent. . . . I thought I hated her, yet I wanted her to tell me how to be just like her."

The story takes place in a hospital room, where Hester's mother is recuperating from surgery. Every evening Hester surprises herself by preparing and eating liver, the daily meal her mother must eat to regain her strength. Given Hester's acknowledgment that her mother "was as much the core and blood juice of our lives as that piece of liver . . . was temporarily hers," Hester's nightly ritual takes on a near-sacramental quality. When her mother learns of Hester's actions a major shift takes place in their long, adversarial relationship: "She was a woman of reserve . . . but this was one of the few times in our life together that I could be dizzyingly sure I had pleased. . . . I saw that I had confused her, not as the chick can sometimes confuse an adult, but as the grown confuse the grown. She had lost her pure version of me. I was opaque."

Hester experiences a surprising reversal when, visiting her mother, she hears a voice from next door saying "Olordletnotmywillbutthinebedone." Her mother's sharp rejoinder–"Listen. . . . When are you ever going to start listening and looking at the world around you!"–jolts Hester into listening attentively: "'O Lord,' it said. 'Let not *thy* will . . . but MINE . . . be done.'"

The narrator of "Gargantua" remembers these events years later, while she is hospitalized. In the wry and moving conclusion of the story the young Hester has come to escort her mother home from the hospital on the same day that Gargantua is leaving Madison Square Garden. The narrator, just out of surgery, re-creates that moment:

> So listen, neighbor, and I'll finish the story of how my mother told me who Gargantua was, how she tells me now. . . . "The beast that haunts us, the nameless," she says, "why it's nothing but an old slice of liver. Or, while I say it is, in this merry-dark way whose lilt you hear yet–it *is* only that. . . . There are things I can't decree away from you–*such things,* my darling. But while I say it is only that, I hold back the beast."

Occasionally serving the same "old dull meal" of liver to her own children, the narrator, following in her mother's footsteps, wants to both protect and prepare those she loves: "I'm the scourge, but *listen. Look about you in the world!*" As in the best of Calisher's stories, narrative and character, image and symbol, past and present, are seamlessly interwoven in "Gargantua."

Saratoga, Hot was followed by two novels in rapid succession: *The Bobby-Soxer* (1986) and *Age* (1987). The protagonist of *The Bobby-Soxer* is a young woman discovering the ambiguities in the world and within herself. As is true throughout Calisher's fiction, change is the only constant. When she revisits her childhood haunts as an adult, the narrator muses, "All lives are legendary. I haven't yet gathered in all the threads of my own, nor will I ever." The same determination to keep on as "a beginning animal," even to the brink of death, informs *Age,* a lean and elegant novel about growing old, written in diary form. A long-married couple–he an architect, she a poet–each keeps a diary to be read by the survivor, while hoping against hope they will "die in absolute yoke." However much death occupies their minds, renewed love and work ultimately triumph. Deciding to leave the womb of their apartment, they are about to set off for parts unknown. They are also working again; he is designing a new house, and she is writing poems. Both are determined to "use the whole house of ourselves. . . . Not close up room after room in us, and live in one. As old people do. And we must let history in."

In 1993 Calisher produced *In the Palace of the Movie King,* a 423-page novel detailing an Eastern European moviemaker and dissident's transition into American life. Her 1996 novel, *In the Slammer with Carol Smith,* also dramatizes an outsider in America, but this time the protagonist is native born. As in the novella *The Railway Police,* the protagonist of this novel has slipped out of her middle-class existence. Accessory to the botched bomb-building scheme of some college friends in the 1970s, she served time in prison and in a mental hospital. The novel charts her tentative forays back into the mainstream, "the calendared life. . . . conducted behind a curtain of numerals: bank statements, salaries, taxes, that sound their warning bells morning to evening, a background music that some repress, many enjoy." At the end of the novel she has tentatively moved back into the fold, but she recognizes a counterimpulse: "There is a need . . . for–could one call it 'singletude,' as apart from living single? One would slip away now and then from the doubleness. . . . To walk, waist untwined, swinging in the alpine air of the lone meditation." This yearning to be both one way and another is a quintessential moment for a Calisher protagonist.

In "Short Novel on a Long Subject: Henry James," an essay that first appeared in the Summer 1967 issue of *Texas Quarterly,* Calisher celebrates James's "extraordinary affirmation of human consciousness. . . . [He] never for a moment underestimated the intelligence of his readers. There are some who will never forgive him for it." The same can be said of Calisher. Whether she is piling detail upon detail in her densely textured accounts of childhood or weaving fables and fantasies, consciousness–most notably her own–is the focal point of her fiction. In his review of *The Bobby-Soxer,* Morris Dickstein sums up Calisher's achievement:

> There are many writers who feel that the prose of a novel should be a transparent window on the world, that the novelist should never draw attention to himself or stand between his readers and his characters. . . . [Calisher] belongs to a different tradition descending from Henry James, in which the writer's own complex intelligence–his humming eloquence, his subtle knowingness–becomes essential to his equipment as a storyteller. Far from holding the mirror up to life, this kind of writer diffracts it through the prism of his sensibility, as if to show how many-faceted it is. (*The New York Times Book Review,* 30 March 1986)

Never writing down to her readers and never content with past successes, Calisher remains a formidable presence in the world of American literature. In *Herself* she wrote, "Each stage of my life seemed to me somehow an ascent, and a surprise–since here in my country one is supposed to decline toward the grave at an acute angle." Then she characterized herself as still "Waiting for More"; the same holds true more than two decades later.

Interviews:

Harvey Breit, "Talk with Miss Calisher," *New York Times Book Review,* 25 November 1951, p. 40;

Eliot Fremont-Smith, "Interview with Calisher," *New York Times Book Review,* 12 May 1963, p. 5;

Roy Newquist, "An Interview with Hortense Calisher," *Writer's Digest,* 49 (March 1969): 58–60, 94–96;

"Interview with Hortense Calisher," *Grain* (Scripps College), 9 May 1969, pp. 33–34;

Cleveland Amory, "Trade Winds," *Saturday Review,* 54 (8 May 1971): 6;

Israel Shenker, "Hortense Calisher Talks About Writing and Herself," *New York Times,* 28 September 1972, p. 54;

John Noble Wilford, "An Author Thrusts Into the Cosmos," *New York Times,* 8 November 1983, C1, C4;

Allan Gurganus, Pamela McCordick, and Mona Simpson, "The Art of Fiction C: Hortense Calisher," *Paris Review,* 105 (Winter 1987): 157–187.

Bibliography:

Kathleen Snodgrass, "Hortense Calisher: A Bibliography, 1948–1986," *Bulletin of Bibliography,* 45 (March 1988): 40–50.

References:

Brigid Brophy, Reviews of *Extreme Magic, Tale for a Mirror,* and *Textures of Life,* in her *Don't Never Forget: Collected Views and Reviews* (New York: Holt, Rinehart & Winston, 1967), pp. 158–162;

David K. Kirby, "The Princess and the Frog: The Modern Short Story as Fairy Tale," *Minnesota Review,* 4 (Spring 1973): 145–149;

Kathleen Snodgrass, *The Fiction of Hortense Calisher* (Newark: University of Delaware Press, 1993);

Snodgrass, "Hortense Calisher," in *Jewish Women in America: An Historical Encyclopedia,* edited by Paula E. Hyman and Deborah Dash Moore (New York & London: Routledge, 1997), pp. 201–202;

Snodgrass, "Hortense Calisher: 'A Beginning Animal,'" *Confrontation,* no. 41 (Summer/Fall 1989): 63–82.

R. V. Cassill

(17 May 1919 -)

Stephen Balmer
Spring Hill Waldorf School

See also the Cassill entry in *DLB 6: American Novelists Since World War II, Second Series.*

photograph by Kay Cassill

BOOKS: *The Eagle on the Coin* (New York: Random House, 1950);
Dormitory Women (New York: Lion Books, 1954);
Left Bank of Desire, by Cassill and Eric Potter (New York: Ace, 1955);
A Taste of Sin (New York: Ace, 1955; London: Brown, Watson, 1959);
The Hungering Shame (New York: Avon, 1956);
The Wound of Love (New York: Avon, 1956);
An Affair to Remember, as Owen Aherne (New York: Avon, 1957);
Fifteen By Three, by Cassill, Herbert Gold, and James B. Hall (New York: New Directions, 1957);
Man on Fire, as Owen Aherne (New York: Avon, 1957);
Naked Morning (New York: Avon, 1957);
The Buccaneer (New York: Avon, 1958);
Lustful Summer (New York: Avon, 1958);
Tempest (Greenwich, Conn.: Fawcett, 1959; London: Muller, 1962);
The Wife Next Door (Greenwich, Conn.: Fawcett, 1959; London: Muller, 1960);
My Sister's Keeper (New York: Avon, 1960);
Nurses' Quarters (Greenwich, Conn.: Fawcett, 1961; London: Muller, 1962);
Clem Anderson (New York: Simon & Schuster, 1961);
Night School (New York: Dell, 1961);
Writing Fiction (New York: Permabooks, 1963);
Pretty Leslie (New York: Simon & Schuster, 1963; London: Muller, 1964);
The President (New York: Simon & Schuster, 1964);
The Father and Other Stories (New York: Simon & Schuster, 1965);
The Happy Marriage, and Other Stories (West Lafayette, Ind.: Purdue University Studies, 1966);
La Vie Passionnée of Rodney Buckthorne: A Tale of the Great American's Last Rally and Curious Death (New York: Geis, 1968);
In an Iron Time: Statements and Reiterations (West Lafayette, Ind.: Purdue University Studies, 1969);
Doctor Cobb's Game (New York: Geis, 1970);
The Goss Women (Garden City, N.Y.: Doubleday, 1974; London: Hodder & Stoughton, 1975);
Hoyt's Child (Garden City, N.Y.: Doubleday, 1976);
Flame (New York: Arbor House, 1980);
Labors of Love (New York: Arbor House, 1980);

Three Stories (Oakland, Cal.: Hermes House Press, 1982);
After Goliath: A Novel (New York: Ticknor & Fields, 1985);
Patrimonies (Bristol, R.I.: Ampersand, 1988);
Collected Stories (Fayetteville: University of Arkansas Press, 1989);
The Unknown Soldier (Montrose, Ala.: Texas Center for Writers Press, 1991);
The Man Who Bought Magnitogorsk (New York: London Company, 1994);
Late Stories (Montrose, Ala.: Texas Center for Writers Press, 1995).

OTHER: *Intro #1,* edited by Cassill (New York: Bantam, 1968);
Intro #2, edited by Cassill (New York: Bantam, 1969);
Intro #3, edited by Cassill (New York: McCall, 1970);
Intro #4, edited by Cassill and Walter Beacham (Charlottesville: University Press of Virginia, 1972);
The Norton Anthology of Short Fiction, edited by Cassill (New York: Norton, 1978; sixth edition, 1999);
The Norton Anthology of Contemporary Fiction, edited by Cassill (New York: Norton, 1988; second edition, 1997).

For more than four decades R. V. Cassill has written short stories that place him squarely in the mainstream of American short fiction. For the most part his stories are not marked by formal experiment. Rather, as Vincent Stewart has noted in *Survey of Contemporary Literature* (revised edition, 1977), Cassill writes "well-made stories . . . about the normal people who occupy the broad middle class of American life, people who would under ordinary conditions not be remarkable. . . ." Cassill has not, however, been entirely bound by tradition. Describing the aesthetic of a fictional group of writers, the narrator of Cassill's novel *Clem Anderson* (1961) offers an explanation of the aims of Cassill's own short fiction: "The story was to be a consolidation of the gains made by Joyce, Crane, Porter, Hemingway and Faulkner. As I recollect the eager theorizing, the new story was to be as compact as poetry. . . . It was to keep the suppleness and reportorial virtues of traditional fiction while it added a range of subtleties unknown before the twentieth century." In his foreword to *Fifteen By Three* (1957), a collection of stories by Cassill, Herbert Gold, and James B. Hall, publisher James Laughlin notes that Cassill, like other young writers of the 1950s, was attempting "to keep the short story from going stale and keep it growing as a form. . . ." These writers, Laughlin observes, tend to "let the particular content declare the approach that will bring through all that is in it."

In addition to short stories Cassill has written novels, novellas, and two nonfiction books–*Writing Fiction* (1963) and *In an Iron Time: Statements and Reiterations* (1967)–as well as many articles, reviews, and critical essays. While some of Cassill's novels have received critical acclaim, David Roberts has called Cassill's short stories his "most insightful and esthetically complete accomplishments to date" while expressing the reservation that "his novels, despite their considerable merit and consistently similar thematic concerns, do not manage to present that essence of embodied vision necessary to the finest artistic performance."

In an interview with William Jaspersohn published in the special Cassill issue of *December Magazine* (1981), Cassill suggests the effort required to produce the transparent and seemingly natural voices of his fiction: "I used to [revise] a whole lot. But what I'm doing in later years is throwing away the whole page and rewriting it. I have a superstition that revision clogs the movement of the prose. It may produce good sentences, but good sentences are not the art of fiction." This attempt at honest revelation of character raises Cassill's short stories above "mainstream" fiction. As Stewart remarks, "at those points of crisis which mark all lives they become remarkable and normality is revealed as the facade that it is."

The central motif in Cassill's fiction is the unavoidable conflict between the possibility of raised consciousness and the impossibility of self-knowledge. His pellucid and seamless style conveys a poignant commentary on failed communications between his characters. Those who learn the art of "listening to the void" find consolation in that silence. His stories resonate with an ever-present sense of loss and a paradoxical expectation of being made whole. As his bereft characters perpetually sense exaltation awaiting them beyond an ever-receding horizon, his stories recount their quests for that elusive sanctuary of enlightened wholeness. The pathos of Cassill's carefully wrought explorations of radical estrangement from life and self is intensified by the Midwestern "normalcy" of his fictional settings, for which Cassill draws on his own experiences of growing up in Middle America.

The son of Howard Earl and Mary Glosser Cassill, Ronald Verlin Cassill was born on 17 May 1919 in Cedar Falls, Iowa. He and his older brother and younger brother and sister spent their childhood in small Iowa towns as their father, a school superintendent, changed jobs every four or five years. Cassill graduated from high school in Blakesburg, Iowa, in 1935, and that fall he enrolled at Iowa State Teachers' College (now University of Northern Iowa) in Cedar Falls. After one year, he transferred to the University of Iowa, earning a B.A. in 1939. At Iowa State Teachers'

R. V. and Kathleen Cassill, 1943

College, Cassill had discovered art. As he wrote later, in a memoir published in the *Contemporary Authors Autobiography Series* (volume 1, 1984), "its claims on me were primal."

During his first two years at the University of Iowa, Cassill went through a period of intellectual and emotional evolution. He remembers this time with pain: "I knew myself to be fearfully alone, alienated as never before or since." He was rescued from what he has called "a para-psychotic withdrawal" by several close student friends who, in his words, "opened the way for me to re-enter the daylight world without giving up what I had stumbled on in the remote dark." His experiences during this period underlie Cassill's central motif, the search for a heightened self-knowledge. This quest becomes all the more poignant when the Cassill protagonist finds himself facing the solemn Midwestern rectitude of the 1920s and 1930s.

In the spring of 1940, having earned recognition for his paintings and drawings at the university, Cassill went to work for the Iowa Art Project of the Works Progress Administration (WPA), first in Des Moines and later in Sioux City and Mason City. His career with the WPA was marked by periods of alcoholic binges and indirection in life, but his meeting his future first wife, Kathleen Rosecrans, in Sioux City, marked the end of this period of youthful anguish and excess. As he later recalled, he began "to feel decidedly responsible and as if I must try hard to live up to Kathie and all her first-rate family."

Several months after their wedding on 4 June 1941, the United States entered World War II, and Cassill was inducted into the army. He was trained as a medic, and after various other postings he was sent to the South Pacific, where he was stationed at Espirito Santo in the New Hebrides. There, he later remembered, "We moved into a rain forest in the midst of a nearly perpetual rainy season to encounter a siege of boredom, jungle rot, and institutional friction that was to last for nearly two full years." Cassill also recalled his shocked reaction to news of the atomic bombing of Hiroshima and Nagasaki in August 1945 and to what he saw later when stationed in Japan and Okinawa: "I was called now to the study of power as it plays behind the screen of ideological falsehood." These wartime perceptions surface in the human intrigues of his later fiction, while the enduring boredom of the jungle is echoed in Cassill's core motif of the existential experience of "being and nothingness."

After the war, Cassill turned to teaching English and writing, completing his first novel, *The Eagle on the Coin* (1950), and publishing short stories with some regularity in little magazines. His story "The Conditions of Justice" won an *Atlantic* "Firsts" Award and was published in the December 1947 issue of *The Atlantic Monthly*. Cassill worked as an instructor at Monticello College in Godfrey, Illinois, in 1946–1948. After earning an M.A. at the University of Iowa in 1949, he was appointed an instructor on the regular staff in the Writers' Workshop there in fall 1949, conducting the graduate fiction workshop with Paul Engle, Hansford Martin, and, later, Ray B. West Jr., founder of *The Western Review*. In 1951 and 1952 Cassill also served as an editor of this journal.

When *The Eagle on the Coin* was published by Random House in 1950, Cassill felt that in some ways he had compromised his artistic integrity in making the revisions requested by his editor, and he reacted in disgust to the book when he received the first printed copy. As he later wrote, "I had to struggle against too many inward mutilations while I tried to write a second novel–which, for sufficient reasons, was rejected by Random House when it was finally offered."

While he was working on the novel, his mother lost her job for teaching "Communist ideas" to her elementary-school pupils, an event that later became subject matter for one of Cassill's short stories, "Where Saturn Keeps the Years" (*Missouri Review,* 1978). At around the same time, in September 1951, Cassill was upset by the suicide of Louis Adamic, a political activist, writer, and editor of the periodical *T & T,* to which Cassill contributed regularly in 1947 and 1948. After Adamic's death, Cassill experienced what he has called a "disaster within" (borrowing the phrase, he has said, from E. M. Forster). In 1952 he left his wife, from whom he was subsequently divorced, and went to Paris with another woman.

Supporting himself in Paris on a Fulbright fellowship, Cassill wrote fiction as he moved from one hotel room to another and made the acquaintance of Richard Wright, Terry Southern, painter Leon Goldin, and bookseller George Whitman. Cassill returned to New York City in June 1953, and by 1954 he had begun supporting himself by writing novels for paperback publishers, by part-time teaching, and by working as an editor for *Collier's Encyclopedia.* During this period James Laughlin of New Directions proposed that Cassill, Herbert Gold, and James B. Hall each contribute five short stories to a collection that was published in 1957 as *Fifteen By Three.*

In spring 1956 Cassill returned to France, taking with him Kay Adams, who became his second wife in Rome on 23 November 1956. In France he quickly wrote the first draft of his most-successful novel, *Clem Anderson* (1961), which he has described as "a transformed autobiography, grafted, of course, onto the design of Dylan Thomas's life and death." After their wedding the Cassills returned to New York City, where their first son, Orin, was born in 1957. The Cassills subsequently had two more children, Erica and Jesse. Cassill supported his family by lecturing part-time at Columbia University and the New School for Social Research (1957–1959) while continuing to write paperback novels. Despite commercial and editorial restraints, Cassill believes "At least two of these still seem to me among the best of the novels I have thus far produced." In 1958 he also worked as an editor for *Dude* and *Gent* magazines. Nearly three years after his rapid drafting of *Clem Anderson* in France, Cassill completed his laborious reworking of it in December 1959. The novel was published by Simon and Schuster in 1961.

In 1960, with a growing family, Cassill returned to teach at the Iowa Writers' Workshop, where his colleagues included George P. Elliott, Hortense Calisher, and Donald Justice. Cassill began a pattern of publishing a novel or short-story collection about every two years. Unhappy with political discord and intrigues in the English department at Iowa, Cassill spent the 1965–1966 academic year as writer in residence at Purdue University and then became an associate professor at Brown University. He was promoted to full professor in 1972 and retired from Brown in 1983.

Relative financial prosperity came to Cassill with the publication in 1970 of his novel *Doctor Cobb's Game;* the enthusiastic reception of this work also led to substantial advances on his next two novels. In 1974 he assumed responsibility for editing *The Norton Anthology of Short Fiction* (1978), which had gone through six editions by 1999, and during the 1980s he also took on *The Norton Anthology of Contemporary Fiction* (1988). Throughout this decade, he was frequently invited to teach at various writers' conferences.

In his introduction to his five stories in *Fifteen By Three* Cassill makes an illuminating observation about the difficulty of capturing truth through the writing process: "the work finished appears to be only a brief homage to the things by whose recall an illusion of permanence was glimpsed in passing." Commenting on "The Romanticizing of Dr. Fless," he adds that humankind needs art for "some fabulous affirmation of meaning in mortality which will protect us from the intolerable lack of meaning in the non-fable of existence." His stories may thus be seen as heroic attempts at revealing glimpses of truth.

Described by Cassill as an effort to "demonstrate some of the responsibilities of a writer," "The Romanticizing of Dr. Fless" is a story of two young men, the narrator and Dick Samson, during an uneventful summer in their hometown of Chesterfield. Dick has returned home from his first year of college determined to become a writer. As the two boys hang out at the service station where the narrator has a job, Dick engages his friend in wild imaginings about the house across the street and its occupants, the aged Dr. Fless and his aging, homely daughter. To their surprise, and Dick's consternation, Miss Fless turns out to be a commercially successful writer of western fiction. Indeed, she has "a letter from the president of a railroad division telling her what a great writer she is." Cassill observes in his introduction that Dick learns "to succeed; that is, to force his family into admitting his status as writer." Yet, when Dick Samson abandons writing at the end of the story, Cassill explains, it is "the forsaken narrator who is dumped into the present world" and who learns that the ultimate responsibility of the writer is "never to stop any part of his function except, perhaps, the mechanics of putting words on a page. The writer has

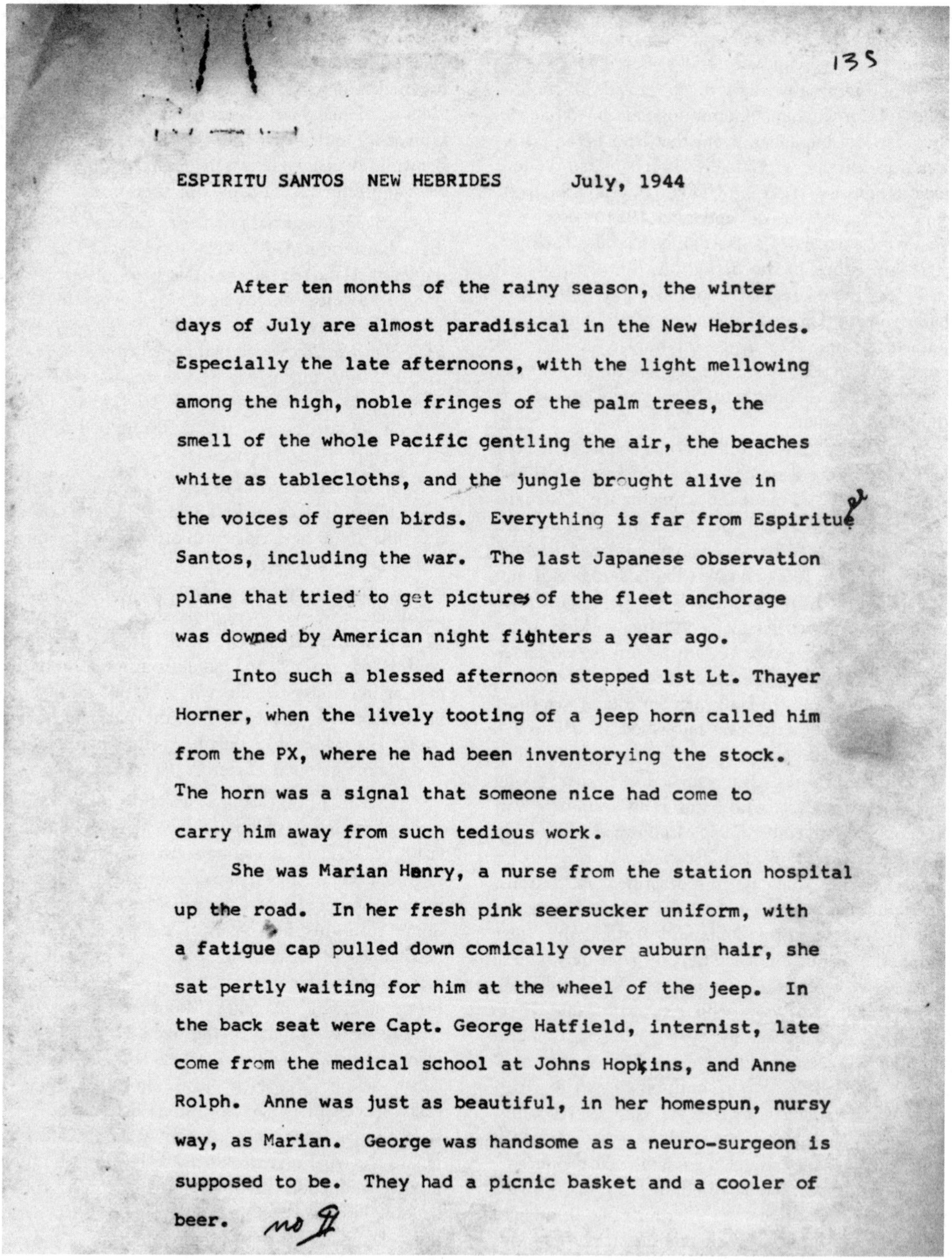

135

ESPIRITU SANTOS NEW HEBRIDES July, 1944

After ten months of the rainy season, the winter days of July are almost paradisical in the New Hebrides. Especially the late afternoons, with the light mellowing among the high, noble fringes of the palm trees, the smell of the whole Pacific gentling the air, the beaches white as tablecloths, and the jungle brought alive in the voices of green birds. Everything is far from Espiritu Santos, including the war. The last Japanese observation plane that tried to get pictures of the fleet anchorage was downed by American night fighters a year ago.

Into such a blessed afternoon stepped 1st Lt. Thayer Horner, when the lively tooting of a jeep horn called him from the PX, where he had been inventorying the stock. The horn was a signal that someone nice had come to carry him away from such tedious work.

She was Marian Henry, a nurse from the station hospital up the road. In her fresh pink seersucker uniform, with a fatigue cap pulled down comically over auburn hair, she sat pertly waiting for him at the wheel of the jeep. In the back seat were Capt. George Hatfield, internist, late come from the medical school at Johns Hopkins, and Anne Rolph. Anne was just as beautiful, in her homespun, nursy way, as Marian. George was handsome as a neuro-surgeon is supposed to be. They had a picnic basket and a cooler of beer. no ¶

Page from the corrected typescript for "Jack Horner," an early novel that was published in part as The Unknown Soldier *in 1991 (Collection of R. V. Cassill)* to realize that the time for his success is in the fullness of time."

Another story in *Fifteen by Three,* "The Life of the Sleeping Beauty," demonstrates Cassill's involvement in his contemporaries' efforts to renew and expand the short-story form. Roberts has described the glosses that appear alongside the main text of the story as "an astonishing and radically effective innovation" that creates "a final and authoritative perspective on a perspective-ridden narrative." Cassill has acknowledged the influence of Marshall McLuhan, whose "*The Mechanical Bride* [1951] was a terrific aid in learning to read the journalism (with its eight types of ambiguity) on which so much of 'Sleeping Beauty' is based. . . . If there is a central reality in 'Sleeping Beauty', one must come to it by descending through the reality of contemporary journalism." Through a series of almost dreamlike vignettes, "The Life of the Sleeping Beauty" presents the life of Miranda as it might unfold outside ordinary consciousness, unlimited by the constraints of a linear, time-bound world. In so doing, Cassill risks losing the reader, and himself, in a vortex of unknowingness, like that Miranda experiences: "If I am not Miranda–she thought once while brushing her teeth–then what, what, what, what, what have you made out of me." Cassill's marginal notations create a dynamic authorial voice that expresses what Cassill sees as the essentially ambiguous experience of human self-consciousness: "the sin of worldliness becomes the sin of emptiness" and those who recognize this truth "live in a weedy hollow between two ramshackle conditions."

Three of the five Cassill stories included in *Fifteen By Three*–"The Biggest Band," "Larchmoor Is Not the World," and "The Goldfish"–also appear in his 1965 collection, *The Father and Other Stories.* "The Biggest Band" portrays an underlying sadness in Midwestern life during the 1930s through its wistful telling of the creation of "the biggest band in the world" for a trip to the Chicago World's Fair. The story begins: "The Corn State Southern Band was a forlorn hope from the beginning, and like other forlorn hopes, it moved within an aura of enthusiastic propaganda." The thirteen-year-old narrator joins the band, naively dreaming that he will discover a fuller life in Chicago, but he finds only bitter disappointment. After a disappointing concert in Chicago, he goes to sleep "on the hotel room floor feeling the misery of those who have tried to sell their souls and have found no taker." At 6:15 the next moring the band performs again, playing well for "a handful of early-rising janitors." The narrator is saved from unrelenting sadness about the band by his humorous perspective, having "In all the years since the fair . . . told the story of our band a number of times, for laughs." The story ends with the narrator imagining how he would have told the story to Mrs. Packer, a woman who was too ill to attend the fair and died soon after. In this version he emphasizes the beauty of the setting and concludes: "It was only the empty sky that watched us–but my God, my God, how the drums thundered, how we blew!"

"Larchmoor is Not the World" and "The Goldfish" are set in the insular world of the college professor and are informed by Cassill's own experiences. "Larchmoor is Not the World" tells the story of Dr. Cameron, a professor who is comfortable in his office-sanctuary, "which he had been seven years in building." He is torn from this familiar setting by his genuine concern for a student, Shirley Bridges, who faces possible expulsion over personal and academic behavior (further complicated by her allegation of brutal treatment by her father, a charge the college president refuses to believe). Displaying unexpected integrity, Cameron protests the president's decision to send Shirley home with her father, and as a result he finds himself "tossed, into the cold, where an old scholar had to worry about rent." The professor was galvanized, not by Shirley but by the fate of a character in Percy Bysshe Shelley's verse play *The Cenci* (1819, 1821): "It was not Shirley who had lured him out of his warm corner. . . . The realer Beatrice, the gold-embroidered princess, the beautiful lady without mercy and without hope had brought him out of the door."

"The Goldfish" is the story of a teacher who searches out a former student with whom he feels an important bond. She represents the possibility of transcending his life as a teacher, which amounts to "Nothing. There's the ultimate grief of being a teacher." He seems unable to understand if he loves her or if he is only projecting onto her the possibility for real human communion that might heal his disaffection from life.

Joyce Carol Oates has written that *The Father and Other Stories* established Cassill "as one of the masters of the contemporary short story," praising his "evocation of people forced into various encounters with one another and with a kind of nameless, inexplicable destiny–something as pervasive and vague as the Midwestern landscape itself." The characters in the title story, "The Father," are among those Oates describes. For this reason the story is both central to the collection and one of its strongest. It begins with a four-year-old boy, Bobbie, catching his hand in the unguarded gears of the corn sheller in his family's barn. To extricate his son from the machinery and save his life, Cory amputates Bobbie's hand "With a three-inch blow" from his hatchet. His act is accepted as rational, and family life continues with outward normality. Bobbie grows up well-adjusted, begins running the farm, marries, and fathers a son. Yet, Cory is plagued by a nameless, irra-

R. V. and Kay Cassill at their wedding in Rome, 23 November 1956

tional shame: "What he could never face–could never understand–was that he was guilty in taking that hatchet down from its hanging place on the wall and cutting off his son's hand." The enduring horror of that day remains more real to Cory than his everyday life. At the end of the story Cory cuts off the hand of his grandson, hoping to be punished "for this repetition of his guilt." Before his transgressive act he can sense the beauty of the natural world (a pervasive presence in Cassill's fiction) and the potential comfort of the human community: "He could hear the tree frogs dinning in the yard. . . . He heard the intermittent traffic of his neighbors . . . going late into Boda or the county seat. . . ." After the act, "he found himself straining to hear the tree frogs. To hear anything." He has cut himself off from the world, and unless he is punished, he believes, "there was no hope for him in all this vast gleam of silence." Oates makes the telling observation that Cory's tragic fixation "never seems a totally irrational obsession." Thus, the nightmarish aspect of Cory's dark logic carries an authority it would not otherwise have.

"The Prize" extends the motif of inexplicable destiny set against the felt presence of the natural world, which both amplifies the young male protagonist's sense of personal estrangement and offers the possibility of redemption from his isolation. Set during the Great Depression of the 1930s, the story focuses on a Midwestern family forced by painful circumstances to leave the city (exiled, according to the protagonist) to a life "near Chesterfield." The boy describes the often-humorous travails of the family after they enter a contest sponsored by the Goodyear Tire and Rubber Company. Contestants are to list as many words as possible that can be made from the letters in the name of the company. The grand prize is $25,000. Through the first quarter of the story, the boy's feeling of disenfranchisement dominates his narrative: "I concentrated fiercely and stupidly on the problem of our expulsion from the city and began to see it as an omen of a world committed totally to sorrow." His mother's desperate determination to win the contest at all costs imparts a climate of doom to her sons as she pathetically drives their feverish construction of anagrams. One evening, the boy relates, "My father came into this intensity." Recoiling, he flees from his family, but he does not get far. The narrator sees him hiding in a nearby culvert. Against the backdrop of the natural world he experiences conflicting emotions about his parents:

> The road was wet. Now at sundown it was beginning to freeze, and I could feel the delicate ice crunch under every step with a beautiful sound and sensation of touch. The rosy light over the cornfield, reflected in a thousand puddles islanded in the loam, seemed to me too strongly and unhappily beautiful for me to stand, and it occurred to me that I might die right then, being so divided by feelings I had never encountered before, wakening to my first realization that living was something that one must choose against hardship to do.

Of course, no one in the family wins the contest, but the parents buy one of the secondary prizes, a toy dirigible, from a winner and give it to the boy. As his mother explains, "Your father and I thought that you'd worked so hard that you *were* a winner." The boy is not consoled: "I had nothing to face except–as on the evening of my father's flight–the width of sundown and spring air, empty but nonetheless resonant with things learned and half-learned, again multiplying by its beauty and silence the real threat of death if I turned away from my family and their organized ways of stinging me. I could see then that I would have to keep pretending the dirigible was fine, and I have never learned what else I could have said." As the story closes, the boy is resigned to the impossibility of ever truly meeting others, or the world, in love and freedom.

"This Hand, These Talons" was surely influenced by Cassill's wartime experience. The intense narrative is the story of the profound sadness and suicide of a young pilot and husband, who has recently returned from war. Cassill's finely crafted prose depicts penetratingly tender and beautiful scenes that are nevertheless made poignant by the young man's pervasive feeling of emptiness. There is solace in the natural world and in the comforts of the made world. Yet, in the end they are not enough. Again in this story, as in "The Father," human relationships fail to make a difference in the protagonist's state of mind. In fact, it is the love of his wife that leads to his decision to end his life. Roberts has praised this story for its "masterly restraint, the control of both emotion and the manifold techniques which contribute to the modulations called point of view," adding: "Here is writing which fully masters the obliquities of the ironic mode."

The sense of inexplicable destiny and profound estrangement in "This Hand, These Talons" is also apparent in "The Inland Years," in which a husband and wife, after nine years of marriage, return for a vacation at the lake where her family once summered, a place the wife feels will serve as "a well-understood point of reference from which we could orient the departure of our lives." A series of incidents and recollections, however, lead to a re-evaluation of an emptiness in their marriage. Meeting an old acquaintance who is drunk, the wife "kept talking, piling up more and more the whole story of her life," and, as the husband describes the scene, "The details of the story were ordinary enough, yet among the three of us we managed to qualify them so it seemed to be an endless record of failure." This distressing reunion transpires against the backdrop of an historical event. Years ago, eighteen high-school students had drowned in the lake. As Oates observes, while according to legend the drowning teenagers faithfully tried to save each other, the husband and wife recognize that between one another there exists only "a general failure that cannot be forgiven."

"And In My Heart" is about an introspective professor, who "Quite a lot of years ago . . . published two volumes of poetry" but has long since realized "that his ability to write had been exhausted." In his writing class he meets two students, a beautiful but limited young woman and her husband, who has serious intentions as a writer. The young woman seeks first to establish her own identity through her husband and then, after he leaves her, through his manuscript novel about their failed marriage and through the perceptions of the professor, who reads the manuscript. To the professor she seems to be saying, "See me. Make me real." As he reads the young man's novel, the professor begins to think of himself as a voyeur of sorts. His insight into their marriage leads the professor to the realization that he can never meet them on fully human terms, "that he could never say to her with the imperial emphasis required to establish all it meant, 'I saw you.'" His conclusion expresses Cassill's recurring theme of estrangement: "What could he say except that time would have its way with them and their stories, fictionalized or real; that on either side of its narrow course remains the same primitive wall of darkness that has rimmed it from the beginning?"

In his introduction to Cassill's 1966 collection, *The Happy Marriage, and Other Stories,* George P. Elliott observes that Cassill sometimes expresses his characters' struggle for meaning in gothic tones. In "The Covenant," for example, the third-person narrator sets the scene with the comment, "It was like it had stayed hot on purpose through July of that year, and when Harlan Casey's Uncle Luke was killed in a highway crash the day before the miserable heat wave broke, it seemed to Harlan, who was thirteen, that whoever had been punishing them in Gath and on the farms around should be satisfied now and might let them alone." This nameless being who "had been punishing them" may be seen as a sign of an underlying horror that is only intensified by the austere Midwestern landscape. At the funeral Harlan's mother compels his five-year-old brother, Chris, to kiss their uncle's corpse. While his mother is unaware of the trauma she has caused, Harlan is filled with guilt, feeling that he should have protected his brother, and he takes it on himself to rescue Chris from his preoccupation with death. By the end of the story their mother knows "She had blundered with her children." According to Elliott, the horror of the story is heightened by the realization that there will always be an essential bewilderment in the characters' lives because they lack a "language for what counted most." They are left with only the expectation that "through the night, by their sleep and their silence, they would forgive each other for being of the same family."

Another of Cassill's experiments with form, "The Happy Marriage" is a first-person narrator's reverie on his marriage and wartime experiences. His narration reveals his fragmented consciousness. He has been out of touch with reality and come back to it "Out of sheer habit."

"The Sunday Painter" is informed by Cassill's undergraduate ambitions to be a painter. The narrator, Joe, has been a student of Grant Wood, one of Cassill's painting teachers, who once commented to Cassill, as the fictional teacher says to Joe, "You've got more speed and less control than any student I ever had." Joe gives up art to enter the world of commerce, only to start painting again some twenty years later. While he is tempted to risk his comfortable life and family for a career as a painter, he ultimately withdraws again from "the adventure of art." He has become haunted by the "withering composure" and penetrating comments of a neighbor's babysitter, who observes that he does not

Dust jacket for Cassill's 1965 book, which, according to Joyce Carol Oates, established him as "one of the masters of the contemporary short story"

"seem to have anything to express." She comes to represent the unanswerable, metaphysical questions painting raises for him. At the end of the story he attacks her with his paintbrush and is taken away in an ambulance. The story is an exploration of the self-doubt any serious artist faces.

"The Crime of Mary Lynn Yager" is the sad story of a young second-grade teacher, Clarissa Carlson, who blames herself for the drowning death of Mary Lynn Yager, one of her students, on a class outing. Clarissa's guilt, deepened by the fact that she did not like Mary Lynn, is a corrosive force throughout the rest of her life. At the end of the story she turns the blame for her unhappiness on the dead child: "Mary Lynn's play with her teacher's life had been foul play, and she had got away with it." The dead child has somehow achieved a release that will forever be denied Clarissa: "Believing this fully at last, holding on the concrete railing, wanting to let go, holding onto her tongue, wanting to scream with rage, Clarissa waited."

The narrator of "The Swimmers at Pallikula" is a junior marine lieutenant fighting boredom on an island south of Guadalcanal "in the middle months of the war." Against his better judgment, he accepts a challenge to make a long-distance swim to a string of barrier islands. His friend's brush with death during the swim illuminates the lieutenant's character in an unflattering light and forces his and the reader's acknowledgment of mortality.

"The War in the Air" is the beautifully told story of Jimmy Stark, a young boy who dies a mysterious death after a feverish illness. In the process of dying he achieves a vision of his life, a transcendent awareness of his and the world's being. Early in the story, on seeing older boys flying a model jet on a tether, ten-year-old Jimmy has a moment of "recognition": "For a stunning second it seemed to be a real plane and to be his." This fantasy becomes a refuge from the knowledge of his mother's affair with a neighbor and the subsequent disintegration of the family. The story achieves its peculiar strength through the dreamlike quality of the world depicted through Jimmy's eyes. Despite the pervasive sadness of the story, Jimmy achieves in his fantasy an "amazed acknowledgment of intimacy so fierce that it could never be glimpsed except in its own light."

Three Stories (1982) includes "The Castration of Harry Bluethorn," a memorable story set during the presidency of Warren G. Harding (1921–1923). A cuckolded husband, Ham Snider, enlists the aid of his brother-in-law, Wayne, to help him castrate his wife's lover, Harry Bluethorn, who "had taken pride in his covert, rumored reputation as a sporting man with a good score among farmers' wives." The characters act out the same sort of inexplicable destiny as other characters in Cassill's fiction. Harry Bluethorn is castrated. Ham Snider returns to his wife, raises a family, and lives for nearly thirty more years. At the end of the story Cassill leaves the reader with unresolved questions: "Was their later life good? Were they happy? Had he done the right thing? They never knew, nor does anyone who told me this part of their story."

The extent of Cassill's accomplishment in the short-story form is impressively demonstrated by his *Collected Stories* (1989), which brings together thirty-nine of his short stories, several of which have not appeared in his earlier collections. Human estrangement is expressed through a variety of means, including Cassill's repeated use of the metaphor of the airplane, which he has described as "the dark alternative to the illuminations of art." In "My Brother, Wilbur," for example, the "day in 1930 when Speed Holman died in his Laird biplane at the Omaha air races" is the moment of revelation at which a young boy envisions the possibilities and the despair of life. In "The Invention of the Airplane" the suicide of a college professor's disfigured wife leads him to a kind of self-exile in which he reimagines building the first airplane: "He had his own reasons for settling on the airplane as a symbolic focus of the times we live in." Through his imaginative fiction, he reconstructs his personality and the world.

Along with "The Father" and "This Hand, These Talons," Roberts names "The Outer Island" as a story that accurately portrays a psychic disorder as a valid experience in a meaningless world. In "The Outer Island" Captain Stern is assigned to evaluate the suicide of an officer who was stationed on a little jungle island and is forced to acknowledge his own mortality. Arriving there, the captain finds a sun-baked beach,

> flinging up a heat and light as sterile as the sand, and the little camp above it. On three sides of the clearing there were trees matted from ground to top with vines; so the whole space was like a green quarry pit open to the sun. The floor of the pit, an area grown with brush and irregular formations of banana trees, held the tents and two buildings. A few trunks of girdled trees pointed up into the glaring sky.

Against this spare and unrelenting background, Stern meets a major whom he at first views as "what you expected of a good C.O. . . . You wanted an even temper and decisiveness and some intelligence." The major entreats him to rule that the suicide was the result of temporary insanity, so that insurance money will be paid to the surviving family. Stern agrees, while actually believing that the true cause was "the whole catechism of loneliness while you were shut on this worthless acre and knowing that you would always have it at the tip of your mind wherever you went after this." The suicide is not a product of mental disorder but rather an honest response to a fractured and meaningless world.

"The Suicide's Cat" is an intense investigation of this breakdown of meaning. After taking in a cat left homeless by its master's suicide, Vernon Reiss begins to see the cat as somehow connected to the misfortunes that disturb his family's otherwise ordinary life. Finally Vernon decides, "The goddamn cat has got all the time in the world to wait and let you use up your time and get nothing for it."

A similar strangeness pervades "The Waiting Room." On her way back to college in Iowa City, Mary Adams expects a ten-minute wait at the Marengo Junction bus station before she is on her way back to the security of her dorm room, where she can "sleep with the knowledge that the years of anxiety . . . were quieting away behind her." She has just become engaged and feels that she is "not only going to marry a nice boy . . . but marry the solid years of the future as well." But she misses her connection and is forced to wait several hours at Marengo Junction in a waiting room that is "a dark green place and hardly lighted at all." Mary finds herself among people who seem diminished as human beings. As she waits, her perceptions become increasingly unmoored from reality. She begins to feel threatened by the others in the bus station, noticing people with missing limbs and other afflictions. Hiding in the restroom, she cuts the palm of her hand with a nail, thinking, "They'll let me out with them now." At this moment Mary is reacting to the broken world in which she finds herself, but later, as she imagines meeting her friends in the dormitory and their curiosity over her bandaged hand, she realizes, "There would be no way in this world to explain it to them, but that was all right. It seemed to her that far away in the secret of their future lives they would come to understand it and then remember."

Cassill's accounts of the human condition have been praised by noted writers such as James Dickey, who in an essay for the special Cassill issue of *December Magazine,* praises Cassill's "daring" and adds, "in his literary work there is also, central to the blooming buzzing disorder of experience, an idiosyncratic artistic scrupulousness very nearly superhuman and yet fully human. . . ." For the same issue Donald Justice wrote, "Certain passages of great dread and terror in Verlin's fiction haunt the memory. . . . His fiction has been for me full of the wisdom and the awfulness of experience." Cassill has created a fictive world full of wisdom and terror in short fiction that exhibits polished technique and solid structure. Cassill's emphasis on the human alienation from true knowledge of self or others marks his stories as his own. He believes that fiction writing is the one art "which most broadly connects the homely, private, errant, ridiculous and immature phases of our lives with the ripened abstractions of philosophy. . . . The type of consciousness invested in and replenished by fiction is simply the realistic orientation of the race to being and nothingness." His characters' search for an orientation to "being and nothingness" is Cassill's signature; his reputation as a short-story writer rests on his depictions of this existential dilemma.

References:

Kay Cassill, Orin E. Cassill, and Curt Johnson, eds., *R. V. Cassill,* special issue of *December Magazine,* 23, nos. 1–2 (1981);

David Roberts, "The Short Fiction of R. V. Cassill," *Critique: Studies in Modern Fiction,* 10 (1966): 56–70.

Papers:

R. V. Cassill's manuscripts are in Special Collections at the Boston University Library.

Laurie Colwin

(14 June 1944 - 24 October 1992)

Patrick Meanor
State University of New York College at Oneonta

See also the Colwin entry in *DLB Yearbook 1980.*

BOOKS: *Passion and Affect* (New York: Viking, 1974); republished as *Dangerous French Mistress, and Other Stories* (London: Chatto & Windus, 1975);

Shine On, Bright & Dangerous Object (New York: Viking, 1975; London: Chatto & Windus, 1976);

Happy All the Time (New York: Knopf, 1978; London: Chatto & Windus, 1979);

The Lone Pilgrim (New York: Knopf, 1981); republished as *The Lone Pilgrim and Other Stories* (London: Collins, 1981);

Family Happiness (New York: Knopf, 1982; London: Hamilton, 1983);

Another Marvelous Thing (New York: Knopf, 1986; London: Hamilton, 1987);

Home Cooking: A Writer in the Kitchen (New York: Knopf, 1988);

Goodbye Without Leaving (New York: Poseidon Press, 1990; London: Hodder & Stoughton, 1990);

More Home Cooking: A Writer Returns to the Kitchen (New York: HarperCollins, 1993);

A Big Storm Knocked It Over (New York: HarperCollins, 1993).

Laurie Colwin (photograph by Nancy Crampton; from the dust jacket for Another Marvelous Thing, *1986)*

During her shortened life, Laurie Colwin published five novels, three collections of short stories, and two cookbooks. The major themes of her novels and short stories are love, happiness, and privacy, treated primarily within the contexts of tightly knit family structures. Within these themes, however, she also explores motifs such as the loss of innocence, the relationship between memory and romantic longing, the conflict between order and disorder, the emotional rise and fall of couples from Edenic happiness into emotional wastelands, the necessity of constructing "fictions" within which life can be understood or endured, and finally, the search for metaphors that counteract the ravages of time through art, which permanently preserves experience by making it available to memory.

Laurie Colwin was born in New York City on 14 June 1944 and raised in Chicago and Philadelphia. Her father, Peter Barnett Colwin, was a fundraiser and director of the United Jewish Appeal. Laurie Colwin attended Bard College but dropped out in 1963. She studied at Columbia University School of General Studies, but again left school, this time to work as an editor for various publishing houses, including Pantheon, Viking, Putnam, and Dutton. She also worked for literary agents Sanford Greenburger and Candida

Donadio (who later became her agent). Her literary reputation grew rapidly when her stories began to appear regularly in *The New Yorker, Mademoiselle, Cosmopolitan,* and *Redbook.* She also became the food columnist for *Gourmet Magazine;* two of her most popular publications were her best-selling cookbooks *Home Cooking: A Writer in the Kitchen* (1988) and *More Home Cooking: A Writer Returns to the Kitchen* (1993). For a time she also served as a translator for Isaac Bashevis Singer. She married Juris Jurjevics, former editor in chief of Dial Press, in 1983; they had one daughter. Colwin died suddenly of a heart attack on 24 October 1992 in Manhattan at the age of forty-eight.

Though Colwin's reputation as a writer of romantic stories with happy endings has not engendered much serious academic criticism, it is evident that her fiction treats some of the most serious philosophical–even existential–topics in contemporary literature. Some critics mistake her genuinely comic imagination for superficiality–there is little question that she is one of the funniest writers of the late twentieth century–but beneath the veneer of humor is a darkness, a sadness that runs throughout much of her fiction. Few moments of ecstatic love are completely free of the subtle intrusions of fate.

Colwin's persistent theme of privacy is usually treated within a romantic context, and sometimes becomes the issue that threatens relationships, especially in the stories in Colwin's last collection, *Another Marvelous Thing* (1986). But what regularly threatens love and happiness are the brutal onslaught of time and the relentless conflict between order and disorder. Many of her stories show couples transformed by the necessity of modifying their overly romantic ideas of true love.

Colwin began her literary career with a critically acclaimed collection of short stories, *Passion and Affect* (1974). Ten of the fourteen stories in the collection had appeared in magazines and journals such as *Anteaus, Cosmopolitan, Mademoiselle,* and *The New Yorker.* The first story in the collection, "Animal Behavior," clearly presents her most consistent theme: the relationship between love and privacy. The story concerns the world of Raiford "Roddy" Phelps, a curator for the American Naturalist Museum and a recognized authority on the social behavior of caged finches. The connection between Roddy's pet pairs of finches and his own pairing with Mary Leibnitz, a graduate student in ornithology, immediately creates a quietly comic situation and invites the reader to look upon human actions as just another form of animal behavior.

Mary accidentally wanders into the museum greenhouse and catches Roddy napping among the birdcages. His immediate response upon awakening is angry petulance: "I don't like this," he says, "being spied on . . . I don't like my privacy invaded." The greenhouse is the first of many Edenic locations found among Colwin's stories. Colwin uses John Cheever's favorite literary technique, "mythologizing the commonplace," almost as frequently as he did. In this garden a Peruvian assistant and janitor, Mr. Flores (whose last name means "flowers"), captures escaped birds and places them gently back into their cages. Roddy quips: "He's a regular Francis of Assisi." Other mythic references abound in the setting: "Her [Mary's] apartment looked over a garden in whose center a cement Cupid with a broken-off right arm was standing in a pool of watery dead leaves. . . . In the corner of the garden grew a catalpa tree, whose dried pods hung like snakeskins amid green emerging buds. . . . 'It's bliss here,' Roddy said." Even Roddy unconsciously acknowledges the landscape of Eden in which a seduction is taking place. The fact that Roddy is married (and suffering from the depressing effects of the recent separation from his wife, Garlan) transforms the pods like snakeskins into traces of the tempting serpent.

Colwin continues to mythologize the commonplace when Mary descends into Roddy's wasteland home:

> His apartment was on the ground floor of a dingy brick building near the river. In the living room was an aluminum work table, piled with paper, two cheap chairs and a matching sofa. . . . In the kitchen was a small Bunsen burner and a pegboard hung with hammers, ratchets, wrenches, and drills. On the Formica sideboard was an acid beaker that functioned as coffeemaker.

The contrast between the two homes could hardly be more striking: Mary's is Cupid's abode in an Edenic setting, while Roddy's is a Hawthornean, Hades-like science lab in which a passionate affair ensues and happiness transforms their lives.

As their relationship develops, Roddy begins to analyze their seemingly perfect affair and, in classic Colwin fashion, his intellectualizing begins to create doubts about the durability of love. Roddy's happiness is so intense that he begins to feel unworthy of her love and becomes edgy and obtuse: "You are a blessing I don't deserve. I'm trying to see what this will look like in memory. . . . We're not living in real time." Mary protests the dark direction that Roddy's self-defeating philosophizing is taking him; he is haunted by time, the most durable destructive force for Colwin's characters. In spite of Mary's heartbreaking protestations, Roddy continues to speak of their love in apocalyptic terms: "I want to maintain the time we have. . . . The earth spins on its axis and everything changes. You can't freeze things, not things as delicate as this, and hope they'll survive a thaw." Mary vigorously asserts that time need not become the ultimate enemy: "Time is the easiest thing in the world to arrange." When Roddy blames the "messy world" for destroying their relationship, Mary announces the major lesson of the story: "You're not talking about the world. You're talking about yourself. The world is outside us. This is an inside job." Colwin thus lucidly presents another of her recurring themes: the inability or unwillingness to distinguish the outside (objective) from the inside (subjective)–passion from affect–becomes a consistent conflict throughout many of her stories.

Roddy seems unable to envision great, passionate love as a permanent condition; it seems too good to be true and simply cannot last: "Look, life has lots of holes in it. This is going to get worse, not better. That's why all this time was so beautiful." Their affair ends when Roddy returns from a trip and ignores her: "When two months passed, she realized he was going to do nothing about her and she was filled with a sense of pain so intense it astonished her."

One of the many ways Colwin's characters assuage the pain of lost love, or the lovers' fall from their perfect Eden into a time-bound wasteland, is to seek out the consolations of art and myth for their healing properties. In her agony, Mary searches among permanent images and artifacts for emotional sustenance:

> She fled to one of the galleries. A group of quiet children was standing in front of a bronze stork. At the far end of the gallery was a small tapestry behind a glass shield. A brass plaque announced that it had been woven by the nuns of Belley in the sixteenth century. In the lush green field . . . was a heron–pure white and slightly lopsided. . . . As she walked closer, she saw that on its face was embroidered an expression of almost human mournfulness. The room filled up behind her as she stood. Tears came into her eyes and her mouth twisted. When she turned, the room was swimming with children.

Mary is able to connect her sorrow with anonymous sixteenth-century French nuns because of the ability of art to make the transitory eternal and relevant, a gift of the imagination that enables human beings to transcend their animal behavior.

This first story in Colwin's first book treats three themes that recur regularly through all of her story collections: the fall of an innocent into the realization of time as the destructive element; the function of art in redeeming time; and the transformation of one person's paradise into another person's wasteland or hell. It is also clear that Roddy's exclusive sense of privacy reveals his inability to see that only love, passion, and the power of the imagination can redeem him from his overwhelming sense of time-bound unworthiness–actually a form of guilt.

The story "Dangerous French Mistress" depicts protagonist Phillip Hartman as sharing similar psychological and emotional weaknesses with Roddy Phelps, especially the limited ability to understand the mysteries of life only in rational terms. This work is also one of Colwin's few stories narrated in the first person by a male. Phillip teaches aesthetics at an unnamed college that resembles Columbia University. Like many of Colwin's characters, he is still working on his dissertation and is in frequent contact with his director, Professor Alden Marshall. Phillip inherited a large and expensive apartment from a lady admirer and shares expenses with a young and charming Egyptian Barnard professor, Anwar P. Soole. Hartman's surname belies his character–he is not a man of the heart and is emotionally threatened by even the hint of strong passion. He is a scholar and lives an obsessively ordered life. He plans to marry an American woman he met in Paris, Jane Pinkham, and he characterizes her as he does himself: "mild, scholarly, cerebral. 'Intellectual sensualists' is the term the girl in Paris invented for people like us."

Into his well-ordered realm enters a major agent of disorder, Lilly Gillette, whose first name ironically embodies the innocence she lost long ago. She is typing the book that Phillip and Alden Marshall are finishing and shows up at the apartment unannounced one day. She immediately seduces Phillip with barely a word, and they continue their strictly sexual relationship until she quits working for Alden. She lets herself in; they make love; and she leaves immediately. Phillip accepts her sexual role in his life with equanimity but little enthusiasm. Problems arise only when she introduces disorder into Phillip's life. After each encounter Phillip finds his books–always neatly and logically arranged–out of order. He initially blames the cleaning woman, who adamantly denies the charge; but chaos pushes him to the edge of despair: "I felt I had been vandalized maliciously, gratuitously. Although my books stood gleaming on the shelves, none of them missing, they were out of order." After he confronts Lilly, she casually admits that she took them off the shelves to peruse them and simply forgot to put them back in their proper place; her explanation does little to assuage Phillip's sense of violation. His overreaction disturbs him to such an extent that he begins to question the basis of his relationship with Lilly.

As with many of Colwin's agonized protagonists, Phillip attempts to find a rational explanation: "If this had happened to someone else, and had been told to me as a story . . . if I could *see* it, I would have . . . said: 'Things like this happen in books and movies, not in

Dust jacket for Colwin's 1974 book, stories in which she began exploring the themes of love and privacy

my life.'" Earlier in the story, Anwar had suggested that Phillip needed some romance in his life and had read to him an account from a Parisian newspaper about a French mistress who had wrecked the car of her lover: "That's what you need, Filipo, . . . a nice dangerous French mistress type, cut from the pages of *France-Soir*." Phillip cannot make the connection and so continues to search for a "story" that might satisfy his rage for order.

During his search he asks Lilly why she had initially come to him. She coolly explains that it was actually Anwar she had been looking for because she had been carrying on an extended affair with him: "He had gone to school and she had simply transferred herself to me." Though her explanation should restore order to Phillip's life, it does not. Even after Lilly ends her visits, he feels compelled to find a "literary" form to unravel the mystery of their relationship: "If I think about it it is like a dark fairy tale in which the magic word is said and the riches disappear, except there were no riches to disappear." Only by envisioning the affair through the lens of a fairy tale can he begin to understand what it meant to him and what role he played in it: "Did I misunderstand, perform a cruelty? Was she in some form of acute distress and I unable to help her?" Once he asks these questions, he begins to move beyond his narrow, narcissistic life; and there may be some dim hope that he may someday discover a world outside his own limited imagination, even though her disconcerting presence in his life had been "only one short step away from carnage and chaos."

While "The Water Rats" bears little resemblance to the characters and situations in "Dangerous French Mistress" and "Animal Behavior," the main character, Max Waltzer, is obsessed with the order of his household. Just as Lilly's careless handling of Phillip's books activated his terror of disorder, Max's fear of water rats transforms him into a medieval knight defending his home from a barbaric siege. Max and his family are genuinely happy and prosperous in their large, comfortable, and expensive home on Long Island Sound. He sends his family to New York City while he and a neighbor declare war on some water rats that have invaded the water line on his property. Clearly, Max views his home as his paradise, and he is willing to go to any lengths to protect his family from these rodents, which begin to take on symbolic dimensions far beyond physical threat.

Max is thrown into chaos after his family departs: "Alone he felt suspended between restlessness and calm. Even when Alice and the children were there, he thought about them constantly. He felt that they lived in his heart . . . he felt his life was filled with a loveliness so intense he wondered how he contained it . . . he couldn't get over them." His fear of the rats grows far beyond reasonable bounds. Max patrols his home three times a day with a gun, but he is nonetheless assailed with a terrifying sense of the fragility of life and an obsession with his absent family's well-being. He begins to see that this anxiety is the price he must pay for such a happy and fulfilling life. The story reaches its climax when Max moves to the edge of the water, aiming his gun at what turns out to be a harmless raccoon, and he realizes that his fears have disengaged him from reality: "he walked to the edge of the water, knelt down, and began to cry. Then he got up and hurled the gun out into the sound as far as he could throw."

Roddy Phelps ruins his happiness by his dark, deterministic worldview and blames "time" for causing him to feel unworthy of love. Though Max Waltzer–who has up to this point blithely "waltzed" through life–flirts with similar kinds of self-destructive rationalizations, he is saved when he sees that his imagination has created this absurd scenario and that the water rats of his own mind are much more dangerous than the actual ones. The principal revelation of the story is that Max discovers the true nature of his fear: it is an "inside job."

Both "The Girl with the Harlequin Glasses" and the title story of *Passion and Affect* became the central stories upon which Colwin built her second novel, *Happy All the Time* (1978). Guido Morris and Vincent Cardworthy first appear in these two stories as best friends who shared privileged childhoods. They are affluent, fashionably bored, upper-middle-class denizens of New York City who hold pleasantly nondemanding jobs: Vincent with the city of New York, and Guido with a private foundation. Guido is temporarily separated from his wife, Holly, who is traveling in Europe with her mother. When she returns in "Passion and Affect," she insists that they move to another apartment: "I don't think we should live amongst our separateness. . . . It means that this is where we started, and this is where things didn't work out. Besides I never liked the kitchen."

The major event in "The Girl with the Harlequin Glasses" is that Misty Berkowitz and Vincent fall in love, but not before Misty creates havoc in his life by her seemingly callous behavior toward him. When Guido demands to know why she treats Vincent that way, Misty explains: "He has an easy life. Part of my function is to give him a hard time. It makes him feel alive. . . . He gets what he deserves, and he gets what he wants. We all do."

The relationships of both couples deepen significantly in "Passion and Affect," and this story is one of the first that established Colwin's reputation as a writer of romantic comedies. While love is the principal theme of the story, the behaviors of the characters are genuinely amusing. Misty becomes even more puzzling in this story because Vincent does not seem to understand how crucial Misty's privacy is to her sense of identity. When he pressures her to let him know exactly how deeply she loves him, she cannot believe that he has not been able to read her signals: "Wasn't he a cretin not to know how loaded every one of her gestures was? . . . Accused of nastiness, Misty said to Vincent: 'If I expressed even a small amount of my tenderness, I'd be sobbing on your shoes eighteen hours a day. Don't you know when you got a good deal?'" She warns him that she does not respond the way most women do to romantic love. Once the emotional ice is broken by Misty's courageous candor and she explains the importance of privacy in her life, she and Vincent embrace and make plans to marry: "In love with Vincent, she was willing and almost helpless, to love Holly, Guido, the rugs on the floor, the postman, telephone operators." For Misty, love can never be an abstraction: it must be specific to one person, and once that occurs she can allow herself to embrace the world and, in effect, release herself from the prison of her fragile and overprotective privacy.

Though the next story, "The Man Who Jumped into the Water," seems at first to be about two teenagers in love, it is actually about the emotional and spiritual mentoring of two young people by an older, caring adult. The unnamed narrator is a teenage girl who seems to be in love with Jeremy Flowers, who is going off to Dartmouth at the end of the summer. The main character, however, is the narrator's neighbor, Charlie Hartz, who has built a large swimming pool in back of his home. The pool becomes a neighborhood center and a kind of refuge for teenagers seeking privacy. Charlie loves to initiate diving contests for his guests, and his own specialty is diving with "a solemn clumsiness." Mythically, the pool is an Edenic location where time stands still and people can be themselves; and Charlie, as "the man who jumps into the water," is the only character in the story who is in touch with the vital energies of life, serving as an ideal for the narrator and Jeremy to ponder.

Charlie's last name, Hartz, is a fairly transparent symbol of the love and concern that he shows for the confused couple, and he becomes the archetypal wise guide. He asks honest questions of the narrator: "Is your heart going to break when the White Hope goes off to Dartmouth?" Charlie is also the only adult to accurately analyze Jeremy's character flaws and offer some solutions: "that punk's got a great future ahead of him if he can tell his parents to go to hell and someone don't knock him off for his affectations." The narrator explains why young people trust Charlie in spite of his directness: "We wondered why we took it, and we did because Charlie found some mutual ground between you and him, and fought an honest battle there." The narrator's uptight father criticizes Charlie because he does not seem to take anything seriously: "but it never occurred to me then that he was the only person I have ever known who knew how to play, and he put himself entirely into what he was doing. He rarely laughed, but when he did it was like a meal."

Charlie also allows the teenagers unlimited use of the pool even when he is not at home; understanding the urgency of teenage desire, he allows the pool to become a place where temptation could occur. Imitating Adam in the garden, Jeremy suggests to the narrator that they should swim naked, which they do; but they preserve their innocence: "We became very modest, and dressed in the garage with our backs to each other."

However, the narrator's devastating fall from innocence comes when she hears that Charlie has committed suicide. Her sister tells her the grim facts: "He shot himself this morning in the car." No note was found, nor were any of the usual reasons for suicide uncovered: "his business was in order . . . his health was good." When the narrator calls Jeremy to beg him to come home for the funeral–he had adamantly refused when his family told him the news–he is semi-hysterical and shocks her with his dark interpretation of the suicide:

> "It's corny," he said. His voice was ragged. He was very near tears. "Don't you know where he did it? He drove to Paradise Lane. *Paradise Lane.* That's very corny. He did it deliberately." He went on and on, about how Paradise Lane was the suicide note he didn't leave and about how it was an existential gesture. He was babbling and I was crying.

Not only has the suicide severely damaged the narrator's fragile innocence, but the possibility that Charlie planned it as a grotesque gesture exacerbates her despair to an almost unbearable degree. She confronts her father with Jeremy's cynical view of the suicide and asks him if it could have been Charlie's last joke on human existence, that he killed himself on Paradise Lane: "He looked at me with the sort of worldliness that spans humor and outrage. 'Not a damn thing,' he said. 'Just a place to park his car.'" Colwin leaves the answer to the reader; whatever drove Charlie to his desperate act has gone with him to the grave. His last and most intimate secret will remain utterly private. By the conclusion of the story, its title takes on a much deeper significance: Charlie's jump into the water becomes his leap into the existential abyss of a meaningless world. Though Colwin is usually thought of as an inveterate celebrant of love and happiness, several of her stories in this first collection are often dark meditations on loss, the failure of love, self-delusion, and the necessity of fictions–themes that occur regularly in the work of the author to whom Colwin is most often compared, John Cheever. Certainly "The Man Who Jumped into the Water" can be read as her version of one of Cheever's most famous stories, "The Swimmer" (1964).

Even more unflattering than her portrait of Phillip Hartman in "Dangerous French Mistress" is Colwin's depressing depiction of Professor Richard Burr in "A Road in Indiana." The aptly named Burr is her clearest indictment of a cold, emotionally disengaged, intellectual male who psychologically and emotionally abuses his wife, Patricia. He, like Phillip, is obsessed with order, and teaches Shakespeare at a large, unnamed university in Indiana. Patricia, an Easterner, feels lost in the Midwest, and adding to her feelings of homesickness are notes from her husband on the refrigerator: "P. Fac. meeting today. Home 6:30 or thereabouts. Fridge filthy, I might add. R."

Patricia has, however, found one consolation in the flat, dull landscape of the Midwest: "Rod McClosky was Patricia's only happy discovery in Indiana." McClosky's country-western music immediately appeals to Patricia; it is the kind of emotionally open music she has never noticed before. She becomes deeply attached to McClosky's latest hit album, *Closing Doors,* and plays it repeatedly. The title song laments lost love and unfulfilled longing, two of Colwin's most important concerns throughout her stories. When Richard returns home from teaching, Patricia plays the album for him, hoping that he will be similarly moved by its heartfelt melancholy. Instead, he asks her not to play it when he is home. In spite of her husband's icy rejection, Patricia listens to it even more, allowing it to speak to her emotional turmoil: "The guitar was so sharp that Patricia felt her heart being sliced. Tears came into her eyes. . . . She was dazzled and rapt, anxious to memorize all the songs at once."

The title of the album becomes a metaphor for Patricia's relationship with her husband, whom she had met when she was an undergraduate and he was her graduate student instructor. She had believed that he possessed "a higher wisdom, and that her own chief flaw was failure of vision." In spite of Richard's accusa-

Dust jacket for Colwin's second novel (1978), which developed from two stories in Passion and Affect

tion that listening to McClosky's music is a form of "emotional sloppiness," she continues to be moved by its powerful emotional effect, and the lyrics depict her condition quite accurately. She has tried unsuccessfully to read the book Richard begged her to read, Charles Dickens's *Bleak House* (1852–1853), another title that defines the dismal emotional climate of their domestic life. Richard also demands absolute quiet after dinner so he can work on his novel in progress, "Pain in Its Simplicity," a title that, once again, describes their life together. Colwin rarely loses an opportunity to add comic touches even in serious stories such as "A Road in Indiana."

One particular incident defines Richard's emotional cruelty: it is about a birthday gift that Patricia purchases for him. The gift is an expensive used set of the Arden edition of Shakespeare, and she secretly takes a part-time typing job to earn the necessary funds. When she gives it to him, he insists on knowing where she acquired the money and rejects the gift because it is much too expensive. He wants her to return it, but she cannot because it is used. His explanation as to why he cannot accept it is the epitome of arrogant psychobabble: "If you wanted to work, you should work for *you,* not to get things for me. It's a way of buying me. I couldn't possibly keep this knowing that you worked at some awful job to get it for me. It's slavish. . . . I want you to do things for Pat." His inane explanation convinces Patricia that nothing can improve their disintegrating relationship; and when she observes Richard spending the evening rearranging his books to find a fitting place for his Arden Shakespeare, she knows that the marriage is over. Once more he derides her for her taste in music, characterizing her devotion to McClosky's songs as "childish ennui." She breaks the record into pieces and escapes to her car for a long recuperative drive. Following her instinct, she stops to buy another copy of *Closing Doors* and finds herself heading east out of Indiana and, apparently, out of her emotionally stifling marriage.

"A Road in Indiana" interweaves several typical Colwinian themes. Richard, the icy intellectual, insists on order and tries to impose it on his wife's "emotional sloppiness" and "childish ennui." In doing so, he callously dismisses her deepest private needs and denies music one of its principal purposes: to speak to her soul in ways that *Bleak House* cannot. Patricia discovers that she is willing to give up the security and safety of being a faculty wife, and she determines to follow the private dictates of her heart. The lesson of *Closing Doors* is that she has to close the door on this emotionally suffocating marriage in order to discover her own identity.

Probably the strongest stories from *Passion and Affect* in terms of theme and character are the last two in the collection, "Wet" and "The Big Plum." Though "Wet" is one of Colwin's shortest works, it is one of her most effective statements on the importance of privacy. The protagonists are Lucy and Carl, who met at Harvard, where he was completing his doctorate in history and she was working on the *Law Review.* Though the story opens on his first day of teaching at a university in Chicago, the focus is immediately on Lucy's love affair with swimming: "Lucy was a born swimmer: she had been in the water as an infant and swam without water wings by the time she was three." Though Carl and Lucy are deeply in love, her swimming is a separate and distinct activity that she shares with no one, not even her husband. Though she has never tried to hide this pleasure from Carl, he is shocked when he accidentally discovers that she has gone swimming every day since their arrival in Chicago; though he decides not to confront her, his imagination magnifies his feeling of being left out of her private life: "all that time and she had never said a word about it. . . . It seemed so deliberate, so concealed and contrived–it broke his heart to think about it."

After following her to the pool and surreptitiously observing her swimming alone, he casually asks her at dinner that night if he could swim with her the next day; she happily agrees, and all of his confused fear disappears. Later, though, the emotional impact of his inner turmoil erupts when he takes out the garbage: "When the wind hit him suddenly, he leaned against the railings and, to his own amazement, wept." Carl finally understands that Lucy's swimming alone constitutes the core of her spiritual center, a region where she can be herself completely. He can now calmly observe her sleeping in his arms and not feel excluded, even though "she was dreaming in private." Carl can now begin to grow out of his adolescent need to control every aspect of Lucy's life. Her name–which means "light"–becomes a suitable metaphor for Carl's painful revelation: that he is not the sole concern of her life. This story demonstrates Carl's desire for control–a symptom of his need to maintain order–in conflict with Lucy's need for privacy.

The concluding story in *Passion and Affect* is one of the longer ones in the collection. It is also the most psychologically complex, and it is simultaneously the funniest and most serious story in the book. "The Big Plum" is about perception and, in that sense, can be classified as an existential or even phenomenological study. But it is also a story about privacy. The protagonist, Harry Markham, is even more emotionally greedy than the darkly obsessional Richard of "A Road in Indiana," because Harry, though with none of Richard's icy cruelty, tries to coerce an employee, Binnie Chester, into enacting his "fiction" of her personal history and making it "real." Harry seems blind to what he is trying to accomplish, however, and treats the situation as semihumorous. Binnie understands from the onset of his questions exactly what he is after.

Harry Markham is managing his family-owned The Big Plum Supermarket while finishing his doctoral dissertation in art history, titled "Vermeer and the Art of the Impossible." Harry has become obsessed with one of the checkout girls, Binnie, at whom he stares day after day from his manager's perch:

> In his mind he referred to her as the Miracle of Rare Device. She cracked gum authoritatively, and when the supermarket was quiet, Harry could hear it. He had discovered that if he hummed the first movement of the Boccherini cello concerto, she was generally on beat. He wondered what she was cracking time to.

As Harry surveys his world from his panoptic guard tower, he unconsciously assumes the role of the objective artist–a position that places him, he assumes, outside the obligations of time, space, and human contact. What he does not seem to understand is that he is confusing life with his fictions about life, a risk that artists and intellectuals continually run.

Harry's imagination is so fertile that he begins creating scenarios about Binnie's life:

> he had fantasized that she lived in Brooklyn, in an old house of ruined elegance, which had thin lace curtains. Binnie's father . . . was a tall, rakish man with Edwardian sideburns. . . . There was a grandmother, too, a faded, shapeless woman who gazed blankly, but tragically, out the window. . . . There was no Binnie's mother. She had died in some way he had not yet worked out. This made him feel tender and protective toward Binnie.

Harry's obsession becomes so demanding that he arranges to meet Binnie after work. Then his fiction of her as an ignorant, naive shop girl begins to collide with reality. Acting on invented information he mistakes for facts, Harry offers to walk Binnie to her father's house in Brooklyn, until she explains that she lives around the corner and that her father lives in Minneapolis with her mother; she has no grandparents. He is so confused that he accuses her of making fun of him, and she calmly responds: "Listen, Big Plum Markham. You follow me out of your father's store and tell me I live in Brooklyn with my father and grandmother, and then you ask *me* if I'm making fun of you?" After Harry lamely explains that these were assumptions on his part, she asks: "Have you considered a career in fiction?"

After she invites him up to her apartment for a cup of tea, she sardonically enters his romantic fictions when he comments on the spareness of her living-room furniture: "My Edwardian father took it all away." Harry, whose fictions have been damaged, insists on pursuing the actual "facts" of her life. Her response is: "My father is a spy and my mother is a zookeeper. My granny teaches Anglo-Saxon at the University of Uruguay." Though Harry confesses to feeling "sullied and ridiculous," he continues to push for information about her life. At this point the story becomes more than simply a lighthearted tale about an abstracted intellectual: it becomes a psychological case history of an invasion of privacy. Lost in his "version" of her, he continues not only to probe into her private life but also to rewrite her life and, thus, to re-create her in his own image: "Do you have any pearl earrings in the shape of a pear, a sort of round pear? . . . Because there is a painting of a girl who looks just like you, and she has on earrings like that." Binnie is further offended by being treated like an object in a painting and shows him to the door.

The following day, Harry continues to press her for information about her private life, so she decides to play along with his benighted condition and gives him two different versions of her life so that Harry can pick the one he likes best: "Now take the one you want and finish your little dissertation about yourself. . . . Whichever suits you. It's your dissertation. Have both. It has nothing to do with me anyway. . . . I'm very serious." Her bold challenge confuses and troubles Harry deeply, and he begins to question himself in ways he had never done before: "He wondered what he did want to know, and why, and why so much." Binnie's refusal to allow her privacy to be violated forces him to reexamine all of his assumptions about what constitutes "reality."

Though it is one of Colwin's longest and funniest stories, "The Big Plum" shows her work moving into deeper philosophical questions about appearance and reality and the dangers of intellectual abstractions. Harry's blindness threatens not only his relationship with others but also his ability to perceive and understand the world in terms other than his own subjective ones. His penchant for imposing the order of his fictions–which he cannot recognize as fictions–on the chaos of the world as viewed from his Olympian perch of the Big Plum moves him dangerously close to living in his own solipsistic realm. Harry also runs the risk of becoming another Colwinian emotionally disengaged intellectual like Roddy Phelps, Phillip Hartman, and Richard Burr.

The only emotionally open, intellectual male in *Passion and Affect* is the vulnerable cartographer Richard Mignon of "Children, Dogs, and Desperate Men." (*Mignon* in French means "dainty" or "sweet.") Unfortunately for the protagonist of the story, Elizabeth Bayard, Mignon is unavailable as a potential lover because he is married, has children, and is a good-natured but nonetheless desperate alcoholic.

Colwin wrote and published two novels between *Passion and Affect* and her second collection of stories, *The Lone Pilgrim.* The first novel, *Shine On, Bright & Dangerous Object* (1975), tells the romantic story of a widow, Elizabeth Bax, whose daredevil husband, Sam, dies in a sailing accident. She then falls helplessly in love with Sam's brother, Patrick, and problems abound. Colwin's second novel, *Happy All the Time,* grew out of "The Girl with the Harlequin Glasses" and "Passion and Affect." While many of the same themes of *Passion and Affect* resurface throughout *The Lone Pilgrim*–privacy, the conflict between order and disorder, the loss of innocence, the necessity of fictions, and love and happiness–Colwin also includes stories about adultery, the past, and longing.

The stories in *The Lone Pilgrim* are generally longer and more carefully developed; they are also darker, more introspective, and psychologically complex, and in several instances they are quite consciously mythical. As a result, these stories are more intellectually challenging and emotionally richer than most of those from *Passion and Affect.* Love, her major preoccupation, becomes considerably more complicated and painful in the later stories because many of them deal with what psychologist James Hillman calls "the suffering of impossible love." Colwin's most perceptive critic, Amy Richlin, correctly claims: "This longing for what you cannot have lies at the center for Colwin. . . . Her texts are *about* the intersection of pleasure with romance and comment as they go on the aesthetic satisfaction of romantic pain–the beauty of longing."

A necessary component of romantic pain is the solitude that many of her suffering women share even in the midst of ostensibly happy family lives; their loneliness makes these stories darker but richer. Colwin's exploration of solitude and loneliness, one of the principal themes in the history of the American short story, puts her in the ranks of nineteenth-century writers such as Edgar Allan Poe and Henry James and twentieth-century exponents of the form such as Cheever, Raymond Carver, and Richard Bausch. Many of their characters, along with Colwin's, suffer from what G. K. Chesterton called "the morbid life of the lonely mind."

Certainly Paula Rice in the title story comes as close as any Colwin character to embodying the "morbid life of the lonely mind." Paula (Polly) analyzes her plight with brutal honesty: "The solitary mind likes to reflect on the pain of past love. If you are all alone, it gives you something to react to, a sort of exercise to keep the muscles flexed." Polly is an illustrator for children's books and characterizes herself as "a charming girl . . . a housepet to several families, I have an acute sensitivity to the individual rhythms of family life. I blend in perfectly without losing myself." Her life as an artist reinforces her need for order, although early in the story she questions herself as to why she is so solitary. Polly's life changes radically when she meets and falls in love with Gilbert Seigh, a publisher and editor of fine editions, whose family has been in the business for three generations. He wants Polly to illustrate two texts that virtually defined romantic love for the Western psyche: *Liber de arte honeste amandi et reprobatione inhonesti amoris* (*The Art of Courtly Love,* ca. 1185) by Andreas Capellanus, and an edition of the works of Marie de France, whose thirteenth-century collections of poems about unrequited love also helped formulate the tradition of romantic love in Europe in the Middle Ages.

Though Gilbert is divorced, he has been keeping company with a lady attorney, a circumstance that makes loving him seem impossible. However, Polly begins doing her best work for Gilbert because she has fallen in love with him. Two of the rules of the courtly love tradition were that the relationship with the beloved be nonsexual and adulterous. The lover could only yearn for or sigh after the beloved–certainly a pun on Gilbert's surname, Seigh. Predictably, her unrequited desire works to her benefit both emotionally and artistically: "Being in love with him brought me all the things in life I counted on: a sense of longing, something to turn over in my mind, and that clear slightly manic vision you get with unrequited love."

Strangely enough, all the time she is dedicating her work to Gilbert, she is haunted by the memory of a painful affair three years earlier with a man named Jacob Baily: "It was love at once–hot, intense, brilliant, and doomed to fail." Though she is still mourning its painful conclusion, she realizes that the experience changed her: "I worked with what I felt was new depth, and carried Jacob around as a secret in my heart." As a result she learns why nineteenth-century poets treated love as a disease. And while illustrating Marie de France's poems–"poems about love in vain"–she often thinks of Jacob and longs for his passionate love.

A delightful surprise at the conclusion of the story is that Gilbert confesses that he too had fallen in love with Polly; they decide to marry within a year. The last pages of the story present a new twist in Colwin's fiction. Polly reflects at length on how lost love qualifies her as a "lone pilgrim" searching for love but at the same time learning to live in a condition of permanent longing. She worries that once married to Gilbert, she will have nothing to long for. Sometimes "fulfillment leaves an empty space where your old self used to be, the self that pines and broods and reflects. . . . What is left to you?" Polly seems to be afraid of letting go of all the despair that has constituted the center of her life up to then. This story is one of many in the collection demonstrating that Colwin's art was becoming more complex and mature.

In "The Boyish Lover" she brings back a character type she had examined closely in three earlier stories in *Passion and Affect:* the cerebral intellectual who has not the remotest notion of what genuine romance–true love–might entail. Further, what Roddy Phelps of "Animal Behavior" and Cordy Spaacks of "The Boyish Lover" share is a deeply masochistic streak that will not allow them to maintain a permanent loving relationship with a woman. The same emotionally crippled character type reappears in the person of Andrew Dilks in "The Smile Beneath the Smile."

Again, Colwin uses names to define character. The etymological root of Cordy Spaacks's first name is the Latin word *cor* or *cordis,* meaning "heart," the symbol of love; yet, love is an emotional condition that Cordy seems utterly incapable of understanding on any level. Once his icy parents appear, however, there seems to be no secret as to how he became a "heartless" lover.

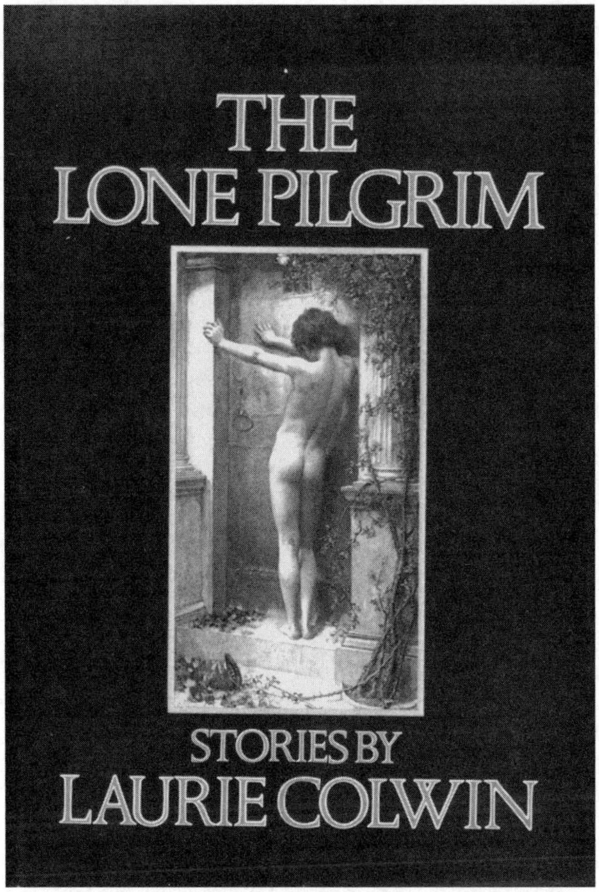

Dust jacket for Colwin's 1981 book, stories that depict love, adultery, and longing

Cordy is a physics professor still working on his dissertation when he meets Jane Mayer, an English professor who teaches at the same university. Cordy is recently divorced and comes from a wealthy family with multiple residences throughout the East. Though Jane's love for him is genuine, part of it comes from her pity for his loveless childhood. Because of that, she sees their relationship as a kind of union of opposites: "Fate had handed her the perfect other." They fall in love and begin an ardent affair. As in "Animal Behavior," their homes become metaphors for their emotional conditions: Cordy's apartment is a wasteland full of Salvation Army detritus; Jane's is Eden "crammed with artifacts: watercolors, family photographs in velvet frames, teapots, pitchers, and beautiful plates."

What appeals to Jane most about Cordy is that he is "a man deprived, and there is no greater magnet for a generous woman than a deprived man." As the relationship continues, though, she begins to see that Cordy regards romance and marriage as mutually exclusive, and she becomes troubled and angry over his penuriousness: there is no generosity of any kind in the man.

She tells him, after he accuses her of living above her means, that he lives in "a needlessly horrible way." He explains: "I live simply. . . . It's very dangerous to become used to luxury." She counters with: "You have a mania for deprivation." He then reveals his real attitude toward life when he criticizes her need to create a warm and comfortable home: "The point is that things give you a false sense of life. If you have a nice house, you begin to think that life *is* nice." When Jane asks, "Isn't it?," Cordy responds, "Not for long."

After this exchange their relationship starts to unravel as they fight over "meeting places, time spent together, and the cost of lambchops." Though they both confess their undying adoration for each other, Cordy insists on ending the relationship; and Jane realizes that his masochism obligates him to deprive himself of her love: "To feel that you have never been given a present is almost as good as having been neglected. Cordy thrived on this form of loss." Colwin called the story "The Boyish Lover" because she considered Cordy's deprivation a form of adolescent self-pity and thus a sign of emotional immaturity and fear of what happiness might bring.

Though one of the shortest stories in the collection, "A Girl Skating" is undoubtedly one of Colwin's most impressive works. Its theme is, not surprisingly, privacy, but a kind of privacy deeply embedded in the innocence of childhood and early maturity. It is also the story of the relentless emotional and psychological stalking of a young girl by an older man who happens to be a nationally known poet and the unquestioned star of the college where he and her parents teach. He is also one of the family's closest friends. Richlin analyzes the story as a case of unfulfilled longing in the guise of "a meditation on the male gaze from the point of view of its object." Like Harry Markham in "The Big Plum," James Honnimer spends his life gazing longingly–and probably lustfully–but without Harry's naiveté. As Bernadette Spaeth, the object of Honnimer's gaze, puts it: "I grew up in the shadow of a great man–James Honnimer, the famous American poet." She then outlines the contours of their complex relationship from her childhood until she was twenty-two.

As an only child, Bernadette relishes her privacy the way her parents do. Though Honnimer and his wife, Lucy, are the most adored couple at the college, Bernadette hates him for his constant attention to and affection for her:

> I was the child he loved best, and there was no escaping him. . . . He was an adult and I was a child. His attentions made me more quiet and solemn than I generally was. When I did not respond as other children did, Honnimer was further delighted by what he called my "infant seriousness."

It becomes clear as her monologue continues that the poet's attentions are suffocating her emotional life. He names everything for her, a habit that deprives her of having to use her imagination. Wherever she happens to be, he somehow mysteriously appears, especially when she is practicing one of her most private activities, skating; it is the one time when she feels completely free to be herself in anonymity. When she is fifteen and skating happily at the rink, she looks up into the bleachers and sees Honnimer staring at her and obviously studying her: "Of course he published a poem called 'A Girl Skating.' That was the title of his next collection, which my parents kept on the table in the study, with all his other books."

Bernadette feels trapped within his paralyzing gaze and at his mercy emotionally: "If I withdrew, I felt him appreciating my withdrawal . . . my absence interested him . . . I felt I had another life beside the one I was living–a life in Honnimer's mind. . . . He deprived me of the right to know when I was alone." That observation explains better than any other why Colwin considered privacy so important.

Honnimer's attentions become even more emotionally threatening when he sends Bernadette his latest book of poems, *The Black Bud.* With a kind of horror, she recognizes that she is the black bud:

> Half flower, half girl wearing a dress that I realized was the one I had worn at my parents' Christmas party the year before. In the last poem, the poet took the flower to what appeared to be a motel, and removed its petals one by one. By that time in my life, I had not yet been in love. I had never had a lover or had a love affair. Honnimer's poems made me feel how my legs might move, what words I might say, how my mouth might look after hours of kissing. I could not accomplish the end of my own innocence. Honnimer had done it for me. Honnimer shot himself ten days after my twenty-second birthday.

Honnimer had become mysteriously depressed, and his wife had left him. Her parents' letter informing her of his suicide brings back the last time she saw him alive; it was at the college museum. As she was studying a painting of the Pietà and two nativity scenes, he had crept up next to her. After declaring that these, too, were his favorite, "He bent down and kissed me on the forehead. . . . I was more frightened than I had ever been. . . . As soon as he was out of the building, I walked home, rubbing the spot on my forehead where he had kissed me."

Few of Colwin's stories are so sensitively rendered as "A Girl Skating," and it concludes with an image that powerfully fuses the loss of innocence and the loss of privacy. But the story also illustrates a deeper, more sophisticated presentation of the place of art in Colwin's later work.

The later stories evolve into increasingly complex texts that include myth, paintings, Christian saints, and medieval topics as corollary but nonetheless enriching elements. By the time she wrote most of the stories in *The Lone Pilgrim* Colwin had moved beyond the witty, sophisticated, and generally lighthearted romantic love comedies about couples such as Misty Berkowitz and Vincent Cardworthy or Guido Morris and Holly Sturgis.

The story "Intimacy" is exactly what its title indicates, but it could as well be called "Solitude" or "Privacy." The story opens with the possibility of adultery between renowned archaeologist William Sutherland and a former student, Martha Howard, a happily married woman. They had been lovers six years earlier, before Martha was married and while she was a graduate student of his. Their passionately rewarding affair had lasted four weeks, and they felt fortunate that when it ended they remained friends and continued to write to each other regularly. Professional circumstances have brought them together after six years, and the story opens as they discuss the distinct possibility of renewing their amorous affair, even though Martha is quite satisfied in her marriage to Robert Howard, a successful economist who works for the Federal Trade Commission. She adores Robert, "but her desire for William had hardly died down. . . . Whatever had been between them was not past."

Martha clearly understands the awkward situation, and Colwin encapsulates the theme of the story: negotiating adultery. Before her marriage Martha's few romantic liaisons had always involved pain and suffering, usually in the form of "unrequitedness or separation"; and, once again, a Colwin character finds herself a victim of deep longing for forbidden love. In "Intimacy" the longing is intensified by the memory of their earlier affair, which had been the most fulfilling romance she had ever experienced; he had become an emotional threshold figure for her, leading her "out of the darkness and into the light." Nonetheless, her happy life with her husband grounds her: "The life she had with Robert was real life to her."

While in the process of deciding to commit adultery, Martha begins to understand the crucial significance of her decision: that it is solely her choice. She also realizes that this choice can be made only in the privacy of her own soul, the loneliest place in the world. Because she knows herself so well, she makes the right choice, because the adultery will not destroy her present happy marriage. It will deepen and enrich it: "It seemed to her the first real moment of her marriage–not her marriage to Robert, but her sense of herself as a married person." The free act of adultery has an efficacious effect on her because she realizes that the essence of her humanity derives from choices. Richlin summarizes the ameliorating effect of adultery in many of Colwin's stories: "In most of these cases, the extramarital passion acts to confirm the strength of the couples' marriage, provides a deeper love unavailable within the marriage without threatening the marriage or degrading it, and/or simply offers another pleasure in life's buffet."

However, a new pattern of furtiveness emerges in this story, because the adulterers become more consciously secretive; but their furtiveness also enables them to share their intimacies more completely. Certainly the couple in "Travel," Marguerite and her famous pianist husband, enjoy traveling together to remote and romantic locales where they can share pleasures that their professional lives will not permit. But his almost desperate need to protect his privacy is instantly recognized by Marguerite after they are married when he, a Vietnam veteran, "opened up a battered wicker case and put on the bed an ammunition pouch, a dog-eared copy of the 'Italian' Concerto, a leather-bound diary, and his army belt–his relics of war." She knows better than to pry into his past life, especially his wartime experiences. Only when they travel together can they share beloved memories "with exclusive understanding."

One of the longer and more intricately structured stories in *The Lone Pilgrim,* "Delia's Father," is about a young girl growing from childhood into adolescence; it is told in the first person. One of the narrator's classmates in their wealthy Upper East Side private school is an exotic girl named Delia Schwantes, whose mysterious family comes from Czechoslovakia. Though the name sounds German, her father came from Prague; the family's surname sounds like the German word *schwanz,* which has unmistakably phallic overtones. The focus of the story is on Delia's exotic and, it turns out, erotic father, who is rumored to have been part of a group of radical artists and poets who fought in the anti-communist resistance of 1968. Indeed, at the conclusion of the story, the narrator, Georgia Levy, after permitting him to kiss her, actually identifies him with Eros himself.

The story opens with Georgia innocently admitting that she and several of her girlfriends have crushes on both Delia and her mother, a teacher in their private school. But what mesmerizes the schoolgirls, especially as they enter adolescence, is Mr. Schwantes, a seem-

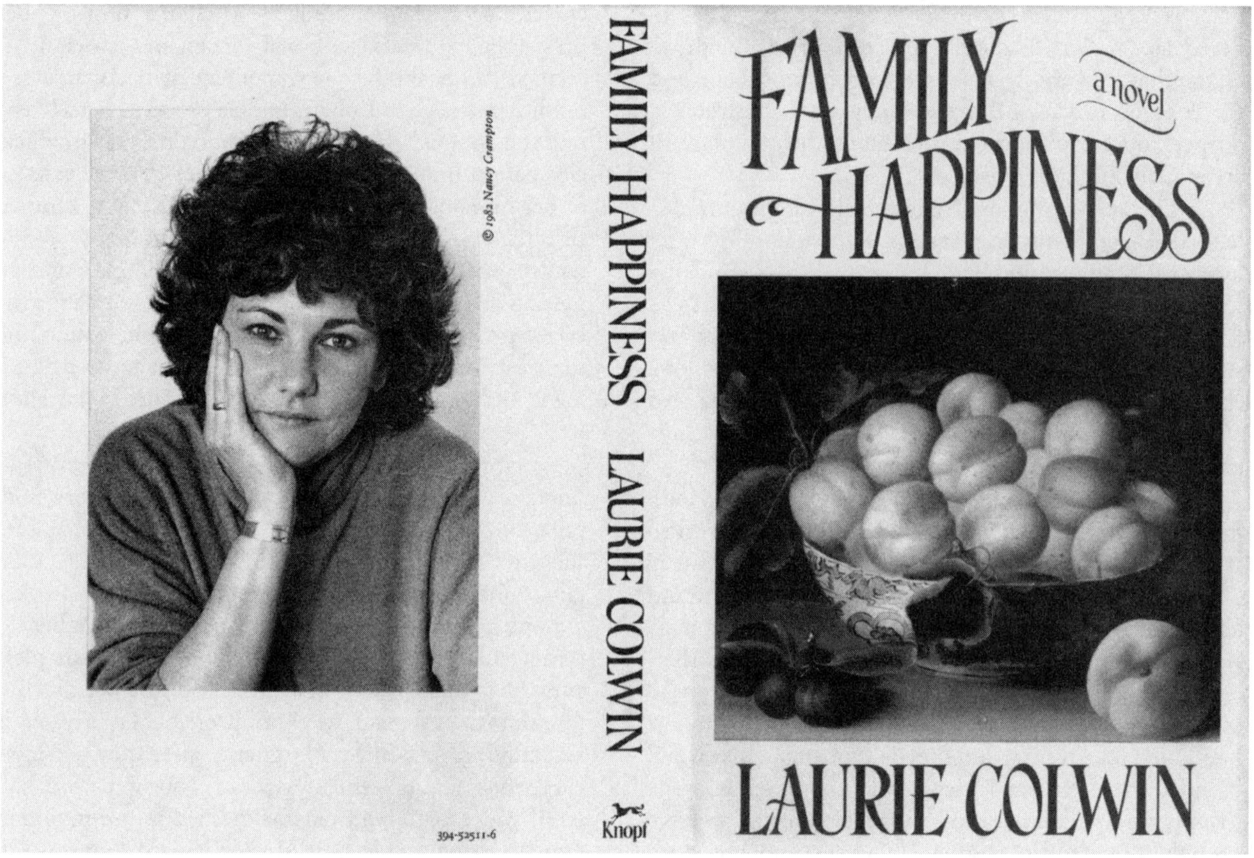

Dust jacket for Colwin's 1982 novel, an expanded version of a story in The Lone Pilgrim

ingly shiftless, utterly charming intellectual who is unemployed even though the family seems to have no money. He is regularly seen around town coming out of restaurants or cafés with a variety of women, never his wife. Everything about the family is culturally exotic, and all the young girls love to visit their home to sample the European cuisine. What Georgia notices most of all is "They were delicate. They had depth and patina like nineteenth-century pottery. Their apartment had a dark, murky golden light which suited them." They are also Roman Catholics in a predominantly Jewish and Episcopal neighborhood.

As Georgia grows into her teens, she hears stories about women who spent time with Mr. Schwantes. She wanders around her neighborhood hoping to run into him because she has fallen in love with him. They meet, and he invites her to take a walk with him. At this point Georgia begins to detect the mythic appeal beneath his Eastern European charm: "His small, beaked features seem to have been made only for seduction and observation. For some people life divides undeniably into childhood and adulthood, and I knew I was one of them. . . . He moved a step or two closer to the promenade wall, and there he kissed me as I knew he would. I kissed him back." She immediately identifies him as Eros, the sexual threshold figure, and becomes more than willing to lose her innocence: "To the virtually untouched girl I was, Eros reared up like a bobcat, clawing at its cage with great strong claws and dangerous teeth." Mythically speaking, Georgia has been seduced by Eros in a public park–an Eden–and she welcomes him with open arms. She also quite consciously acknowledges her transformation–her "happy fall"–because she no longer understands the "tribal language" of children and she knows that when she meets her former playmates, they will neither understand nor recognize her.

Colwin's unambiguous use of mythical characters and themes in "Delia's Father" should prepare the reader for the next story, "A Mythological Subject." The title is actually that of a painting by sixteenth-century painter Piero di Cosimo. The subject of the painting is Procris, the nymph accidentally slain by her husband, Cephalus, a hunter whose spear missed its mark: hearing what he thought was a wild beast in the forest, he took aim and killed his wife instead. Nellie Felix, the narrator's cousin, explains: "That picture is full of the misery and loneliness that romantic people suffer in love." However, Colwin reserves the full explanation of the title until the end of the story to give the reader a mythic analogue with which to understand the deeper meaning of the story. The main subject is Nellie's rage for order, a familiar theme throughout Colwin's stories. Nellie's surname, "Felix," means "happy" in Latin; but without order there is little happiness in her life. After two dramatic love affairs, she meets and falls in love with a lawyer, Joseph Porter: "With him Nellie found what she had been looking for. . . . Nellie believed in order, in tranquility, in her household as a safe haven." She relishes her orderly life with Porter but cannot forget that her two earlier romances had seriously threatened her emotional stability; they also revealed the part of her self that yearned for chaos. The "neat and tidy surface of things warded off misery and despair" and made her unusually vigilant about maintaining a balanced life. On her honeymoon in Barcelona, Nellie finds an objective correlative that virtually defines her philosophy of life:

> It was an ornamental fountain that shot up a constant jet of water. On top of this jet bobbed an egg. This seemed to Nellie a perfect metaphor to express the way she felt about life. Without constant vigilance, self-scrutiny, accurate self-assessment, and a strong will, whatever kept the egg of her life aloft would disappear and the egg would shatter.

Nellie, who teaches three days a week at a women's college an hour from her home in New York City, meets a fellow professor, Dan Hamilton, an historian who shares a ride with her. Almost immediately, they kiss on impulse and, after a late dinner, realize they are in love. As in most of Colwin's adulterous love stories, they are reasonably happy in their present marriages, but are sick with desire for one another. Though they decide not to go to bed with one another–both their mates are away–Nellie awakens the following day transfixed with love. Observing a buzzing fly, she is overwhelmed with the "complexities and originality of things, the riches of the world, the amazing beauty of being alive. . . . Love, even if it was doomed, gave you a renewed sense of things: it did hand life back to you." Though Nellie's tidy life suddenly looked precarious and unstable, she and Dan decide they must become lovers.

The effect of the affair on Nellie is profound because it radically divides her heart. Though she feels great emotional and moral pain, her love for Dan "opened the world up in a terrible and serious way and caused her to question everything: her marriage, her ethics, her sense of the world, herself." Every aspect of their lives becomes intensely complex and painful, except for the times they are in each other's arms. But as the indefatigably logical Nellie confesses to her narrator cousin, what torments her the most is that she can find no meaning for it; she simply cannot believe that events simply happen by chance. Falling in love, then, meant that she had been unconsciously searching for it. Then the narrator confesses that she too, though quite content in her marriage, has had several wonderful affairs during her life and is delighted that Nellie has also become a fellow adulterer: "I knew she divided the world into the cheerful slobs like me and the emotional moralists like herself." Her cousin offers Nellie an alternate view of life and love, hoping that it might open her up and lessen her dependence on order and rigidity: "I'm not beautiful and I'm not so lovable, but I'm interested in love and so it comes to find me." This idea astonishes Nellie, a proposal she has never considered.

The story ends with the narrator contemplating the exhausted and love-torn Nellie sleeping on her couch. She suddenly remembers di Cosimo's painting "A Mythological Subject" and places her beloved cousin's plight within an aesthetic context, thus discovering a new application for the ancient painting: "A love affair is like a shot arrow. It gives life an intense direction, if only for an instant. . . . Well, she had gotten what she wanted. There she lay, wiped out, fast asleep, looking wild, peaceful and troubled all at the same time. She had no dog to guard her, and no bed of wildflowers beneath her like the nymph in the painting."

The narrator understands her cousin's present dilemma more accurately when she finds the same beauty of longing rendered in an aesthetic form four hundred years old. Colwin's increasing dependence on the resonance of ancient myth expands the emotional range and thematic content of her later stories by connecting them to earlier traditions in both ancient Greek myth and Italian Renaissance paintings.

No story of Colwin's is as obsessed by the conflict between order and disorder as "Saint Anthony of the Desert," perhaps her single most accomplished story. In it she subtly interweaves many of her recurring themes with a literary maturity found in few of her earlier stories. Important secondary themes also include the loss of innocence, falling in love, and the construction of a sense of self. The first sentences of the story begin after a love affair is over and also announce the primary theme: "Haphazardness, as a condition of life, has its usefulness but is of fixed duration. At the time of which I am writing, my life was entirely the product of haphazardness, and I had encountered no reason not to enjoy it. Along with being haphazard, I was lucky." By naming the narrator Miss Greenway, Colwin is suggesting that she may possess the potential to grow and be cultivated by life experiences. As it happens, she does grow throughout the narrative, somewhat like an English garden–that is, in the most unexpected ways.

The first half of the story charts the narrator's path from disorder to order with the assistance of several wise guides who help her discover and develop parts of herself of which she was hardly conscious. Though a college graduate, she is barely able to balance her checkbook, but she somehow manages to find employment in a museum gift shop and, after two years, saves up enough money to travel to Paris to visit her cousin, an architect working for UNESCO. Since she has no direction, he sends her on a walking tour of some of the churches and cathedrals in and around Paris. She falls in love with the Benedictine Abbey of Saint Wandrille de Fontenelle, not only because of its impressive medieval architecture but also because it is filled with living Benedictine monks singing the Divine Office daily. By observing a spiritual way of life she is unfamiliar with, she begins to understand the idea of order in a fresh and compelling way.

After she returns to New York, she takes a job in a bookstore that specializes in books on travel and architecture and begins to read works on medieval monastic orders and architecture. She also loves the order of her workplace, even though her domestic life remains aimless and haphazard. She begins to understand why she is fascinated by monasticism: "I felt that this subject had the appeal of the substantial, the enduring, the traditional–three things notably lacking in my life. The idea of permanence, of a fixed course of life, was consoling to me."

Her reading reveals to her aspects of her life she has never encountered before. While Miss Greenway is reading a book titled *English Monastic Life,* an acquaintance suggests that she delve deeper into the origins of Christian monasticism, and specifically into the life of Saint Anthony of the Desert, a third-century, pre-Benedictine Egyptian desert father considered the founder of Christian monasticism. In examining Saint Anthony's life, Miss Greenway makes several important discoveries. Anthony's purpose in life was giving his wealth away to the needy; once freed from the burden of possession, he moved to the Egyptian desert to live in total solitude, a condition that enabled him to contemplate the divine mystery and to escape the temptations of the secular world. Saint Anthony created his own private hermitage; and the more the narrator reads about him, the more she identifies with him. She is also charmed by the way he warded off the devils who tormented him with the most sensuous temptations; many medieval and Renaissance paintings depict him in painful conflict with these grotesque demons. Finally, Miss Greenway comes to realize that Saint Anthony's greatest accomplishment was his genius for being–that is, his ability to exist in serenity and peace in his own garden in the desert of the world.

Through her aptly named friends, the Bridges, she meets the man she immediately falls in love with: Alden Robinson, a professor and highly regarded socio-economist who is also Miss Greenway's opposite in every way: to her, "His orderly life seems to be the result of daring and risk," but he interprets her chaotic life as evidence of "flexibility, espirit, lightness." His loving her as she is transforms her vices into virtues, and she in turn uses her virtues to release him from his over-determined sense of order: "She taught him how to dance and . . . how to float, how to relish life without such strict rules for it." Increasingly in Colwin's later fiction her metaphors become more penetrating and embody more succinctly the emotional center of her characters as they aspire to express themselves in some sort of aesthetic form. For example, Miss Greenway describes her life as "a relief map full of valleys, hills, and moraines," while Alden's life is "a hard, straight road that got you to an appointed city."

Once again, the narrator's love affair is, in the courtly love tradition, necessarily adulterous. Alden is separated, not divorced, so the authenticity of her love depends on it being both forbidden and unfulfilled. But when he informs her that his estranged wife wants to try to patch up the marriage, Miss Greenway is not prepared to fall into the deepest depression of her life. In this great despair she identifies with Saint Anthony: "I was beset by devils I had not known existed: grief, rage, longing and pure desire." After Alden calmly explains to her that he and his wife have worked things out, she is devastated: "His ease in my apartment broke my heart. I wanted to say, like Saint Anthony of the Desert: 'Why do you do harm to me when I harm none of you? Go away, and in the Lord's name, do not come near these things again.'" She never sees him again.

In the concluding paragraphs of the story Colwin explains more clearly than in any previous story its exact meaning: "For months I had been in a cave with my own small demons. Now I was ready to go out into the desert, which was my life." Walking near her apartment, Miss Greenway encounters a pathetic, homeless cat. When she picks it up, it kisses her, and the chance encounter creates the occasion for her full epiphany. Miss Greenway sees that she is still alive, though in terrible pain: "My tears over that cat were simply tears of envy over what would never be mine to give again: that witless, spontaneous affection; that hungry, purposeless availability; that innocence." She had experienced the tormenting power of love–its dark enchantment–and realizes that it is gone. She consciously identifies her plight with the legendary Anthony, but also sees a crucial distinction: "Unlike Saint Anthony, I had no militancy of faith to bear against pain. A good bout with the devil does not leave you free of temptation and pain."

"The Smile Beneath the Smile" is, like "Saint Anthony of the Desert," one of Colwin's darkest love stories. The love between Andrew Dilks and Rachel Manheim is both passionately obsessive and desperately sad. The professional situations of both characters is typically Colwinesque: Andrew comes from a family of wealth and privilege and teaches pure mathematics on the graduate level, and Rachel works in a rare-book store. The story opens with the couple and Andrew's son, William, having lunch while admiring women gaze at the seemingly happy trio. What the admirers do not know is that Andrew is in the middle of a messy divorce from his wife, Carol, William's mother. The trio make a beautiful image, an emblem of perfect contentment as observed by the onlooking women, who view them with envy. But because of the legal implications of Andrew's divorce, they can only meet at his convenience and only in the most guarded places. Richlin remarks that "The Smile Beneath the Smile" is a meditation "in which female bystanders admire the visual effect of a couple tormented by romantic longing." Colwin's later stories are increasingly concerned with the impossibility of love, the principal response to which is "the beauty of longing."

What makes their love even more poignant is that they can barely stay away from each other because of the passionate power of their physical attraction. When they are together, their love transforms them into semivisionary beings. Rachel feels the pain of longing deeply but knows it will never find permanent form in marriage or some other kind of stable situation. And, as Miss Greenway found an emotional and aesthetic analogue in the figure of Saint Anthony, Rachel finds her dilemma defined in Thomas Wyatt's sonnet "They flee from me, that sometime did me seek," which she has recited to Andrew in the bathtub. She finds profound meaning and relevance in the connection between her life, the poem, and her obsession with a medieval literary tradition: "Courtly love is, after all, a tradition of thwarted love." Like Miss Greenway, Rachel understands herself through reading and envisions her present dilemma within an historical and literary context: "If Rachel lived in a tower and Andrew were a gallant courtier, she would be perfectly happy to receive a caged nightingale from time to time, wouldn't she?" She realizes with sadness what their relationship is actually about: "All she got was an education in yearning . . . a four-point course in futility."

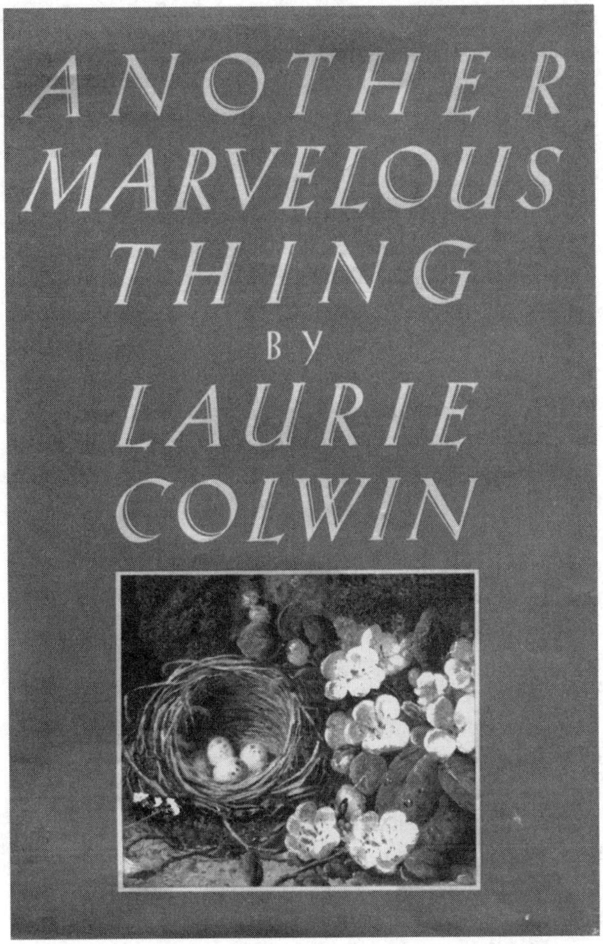

Dust jacket for Colwin's 1986 collection of eight related stories that chronicle an adulterous relationship

The story concludes where it began: with women in the restaurant gazing on what looks like a scene of familial happiness. However, Rachel comes to the stark realization that their furtive and mournful meetings are the only thing they share, a condition that leaves "him satisfied and her bereft." He, like several masochistic males in other stories, chooses to live within the romantic agony of his unfulfilled relationship, seeming to enjoy its "poignant sadness." Rachel knows that any attempt to move her dream of love out of its timeless, mythic realm and into reality will destroy it utterly. "The Smile Beneath the Smile" may be Colwin's most brilliant psychological love story because of her ability to contextualize love within specific historical and literary traditions.

Though Colwin's stories became longer, more serious, and more complex, she lost none of her capacity for comic treatments of romantic relationships. The story "The Achieve of, the Mastery of the Thing" returns to the humor and lightheartedness of her earlier stories. The comedy begins with the ironic use of the title, which is a line taken from the English Jesuit poet Gerard Manly Hopkins's poem "The Windhover" (1877). The poem embodies the preternaturally magnificent flight of that bird as it rides on the wind, its flight combining stasis and process, flux and stability–in short, perfection in divine, natural, and aesthetic form. What makes Colwin's title so humorous is that the story is about a young and charming faculty wife, Ann Speizer, who has been stoned on marijuana since she was in high school. That is the achievement that the story memorializes, and even celebrates, to some extent.

The narrative begins in the first person and in the fallen world of Ann's presumed divorce: "Once upon a time, I was Professor Thorne Speizer's stoned wife, and what a time that was." She admits her great love for marijuana and harkens back to a time when it was readily available and in general use by young college students. She also recalls the romantic pursuit of her husband, who was her graduate student instructor in a history class. She was twenty-two and a pothead, while "Thomas was older and had a job. That made him a real citizen in my eyes." They fell in love; he finished his Ph.D.; and they moved to "a pastoral men's college where there was sure to be no drugs. . . . However a brief scan of the campus turned up a number of goofy stares, moronic giggles, and out-of-it grins. It did not take me long to locate my fellow head."

Ann's major problem throughout the story is that her serious-minded husband does not have the foggiest suspicion about her long-term drug use; in fact, he has never seen her straight.

Ann is, understandably, unable to relate to the other faculty wives because of age and divergent interests; but finally she meets Lionel Browning, a student who becomes her drug supplier. Stoned though she is, her summary profile of the faculty and their wives rings true: "These women drank too much sherry at parties and became very, very still . . . it was plain to see how much professors hated students who, since they had not yet passed through the heavy gate of adulthood, were considered feckless, stupid, with no right to anything." After a time her husband accuses her of having an affair with Lionel because they spend so much time together. She adamantly denies the accusation and feels that it is time to tell her husband the truth: "I smoke marijuana unceasingly and always have." After Thorne gets over the initial shock and realizes that nothing can alter the past, he decides to smoke some grass with her. As he begins to feel the effects of the drug, Ann meditates on the connection between poets and grass and notes that many of her pothead friends were utterly convinced that both William Blake and Hopkins had to be high when writing their visionary poems. As Thorne's eyes begin to glaze over, Ann recalls the title of her favorite Hopkins poem and applies it to her victory in getting her serious history-professor husband stoned: "I felt full of achievement and mastery–Thorne being the victim and beneficiary of both. Getting him stoned was a definite achievement of some sort or other."

"The Achieve of, the Mastery of the Thing" is both a reminiscence and a parable about the impossibility of creating and maintaining an Edenic paradise free from the destructive effects of time. Being "stoned" implies that time has stopped, but the experience proves to be illusory and, over a period of time, depressing. The story is one of Colwin's funniest even though it ends on a sad note.

The concluding story in the collection, "Family Happiness," is also its longest. Colwin later developed it into a novel with the same title in 1982. It is also the least painful story in *The Lone Pilgrim.* Once again, its subject is an adulterous affair, this one involving a happily married woman from a wealthy but idiosyncratic family. Richlin claims that, more than any other Colwin story, "the extramarital passion acts to confirm the strength of the couple's marriage." Polly Solo-Miller's family is an old Jewish, New York City one that loves and supports art and music and specializes in sumptuous family celebrations; its members like to refer to themselves as a "tribe." Polly deeply loves her lawyer husband, Henry Demarest, and their two children, Pete and Dee-Dee. After getting through a lengthy description of Polly's heaven-on-earth marriage, the reader is taken aback to learn of her affair with a well-known artist, Lincoln Bennett, whom she met at his fancy gallery.

The story chronicles the course of their many furtive meetings, usually at Lincoln's studio. Though Lincoln cannot convince Polly to spend a week with him in Paris, their affair runs a fairly smooth course. Polly is surprised, however, at how desperately she misses him while he is in Paris. Absent from the affair is Colwin's usual conflict between the "tidy" and the "chaotic," because both participants are quite orderly and coordinate their elaborate plans with admirable skill. However, one of the reasons why Polly is able to get away with her affair is that no one seems to notice what she is doing or where she is at any given time. She is the least temperamental member of "the tribe" and the unofficial family listener: "That's the bliss of it. I never even have to lie. No one ever asks me what I do." Though Polly relishes, and even celebrates, her role in the family, she has other needs: "She wanted family life, although now she had learned that she wanted privacy as well: Lincoln was her privacy."

Another gift that Polly discovers only in Lincoln's painful absence is the transforming effect he has on her self-image: "Without Lincoln, her life was not natural. He made the Polly everyone doted on visible to Polly–there was no way to thank someone for such an amazing gift." Only in the final scene of the story (and also of the novel) does Polly experience one of the truly great revelations of her life. She is watching her husband and two children flying kites in Central Park, a sport she and Lincoln also love. She is unable to stop her interior dialogue with Lincoln, even in the midst of affectionate family activities. The sight of her family's kites darting and zigzagging in the sky brings her to tears: "Polly felt her heart break open to love and pain. No kite, of course, had been given to her to fly, but she felt as overexcited and grateful as if it had." Though privacy is one of the principal themes of the story, it is a specific kind of privacy that enables her to be herself completely: "Wasn't it odd that not one of them knew anything about what was closest to her heart."

All eight stories in Colwin's third collection, *Another Marvelous Thing,* are linked; they concern the place of privacy in the adulterous relationship of the protagonists, Josephine Delielle (Billy) and Francis Clemens (Frank). As a critic for *The New York Times Book Review* (13 April 1986) explained:

> The stories in this slim volume are connected, and they often relay the same event from different perspectives, but each one is complete unto itself, and because of the frequent repetition of information, the book does not profit from being read straight through as if it were a novel. . . . These [stories] should be read one at a time, perhaps just before bed as a respite from an especially trying day.

Even though the individual stories appeared in various journals over a period of years, the cumulative effect is one of Colwin's most artfully constructed private worlds, a mythopoeic setting created and sustained by the writer's favorite energy source: adulterous love. Rarely has Colwin been so straightforward about the connections between love and privacy and sadness. Two of the stories, "A Country Wedding" and the title story, barely allude to Frank; however, the other six emphasize the critical importance of privacy as a necessary ingredient for their love to exist and flourish.

The narrator of "My Mistress" is Frank (though in most of this story he is called Francis), one of the few male narrators in Colwin's stories. Frank, an emotionally open older man, is a model of tidiness in both his life and his professional work. The opening paragraph shows him comparing his mistress, Billy, a tough-minded young lady, to his elegant, well-dressed, and impeccably organized wife, Vera. His continuous repetition of the word "mistress" undoubtedly alludes to the figure in one of William Shakespeare's most popular sonnets. Indeed, this story is a kind of prose version of Sonnet 130; Billy is as much a mess as the Bard's imperfect but nonetheless irresistible mistress. This story is the first in which Colwin deliberately uses phrases from another writer to structure the story. Both Frank and Billy are happily married and find fulfillment in their legal families. They are equally content in their professional lives; Frank is a successful investment banker, and Billy an economic historian. She, like so many Colwin characters, is still working on her doctoral dissertation. They meet at a cocktail party for one of the journals they both write for, the *Journal of American Economic Thought.*

They carry on their affair almost every weekday afternoon, most of the time at Billy's Spartan but messy townhouse. Frank calls Billy "an absolute fact in my life. . . . Thinking about her is like entering a secret room to which only I have access." The circumstances of their love affair shape six of the stories in the collection, but privacy is the theme of all eight stories. New to Colwin's view of her characters' adulterous affairs is her treatment of them as genuine works of art; these narratives record in a real way the art of courtly love–adulterous and furtive–within a modern context. Indeed, only within the mysterious realm of their adultery are they able to consciously move in and out of romantic roles and assume seemingly contradictory opinions and points of view.

Though Billy sometimes refers sardonically to their affair as "the rapturous consummation," she also summarizes her feelings toward it as "sorrow, guilt, horror, anticipation." Both of them enjoy imagining their affair as something out of a French movie, which is the title of another story in the collection. Billy describes their audacious week-long trip to a cottage in Vermont as "sneaking off to a love nest with your lover," a phrase that lends the occasion an even sexier connotation than mere adultery. Once they arrive at their cabin, they re-enact roles from their youth: "We lived like graduate students or mice and not like normal people at all. We kept odd hours and lived off sandwiches. We stayed in bed and were both glad when it rained." Assuming such roles becomes an important ingredient in constructing and maintaining their affair as a conscious work of art which, in turn, enables them to explore each other with greater freedom and passion. Part of their erotic exploration involves arguing over who is the tempter and the temptee; but the persistent question they never stop asking is why they are together. Billy does come up with a plausible answer that brings the concerns of art and love together: "It's an artistic impulse. . . . It takes us out of reality and gives us an invented context all our own." Frank had earlier offered an alternate explanation of their affair: "It often seems that the function of romance is to give people something romantic to think about."

"My Mistress" concludes with a visual image reminiscent of a 1914 painting by Oskar Kokoschka called "The Tempest." The painting shows a man and woman in a boat grasping each other and protecting each other from the furious storm raging about them. At the conclusion of the story, Frank and Billy are embracing each other under a quilt in desperate intimacy: "If we hold each other close enough, that darkness is held at bay." Their shared view of their love as a work of art helps them fathom the profoundly existential nature of their actions.

In the next story, "Frank and Billy," Colwin continues to develop and expand the metaphor of art as the most accurate delineation of the function of love. The plot is basically the same as "My Mistress," though several details are added, such as the precise moment their affair began. Though the illicit affair continues in "French Movie," Billy begins to feel deep guilt over it; she is also becoming increasingly troubled by Frank's pressuring her to reveal details of her private life with her husband, Grey. Frank, on the other hand, never stops talking about his perfect wife, Vera. Yet, both realize that "the things they really wanted to know were unaskable." Billy continues to examine their relationship and find metaphors that might uncover their reasons for being together: "That was the thing about a love affair. It went by frame by frame. . . . The time Billy and Francis spent together had a beginning and an end. The middle was full of moments, of one sort or another. It was like a movie–it was like a French movie." Colwin brings together memory, time, and art in "French Movie" in ways she had not previously. Without the motion picture metaphor to give their affair a specifically modern context, their relationship would be just another tawdry coupling, full of desperation and fear. Art ennobles the commonplace and gives it meaning. The tale ends in a local park where they had regularly met early in their relationship and where they decide to end the affair, at least for a while. Colwin transforms the park into a mythical Garden of Eden free from the constraints of time–and thus responsibility–and replete with crab-apple trees. The last scene could easily come from a romantic French movie by François Truffaut and epitomizes the regeneration of the mythic garden starring the gloriously transformed Billy and Francis as Adam and Eve.

In "A Little Something," however, their affair is still going on, and the story is about Frank's fear that their affair will soon end. The major threat to their union is Billy's increasing sense of guilt. She shocks Frank by articulating her real feelings about adultery: "Obviously I can't triumph over my immoral side." The story concludes with an afternoon nap that may be their last: "He felt he was laying in a store of memories almost as you stock a pantry with emergency supplies. . . . This afternoon would be as if etched in glass: bright, hard, and clear. It was his to have: he could conjure it up whenever he wanted, wherever he was." Remembered or conjured images from the past increasingly recur in Colwin's late stories and demonstrate her serious concern with time as a destructive force and art as the only antidote.

"Swan Song," as the title suggests, is another version of the end of the affair. However, the rift is caused, once again, by Billy's intractable sense of guilt and defilement over the shoddy circumstances of their affair. Frank continues to press her for intimate details of her life with her husband. He also becomes jealous over Billy's private obsession with reptiles and birds, disturbed that she has a satisfactory life that does not include him.

The last story in the collection, "A Couple of Old Flames," tells of their chance meeting two years after they parted. They lightheartedly exchange accusations as to who actually ended the relationship: Frank claims she threw him out and left him in the dust, while Billy laments that her life was ruined. Though there may be some truth in their witty accusations, both seem content to be back in their legal and happy family lives. Though they part amicably, they still mourn the loss of the most unforgettable part of their lives. The following day, Billy takes her newly born son to the park–another Edenic location–and experiences a semivisionary revelation over the deeper meaning of their love. She finally sees that, though they had nothing in common, they had fallen deeply in love; she finally understands the link between love and the imagination: "A love affair was another amazing product of human ingeniousness, like art, like scholarship, like architecture. It was a created thing with rules, language, and reference. When it was finished it lived on in its artifacts: a million memories and gestures." Nowhere does Colwin detail more comprehensively the complex interconnections among love, time, and memory: art transforms them into artifacts, into enduring and permanent truths in human lives.

Few American short-story writers developed as rapid or as impressively as Laurie Colwin. From the lighthearted romantic comedies of *Passion and Affect,* her work matured into the later, psychological and mythically textured stories that have secured her place in contemporary American literature.

Reference:

Amy Richlin, "Guilty Pleasures: The Fiction of Laurie Colwin," *New England Review,* 13, no. 3–4 (Spring/Summer 1991): 296–309.

Rick DeMarinis

(3 May 1934 -)

Thomas H. Schmid
University of Texas at El Paso

BOOKS: *A Lovely Monster: The Adventures of Claude Rains and Dr. Tellenbeck* (New York: Simon & Schuster, 1975);
Scimitar (New York: Dutton, 1977);
Cinder (New York: Farrar, Straus & Giroux, 1978);
Jack & Jill: Two Novellas and a Story (New York: Dutton, 1979);
The Burning Women of Far Cry (New York: Arbor House, 1986);
Under the Wheat (Pittsburgh: University of Pittsburgh Press, 1986);
The Coming Triumph of the Free World (New York: Viking, 1988);
The Year of the Zinc Penny (New York: Norton, 1989);
The Voice of America (New York: Norton, 1991);
The Mortician's Apprentice (New York: Norton, 1994);
Borrowed Hearts: New and Selected Stories (New York: Seven Stories Press, 1999).

Rick DeMarinis (photograph by Carole DeMarinis)

After he won the 1986 Drue Heinz Literature Prize for his first collection of short stories, *Under the Wheat,* Rick DeMarinis told an interviewer about his career-long interest "in the demonic underpinnings of everyday . . . events": "in things that appear rather normal and rather wholesome," DeMarinis noted, "there's always an element of darkness." The ordinary and the troubling are the twin poles of many of DeMarinis's short stories, which have been published in magazines such as *The Atlantic Monthly, GQ,* and *Harper's* for more than twenty years. An accomplished novelist as well, DeMarinis has been critically acclaimed for the humanity, generosity, and incisiveness of his portrayals of "ordinary" characters whose lives somehow spin inscrutably toward the edges of various forms of human darkness–including violence, drug addiction, voyeurism, professional failure, and failed relationships. For DeMarinis's characters "the fix is in"; he told *The New York Times* (30 October 1988): "[my characters] are not doing much more than surviving. What do we get beyond that anyway? We survive."

DeMarinis is a survivor. The son of Alphonse and Ruth Siik DeMarinis, Rick DeMarinis was born in New York City on 3 May 1934, the only child of a minor New York mob figure, who was also prizefighter Rocky Graziano's first professional manager. Growing up in the 1930s and 1940s, DeMarinis learned early in life the painful lessons of parental abandonment and of the child's need to adapt, often heroically, to constantly shifting environoments, new schools, his parents' broken marriage, and his mother's string of moves, temporary jobs, and boyfriends after her divorce from Alphonse DeMarinis in the late 1930s. He also learned rebellion. Leaving home for good in 1952, DeMarinis spent two years as a listless student at San Diego State College before enlisting in the U.S. Air Force in 1954 on a drunken pact with a college friend. He was stationed in Montana as a radar operator until his discharge in 1958. Entering the University of Montana as a mathematics major, DeMarinis graduated with a B.A. in 1961 and took a job with Boeing as an engineer at the Minuteman Missile project in Great Falls, Montana, where he spent the next three years gritting his way through an unfullfilling career and an unhappy first marriage. In 1964, inspired by Federico Fellini's motion-picture classic, *8 1/2* (1963), DeMarinis returned to the University of Montana and entered the M.A. program in English, where he studied writing under Richard Hugo and began developing the fictional craft that has been his life's work ever since. Since earning his M.A. in 1967, DeMarinis has been a full-time writer and teacher of creative writing, holding faculty positions at the University of Montana (1967–1969), San Diego State University (1969–1976), Arizona State University (1980–1981), and the University of Texas at El Paso (1988–1999). Happily married since 1966 to his second wife, Carole Joyce Bubash (also a writer and teacher), DeMarinis continues to write from his home in Missoula, Montana, where he has retired as an Emeritus Professor of English from the University of Texas at El Paso and where he can be near his three grown children and their families. He has received many honors and awards, including two National Endowment for the Arts Fellowships (1976, 1982), the Drue Heinz Literature Prize (1986), a Literature Award from the American Academy of Arts and Letters (1991), and The Anioch Review Award for Best Prose (1999). DeMarinis has indeed survived his early struggles and made a major contribution to American fiction.

DeMarinis's short stories often explore the pathos and humor of people's haphazard attempts to survive, to live through the darkness and the knowledge of failure. DeMarinis's fiction embodies his philosophy that "the best thing you can wish for anyone is a second chance," as he told an interviewer on the NPR *Morning Edition* in June 1991, even if individual characters in his stories, as in life, do not always get second opportunities. Such honest empathy with failure gives DeMarinis's stories an undeniable humanity and a distinctly post–World War II sensibility: the feeling that individual will is most often powerless against the inertia of institutions, that individual success often comes at the cost of self or relationships. As DeMarinis told an interviewer on NPR *Performance Today* in 1988, "what we do to each other [is] often grotesque and often result[s] in life dilemmas that are almost insoluble."

Though it is uncharacteristically detached in tone when compared with later stories, "Under the Wheat" is a good example of this sensibility. First published in a 1974 issue of *The Iowa Review,* the story takes the reader beneath the placid wheat fields of North Dakota in 1962, deep into the steel and concrete pits of intercontinental-ballistic-missile silos, as seen through the eyes of Lloyd, an unimpassioned systems inspector. Despite his surface calm, the narrator's personal life is disintegrating. His emotional stress is skillfully objectified through contrasting imagery: the endless miles of gently undulating wheat contrast strikingly with the threatening missile chambers beneath the surface and dark anvil-shaped clouds above, with their potential for becoming tornado funnels. The natural vitality of the North Dakota farmland is juxtaposed with the lifeless streets and broken building facades of the ghost town through which the narrator compulsively wanders on his rare days off. Lloyd drives for hours from silo to silo on his inspection rounds, checking the sump pumps required to keep water out of the holes, while his wife becomes more and more distant and eventually leaves him altogether. He takes up with Myrna, a local woman whose primary sexual stimulation seems to derive from the destructive potential represented by the empty silos, in the bottoms of which she and Lloyd make love, ninety feet below the surface and seemingly light years away from what Lloyd terms the "rules." Lloyd's life becomes as empty of meaning as the temporarily vacant silos are of their missiles.

Yet, in a way that is typical of DeMarinis's stories, "Under the Wheat" avoids placing blame or moralizing about the way things are, and it ends with a moment of human tenderness, provisional and fragile though it may be. At the conclusion the possibility of human connection and communication opens up for Lloyd and Myrna as they stand in one of the abandoned houses in the ghost town. Lloyd nervously watches a dark funnel cloud in the distance:

> The funnel is behind a bluff, holding back. But I can hear it, the freight trains. Myrna is standing behind me, running a knuckle up and down my back. "Hi, darling," she says. "Want to know what I did while you were out working on the dam today?" The dark tube has begun to move out from behind the bluff, but I'm not sure which way. "Tell me," I say. "Tell me."

Lloyd's simple imperative and the potential for intimacy it opens up contrast sharply with the indifference and avoidance that plague his marriage, in which he and his wife "are like two magnetic north poles, repelling each other for invisible reasons." Invisible reasons haunt many of DeMarinis's characters.

"Under the Wheat" provides an initial clue to many of DeMarinis's key tendencies, including an intense focus on character over plot; a restrained, patient style; a relentless honesty learned from Hugo; and an overriding concern with personal relationships as the stuff of humanity's sins, its perverse grotesqueries, and its redemption. It is also an apt title story for DeMarinis's 1986 collection as a whole. The stories all explore in various ways the potential for perversion that lurks beneath the surface of human "normalcy." Several stories, in fact, ironically question the legitimacy of "normalcy" itself, asking how abusive or controlling aspects of human behavior can become comfortably "ordinary." All tell the stories of individuals who find themselves in untenable situations.

In "Good Wars," a vaguely autobiographical story of a boy's coming of age and adulthood in the years following World War II, the first-person narrator must deal with personal "wars" set against the backdrop of American engagement in World War II, the Korean War (implicitly), and the Vietnam War. Unlike Lloyd in "Under the Wheat," Bernard in "Good Wars" is less detached and more innocent, though nevertheless caught up in the struggle to understand the mysteries of human conflict and the stakes involved in taking up a position and having to defend it. He and his brother Woodrow witness their father's transformation from a jovial jokester to an empty automaton (who eventually simply disappears) after he returns from World War II, the last "good war." Bernard deals with a schoolyard bully, Dolph Hubler, but only after learning the grim truth that bullies like Dolph "existed in the world as a *principle,* a mindlessly vengeful force," and only at the cost of separating himself irrevocably from his usual group of play-it-safe friends, who "had already become experts in their mid-teens at cutting their losses." Bernard endures and tries to bond with his mother's succession of boyfriends, all negative authority figures: one uses words such as "cruelly sharp instruments"; another tells transparent lies about a war record he never earned; and another insists on giving Bernard a boxing education he does not want. He marries, divorces, and falls in love with Inez, a younger woman whose ferocious involvement in the anti-Vietnam War movement he cannot completely share. At the end of the story he becomes a security guard at a department store, where he is forced to deal with a lunatic who begins a rampage in the sporting-goods department for no apparent reason.

For Bernard, and ultimately for the reader, the distinction between "good wars" and "bad wars" is rendered defunct: there are only "wars," whose causes always remain partially hidden. Vietnam, a "bad" war for Inez, becomes also her "good" war in the sense that it provides her with the "ready yoke of righteousness." Yet, in the process of grafting her passion to the adrenaline-pumping cause of revolution, Inez draws away from Bernard: he becomes the enemy, a "doubtful hero," as Bernard himself recognizes, "who would never fight for the cause of the moment–unless . . . caught in its feverish arms and *combat* was the only way out of that sweaty embrace." Wars, like life itself, are personal things for Bernard, and, generally, for DeMarinis. People fight for private and selfish reasons, according to the world of DeMarinis's fiction. Lofty ideals, while not "wrong," tend to become part of what separates people and leads them to do "grotesque" things to each other.

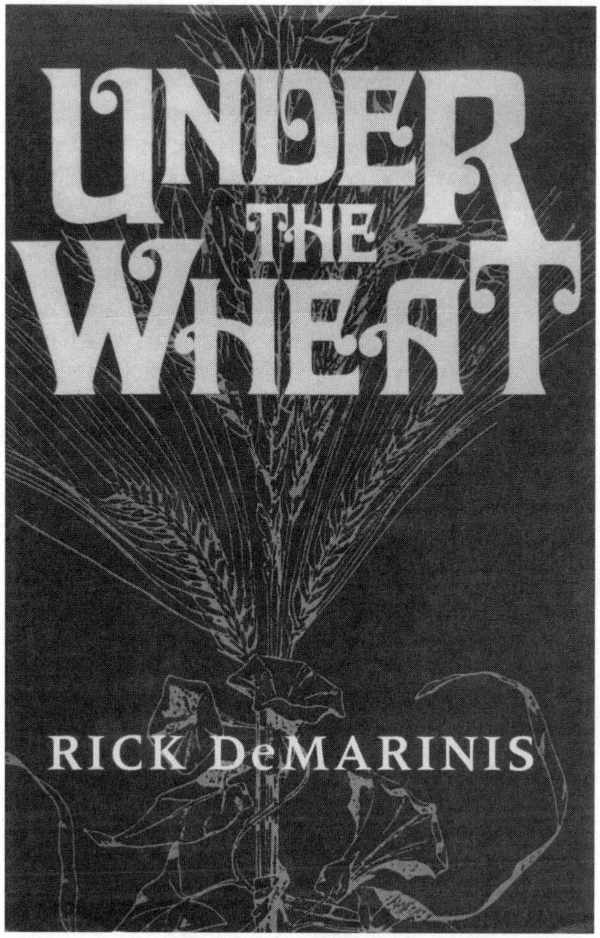

Dust jacket for DeMarinis's first collection of short stories, which won the 1986 Drue Heinz Literary Prize

"Good Wars" is an important story in DeMarinis's canon for several reasons. Thematically, it explores territory to which the author returns in several other stories as well as full-length novels such as *The Year of the Zinc Penny* (1989) and *The Mortician's Apprentice*

(1994): America's coming of age after World War II; the pitting of the individual against larger, partially unknowable social forces; the struggle of youth against authority; and the emotional turmoil of parental abandonment. "Good Wars" also introduces readers to recurring character types: overbearing adults; shy, introspective boys or young adults who deal with life stoically and with a touch of sardonic humor; and supporting characters who have resigned themselves to varying degrees of personal and professional compromise. Stylistically, the realism of the story, its darkly comic tone, and its slightly bewildered first-person narrator define artistic contours DeMarinis continues to shape with originality and vision.

In "Weeds," for instance, DeMarinis again uses a loosely autobiographical first-person narrator this time to tell the story of a young man faced with the death of his father, the looming dissolution of the family farm, and his mother's last-ditch alliance with a neighboring farmer, a widower who is clearly most interested in adding their land to his own. In this story, however, DeMarinis combines the protagonist's realistic narration with elements of fairy-tale fantasy in a brilliant play on "Jack and the Beanstalk," a technique he again uses effectively in "Your Story," in his 1988 collection, *The Coming Triumph of the Free World.* The painful truth of "Weeds" is that "Jack" cannot save the farm or prevent his mother from remarrying any more than he can prevent the aerial spraying of toxic herbicides that hastened his father's death. His selling of the family cow for a sack of seeds leads only to the proliferation of frightening, opportunistic weeds that magically mature overnight and spread "black clouds of seed in grainy spirals . . . far and wide, across the entire nation." As Alison Lurie, one of the judges for the 1986 Drue Heinz Literature Prize, commented, "Weeds" is a "comic fantasy of ecological disaster"; it is also a devastating vision of the indifferent weeds of chance, "progress," and self-interest that threaten to choke out human life everywhere.

Lurie's perceptive recognition of the comic dimension to "Weeds" hits on a tonal vein that runs throughout DeMarinis's fiction. In his review of DeMarinis's second short-story collection, Russell Banks has called it "the comedy of a decent heart enraged," a comedy "rooted in the everyday" (*The New York Times,* 30 October 1988). DeMarinis's comic instinct, akin to John Cheever's and at times to Joseph Conrad's dark vision of the absurd, finds a little something to smile at in the fragility of human constructs and in the wide gap that exists between individual will and the roadblocks to its fulfillment that reality throws up with careless persistence. The tragicomic heroes and villains of DeMarinis's stories are eerily ordinary characters, who either resolutely maintain the absurd illusion of control in a world of "invisible reasons" or who perceive and surrender to their inevitable powerlessness. The former tend to be the villains, authority figures manqué, who bolster their deluded perceptions of control with verbal tics, clichés, or other trappings of position such as clothes, uniforms, or brand-name products. The latter (often the first-person narrators) tend to be the heroes, bare survivors who come to know, like Bernard in "Good Wars," that the fight never stops and that real, unequivocal, permanent victory never comes.

DeMarinis's bad guys tend to be the funniest, if also the most perverse and despicable, of his characters. Yet, DeMarinis's empathy tends to make these characters understandable to readers, if not sympathetic. He has the ability to create extreme characters that are shockingly realistic rather than parodic and, in some small corner of their existence on the page, vulnerable. They are the bullies, the self-aggrandizing stepfathers, the petty bureaucrats, the scam artists, and the pretenders of all kinds, people who tend toward self-protective delusion, hypocrisy, and general dishonesty. They are grotesques, such as the self-styled "Commodore" of "Life Between Meals," an uncontrollable overeater who controls women through food, wears ludicrous nautical uniforms, and prefaces his most self-satisfied observations with "Now hear this." They include ordinary, intellectually pretentious people such as Bernard's mother's critical boyfriend in "Good Wars," who "once said out loud that criticism was his gift" and "looked as though he was waiting for someone to pin a medal on him after he said this." They also include outrageous hucksters, such as Billetdoux in "Billy Ducks Among the Pharaohs," who pronounces his own last name as in the story title and who runs a door-to-door photography scam that allows him access to the houses of the comfortable middle class and, more important, to their antiques, trinkets, and even refrigerators. ("I'll say this," he tells the narrator while munching a purloined pork chop at one house, "the lady of the house knows how to fry a chop.")

These characters are thoroughly American, warped by a world of tarnished American values such as "freedom," "opportunity," and "individualism," and are set in an American near past that is at once nostalgic and urgently contemporary, both affirmative and repellent. "Billy Ducks," in fact, carries on the grand American tradition of the literary huckster established by the title character in Herman Melville's *The Confidence-Man* (1857) and Mark Twain's various versions of the con artist and doubtful opportunist in novels such as *Huckleberry Finn* (1884) and *A Connecticut Yankee in King Arthur's Court* (1889). Like his predecessors, DeMarinis uses such characters, who reside somewhere along the edge of the mainstream, to hint at the treacherous currents concealed beneath the "normal" flow of American life. By his own comparison, his characters and stories thus function like the fish-eye security lens sold by a huckster character in "The Smile of a Turtle," who claims that the lens "puts a bend in the world" so that "you get to see more of it that way." The key to DeMarinis's comic vision is precisely this skewed, sweeping, inclusive view, which takes in what Billy Ducks calls the "Pharaohs"–the comfortably wealthy–but tends, finally, to center on the masses in the middle, the blue-collar, nonacademic hordes with which the author identifies. DeMarinis's characters tend to be the ekers-out of livings rather than the lofty and successful. They suffer from reality, not ennui.

The stories collected in *The Coming Triumph of the Free World* (1988), DeMarinis's second collection, envision other convex distortions of "normal" life, those enabled by such things as madness, psychoactive drugs, shamanism, the thick bottoms of shot glasses, and the burden of knowing the world's indifference, which the narrator of one story describes as "seismic disregard." *The Coming Triumph of the Free World* centers on bare survival, taking the reader further toward the end of the rope from which DeMarinis's characters perennially seem to swing. The characters in these stories tend to be somewhat older than those in *Under the Wheat,* and consequently they are more alienated, more entrenched in untenable situations such as tense marriages, disillusioning jobs, and various forms of emotional crisis. These stories are both more stylistically "experimental" and more troubling than the earlier ones; yet, they retain a comparable insistence on what Russell Banks calls "the details of everyday life, the same details that make the stories of Richard Ford and Raymond Carver, for example, so believable." These stories are certainly believable. They are also chilling, at times desperate, and always reflective of the oddities that "everyday life" reveals to the sharp observer.

The stories in *The Coming Triumph of the Free World* are brilliant mixtures of the real and the surreal, as if to suggest that the "ordinary" is always tempered by the bizarre and unexplainable. These stories tend to be among DeMarinis's most narratively complex, most visionary, and, occasionally, most hallucinogenic. Madness–and the mind-altering drugs used (often brutally) to treat it–pervade several of the stories, many of them narrated by an anonymous recurring character, who is unemployed, is being medicated for depression by a prescription-happy psychiatrist, and is frantically trying to hold together his marriage to a woman named Raquel. This massively unreliable narrator bears witness to the darkly comic forces of the absurd that grow alongside man's attempts to order the world rationally

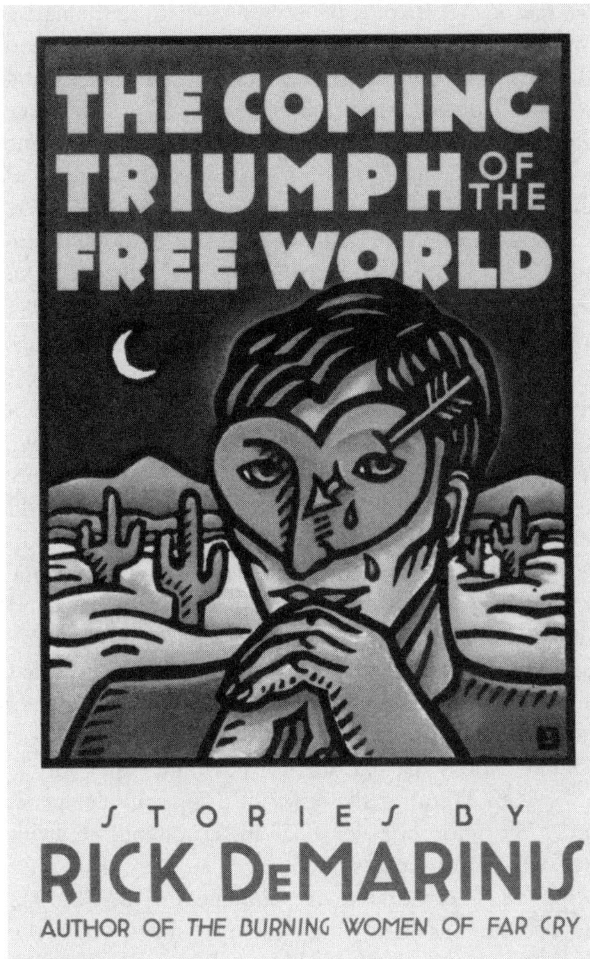

Dust jacket for DeMarinis's 1988 book, in which the narrator of the title story muses that James Bond's "wars were often fought in the Bahamas, as if the coming triumph of the free world were tied, somehow, to white sand, blue water, and submarine sex"

and that perhaps can be glimpsed only from the edge of madness, or at least from some psychological and emotional stress point beyond "normal" parameters.

"The Handgun," the opening story in the collection and the first to feature this narrator, provides the first chilling peek at one such stress point: the sleeplessness and marital tension created by the mindlessly quotidian barking of a neighborhood dog each morning at 3 A.M. The premise is simple: driven to madness by the hound's daily serenade, Raquel insists that the narrator buy a gun with which to shoot it dead. Yet, it is handled with finesse and psychological insight, worthy of Cheever's sharpest tales of personal crack-up or Edgar Allan Poe's best suspense stories. The point of "The Handgun" lies not in the gun itself, but in what the situation reveals about the characters and their lives together. The story mercilessly lays bare the subtle shifts and power plays of a failing marriage, the "invisible reasons" that come between people as, in the narrator's final simile, the gun comes between him and Raquel: "The gun caught my eye again. It had a tight, self-satisfied sheen, like a deceptively well-groomed relative from a disgraced branch of the family who'd come to claim a permanent place in our home." Like many of the stories in *The Coming Triumph of the Free World,* "The Handgun" objectifies the mysteries of internal alienation and aggression through external "things" and phenomena. In DeMarinis's fictional world, both have a way of thwarting efforts to maintain control.

The stories in *The Coming Triumph of the Free World* repeatedly accomplish such acts of revelation through a kind of poetic defamiliarization of the ordinary. Strange things happen and are thought in these stories, but they are things both permitted and encouraged in a world characterized chiefly by deception on a cosmic scale. In this world nearly everyone is in denial; nearly everyone is cheating or is compromised in some manner; and almost no one actually realizes it. Such unknowing complicity with the world's counterfeits can be revealed only from the vantage point of the extreme. In the title story, for example, the maniacal laughter of a homeless person (whom the narrator calls "Muni," after movie actor Paul Muni) in the aisles of a supermarket penetrates the narrator's denial of his crumbling life with Raquel, and becomes *his* manic laughter, the only response he can find to the emptiness of his life: his depression, his long-term unemployment, and the growing distance between him and his wife. Yet, the presence of Muni in the Safeway aisles, a mocking comment on the unsafe way of the world, leads also to a revelation of a sort, the revelation of the "black world" the narrator perceives beneath the tissue of safe lies about the "good life." Alone, the narrator stays up all night watching television, marveling at the absurdity of a James Bond movie: "his wars were often fought in the Bahamas, as if the coming triumph of the free world were tied, somehow, to white sand, blue water, and submarine sex."

The reappearing narrator of "The Coming Triumph of the Free World," "The Handgun," and another story of note, "Pagans," feels himself caught in a middle realm of existence that is emotionally crippling and oddly prophetic. As he puts it in "Pagans," he knows he is "still a half-turn out of tune" with the world around him, despite the heavy doses of psychoactive drugs his psychiatrist insists will make his brain and the world "mesh." Yet, he nevertheless perceives that the world as a whole runs perpetually and blindly a half-step out of whack with itself. It is "yoked to a rhythm," he concludes in "The Coming Triumph of the Free World"; "it [can] neither escape nor follow." For this character, as for many of DeMarinis's characters, the world is by definition an untenable proposition.

This perception leads this particular narrator to the collapsing visions of near-psychosis, in which he becomes inseparable from Muni in "The Coming Triumph of the Free World," or in which the three New Year's Eve parties he wanders through in "Pagans" fuzzily merge. But in a sense such mergings accurately depict reality for the narrator, and, more important, for the reader. The narrator really is as alone and as unable to deal with his isolation as Muni. The three parties in "Pagans"–his own, where he catches Raquel flirting with the milkman; his psychiatrist's, where the patients keep their separate mad vigils and never connect; and an anonymous computer-dating party, where he is mistaken for a man who is sexually aroused by "small features" in a woman–really are equally alienated, incommunicative rituals. The weapon in "The Handgun" really does become a sinister part of the family. It is not that "reality" and "fantasy" meet, nor that these stories explore some obvious point about the world being essentially "insane." On the contrary, these stories insist on just how ordinary such occurrences are.

Another crucial point about these stories, however, is that the narrator does survive, though barely. He and Raquel do not shoot one another, though that possibility–the sheer plausibility of it–hangs latent in "The Handgun." By the end of "The Coming Triumph of the Free World" he is able to stop laughing hysterically like Muni, though he is left empty and unable to explain to Raquel–or to himself–the reasons for his hysteria. At the end of "Pagans," after a night of bolting from one party to the next and feeling equally alone in each, he does hurry home to Raquel, in spite, or because of, the knowledge of her infidelity. Survival in DeMarinis's stories is another precondition of the world's "rhythm," as well as another aspect of his essentially comic vision. Few stories end in death or utter dissolution. Most reaffirm that the world spins on, crazily and fraught with accident, but, at least, reliably.

Not every story in *The Coming Triumph* takes its characters to the brink of psychotic collapse, though that possibility indeed hovers around the edges of many. Several stories play comically and insightfully with fictional structure itself, as in "Romance: A Prose Villanelle," in which DeMarinis rewrites the Western romance in terms of an East Coast woman's search for identity as a ranch cook, who lacks previous experience and who ends up falling in love with another cook rather than the dashing owner. But the final story, "Medicine Man," is the most uplifting and affirmative in the collection while also its strangest and most visionary. Like "Romance," "Medicine Man" takes place in the West, in Montana. Unlike "Romance," however, "Medicine Man" tells a serious tale. A mixed-blood Assiniboin healer with miraculous powers by turns angers, amazes, and cures the faded, hard-drinking residents of a small town. Where most of the stories in *The Coming Triumph of the Free World* work by casting doubt on conventional certainties, "Medicine Man" works by instilling belief in the unseen and mysterious. It shares with nearly all DeMarinis's short stories a sense of the overwhelming folly of what the medicine man, Louis Quenon, calls "the world that men have made," in which they "can't tell the difference between the urge to grin and the urge to spit." Yet, the story concludes in the narrator's moment of transcendent belief–in Quenon and in his life-affirming power, which is expressed ultimately in a silent smile: "a smile that could make you feel that you'd finally gotten the point after years and years of pretending there wasn't one." It can be argued that DeMarinis's stories do the same thing for the reader. They take readers to the edge of the place where belief systems break down, putting readers face to face with "seismic disregard" but also somehow bringing them back to a renewed sense of reality, of the "rhythm" that pulses through the fabric of things with or without human consent. Pretense no longer remains an option when reading DeMarinis's stories, including those–like "Medicine Man"–that appear to abandon empirical reality for the mystical and mysterious.

While "Medicine Man" is rather mystical, it also is rooted in the bedrock realities of small-town Western life and in this sense looks forward to the predominantly realistic stories in DeMarinis's third collection, most of which were written after the author's move to El Paso in 1988. The stories in *The Voice of America* (1991) tend to be set in the West–in Arizona, Texas, Montana, California, and points in between. They still stress the inner workings of characters "living on some kind of edge," a focus that lifts these stories above any facile "regionalism." The scope of this collection, indeed, is as wide as America itself, as DeMarinis continues, with a fully matured craft, to expose the cracks beneath the shining illusions of postwar American prosperity and freedom, through stories about individuals (mostly men) who must face the disintegration of an American way of life that has become what reviewer Melissa Pritchard called "toxic and untrustworthy" (*Chicago Tribune,* 2 June 1991). The stories in *The Voice of America* are full of broken promises, including that of the American dream itself, supposedly reaffirmed and guaranteed by the glorious victory of World War II. For most of the characters in these stories, there are no guarantees.

In many respects *The Voice of America* returns to the style and content of *Under the Wheat,* taking the characters and themes of those stories and infusing them into new, distinct stories of increased depth and power, most of them once again narrated by protagonists undergoing the stresses of dysfunctional family life, personal loss, and professional failure. "Safe Forever" features another version of Bernard in "Good Wars," a vulnerable youth whose dreams of heroic combat are dashed by the end of the war and who finds that the American victory leaves his life sadly unchanged and still dominated by thoughtless and abusive adults. Stories such as "The Voice of America," "Horizontal Snow," and "An Airman's Goodbye" are told by disenchanted young adults of the 1940s and 1950s, who range from mildly disaffected to violently enraged and who bring into focus new aspects of characters first developed in stories such as "Good Wars" (with respect to the older Bernard), "Weeds," and "Billy Ducks Among the Pharaohs." "Desert Places" and "Her Alabaster Skin" partially reinvent the lost and career-challenged middle-aged men of stories such as "Under the Wheat" and "Flowers of Boredom" (in *The Coming Triumph of the Free World*). Such stories continue exploring familiar subjects–broken families, the ravages of addiction, the deflation of belief in the American dream–but with an increased lyricism and an even greater sense of compassion than in DeMarinis's earlier work. *The Voice of America* speaks to a deep universal need for a second chance in life, something DeMarinis rightly claims to "know a little bit about." To read these stories is devoutly to wish, along with the writer, for the world's second chance.

In *The Voice of America* DeMarinis probes human needs and failures with remarkable tenderness, honesty, and humor, the hallmarks of his fictional craft throughout his writing career. Some stories are more hard-edged than others, such as "The Voice of America," whose 1950s teenage narrator adopts a desperate stance of reckless delinquency in response to the alcoholic violence of his home life, and "Wilderness," a creepily tense homage to Ernest Hemingway's "The Short Happy Life of Francis Macomber" (1936). Most of the stories in the collection, however, are gentler, more forgiving than "Wilderness." "Desert Places," for example, is a thoughtful, lyrical tale of a man trying heroically to understand his failures with his family, his dead father, and with the bottle; and "Paraiso: An Elegy" is a gritty look at a beloved friend's death from cancer, which leaves the narrator convinced that "all of us are moving to the drumbeat of some privately realized dance." Even the hilarious "Her Alabaster Skin" generates great tenderness for its pulp-romance-writing protagonist, who tells his own story of selling out, burning out, failing at marriage, and eventually being given the possibility of a second chance at romance with, of all people, a woman who publically impersonates his pseudonymous identity, "Veronica LaMonica." At the end of the story, pursuing "Veronica" and dropped at the airport by his ecology-minded son, the cynical writer reflects on the meaning of his newfound interest in romance in words that epitomize DeMarinis's own philosophy:

> I give him a bear hug and a kiss, for he is my son and I love him more than Donahue and Oprah do and he

> needs to know it. He wants me and the planet to have a second chance. And a second chance is the sweetest blessing any of us can hope for.

Throughout his fiction DeMarinis gives urgent voice to the need for second chances, a need that arises spontaneously from the very American ethics created supposedly to fulfill human needs. Historically grounded in the postwar optimism and hucksterism of the 1950s, this America has a "rhythm" that its citizens can "neither escape nor follow," themselves having set it in motion. DeMarinis's fiction pinpoints the stress points in current American life with unfailing accuracy and without postmodern posturing. His characters and his writing style remain rooted in the light of everyday life, with its dark shadows of bloodthirsty competition, personal inadequacies, abusive relationships, and financial ruin. (The couple in "Your Story," for example, suffers from debts that "at twenty-two percent interest . . . took on an unearthly life of their own and became a fiscal Frankenstein monster that sought to destroy its creators.") His stories use the language of everyday life to expose Americans' vanities, posturings, and all-too-human predilections for dissembling.

DeMarinis continues to write stories that force his readers to see the ordinary with new eyes and that will continue to be read and considered as significant contributions to American literature. As Banks has noted, DeMarinis has "a gifted ear for American speech, a crush on all kinds of slang . . . a wry appreciation of brand names, the detritus of contemporary life," and this ear gives DeMarinis's stories a rootedness in historical American life as well as a timelessness that comes from the preservation of the different voices of America. It is a mark of the continued relevance of DeMarinis's fiction, as well as of the unerring way it reflects cultural moments, that his stories continue to be published in many anthologies, including *Writers of the Purple Sage* (1984), *The Graywolf Annual* (1985), *Soldiers and Civilians* (1986), *The Year's Best Fantasy* (1989), *Lives and Moments: An Introduction to Short Fiction* (1991), *Dreamers and Desperadoes: Contemporary Short Fiction from the American West* (1993), *Science and Technology: Readings for Writers* (1995), *Caught in the Act: The Photographer in Contemporary Fiction* (1996), and *The Portable Western Reader* (1997).

Finally, however, it is DeMarinis's affection for his fictional characters and his living readers that continues to gain him a wide audience. For DeMarinis, writers and readers together must search for meaning, significance, order, and a second chance. DeMarinis's stories are the reader's stories, and that fact makes the opening lines of the appropriately titled "Your Story," one of DeMarinis's personal favorites, an apt summary of his writing philosophy:

> This story happened early in the history of the human race, a few years from now. It is your story, though you may have some quibbles. It's the writer's story too, but he wants to camouflage it. (The form he's chosen confirms this.) Look at it this way: he offers a parable of a parable, nut and shell, easily cracked and eaten. But the question is, will it nourish or poison or just lie suspended in the gut like a stone? It points no finger of blame, pats no one on the back, gives no guarantees beyond asserting the commonality of its long-lost roots, which are transplantable anywhere. To make matters worse, the writer (never applauded for his penetrating insights and infamous for his lack of convictions) probably won't get it right. He'll need your open-minded help. . . .

DeMarinis's short stories continually provide the chance to get it right. As the conclusion to "Your Story" once more reminds readers, they "are always in the middle" of DeMarinis's stories. From that vantage point readers can share DeMarinis's visions of ordinary life.

Interviews:

Gordon Dillow, Interview with DeMarinis, *Missoulian,* 4 June 1979;

Deirdre McNamer, Interview with DeMarinis, *Missoulian,* 27 April 1984;

Patricia Sullivan, Interview with DeMarinis, *Missoulian,* 16 August 1985;

Michael Moore, Interview with DeMarinis, *Missoulian,* 28 November 1986;

Steven Almond, Interview with DeMarinis, *El Paso Times,* 30 September 1990;

S. Gail Miller, Interview with DeMarinis, *Horizons* (UT-El Paso), 1 February 1991;

Wendy Smith, Interview with DeMarinis, *Publishers Weekly,* 10 March 1991;

Ginny Merriam, Interview with DeMarinis, *Missoulian,* 21 August 1994;

Thaddeus Herrick, Interview with DeMarinis, *Houston Chronicle,* 26 March 1995;

Sherry Jones, Interview with DeMarinis, *Missoulian,* 15 June 1999;

Sarah Schmid, Interview with DeMarinis, *Missoula Independent,* 17 June–24 June 1999.

Papers:

The Brigham Young University Library in Provo, Utah, has manuscript drafts and galley proofs for some of Rick DeMarinis's novels and short stories.

Stanley Elkin

(11 May 1930 – 31 May 1995)

David Dougherty
Loyola College in Maryland

See also the Elkin entries in *DLB 2: American Novelists Since World War II; DLB 28: Twentieth-Century American-Jewish Fiction Writers;* and *DLB Yearbook: 1980.*

BOOKS: *Boswell: A Modern Comedy* (New York: Random House, 1964; London: Hamilton, 1964);
Criers and Kibitzers, Kibitzers and Criers (New York: Random House, 1966; London: Anthony Blond, 1967);
A Bad Man (New York: Random House, 1967; London: Anthony Blond, 1968);
The Dick Gibson Show (New York: Random House, 1971; London: Weidenfeld & Nicolson, 1971);
Searches and Seizures (New York: Random House, 1973); republished as *Eligible Men: Three Short Novels* (London: Gollancz, 1974); republished as *Alex and the Gypsy: Three Short Novels* (Harmondsworth, U.K. & New York: Penguin, 1977);
The Franchiser (New York: Farrar, Straus & Giroux, 1976);
The First George Mills (Dallas: Pressworks, 1980);
The Living End (New York: Dutton, 1979; London: Cape, 1980);
Stanley Elkin's Greatest Hits (New York: Dutton, 1980);
George Mills (New York: Dutton, 1982);
Early Elkin (Flint, Mich.: Bamberger Books, 1985);
Stanley Elkin's The Magic Kingdom (New York: Dutton, 1985);
The Rabbi of Lud (New York: Scribners, 1987);
The Six-Year-Old Man (Flint, Mich.: Bamberger Books, 1987);
The MacGuffin (New York: Linden Press, 1991);
Pieces of Soap: Essays (New York: Simon & Schuster, 1992);
Van Gogh's Room at Arles: Three Novellas (New York: Hyperion Press, 1993);
Mrs. Ted Bliss (New York: Hyperion Press, 1995).

OTHER: *Stories from the Sixties,* edited by Elkin (Garden City, N.Y.: Doubleday, 1971);
The Best American Short Stories 1980, edited by Elkin and Shannon Ravenel (Boston: Houghton Mifflin, 1980).

photograph by Miriam Berkley; from the dust jacket of Van Gogh's Room at Arles, *1993*

When Stanley Elkin died in 1995, he had already fallen into the dreaded category of "a writer's writer." Although literary critics and fellow novelists continued to celebrate his daring, zany innovations in fictional form, his books were falling rapidly out of print in his later years. He was eager for public acceptance and good sales, but he steadfastly refused to compromise his art and vision to gain the public recognition he craved. Even as his earlier books drifted out of and back into print, he continued to produce the kind of idiosyncratic, funny, and thoughtful novels that had been the source of his reputation among the writers and critics who looked to his stylistic innovations for inspiration. He responded to a question about literary influences with uncharacteristic modesty in an interview for a special issue of *Delta* (February 1985), saying that he hoped no one was doing what he was doing, but that he hoped at least he was doing what he was doing.

Elkin's aim was to restore to literature the primacy of style and rhetoric. Respected poetry critic Helen Vendler and novelists as diverse as William Gass, Robert Coover, and Cynthia Ozick have praised the exuberance and originality of Elkin's prose. He joked once that he would "rather have a metaphor than a good cigar" and that fiction "gives an opportunity for rhetoric to happen." It is as a wordsmith, a crafter of syntax and a fracturer of readers' expectations, that Elkin made his most powerful impact on his fellow writers and on general readers. In his early novels he was willing, and at times eager, to subordinate all the traditional elements of fiction–plot, characterization, setting, even verisimilitude–to the exigencies of rhetoric. As his art matured and his vision deepened, he came to value ideas and themes in his fiction, but even as late as *Van Gogh's Room at Arles: Three Novellas* (1993), the rhetorical energy often pushed aside the more orderly elements of plot and characterization.

Elkin published only one volume of short stories, *Criers and Kibitzers, Kibitzers and Criers* (1966), and that was early in his career. He continued to write and publish short fiction, but for the most part it was later recast as episodes in his novels. His whimsical collection *Stanley Elkin's Greatest Hits* (1980), for example, includes chapters from *Boswell: A Modern Comedy* (1964), *A Bad Man* (1967), *The Dick Gibson Show* (1971), and *The Franchiser* (1976), standing alone as autonomous stories, as well as one story from *Criers and Kibitzers, Kibitzers and Criers* and two novellas. The first section of *George Mills* (1982) appeared complete in *Antaeus,* then in a small chapbook in 1980, before being included in the novel. However, since the author considered these stories parts of larger aesthetic units, it would be inappropriate to consider them under the rubric of short fiction.

Stanley Lawrence Elkin was born in New York City on 11 May 1930, while the United States was swamped in a worldwide economic depression. His father, Philip, was a traveling salesman, and his pitchman's zeal assured the family of an excellent income, especially after he relocated to Chicago when his son was three. Elkin's love of language was assured by the stories his successful, dapper father told after his trips through the plains states, selling costume jewelry to stores and vendors. As Elkin lovingly recalled in "My Father's Life," a 1987 essay collected in *Pieces of Soap* (1992), Philip's rhetoric, manner, and enthusiasms were infectious, larger than life:

> It's the language of myth and risk and men sizing each other up. It's steely-eyed appraisal talk, I-like-the-cut-of-your-jib speech, and maybe that's not the way it happened. But that was the way my father told it and it became The Story of How They Gave Him the Central Time Zone . . . of how he moved west and took up his manifest destiny in the Chicago Office.

This environment, with a love of spoken and written language as a means of transforming the ordinary to the mythic, encouraged Elkin's creative tendencies. The heroes of many of his novels are pitchmen who sometimes get tangled in the labyrinths of their own pitches, such as marketers Ben Flesh in *The Franchiser* and Leo Feldman in *A Bad Man,* the radio personality of *The Dick Gibson Show,* or politician Bob Druff of *The MacGuffin* (1991).

Upon completing his B.A. (1952) and M.A. (1953) at the University of Illinois, Elkin served in the U.S. Army from 1955 to 1957, then returned to Illinois for his Ph.D. (1961). By the time he had completed his dissertation on religious symbolism in the works of William Faulkner, Elkin had published stories of his own and was well on his way to a career as a writer and teacher. Although he accepted visiting appointments at several universities, most of his academic life was spent at Washington University in St. Louis, where he became Merle Kling Professor of Modern Letters in 1983.

After a vigorous and even athletic youth and early adulthood, Elkin was diagnosed as having multiple sclerosis in 1972. He transformed his own physical condition into the raw material of art on two occasions. The hero of *The Franchiser,* Ben Flesh, suffers from early symptoms of the disease as he madly seeks to build an economic empire while franchising America before his own demyelination renders him unable to travel and barter. Professor Jack Schiff, the hero of "Her Sense of Timing" in *Van Gogh's Room at Arles,* who also makes a cameo appearance in the title story, represents a late stage of the illness; he is incapable of self-sufficiency and independent living. Elkin died on 31 May 1995 of complications from heart surgery. His posthumous novel *Mrs. Ted Bliss* (1995) won the National Book Crit-

Dust jacket for Elkin's 1966 collection of stories about protagonists learning to cope with suffering and sorrow

ics Circle Award, as had his personal favorite among his books, *George Mills,* in 1982.

Elkin's early stories, those collected in *Criers and Kibitzers, Kibitzers and Criers,* reveal sadder themes than his early novels, which exhibit a spirit of defiance and celebration. The stories reveal a more somber Elkin, a writer concerned with the fragility of life and man's susceptibility to sorrow and suffering. Except for "A Poetics for Bullies," which is in many ways a companion text for *A Bad Man,* the stories in *Criers and Kibitzers, Kibitzers and Criers* consider the lives of heroes and even communities that learn to endure human suffering without the defiant humor of the exuberant protagonists of the novels.

"Cousin Poor Lesley and the Lousy People" recalls youths whose expectations have been almost systematically dashed. The title character, a nerd who studied photography at a Midwestern college, then joined the Marines and died in a freak accident, is mourned by his equally nerdy sister, who in turn imposes her grief on the narrator. This narrator had resisted introducing Lesley to his circle of friends, a group of street toughs who insulted everyone with tough-guy disrespect and would have devastated Lesley. This gang has ultimately fared no better, however. Danny, the leader of the "Lousy People," the "taste-maker" who "encouraged aberration for its own sake," has as an adult been confined in a rehabilitation home and, when visited by the narrator, passes a despairing verdict on all experience: "It's a pile of crap. . . . It's no deal at all." Danny's legacy counters the Lousy People's expectations. Instead of being a defiant hero in the James Dean mode, Danny is vegetating in cynicism. Other Lousy People have followed suit: one is incarcerated for turning violently on his mother; another has become a petty insurance agent. Although the case might be made that the narrator has not succumbed to death, madness, or mediocrity, the story offers no substantial evidence that he has crafted a meaningful life. At one extreme among the early stories, then, "Cousin Poor Lesley and the Lousy People" is an elegy for lost youth and hopes. Thematically, it hardly matters whether one is a "straight man" like Lesley or a rebel without a cause like Danny. One's youthful expectations and hopes are destined to be frustrated in one's adulthood. In this story, perhaps more than in many of the stories in the collection, Elkin's irony is cosmic, but hardly comic.

The title story is a more powerful example of the sorrow dominating Elkin's early short stories. The protagonist, merchant Jake Greenspahn, suffers more like a character out of a Bernard Malamud or Edward Lewis Wallant novel of the American diaspora than the vigorous, engaging hustlers of *A Bad Man* or *The Franchiser.* Jake's day–the scope of his story–involves acknowledging and dealing with many griefs. Weary of the grind of selling, he views his inventory as a burden. In a changing neighborhood, he wishes that he could sell the business and be done with it. His business reversals are compounded by personal griefs, for he has recently buried his only son. He feels painfully the loss of his familial future and his business enterprise. His life stretches before him as an unending sequence of sad days like the one he undergoes in the novel.

Unlike Malamud's Morris Bober in *The Assistant* (1957), the prototype of the suffering Jewish American grocer, Jake is no long-suffering saint. He carries his resentment and disappointment with him as surely as he suffers the constipation that crudely symbolizes his repression of his many griefs. He resents even his friends and associates, categorizing them in either the "criers" camp, people who merely complain about their lives, or the "kibitzers" camp, people who live vicariously on others' experiences. Elkin's most bitter irony is that, although Jake uses these labels to disparage the people with whom he associates, he is himself both a crier, missing few opportunities to practice a form of passive aggression and thereby to impose his grief on others, and a kibitzer, someone who holds no real cards of his own but lives through others, whether in the form of his dashed expectations for his son, Harold, or his voyeuristic suspicions that his butcher and his cashier are carrying on a torrid sexual affair even in his store.

Although Jake's sorrows focus mainly on Harold's death and the declining business, he displaces his grief by means of cruel treatment of others. He fires Frank, his produce man, for a trivial cause, although Frank has been instrumental in keeping the store from going under. Jake, however, suspects that Frank has been stealing from him. Moreover, he alienates a wealthy customer whom he believes came into the store to cheat him by asking for a discount on a loaf of bread after deliberately mutilating the wrapper. Despite the fact that the shopper is a doctor's wife (therefore well-to-do), a long-term customer (with, however, a history of stunts such as the one with the bread wrapper), and someone bringing an abundantly loaded cart to the miserably unbusy checkout, Jake chases her out of his store as a *podler* (thief). He is thus doing injury to himself simply to assert his identity and proprietorship. Throughout the story Jake also feels victimized by the chain store that has opened nearby and by the customers who buy most of their groceries at the supermarket, then come to his store to take advantage of the loss-leaders he advertises to entice shoppers away from the chain store.

Thus alienated from his business, his associates, his fellow merchants, and his personal life, Jake faces with dread the minion he will observe for a year in Harold's memory. His grief is exponential: Harold, his beloved son, has died childless and without having the chance to experience life for himself–another "kibitzer" in Jake's classification system. But life has yet one more brutal truth for Jake to face and suffer. While Jake is firing Frank for disagreeing with him, the produce man inadvertently blurts out that Harold was looting the cash register. After this revelation, evidence accumulates indicating that, no matter how much Jake may seek to deny it, his son was indeed responsible for the thefts Jake has blamed on others. Gradually he comes to accept this truth, and that evening in shul he grieves for his son, "twenty-three years old, wifeless, jobless, sacrificing nothing even in the act of death, leaving the world with his life not started"–and a thief. There is no end to Jake's sorrow, only expansion. Although it would be an exaggeration to call Jake a "loser" because of his sorrow and his ineffectual response to it, he has none of the dynamism, confrontational energy, or defiance of the heroes of Elkin's novels, who can be depended upon to fight back against circumstance.

This general tenuousness is true of many of the protagonists in *Criers and Kibitzers, Kibitzers and Criers.* Feldman, the protagonist of "In the Alley," faces his terminal illness by insulting a whore and getting himself beaten almost to death–almost but not quite taking control, if not of his life, then of his death. By contrast Bertie, the moocher of "The Guest," feels paradoxically that "dependence gave him energy. He was never so alert as when people did you favors." Bertie forces himself on acquaintances as a house sitter, then spends much of his two-week stay fantasizing about roles that could bring him the illusion of importance and power. Planning to commit suicide before the tenants return, Bertie turns to drugs to induce "visions" as his fantasies become increasingly morbid. In his final hallucination it occurs to him that he has one recourse other than suicide to force others to acknowledge his presence. He robs the family, then desecrates some of their artworks. When real robbers show up in the night, Bertie's role as a petty thief is challenged. By fleeing before the owners return, he attempts to claim responsibility for the real robbery as well as his own gestural one. With a strange joy born of self-loathing, Bertie takes satisfaction in the knowledge that he will be hunted down and punished, that he can matter to someone outside one of his fantasies as an outlaw. In fact, however, even the robbers were not interested enough in him to make any effort to prevent him from being a witness to their crime.

The most extreme example of Elkin's sad tale of the proverbial schmuck is the often-anthologized "I Look Out for Ed Wolfe," a narrative about Ed Wolfe's vocational and philosophical crisis. The central character is dismissed from his job, sells all his belongings, and creates an unnerving scene when he attempts to sell a woman in an African American nightclub. Wolfe's progress through the story may on one level be viewed as a devolution from obsessive behavior to destructive actions harmful to others as well as himself. At the same time Elkin's tone suggests that readers should mix compassion with judgment for Wolfe, whose experience may be a paradigm for the existential crisis awaiting those who define themselves in terms of jobs, or objects, or associations. Elkin uses a controlling theme, the often-repeated reminders that Wolfe is an orphan. Although this fact does not fully explain Wolfe's behavior in the story, it does suggest a synecdoche in which Wolfe's predicament represents the rootless alienation of modern commercial culture.

After he has sold all his possessions–he calls this process "liquidating [his] inventory," using a term with overt commercial associations–Wolfe develops a balance sheet that explicitly associates the status of being an orphan with the logic of business culture. Amortizing his assets, life insurance, automobile, spare clothing, and furniture, Wolfe concludes that his net worth equals "the going rate for orphans in a wicked world. Something under $2500." While this sum may have seemed less paltry to Wolfe than it does to the reader at the end of the twentieth century, the problem is that Wolfe feels compelled to equate his worth with a material sum. Again and again, he identifies his special grief as that of the orphan and at one point even goes so far as to suggest an equation (perhaps more problematic than Elkin intended) between orphans and African Americans.

The tenor of Elkin's emphasis on Wolfe's orphan status is suggested in the first paragraphs of the story. Wolfe always thinks of himself as looking and acting like an orphan, with the "ruthless isolation, the hard self-sufficiency" of loners and isolated persons. Readers should note immediately the dual registers of these descriptions. When viewing himself as a loner, he notes powerful qualities such as "ruthlessness" and "self-sufficiency." Yet the dominant impression of Wolfe's claim of orphan status is his sense of victimized dispossession and the absence of a history behind his personal experience. Because he sees his life as lacking roots or history, Wolfe looks to alternative sources for his identity, his sense of being. As the title suggests, Wolfe depends on others to "look out for Ed Wolfe" psychologically. The result of this existential dependency is a series of assaults on his ego that ultimately results in a desperate symbolic gesture in which Wolfe associates his orphan status with the Middle Passage heritage of the black people in the nightclub, whose ancestors were cut off from their African heritage by the commercial ruthlessness of the slave trade. Rather than empathizing with these persons, however, the drunken Wolfe re-enacts the worst roles available in the commodified, dehumanized heritage of slavery, claiming the role of slave-auctioneer over Roberta Mary, whom he seems genuinely to like, thus insulting the collective memory of every person in the club. He compounds this insult by giving all his money to "buy" Roberta Mary. Although his motive is to continue his personal process of dispossession, the effect can be none other than to claim illegitimate power based solely on race.

Even before this disastrous misapplication of what may indeed be a productive intuition of the similarity between any orphan, who in Wolfe's case knows neither his family history nor even his cultural association (he grew up in a Jewish orphanage, but no one was sure whether he was born of Christian, Jewish, or even atheist parents), and descendants of slaves whose ancestors were systematically denied traditional family associations, Wolfe has compensated for his orphan status by throwing himself uncritically into those concepts of himself that others created for him. Working at the ironically named "Cornucopia Finance" company, which subverts its horn-of-plenty allusion by making petty loans to the down and out, Wolfe has discovered his role in life as a bill collector–really a bully with a telephone. To validate himself and give himself assurances of his power, he compulsively abuses and insults the deadbeats who cannot meet their financial obligations, at one point threatening a client (whom he labels a Pole, thereby slurring immigrants of Polish origin by insinuating that all Poles are bad credit risks) with both "lawyers and the machine guns" to collect a bad debt.

Elkin's simplest irony is that Wolfe is so good at what he does that he gets himself fired. His employer, who advises that Wolfe watch out for himself by adopting the businessman's credo of "detachment and caution," admits that he is firing Wolfe not because he is inept, but because he takes his job too seriously: "An artist. You had a real thing for the dead-beat soul. . . . But, Ed, you're a gangster." Wolfe's boss may or may not realize that Wolfe throws himself so savagely into his job because it is his only source of self-esteem. Grasping for selfhood, Wolfe loses all restraint. His campaign against deadbeats is a way he can assert him-

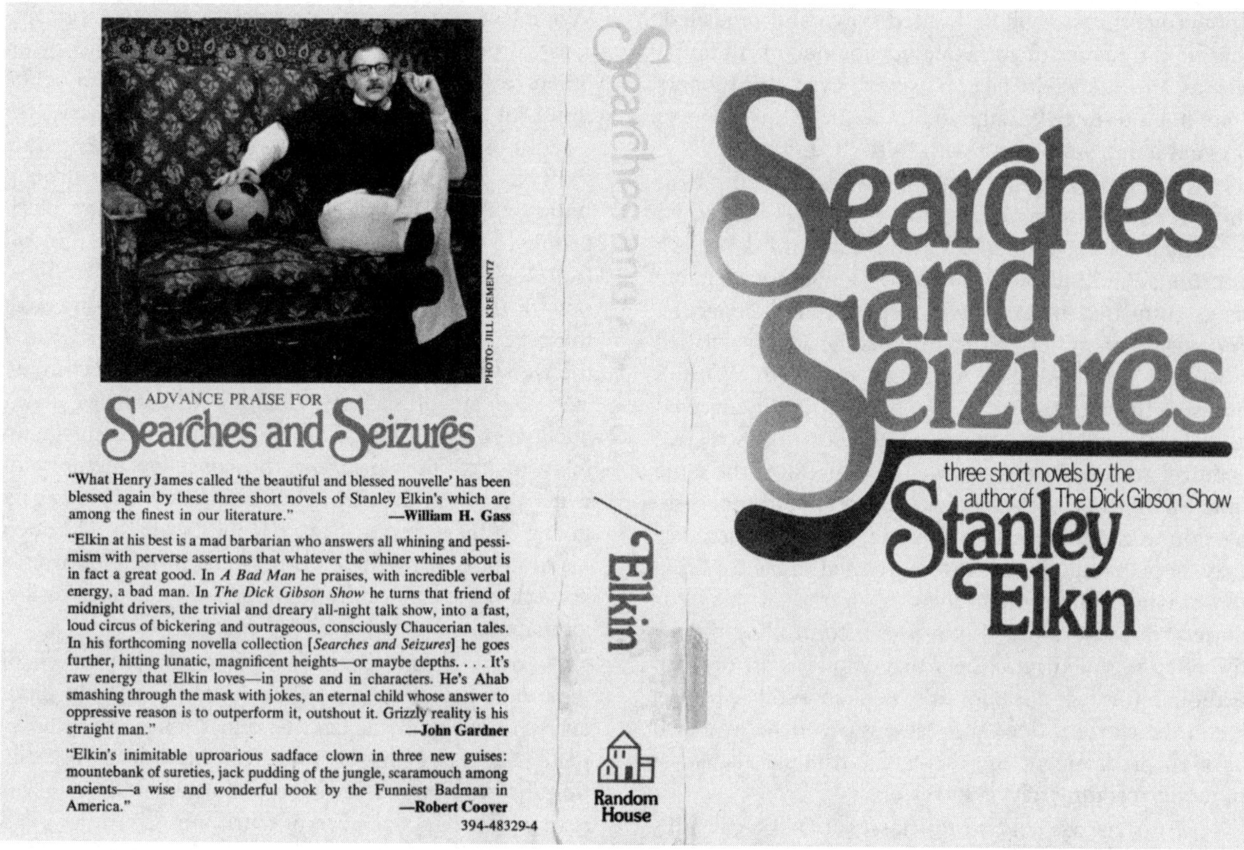

Dust jacket for Elkin's 1973 collection of novellas; the title alludes to the Fourth Amendment of the U.S. Constitution

self and at the same time win company approval, or so he thought.

On being fired, Wolfe takes his orphanhood, as he conceives it, to a different and somewhat more desperate level. Wolfe discovers through a series of accidents a new vocation as a "born salesman." He finds in the pitchman's rhetoric an outlet for his creativity and in the strong-arm tactics of salesmanship a new validation of his identity. Paradoxically, this activity of selling evolves into a strategy for dispossessing himself of that new validation. When he sells his record collection, Wolfe says he is giving up his "ears." His books he associates with his mind. He calls cashing in his insurance policy selling his future. Wolfe is liquidating not just his material assets but also all the signs and signifiers of his personality as he can define it. But, having converted his identity to capital, he finds that he faces a dwindling resource. The recognition that selfhood, thus commodified in quantifiable terms, is a finite resource leads Wolfe to his final, insane grasp for significance.

Wolfe has become so alienated within his definition of his orphanhood that he can think of human interdependency only in terms of power and possession. Thus his drunken effort to auction off, then to buy, Roberta Mary suggests two central yet paradoxical issues in "I Look Out for Ed Wolfe": first, it is a logical summary of Wolfe's association of personal qualities with material assets, one compounded by his cultural heritage of racism leading back to slavery. Conversely, Wolfe's buying Roberta Mary, then taking leave of her, suggests that he has completed the process of self-divestiture. He no longer sees money as a metaphor for self. But the reader is left to wonder whether Wolfe is better off, whether will he get out of the club alive after the insults he has handed out, and how he will survive without money or a job. Of course, it can be argued that what he had, even as a bill collector, can hardly be called a life because it was lived under an illusion.

One exception to the stories that narrate events in the lives of unhappy, unreconciled, passive characters is "A Poetics for Bullies," the central first-person narrative of a neighborhood punk who has elevated bullying to a self-defining art form. The protagonist, "Push the Bully," makes it his life's work to push others' faces in their weaknesses, to make people acknowledge and regret their imperfections. At one level, Push is a seething well of resentment: "I love nobody loved." At a competing level, however, Push is, as the title implies, an artist. He treats bullying not as a matter of brute strength but as a dramatic art of rhetorical intimidation. He has given up physical training, for he feels that bullies who have greater strength than those they torment do not qualify as bullies at all: "they're *athletes.*" Push defines a true bully as one who risks much, one whom his victims might beat up. He creates his own nature by proving to himself that he can manipulate his victims through force of will and sheer verbal skill, not through physical domination.

Elkin's strategy is to insist that the reader give a hearing to a character who defines his worth by impressing others with their weakness. By limiting the point of view to what Push sees and feels, Elkin tries to give Push sole claim upon the reader's allegiance. When Push's challenge for leadership on the playground comes, readers have no choice but to accept his version of the events he narrates. Push's adversary, the new kid, is like someone directly out of a Horatio Alger story, a Boy Scout manual, or a parent's fondest daydream. The generically named John Williams represents everything Push is not and will not become. Williams is a scholar-athlete, excelling in all the arts appropriate to students. Moreover, he has a rich stock of exotic adventures and a fund of esoteric knowledge, all of which he is eager to share with Push's victims. Worse yet, from Push's perspective, Williams practices charity in the community and in the schoolyard. To the losers Push has tormented, Williams gives palliatives and tactics to cope with their weaknesses and deformities. He even offers to befriend Push.

There is little that explains Williams's motives except that he is "good." Thus the story becomes a classic confrontation between "virtue" and "malice." But readers find themselves impressed on the side of malice, which in this context seems no less arbitrary or insidious than virtue. Whether Williams's motives are simply to do good, or to create dependence on the part of those who benefit from his kindness, his actions seem to threaten Push's very essence. So Push provokes a confrontation–one he knows he is destined to lose, since Williams has not stopped working out. In spite of his ethic that strength is alien to true bullying, Push hits Williams knowing that his only hope is that Williams will strike back, show anger, and lose credibility with the other children. But Williams has an excellent right cross; the other children approve of Williams's self-defense; and Push is doubly defeated when Williams offers to help him rise, a gesture of reconciliation, after decking him. Push's gamble has backfired. All he has left is his defiance, his refusal to be reconciled, and this sole value alienates him even further from the playground community. Yet, Push feels surprisingly vindicated by his "bully's sour solace. It's enough, I'll make do." In this story, as in *A Bad Man,* Elkin forces his readers to consider the integrity of the bully's self-conception in the face of the challenges presented by model citizens such as Williams who in fact embody fairly ubiquitous bourgeois virtues.

The title of Elkin's first collection of novellas, *Searches and Seizures* (1973), alludes to amendment four of the Bill of Rights, which protects citizens against unlawful search and seizure. Elkin offers one representative of each of his classes of typical protagonists. Preminger, the hero of "The Condominium," resembles the sorrowful middle-class hero of many early stories. He accepts passively the condo his father willed to him, and after making several futile efforts at reconciliation with the artificial, phony life his father had created for himself there, the son commits suicide. Preminger is one of the few characters in all Elkin's fiction to submit to despair and the only major character who chooses death over life. Although the attitudes of the condo association and the father's former girlfriend are roundly satirized as empty and pretentious, Preminger's reaction is far less than defiant. His death is really an admission of his inability to cope with the other tenants' bourgeois mediocrity.

The hero of the strange novella "The Making of Ashenden" is a variation on the John Williams type in "A Poetics for Bullies," a refined, kindly aristocrat who seems to spring from one of Henry James's novels of innocence coming to terms with the possibility of misery. Telling his own story, Brewster Ashenden considers himself a "heroic man" who knows "literature and math and science and art"–in short, he says, "I know everything." Like most romantic heroes, Ashenden at last finds his true love, a perfect woman–wise, beautiful, gentle, nauseatingly virtuous, and sick to the point of dying. This mixture of a send-up of romantic sentimentality and a spin-off of the James novel of innocence turns to a typically Elkin experience when the hero finds the world of art encroaching on reality. Set the ridiculous task of recovering his sexual innocence by Jane so that they may marry chastely before she dies (although he is not totally innocent, he is perversely altruistic), Ashenden finds himself entering a world in which reality imitates art. Walking in his friend's English manor garden, he sees manifestations of paintings by several masters.

"The Making of Ashenden" turns from satiric realism to metafictive zaniness when Ashenden encounters a bear in estrus and decides that in order to save his life he must service her. At first he believes this act is part of the test his fiancée had in mind. As he wryly puts it, "I was in art and now I'm in allegory." But the "allegorical" relation between nature and art reaches its apotheosis when Ashenden overcomes his natural aversion and couples successfully with the she-bear, thus initiating his own transformation from an advocate of the civilized, refined, and intellectual to a devotee of the wild and the coarse. The novella becomes a send-up of Henry David Thoreau's statement in *Walden; or, Life in the Woods* (1854): "I love the wild not less than the good." The pun implicit in the title–Ashenden is "made" in that he is seduced, sort of, by a bear and he is moreover "made" in that he devolves from a man who loves artifice and refinement to one who relishes coarser pleasures–is reinforced by the final, cruder pun that signifies his transformation. Ashenden redefines the classic table of the elements: "Air. Water, he thought. Fire, Earth, he thought . . . and *honey*."

Beyond a doubt, however, the masterwork of *Searches and Seizures* is "The Bailbondsman," a funny and compelling novella about a lower-class, obsessive hero who exists on the periphery of the law enforcement system and who, as do so many protagonists of Elkin's novels, lives for his work and defines his character as an extension of his vocation. The author told an interviewer in 1991 that his inspiration for this novella was a piece by the late Chicago columnist Mike Royko, in which he claimed that the bailbondsman is not merely on the periphery, but actually outside, the law. According to Royko, these individuals have literal power of life and death over those who jump their bonds. Whether or not that is true, the premise interested Elkin. Such a role would undoubtedly appeal to obsessive characters, his specialty.

Whether it be in his associations with his clients, with his professional organizations, with his employees, or even with his nemeses, the two crooks he could not catch, Alexander Main acts with single-minded, comic assertiveness. Elkin casts bailbondsmen as connoisseurs of the outré, "men who had never tired of the infinite eccentricity that came their way." Even Main's short-term memory, which is like a computer, manifests his vocation. He takes pride in recalling every detail about anyone he encounters professionally, then discarding the information when it no longer serves any purpose: "chuck it in the mind's wastebasket as you'd throw away a phone number . . . when it no longer has any meaning." This professional pride is the first clue to Main's personality: he objectifies people; he recalls them in detail as long as they are professionally relevant, but when they cease to matter as clients, they cease to matter at all. He wonders if a guard at the city museum is his friend because Main includes the guard on his Christmas list for petty officials of the court system. This ambiguity about the nature and terms of friendship confirms that Main simply has no life outside his role as a bondsman. In that role he is even more compulsive than most typical Elkin protagonists. Like Feldman in *A Bad Man,* who hungers to make the impossible sale and thereby to define himself, Main obsesses on the perfect criminal–not the garden-variety petty thief or pimp but an honest-to-badness criminal with the capacity to jump bail and make a magnificent break for it. Until that ideal felon comes along, Main contents himself with bullying and chasing petty crooks and hustlers set up by collusion between the mob and the courts.

The novella is a series of conflicts with petty Mafia-types, pimps, and crooked judges, but in his dreams Main hunts down his two idealized nemeses, the oddly named Oyp and Glyp, "fugitives from fugitiveness itself, . . . limits to his power and his precious freedom." In his dreams he hounds these fugitives, the only ones ever to jump bond successfully on him, as far as the pyramids to haul them back to justice or simply kill them. In his strangely erotic dream Oyp and Glyp are elevated to mythic status: as robbers of a pharaoh's tomb, caught red-handed (one actually has the mummified heart in his pocket), they are the ultimate challenge to a bondsman, archcriminals whose escape from Main proves their skill, not his ineptness. But waking, Main sadly realizes that he has mythologized these petty criminals, who were not "masterminds, not arch criminals, just ordinary car thieves"–just small-time crooks who escaped by dumb luck. Thus Main's dream is a compensation for his one failure in the bring-'em-back-dead-or-alive ethos of the bondsman.

The novella ends with a mad, compulsive transformation. Main converts his usually meek associate Crainpool into the master prey he needs to fulfill himself as a bondsman, to give him a surrogate for the lost personal myth of Oyp and Glyp. Although Crainpool is victimized and objectified, Elkin's aggressive, assertive hero is once again animated by the need to track down a master fugitive, even if one of his own creation.

Probably the most commercially successful collection of short fiction by Elkin is also his most controversial. His 1979 "triptych," *The Living End,* is composed of three stories with closely wrought intertextual links among the characters and themes. The collection brought Elkin an audience unprecedented before and after in his literary career, but it also challenged and even insulted many people's beliefs about heaven, hell, the afterlife, the moral life, the nature of God, and the possibility of cosmic justice. Taken collectively, the three stories constitute a dark, funny, outrageous reflection on many beliefs people hold, with whatever degree of seriousness, about life and the hereafter.

The best story, "The Conventional Wisdom," is Elkin's version of the book of Job, which asks that profound biblical inquiry, "Why do good people suffer?" The biblical answer is that God permits people to suffer in order to test their faith; for twentieth-century writers, this answer has proved inadequate. Elkin's saintly hero, the merchant Ellerbee, does everything in his power to live a virtuous life. Although he is a purveyor of liquors, Ellerbee builds his business around his employees' best interests. One, shot in a robbery and incapacitated for life, has never missed a paycheck because of his boss's sense of duty; neither has another former employee's widow. Ellerbee also provides for his aged parents, although as an adopted orphan he has no biological obligation to them. Even his decision to relocate his store to a suburban mall is motivated as much by his concern for his employees' safety as it is for potential profitability. Elkin's first cosmic irony is that in this presumably safe location, Ellerbee is robbed and quite deliberately murdered. The ultimate measure of Ellerbee's moral decency is that, even as he faces the weapon that will take his life, he takes comfort in knowing that his attackers are white, so the racist clichés of others in the business community will be proven incorrect by his death.

John Milton–whose rhetoric Elkin invokes when God calls the damned in hell "iambic angels in free fall"–set out "To justify the ways of God to Man" in *Paradise Lost* (1667). Elkin suggests the irrelevance of any such justification with the way Ellerbee is treated in eternity. Any reasonable person would expect such a good man to go to heaven; but Ellerbee is cruelly damned. Even Job was reconciled, and Ellerbee eventually demands that God give him an explanation, not a "Job job." Not only is Ellerbee denied perpetual bliss, but the process of his denial reveals cosmic sadism. After his murder he gets a grand tour of heaven, and all the clichés ever heard about heaven are true: the streets are gold, and the blessed enjoy blissful reunions purged of their fleshly imperfections. Ellerbee is excluded only after he has learned what he stands to lose by being consigned to hell. How, readers wonder, can this be divine justice?

In hell Ellerbee continues the efforts of a decent person to be reconciled to injustice. He tries to become a model citizen of Hades. He tries to make work, in order to avoid the boredom of eternity; to learn, like the hero of Albert Camus's *Le Mythe de Sisyphe* (The Myth of Sisyphus, 1942), to love his pain; to explain his punishment by reverting to paranoia and believing that God had something against him specifically; and even to pray in hell, to demand that God (whom Ellerbee, after sixty-two years of undeserved damnation, calls "Old Terrorist, . . . God the Godfather") explain His purposes to Ellerbee. The explanation he gets, while technically valid, is anything but satisfactory. Ellerbee challenges, "Where were *You* when I loved my neighbor as myself? When I never stole or bore false witness? When . . . I never even raised a finger in anger?" God responds that He finds Ellerbee technically guilty of breaking four commandments: swearing, failing to observe the Sabbath, failing to honor his parents, and feeling adulterous lust. All are literally true: Ellerbee cursed, but far less than most people do; he kept his store open on Sundays to keep up payments to former employees; he provided for his adoptive parents but did not know his birth parents and therefore could not have honored them; and he became sexually aroused when the attractive widow of a former employee became amorous in expressing her appreciation, though he repressed his sexual desire. He has been assigned to hell on a series of technicalities, but mostly because he inadvertently insulted God by associating the beauty of heaven with a theme park.

Dust jacket for Elkin's last collection of novellas (1993), which includes "Her Sense of Timing," about a professor with multiple sclerosis

All this mistreatment of Ellerbee-Job foregrounds the most controversial theme in Elkin's triptych: the nature of God, who seems petty in sending Ellerbee to hell and sadistic in his address to the inhabitants of hell. Moreover, in the second story, "The Bottom Line," God makes a mistake when he visits (but not to harrow) hell: He further banishes one of the damned from hell to a permanent limbo and eventually grants heaven to a sadistic, whining loser named Quiz. He takes a child because the child plays beautiful music, and God wants that praise in heaven, not on earth. So God is capricious, unfair, sadistic, and extremely egocentric, every inch a verbal exhibitionist. With a Holy Family that resents Him and a Creation that cannot appreciate Him, God decides at last to annihilate all He has created. His caprice and egocentrism are manifested when he explains the doctrine of original sin: "It was all Art. *Because it makes a better story is why.*"

This emphasis on God as narrator of his own story has provoked many readers to see *The Living End* as a metafiction in which the role of the creator is analogous to that of a writer who creates characters and events for the purpose of the narrative itself. In Elkin's triptych, however, it is the creatures who suffer so the creator may enjoy watching His narrative unfold. While this spin is an extrapolation from the orthodox religious notion of earthly life as a test to prove our worthiness to enjoy eternal bliss, the God of most religions is neither as capricious nor as error-prone as this one. His decision to end creation itself because "I never found my audience" provides conclusive proof that the parable of God as writer/creator can be pressed to a reductio ad absurdum. Although Elkin vigorously defended his creation as an extension of the orthodox notion that God is omniscient (he once told an interviewer, "He's entitled. He's God"), there is something whimsical, but funny and engaging, about the doomsday of *The Living End.* It makes readers laugh, and if they are intellectually up to it, they are challenged to reconsider all the conventional wisdom about religion and eternity.

One of Elkin's final fiction collections was *Van Gogh's Room at Arles.* In the first story, "Her Sense of Timing," which is quasi-autobiographical, the wife of a professor suffering from multiple sclerosis announces her intention to leave her husband on the day of his annual party for his graduate students. Claire leaves Jack Schiff to get along as best he can with his walker, a stair-glide his students later break in a drunken roller-coaster prank, and an aggressive, older, pushy graduate student whom Schiff briefly hopes may have amorous interest in him.

The many threats to Schiff's independence leading up to and during the party subvert his authority as a teacher and take away his personal privacy as some students eventually put him to bed and discover the inconveniences of his illness, such as his bedside urinal. Elkin concludes the story by alluding to a popular television commercial of the early 1990s, when Schiff shouts toward his new security system, "I've fallen and I can't get up!" When he decides on this catchphrase as the greeting for the answering machine he must buy because of his immobility, Schiff admits to himself how little autonomy he has left.

"*Town Crier* Exclusive, Confessions of a Princess Manqué: 'How Royals Found Me "Unsuitable" to Marry Their Larry'" is proof that Elkin's comic genius did not wane as his health deteriorated. In 1989 Elkin called this work-in-progress a novella "about the vocation of being a princess," a clear allusion to the early stages of the troubles the current British royal family has endured. The years between the plan and the publication only brought more public data to support Elkin's narrative of royal humiliation. Until it was implicated in the 1997 car crash that killed Princess Diana, whose early conflicts with the royal family probably inspired parts of this story, tabloid journalism flourished as one of the seamier aspects of pop culture. Royal family antics embarrassed the monarchy and the British Commonwealth while creating financial empires for certain tabloid publishers. "Confessions of a Princess Manqué" deftly sends up the commercial prurience of the tabloids, the pretentiousness of royalty, and the phony dignity of public figures.

The spurned princess, Lulu, tells her own story, an uncharacteristic Elkin technique–except for "A Poetics for Bullies" and the novel *The Rabbi of Lud* (1987), he generally preferred omniscient or limited omniscient narrative. The story is told as a series of weekly installments that Lulu has sold to a London tabloid for £50,000; Elkin thus takes a potshot at those tabloid editors who pay handsomely for lurid stories and are concerned less with truth than with convenience. Lulu assures her readers and her publisher of plenty of prurient and salacious gossip, yet she is more like Victorian writers in her verbal reticence. She even uses dashes to replace vowels in certain naughty words.

As a character, and as a source of information, Lulu is a fascinating variation on the Victorian stereotype of the scorned woman. Her revenge, however, is not directed at her prince, or even at the royals, who certainly discouraged the prince in his courtship, but at the brash, nouveau riche tabloid editor, who turns out to have dumped Lulu before she met the prince, and with whom many of her revelations constitute a conversation of sorts.

Prince Larry is one of Elkin's saintly characters, a comic version of the Ellerbee character in *The*

Living End. The joke is that this prince, unlike most contemporary royals, really is a prince of a guy; he has sacrificed everything for his duty to the crown, while his hedonistic brothers and sisters supply tabloid publishers with profitable fodder. Larry is kind and thoughtful to everyone, Lulu included. He even loses deliberately at a famous casino so the proprietor will not take advantage of his weaker siblings. But his love for Lulu, which is genuine, must be sacrificed to an artificial version of royal dignity and noblesse oblige. Elkin's verdict on the utter ridiculousness of concepts such as noblesse oblige in the postmodern, tabloid era is manifested when the prince decides he must bow to family pressures and repudiate Lulu–not because she is not a virgin but because her previous sexual partner was a peer, and a nouveau riche one at that. At one point he actually regrets that Lulu did not sleep with a commoner.

In "Confessions of a Princess Manqué" Elkin confirms his own commitment to language as a means of manifesting the folly of the human condition, making this late story a representative example of his overall achievement. His eccentric, ironic, obsessive view of the human condition is a healthy antidote to depression and to self-importance. He taught readers much about the richness of language and about the art of laughing at themselves.

Interviews:

Scott Sanders, "An Interview with Stanley Elkin," *Contemporary Literature,* 16 (1974): 131–145;

Phyllis and Joseph Bernt, "Stanley Elkin on Fiction: An Interview," *Prairie Schooner,* 50 (1975): 14–25;

Thomas LeClair, "Stanley Elkin: The Art of Fiction LXI," *Paris Review,* 17 (Summer 1976): 53–86; republished in *Anything Can Happen: Interviews with Contemporary Authors,* by LeClair and Larry McCaffery (Urbana: University of Illinois Press, 1983), pp. 106–125;

Jay Clayton, "An Interview with Stanley Elkin," *Contemporary Literature,* 24 (1983): 1–11;

Richard B. Sale, "An Interview with Stanley Elkin in Saint Louis," *Studies in the Novel,* 16 (1984): 314–325;

David C. Dougherty, "A Conversation with Stanley Elkin," *Literary Review,* 34 (1991): 175–195;

Peter J. Bailey, "'A Hat Where There Never Was a Hat': Stanley Elkin's Fifteenth Interview," *Review of Contemporary Fiction,* 15 (Summer 1995): 15-26.

Bibliographies:

Larry McCaffrey, "Stanley Elkin: A Bibliography 1957–1977," *Bulletin of Bibliography,* 34 (1977): 73–76;

William M. Robbins, "A Bibliography of Stanley Elkin," *Critique,* 26 (1985): 169–184.

References:

Peter J. Bailey, *Reading Stanley Elkin* (Urbana: University of Illinois Press, 1985);

Bailey, "Stanley Elkin's Tales of Last Resorts," *Mid-American Review,* 5 (1985): 73–80;

Doris Bargen, *The Fiction of Stanley Elkin* (Frankfurt: Lang, 1980);

Robert Edward Colbert, "The American Salesman as Pitchman and Poet in the Fiction of Stanley Elkin," *Critique,* 21 (1978): 52–58;

Robert Coover, "Preface," in *Stanley Elkin's Greatest Hits* (New York: Dutton, 1980), pp. ix–xii;

Delta, special Elkin issue, 20 (February 1985);

John Ditsky, "'Death as Grotesque as Life': The Fiction of Stanley Elkin," *Hollins Critic,* 19 (June 1982): 1–11;

Kurt Dittmar, "Stanley Elkin, 'I Look Out for Ed Wolfe,'" in *Die Amerikanische Short Story der gegenwart: Interpretation,* edited by Peter Freese (Berlin: Schmidt, 1975), pp. 252–261;

David C. Dougherty, *Stanley Elkin* (Boston: Twayne, 1991);

Harry G. Edinger, "Bears in Three Contemporary Fictions," *Humanities Association Review,* 28 (1976): 141–150;

Thomas LeClair, "The Obsessional Fiction of Stanley Elkin," *Contemporary Literature,* 16 (1974): 146–162;

Larry McCaffrey, "Stanley Elkin's Recovery of the Ordinary," *Critique,* 21 (1978): 39–51;

Melvin Raff, "Wyndham Lewis and Stanley Elkin: Salvation, Satire, and Hell," *Studies in Contemporary Satire,* 8 (Spring 1981): 1–8;

Review of Contemporary Fiction, special Elkin issue, 15 (Summer 1995);

Arthur M. Saltzman, "Ego and Appetite in Stanley Elkin's Fiction," *Literary Review,* 32 (1988): 111–118;

"Stanley Elkin and William H. Gass: A Special Feature," *Iowa Review,* 7 (1975);

Alan Wilde, "A Map of Supersensitiveness: Irony in the Postmodern Age," in his *Horizons of Assent: Modernism, Postmodernism, and the Ironic Imagination* (Baltimore: Johns Hopkins University Press, 1981), pp. 127–165.

Irvin Faust

(11 June 1924 -)

Julia B. Boken
State University of New York at Oneonta

See also Faust entries in *DLB 2: American Novelists Since World War II, DLB 28: Twentieth-Century American-Jewish Fiction Writers,* and *DLB Yearbook: 1980.*

BOOKS: *Entering Angel's World: A Student-Centered Casebook* (New York: Bureau of Publications, Teachers College, Columbia University, 1963);

Roar Lion Roar and Other Stories (New York: Random House, 1965; London, Gollancz, 1965);

The Steagle (New York: Random House, 1966);

The File on Stanley Patton Buchta (New York: Random House, 1970);

Willy Remembers (New York: Arbor House, 1971);

Foreign Devils (New York: Arbor House, 1973);

A Star in the Family (Garden City, N.Y.: Doubleday, 1975);

Newsreel (New York & London: Harcourt Brace Jovanovich / Bruccoli Clark, 1980);

The Year of the Hot Jock and Other Stories (New York: Dutton, 1985);

Jim Dandy (New York: Carroll & Graf, 1994).

OTHER: Paul Cain, *Fast One,* afterword by Faust (Carbondale: Southern Illinois University Press, 1978).

SELECTED PERIODICAL PUBLICATIONS–UNCOLLECTED: "Action at Vicksburg," *New Black Mask Quarterly,* no. 5 (1986): 101–128;

"The Empire State is Number Three?" *Confrontation,* no. 37/38 (Spring/Summer 1988): 25–40;

"Artie and Benny," *Michigan Quarterly Review,* 30 (Spring 1989): 236–257;

"The Blue Seats," *Confrontation,* no. 42–43 (Spring/Summer 1990): 50–64;

"Bootsie Wants Harvard," *Four Quarters,* 5 (Fall 1991): 13–27;

"Let Me Off Uptown," *Fiction,* 10, no. 1–2 (1991): 73–105;

"Enemy Propaganda," *Confrontation,* no. 48–49 (Spring/Summer 1992): 30–50;

"The Combat Zone," *Descant,* 33, no. 1 (1993): 2–28;

"Black Auxiliaries," *Literary Review,* 37 (Summer 1994): 545–567;

"Journey into War," *Dimensions: A Journal of Holocaust Studies,* 9, no. 1 (1995): 15–21;

"Paradise," *Confrontation,* 58–59 (Spring/Summer 1996): 83–107.

Irvin Faust was still a teenager in 1940, when the German invasion of France reshaped his personal universe. As he recalled years later in "Journey into War" (1995), "I experienced the worst culture shock of my young life. France fell in six weeks. The greatest army in the world, my heroes of 1914–1918, collapsed overnight." Most young men in their midteens do not take global crises personally, but Faust had been nourished in a household where history held a bitter legacy. His father, Morris, had left his native village near Kraków in Galicia to escape anti-Semitism at a time when that part of Poland was under the domination of the Austro-Hungarian emperor Francis Joseph I. As Faust wrote in 1995, "With or without the Emperor, the Polish were as bad as the Austrians, and the Austrians were even worse than the Germans–look at Hitler." Leaving behind his parents and his sister, Morris Faust and his three brothers immigrated to the United States, where they settled on the Lower East Side of Manhattan. Morris Faust joined a Galician support network and began, like many other European immigrants at this time, to realize the so-called American Dream. He sent packages to his parents and sister until 1939, when the Germans initiated World War II by invading Poland. Never heard from again, those three relatives probably lost their lives early in the war at the nearby Auschwitz concentration camp. After the invasion the elder Faust lost his customary gusto for life.

The stories told by Morris Faust and the subsequent events in Europe created in Irvin Faust a lifelong awareness (perhaps even an obsession) with history. Another family narrative dear to Faust stems from his mother's side of the family. Like her father and grandfa-

Irvin Faust (photograph by Jean Faust)

ther, Pauline Henschel Faust was born in the United States. According to family legend Faust's maternal grandfather, Louis Henschel, was the only Jew who fought with the U.S. Army in General George Crook's 1883 expedition against the Apaches led by Geronimo.

Faust spent his early life in Brooklyn and Queens in a household that revered Judge Benjamin Nathan Cardozo, Sol Bloom, Emanuel Celler, and Judge Samuel S. Liebowitz, all noted liberals. Faust enlisted in the Signal Corps Reserve at the age of eighteen, received training, and was called up to active duty at nineteen. He chose to serve in this branch of the U.S. Army because he was inspired by the signal man in the movie *Wake Island* (1942), who served under the heroic leader played by actor Brian Donlevy. Dropping out of Queens College of the City of New York (now Queens College of the City University of New York), Faust entered an army training program that developed him, he says, into a "slick (Donlevian) Morse Code man." In 1944 he was shipped out on a converted Liberty ship that took fourteen days to reach England through the heavily mined North Atlantic. Faust was eventually posted to the Sixty-Fifth Division of General George S. Patton's Third Army in Luxembourg. As the German army disintegrated, the stream of surrendering prisoners "turned into a flood, [and] we simply waved the *Übermenschen* back toward our rear lines. It was heady stuff for the kid" (who was then twenty years old). In April 1945 units of the Sixty-Fifth Division reached the notorious concentration camp at Buchenwald. There Faust found the emaciated bodies of the survivors as disturbing as heaps of corpses: "This, even for the Hun, was out of bounds. As a soldier, *I* felt more degraded." These searing memories haunt him still. During the remainder of his military service, Faust participated in the liberation of the Philippines and then served in the Army of Occupation in Japan.

After demobilization from the army in 1946, Faust entered City College of New York (now City College of the City University of New York). He majored in physical education and biology, earning a B.S. in 1949. Faust's passionate interest in sports is apparent in his fiction, which is also informed by his experiences teaching at a junior-high school in Harlem (1949–1953), where he encountered a rich mixture of African American, Puerto Rican, and Asian American cultures. During this time he also studied guidance and counseling at Teachers College of Columbia University, receiving an M.A. in 1952. In 1960 he earned an Ed.D. from Columbia with a dissertation that was later published as *Entering Angel's World* (1963).

Faust became a guidance counselor at Lynbrook High School in 1956 and then guidance director at Garden City High School in 1960, successfully combining careers as an educator and a fiction writer until 1997, when he retired to devote all his time to writing. He has published seven novels and two collections of short stories. A motion picture version of his novel *The Steagle* (1966) was released in 1971.

On 29 August 1959, Faust married Jean Satterthwaite, a native of North Carolina who became the first president of NOW-NY (1967), the first chapter of the National Organization for Women. A major action of NOW-NY was bringing a suit with the New York State Human Rights commission in May 1967 against all the major New York City newspapers for classifying job listings by gender. *Faust et al* vs. *New York Times et al.* was settled in January 1969, when the papers began listing jobs alphabetically by category. Since their marriage, the couple has lived in New York City, where they are deeply engaged with the culture of the city.

Faust draws on the vibrant diversity of Manhattan for stories that examine with humor and compassion what he calls the "terrible miserable blessed city." Drawing on his knowledge of sports and American history, Faust often writes about poor, disenfranchised young people whose struggles to survive or achieve the ever-receding American Dream invariably elicit the reader's compassion, admiration, and empathy.

Roar Lion Roar and Other Stories, Faust's first published volume of fiction, appeared in 1965. Reviewing the book for *The New Republic* (30 January 1965), Stanley Kauffman exclaimed: "Opening his book is like clicking on a switch; at once we hear the electric hum of talent." The reader encounters a wide range of characters–including eccentrics, idealists, paranoids, and political activists. Many are obsessed with radio, movies, and fame; most face the consequences of blind trust in fantasies.

"Philco Baby" portrays a pleasant young man living deep in a fantasy world. A worker in a stockroom, Morty derives his sense of identity from what he hears on a Philco portable radio that he carries everywhere in his shirt pocket. A counterman at the restaurant where Morty eats lunch compares him to "a mother kangaroo" carrying her baby in her pouch, and he is an obsessive "mother," completely enthralled by the popular music and announcers of the day, occasional newscasts, and all the advertisements with their bromides and hyperbolic promises for solutions to problems such as headaches, hair, halitosis, and body odors. Morty delights in this radio world, which is more real to him than the mundane stockroom and city streets. Miss Mandell, an unattractive fellow worker, intrudes on Morty's fantasy world, trying to form a romantic relationship with him. The denouement takes place in Coney Island, where she begins to seduce Morty on the beach. After his fantasy self resists her advances and her demands that he turn off his radio, she pulverizes it as it plays Connie Francis's recording of "Come Back to Sorrento" in Italian. Morty's protected universe is splintered, while a new fantasy world coalesces. In the sort of suspended ending that is a hallmark of virtually all his stories, Faust leaves his readers to draw their own conclusions. Will Morty succumb to the world of the flesh or run out and buy another radio? Media technology has offered Morty an avenue of escape, one in which he risks losing himself.

"Jake Bluffstein and Adolph Hitler" enters a darker, more hallucinatory realm of fantasy, as Faust explores the Jewish experience of the Holocaust. Crippled by the burden of survivor's guilt, Jake Bluffstein perversely expresses his self-loathing by painting "Juden" (Jew) on a refugee butcher's shop and spends days verbally abusing his wife, projecting his self-hatred against people in the subway whom he believes to be Nazis, and searching historical accounts of pogroms and courageous Jews who strike back at their persecutors. The story climaxes with Jake's preaching in the synagogue, empathizing with his fellow Jews and their centuries of suffering and praising their "perfection, purity and beauty." Suddenly, Jake feels himself to be like Adolf Hitler, mesmerizing his troops from the balcony as the German dictator did during the war. Suddenly envisioning Nazi Storm Troopers coming toward him, he roars "SIEG" and hears the uniformed men shout "HEIL." Jake's guilt finds expression in anger at the passivity of the Jews. He assumes the role of the Nazi victor by painting obscene graffiti, and he finally fuses the role of the conquered and the conqueror by imitating the Storm Troopers' cry of victorious superiority. At the end Jake feels free, but the reader is left with distaste for his repellent actions and tortured misperceptions, the consequences of self-hatred.

In an unpublished 1998 interview Faust expressed the belief that every Jew "is living on the edge of the Holocaust today." He is convinced that Jews have been liberated to a degree by the existence of Israel, which stands as commemoration of those lost in Europe. Faust believes that his fiction must create a "resonance with the intelligent reader who may or may not be a student of the Jewish experience."

After the publication of this story, Faust received some complaints from Jewish readers who criticized him for depicting a self-demeaning Jew. When asked to comment on Jake's anti-Semitism, Faust explained, "I

IRVIN FAUST was born in Brooklyn, was educated in the city public schools and graduated from CCNY. He holds a doctorate in the field of guidance from Teacher's College, Columbia University, where he has also taught. Mr. Faust was a teacher for five years, and for the past four years has been Director of Guidance at Garden City High School.
His case studies, *Entering Angel's World*, were published recently by Teachers College Bureau of Publications. Short stories have appeared in *The Paris Review*, *The Sewanee Review*, *The Saturday Evening Post*, *Transatlantic Review*, *San Francisco Review Annual* and *The Carleton Miscellany*.
ROAR LION ROAR
Irvin Faust
RANDOM HOUSE
ROAR LION ROAR
and other stories by
Irvin Faust
A RANDOM HOUSE BOOK

Dust jacket for Faust's 1965 collection of short stories, most of which deal with New York City teenagers whose fantasy lives have been shaped by the mass media

felt that it was important to talk about self-hatred. I think it's important to bring it out in the open, even to the extent that it becomes a psychosis, which it did in Jake's case."

"Into the Green Night" also employs interior monologue, in this case the thoughts of Armand LaRue, a young adolescent during the 1930s. Armand spends most afternoons in the "green night" of a darkened movie house known as Skouras' Oasis, where he fantasizes about movie stars such as Robert Taylor, John Garfield, Clark Gable, Alice Faye, and Jeanette MacDonald. He considers himself not only precociously clever and supersensitive but also gifted with extrasensory perception and immortality. His escapism also draws on mythology, and he identifies with Loki, the tricky, temperamental, devious Norse god of mischief.

One day, having read a description of puberty in *The Boy Scout Handbook*–which explains euphemistically that when a boy is twelve or thirteen, "A magical substance is manufactured and runs through his body and changes him and he is no longer a boy, but a youth"–Armand becomes exhilarated. He decides, "I am a special kind of youth. With a magical substance!" Painfully shy with girls, he wills himself to talk with them. He embraces life outside the movie house and rejects the movie stars he has adored: "Thank you and goodbye." As he walks out of the theater, he tries to focus on "real" life. He fantasizes about his English teacher's legs and thinks "he was no longer afraid of Armand or of life." He will "Maybe start a few fights on the street, especially with the wise guy who called him a Mockey. He was no Mockey; he was Armand LaRue. . . . That wiseapple better watch it." He has ransacked the mythologies of Viking lore and Hollywood dreams to construct an idealistic identity for himself: "Lucky" LaRue, superhero.

"Googs in Lambarene" is the story of a young idealist hell-bent on improving his world, beginning with Central Park in Manhattan. Inspired by the humanitarianism of the famous missionary Albert Schweitzer, who improved the welfare of Africans in the West Gabon village of Lambarene, Siegfried "Googs" Korngold, a lowly worker in a bank, enlists his reluctant roommate Alfred to challenge Central Park, where they plan to train and prepare themselves to help the unfortunates of New York City. Their problems begin after Googs, who has volunteered to umpire a blacks-versus-whites baseball game, makes an unpopular call. Alfred has to rescue him from a beating. In their urban odyssey they attract some followers: a young black boy; a prostitute they rescue from would-be rapists; a homeless, elderly thief; and an agoraphobic teacher. The boy's mother reclaims him and accuses the do-gooders of kidnapping. The prostitute leaves, attaching herself to a policeman. The thief absconds with the duo's haversacks, canteens, web belts, and razors. The teacher accuses Googs and Alfred of shaming him in front of his students. Googs's pathetic failure to emulate Schweitzer is complete.

Faust's ironic narrative utterly deflates Googs's and Alfred's idealistic intentions. New York City is unreformed by these self-appointed domestic missionaries, but Googs remains idealistic. At the end of the story they encounter a mad pornographic street painter whom Googs identifies as a "true down and outer. The real thing. A project for all time." He chastises this derelict, who responds, "Say boo and I'll kill you." Googs says "Boo," the last word in the story. Typically, Faust lets the reader infer Googs's fate.

Like "Googs in Lambarene," "The Madras Rumble" charts the failure of a would-be mentor with good intentions. Larry Cohen, a candidate for a business degree at Columbia University, finds a job as activities coordinator for a neighborhood group of culturally underprivileged teenagers. As part of his duties he is to help Wilmat Shankar, a student from Madras, India, who yearns to work with children. Cohen puts this idealistic young man to work with a group of streetwise teenagers and discovers, "I have not seen anyone with more pure, spontaneous ability to relate to kids. . . ." Cohen gradually gives Shankar complete control of the group. In time Shankar collects an entourage of social activists who, infected with his zeal, block traffic on Riverside Drive by picketing with signs such as "COLOR IS MERELY A PIGMENT: IT IS NOT AN ORGAN." Shankar carries the largest sign: "LIBERATE YOUR BROTHER AND YOU LIBERATE YOURSELF." Cohen removes Shankar from the scene before the police arrive, advising him that "you can't stop traffic with brotherhood." Next Shankar proceeds to lead a cadre of protestors who position themselves on the subway tracks. Just moments before the protestors would be pulverized, Cohen again comes to the rescue. He advises the young Indian against Gandhian passive resistance, exclaiming: "To be down, not to strike, is gutless. One must strike back." Eventually, having taken Cohen's advice literally, Shankar and his cohorts become embroiled in a protection racket. When he hears about their illegal activities, Cohen has no choice but to turn Shankar in to the authorities. He is sent back to Madras, and the episode ends Cohen's brief career in social work.

The humor of the story arises not only from Cohen's loss of control but also from Shankar's appropriation of Cohen's power. Shankar acts on his mentor's principles while comically adopting the argot and values of his streetwise followers. As Cohen hoped, Shankar has become culturally assimilated but not in the way Cohen planned.

"Miss Dorothy Thompson's American Eaglet" again depicts youthful idealism confronted with corrosive reality. The story is the first-person narrative of Myron Leberfeld, a city high-school student flushed with patriotism during World War II. It is 1942, and many agricultural workers have left their farms to serve in the military. Intrigued by a pamphlet written by Dorothy Thompson, a well-known journalist and then the wife of novelist Sinclair Lewis, Myron heeds the cry "The Volunteer Land Corps Wants YOU!" and volunteers for summer farm work.

Myron is assigned to a farm in Charlotte, Vermont, where the taciturn Leicester family ekes a marginal, hardscrabble existence. When the family discovers soon after Myron's arrival that he is Jewish, they stare at him in surprise, and the father says he has not seen a Jew in years. Morty says, "There are three million in New York. . . . More than in *all* of Palestine."

Her curiosity piqued, the Leicester daughter asks him to "talk Jew to me." Myron responds, "Ish leeba Dick," which he then mistranslates as "I love you, Dick," prompting the daughter to address him as "Dick" through the rest of the story. (The actual translation of "Ich liebe dich" is "I love you," *dich* being the informal German for "you.")

Eventually Marvin tricks a reluctant neighbor into helping the Leicesters mow their hay, using the neighbor's farm machinery to complete the job in time to save the hay from ruin in an untimely rainstorm and effectively staving off the collapse of the farm for another year. At the end of the summer the emotionally reserved Yankee family insists on escorting Myron to the railroad station as he departs for home, and Myron realizes that the woebegone Leicesters have unwittingly, unexpectedly initiated his transformation into a mensch, introducing him to "rectitude, dignity, and a sense of what is right," about which Myron's father has always talked. Faust here departs from his usual reserved ellipticism in articulating Myron's deep emotions on leaving the farmers, who will always remember 1942 as the year when that Jewish fellow appeared.

The story clearly captures the atmosphere of rural farm life, with the contrast between the rustic Leicesters and the sharp-witted city boy Myron, contributing humor to the narrative. In a 1978 interview with Matthew J. Bruccoli, Faust described the autobiographical roots of the story, explaining that like Myron, he had served in the Volunteer Land Corps in 1942, adding: "There was this three-day convention in Burlington. I can remember Thompson getting up and talking to us and seeing Sinclair Lewis kind of wandering around. To me, at that time, Sinclair Lewis didn't mean much, except that he had written *Arrowsmith,* which I was required to read in high school. So this farm project was part of the pre–World War reaching."

Thematically reminiscent of "Into the Green Night," "The World's Fastest Human" introduces the reader to Calvin Coolidge Delaware, a twenty-two-year-old runner who derives his sense of manhood from his running. After a slow beginning at college, where he has an athletic scholarship, Cal suddenly begins breaking records, becoming the fastest sprinter in the world and discovering "Victory . . . is the only true gestalt. . . ."

In Manhattan to train with fifty of the best American athletes for an important international track-and-field meet, Cal joins with a shot-putter and a decathlon winner to become the three musketeers. One evening the three men pick up some women in a ballroom, and, planning a one-night fling, they identify themselves with false names. Cal pretends to be a Vietnamese athlete.

Cal drives his friends and the three women to the Cloisters, a medieval museum perched on a bluff in Fort Tryon Park near the northern end of Manhattan, overlooking the Hudson River. While Cal's two friends, who have engaged in sex with their dates on the way to the Cloisters, cavort with them around the park, Cal is rejected by Muriel, his date for the evening. Pressing his suit, he tells her that he is really "white trash" from South Carolina and will be leaving in a few days to represent the United States in Europe. Then, leaping from the car, he sprints wildly around parapets and ramparts, jumping over the car and imagining himself in fantastic, faraway medieval battles and calming his sexual frustration through his athleticism. Returning to the present, he sees Muriel, running toward him completely naked and eager to join the frolic. Cal finds "the big second effort," and the story ends with Cal's confident double entendre: "I am ready for the stiffest competition Europe can offer. From the Place Pigalle to the Via Veneto." Faust leaves the reader with images of three adventurous, athletic musketeers, eager to engage in the rituals of sexual jousting before going on to other kinds of competitions.

Unlike most of Faust's short stories, which usually employ first-person narrators, "Justice for Ladejinsky" has a third-person, restricted center of consciousness. The focus is on Maury Stein, a New Yorker who goes to Indian Lake in the Pocono Mountains of Pennsylvania to act in summer stock. Maury envisions peaceful, bucolic surroundings and the pleasure of performing plays by William Shakespeare, Anton Chekhov, and Tennessee Williams, but he encounters a reality embroiled in politics. Members of the company frequently ask him to sign petitions favoring liberal causes such as support for a nuclear-test ban and opposition to Senator Joseph McCarthy's investigations into Communist infiltration of the federal government. Some of the actors praise dramatist Arthur Miller's courageous refusal to cooperate at the hearings and condemn Clifford Odets and Elia Kazan, who agreed to testify. Company members also collect funds for the children of Julius and Ethel Rosenberg, who were found guilty of giving atomic secrets to the Soviet Union and were executed in 1953. The troupe also takes up the cause of Russian American Wolf Ladejinsky, a noted agricultural specialist denied security clearance by Ezra Taft Benson, secretary of agriculture during the Eisenhower administration. (Ladejinsky was eventually exonerated.) Maury, who had reservations about some of these political issues, finally admits that he has "measured for the first time the appalling scope of his political naïveté."

Also disrupting the tranquility of Indian Lake is the fickle Gail Kern, who has an intermittent affair with Maury. Other company members have warned him about Gail's neurotic instability on political issues, and he learns that she is romantically unreliable as well. The final lines of the story suggest that even at Edenic Indian Lake, there is no escape from personal, professional, and political problems.

The title of the brilliant "Roar Lion Roar" comes from a line in the Columbia University fight song. The story opens with Ishmael Ramos, from Ponce, Puerto Rico, lying paralyzed in a Manhattan hospital. His problems began when he got the job of his dreams: working as a janitor in the Columbia gymnasium building.

Romantically obsessed with the Columbia football team, Ishmael buys a Columbia jacket and a pair of the white shoes favored by Columbia students. He begins to restructure his identity around the Columbia team, which is well known for its long losing streaks. After Columbia loses to Princeton, Ishmael's dream world collapses. In despair, he jumps from the cliffs near the football field into the Hudson River, attempting to atone for the team's failure by making the ultimate sacrifice. No one at Columbia recognizes his motivation. Ishmael's last words as he dies are poignant

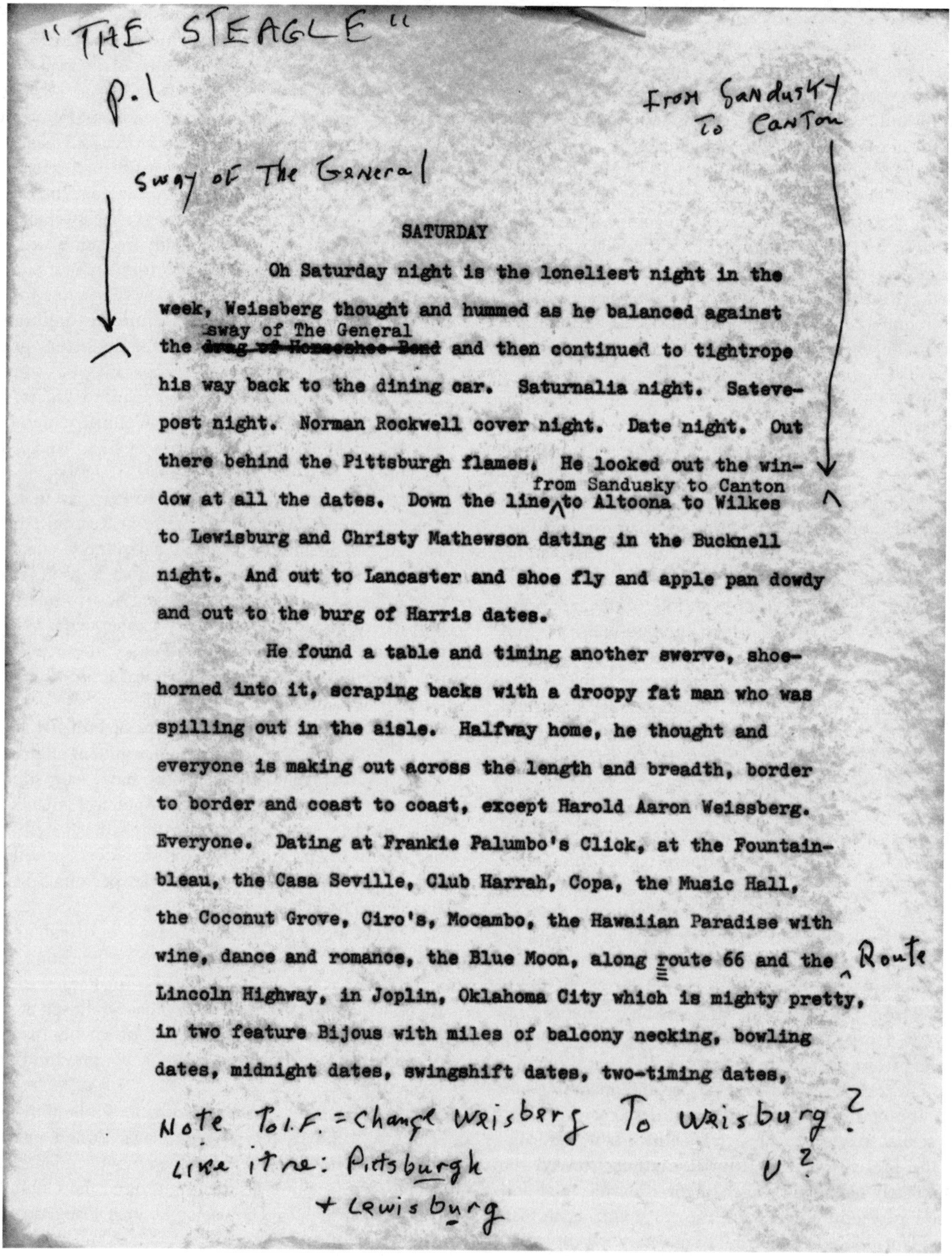

"THE STEAGLE"
p. 1

sway of The General

from Sandusky To Canton

SATURDAY

Oh Saturday night is the loneliest night in the week, Weissberg thought and hummed as he balanced against the sway of The General ~~drag of Horseshoe Bend~~ and then continued to tightrope his way back to the dining car. Saturnalia night. Satevepost night. Norman Rockwell cover night. Date night. Out there behind the Pittsburgh flames. He looked out the window at all the dates. Down the line from Sandusky to Canton to Altoona to Wilkes to Lewisburg and Christy Mathewson dating in the Bucknell night. And out to Lancaster and shoe fly and apple pan dowdy and out to the burg of Harris dates.

He found a table and timing another swerve, shoehorned into it, scraping backs with a droopy fat man who was spilling out in the aisle. Halfway home, he thought and everyone is making out across the length and breadth, border to border and coast to coast, except Harold Aaron Weissberg. Everyone. Dating at Frankie Palumbo's Click, at the Fountainbleau, the Casa Seville, Club Harrah, Copa, the Music Hall, the Coconut Grove, Ciro's, Mocambo, the Hawaiian Paradise with wine, dance and romance, the Blue Moon, along route 66 and the Lincoln Highway, in Joplin, Oklahoma City which is mighty pretty, in two feature Bijous with miles of balcony necking, bowling dates, midnight dates, swingshift dates, two-timing dates,

Route

Note To I.F. = change Weisberg To Weisburg?
like it re: Pittsburgh + Lewisburg
✓?

Page from the revised typescript for Faust's 1966 novel (Collection of Irvin Faust)

proof of his loyalty and his insanity: "Les go Li-yons, we number one in the Ivory Leak." "Roar Lion Roar" not only conveys the specificity of the New York experience and the particular madness of one obsessed fan, but it is also a parable of the American Dream shattered.

Throughout *Roar Lion Roar and Other Stories,* Faust captures the essence of New York, both through his characters' language and his evocations of specific locations. Writing in 1995, Neil D. Isaacs praised the stories for showing "how popular culture touches lives in ordinary and extraordinary ways while most refer to what evolves as a dominant theme in Faust's work–the problematic nature of the 'self' in a complex world." The stories continue to appeal to readers, who appreciate Faust's powerfully rendered, colorful characters, his finely tuned ear for the vernacular, and, above all, his multilayered comic technique.

By the time *The Year of the Hot Jock and Other Stories* was published in 1985, several critics had pronounced Faust "a writer's writer." Writing for *Columbia* (December 1985), fiction writer David R. Slavitt noted the particular appeal of Faust's fiction to readers who recognize its Manhattan settings; yet, even among readers unfamiliar with these places, Slavitt notes, "A new book of stories from Irvin Faust is an occasion for general rejoicing."

"The Year of the Hot Jock," which Faust first envisioned as a novel, is the first-person, interior monologue story of Pablo Diaz, a Panamanian American jockey flourishing in the world of horse racing. In thirteen years of racing he has become one of the best jockeys in the sport and one of the richest. His Cuban-born wife, Ramona, enjoys their wealth but hates Pablo's constant traveling to racetracks in Florida, New Jersey, and California, during which he engages in a series of transient sexual encounters with women.

Above all, Pablo has achieved his definition of the American Dream–worldly success. As marital tensions mount, Pablo reflects on Ramona's view of him: "never satisfied, more I get, more I want, million this year, fifteen next. Just the money? No, just *more.*" While Pablo may seem self-centered, smug, and devoid of human values, he is redeemed in the eyes of the reader by an incident that reawakens his sense of morality. When a friend tries for a second time to involve him in fixing race results, Pablo turns him in to the authorities.

Pablo usually exerts control over his personal life, but now he is faced with a situation that he cannot shape as he wishes. As he rides in a race, his horse breaks a leg, unseating Pablo, who thinks "I'm sailing into space, like a lazy cloud, roll over in air, slow easy." His final thoughts are "please pray for me Ramona. . . ."

Throughout this story of the life and death of a simple, unlettered, humorous "hot jock," the narration of Pablo's thoughts reveals Faust's ear for dialect. The story won an O. Henry Award in 1986.

In "Bar Bar Bar" a widower and a widow, Howard Fu and Carrie Greenbaum, meet on a bus bound for the casinos in Atlantic City, New Jersey. While Howard is an experienced gambler, Carrie is an amateur. After Carrie gets lucky playing the slot machines, they return to Atlantic City five days in a row. They eventually broaden their circuit to include the racetrack at Belmont, Long Island, and other gambling centers such as Saratoga. Carrie most often wins while Howard customarily loses.

As the couple's relationship evolves, Howard's son and daughter-in-law worry that Howard may be subsidizing Carrie's gambling, and Carrie's son worries that Carrie has fallen under the spell of a gambling Svengali. All the children expect problems to arise from differences between Howard's Chinese background and Carrie's Jewish background. One day the children from both families demand to know if Howard and Carrie are planning to marry. Spurred by this inquiry, Howard proposes to Carrie on the spot, and she accepts immediately. Unfortunately, Howard suffers a serious stroke just before their wedding.

The metaphor of gambling, which runs through this story, correlates the world of the casinos and racetracks with the larger arena in which all choices require some of the gambler's courage. Reviewing *The Year of the Hot Jock and Other Stories* for *The New York Times Book Review* (14 July 1985), fiction writer Herbert Gold found the ending of "Bar Bar Bar," in which the faithful Carrie is at Howard's bedside, excessively "pathetic," but he praised the "uncondescending compassion" of Faust's characterizations. While the ending leaves Howard and Carrie's future together ambiguous, the title of the story offers hope: bar-bar-bar is the slot-machine combination for winning the jackpot.

"Operation Buena Vista" presents another instance of torpedoed dreams. While betrayal is the central motif, Faust interlaces his tale with humor, irony, and poignancy. A young black boy living in the neighborhood around Columbia University, Henry Armstrong Strothers (his first and middle name taken from the well-known welterweight) becomes enamored of American history and the larger mainland. His father refuses him permission to accompany his school class on field trips to Princeton, New Jersey, and Philadelphia, Pennsylvania. He argues that Henry's future and well-being will be rooted in Manhattan. Having been a victim of racism, Henry's father wishes to protect his son and fears that Henry will reject his father's warnings as the product of a limited mentality.

The "Operation Buena Vista" (Operation Good View) of the title is a school-sponsored project to send urban students to other parts of the country to "provide meaningful experiences outside their life framework." Mr. Strothers objects to the program, insisting that Manhattan "is *his* Bona Vista." When he hears that Henry has been corresponding with Lance Olson of Duluth, Minnesota, and is expecting to spend the summer with the Olson family, Mr. Strothers asks the school guidance counselor whether the Olsons know "all about Henry" (that is, whether they know that Henry is black). Faust extracts much humor from the contrast of Mr. Strothers's vivid dialect and the uncommunicative professional jargon of the guidance counselor.

When Lance informs Henry by letter that their summer plans must be canceled because the Olsons are going to California, the guidance counselor reveals to Henry that his brother has written to the Olsons about Henry's race. Betrayed by his family, his counselor, and Lance, Henry chooses not to believe Lance is racist. At first he concentrates his anger on his brother, comparing him to Aaron Burr, Thomas Jefferson's vice president who killed Alexander Hamilton in a duel and later conspired to overthrow the U.S. government. Subsequently, during a moment of epiphany on the George Washington Bridge footpath, Henry wonders, "Was Lance a goddam fuckin Aaron Burr?" He looks down, and instead of a *buena vista,* he sees the murky waters of the Hudson River. He is overwhelmed by a bitter sense of universal betrayal. The moment seals the end of his innocent, romantic plans to cross the great divide between Manhattan and Minnesota. Again, Faust leaves the reader uncertain: will Henry leap to his death or return home? Will he accept the reality of racism and betrayal?

The main character of "The Dalai Lama of Harlem" is a black man named Daddy Thomas Heavenly, a spiritual leader and a megalomaniac who chooses for his successor Samson DeBaron, a raffish Harlem African American boy. For a sum Samson's alcoholic mother agrees to let Daddy train Samson to be the next Dalai Lama of Harlem. Promising Samson a glorious future, Daddy takes the boy to Starry Acres, the estate north of Manhattan where Daddy runs a retreat for the tough urchins of Harlem. Samson does not want to become the Dalai Lama. He leaves Starry Acres on his first night at the retreat and breaks into Sing Sing prison in Ossining, New York. Found sleeping in a prison recreation area, he resists returning to the estate. When Daddy promises to make Samson "the biggest Lama in this entire *country,*" Samson responds with an obscenity and screams, "*I don't wanna be no god.*" Samson runs away again and is found at "the bottom of a slag pit near Briarcliff. His neck was broken."

Clearly, Faust is making fun of Daddy and his hubris. Early in the story Daddy seems materialistic and manipulative; yet, as the story progresses, he builds sympathy for Daddy as a survivor of Southern racism, just as the Dalai Lama of Tibet is a survivor of Chinese brutality. Daddy, however, lacks the spiritual transcendence of the real Dalai Lama. Eventually disgorging the "sugar of all the plush, lost years," and apparently cleansed, Daddy walks out of his mansion and heads "toward all the magnificent bone-misery of the city." Daddy remains a complex enigma–helping many impoverished black boys while hating and envying Martin Luther King Jr. and enjoying power and wealth while indirectly causing a tragedy.

"The Double Snapper" is a fast-paced story combining situation comedy with serious intellectual questions. Having critiqued radio and film fantasies in earlier works, Faust takes on another fantasy medium: television. Grayson MacBean, well read in literature, philosophy, and especially in history, is the executive producer and first vice president of a television network. The story details Grayson's interactions with P. Nelsma, his boss, and Harry Braxton, one of the network writers, who proposes a series of programs about General Benedict Arnold, the American Revolutionary War traitor who was also one of George Washington's confidantes. Braxton convinces Nelsma that Arnold was complex, brilliant, and sensitive–a worthy subject for a television biography. MacBean supports the idea of airing a genuine portrait of Arnold, "with every wart and wen thrown in. The sweet and sour. It's ultramodern." He then wryly proposes spinoff programs rehabilitating other antiheroes (such as Aaron Burr, Adolf Hitler, and Emperor Maximilian of Mexico).

The first episodes of *The Benedict Arnold Show* break all records: ratings are meteoric, and two million viewers love the show. When Braxton wants to change the ending to please the growing audience, MacBean protests, "What about *history,* Harry?" but Braxton retorts, "I've thoroughly analyzed all the social and psychological factors, all the centrifugal and centripetal forces at work here, and everything adds up irrevocably to a heroic denouement for Arnold." MacBean holds out for historical accuracy, but Nelsma approves of Braxton's crowd-pleasing revisionism: the show, Nelsma observes, is "a *double* snapper." Nelsma's use of comic terminology places the whole television enterprise in the realm of gamesmanship and makes rewriting history no more consequential than any other game strategy. The point is not to preserve historical truth but to perpetuate a profitable lie, making the viewers feel good about themselves. "Every loser out there," Braxton observes, "becomes a *winner.*" Only MacBean continues to feel a responsibility to the patriots, the nontraitors who lost their lives fighting for their country. Though the ending is typically inconclusive, MacBean seems to be deciding to save his inflated salary by following those who crumpled under the pressure of Nielsen ratings rather than revealing to the public that the show is "a complete, calculated fraud." Compromise and betrayal are a fact of adult life in Faust's fictional universe.

"Simon Girty Go Ape" focuses once again on urban teenagers. Depicted in a tableau at the Museum of the American Indian in Manhattan, Simon Girty is an historical figure who was labeled a "renegade" after he left his village, married an Indian woman, and fought against his fellow whites. Joseph, a black teenager visiting the museum with a white friend, looks at the tableau and concludes "this cat pack it in and go ape."

The boys are observed by two adult museum visitors, Leonard and Sylvia. Leonard is delighted with the boys' enthusiasm and intrigued by their re-enactment of the Indians' sale of Manhattan Island to the Dutchman Peter Minuit. Leonard reveals his tendency to romanticize reality when he thinks, "Oh, if he could only turn impresario and present them in this scene on every street corner from Harlem to Birmingham." During their playacting the white boy, who is playing the part of the Indian, snatches a piece of valuable antique wampum and runs about gleefully as he haggles with his friend over the "sale."

When a sleepy museum guard finally notices the rumpus and chases the boys, Leonard exclaims that the boys "are just *playing,*" tackles the man, and cautions him: "You must stop being a . . . bully." Meanwhile, however, Joseph's white cohort grabs Sylvia's purse from her hand, and the two boys run from the building. The story ends with the guard asking, "Okay buster, you happy now?" The tale follows a familiar pattern of reversal. Leonard, so knowledgeable about Indian history and somewhat condescending to Sylvia, has been outwitted by two street-smart hoods, one of them a young white "renegade" replicating the treason of Simon Girty against his own race.

"Gary Dis-Donc" concerns a young American Francophile spending a year in Paris on a "Students Across the Sea" scholarship. Gary Donk (né Donkleberger) is ecstatic about living in the City of Light with the Boncoeur family, which includes Jean-Pierre, the son who nicknames Gary "Dis-Donc" (which may be translated idiomatically as "Do tell me" or "So tell me, already!"). The story comprises Gary's interior monologues, which are sprinkled with French phrases and bilingual wordplay.

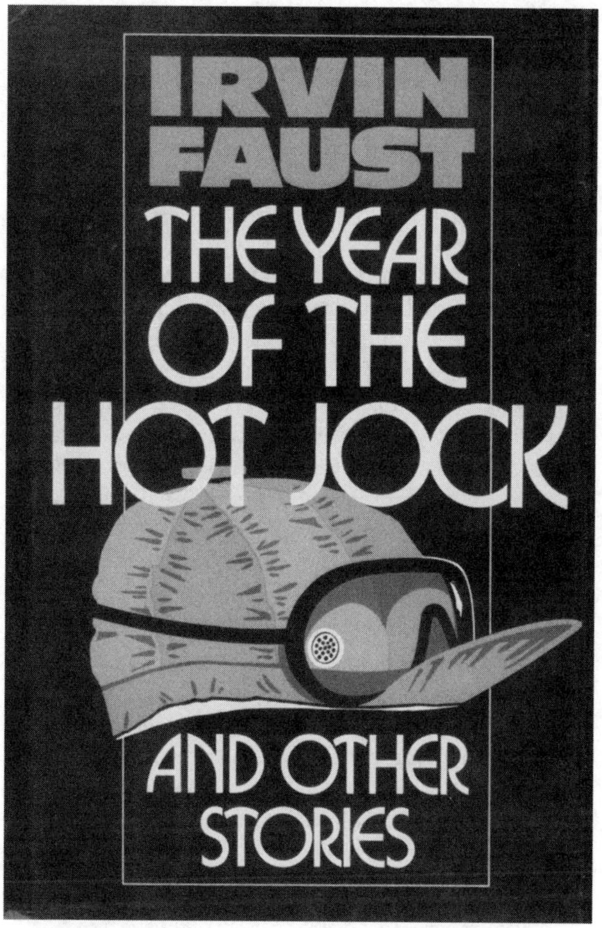

Dust jacket for Faust's 1985 book, in which the title story is an interior monologue charting the life and death of a successful jockey

Gary attends classes at the lycée Victor Hugo, but Jean-Pierre, who was a maquis (a member of the French underground) during World War II, does nothing. The family endlessly replays their wartime life under German occupation. Jean-Pierre gives Gary several letters to deliver, and their delivery is soon followed by bombings, leading Gary to conclude that he has become involved in a secret revolutionary group. In the last portion of the story the boundary between reality and fantasy has been crossed: Gary and Jean-Pierre flee to Belgium, where they are captured and returned to France to face the guillotine, with Gary intoning:

> Vive la France eternelle,
> Vive la gloire
> Vive Gary Dis-Donc.

The bookish American is transformed into a French revolutionary, a street fighter prepared to conquer all oppressors, as his rapidly cascading linguistic rhythms evoke the overheated imagination of youth, the heroic energies of French libertarianism, and the linguistic experiments of James Joyce.

In "Melanie and the Purple People Eaters," which was selected for inclusion in the *O. Henry Prize Stories of 1983,* Mel Horowitz and his wife, Marcia, have been called to their five-year-old daughter Melanie's school because she has been using strange vocabulary, such as the word "horsebleep." The school authorities refer the family to the "Bunny Development" specialist, guidance counselor Milton Sitkin, whom Melanie dismisses as a "superstiff." When Sitkin says that Melanie may be exhibiting a form of glossolalia, Mel asks, "Do you mean religious double talk? . . . We don't even talk religion with her. . . . We're orthodox atheists." Like the guidance counselor in "Operation Buena Vista," Sitkin speaks in an incomprehensible professional dialect as he discusses Melanie's private language: "Regardless of how fascinating the tongue thing may be, it rates nowhere in the taxonomy of cognitive functions." Melanie is also reported to have said, "It is not over till it's over." Sitkin believes the remark to be "Kierkegaardian," but the reader is becoming increasingly aware that most of her so-called private language is sports talk she has picked up from her father and television sportscasts and used out of context. As Mel and Marcia squabble, more dialects clash, with Mel spouting sports argot such as "You need the mo to get an O," which means, "You need the momentum to get an ovation."

Melanie is next subjected to a psychologist who speaks a different professional psychobabble. Marcia subsequently leaves home, taking Melanie and writing Mel a note insisting that "*the child must give up your world,*" or she will be forever trapped by sports talk. Mel cannot accept this conclusion. He takes Melanie from her school against the objections of her teacher and drives her to North Carolina for the ACC basketball tournament. They pass the time on the road playing a car game, each quizzing the other with cryptic sports references that must be identified. For example, Melanie offers the epithet "Purple People Eaters," and her father identifies them as the Minnesota Vikings football team. As Melanie demonstrates her fluency in her father's sports dialect, Faust tweaks the presumptions of teachers, counselors, psychologists, spouses, and parents.

In "Bunny Berigan in the Elephants' Graveyard" Faust again examines the impact of motion pictures on impressionable fans. The story begins in 1984, on the day of Johnny Weissmuller's death. A well-known Olympic swimmer, Weissmuller is best known for his starring roles in twelve Tarzan movies during the 1930s and early 1940s.

Axelrod, the central consciousness in this story, roams around Manhattan and the Bronx, obsessively talking with strangers about Weissmuller's death. During his odyssey Axelrod meets the teenaged Juanita, with whom he visits his old high school, Lewisohn Stadium, and the Polo Grounds, all changed since he visited them last. Axelrod tells Juanita that he is Bunny Berigan (a jazz trumpeter, who died in 1942), assuming that name because he played the trumpet fairly well until his father forced him to change to the violin.

Axelrod/Berigan and Juanita then visit the Church of the Holy Word, run by Reverend Mickey, a black preacher and ex-convict whose church now occupies the building that Axelrod remembers as The Castle, a movie theater he frequented in his youth. The movie marquee no longer announces the newest Tarzan movie, but rather Reverend Mickey's current homiletic theme: "REVEAL, REPEAL, REPENT, RELENT." Later, Axelrod returns to the church, where he listens to the testimonies of the repentant and feels compelled to add his own recitation of misdemeanors. "Welcome to the elephants' graveyard," Reverend Mickey responds. In the church Axelrod is no longer a spectator at the movies, but an actor.

Reverend Mickey's gnomic allusion to the "elephants' graveyard" seems to be a comment on the decayed condition of the Bronx neighborhood around his church. The phrase also reminds the reader of the death of Weissmuller, the death of adventure, and the irremediable changes in the setting of Axelrod's lost youth. The preacher's sardonic welcome also signals his moral decay, which is confirmed by his manipulation of his flock in the movie emporium he has transformed into a religious theater. As in other Faust stories nostalgia is muted by humor and irony.

As a whole, *The Year of the Hot Jock and Other Stories* presents an engaging cast of New York characters: African Americans, Jews, Asian Americans, Hispanics, ministers, television hucksters, and teenage hoods, many of them older than the characters featured in *Roar Lion Roar.* Isaacs has noted that these stories demonstrate "a storyteller's mastery of his narrative art. Each is a uniquely faceted gem; taken together they are a dazzling display of Faust's characteristic materials and methods . . . and [display] an ear sensitive to the revealing nuances of dialogue that catches the manifold variety of New York voices and tones."

Faust's short stories cohere to characteristic themes and patterns. His protagonists are obsessive, addicted to sports, movies, and history. They are aware of institutional flim-flam and the effects of urban blight, even as they are victimized by unqualified professional authority figures and the economic forces that have reduced their neighborhoods to crime-ridden rubble. They do not build empires or fortunes. They struggle to survive in a world of poverty, mass-media propaganda, racism, hypocrisy, betrayal, and seemingly inescapable anonymity. Some are defeated, but most survive, hurled from fantasy into the real world, moving beyond idealism, naïveté, innocence, and credulity to engage in a daily struggle with the reality into which they are thrown.

In an unpublished 1998 interview Faust described his writing as an attempt to make his readers feel that they get "into the other person's skin deeply, not superficially." He considers his dialogue one of his strengths: "I'm not afraid to depart from straight narrative use. I try to use forms and methods appropriate to my design." Although some critics have called him a social realist, he has rejected that label: "I like John O'Hara's stories and write somewhat in that tradition, except that instead of social realist, I consider myself a psychological realist and am, perhaps unconsciously, aware of the psychology of Carl Rogers," who developed theories in indirect counseling and interpersonal relationships. "Always," Faust continues, "I am dealing with a psychological undergirding. [While] some people consider characters' being undone by their neuroses, my characters adjust to their neuroses. What is considered abnormal behavior by others is normal to them." Because Faust's narratives are often elliptical, he is sometimes considered a postmodernist. No matter what direction his fiction takes, Faust continues to surprise the reader with his joyous linguistic play, his cinematic effects, and his omnipresent humor.

Interview:

Matthew J. Bruccoli, "Irvin Faust," in *Conversations with Writers II* (Detroit: Gale Research / Bruccoli Clark, 1978), pp. 46–72.

References:

Neil D. Isaacs, "*Jim Dandy* to the Rescue," *Virginia Quarterly Review,* 71 (Autumn 1995): 750–755;

Stanley Kauffman, "The Electric Hum of Talent," *New Republic,* 152 (30 January 1965): 22–23.

Papers:

The Mugar Memorial Library at Boston University has a collection of Irvin Faust's papers.

Merrill Joan Gerber

(15 March 1938 -   )

Charlotte Zoë Walker
State University of New York College at Oneonta

BOOKS: *Stop Here, My Friend* (Boston: Houghton Mifflin, 1965; London: Hutchinson, 1966);
An Antique Man (Boston: Houghton Mifflin, 1967);
Now Molly Knows (New York: Arbor House, 1974);
The Lady with the Moving Parts (New York: Arbor House, 1978);
Please Don't Kiss Me Now (New York: Dial, 1981);
Name a Star for Me (New York: Viking, 1983);
Honeymoon (Urbana: University of Illinois Press, 1985);
I'm Kissing as Fast as I Can (New York: Fawcett Juniper, 1985);
The Summer of My Indian Prince (New York: Fawcett Juniper, 1986);
Also Known as Sadzia! The Belly Dancer! (New York: Harper & Row, 1987; London: Pan, 1988);
Marry Me Tomorrow (New York: Fawcett Juniper, 1987);
Even Pretty Girls Cry at Night (New York: Crosswinds, 1988);
I'd Rather Think about Robby (New York: Harper & Row, 1989);
King of the World (Wainscott, N.Y.: Pushcart Press, 1989);
Handsome as Anything (New York: Scholastic Press, 1990);
Chattering Man: Stories and a Novella (Atlanta: Longstreet Press, 1991);
The Kingdom of Brooklyn (Atlanta: Longstreet Press, 1992);
This Old Heart of Mine: The Best of Merrill Joan Gerber's Redbook *Stories* (Atlanta: Longstreet Press, 1993);
Old Mother, Little Cat: A Writer's Reflections on Her Kitten, Her Aged Mother, and Life (Atlanta: Longstreet Press, 1995);
Anna in Chains, Library of Modern Jewish Literature (Syracuse: Syracuse University Press, 1998).

SELECTED PERIODICAL PUBLICATIONS–UNCOLLECTED:

FICTION

"Yom Kippur," *Florida Quarterly* (Fall 1967);

Merrill Joan Gerber (photograph by Lou Mack; from the dust jacket for The Kingdom of Brooklyn, *1992)*

"Inside the Castle," *Ladies' Home Journal,* 89 (February 1972): 96, 120–122;
"At the Fence," *Sewanee Review,* 93 (Winter 1985): 5–19;
"Cleopatra Birds," *American Voice,* 1 (1985): 57–65;
"Mozart You Can't Give Them," *Sewanee Review,* 94 (Summer 1986): 352–360;
"Night Stalker," *Shenandoah,* 37 (Summer 1987): 65–75;
"This is a Voice From Your Past," *Chattahoochee Review,* 17 (Summer 1997): 54–61.

NONFICTION

"Letting the Well Fill," *Writer,* 86 (March 1973): 14–15;
"Through the Maze to the Story," *Writer,* 88 (April 1975): 9–11, 46;
"The Process of Writing a Story," *Writer,* 94 (November 1981): 16–18, 45;

"Following the Thread into the Labyrinth: A Fond Recollection of Andrew Lytle," *Chattahoochee Review,* 8 (Summer 1988): 24–27;

"Staying With It," *Writer,* 102 (October 1989): 9–11;

"The Treasures We Held," *Sewanee Review,* 103 (Fall 1995): 507–521;

"Remembering Wallace Stegner," *Sewanee Review,* 103 (Winter 1995): 128–135;

"The Lost Airman: A Memoir," *Commentary,* 105 (June 1998): 51–56;

"Getting Mother Buried," *Chattahoochee Review,* 19 (Fall 1998).

Merrill Joan Gerber is a distinguished writer of short fiction whose work has won honors such as *The Sewanee Review* Andrew Lytle Fiction Prize (1985), an O. Henry Award (1986), and the Pushcart Press Editor's Book Award (1990). She has published five volumes of short stories, as well as five novels for adults, a memoir, and nine novels for young adults. Gerber's realistic style is often painfully honest and sardonically humorous. Her work is known for its perceptive observations about family relations, particularly in Jewish families, and about the changing lives of women during the second half of the twentieth century. Her 1998 volume of short stories, *Anna in Chains,* was published as part of the Syracuse University Press Library of Modern Jewish Literature, which also includes works by distinguished writers such as Cynthia Ozick, Tova Reich, Daniel Stern, and Arthur Miller. In 1993, when she presented Gerber the 1992 *Hadassah Magazine* Harold U. Ribalow Award, Ozick praised Gerber's writing as "strong plain prose that shines with the clarity of absolute probity, mixed with all the rubble, pain, and debris of things-as-they-are." Ozick added,

> You will not find a fashionable "magic realism" in Merrill's tales. What you *will* find is realism acutely devoted to the inner life without ever sacrificing full observation of the outer life. In a time overcome by fictive inconclusiveness and confusion, Merrill Joan Gerber writes in pursuit of illumination and penetration.

Merrill Joan Gerber was born on 15 March 1938 in Brooklyn, New York, to William and Jessie Sorblum Gerber. Her father, an antiques dealer, was memorialized in her first novel, *An Antique Man* (1967). Gerber also drew on her childhood for her novel *The Kingdom of Brooklyn* (1992), which depicts a dysfunctional family through the eyes of a young child.

In her essay for the *Contemporary Authors Autobiography Series* (volume 20, 1994), Gerber wrote, "My household was volatile: my mother explosive, my father conciliatory (he had to be), my aunt and grandmother (who lived upstairs while I lived with my parents downstairs) acting as buffers or mediators or simply 'flies on the wall.'" In a 1996 interview with Mario Materassi (published in part in *Sewanee Review,* Summer 1999), Gerber explained that, as an only child for the seven years before the birth of her younger sister, she "was the point of battle" between her mother and her mother's younger, unmarried sister, Greta Sorblum:

> My aunt wanted to teach me how to bake and cook and sew. My mother had contempt for those household joys and she wanted to teach me rhyming and Beethoven and what little culture she had. She didn't have very much culture but she had a great desire to be a cultured American, whereas my aunt had a great wish to make me aware of my Jewish background.

Gerber told Materassi that she began writing at age seven, composing little poems about the customers in her aunt's beauty shop. When she was still quite young, her father gave her a typewriter. She took it to the basement, where she could escape "from the tumult of the household" and "write to someone who really understands." Her first publication was a jingle that appeared in her eighth-grade school magazine.

In 1952, when Gerber was fourteen, she moved with her parents and younger sister to Miami Beach, Florida. There, when she was fifteen, she met her future husband, Joseph Spiro. She attended the University of Miami briefly in 1955 and transferred at the end of the fall semester to the University of Florida, where she studied with Agrarian writer Andrew Lytle, whom she calls "the great writing teacher of my life." In his class Gerber "first understood I had a serious calling," and she still recalls some advice he gave her in a private conference: "Merrill, there is only one way to write: you must follow the thread back into the labyrinth; there and only there you will find the meaning."

After earning a B.A. in 1959, Gerber began graduate work at Brandeis University, where Spiro was already enrolled as a graduate student in history. The two were married on 23 June 1960. They subsequently had three daughters: Becky, Joanna, and Susanna. Gerber completed the course work for a master's degree in English but left before taking her oral examinations, in part because she felt she was being discriminated against as a woman. In her essay for the *Contemporary Authors Autobiography Series* she explains that Irving Howe, who was head of the English department, told her she was "only a girl and only a writer," and, despite her good grades, the fellowships were earmarked for men. Years later, Gerber re-applied for her M.A. at Brandeis, and after taking a written examination (orals no longer being required for the master's degree), she earned the degree in 1981.

Gerber (second from left) with her father, William Gerber, mother, Jessie Gerber, grandmother Beckie Sorblum, and aunt Greta Sor blum, 1944

In 1961, while her husband continued his graduate studies at Brandeis, Gerber went to work as an editorial assistant at Houghton Mifflin. In April 1962, when she was in the ninth month of her first pregnancy, she received a Wallace Stegner Fiction Fellowship at Stanford University for the 1962–1963 academic year. She and Spiro moved to Stanford, where the other Stegner Fellows included Robert Stone. In autumn 1963 Gerber and Spiro moved to Riverside, California, where Spiro took a job teaching history at the local branch of the University of California. Two years later they went to Monterey Park, California, and Spiro joined the faculty of Pasadena City College. In 1968 Gerber and Spiro bought a house in Sierra Madre, where they continue to live. Gerber teaches creative writing at the California Institute of Technology (Cal Tech) in Pasadena.

While still in Boston, Gerber had sold a story to *Mademoiselle,* and within months of beginning work at Stanford, she sold two more stories: one to *The New Yorker* and the other to *Redbook.* When she had her first book offer, Wallace Stegner told her the terms were not "respectable" and urged her to "hold out for what you're worth." By the end of that same year Houghton Mifflin had offered her "nearly fifteen times the amount of the first offer." Stegner continued to be a mentor and friend to Gerber until his death in 1993.

Gerber's first published book, the short-story collection *Stop Here, My Friend* (1965), includes stories that had previously been published in *The New Yorker, The Sewanee Review, Redbook,* and *Mademoiselle.* "We Know That Your Hearts Are Heavy," which first appeared in *The New Yorker* (20 April 1963), focuses on a family funeral. The story opens with a description of pigeons outside the Boston office of Janet, the young, married female narrator:

> Pigeons are crowding the window sill to keep out of the rain. The drizzle has just turned to downpour, and the birds have flown up from Boston Common. They are stepping on each other's toes to find a footing on the two-inch ledge. The victims of missteps do not fall six stories and spatter their blood on the pavement; they merely hang in midair, flutter a hundred wet black feathers, and immediately land back on the ledge, dancing a wild two-step to get dry.

These lines suggest not only the complex family situations that Janet encounters at her uncle's funeral but also the tentative optimism that she has developed by the end of the story. Returning home for the funeral,

Janet experiences the irritation of conflicting personalities and the comfort of traditions within her large Jewish family, along with a shocked recognition of the reality of death.

The story also presents the almost claustrophobic closeness of family members gathered from distant places for a funeral and sleeping together in crowded, uncomfortable quarters. Janet's patient, loving husband, Danny, is with her throughout the ordeal of family fighting, discussions of the will, and a painful burial scene, during which questions about religion and death run through Janet's mind. Yet, in the end the focus returns to youth, to the new life Janet and Danny are making together, and to the pigeons:

> Nothing matters. . . . I want to go back to my tiny office and watch the pigeons strutting on my windowsill, which overlooks the Common. There are things to do–many things to do–and I understand that that is the only answer I shall have to all my questions.

Janet and Danny–and Janet's parents, Abram and Anna Goldman–also appear in many of the forty-two stories Gerber has written for *Redbook* magazine. Gerber, who has published more stories in *Redbook* than any other fiction writer, collected twenty-five of these stories in *This Old Heart of Mine* (1993).

Stop Here, My Friend also includes Gerber's first *Redbook* story. "A Daughter of Her Own" (January 1964) describes the conflict between a new mother and her own mother, reversing the myth of the idyllic bonding between mother and daughter at such a time. In its final moments, however, this wrenchingly honest story reveals the strength of the love underlying the conflict: As her mother walked through the gate at the airport, the narrator reports, "I ran after her and threw my arms around her and hugged her, crying 'I love you, Mother, I love you,' and we embraced desperately, as though this were the last time we could ever express our love, and then she went through the gate, her head down, her hand to her eyes."

In the final paragraph, as the narrator, her husband, and the baby start to leave the airport, the wind blows off the baby's cap, proving to the young woman that in at least one instance her mother, who had said the day was "too windy for the baby," has been "right."

Throughout her career Gerber's close connection with *Redbook* has caused many critics to look disparagingly at all her fiction despite the publication of some of her short stories in prestigious magazines such as *The New Yorker, The Atlantic Monthly,* and *The Sewanee Review.* In fact, the level of craftsmanship is consistently high in all her short fiction. Especially in the 1960s, Gerber has said, there was another reason that her work was not taken seriously. In an unpublished 1998 letter she commented, "I didn't realize for a long time that serious writers weren't women. That is, in college, I thought I was not a "woman" writer but a "serious" writer. . . ." Yet, she added,

> I began to have my doubts at Stanford, where the men in the class, who wrote about drugs, drink and war seemed to be taken more seriously than, say, myself, who wrote about childbirth and a family funeral. . . . (Women writers innocently aspired to be published in women's magazines then. Think of Sylvia Plath, who wanted more than anything to sell a story to the *Ladies' Home Journal!*) I truly don't know where it all went wrong; how I became invisible.

Gerber's second collection of short stories, *Honeymoon* (1985), includes stories published in *The Sewanee Review, The Virginia Quarterly Review,* and *The Atlantic Monthly*–as well as one story from *Redbook.*

The extraordinarily accomplished opening story, "Honeymoon," is a relentlessly unromantic third-person story told from the viewpoint of Cheryl, a naive young woman who has just married Rand, a much-older professional gambler. Her circumstances have clearly led her to settle for much less than she has hoped for in her romantic dreams. Though she tries to make the best of her situation, the story gradually reveals how unhappy she is, while brilliantly contrasting the beauty of the southwestern landscape with the grimness of gambling casinos. The difference is apparent in a passage describing Cheryl's lonely trip to see Hoover Dam while her husband continues to gamble. Riding on the tour bus, she thinks, "Sometimes Rand looked like an old bird with his skinny shins, the way the skin on his legs seemed scaly. She was glad he was cooped up in some casino, in the dark daytime inside of those places. She was going out into the sun . . . where she could thaw out." Cheryl also begins to recognize the situation in which she has placed herself:

> Sometimes she thought she had seen everything, thought everything she was ever going to think, and the next eighty years of her life were going to be exactly the same as the first twenty. But once in a while she saw something new and got a different feeling, and when that happened, it gave her hope again. At first, being with Rand had given her a thousand new thoughts and feelings, but now she was having no new ones. Like everything else, it had gotten old–and she had only married him yesterday. If, as her mother said, the marriage–considering his record–was sure to be a short-term thing, then *that* was rotten. And if it was to be forever, till death did they part, that seemed rotten too.

Gerber with her husband, Joseph Spiro, and their three daughters: Susanna, Joanna, and Becky, 1967

This realization does not conclude the story. On this visit to Hoover Dam, Cheryl meets and befriends a couple she envies for their sexiness and apparent happiness. In a beautifully rendered scene in a tunnel under Hoover Dam (another "dark daytime inside" like the casino), Cheryl playfully guides the other couple with her "Love-Lites" light-up earrings, and when the young man invites her to travel with them, she readily agrees. Her renewed hope does not last long. At the end of the tour the couple manages to evade her.

The second story in this distinguished collection, "At the Fence," was originally published in *The Sewanee Review* (Winter 1985) and earned the Andrew Lytle Prize for 1985; while "I Don't Believe This," which first appeared in *The Atlantic Monthly* (October 1984) was selected for inclusion in the 1986 O. Henry Awards collection.

One of Gerber's best stories, "I Don't Believe This" explores the relationship between two adult sisters. One of the sisters has been a victim of domestic violence, and the entire family is trying to cope with guilt and anguish over her husband's suicide. The story concludes with the children's macabre response to their father's death and their mother's traumatized denial of their true feelings. At Halloween her sons build a mock graveyard at the foot of a tree in the front yard and hang from the tree a dummy wearing their father's sweatshirt. When the dummy is still there long after Halloween, the boys' mother insists, "I don't think they're thinking about him. I think they just made it for Halloween, and they still like to look at it."

Beginning in the mid 1980s Gerber has received increasing recognition for her work. In 1985, the year in which she won the Andrew Lytle Award, she also received the Fiction Network Fiction Competition Prize for "Hairdos." Her 1989 novel, *King of the World,* won the 1990 Pushcart Press Editor's Book Award. In 1992 her story "Honest Mistakes" was cited as a "distinguished story" in *Best American Short Stories 1992,* and the following year her novel *The Kingdom of Brooklyn* earned her the *Hadassah Magazine* Harold U. Ribalow Award for 1992.

Gerber's third collection of short stories, *Chattering Man* (1991), includes an eight-part novella that features Anna Goldman, a recurring character in Gerber's Janet and Danny stories. Based on Gerber's mother, Anna, now elderly, it is a great literary portrait of an aging protagonist in all her complexity.

This Old Heart of Mine: The Best of Merrill Joan Gerber's Redbook *Stories* (1993) demonstrates Gerber's accomplishment in a series of stories that depict three decades of a family's history with honesty, tenderness, and humor. The Janet and Danny stories begin shortly after the couple's marriage and end with "This Old Heart of Mine," after the youngest of their three daughters has left for college. Gerber has described them as:

> a kind of limited history of my life. I had never, before I sold my first story to *Redbook* as a Stanford Stegner Fellow, read "women's magazines" and thus felt myself untainted by the "stigma" that seemed to attach itself to that label throughout my career. . . . I loved writing the *Redbook* stories. . . . I felt every one of them was real and true (within the limits of what I knew I could discuss in that environment). There were limits, yes, and I was often asked to change the endings, to make them "clearer"–to make them happier.

Writing about her mother's work for *Contemporary Jewish-American Novelists* (1997), Becky Spiro Green comments that it "has predominantly centered on family life in all its manifestations, including love, conflict, and sometimes terror. Her families are Jewish families; her characters' commitment to their Jewish identity varies as widely as does the commitment of American Jews in all walks of life."

Considering Gerber's emerging reputation as a Jewish writer, it is interesting that this important dimension of her work was sometimes suppressed by *Redbook* editors. "I wasn't so much editing myself when I repressed the ethnic content of the stories," Gerber explains, "as trying to understand what it would take to be published. It was clear to me that Jewish thinking was not for *Redbook* or any of the other women's magazines in which I published." She says, however, that she never differentiated between her *Redbook* stories and her "serious literary stories," adding that "after one story appeared in *Sewanee Review, Redbook* offered to buy second serial rights, and published it! (They said they wished I had sent it to them first.)" Later Gerber was able to stop "concealing the Jewish content of my stories" and wrote the Anna stories that were first published in *Chattering Man* and later in *Anna in Chains.*

Cynthia Ozick criticized the repression of Jewish content of Gerber's stories in her review of *Stop Here, My Friend* for *Midstream* (June 1965). While praising Gerber's style, Ozick found fault with the stories for being "without . . . Jewish consciousness." Years later the two women met and, as Ozick remembered in 1993, "we instantly fell into a quarrel, which I'm afraid I started, on the whole question of Jewish viewpoint. It was, I confess, less a quarrel than a scolding–a one-sided assault on my part, aggressively intolerant." After this unpromising beginning, Ozick and Gerber continued their exchange in a correspondence and eventually developed a strong friendship. Ozick's initial reservations grew into admiration for Gerber's "crucially honest" writing. In her 1993 presentation speech Ozick commented on her change of opinion, pointing to Gerber's complex portrayals of Jewish families in books such as *King of the World, Chattering Man, The Kingdom of Brooklyn,* and *This Old Heart of Mine:* "All these volumes reveal the lives of contemporary Jews as they sometimes really are." Ozick concluded her remarks by calling Gerber "one of those writers who discover us to ourselves, and move us almost more than we can bear."

These words seem a particularly apt description for Gerber's 1998 book, *Anna in Chains.* Perhaps her most accomplished work yet, it examines with wit, honesty, and complexity the later life of Anna Goldman, now a spirited and eccentric elderly widow. The stories follow Anna on the downward path of aging as she moves from an independent life in her apartment to an increasingly restricted existence in a retirement home and then a nursing home. Paralyzed after a stroke, she is reduced to a life "in chains," which she finds nearly unbearable. Despite the sadness of Anna's story, the reader becomes entranced by Anna's fierce spirit and the surprising humor of the stories.

Andrew Lytle, Gerber, and Smith Kirkpatrick at an event honoring Lytle, Gerber's first writing teacher, De Kalb College, Georgia, 1989

In "Tickets to Donahue" Anna and her sister Gert argue about sexuality. Gert accuses Anna, who is nearly eighty years old, of using her "glamor-girl look" to flirt with the tour-bus driver and warns, "Someday you won't get away with that. Men used to follow you home from the subway for that look. So don't act so innocent. That look of yours fooled Abram into marrying you, and then you made him beg for love all his life."

In "The Next Meal is *Lunch*" Anna, who has recently moved to a retirement home, meets a man whom other women have warned her against because of his interest in sex. He gives her a copy of an article to prove that he is a famous architect, initiating the following exchange:

> "I'm not impressed," Anna said, handing it back. "At this point in my life, only Arthur Rubinstein could impress me."
> "I have it over him," said the man. "I'm still alive."
> "Maybe, but only barely," Anna observed. She ordered from the waitress. "Easy on the onions," she said. "I might have a date later on."

In "Hear No Entreaties, Speak No Consolations" Anna has had a stroke and been moved to a nursing home. The point of view places the reader inside a body that is completely confined: "Anna was shackled: straps and ropes and chains and tubes entrapped and surrounded her; Houdini couldn't have got out of this place." Yet, Anna's mind and spirit continue to fascinate the reader. In the nursing home Anna's Jewishness is continually assaulted by the assumption that most residents are Christians. One afternoon, for example, the only entertainment available turns out to be a religious meeting, which she chooses over boredom. To her astonishment, she discovers that most of the people there are young people with terrible diseases. Moved to sympathy for them, Anna turns to her daughter, Janet, to express gratitude for the life she has lived:

> "Everyone here is young," Anna whispered to her, "but I'm very old. I've lived my whole life."
>
> "Yes, you're very old, Ma."
>
> "I've had the whole thing," Anna said, amazed. She actually felt peace descending on her, heavily, without grace, like a pelican coming to land on a rock. "There's nothing more for me to do. I just realized, darling–I'm at the very end. I don't have to worry anymore. That's all there is to it."

The next story, "Anna in Chains," takes the reader a step further on Anna's journey toward death. Anna's old competitiveness with her sister Gert is revived when she learns that Gert has attempted suicide and is seeing a psychiatrist. By the end of the story Anna is also talking to a psychiatrist–in an act of one-upmanship that adds levity to this sorrowful story. She tells the kindly young Jewish psychiatrist:

> "Look, so I'll cooperate, Medicare will pay you. I'll let you come and keep me company and talk till your half-hour or whatever is up. But you should know I don't really believe in this psychology baloney. You talk but I don't have to listen. I'll ignore you, which is exactly what I do when my daughters come to see me. But I want you to understand, Arthur-the-psychiatrist: there's nothing you can teach me about life. I've lived three times as long as you have. So if I'm not paying attention, you'll be kind enough not to force yourself on me. Maybe I'll be thinking about how I danced with Abram at my wedding, how the gardenias he gave me smelled like the entire Brooklyn Botanical Gardens in springtime, how the edges of the corsage were already turning brown when we got to Atlantic City for the honeymoon. You can rest assured–I have enough to think about till the end of time."

Gerber is at work on a sequel to *Anna in Chains,* about Anna in the afterlife. As novelist Robert Stone noted on a publicity brochure for *Anna in Chains,* Gerber's fiction is characterized by a "deceptively forthright style" and precise depictions of "the complications and frustrations of ordinary lives." Her extraordinary stories deserve a wide readership.

Interviews:

Lisa See, "Merrill Joan Gerber: A Veteran of the Short Story (and More) Collects Some of Her Strongest Stories," *Publishers Weekly,* 240 (8 November 1993): 54–55;

Mario Materassi, "On the Edge of the Action: A Conversation with Merrill Joan Gerber," *Sewanee Review,* 107 (Summer 1999): 438–439.

William Goyen

(24 April 1915 – 29 August 1983)

Reginald Gibbons
Northwestern University

See also the Goyen entries in *DLB 2: American Novelists Since World War II,* and *DLB Yearbook 1983.*

photograph © by J. Gary Dontzig; from the dust jacket for Had I A Hundred Mouths, *1985*

BOOKS: *The House of Breath* (New York: Random House, 1950; London: Chatto & Windus, 1951);

Ghost and Flesh: Stories and Tales (New York: Random House, 1952);

In a Farther Country: A Romance (New York: Random House, 1955; London: Peter Owen, 1962);

The Faces of Blood Kindred: A Novella and Ten Stories (New York: Random House, 1960);

The Fair Sister (Garden City, N.Y.: Doubleday, 1963); republished as *Savata, My Fair Sister* (London: Peter Owen, 1963);

Short Stories, edited by Erwin Helms (Göttingen: Vandenhoeck & Ruprecht, 1964);

My Ántonia: A Critical Commentary (New York: American R. D. M. Corp., 1966);

Ralph Ellison's Invisible Man: A Critical Commentary (New York: American R. D. M. Corp., 1966);

A Book of Jesus (Garden City, N.Y.: Doubleday, 1973);

Selected Writings of William Goyen (New York: Random House, 1974);

Come, The Restorer (Garden City, N.Y.: Doubleday, 1974);

The Collected Stories of William Goyen (Garden City, N.Y.: Doubleday, 1975);

Nine Poems (New York: Albondocani Press, 1976);

Arthur Bond (Winston-Salem, N.C.: Palaemon Press, 1979);

Wonderful Plant (Winston-Salem, N.C.: Palaemon Press, 1980);

Precious Door (New York: Red Ozier Press, 1981);

New Work and Work in Progress (Winston-Salem, N.C.: For private distribution by Palaemon Press and TriQuarterly, 1983);

Arcadio (New York: Potter, 1983; London: Serpent's Tail, 1989);

Had I A Hundred Mouths: New & Selected Stories 1947–1983, edited by Reginald Gibbons (New York: Potter, 1985; London: Serpent's Tail, 1988);

Half a Look of Cain: A Fantastical Narrative, edited by Gibbons (Evanston, Ill.: Northwestern University Press, 1994).

PLAY PRODUCTIONS: *The House of Breath, A Ballad for the Theatre in Four Scenes,* New York, Circle in the Square Theatre, April 1957;

The Diamond Rattler, Boston, Charles Playhouse, May 1960;

Christy, New York, American Place Theatre, March 1964;

House of Breath, Black/White, Providence, R.I., Trinity Square Repertory Company, November 1969;

Aimee, book and lyrics by Goyen, music by Worth Gardner, Providence, R.I., Trinity Square Repertory Company, December 1973.

PRODUCED SCRIPTS: "A Possibility of Oil," television, *Four Star Theatre,* CBS, 1958;

"The Mind," television, *Directions '62,* ABC, 1961.

OTHER: "A Parable of Perez," in *New Directions in Prose and Poetry,* no. 11, edited by James Laughlin (New York: New Directions, 1949), pp. 240–243;

The Left-Handed Gun, motion picture, ballad lyrics by Goyen, Warner Bros., 1958;

"Simon's Castle," in *Simons Burg und andere Erzählungen,* translated by E. Schnack (Munich: Deutscher Taschenbuch Verlag, 1978), pp. 80–92.

TRANSLATION: Albert Cosséry, *The Lazy Ones* (New York: New Directions, 1952; London: Peter Owen, 1952).

SELECTED PERIODICAL PUBLICATIONS–UNCOLLECTED:

FICTION

"Right Here at Christmas," *Redbook* (December 1977): 77–78;

"The Storm Doll," *Ontario Review,* no. 7 (1977–1978): 28–34;

"The Seadown's Bible," *Delta,* no. 9 (November 1979): 113–119;

"Black Cotton," *Ontario Review,* no. 17 (1982–1983): 80–86.

William Goyen remains one of the most original and important American short-story writers of the twentieth century. Known also for his novels and plays, Goyen was a productive short-fiction writer whose particular gift was at its highest level in that genre. Even his novels *The House of Breath* (1950), *In a Farther Country* (1955), *Come, the Restorer* (1974), and *Arcadio* (1983) are constructed of sections that tend to be the length of a short story and to have the emotional and rhetorical intensity and shape of that genre–a construction that is essential to Goyen's accomplishment in inventing new forms of the novel. The preoccupations of Goyen's stories distinguish them from those of other Southern writers and from regional writers in general, while his experiments with the genre distinguish his work from that of either the traditionalists or the more cerebral experimentalists (the "metafiction" writers) of the four decades following World War II.

Technically, Goyen perfected a meditative form for the story, often in the voice of a first-person narrator. His narrators not only tell their own stories but also frequently tell them to another character in the story, whether that other character is explicitly described or only implicit. Late in life Goyen often spoke of this "teller-listener" dynamic between two persons. Furthermore, his short-story structures often establish certain motifs or ideas or simply words that are filled with feeling, to which they return like musical compositions that return to certain phrases and harmonies.

Charles William Goyen was born on 24 April 1915 in the small east Texas town of Trinity to Mary Inez (née Trow) and Charles Provine Goyen. His father was a lumber salesman, and nearly all of Goyen's fiction is permeated with the atmosphere of the east Texas pine woods and small towns of his father's world. Goyen's early childhood gave him the rhythms of rural speech and those of the Bible. When Goyen was eight, his parents settled in Houston after a brief period in Shreveport, Louisiana. Goyen grew up at 614 Merrill Street in the section of Houston known as "The Heights"; he attended public schools, then Rice Institute (now Rice University), where he received a B.A. in 1937 and an M.A. in 1939. He taught at the University of Houston from 1939 to 1940, then entered the U.S. Navy; during World War II he served on an aircraft carrier, although he suffered from chronic migraines and seasickness. Discharged from the navy after the end of the war, he returned briefly to Texas, then spent time in New Mexico (where he built a small house and where he returned to live sporadically over the next decade), California, Chicago, and New York City. He completed his first novel, *The House of Breath,* in London. This novel and his first collection, *Ghost and Flesh: Stories and Tales* (1952), won him successive Guggenheim fellowships in 1952 and 1954, and he spent time in Rome in 1954–1955. After he returned from Europe, he remained in New York City for many years; there, on 10 November 1963, he married Doris Roberts, a stage, motion picture, and television actress; a few years before his death he moved to Los Angeles, where she was working. He died of lymphoma on 29 August 1983.

Goyen's works explore both fleshly and spiritual experience; his work often represents an inquiry into the self-contradictory human spirit. He also writes with a robust delight in the scenes and things of humble

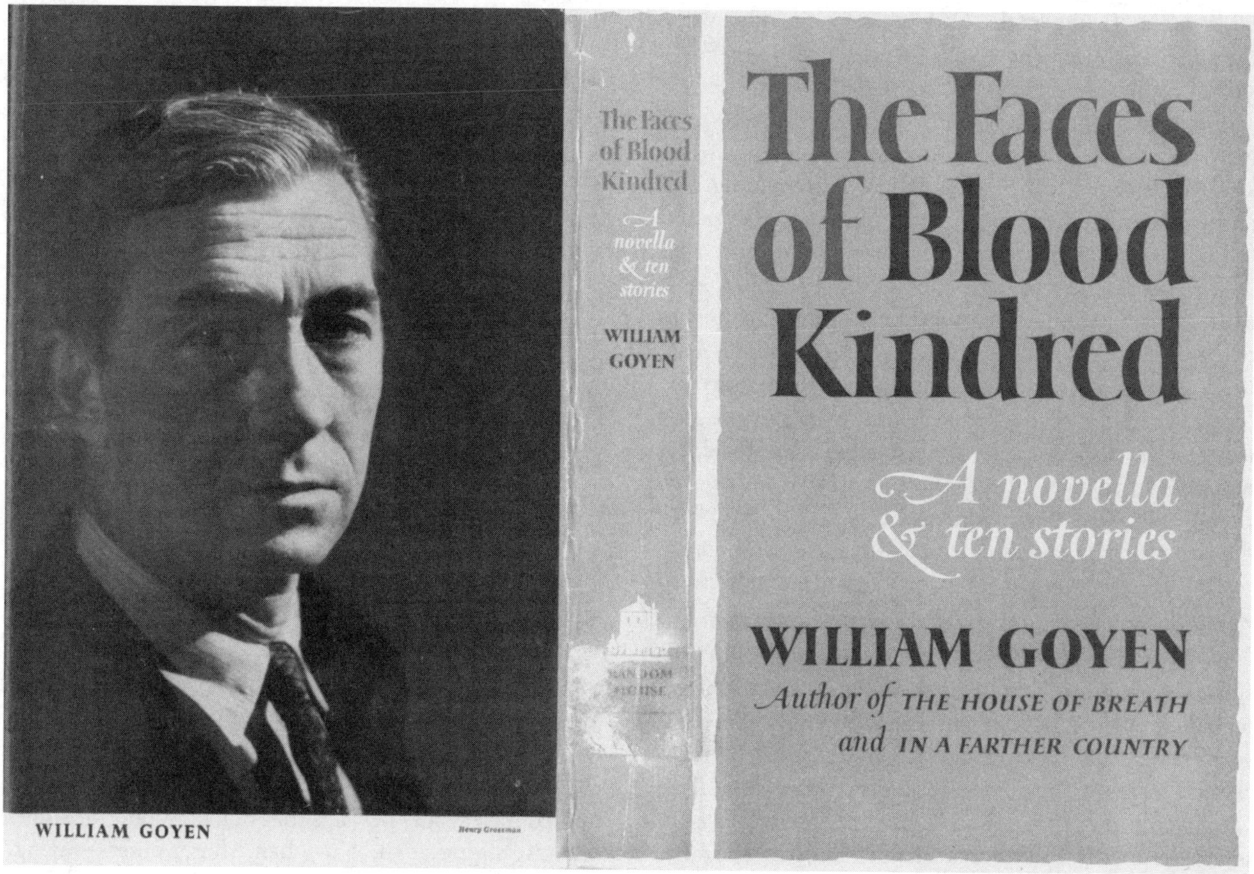

The Faces of Blood Kindred
A novella & ten stories
WILLIAM GOYEN
Author of THE HOUSE OF BREATH and IN A FARTHER COUNTRY
WILLIAM GOYEN
RANDOM HOUSE

Dust jacket for Goyen's 1960 book, in which he continued to develop the technique of telling stories within stories

daily life, in quirks of character and appearance, and in the impassioned, unselfconscious speech of the humble and poor rural folk among whom he spent his early years. In his fiction he sometimes follows those folk as they move into Houston, Dallas, or New York and try to cope–not always successfully–with the pace and intensity of urban life. Goyen was dedicated throughout his artistic career to the power of storytelling as a way of discovering or even establishing meaning in human life. Deeply immersed artistically in works of European, English, and American modernism (by such writers as Marcel Proust, Samuel Beckett, T. S. Eliot, Ezra Pound, and Katherine Anne Porter), Goyen joined the technical sophistication of these writers with the humble materials of ordinary persons living small-town Texas lives.

The stories in *Ghost and Flesh* should be considered not only for their individual merits but also for the way they are linked formally and thematically to form a collection. The book progresses by stages from the plot-driven "The White Rooster" to meditative stories, and from third-person narration that is fairly distant from the fictional characters to the close third-person and first-person intimacy of the meditative stories. Finally, it moves from amusement toward the most profound aspects of being.

In the darkly comic "The White Rooster," with the technique of third-person narration, Goyen pursues a gentle satire and an image–in both a rooster and an old man–of defiant individualism. The next three stories ("The Letter in the Cedarchest," "Pore Perrie," and "Ghost and Flesh, Water and Dirt") are narrated in the voices of their principal characters; then come two stories ("The Grasshopper's Burden" and "Children of Old Somebody") with third-person narrators who are close to the central characters. "Nests in a Stone Image" attains the unusually close third-person narrative voice also evident in "The Horse and the Day-Moth." The final story, "A Shape of Light," goes beyond the others in two ways–its language is a kind of "aria" (Goyen's own term, late in life, for much of his fiction), and its structure is as unplotted as possible. Thus the sequence of stories in *Ghost and Flesh* advances through the possibilities of narrative voicing from the least intimate to the most.

Throughout *Ghost and Flesh,* the title words appear repeatedly, often in a tone of melancholy. Even the fairly antic "Letter in the Cedarchest" concludes with the idea that everyone has a "ghost story or a flesh story." When the first voice to speak in "Pore Perrie" asks to hear a story, the second voice says, "The flesh of it is buried, but we have the ghost of it again." These key words signal a preoccupation with recovering the past–a recovery that is only partial, and therefore painful, but nonetheless desired. The presence, or absence, of the past in the lives of the living is one of Goyen's main themes. Another is the paradox of the experience of leaving home and returning again–the home has been changed by time, and thus defeats one's desire to return to a place that is still as it was, even though one was anxious to leave it for the very reason that it does not seem to change. Those who have read *The House of Breath* will not be surprised that the loss of the past and the attempt to recover it in a realm of language, if not in reality, are at the heart of Goyen's first story collection as well.

In "Pore Perrie" it is clear that the recovery of sad stories is painful, and that some who know them, including Aunt Linsie in this story, would rather not speak them; but there are others who must know, who clamor to know. Formally, this story nests narratives within each other to a dizzying degree, making use of quotation marks and distinct sections in order to show what a journey it is for the teller and the listener to return through stages to the unknowable past and to imagine it as it might have been.

"The Grasshopper's Burden" links the key word *ghost* to the sad figure of George Kurunus, the deformed boy who fascinates and repels the main character, the schoolgirl Quella. Frequently in his fiction Goyen treats those who are deformed or outcast, or both, marking and honoring their differences from others and their special burdens of consciousness. In Quella's world, George is a "ghost" haunting the security of the apparently normal world. "Children of Old Somebody" explicitly raises the theme of the past: "there is this loss to recapture, to salvage up from fathoms, hovering over the depths to rescue the shape when it rises." This story also broadens the idea of the "ghost" to include the child who is "the ghost" of the passion of its parents; and in the figure of "Old Somebody," an evanescent shape of change and mystery and death, the story invests the power to return the past to the present. In this story, every strange figure–a beggar at the back door or a face at the window–is a reminder, even an embodiment, of the lost past, which can either frighten like death or restore like a remembrance of love.

The central character of "Nests in a Stone Image" says out loud to himself:

> What vanishes returns, again and again in any room at any hour; there is no room in the wide world will shelter you from it, no place to go into out of it, no refuge, no asylum. Stand and face it and endure it, the vision; but tell of it, in its multifarious ways and changes and appearances, its hundred faces and cries and sounds, its infinitely elaborate wardrobe of masks and costumes; everything contributes to the whole image, there is the total contribution, there is the listening and the speaking.

The structure of this story is perhaps the most meditative or musical, as it moves from and returns to idea after idea in order to capture a complex, elusive feeling.

The title of "Ghost and Flesh, Water and Dirt" announces the presence of the past. In this story Margy Emmons tells of her own tragedy as if her purpose is not simply to tell the story but to live in it again through the language with which she shapes it. She passes on to her listener the wisdom that she has gained from her friend Fursta Evans and that she has made her own: "Now I believe in *tellin,*" she says, adding, "There's a time ta tell and a time ta set still ta let a ghost grieve ya." Unlike Aunt Linsie of "Pore Perrie," Margy believes that one should tell the stories of sadness. The structure of this story is simple: it opens with an unidentified voice–perhaps that of a bartender or someone else sitting at the bar when Margy enters–saying, "Was somebody here while ago acallin for you." The story then plunges into Margy's voice, in which it stays. Goyen adjusts the readers to the urgency of Margy's speech by presenting the first paragraph (her immediate reaction, her muttering to herself) in italics; then she settles down, presumably having found someone to talk to, next to her at the bar, and she tells the tale from beginning to end.

She is troubled by the ghost of her first husband, who killed himself out of grief after their only child was killed in a riding accident. At some points in the story she goes back into her own mind; then her speech is represented by italics. Mostly she tells her listener of the aftermath of the accident: of her great grieving; of her decision, at Fursta's urging, to start life over again; of moving to California (the time is World War II), working in shipbuilding, and meeting a sailor with whom she falls in love; of her grief at his death at sea during the war; of her return to Texas; and of her alternating rounds, now, of quiet grief, when she lives with the ghost of her first husband and is lost in images of the past, and her "time a tellin," when she bursts out of this grief and is among other people and telling her story.

The plot is powerful, but what is even more remarkable is the language with which Goyen creates his main character through her own words–her convincing intimacy, her great grief, her good humor, the depth of her wisdom about the course of strong feeling, her verbal mannerisms and habits, and her diction. She is fully immersed in a rapture of the tragic, and although she says that things are funny and can laugh about them, she never breaks out of that rapture, which is what drives her intense language forward.

The Faces of Blood Kindred: A Novella and Ten Stories (1960), Goyen's second collection, continues to develop the fictional techniques and the ideas already laid out in *Ghost and Flesh* and in *The House of Breath.* In the time between Goyen's first two books and this book, he also completed a second novel, *Half a Look of Cain: A Fantastical Narrative,* but was unable to find a publisher for it; the book was published posthumously in 1994. This novel advanced the techniques of nesting stories within each other, and of relating them by theme and image, which Goyen had begun in "Pore Perrie" and *The House of Breath.* In subtitling *Half a Look of Cain* "A Fantastical Narrative," Goyen announced that he was exploring and creating a fictional technique that had left naturalism completely behind. The novel also furthered his exploration of erotic life, both in and of itself and as it relates to elation and suffering of the human spirit. He continued these explorations in his second collection.

"Old Wildwood" is the central story of *The Faces of Blood Kindred,* serving as a kind of midpoint of feeling and technique, as "Ghost and Flesh, Water and Dirt" serves the first collection. Making use of close third-person narrative, Goyen presents the central, unnamed character, "the grandson," who receives a letter from home while he is in Rome–a letter that awakens profound memories as it informs him that his grandfather has died. Returning to memories of that man, he also discovers a memory of a moment of self-understanding, of self-making, of that threshold of knowledge in his childhood when he began to understand what his hopes for himself might be. "Old Wildwood" concludes by returning to the moment when the grandson has received the letter in Rome; while readers have been "listening" to these memories, the grandson has been sitting on the Spanish Steps, "supporting himself upon the opened palm of his hand." Now, "engraved in the palm of the hand he had leaned on, was the very mark and grain of the stone, as though his hand were stone." This feeling sparks in him the realization that from the past, from the life of his grandfather, he must seize what he would make himself in the present: "He would not have a hand of stone! He would carry a hand that could labor wood and build a house, trouble dirt and lay a highway, and blaze a trail through leaf and bramble; and a hand that could rot like wood and fall into dust." Also worth noticing is that the grandfather has a Goyenesque physical deformity–in his case, a twisted foot–

Goyen and his wife, actress Doris Roberts, whom he married in 1963 (photograph by Ben McCall)

which in Goyen's fiction marks him as a figure of power.

Another especially important story in this volume is "Rhody's Path," which begins with signs of the rhetoric of orality: the intimate "you" and "us," the colloquial "twould," and a confiding tone and syntax. The tone of voice is folksy, but this style does not, in Goyen's work, mean that the author is distancing himself with irony from his narrator. The busy scenario of this story–a revivalist, a plague of grasshoppers, a rattlesnake, a flagpole sitter, and Rhody and her large family–give it almost the scope of a miniature novel. The main ideas are that of leaving and returning–which Rhody does repeatedly, by "her path"–and erotic life. Rhody is forever in search of an elusive excitement, no doubt partly erotic, that will free her from the claustrophobic imaginative and moral confines of small-town and family life. The revivalist is in some ways a familiar figure in Goyen's work, not because Goyen often writes about preachers but because he so often portrays characters whose spiritual ambitions or hopes are thwarted or–perhaps more interestingly–fed by their pleasure in the senses: they are torn between spirit and body, and not infrequently they combine excesses of both.

Several previously uncollected stories appeared in *The Collected Stories of William Goyen* (1975), including older works such as several chapters of the then-unpublished novel *Half a Look of Cain* ("The Enchanted Nurse," "The Rescue," and "Figure Over the Town")

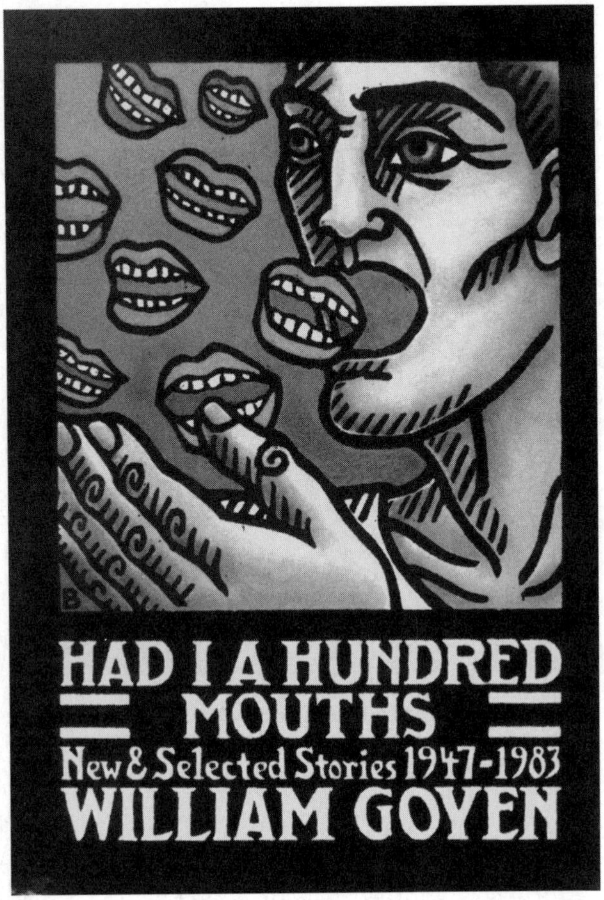

Dust jacket for the posthumously published book that includes most of Goyen's last stories, including the title story, a tale of lust and violence told by an uncle to his young nephews

and "Tapioca Surprise," which belongs to the period of "The White Rooster." There is also an important newer story, "Bridge of Music, River of Sand," in which Goyen addresses another of his major preoccupations: the harsh destructiveness of industrial and urban society, which causes human suffering, estranges people from each other, and also despoils the natural environment. A meditative, first-person piece, this story makes central symbols of the bridge and the river. The river in *The House of Breath* was ungovernable by human beings; it was the very life of fertility and eros. But in "Bridge of Music, River of Sand," it is dry; it has disappeared or been destroyed somehow. Not only is the river dry but also the town beside it is filled with the acrid fumes of the mill. The fouling of the natural world is connected in this story to an end of feeling, an end of the rushing current that spoke to the narrator of *The House of Breath* of raw, sopping life, both intoxicating and frightening him with it. Reflecting the narrator's bewilderment and despair in "Bridge of Music, River of Sand," perhaps, is another character in the story–the anonymous man who throws himself off the bridge only to plunge to his death not in water but in dry sand below.

Most of Goyen's last stories were collected posthumously in *Had I A Hundred Mouths: New & Selected Stories 1947–1983* (1985), published two years after his death. This group of stories displays an extraordinary late adventurousness of form and feeling. "Arthur Bond" is a supremely intense and compressed performance that asks, and cannot answer, the meaning of obsessive lust. The dark fable "In the Icebound Hothouse," which circles around the same theme, adds to it a typically Goyenesque self-interrogation with regard to the past and the feeling of isolation and loneliness. "The Texas Principessa" is a humorous monologue in which death and sex are only way stations on the road to the inexplicable good fortune of the narrator. The dark comedy of alcoholism and recovery dominates "Where's Esther?," while anger, violence, and reconciliation prevail in "Precious Door." Perhaps the two most extraordinary of Goyen's stories are "Had I A Hundred Mouths" and "Tongues of Men and of Angels." In these two stories, all of Goyen's gifts, preoccupations, technical achievements, and emotional intensity are focused and dramatized.

In "Had I A Hundred Mouths" Goyen seems to fully realize the possibilities that were waiting to be accomplished in his earlier work. The tale is one of ungovernable lust, racial hatred, and suicidal despair, but also of love and reconciliation. At another level, Goyen eroticizes, although not at all crassly, the teller-listener situation, for he frames the story as a tale told long ago to the narrator by his drunken uncle while the uncle and his two nephews, in hot weather, were lying nearly naked in a bed, resting. The frame also establishes that the narrator, looking back at this moment of telling and listening from his adult perspective, understands it to have marked his whole life with the quest to live his feelings fully and freely. The language itself is seductive, as it engages one in the ceaseless cycles of telling and listening.

While the older nephew, the boy at the uncle's side, is troubled deeply by what he hears his uncle tell, the uncle himself speaks casually of the most shocking and barbaric violence, leading to his story of what happened to the woman Louetta. To the two small boys, the uncle incongruously, almost abusively, recounts the long-ago rapes of Louetta–by a black stranger, then by himself, and then, years later, by her own son, Leander, who does not know she is his mother. Goyen takes no note of the shock that must have been felt by the two boys at hearing the uncle's tale, for the story has moved out of the frame of the older nephew's point of view entirely and now adopts the uncle's point of view. Here Goyen finds the richest expression of the mysteries and complexities of point of view itself, of how the human angle of vision is what it reveals. From time to time readers are reminded of the presence of the two silent, presumably spellbound and even frightened boys: "And now I'm going to tell you something," the uncle says in the middle of the tale. With a deft technical touch, Goyen keeps the story within the uncle's voice and yet at the same time shows that the story is simultaneously a remembering by the uncle, a telling to the two boys, and a subsequent retelling by the older of the boys to himself years later.

When the uncle finishes his tale, the older nephew asks him what became of Leander, the tormented boy turned violent. The uncle says he does not know, and the story returns once again to the scene of the man and two boys lying together, the man sleeping now, the boys awake. Then the narration takes a surprising turn. The framing voice with which the story began–a close third-person narration focused on the older nephew–now recurs as the story leaps ahead in time to the uncle's funeral. The older nephew is shocked by the sudden appearance of several hooded members of the Ku Klux Klan–those who had destroyed Leander. One of them lifts his mask and reveals himself as the younger nephew, and the older nephew feels "terror and rage."

The voicing of the story reveals how the social and psychological situation of storytelling, which this story dramatizes, transmits not only a tale but also moral values–positive and negative, depending on who is telling and who is listening. The same story may transmit contradictory values: the older nephew feels something of himself being formed in the experience of listening to the uncle, which makes him identify with both Leander's suffering and the uncle's own youthful passion; but the younger nephew instead absorbs the racial hatred that pursued the rapist of Louetta and the child of that crime, who also rapes–Leander.

Finally, the older nephew has a vision of the return of Leander on his own city street–a ghostly presence and reminder of the past. This revelation is a key to the older nephew's self-understanding, his longing, and his hope.

"Tongues of Men and of Angels," a sequel to "Had I A Hundred Mouths," shifts the narrative voice into the first person–that of an anonymous narrator who, seeking the meaning of dramatic crises and violent episodes in human lives, goes back through the stories of the characters in "Had I A Hundred Mouths" and adds to them a series of fantastical tales that leave the reader not knowing what in those characters' lives was real and what was imagined. The fantastical aspects of *Arcadio*–the novel completed by Goyen around the same time that he was drafting these two stories–are similarly indeterminate. In "Tongues of Men and of Angels," the last writing that Goyen completed before his death, he addresses, in a way, all the technical and emotional issues he has explored throughout his artistic career, completing his body of work with the wildest, most bizarre tale of them all.

Goyen's accomplishments as an artist include the distinctness of his conception of the short story and his genius for narrative voices. He will also be remembered for his tolerant and humane sympathy for all those who are marked as different from others, his sensitivity to the life of feeling, and his alarm over the fate of the natural world. His work constitutes one of the most memorable artistic visions in American short fiction.

Letters:

"Letters to Zoe Leger" and "Letters to Maurice Coindreau," *Delta,* no. 9 (November 1979): 49–99;

"Like a Buoy: Letters from William Goyen to John Igo 1952–1983," *Pax,* 3, nos. 1–2 (1985–1986): 41–59;

William Goyen: Selected Letters from a Writer's Life, edited by Robert Phillips (Austin: University of Texas Press, 1995).

Interviews:

Harvey Breit, "Talk with William Goyen," *New York Times Book Review,* 10 September 1950, p. 12;

Robert Phillips, "The Art of Fiction LXIII," *Paris Review,* no. 68 (Winter 1976): 58–100;

"Portrait of the Artist as a Young Texan: An Interview with 1977 Distinguished Alumnus William Goyen," *Sallyport,* 32, no. 5 (June 1977): 6–8;

Rolande Ballorain, "Interview with William Goyen," *Delta,* no. 9 (November 1979): 7–45;

John Igo, "Learning to See Simply: An Interview with William Goyen," *Southwest Review,* 65 (Summer 1980): 267–284;

"William Goyen: A Poet Telling Stories," in *Talking with Texas Writers: Twelve Interviews,* by Patrick Bennett (College Station: Texas A & M University Press, 1980), pp. 227–247;

"William Goyen: une réédition de *La Maison d'haleine*: un entretien réalisé par Jean-Michel Quiblier," *Masques,* no. 14 (Summer 1982): 16–22;

Reginald Gibbons, "An Interview with William Goyen," *TriQuarterly,* no. 56 (Winter 1983): 97–125;

John F. Baker, "PW Interviews: William Goyen," *Publishers Weekly* (5 August 1983): 94–95.

Bibliographies:

Clyde L. Grimm Jr., "William Goyen: A Bibliographic Chronicle," *Bulletin of Bibliography,* 35, no. 3 (1978): 123–131;

Grimm and Patrice Repusseau, "Oeuvres de William Goyen," *Delta,* no. 9 (November 1979): 219–250;

Stuart Wright, *William Goyen: A Descriptive Bibliography, 1938–1985* (Westport, Conn.: Meckler, 1986).

References:

Leonard Ashley, "'Tightly-Wound Little Bombs of Truth': Biblical References in the Fiction of William Goyen," *Literary Onomastics Studies,* 8 (1981): 147–165;

Pierre Brodin, *Vingt-cinq americains: littérature et littérateurs américains des années 1960* (Paris: Nouvelles éditions Debresse, 1969), pp. 71–82;

Ernest R. Curtius, "William Goyen," in *Essays on European Literature,* translated by Michael Kowal (Princeton: Princeton University Press, 1973), pp. 456–464;

Erika Duncan, "William Goyen," in her *Unless Soul Clap Its Hands* (New York: Schocken Books, 1984), pp. 17–30;

Reginald Gibbons, *William Goyen: A Study of the Short Fiction* (Boston: Twayne, 1991);

Louise Y. Gossett, "The Voices of Distance: William Goyen," in her *Violence in Recent Southern Fiction* (Durham, N.C.: Duke University Press, 1965), pp. 131–145;

Frederick J. Hoffman, "Varieties of Fantasy," in his *The Art of Southern Fiction: A Study of Some Modern Novelists* (Carbondale: Southern Illinois University Press, 1967), pp. 124–129;

Brooke Horvath, Irving Malin, and Paul Ruffin, eds., *A Goyen Companion: Appreciations of a Writer's Writer* (Austin: University of Texas Press, 1997);

Michel Lucazeau, *Surrealism in William Goyen* (Bordeaux: Diplome d'Etudes Superieures, Faculté des Lettres et Sciences Humaines de Bordeaux, 1963);

Gabriel Merle, "Les Liens du sang et les liens du temps dans *The Faces of Blood Kindred,*" *Delta,* no. 9 (November 1979): 187–194;

Mid-American Review, special Goyen issue, 13, no. 1 (1992);

Joyce Carol Oates, "Introduction," in *Had I A Hundred Mouths: New & Selected Stories, 1947–1983,* by Goyen (New York: Potter, 1985), pp. vii–xii;

Jay S. Paul, "Marvellous Reciprocity: The Fiction of William Goyen," *Critique* (1977): 77–91;

Paul, "Nests in a Stone Image: Goyen's Surreal Gethsemane," *Studies in Short Fiction,* 15 (Fall 1978): 415–420;

Robert Phillips, *William Goyen* (Boston: Twayne, 1979);

Patrice Repusseau, *An Approach to William Goyen's The House of Breath* (Paris: Mémoire de Maitrise, Institut d'Anglais Charles V, Université Paris VII, 1971);

Repusseau, "The Concentrated Writing of William Goyen: Reflections on *Come, the Restorer,*" *Delta,* no. 9 (November 1979): 197–216;

Repusseau, ed., *William Goyen: De la Maison vers le Foyer* (Pantin, France: Le Castor Astral, 1991);

Stephen Spender, "The Situation of the American Writer," *Horizon,* 19, no. 111 (March 1949): 162–179;

Simone Vauthier, "The True Story: A Reading of William Goyen's 'Pore Perrie,'" *Les Cahiers de la nouvelle: Journal of the Short Story in English,* 1 (1983): 139–158;

Allen Wier, "William Goyen: Speech for What is Not Spoken," *Black Warrior Review,* 10, no. 1 (Fall 1983): 160–164.

Papers:

The major collections of William Goyen's papers are in the Fondren Library at Rice University in Houston and the Harry Ransom Humanities Research Center at the University of Texas at Austin.

Shirley Ann Grau

(9 July 1929 -   )

Ellen Burton Harrington
Tulane University

See also the Grau entry in *DLB 2: American Novelists Since World War II.*

BOOKS: *The Black Prince and Other Stories* (New York: Knopf, 1955; London: Heinemann, 1956);

The Hard Blue Sky (New York: Knopf, 1958; London: Heinemann, 1959);

The House on Coliseum Street (New York: Knopf, 1961; London: Heinemann, 1961);

The Keepers of the House (New York: Knopf, 1964; London: Longmans, 1964);

The Condor Passes (New York: Knopf, 1971; London: Longman, 1972);

The Wind Shifting West (New York: Knopf, 1973; London: Chatto & Windus, 1974);

Evidence of Love (New York: Knopf, 1977; London: Hamilton, 1977);

Nine Women (New York: Knopf, 1985);

Writers and Writing: The Flora Levy Lecture in the Humanities 1983 (Lafayette: University of Southwestern Louisiana, 1988);

Roadwalkers (New York: Knopf, 1994).

photograph © Jerry Bauer; from the dust jacket of Roadwalkers, *1994*

In her 1983 Flora Levy Lecture in the Humanities at the University of Southwestern Louisiana, Shirley Ann Grau commented, "A writer is an evangelist whose preaching is subtle and utterly disguised–often from himself." This statement strikes at the heart of the contradictions in the work of this writer whose objective style belies the moral force of her narratives. At once worldly and quintessentially Southern in her sentiments, Grau professes surprise at the multiple, complicated responses that her texts inspire in critics. Her stories present a mysticism that underlies everyday reality, the unshakable vestiges of inherited (sometimes cursed) tradition that persist from generation to generation. Grau's fiction covers a surprising narrative range, giving voice to nostalgic adults and pampered children, to the poverty of the South and its wealthy grandeur, to the concerns of aging summer cottagers on the East Coast and to whites and blacks in the uncomfortable racial reality of the twentieth century.

Her three collections of short fiction, spanning the length of her writing career, depict the full range of Grau's talents and subjects. *The Black Prince and Other Stories* appeared in 1955 to considerable acclaim only nine years before her Pulitzer Prize winning novel, *The Keepers of the House* (1964). The striking depiction in the novel of personal conflict based on race and inheritance finds its roots in the brief, intense themes of her first collection. Her second volume of short fiction, *The Wind*

Shifting West (1973), deals with the difficult issues of alienation and miscommunication in families and marriages, with special attention to the ravages that war wreaks on those left at home. Grau's 1985 collection, *Nine Women,* focuses on the struggles of daughters, wives, and mothers to handle memories of the past, widowhood, the alienation of aging, and death.

While not an avowed feminist, Grau addresses gender issues throughout her fiction, depicting women who struggle with propriety and their expected roles as wives, mothers, lovers, and often providers. Indeed, many of her characters fight the weight of tradition and expectation, often only to succumb in the end. Grau's own experience reflects the complicated pressures on women in the middle of the twentieth century. Shirley Ann Grau was born in New Orleans, Louisiana, on 9 July 1929 to Adolph E. Grau, a dentist, and Katherine Onions Grau. She divided her childhood between New Orleans and Montgomery, Alabama, moving back to New Orleans after World War II to finish high school at an all-girls boarding school. After graduating from Ursuline Academy, she went on to Sophie Newcomb College, the only undergraduate division of Tulane University to which women were admitted then. Scholar Paul Schlueter quotes her comment that Newcomb acted as a kind of glorified "finishing school" that produced not scholars, "only mothers." Grau's first story publications came in *Carnival,* a student magazine, and *Surf,* a local literary publication. Despite her literary promise, she interrupted her graduate studies at Tulane when she realized that women were not allowed to be teaching assistants there. Grau continued writing and individually published three of the stories (one of these in *The New Yorker*) that eventually formed part of *The Black Prince and Other Stories.* Her 1955 marriage to the considerably older philosopher and respected Tulane professor James K. Feibleman marked the beginning of a comfortable domesticity that established Grau's continuing tradition of summering in Martha's Vineyard and wintering in a suburb of New Orleans, two locales consistently reflected in her short fiction. Grau and Feibleman have four children. When it appeared, *The Black Prince and Other Stories* was heralded by a critic for *Time* (24 January 1955) as "The most impressive U.S. short story debut between hard covers since J. D. Salinger's *Nine Stories* [1953]."

Beginning with *The Black Prince and Other Stories,* Grau has made a point of taking up in her fiction the difficult cultural issues of the southern United States, especially gender and race. This collection is especially concerned with the primal forces and folkloric influences that drive human beings, sometimes in spite of themselves. Her characters deal with the constraining psychological remnants of the old Southern regime, trying to redefine their gender and racial roles in the light of new standards and opportunities. The heavy use of dialect and colloquial speech patterns lends the stories a sometimes troubling intimacy with their frustrated, and at times violent, subjects.

The title story (originally published in summer 1953 in *New Mexico Quarterly* as "The Sound of Silver") sets the earthy, disquieting tone for the collection. The Lucifer-like main character, Stanley Albert Thompson, is a locus of violence and desire, inspiring infighting and jealousy within a rural black community. Grau's epigraph describing the angel "fallen from heaven" adds to Stanley's menace and his mystical allure as he slowly seduces the unfeminine Alberta by turning drops of wax into silver coins. Stanley establishes himself as an undefeatable fighter whom the men fear to challenge, instead bickering and picking fights among themselves; he is also a suave, handsome man with an endless supply of money, who is extremely desirable to women. The perceived discord that Stanley unleashes in the community lasts even after he and Alberta disappear: "when women talk–when there's been a miscarriage or a stillbirth–they remember and whisper together." The timeless, mythic feel of this story belies its subtle commentary on current racial and economic issues: it effectively portrays the tendency in some poor communities to express frustration with outside forces through violence enacted within the community. In "The Black Prince," money has replaced community as the most valuable commodity.

Grau's reliance in this story on superstition and a tradition of inherited knowledge and value is true to the overarching themes of the collection: in a 1987 interview with John Canfield, Grau commented, "In *The Black Prince and Other Stories,* I was trying to create a kind of legendary, mythological time, a non-real approach, a storytelling in the legendary sense of storytelling." Other stories in this collection pick up the theme of a much desired but usually failed metamorphosis; characters often find that they are more shaped and determined by their pasts and their heredity than they ever realized. When Lena of "Miss Yellow Eyes" commits to go with Chris to "cross over" in Oregon, since they can both pass for white, she has agreed to cut her ties to the past and start a new life without the implication of her blackness. In the words of Chris to her brother, Pete, "You plain crazy to stay a nigger. I done told you that." Pete fears going to fight in the Korean War so much that he mutilates himself to make himself unfit for service, bitterly asserting that in his cowardice he has preserved his life. The more noble Chris dies in combat, leaving Lena in the role her mother had held, that of a war widow, rather than allowing her to assume a more liberated, white identity in the less racially defined Oregon. The story ends as Lena, unable to handle her brother's taunts that he is cowardly but living, slams the picture of her revered father into Pete's newly injured arm. She is no longer the disquieting model of restraint that she has been throughout the story.

"White Girl, Fine Girl," the opening story in the collection, presents a similar vision of racial frustration and intra-family violence. The protagonist, Jayson, recently released from prison and brutally rejected by the black woman for whom he killed, takes pleasure in a promised sexual union with a red-haired woman who is almost white. This image of desire for a white-looking woman is counterbalanced by the frustrated Aggie, Jayson's former lover, who has given up on relationships with men because they leave her nothing but children. Thus, she has trained her three daughters, each of whom has a different father, to throw stones and bits of bricks at the men to prevent them from approaching Aggie when they enter her street. Though the daughters forcefully repel the determined Jayson, their blows causing him almost to lose consciousness, Jayson's daughter eventually recognizes their kinship and follows him pleadingly. Fulfilling Aggie's cynicism, Jayson tosses a stone back at his daughter and then ignores her, leaving her in the road as he strides toward the sexy redhead.

Another story, "The Way of a Man," also addresses parent-child relationships, showcasing the isolation and misrecognition that can come out of broken families. William's father, an unambitious, peaceable man and a war veteran, had married a young, attractive woman who believed the rumors that the older man has hidden a large sum of money. The marriage soon fails, and the son's return to his father as a young adult does not spark a reunion or even land the youth a few dollars but, instead, leads to a rivalry between the two men. Each longs for possession of a nice skiff that is overturned and floating abandoned in the water. Even the discovery of the body of a young white woman entangled with the boat does not dampen their enthusiasm, though the father criticizes William for his weakness in being disturbed by the dead woman. William returns later as a fugitive, but his father taunts him again about his manhood–"You supposed to be a man and you afraid. You plain afraid"–and laughs at the young man. William abruptly, unthinkingly kills him in frustration. He cries, then searches for the old man's money, finding only seven silver pieces, the pathetic "fortune" for which William's mother had married his father, ultimately the price on his father's head. William stalks off in fear, scared of the events that he has put in motion, ironically not yet a man.

The last story in the collection, "Joshua," set in the Gulf of Mexico during World War II, picks up this theme of uneasy maturation. The title character is forced by his father to take out the father's fishing boat. His parents are fighting because his father refuses to use the boat to earn a living or get food since another fisherman was killed by a German U-boat. Joshua and his friend are terrified of the trip, but Joshua insists on going still further out because he is ashamed that his friend has seen his fear. As Joshua pushes on, remembering the fearsome legends that belong to the area, he finds the body of a dead German soldier. Putting aside his revulsion at touching the corpse, he takes the soldier's leather coat for himself, a badge of his own bravery and the provision for his family (in the form of a much-needed new coat) that his father is too frightened to make.

Dust jacket for Grau's first book, which Time *called "The most impressive U.S. short story debut between hard covers since J. D. Salinger's* Nine Stories*"*

Other stories in *The Black Prince* adeptly deal with the generational difficulties of middle-class white Southern families, offering glimpses of what lies behind a seemingly genteel veneer. "The Girl with the Flaxen Hair" showcases the burden of an ugly past. A mother and daughter live behind a facade of an illustrious family history; rather than dealing with the hideous financial need of their present situation, they struggle to preserve a proper appearance. Only when the daughter is struck by a train and killed while stealing coal from the train-yard do the neighbors become aware of the full extent of the women's poverty and their desperate clinging to their past status. "One Summer" depicts another kind of hidden Southern heritage. A teenage boy experiencing his own first romance makes a discovery at his grandfather's death: the black woman who had lived with his grandfather since his grandmother's death, ostensibly as a housekeeper, was really his grandfather's lover. Their long-term relationship forces the boy to reconsider his simpler ideas of love, even as he tries to make sense of his grandfather's death and what it means for son and grandson. Throughout *The Black Prince,* the burdens of familial heritage appear inescapable.

"Fever Flower" seems to depart from the earlier generational struggles, portraying a modern woman who wants to keep her liaisons limited to evenings so they do not clutter her days. The story, however, focuses on the long-term implications of a broken marriage. Katherine is infuriated by the marriage settlement that requires her to vacate her house one day each week as her former husband comes to spend time with their child, Maureen. She cannot amuse herself knowing that she is not free to return home, and so she makes a difficult weekly visit to her mother as a kind of penance. Meanwhile, Maureen's father, Hugh, struggles with his love for, and alienation from, the young daughter who is also the child of his former wife. These battle-worn characters cannot let down their emotional barriers enough to become truly close.

Grau's second collection, *The Wind Shifting West,* is another diverse offering that presents issues of estrangement and miscommunication within families. Unlike her other two short-story volumes, *The Wind Shifting West* includes stories of varying lengths, often quite brief; there are twice as many stories as in the other collections, ranging from short sketches to the more lengthy psychological studies typical of her other work. More thoroughly grounded in the present than her first collection, this volume also depicts the multifaceted effects of tradition and alienation on recognizably modern lives. In "Pillow of Stone" a young pregnant woman who has left her own family to marry into an isolated Cajun family braves stormy waters in a rickety boat to return proudly to the wake of her father. Her child moves within her as she claims her "rightful" place at the wake that night; her head is high because "My papa he can rest, now I have come with one to take his place." Her pregnancy and the role that it holds for her are not just aspects of the new life she has entered: they gain their meaning through the past, the familial ties that she has hitherto shirked.

Troubling ties also characterize the opening story of the collection. "The Wind Shifting West" depicts a married couple whose relationship is slowly becoming more distant; the wife, Caroline, recalls, "They did not kiss in front of Guppy anymore, it embarrassed the child." Her cocky husband, a recreational sailor, has lost his mast on a rough day and needs a rescue. His and Caroline's increasingly disconnected relationship is symbolized by their broken ship-to-shore phone call, during which neither can really understand the other. Caroline agrees to ride with her brother-in-law, the European expatriate Giles, to pick up her husband. Giles insists on stopping for a swim, trying to seduce Caroline and allowing her to see the swimsuits in his boat for all sizes of women, a measure of his frequent infidelities to his wife. She goes ahead with the fling, realizing its banality: "There isn't ever much left when it's done." However, she realizes that her husband will never recognize the residue, the seaweed left on the anchor and the salt on their skin, since their estrangement has become a foregone conclusion.

The sea is also the setting for "The Land and the Water," which develops the familiar Grau theme of a young girl's emotional coming-of-age. The narrator's father and brother go out in their boat, not for pleasure, but to search for a group of teenagers who did not return before a storm; they are forced back by the weather. The narrator must alter her companionable view of the sea as unthreatening and hospitable when she has a vision of being entangled "down in the sand and mud with the eel grass." She visits the shore early the next morning, running back to her mother's kitchen with the impression that there was "Something that had reached for me, and missed"; she no longer has an innocent apprehension of the water.

"Beach Party" describes a similar emotional crisis for an older girl. Frieda has gone to a beach party with her brother and has ambiguous feelings about the attentive boy she has just met who has been holding her hand and kissing her. The tone of the group changes abruptly when a boy asks the group for help locating his brother, who had gone diving but never come up. All of them are affected by the discovery of the diver, who has been under water too long to be resuscitated despite their efforts. Frieda moves down the beach to be alone with her feelings, only to find the party has left her there, unaware she is missing. Abandoned by both her brother and her potential lover and unable to stay at the site any longer, she chooses to walk home, knowing it will take most of the night. The dependency she has been hitherto encouraged to have on men is unfounded, since neither man has taken care of her.

The discomfiting story "Homecoming" portrays a young girl's refusal to be placed in the role her mother plays, in this case the mournful resignation of a war widow. The narrative commences at a wake for a young man who died in combat; his girlfriend's frustration and callousness seem out of place in the serious setting. Soon, however, the reader discovers that the girl is disgusted with the hypocrisy around her. She had worn the ring of a boy she barely knew, whose family lived across the country. Though she regrets his death, she regrets it along with all war deaths and the hideous violence of war. The mother is determined to make her daughter enact the ritual of mourning that the mother went through, though no such emotion lies behind it on the part of the daughter. She comes to regret only that her feelings had been so shallow, that one boy of his sort would do for her as well as another.

"Sea Change" shows another side of mourning: a wife left at home struggling with intense feelings of abandonment and frustration, deeply shell-shocked in her own way. The story is interspersed with fragments of remembered conversation with her husband set alongside her present fainting spell at the airport and dialogue with a serviceman who is attracted to her despair and grief. His sexual impulse points to the possibility of a more viable, productive future for the deeply hurting wife. Her emotional state is so precarious that the reader is unable to determine whether she is actually a widow or her projected fears have so intensified her feelings that she anticipates a death which did not really occur.

"Three" also tells the story of a grief-stricken wife who goes on to another relationship after her husband's death. Ann's attachment to her first husband, Jerry, is so great that she sees him as a continued physical presence in her life, and in the last lines of the story she is trying to introduce Jerry's presence to her new husband. The story ends at this ambivalent moment, which casts doubt on the sanity of the character even as it legitimizes her deep emotion.

In the context of these more probing stories, "The Patriarch" seems like a neatly-plotted trick, an unexpected reversal; it evolved into Grau's 1977 novel, *Evidence of Love.* The son of a spoiled, promiscuous, indulgent man has turned to the Unitarian ministry for a deeper sense of the truth than his father's proud transgressions seem to offer. In the wry resolution of the story, the son fears that he has taken the wrong route, that "truth lies beyond the fulfillment of desire, in satiated appetite." At this moment his father appears at the window with his grandchildren, waving in greeting and perhaps benediction.

"The Last Gas Station" offers black humor in a narrative of rural isolation, tapping into the familiar

Dust jacket for Grau's 1985 book, stories that focus on women's experiences of love, family life, aging, and mortality

mode of Southern Gothic. A family made strange by remoteness and the absence of a feminine presence falls apart: a brother leaves with little acknowledgment; the father dies and is casually buried on site; two brothers fight violently and depart. Finally the youngest and most fearful brother is left in the old family gas station without gas to sell or even electricity in the station or his residence. He knows that he too must leave, but he is so disconnected from humanity that his only escape is to put himself in the path of traffic to force it to stop. In his desperation, the chance of death is worth the hope of escape.

"The Man Outside" also emphasizes this fundamental human alienation. When a mediocre farmer leaves his family to fend for themselves while he attends to his "visions" in a shack outside, then disappears altogether, his wife eventually puts her life back together. She remarries a more practical, prosperous man whom she loves. They pull the farm together, and her contentment is such that she even plants decorative flowers in the yard. The change, seen through the eyes of one of the children, is made all the more striking when a tattered man returns to stare at the house from the road. He is sent away from this newly enriched dwelling at the request of the mother. The children retain the tantalizing possibility that this man is their father returned to the home where he is no longer needed.

The plot of "The Thieves" offers another take on disconnection within a relationship, foreshadowing the narratives of feminine experience that make up *Nine Women.* Carrie, dissatisfied with the casual relationship that she has with her lover–from whom she wants more commitment–disaffectedly has a few drinks with him but then heads alone to her apartment in the French Quarter. Watching from her window, she sees a police search in progress and then helps a bungling thief to escape by calling to his attention the gate that he had missed. Her boyfriend, Steve, arrives soon after; he assumed that her earlier mood was because she figured out that his parents have been encouraging him to marry a hometown girl. Even as he assures her that he refused the other girl, Carrie insists that he go home. In the light of her experience with the thief, she realizes her complicity in Steve's casual use of her, his "thieving" and her own need to be loved. Though the ending is ambiguous, Carrie seems assured of herself rather than propelled by events for the first time in the narrative.

Another love story in *The Wind Shifting West,* "The Lovely April," is a kind of wistful romp that highlights the racial barriers that it unrealistically transcends. When the black cook in a white household falls in love with their new neighbor, an eccentric and mentally unstable white man of good family, she disappears with him rather than allowing him to be taken back to his home and respectably managed. In contrast, "Eight O'Clock One Morning" more faithfully captures the racial tensions inherent in the post–civil rights, rural South. When white youths looking for trouble attack a black delivery driver on a street of white families, the father of the narrator risks his own safety to go out and expedite the man's flight. Despite his humane action, the father does not espouse an egalitarian attitude: "'Niggers and white niggers,' my father says. As if that explained everything." This story captures the uneasy position of the white man who cannot fully accept racial equality, but cannot be a party to abuse.

The closing story in this collection, "Stanley," more subtly brings racial tensions into perspective. The main character shares his name with the protagonist of "The Black Prince" but has none of the same mystical associations. In the course of the narrative, Stanley, a valet in the house of a wealthy white man, tries to reconcile his ailing employer's approaching death with his own aging and feelings about mortality. He is no longer young enough to follow through on a fling with Roberta, the attractive, willing nurse in the household. Eventually, Stanley realizes that like the old man, his taste for pleasure and adventure has diminished: "He hadn't thought of himself as like the old man, not in any way. But there it was." Though the story maintains the boundaries of status and race that divide the two men, their aging reaches across these barriers to the looming presence of death, the end awaiting both men. Though published prior to *The Wind Shifting West,* the novel *The Condor Passes* (1971) is an expansion of "Stanley."

Of Grau's three collections, *Nine Women* is the only one to evoke specifically and exclusively the feminine perspective; the unifying element of these stories is women's voices as they detail their struggles with familial roles, aging, and seeking and anticipating death. The collection begins with the nostalgic and evocative "The Beginning," the story of an illegitimate young girl whose mother propagates a forceful and positive perspective, bringing magic into the otherwise dreary routine of poverty. Ironically, the young girl that the mother characterizes as an Indian princess, "the jewel of the lotus," is the product of a one-night stand with "a Hindu from Calcutta, a salesman of Worthington pumps." Her mother becomes a skilled dressmaker, a self-titled "Modiste," whose daughter models the exquisite clothing her mother sews. Despite their difficult situation, the mother's love and determination give her daughter an unflagging sense of her own self-worth: "when I stood naked and revealed as a young black female of illegitimate birth, it hardly mattered. By then the castle and the kingdom were within me and I carried them away." The artificial ancestry and hereditary value that the mother gives her daughter serve as the basis for the young girl's self-sufficiency in the face of her difference.

"Letting Go" profiles another kind of parent-daughter relationship in which the daughter must cut her ties to her confining, rigid parents in order to realize her own potential. Mary Margaret has maintained her steady relationship with her parents, sharing dinner and a novena every Wednesday night, despite their crude rejection of her new husband. After years of the same pattern, she and her husband decide to split amicably, to try for "more than this." Despite her determination to move away to a new job, some of Mary Margaret's strength falters in the face of her parents' powerful determination to ignore anything that makes them uncomfortable. Even as Mary Margaret breaks with them, she finds it hard not to capitulate: "It was a warm night, she thought. As her mother had said, she hadn't really needed to bring her coat."

"Ending" profiles another family crisis: Barbara Eagleton and her husband stay together until the night of their daughter's traditional wedding. Her composure is slowly broken as she contemplates a trio of unions: her daughter's new marriage, the breakup of her own long marriage, and her mother's refusal to marry the Jamaican man who has meant so much to both of them. Her mother's happy self-sufficiency contrasts Barbara's sudden fear of loneliness.

The story "Housekeeper" features another strong woman undergoing a change of roles. Despite her children's objections to the low status of her choice, Mrs. Emmons, a recent widow, decides to work as a housekeeper since it is the job she knows best. She relives her own memories as she carefully cleans Dr. Hollisher's house. A retired psychiatrist, Hollisher has a variety of enthusiasms to fill his days and gradually falls into a rhythm with Mrs. Emmons. Even though she leaves to remarry, finding him another good housekeeper to replace herself, Hollisher pays her the ultimate compliment by leaving the house to Mrs. Emmons, pointedly demonstrating the affection for her that he had hardly expressed.

With a more sophisticated, urban feel, "Home" depicts the familial emotional bond between a lesbian couple. Angela, the older partner, recognizes her lover's tantrum coming on but views it as yet another mood swing. Instead, Vicki, who unlike Angela does not have a child from an earlier relationship, longs to have a child to satisfy her own needs: "At least then my bones and blood will be quiet." After initially countering Vicki's difficult revelation, Angela eventually acquiesces to her partner's legitimate need, realizing that she cannot stand between Vicki and motherhood just because her own need to be a mother has been fulfilled.

"Hunter" and the closing story of the collection, "Flight," are thematically linked; both associate flying and experiencing death. The earlier story tells of Nancy Martinson, the sole survivor of a plane crash that claimed the lives of her whole family. Her eerie, quiet demeanor is explained by her belief that she fell through a flaw in time "and was left behind." She seeks out death by taking flight after flight in the hope of a fatal crash so that she can rejoin her family, convinced that, should she die through other means, she will remain separated from them forever. "Flight," on the other hand, is the subtler rendition of a woman's thoughts as she makes arrangements to be at home for her impending death. She peaceably remembers moments from her long life and mentally drifts to her death as she takes her last flight home with her son: "The raft sailed directly into it, into the dark." This vision of a gentle death overtaking a woman sated by her memories strongly contrasts the desperation of Nancy in "Hunter," as she aggressively seeks the violent death that separates her from her family.

Widely recognized for her novels, Shirley Ann Grau clearly deserves attention for her short fiction as well. Her stories are deeply evocative, making use of the concise form to enable the reader to glimpse moments that crystallize human struggle and motivation. Grau's stories reflect the broad, insistent concerns of the writer, ranging from youthful self-preoccupation and maturation to the complex emotions of women dealing with widowhood, aging, and death. Narrators detail their own earlier, innocent experiences with distance and even nostalgia, though there is no returning to the conditions of the past. Grau's ability to depict the results of past and pending racial tensions, her skillful use of dialect and milieu, and her intense, sometimes bitter awareness of the influence of the past, combine in a series of unforgettable psychological portraits. Though her stories are uncompromising and objective, Grau's distinct sense of morality and of the far-reaching effects of justice comes through in each of them. In his introduction to her 1983 Levy Lecture, Joseph Schwartz heralds this hidden evangelism in an author claiming to have "no cause and no message."

Interviews:

Mary Rohrberger, "Conversation with Shirley Ann Grau and James K. Feibleman," *Cimarron Review,* 43 (April 1978): 35–45;

John Canfield, "A Conversation with Shirley Ann Grau," *Southern Quarterly,* 25 (Winter 1987): 39–52.

Bibliography:

Margaret S. Grissom, "Shirley Ann Grau: A Checklist," *Bulletin of Bibliography,* 28 (July–September 1971): 76–78.

References:

Louise Y. Gossett, *Violence in Recent Southern Fiction* (Durham, N.C.: Duke University Press, 1965), pp. 177–195;

Susan S. Kissel, *Moving On: The Heroines of Shirley Ann Grau, Anne Tyler, and Gail Godwin* (Bowling Green, Ky.: Bowling Green State University Popular Press, 1996);

Paul Schlueter, *Shirley Ann Grau* (Boston: Twayne, 1981).

Amy Hempel

(14 December 1951 –   )

Mitchell Goldwater
State University of New York College at Oneonta

BOOKS: *Reasons to Live* (New York: Knopf, 1985);
At the Gates of the Animal Kingdom (New York: Knopf, 1990);
Tumble Home (New York: Scribners, 1997).

OTHER: *Unleashed: Poems by Writers' Dogs,* edited by Hempel and Jim Shepard (New York: Crown, 1995).

"There's a way in which you can make the readers laugh until suddenly they're crying and they don't know what hit them," says Amy Hempel of her first collection of short stories, *Reasons to Live* (1985). Through three collections, Hempel has pioneered a spare and compressed prose style that blends humor and sadness, grief and the quick one-liner, to create a moving fiction of short moments. Her work, with its reliance on metaphor and the associative leaps of characters' minds, often reads much like poetry. The result, as a critic for *The Washington Post* (7 May 1985) said, is that "Hempel makes small and cryptic moments explode with suggestion."

The fact that her stories are compressed and often short, some no more than a page, has led many critics to associate her work with minimalism. Hempel is mentioned alongside Mary Robison, Ann Beattie, and Raymond Carver–three writers who are considered to have originated the style. Yet, Hempel believes that the label says little about the work it is meant to describe; as she told interviewer Jo Sapp in 1993, "A lot of the writers called minimalists had nothing to do with each other. It was a catch-all. These days, when you see the word *minimalism* in a review, all it tells you is that the reviewer is lazy." Other critics have tried to categorize her work more precisely: one reviewer for *The New York Times* (11 March 1990), for example, called Hempel a "miniaturist" rather than a minimalist, a label that Hempel is more comfortable with. "No one likes to be tagged," she told Sapp, "but I don't mind miniaturist. Yes, I work small, concise, precise."

Amy Hempel (photograph by Kenneth Chen; from the dust jacket of Tumble Home, *1997)*

Typically, Hempel's stories have few plot points, and those may be left for the reader to infer. She relies instead on the humanity of her main characters–their humor, their recollections, their ability to find ways to cope in day-to-day things as they struggle to go on in a world that seems askew. Most of her stories, in the first two collections especially, begin–by design–after a precipitating event to which there may be no reference in the body of the story. "I don't have any great interest in the sort of dramatic writing that would be necessary to give you the wreck, the murder, the whatever," Hempel told Sapp, adding, "I come in when the people are sitting around later with their heads in their hands, just looking around the room, saying, 'Now what?'"

Amy Hempel was born on 14 December 1951 in Chicago, Illinois, to Gardiner and Gloria Hempel. She spent her childhood in and around Chicago; after the third grade, she lived for eight years in Denver, Colorado, before moving to San Francisco. Her time in California, where she spent the next twelve years, significantly influenced her early fiction. She attended several colleges in the state–among them Whittier College, San Francisco State University, and California State University at San Jose, where she earned her B.A. in journalism and developed some of the writing practices that contribute to her lean prose style. The changes in locale were the result of a series of personal and family crises. "I had a nonlinear college education," she told Sapp; "I went from accident to accident, hospital to hospital; I'd walk out of the house in the morning and half look up to see when the Mosler safe was going to fall out of the sky and smash me into the sidewalk." These experiences, which she refers to as "research," offered the starting points for stories that appeared in her first collection.

Hempel cites her friends at that time, particularly members of improvisational comedy groups, as a significant influence as well: "By hanging around with these people for years, I was able to see the slightly skewed way into something." One story in her first collection illustrates this experience most explicitly: "Three Popes Walk into a Bar" takes as its central character a comic on the circuit who is trying to save his marriage. Hempel, however, did not begin making use of these early inspirations until after she left California for New York.

The move to New York marked a turning point in her writing life; there she began to shape her experiences into fiction, and she enrolled in a writing workshop taught initially at Columbia University by Gordon Lish, a former editor at *Esquire* magazine. She worked with Lish for several years, enrolling in or sitting in on his classes; later, as an editor at Knopf, Lish had Hempel's first collection, *Reasons to Live,* published. Hempel credits Lish's workshop with giving rise to many of those early stories. In one case, she talks about how Lish had asked those taking his class to "write up your most terrible, despicable secret, 'The thing you will never live down.'" The result, for Hempel, was her first story, one of the most notable in *Reasons to Live:* "In the Cemetery Where Al Jolson is Buried." Prompted by Lish's suggestion, Hempel returned to her past: "I knew instantly what that [thing] was. I'd failed my best friend at the moment when I absolutely couldn't fail her, when she was dying." Yet, this story also illustrates her ability to synthesize experience and the craft of fiction, to create a truth independent of the facts: "There is not a word of dialogue in that story that either one of us ever said, yet it's a true story." This story represented the beginning of a successful career in short fiction. Over the next twelve years, Hempel published two more collections of stories: *At the Gates of the Animal Kingdom* (1990) and *Tumble Home* (1997).

As Hempel's style has developed over the course of her career, the overarching themes of her collections have changed as well. While *Reasons to Live* and most of *At the Gates of the Animal Kingdom* explore the ways in which various characters cope with loss through an attention to day-to-day things, *Tumble Home* tries to complicate that theme by presenting fiction about characters who are simply being, or, as Hempel puts it, "who had everything they needed and were happy in normal ways."

Each of the fifteen stories in Hempel's first collection involves a character learning to cope with a difficult situation. "The Man in Bogota," for example, is one of Hempel's earliest stories and is, she said in a 1997 interview with Suzan Sherman, "representative of everything I've done since then." In addition to being representative, it is also instructive of how her work is to be read. Only one page long, this piece shares some thematic and technical elements with many of her other stories. The story begins with a woman on a ledge. No one can convince her to come back in. Will she jump? An observer, whose name and gender are not identified, imagines what he or she would say to talk the woman down. The speaker recounts a brief story of a man in Bogota who had been kidnapped and ransomed, and who returns better for the experience, though not by overcoming adversity in the way a typical hero in popular movies might. His betterment is, in a sense, a side effect of his day-to-day life under guard, the unexpected result of dire circumstances. This story-within-the-story is representative of Hempel's stylistic and thematic approach; she often uses striking digressions, ministories that work like metaphors or parables that may have the potential to save–sometimes in surprising but subtle ways. Likewise, placing one story within another suggests how Hempel would like her works to be taken: readers are not told a story so much as they are asked to identify with a speaker who is using a story for himself or herself, or offering a story to another person in need, as a way to go on.

"In the Cemetery Where Al Jolson Is Buried" addresses a similar theme but in a different way. The story is more traditionally linear and makes greater use of Hempel's characteristic humor. The narrator visits her best friend from college, who is in a southern California hospital (which they have nicknamed "Marcus Welby Hospital") and is dying of an unnamed disease. Their exchanges are quick-witted, their banter comfortable; for instance, the friend asks the speaker at the opening of the story to "Tell me things I won't mind forgetting," to "Make it useless stuff or skip it." The speaker tells her one silly fact after another, and comes to a brief story of the first chimp taught to use sign language:

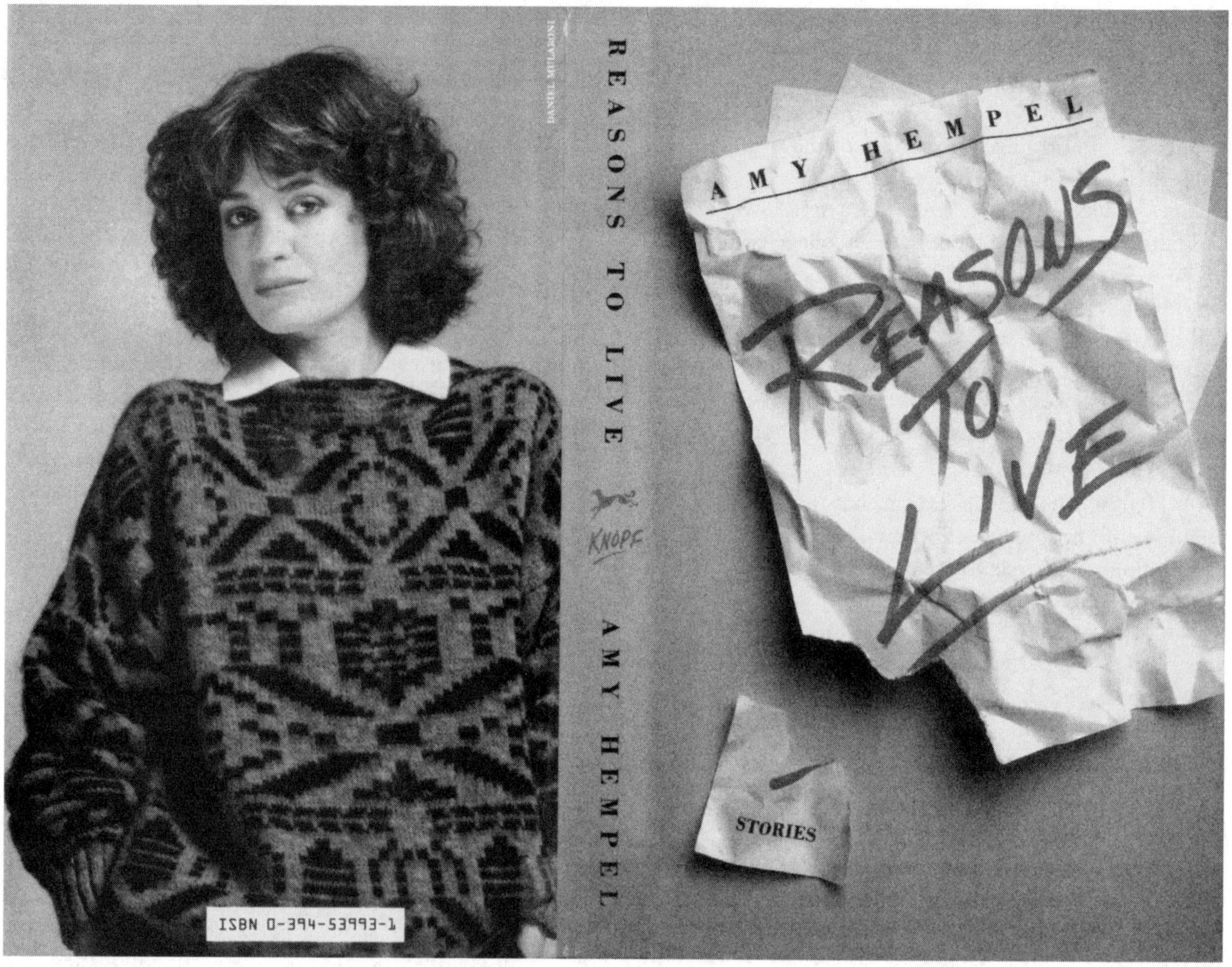

Dust jacket for Hempel's first book, which includes stories begun in writing workshops taught by former Esquire *editor Gordon Lish*

"Did you know that when they taught the first chimp to talk, it lied? That when they asked her who did it on the desk, she signed back the name of the janitor. And that when they pressed her, she said she was sorry, that it was really the project director. But she was a mother, so I guess she had her reasons."

"Oh, that's good," she said. "A parable."

But the speaker's tale is incomplete, and later she reveals more about the chimp, making the "parable" not "useless stuff" at all; it is instead a way for her to come to terms with her grief and the sense that she has let down her friend. At this point in the story, though, it is apparent that the two have been through a lot together, and humor has been part of what has helped them through their tough times in the past. They continue almost as if nothing has changed, and yet readers also see how their joking works differently for the two of them in their different situations. As the dying friend is to meet with her doctor, the speaker describes the situation this way:

She is flirting with the Good Doctor, who has just appeared. Unlike the Bad Doctor, who checks the IV drip before saying good morning, the Good Doctor says things like "God didn't give epileptics a fair shake." The Good Doctor awards himself points for the cripples he could have hit in the parking lot. Because the Good Doctor is a little in love with her, he says maybe a year. He pulls a chair up to her bed and suggests I might like to spend an hour on the beach.

"Bring me something back," she says. "Anything from the beach. Or the gift shop. Taste is no object."

He draws the curtain around her bed.

"Wait!" she cries.

I look in at her.

"Anything," she says, "except a magazine subscription."

The doctor turns away.
I watch her mouth laugh.

The humor allows each friend to confront or avoid aspects of the impending death. On the surface they may quip comfortably, but their different positions become increasingly apparent. As the story progresses, these differences create a tension that drives the conclusion of the story.

Two stories from this collection use similar elements and situations to elicit different feelings. "Celia is Back" and "Today Will Be a Quiet Day" are third-person narratives, which are rare for Hempel; most of her stories are in first person, and the speakers are usually female or unspecified. Both stories involve a father, son, and daughter, all of whom are verbal jousters, and in each story the father is portrayed as responding to some unnamed tragedy behind the narrative. In spite of these similarities, the reader can infer that the families are headed for different outcomes. In "Celia is Back" a boy and his sister enlist their father's help entering cereal box contests. The father encourages with clever platitudes, reminding his children of "the Three P's. . . . Patience, Perseverance, and Postage," for instance. Yet, when the children move on from the simple sweepstakes and push him for help with the essay entries, the father's platitudes degrade into a mishmash of advertising copy. The reader glimpses him losing his humanity. Near the end, in a moment where he blurs his own circumstances with those of his surroundings, the father is reassured by a sign in the local hairdresser's shop: "*Celia, formerly of Mr. Edward, has rejoined our staff.*" By the final line of the story he tells himself that "Everything will be fine . . . now that Celia's back." The reader, of course, knows by this point how tenuous this assertion is.

"Today Will Be a Quiet Day" ends with a similar assertion on the part of the father after he spends the day with his two children, yet at that time readers also see evidence of healing. The father and the two children are capable of kindness in spite of their emotional distance from one another and their troubles: the suicide of the son's friend and the daughter's sensitivity to the death of a pet. The humor in this story is a means to be cruel, but in the end it is the way these characters show their vulnerability and their caring for one another.

Raymond Carver selected "Today Will Be a Quiet Day" for inclusion in *The Best American Short Stories 1986,* one of several honors Hempel received for her first collection. "In the Cemetery Where Al Jolson is Buried" garnered Hempel a mention as an Outstanding Writer in the *Pushcart Prize: Best of the Small Presses* anthology of 1984–1985, and it was later included in the *Norton Anthology of Short Fiction.* The collection as a whole received a silver medal from the Commonwealth Club of California in 1986. Critics praised most of Hempel's stories as moving; one reviewer for *The New York Times* (28 April 1985) remarked that "They can take your breath away." Many touted Hempel as a promising newcomer, as someone to watch, even as they balanced their praise with only a mention of what did not work in Hempel's writing. A qualification in an otherwise positive review in the *Chicago Tribune* (30 June 1985) stating that "occasionally" Hempel's stories were "more punchy than powerful" typified the degree and extent of the negative comments in the press.

The reception of Hempel's second collection, *At the Gates of the Animal Kingdom,* was more varied, if not downright partisan. Now that her work was no longer considered that of a newcomer, some critics became wary of what was referred to as Hempel's "minimalist approach." The title of one review in the *Boston Globe* (8 March 1990) exemplified the sentiment with its request for "A Little Less Minimalism, Please." For many critics, her work became the focal point of a larger battle over what was valuable in fiction generally. One review of *At the Gates of the Animal Kingdom* in the *Chicago Tribune* (29 April 1990), for instance, discusses only a single story, which the reviewer uses to attack what he sees as the failings of minimalism as a whole. Others, however, praised her book, which, like the first collection, continued to develop themes of loss, struggle, and redemption through the small doings of day-to-day life.

Yet, even with this similar focus, stories in this collection have a larger coherence that raises a second issue only hinted at within Hempel's first collection. At the end of "In the Cemetery Where Al Jolson is Buried," Hempel includes a dedication–presumably the name of the friend who died, the person on whom the story is based. This inclusion indicates the fine line between factual and fictional truths. With her second collection, however, Hempel introduces this concern explicitly and invites a reader to see it enacted in several stories working together, with crosshatched details that suggest an underlying narrative between stories. In the fourth story, "Rapture of the Deep," for instance, the speaker's reference to the death of a lover who drowned while scuba diving when the two were on an island vacation suggests that she is also the speaker of the first story in the collection, "Daylight Come," about a couple vacationing on an island. It appears that time and tragedy have passed between these stories, and more importantly, there is a suggestion of a guiding consciousness behind the book as a whole. Perhaps it is a single background story, and readers are offered only pieces. This connection combines with a seemingly autobiographical two-part piece, "The Harvest," to create the illusion of autobiography via the background story. Is it all real? By inviting readers to ask this question, Hempel raises the issue of what truth and fact in fiction writing are.

Although not all of the stories seem to involve this issue–and one could not claim that this collection blurs the line between the short story and the novel in the ways that some of Tim O'Brien's work has–Hempel does address the issue directly in "The Harvest." This unusual story is in two parts, the first in the voice of a speaker, the second in the voice, presumably, of an author who created the speaker. The first part tells of an automobile accident and its aftermath and reads like a typical Hempel story: the female speaker insightfully moves the story along through metaphorical digressions. She is reflecting on what has happened, with the reader as confidant. From the beginning she is even able to talk about changes in the ways she has told the story to others: "What happened to one of my legs required four hundred stitches, which, when I told it, became five hundred stitches, because nothing is ever quite as bad as it *could* be."

The speaker of the second part also comments on the story of the car wreck, yet in this version she sounds like an author who is concerned with the question of truth in fiction. She begins, "I leave out a lot when I tell the truth. The same when I write a story." She is, ostensibly, the writer of the "story" that precedes this confession, this epilogue in which more details, more purported "truths" are offered. Hempel's speaker relates explanations about why things were changed in ways that form a delicate dance with the preceding version. Yet, by the end, these elaborations on the details seem, by design, to be both honest and artificial; they are, in a sense, another story, for even this essay-like piece ends with a similar series of juxtaposed digressions that use the very artifice the piece exposes. In the interview with Sherman, Hempel remarked about this second version, "I could have written a third version that would have revealed everything I changed or made up in the 'true' version. It's an infinite deal." The apparent "truth" behind the second version creates the same effect of the apparently fictional version. Are the facts of the second more true than the first? Hempel seems to ask, why does it matter?

Aside from the emergence of this second theme, the similarities of the first two collections are most noticeable: spare prose, adept humor, metaphorical digressions and associations, nameless speakers obsessed with the fear of earthquakes or other disasters, and the presence of animals. Hempel's love for animals–they appear in many stories–led her to write the title story. She told Sapp that "At the Gates of the Animal Kingdom" is "the only overtly political story I've ever written. . . . I had something I wanted to address before I had the story. Normally that would be a huge danger sign to me, would doom the story to failure." The story begins with an eccentric woman who stays with two boys while their parents are away; her pets, of course, must come along as a condition of her employment. She is haunted by a voice in her head that reports instances of animal torture in the matter-of-fact tone of a nature documentary voice-over. Hempel sets the eccentricities and sensitivities of her main character against the boys' reluctance to show their own sensitivities and caring. In doing so, she creates a new context for facts about the treatment of animals, facts that are typically dulled by the conventions of most media reporting.

The final piece, "The Rest of God," signals a change in direction that is more fully realized in Hempel's third collection. The story is, to borrow a phrase from it, "a lyric seizure that succeeds a close call"; details are listed and layered, creating a poetic density. This phrase also describes the relationship of this story to the rest of the book. While each earlier story is about coping with loss, this one celebrates life in the aftermath. The structure of the story, which involves a group of people on vacation at the beach, has the familiar arc of escalating tension and resolution, but unlike most of Hempel's other stories there is no tragedy looming, no immediate loss from which the characters are recovering. Hempel begins the writing process instead with the questions, "What if there were people who hadn't lost anything? What would they be doing?" To Sapp, she described the significance of this story to her writing as whole: "The work I've done since that story is very different in feel. It's harder in a way, to write about people who are not faced with any threat. There they are, just having their lives. How do you make a story out of that?" This challenge led to many of the stories in her next collection.

In the seven years during which she wrote *Tumble Home,* Hempel jointly edited, with author and friend Jim Shepard, a book of poems written ostensibly by the pets of contemporary writers. *Unleashed: Poems by Writers' Dogs* (1995), a product of Hempel's love for animals, began when writer Bob Shacochis presented a poem he attributed to his dog Frank. From there, Hempel and Shepard encouraged and received submissions from other writers such as Rick Bass, Heather McHugh, Maxine Kumin, John Irving, Edward Albee, and Arthur Miller. With its playfulness, the book struck a positive chord, particularly with mainstream publications such as *People Weekly,* and the reviewers often took the occasion to be playful themselves. Many recognized the book as more than simply funny. A critic for the New Orleans *Times-Picayune* (12 October 1995), for example, wrote that the collection is "by turns hilarious and heartbreaking," while the reviewer for *People Weekly* (25 September 1995) said–with a pun typical of many reviews–that the book "yields more than light-hearted doggerel." The significance of the critical reception of this book to Hempel's career should not be overlooked, because it foreshadowed–if not influenced–the responses of both the reading public and the critics to her next collection. Hempel gained exposure to the mainstream press, and by associating herself with poetry she may have distanced her work from the debate on minimalism that surrounded her previous collection.

Reviews for *Tumble Home,* a collection of seven short stories and one novella, were similar to those for her first collection twelve years before. Many critics praised the work vociferously, with only an occasional remark about the sketchy quality of one story or another. Yet, there were some significant differences in the reception as well: Hempel's work received more attention from the mainstream press, which may have led to its commercial success. *Tumble Home* was on *The New York Times* Best-seller List for three weeks–a rare breakthrough for a collection by any short-story writer. Unlike the reviews of *At the Gates of the Animal Kingdom,* these assessments had little sparring over minimalism and the state of short fiction in general. Hempel was no longer positioned as the standard-bearer or scapegoat for minimalism, which may have been a result not only of her involvement publishing the poetry of *Unleashed* but also the inclusion of her novella, the longest work she has created to date.

Thematically, the change noted in "The Rest of God" is apparent in several stories in *Tumbling Home,* which interviewer Sherman characterized as "a point of departure from Hempel's earlier collections. . . . Her new work dwells less on the losses, focusing more on the celebration of what's good, even in the simplest of terms, of being in the here and now." The opening piece, "Weekend," for example, with its omniscient narration, is a lyrical evocation that conjures the magic of an ordinary weekend day via a description of a ball game and its relaxed aftermath with family, friends, and dogs. Juxtaposed details and actions spark an appreciation for the richness of the day and its seemingly-botched ball game. The first-person speaker of "The Children's Party" describes a similar get-together of families and locals, evoking a similar sense of the magical, but with a more immediate feel.

Other stories, however, return to the theme Hempel worked with successfully in her previous collections. The cryptic "Housewife," only one sentence long, reintroduces the sense of a character struggling to cope. Although more conventional in form, "The New Lodger" shares this theme. The speaker revisits a beach town where she has been three times before, exhibiting the self-consciousness of an outsider alone in a small town. She recounts the dangerous road there and the perils and sadnesses of earlier trips. Without referring to the specifics of her current situation, she remarks that this time she will "stay for as long as it takes." Like so many of Hempel's characters, the speaker struggles to cope with some undisclosed situation, and readers are left to witness the ways in which she manages.

Dust jacket for Hempel's 1997 book, the title novella of which is in the form of a letter written by an institutionalized woman to a famous artist

Hempel's later work is not so much a turning away from what she has done before than it is a complication that enriches her earlier theme. The novella, "Tumble Home," most exemplifies this complication; it is an extended epistle written by a woman in a private sanitarium to a famous artist she had met briefly and only once. She describes her friends at the institution, a former girls' school, and their conversations in the "Hostility Suite" or in "Little Egypt" (so named because as the former smoking room of the school, "it had so many Camels in it"). The letter is a mosaic of recollections and references to her current life; she writes of the tulips she planted that bloomed without stems, or her mother's suicide, or the dogs from a nearby animal shelter that the "guests" of the sanitarium walk. She is funny and serious, and she reveals much to the famous near-stranger to whom she writes as she attempts to follow "the western tradition," which is: "Put your cards on the table." In so doing she both discusses and enacts the paired themes–the struggle to cope and the "celebration of what's good, . . . of being in the here and now." At the end of one recollection, for instance, the speaker reveals this thematic complication. She writes of the only church sermon she can remember, titled "The Blessing of Dailiness." It "had to do with why we should thank God for our toothbrush in the morning. We should thank God that each day must begin with an ordinary ritual, and not go immediately into crisis. It's a time-honored fact that after a close call, we all embrace the ordinary. But that is because it has become miraculous. Or *we* have–alive to see it."

The presence of ordinary objects in the lives of Hempel's characters ultimately serves as the nexus of these themes, where the richness of the everyday meets larger losses. The speaker of "Tumble Home" recognizes as much when she recalls herself as a girl accompanying her mother, a museum docent. The girl has studied the mother's subject and knows that because the Dutch Baroque painters of the seventeenth century did not have the funds, and because their Calvinist religion did not allow them to create garish works, "it was to the objects in the world around him that the Dutch painter turned." The speaker, in a striking moment of self-awareness, later echoes that sentiment as she describes her own life, and her letter. All the important characters in the collection, with varying degrees of self-awareness, turn to the ordinary for consolation and celebration.

Stylistically, Hempel uses many of her trademark techniques and elements, but the result is, in some ways, a more demanding read. The descriptions are more lyrical, and the characters' associations more oblique. Hempel counts on readers' abilities to be affected in more subtle ways by the texture of the language in the work and the associative leaps of its speakers. The reader's role is in part to follow a mind as it tries to understand itself. The speaker of the novella seems to be aware of her–and Hempel's–stylistic techniques when, in writing about the arrangement of slides at an art lecture she once attended, she comments, "Nothing, given time, is random."

In *Tumbling Home* Hempel broadens the canvas on which she works, developing a new thematic pattern that enriches rather than replaces the old. She deepens her abilities, experimenting with more subtle ways to use the techniques that had made her a promising newcomer twelve years earlier. Yet, as her commercial success shows, she has not overreached her audience. Hempel extended her abilities into a new area, and the fact that readers are offered a novella from a "miniaturist" who, even in a longer form, still works with precision, may set a higher poetic standard for future readers and writers of fiction.

Interviews:

Jo Sapp, "An Interview with Amy Hempel," *Missouri Review,* 16, no. 1 (1993): 75–95;

Suzan Sherman, "Amy Hempel," *Bomb,* 59 (Spring 1997): 66–70.

Janet Kauffman

(10 June 1945 -)

Michael Depp
University of New Orleans

See also the Kauffman entry in *DLB Yearbook 1986.*

BOOKS: *Writing Home,* by Kauffman and Jerome McGann (Dallas: Coldwater Press, 1978);

The Weather Book (Lubbock: Texas Tech University Press, 1981);

Places in the World a Woman Could Walk (New York: Knopf, 1983);

Collaborators (New York: Knopf, 1986);

Where the World Is (Ann Arbor, Mich.: Montparnasse Editions, 1988);

Obscene Gestures for Women (New York: Knopf, 1989);

The Body in Four Parts (St. Paul, Minn.: Graywolf Press, 1993);

X Amount of Time/Lines, mixed-media work by Kauffman and Nancy Chalker-Tennant (Rochester, N.Y., 1995);

Characters on the Loose (St. Paul, Minn.: Graywolf Press, 1997);

We Are Moving Words, mixed-media work by Kauffman and Chalker-Tennant (Rochester, N.Y., 1997);

Red Barn Gone Black, handmade, cardboard-cut-out images printed on newsprint, etching press (Ypsilanti, Mich., 1997);

Stain & Suture Book, handmade, cut pages, boxed (Ypsilanti, Mich., 1997);

Behind the Lips, accordion, Polaroid emulsion-transfer images, bamboo-stick frame (Ypsilanti, Mich., 1997);

Telescopic Heavens, montage text on recycled plastic, four double-sided pages (Ypsilanti, Mich., 1998).

OTHER: "An Extreme Ordinariness," in *An Unsentimental Education: Writers and Chicago,* edited by Molly McQuade (Chicago: University of Chicago, 1995), pp. 86–91.

Janet Kauffman (courtesy of Kauffman)

Throughout all her work, Janet Kauffman's professed and persistent interest is in language–its material presence and creative power. Situating her work in conventional genres or forms is secondary to her interest in the physicality of words.

Because the characters of Kauffman's stories, usually rural women, are intelligent, resilient, and determined in harsh circumstances, she has been widely recognized as a feminist writer. Yet, while she readily acknowledges her feminism, Kauffman's later work has veered toward a different kind of politics, more concerned with physical and ecological connections than with gender relations. As a result, her traditionally minimalist work has become increasingly experimental with a sometimes excruciatingly close attentiveness to form, space, and presence. At the same time, her literary focus has widened to encompass characters and their environments in equal measure, and she has exhibited less of an inclination to subordinate this focus to the constraints of linearity or clear-cut divisions of genre or form.

Much of Kauffman's artistic sensibility is informed by her roles as writer, teacher, and farmer. She was born in Lancaster, Pennsylvania, to Chester Kauffman and Thelma Hershey Kauffman, who grew tobacco on a farm in Landisville, a town in southeastern Pennsylvania. Kauffman has revealed little of her family experiences, other than to acknowledge that her father, a Mennonite, left the faith after his marriage and did not raise his children as Mennonites. She has written, however, that the "Mennonite moral debate, plus the . . . pacifist assumption that human behavior doesn't have to be violent, were influences that lingered."

Kauffman's formative years were spent close to the land in her predominately Mennonite community. The effects of this upbringing were critical to her later work. As she revealed to *World Authors* (1995): "it was my early and continued involvement with farming, with the natural world, the social activism and pacifism of the Mennonites, followed by the civil rights and women's movements, that affected my work and writing in crucial ways." After earning a B.A. in French and English at Juniata College in Huntingdon, Pennsylvania, in 1967, she went on to graduate work at the University of Chicago, where she received an M.A. in 1968 and a Ph.D. in 1972. In "An Extreme Ordinariness" (1995), a reflective essay on her graduate-school experiences and writing career, she wrote of her indebtedness to the university for introducing her to contemporary poetry. In studying it, she discovered the possibilities of "language as a material for creating things" and began to appreciate its properties as "plastic and variable and malleable."

After completing her graduate work, Kauffman moved to the farmlands of Hudson, Michigan, and took a job at Jackson Community College in Jackson, Michigan, where she taught from 1976 to 1988. She then went to Eastern Michigan University in Ypsilanti, where she remains as a professor. After her move to Michigan she became a farmer once again, on eighty acres in Hudson, where she grew mostly alfalfa hay. She stopped farming in the late 1980s and has transformed her property into a wildlife and wetlands preserve as part of the Federal Wetland Reserve Program. In an unpublished 1999 interview she explained, "That's been my main work for the last few years since I stopped farming–breaking the drainage tile and restoring wetlands to the site." She is divorced and the mother of two grown sons.

From her first efforts as a poet, farming has played an incalculable role in Kauffman's relationship with language and thematic content. "I'm sure the handiwork of some of the farming I've known–tobacco, hay–has something to do with my determination as a writer to attend to the physicalities of place, person, and language," she has said. "There is a certain kind of attention to what is right in front of you at the moment."

After graduate school Kauffman spent ten years writing poetry before turning her efforts toward fiction. *Writing Home* (1978), written with Jerome McGann, was her first published volume of poetry, and it was followed by *The Weather Book* (1981), which was selected for the Associated Writing Programs Award Series. The book is remarkable for its early thematic engagement with farming and the earth, its particularized brand of feminism (approached through a nontraditional, environmental perspective), and its lyrical, imagistic language.

Places in the World a Woman Could Walk (1983), Kauffman's first collection of short fiction, is a relatively thin volume of twelve stories. It establishes the rural settings, independently minded characters, and precise, minimalist style that distinguishes much of her work to date. Mark C. Harris has observed that the collection retains the same lyric sensibility as her poetry: "the lyricism of her fiction suggests that poetry is never far from her." *Places in the World a Woman Could Walk* was well received by critics, among them Wendy Lesser, who praised the quality of Kauffman's female characters. Writing in *The New York Times Book Review* (8 January 1984), she observed, "These women are strong without being self-sufficient, knowing yet not sophisticated, accustomed to long silences but delighted at the least chance for conversation." Lesser also noted that the language of the stories has a strong affinity to poetry, remarking: "she lends a poet's sense of rhythm and abbreviation to her dialogue . . . [and] the people in these tales speak a language that is both stylized and accurate, rhythmically odd and absolutely convincing." In *Queen's Quarterly* (Spring 1987), Judith Russell also commended Kauffman's poetic economy of language, noting that her stories are "distinguished by taut and complex syntax, poetic rhythm and beautifully observed detail."

Writing in *The New York Review of Books* (31 May 1984), Robert Towers was more withholding in his praise than other reviewers, but he did note that in "her

Dust jacket for Kaufmann's 1983 book, her first and most conventional collection of short stories

successful stories . . . Kauffman achieves her effects with light, deft touches, and a minimum of explanation. She writes elliptically, sometimes quirkily." Categorizing her as a "New Regionalist" for her chosen milieu, Towers was bothered, however, that some stories seemed "too programmatic in their feminism."

In *Places in the World a Woman Could Walk* Kauffman demonstrates a strong, consistent ability to characterize swiftly in a few deft turns of phrase, a quality that illuminates her characters with maximum economy. Likewise, her attention to plot is minimal, and to Harris's reading it serves more as a device to modulate the intensity of her language than to realize an elaborate story. Kauffman has confessed, "I'm not a good storyteller; I have a terrible memory for plot." In an unpublished interview she added, "My fiction doesn't usually have the profile of a story. I'm not very interested in beginnings or ends, especially, so I think what I do is a lot of middle."

Nevertheless, the stories of *Places in the World a Woman Could Walk* mark her greatest adherence to linearity and conventional short-story writing, which is not to suggest that they are all recognizably conventional. In fact Kauffman uses readers' conventional expectations against them. The most vivid example of this phenomenon is in the title story, which begins with a jolt: "The day the tornado hit Morenci was the day Lady Fretts finally put her mind to the slaughter of Susie Hey Susie and her babies. I said good. I said do. Enough of holdover, mournful faces." Only later in the paragraph does the reader learn that the narrator is talking about cows.

The decision to slaughter the cows marks an abrupt turn in life for Lady Fretts, who has been mourning her husband's death for twelve years, confining herself to the environs of his farm. In that time her mourning has been expressed by raising the pair of calves born on the day he died, along with their mother, to their present, profitless heft. Lady Fretts's quiet but acutely observant sister-in-law Molly, the narrator, has connected this surplus grief and love with its physical realization in the cows: "Love manifested itself in expansive forms, and in weight, and in hefty creatures of the world." Having buried the slaughtered cows, Molly is not surprised when Lady Fretts decides to leave for Greece to study sculpting. Molly has never taken the widow's inert facade for granted: "Lady rode a sofa for years; I should have seen it would be no trouble for her to take it from there."

Kauffman gives the animals in her stories a viable presence equal to that of her human characters and the landscape. This tendency is again evident in "Who Has Lived from a Child with Chickens," in which a trio of chickens and a rat named Ratzafratz are responsible for most of the plot. Yet, the narrator, a college-educated woman now working a farm, warns the reader at the outset against rendering her animal tale into fable: "this is no tale of sentiment; it's no *Animal Farm* with sides to jump to or enemies to chuck. A sequence of events occurred. Simply. The way things do."

Many of Kauffman's best characters in this volume share a similar perspective. They bring a literal-minded intelligence to their farmwork and rural existences. They know what they are and how they are but one component in a broader landscape. "Patriotic" includes some of the most engaging of such characters. It is narrated by a farm woman who is left to manage the land herself after her husband has gone on to work in town. To bring in the hay, she enlists the help of Mrs. Bagnoli, whose husband is also working in town, and Floyd, an easygoing neighboring teen. The narrator appreciates Floyd's most estimable qualities and lays them out in a few simple strokes: he "is placid, always in the present moment" and "being goodhearted, will never deeply offend. It is possible he will know happiness." Mrs. Bagnoli, who drives the tractor, is assessed for her other grounded virtues. "It doesn't take long to see that Mrs. Bagnoli is a purposeful, serious-minded woman," says the narrator. "It's clear she commands a world-view."

In the course of baling the hay, the threesome shares a coexistence so connected with the task at hand, so engaged with the direct physical nature of the work, that age and gender distinctions between them fall away. This dynamic defines the extent of the narrator's politics, prompting the patriotism of the title in its most democratic, physically realized sense. The synchronicity of the three is epitomized when they strip off their shirts while working, utterly unselfconscious in their enthusiasm and appreciation of each other's strengths and values. While the narrator knows full well the transience of the moment, her knowledge does not impede her immersion in it. As Lesser observed, "much of the power comes from the narrator's sense that she will remain on the land year after year, but the boy will soon go away to college and beyond."

Another such understanding occurs in "The Alvordton Spa and Sweat Shop." Marabelle, a beautician, lives in the basement of a house left unfinished by her lover, who has deserted her. She offers refuge to women in need of restructuring their lives, stepping away from their entanglements, or planning their next move with a lover. The narrator becomes one such refugee: "When there's trouble, and I want to break down the issues and somehow stay intact, I get myself into a corner of Marabelle's basement for as long as it takes." There, as a harsh Ohio winter bleakly layers snowdrifts outside, the narrator restores herself, soaking up the environment created by Marabelle's simple but wizened understanding. "She sucks anguish," the narrator says, "like lemonade through a straw, all for herself." And although Marabelle might be a little worse for the wear for all of her tautly expressed sympathy over the years, she retains her optimism–"she thinks the world favors human life."

"Harmony" depicts another idiosyncratic kind of optimism in an otherwise dismal environment. After *Life & Living* determines the city of Jackson to be the worst place to live in Michigan, one of its denizens becomes determined to find all its hidden, beautiful vistas. Sherry's backlog of experiences with men, children, and nature has taught her to seek out the sublime in unlikely places. The kind of woman who will speak unabashedly about her enthusiasm for sex, Sherry stands in contrast to Vicki, the far more inhibited and suspicious narrator. When one of Sherry's quests leads her and Vicki on a day trip to an uninviting Jackson swamp, Vicki is angered by Sherry's ability to find beauty there. "Honest to God, she can stretch a view," she says. "I think it's a pity. She doesn't expect enough." Yet, Sherry is an undaunted woman. She is a single mother, a divorcée living with a difficult man, a weathered survivor. Her energy is sustained by what might be self-deception, but it nonetheless fuels her undiminished confidence: "life is sweet; life is incorruptible. She thinks she's living proof."

Like Sherry, Kauffman has the quality of making crucial but subtle distinctions in what sometimes seem to be monochromatic landscapes and impenetrable characters. The color palette of "At First It Looks Like Nothing" is drawn from the "mean metal" grays of a Michigan winter. Yet, as the title suggests, distinguishing features can emerge if one looks closely enough. For instance, Durango, the narrator's lover and an outsider, is markedly distinct from Michigan men "who run their lives on motors, like twenty-first-century jet-shooting backpackers, bodies in mechanized flight." As the two stroll on the bleak landscape, Durango's easy pace is a study in contrast to such men, which suits the narrator fine during their ambivalent affair: "We walk; we make

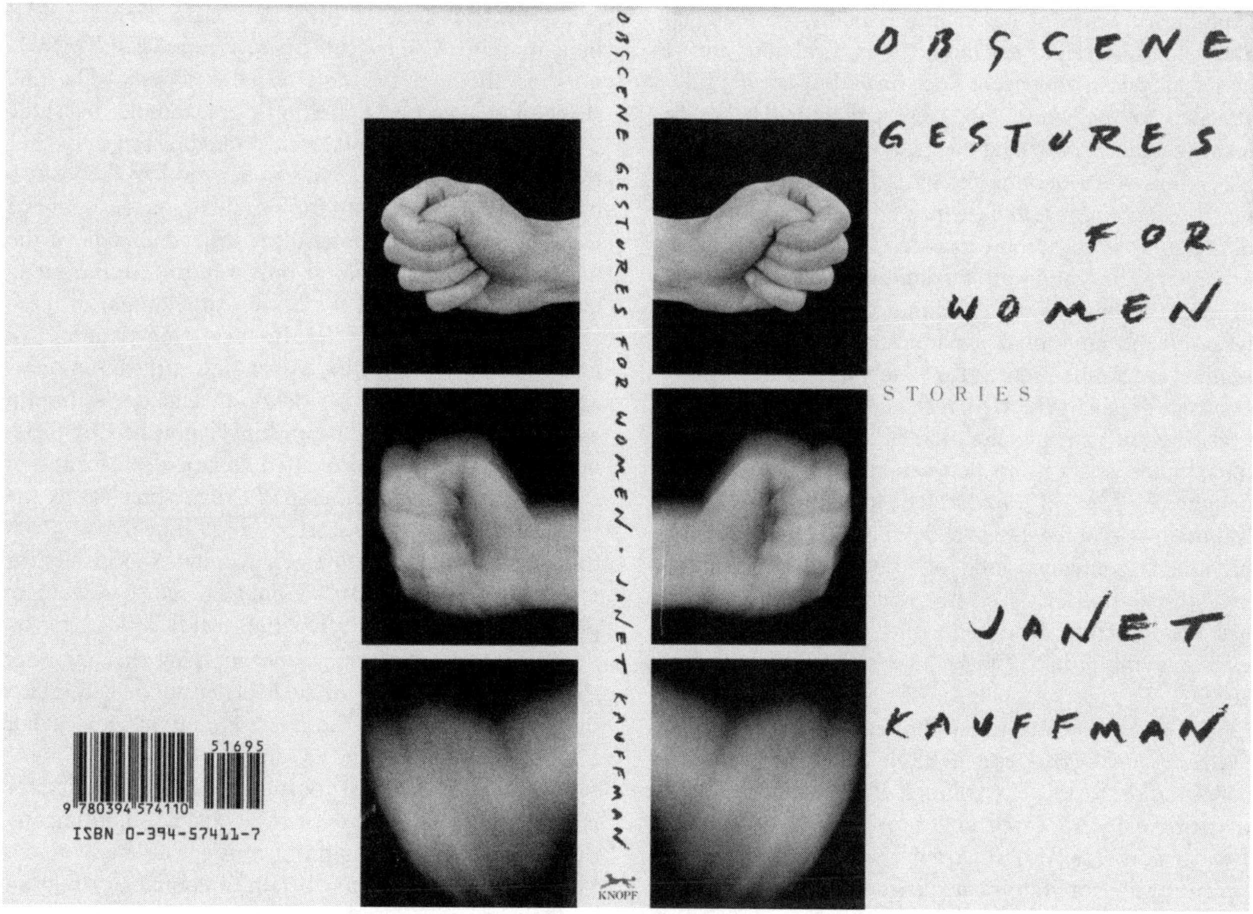

Dust jacket for Kauffman's 1989 book, stories that were praised for their "spare elegance" and "quirky panoply of characters"

the slowest and longest love in the state. It's a love like the care of the dead, like the last wash–full of pity."

While beneficial but temporary relationships of understanding are forged in many of the stories in *Places in the World a Woman Could Walk,* two are distinct for their sense of physical menace and troubling disconnectedness. In "How Many Boys?" two enigmatic wrong numbers disturb a family sitting down to dinner. Remarking on the sense of confusion and panic that follows, Towers noted, "Kauffman has, in fact, placed a serenely smug family under siege: tragedy is a spit away, and nothing can be done about it."

"Isn't It Something?" confronts a more concrete tragedy than "How Many Boys?" Celia Dollop has fled an abusive husband for an elemental existence in a rural Michigan cabin. There she befriends the narrator, a single mother with an abusive partner of her own and a proclivity to keep her troubles unspoken. As Julia Lisella wrote in *The Village Voice* (9 January 1990), "The narrator is fascinated by Celia's willingness to live in deprivation. But it is the narrator who is deprived. On visits with Celia, she is unable to reveal anything about herself." Eventually, Celia's solitary bliss is ended in murder, and the narrator mourns the withholding of herself in their few encounters. Her parting words are advice to her daughters, warning them against such reticence: "You might as well breathe at the same time and let things out in the air. Don't just ask questions, I told them. Give things away. Give yourself away."

There is a peculiar juxtaposition of emotions and the physical notion of words as breath in the air in these last sentences. Indeed, Kauffman has acknowledged her constant attention and interest in the fact that "talking is air, and when you write a word . . . it is physically there. I'm aware of that all the time." Such dual attentions to emotions and the physicality of words pervade "My Mother Has Me Surrounded." It is simultaneously a profoundly attentive meditation on space and form and an exploration of the power struggles in a mother-daughter relationship. The narrator, recalling a girlhood memory of a day at the beach with her Mennonite mother, recaptures the voice of that age and her exploratory sense of her mother's bodily parameters. She defines herself as her mother's physical opposite: "I hover, physically apparent since birth, but not yet fully attached to the world, not weighted with the bodily form she values: working thighs, an emphatic pelvis."

This story became the basis for Kauffman's first novel, *Collaborators* (1986), which repeats the entire text of the story as its second chapter. The novel continues to explore the young girl's relationship with her independent mother, with Kauffman again inextricably weaving the emotional dynamics of the story into a minutely examined sense of spatiality and presence. *Collaborators* was largely well received, and Anne Tyler praised Kauffman's exploration of "the sinewy, tough, often bitter relationship between the mother and her daughter" (*The New Republic,* 21 April 1986). Michiko Kakutani also noted its novel-defying structure, classifying it as "essentially a long tone poem," while expressing reservations, however, regarding its "wordy passages, freighted with ambiguity and a kind of portentous symbolism" (*The New York Times,* 19 February 1986).

Collaborators was followed by the evocatively titled *Obscene Gestures for Women* (1989), Kauffman's second collection of stories. The volume, which includes stories that originally appeared in *The New Yorker, The Paris Review,* and *The Missouri Review,* was met with widespread praise for Kauffman's ongoing experimentation with language and broadening thematic concerns.

"In these short stories Kauffman's ideas about femininity and Americanization take off," wrote Lisella. "Even the landscape is more expansive." Lauding "the amazing generosity of the writer," Robert Kelly, writing in *The New York Times Book Review* (24 September 1989), described *Obscene Gestures for Women* as "fifteen stories of spare elegance, revealing crannies full of unexpected details." Kelly was especially moved by the quality of having "ordinary events blossom with images that seduce the reader to mysterious destinations off the common path." Doris Lynch applauded Kauffman's "quirky panoply of characters" and "rich, sensual language" (*Library Journal,* 1 September 1989), while Gregory L. Morris declared her "a writer on intimate terms with language" (*Prairie Schooner,* Winter 1990).

Not all critics were so enthusiastic, however, as Greg Johnson noted Kauffman's "consistently narrow emotional range" (*Georgia Review,* Spring–Summer 1990) and Sybil Steinberg found even more pervasive flaws in the collection. Writing in *Publishers Weekly* (14 July 1989), she determined, "Ultimately, the lack of discernible plots or deeply realized characters is a handicap the stories cannot surmount. Other than a few instants of crystallized perception, very little occurs here, and the sameness becomes wearisome."

Readers looking for more elaborately realized plots than in *Places in the World a Woman Could Walk* will not find them in *Obscene Gestures for Women.* The title story of this second collection, for example, has little explicit action. Marimba, its protagonist, grinds her teeth at night. On the advice of her mother she visits a hypnotherapist to rectify the problem, and he suggests that she make obscene gestures instead to relieve the nervous energy. The plot is only a frame around meditations on politics and the body. An example of these abstract interests is Kauffman's appreciation of Marimba's ground teeth: "Worn to a surface sameness and sheen, like rocks set down at a glacier's mouth. Fresh. So smooth. An astonishingly polished by-product of a fiercely tormented process." Marimba's response to the hypnotherapist's suggestion opens the political leanings of the story. "I'd ask if he'd ever given thought to obscene gestures for women. Specifically for women," Marimba says, "Could he see that women, physiologically, do not screw the world?"

While Kauffman may be implying that men are the only ones capable of such penetration, her indictment does not follow the lines one might expect. For instance, "Machinery" casts aside the notion that "men" rape the earth with their tools and vehicles. Its narrator is a farmer who disapproves of her son's shoplifting tendencies and his immersion in music. She tries to convince him that there is a beautiful complexity and an elemental truth in machines. "If he knew one machine, knew it backwards and forwards, he'd at least know more than himself," she says. "Machines open up the world and give you a ride through your own territory. You ride a rock; it's another point of view." For the narrator, machines are a natural extension of the lands on which they work, as "outside, in the fields, machinery presents itself, even painted John Deere green, as so many scraps of landscape." This view prompted Patricia Laurence to observe, "Far from being a violation of the land or the spirit, machines are creative in the hands of the women who operate them. They are a metaphor for soaring. . . ." (*The Review of Contemporary Fiction,* Fall 1990).

Considering machinery in equal proportion to the world in which it functions, Kauffman also spends ample energy in this volume observing the corporeal. Lovemaking plays atypical roles in two such stories. In the first, "In the Discorruption of Flesh," the narrator is entirely attuned to the nuances of her lover's form. "I have made a study of all the skin of his body," she explains. "And I have learned a great deal. But his whole skeletal structure, I would say, refuses to give itself repose." This intense degree of observation led Morris to compare their lovemaking to "a form of cartography." In "Where I'd Quit," one of Kauffman's comparatively rare male protagonists, a machine-shop worker, conducts an affair with a married woman. Their couplings, he tells the reader, stem from their need "to see each other to believe. . . . Not so much to believe in each other as to believe in everything else. When we got to our bodies . . . the flesh of them, the scattered patches of hair–well, it wasn't a choice." Johnson wrote that the story evokes "the grace of temporary but genuine human connections," while Kelly found their need to be "a beautiful definition of love."

If such stories manipulate conventional notions of love and physical contact, Kauffman is even more subversive in efforts such as "Women Over Bay City" and "Anton's Album," which have little regard for traditional linearity or storytelling. In "Women Over Bay City," a group of women mythically descend into the male protagonist's cornfield, "synchronous as a flock." His response is a grateful kind of awe before the "thousands" who land, poised but still. "I have seen women pull a lot of stunts, he thought. But nothing like this. I believe I'm a lucky man." Such a remark pierces to the heart of Kauffman's playfulness–having a laugh at her own bizarre, parable-like scenario while not diminishing its vivid, dreamlike imagery.

"Anton's Album" is an altogether different kind of formal experiment, wherein the narrative device is the perusal of a photograph album. The narrator, looking back on a failed affair, flips through pictures, describing them elliptically in sixteen terse, barely translucent passages and recounting the trajectory of her relationship with the photographer. The story lacks the surefootedness of other such experiments, however, and Lisella called it "practically impenetrable" while Johnson said it was crippled by its use of "literary gimmicks."

While similarly experimental, "Marguerite Landmine" met with more critical approval–in all likelihood because of its complex titular figure. A traveling performer, Marguerite also goes by the name of Marguerite Origami, a fitting name for a woman of many complex creases and folds in her character. She is at once mythic and whimsical, cultural fugitive and Congress-sanctioned artist. (She is on her way to give a performance for the combined houses in the Capitol.) Marguerite's apparent paradoxes, like many of the disparate components of Kauffman's work in general, are not in conflict with each other. They are merely evidence of her disregard for remaining categorizable or static in any way. Marguerite is always moving–through landscapes, modes of expression, and even names. When an awestruck motorcycle policeman pulls over her van, "painted in the guise of landscape," he says: "They told me you couldn't be stopped." Her response is the simple truth: "That's right, I can't." This sort of independence also resonates vividly in the strong protagonist of "Marimba, Who Walked Between the Ranch and the Diner." As Lisella observed, Marimba is "an example of a woman who decides to live on her own, and on her intuition, rather than in service to husband and children."

While Kauffman invests an impressive independence in the abstract stories, one of the best in the collection is the considerably more grounded "The Easter We Lived in Detroit," which won her the Pushcart Prize X in 1984. The story is a magnificently observed rendering of a married couple's apparently unremarkable Easter Sunday. Its narrator is a woman whose religious-zealot daughter has just made her "a grandmother at 34" and whose husband has disengaged himself from active life (and his job as a welder). Given quiet, uninterrupted occasion to think and reflect, the narrator has "a whole day to study what was on my mind," and the product of this study is richly absorbing. Kauffman instills a remarkable concentrative power in the narrator, capturing a visceral quality in the language that electrifies her every attention to objects and empty space: "Even a small thing–a book, or a scrap of dust in the corner–took up a quantity of space, and the room seemed full of things to be seen and space to be seen between." Even watching her sleeping, "vacated" husband, the narrator sees how around him "the quiet accumulated; it polished him, waxy and definite. That Easter morning, at a distance of twenty feet, I could see the capsules, like layers of color, around him."

Kauffman's next book is a novel, *The Body in Four Parts* (1993), which continues her experimentation with narrative forms. The novel is divided into four sections–one for each of the elements of earth, air, fire, and water, and the elements also become characters in the minimal story. Writing in *The New York Times Book Review* (29 August 1993), Jonathan Baumbach called the book an "odd, eloquent" novel whose "pantheistic conceit is not quite as whimsical (or off-putting) as a description of it might suggest." Amy Hollywood deemed the novel important for its "attempts to erase dualist forces between women's healing and destructive abilities," observing how the language "takes on its own physicality in a chain of reasoning where language depends on the body" (*New Literary History,* Summer 1996).

Characters on the Loose (1997) is Kauffman's most experimental volume of stories to date. Including fiction previously published in *The New Yorker, Threepenny Review, Antaeus,* and other journals, the collection met with a mixed reception. Writing in the *Library Journal* (15 May 1997), Judith A. Akalaitis praised the "innovative prose" of *Characters on the Loose* as "enticing." Embracing Kauffman's leanings toward abstraction,

Cover for Kauffman's 1997 book, experimental stories praised for their "innovative prose" and "deceptively complex vision"

Akalaitis added, "The characters share a deep sense of intimacy, presented without heavy reliance on context that readers are thus invited to imagine." The reviewer for *Publishers Weekly* (31 March 1997) wrote, "The deceptively complex vision Kauffman expresses in this slim collection . . . will coax readers into territory that is not as homely and familiar as it seems." But A. O. Scott found the volume "especially disappointing." In *The New York Times Book Review* (13 July 1997), Scott wrote, "in too many of these stories Kauffman presses a none-too-precise theoretical agenda at the expense of narrative technique," so that "when it is not gratingly self-conscious, [it] feels slack and diffuse."

Kauffman addresses the nature of words, particularly their physical presence, repeatedly in *Characters on the Loose*. In the first story, "Nightmares for Everybody," a woman sends her alienated homosexual son a letter written in her own menstrual blood. The son's reaction is the source for the title of the volume: "Like a communion thing . . . that's what it sounded like to me. 'Drink, read. Letters for us, characters on the loose.'" Thus, Kauffman invests her words with a tangible physical power in *Characters on the Loose*–the words spring from life (blood) to an unpredictable existence when they find their way to the page. "Girl Games" illustrates another such instance of deliberate attention to words. While its narrator waits for a friend and reads, she observes, "The words look like live things, with arms and legs, appendages, bodies of their own. They move, and lie down. And put together, some of them even make sense."

Nowhere is this physicality more directly and playfully explored, however, than in "26 Acts in 26 Letters," the genre-defying centerpiece "story" of the book. A ten-part engagement with the letters of the alphabet, "26 Acts in 26 Letters" plays with the manifold meanings of the word *character*–seizing on two in particular: as a letter and as a fictive presence. Kauffman's alphabet is a carnal, even hedonistic array of letters that come together in contortionistic orgies, grappling and coupling for pleasure and power. As Kauffman told Carolyn Kuebler in a 1997 interview, "I really wanted the letters to be alive, in a most simple way. I'm very aware of the shape of letters, and I wanted people to think about letters as having shapes in the way we think of our bodies as having shape." She also noted that it was not coincidental that pornography often includes characters with names such as A and O.

The prose of "26 Acts in 26 Letters" is Kauffman's most sexually explicit and even scatological, as unmindful of inhibitions as it is of following any conventional boundaries of the short story. One section, "CDEF," is indicative of the visceral, sexually acrobatic quality of Kauffman's letters: "They're in a circle, naked–shaped and appendaged exactly as you can see: C open at both ends and closing on D; E with all those arms and genitalia hooking easily to D in the middle and to F, top to bottom," while F later observes that in their connection, "We're a four-letter word. . . ."

The sections are accompanied by graphic illustrations of naked, human, alphabet letters. This alphabet is from engravings by Martin Weygel, circa 1560, though Kauffman says in an unpublished interview that her text was written before her discovery of Weygel's alphabet. The book is evidence of her increasing inclination to pair text with images, and it anticipates her recent forays into the visual arts.

While the alphabet letters are the most unusual characters in *Characters on the Loose,* Kauffman certainly provides an ample number of idiosyncratic figures in the other stories: Howie in "Nightmares for Everybody" can write simultaneously with both hands; Kalamazoo in "Kalamazoo Is Where Kalamazoo Is" is named for his hometown and "thinks in the third person"; Eureka Upright in "Eureka in Toledo, Weather Permitting" is named for a vacuum cleaner and is an activist who prefers talking about the weather; Emily Dickinson takes a bicycle ride through the modern world in "Signed Away"; and Delilah in "What Lies Ahead," a detached, self-described "alien girl," gets pregnant, conceals the pregnancy, gives birth alone while her household sleeps, and then buries the stillborn infant in the backyard. Hearkening back in tone to such earlier stories as "How Many Boys?," "What Lies Ahead" illustrated to Scott how "the placid surface of daily life leads suddenly and inexorably to horror."

Kauffman uses some of the stories in this collection to illustrate and articulate ideas that she has been cultivating since her earliest poetry. Among them is her enduring interest in the profound influence of the weather in people's lives. In "Eureka in Toledo, Weather Permitting" Kauffman writes, "With Eureka, weather is not small talk: it's her motive, her parentage, her explanation. Science and eros; roof and floor." Eureka prefers to be outdoors. As she tells the narrator, "Air in a room is as dense . . . as soil to the worm-eye." While Kauffman's attention to weather has always been among the characteristic details in her fiction, she has moved it more to the foreground in this story. As she told Kuebler, "It always surprises me that weather is something people don't notice, or don't seem to feel, or to register, all the time."

Another story, "Baku's Theory," illustrates Kauffman's theory of writing about a place where one lives. The American narrator is a member of an immigrants' support group in Battle Creek, Michigan. Baku Pledhla, the leader, often refers to the theory that "It takes fifteen years to know where you are, and to know if it makes sense to be there." The theory reflects Kauffman's feelings on writing about her chosen home of rural Michigan. "I have to live in a place so long before I feel like I'm really there and can write about it," she said in an unpublished interview.

From the protagonist of "Dream On," who uses dreams to cope with the early deaths of loved ones, to the simple, physical pleasures of tobacco farming in "God Made Him the Way He Is," to the gamelike quality of "What's Wrong with This Picture?" *Characters on the Loose* is Kauffman's most eclectic volume of stories. It may put narrative among its lowest priorities, estranging readers looking for consistent and discernible story lines. The collection nevertheless marks Kauffman's growing disregard for patterning stories along conventional lines and her interests in visual and environmental components in her work.

Kauffman's most-recent work has been in the visual arts, where she has made several mixed-media works both independently and in collaboration with visual artist Nancy Chalker-Tennant of Rochester, New York. Kauffman, who has no formal training in the visual arts, has become increasingly interested in recapturing the pairing of images and words, "to make language very physical and to either have it like image or have it appear with images in an equal way."

Drawing on the convergence of image and text repopularized by the internet, as well as the notion of hypertext, Kauffman has been inspired to translate these ideas in a world outside of cyberspace. "I really love the way [hypertext] disturbs the linearity of text," she said in an unpublished interview; "but I'm still anxious to disturb as much as possible on paper. I just like the physicality of paper and books."

As she continues to explore the visual qualities of language and to disturb conventional expectations, Kauffman presses defiantly forward from her vista in the Michigan wilderness. While it would be difficult to speculate on the directions her future narratives will take, it is certain that her language will progress with increasingly deliberate attention to itself. "I think a lot of times fiction is written so the language is invisible and the story becomes visible," she has said; "and I think with my writing, the language stays more visible. For some people that can be an interference rather than a pleasure. But for me, it's a real pleasure."

Interview:

Carolyn Kuebler, Interview with Janet Kauffman, *Rain Taxi Review of Books,* 2 (Fall 1997): 12–15.

Reference:

Julia Lisella, "Young Americans: Janet Kauffman Faces the Nation," *Village Voice,* 35 (9 January 1990): 57–58.

Michael Martone

(22 August 1955 –)

Paul Maliszewski

BOOKS: *At a Loss: Poems* (Fort Wayne, Ind.: Windless Orchard Press, 1977);

Alive and Dead in Indiana: Stories (New York: Knopf, 1984);

Return to Powers: Prose Poems (Fort Wayne, Ind.: Windless Orchard Press, 1985);

Safety Patrol: Short Stories (Baltimore: Johns Hopkins University Press, 1988);

Fort Wayne Is Seventh on Hitler's List: Indiana Stories (Bloomington: Indiana University Press, 1990; revised and expanded, 1993);

Pensées: The Thoughts of Dan Quayle: Stories (Indianapolis: Broad Ripple Press, 1994);

Seeing Eye: Stories (Cambridge, Mass.: Zoland Books, 1995);

The Flatness and Other Landscapes (Athens: University of Georgia Press, 2000).

OTHER: *A Place of Sense: Essays in Search of the Midwest,* edited by Martone, photographs by David Plowden (Iowa City: University of Iowa Press, 1988);

Townships, edited by Martone, photographs by Raymond Bial (Iowa City: University of Iowa Press, 1992);

The Scribner Anthology of Contemporary Short Fiction: Fifty North American Stories Since 1970, edited by Martone and Lex Williford (New York: Scribner, 1999).

SELECTED PERIODICAL PUBLICATIONS–UNCOLLECTED: "Author's Note," *Notre Dame Review,* no. 5 (Winter 1998): 93–94;

"My Situation," in "The Situation of American Writing," *American Literary History,* 11 (Summer 1999): 307–311.

In the story "Author's Note," published in the Winter 1998 issue of the *Notre Dame Review,* Michael Martone writes about a character named "Michael Martone," who was born in Fort Wayne, Indiana, in 1955. This information is true. The subject of this entry, like the character in the story, was born in that place and year. Although the beginning of "Author's Note" keeps close to the form and language of a real author's note, Martone's story quietly exceeds the boundaries of the form, including, for instance, a detailed retelling of Martone's birth–"it had been a difficult one, sunny side up, where forceps are used." Martone's physician, it turns out, was Frank Burns, the doctor who was the basis for the fictional character Frank Burns in Robert Altman's movie *M.A.S.H.* (1970).

As the story continues, the Martone character fades into the background somewhat. Instead of providing a brief curriculum vita, "Author's Note" relates the subject's memories of the premiere of *M.A.S.H.,* the doctor's heightened celebrity, and the high-school track-and-field successes of the doctor's son, Frank Jr. In Martone's story the people of Fort Wayne come to confuse Frank Burns the character with Frank Burns their doctor, as readers of "Author's Note" may confuse Martone with "Martone." The character from the movie and the later, highly successful television show replaces the original; the mythological replaces the actual.

At the end of this short story the character Martone reappears, revealing in the same dry, affectless language of factual author's notes that his mother died as the result of a botched hysterectomy performed by Dr. Burns. In the hospital waiting room Martone listens to Dr. Burns deliver the news as a television–so instrumental in the construction of the doctor's celebrity and the character's mythology–vies for Martone's attention.

A nonfiction author's note for Michael Martone might include the following information about his family and education. His parents are Anthony Martone, a telephone-company switchman, and Patricia Payne Martone, a public-school assistant superintendent who is, in fact, alive and living in Indiana. After attending Butler University (1973–1976), Michael Martone transferred to Indiana University, where he won the Myrtle Armstrong Fiction Award for his short story "Story

Michael Martone

Problems" in 1977, the same year in which he earned his A.B. degree. He worked for a while in a hotel (1977–1978) before enrolling in the writing seminars at Johns Hopkins University, where his instructors included John Barth, Hugh Kenner, and Richard Howard. A consideration of the work of these three teachers offers interesting perspectives on Martone's work: Barth for his sense of the story *as* story; Kenner for his close attention to literary forms and for his book *The Counterfeiters* (1968), which discusses satire and the increasing ease with which real things can be faked; and Howard for his use of the dramatic monologue. At the same time, however, Martone's writing, particularly his exploration of the short-story form, is clearly his own.

After earning an M.A. from Johns Hopkins in 1979, Martone taught in the writing seminars in 1979–1980. Since then he has taught literature and creative writing at Iowa State University (1980–1987), Harvard University (1987–1991), Syracuse University (1991–1996), and the University of Alabama (since fall 1996). Martone married poet Theresa Pappas on 3 April 1984. They have two sons, Sam and Nick. Pappas and Martone are the publishers of Story County Books.

While Martone's fictional "Author's Note" includes none of the biographical information one might expect, describing what this curious work of fiction is *not* helps to describe what much of Martone's fiction is. "Author's Note" is not a memoir, fictionalized or otherwise. Martone is not using fiction to come to some kind of reconciliation with or understanding of a difficult moment in his life by using *M.A.S.H.* and celebrity as a way addressing it indirectly. "Author's Note" is not chiefly a parody, nor is it just about the intersection of truth and fiction, whereby Martone inserts himself into a largely fictional world in order to describe how his real, nonfictional life is warped and bent by the heavy gravity of celebrity. In "Author's Note" the largely fictional parts, in fact, are those parts having to do with the character Martone. To read the story primarily or even secondarily as autobiographical would severely mislead. To read it all as ironic fiction and believe that none of it is real, however, would be to miss what the story illuminates best: the author's work.

"Author's Note" may be read as a note about Martone's methods and materials, a sly, indirect, and nonprescriptive *ars poetica*. As in nearly all of Martone's work, the people and places of Indiana are present in the story, including some state celebrities, as well as ordinary people who meet celebrities in unlikely moments in history. As in "Author's Note," Martone often uses biography, his or someone else's, as a starting point for fiction. In Martone's work, however, biography is never the primary mode nor is biographical insight much of a consideration.

At a time when the memoir is a popular mode of expression, Martone's fiction is important because it points to another mode of understanding. While there are biographical elements in "Author's Note" and other fiction by Martone, the biographical elements alone do not lead the narrative. Martone's stories do not argue for the primacy of personal, biographical insight. Instead they demonstrate uses for biographical material that are less personal and more broadly cultural than the memoir. As the story "Author's Note" demonstrates in its mingling of biographical meaning and fact with fictional suggestion and artifice, fiction can serve more than the purposes of personal expression.

Mingling of fact and fiction can, in fact, reveal the contours of contemporary mythology and speak to not only how that mythology is constructed over time, by many people acting cooperatively and telling their collective stories, but also how people relate to the larger-than-life mythological figures they have had some hand in creating or, at least, sustaining. Behind each of Martone's stories is his interest in the state of Indiana, specifically how stories construct the state with words and what those stories say about the people who live there. As Martone writes in the preface to the revised and expanded edition of *Fort Wayne Is Seventh on Hitler's List* (1993), "I hope these stories form a kind of Midwestern mythology adding to the complex web of anecdotes and tales we already tell ourselves about ourselves and about this part of the world that is our home." Martone is interested in collecting the stories of Indiana, an enterprise loosely analogous to anthropology or cultural history, and in manufacturing new stories and myths. His Indiana is both real and fictional, at once totally recognizable and slightly distorted, an Indiana composed by using historical accounts and WPA (Works Progress Administration) reports as well as unofficial sources such as family customs, local traditions, agricultural practices, and the received folklore of generations. His state is also an Indiana of the mind. The narrative methods, the sense of biography and place, and the playful appropriation of the historical record for the generation of fiction and the regeneration of myths are all apparent in "Author's Note," as in much of Martone's fiction.

Like later work such as "Author's Note," *Alive and Dead in Indiana* (1984), Martone's first collection of short fiction, explores the complicated intersections between fame and obscurity, truth and fiction, and myths and whatever hard-to-grasp reality and necessity gave rise to the myths. While these intersections are by no means the exclusive property of the people of Indiana, the fact that Martone's stories are set in a state not often considered in American fiction means that the people and places Martone explores are likely to be new to readers. In those areas of the country where the literary property is overdeveloped–places such as literary New York and Los Angeles or the South of gothic fiction–it is often impossible to separate the myth from the precursor of the myth. Few can say the myths of Indiana are so ingrained as to be beyond study. In a 1997 interview, conducted after his move to Alabama, Martone commented: "I had relatively few other stories about Indiana to fight through or absorb or transform. Now that I am in the South what strikes me is how writers wishing to write about it struggle with not only the stories written of the region but the actual enactment of the stories real Southerners have read and now perform."

In writing about Indiana, Martone has comparatively few regional literary influences. James Grove describes Martone's work as being just off the "interstate" of American literary fiction. Grove quotes Martone as saying, "One thing that's sort of interesting about the Midwest is that people write it off as *not* being interesting, and in a way it's pretty easy to make it interesting because so few people visit it and know it."

All the stories in *Alive and Dead in Indiana* are told from the first-person point of view, but they are not first-person stories in which the narrators' voices come from nowhere and tell stories with beginnings, middles, and ends. Rather, these first-person stories are prompted by something or someone else. These narrators accept the "I" with some reluctance. In "Everybody Watching and the Time Passing Like That," a story told by James Dean's high-school drama teacher, the narrator begins with a question: "Where was I when I heard about it?" Someone not in the story is there listening to the teacher talk. Moreover, this listener has prompted her to tell her story by asking her the question she repeats. Her next remark–"Let's see"–reveals that the story as Martone writes it catches her in the act of recollection, not prepared to begin an organized narration.

The drama teacher is also reluctant to talk about James Dean. All her memories of Dean in the school plays come down to one simple, declarative statement. Near the end of the story she says, "He died." She continues with a warning, presumably addressing her remarks to the unseen magazine reporter who prompted her narrative: "Leave his life alone," she says, sounding reluctant to take even the role she has already accepted in making a myth of Dean's life, a process that builds his character, a type recognizable and accessible to people everywhere, from the stuff of her personal memories.

The recollected nature of the story is never far from the reader's consideration. The occasion for the telling of this story–the original question–frames the story and informs the reader's understanding of it. Myths require some original recollection, just as they require many retellings. Martone's story catches the process of myth generation in the middle of one of those retellings. The myths of Dean's early years are formed by gradual accretion, perhaps becoming embellished and changed a bit, but beginning only as the people with whom he came into contact tell their stories to people who ask them questions.

Though his name is never mentioned in the story, the narrator of "Pieces" is Colonel Sanders, the founder of Kentucky Fried Chicken, talking about a time when he was just Harland Sanders, something of an itinerant salesman and cook who sold restaurants a good recipe for cooking chicken pieces. While "Pieces" has a famous narrator, in the other stories–including "Everybody Watching and The Time Passing Like That," "Dear John," and "Greek Letter in Bed"–Martone's narrators are on the outermost edges of celebrity; that is, they know people of whom the reader has heard. While peripheral narration does lend itself to a perspective of useful indirection, stories such as "Pieces" demonstrate that Martone can write also from a more direct perspective, filling in the empty spaces in a mythic fabrication with narrative and the details of human existence. By its conclusion "Pieces" becomes a story about traveling and the itinerant life and the fast yet fragile bonds that form among people who live it.

In "Alfred Kinsey, Alone, After an Interview, Dreams of Indiana" the fictional Alfred Kinsey's distant memories drift in and out of his recollections of more recent events. Martone's version of Kinsey, the famous researcher of human sexual behavior, mixes equal parts method and memory. While many such stories can easily lose their way by making the character's occupation serve as the metaphorical touchstone for every recollection, in Martone's story occupation often informs the narrative, but it does not serve as the only lens through which Kinsey sees himself.

The story is nostalgic but not in the sense of offering up hazy, sentimental memories. Instead it is nostalgia in the manner of Vladimir Nabokov, who wrote that throughout a person's life, nostalgia remains an insane companion, while still nonetheless being tolerated. Kinsey's nostalgia for his Indiana beginnings, when he studied comparative zoology before turning to human sexuality, is complicated by his present reality and circumstances. Hardened by time and the social-scientific method, his nostalgia is one of dispassionate appraisal. Also of interest in the story is the obvious irony that Martone invents Kinsey's fictional memories of Indiana. There is plenty of biographical evidence placing Kinsey in Bloomington, of course, but Martone fills in the spaces between the facts, giving his character rich memories and the sort of reveries people have at the end of a long day. It is characteristic of the tender, unobtrusive ironies throughout all Martone's fiction that in "Alfred Kinsey, Alone, After an Interview, Dreams of Indiana" Martone has created fictional secrets about the youthful romance between Kinsey and his wife, Clara, and attributed them to the man who made it his calling to investigate the secrets of average Americans.

Safety Patrol (1988) departs from Indiana celebrities and those who "knew them when" but remains close to places in Indiana. The collection is unified by themes such as fear and safety, as well as accidents and fate; by considerations of the various perspectives from which people see, including aerial photographs taken from an airplane, the view from an observation deck of the Empire State Building, and X-rays; and by a narrative mode that is familiar to readers of *Alive and Dead in Indiana*.

In *Safety Patrol* some of the stories resemble essays written by fictional characters. For example, "Watch Out"–in which a French teacher who teaches recent French émigrés all the English they need to learn in order to avoid accidents and mishaps–begins, "I will write my story using English only, as my students should do." Her use of the word *story* is significant, for while Martone's story is fiction, the teacher is using the word in its nonfiction connotation. The teacher's statement of purpose is phrased in a form that beginning writers often use to start an essay: that is, "first I'm going to tell you what I'm going to do, then I'm going to do it."

Similarly, in "The Safety Patrol," the final story in the collection, the narrator begins by referring to an illustration in a dictionary: "If you look on page 253 of the New College Edition of The American Heritage Dictionary, there, in the right margin toward the bottom of the page, you will find an aerial photograph of a cloverleaf interchange at Fort Wayne, Indiana." The dictionary citation as rhetorical opening will probably be familiar to anyone who has ever read student papers. The narrator is a sixth-grade teacher, who is in charge of organizing the school safety patrol, which ensures order as students walk to school, all while he carries on a Byzantine series of affairs with fellow teachers and administrators.

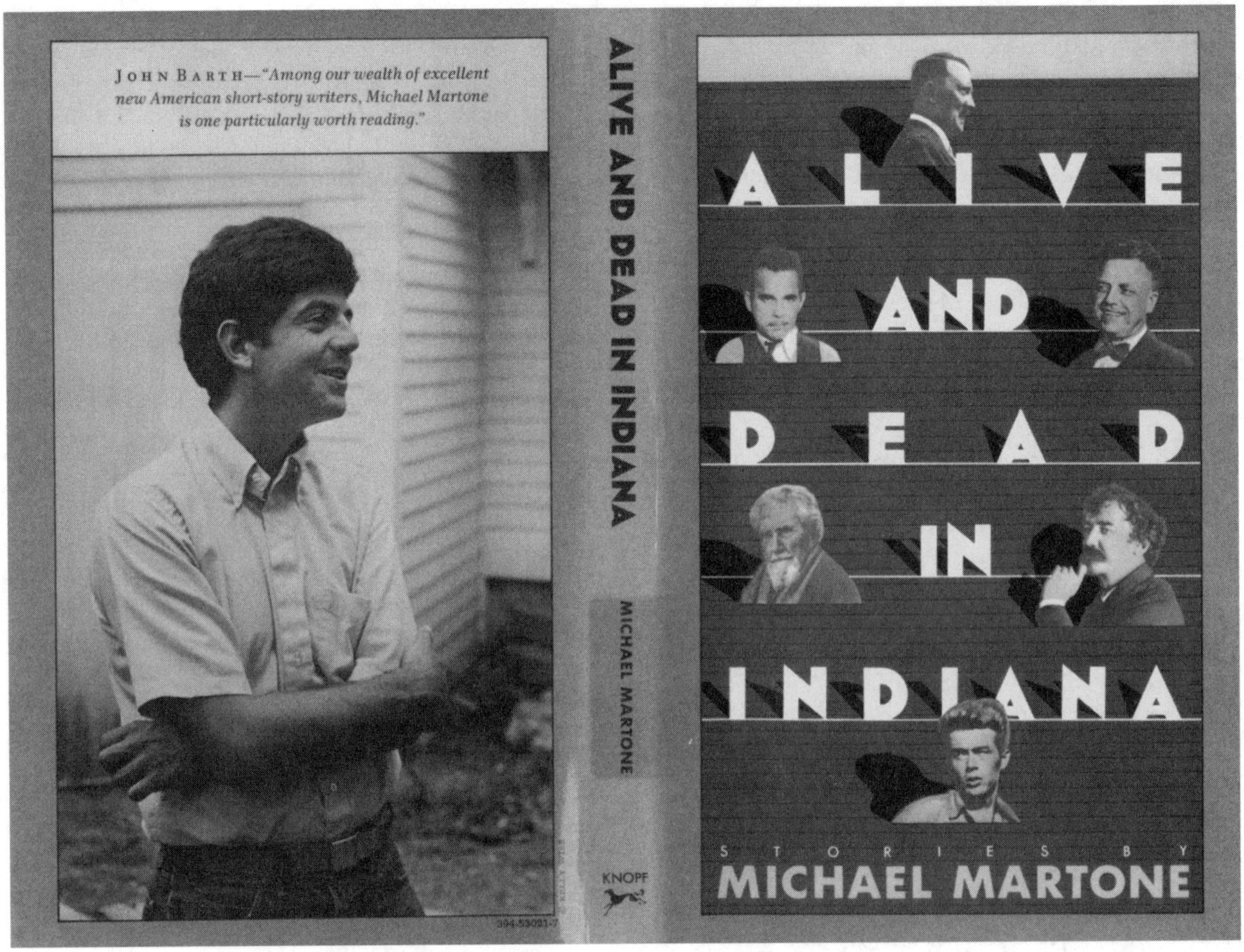

Dust jacket for Martone's 1984 book, short stories that feature real-life celebrities with connections to Indiana

This pattern of order in one area of a character's life while disorder and chaos reign in another holds true for many of the stories in the collection. Safety, as Martone writes about it, can be understood only in terms of its opposite, danger. Working to ensure safety without the presence of danger would be to engage in meaningless actions. If there were no dangerous intersections and rash drivers, there would be no need for the safety patrol. The seemingly limitless permutations of danger define the areas that need to be rendered safe for people, not the other way around. As Martone points out, the color of the industrial yellow paint used to signify danger is derived from lead: a toxic element produces the color that has become associated with signs that direct people along the safest route.

Fort Wayne Is Seventh on Hitler's List (1990) includes the stories published in his first book and three new stories. The title story was published in *Alive and Dead in Indiana* as "Vocation." One of the new stories is "The Teakwood Deck of the U.S.S. *Indiana*," a story about a man visiting the Indiana governor's office to see a piece of the deck of the World War II–era ship that has been fashioned into a desk in the shape of the state. The narrator prides himself on being able to locate the point of his birth on the smooth, varnished finish of the governor's desk. Like many of Martone's stories, this one concerns a person's sense of place and how important it is in the construction of identity. The story also introduces the notion of scale, important not only in reading maps but also in discussing Martone's fiction, which–book by book and story by story–has become an evolving written "map" of the state. The narrator recalls a man in prison who was employing considerable ingenuity to make a scale model of the U.S.S. *Indiana* from scraps of junk. The story concerns the forms of distortion and unreality between scale-model ships and scale maps compared to actual warships and the real landscape. The practice of creating scale representations is necessary to allow perception of things that are too large to be seen as a whole when life-sized, but scale also produces distortions. A significant trade-off underwrites the apparent order produced by scale. Still, Martone's fictions are, when viewed collectively, a series of carefully constructed, finely detailed scale models made in the image of a state.

Another new story, "Schliemann in Indianapolis" is about Heinrich Schliemann, the German archaeologist who discovered the putative ancient city of Troy. He comes to Indianapolis in 1869 to establish residency and get a divorce. At first the story seems in keeping with the stories from *Alive and Dead in Indiana.* Martone appropriates an historical figure and re-imagines the person, providing fictional details to fill out the sketchy historical record and offering an interesting meditation of fame and obscurity. Yet, there is more buried in "Schliemann in Indianapolis."

In the acknowledgments to the collection Martone thanks the Indiana Historical Society for granting him permission to quote from a journal titled "Schliemann in Indianapolis." In a 1997 interview Martone explained that most of the text of the story is quoted from a journal the archaeologist kept while in Indianapolis. To further complicate the relationship between truth and fiction, the journal from which Martone was to quote had been edited by someone else. Just as the archaeologist assembles a whole object from fragments, Martone assembled his story from fragments of an edited, that is mediated, journal. Martone's story is a reconstruction of events based on a reconstruction of Schliemann's journal. Furthermore, journal entries are, after all, reconstructions of the days' events. People do not write their journals as events unfold; they write after memories of events have faded slightly, perhaps days later. Martone's story about archaeology and the process of writing–as well as history, divorce, and marriage–is a creative reconstruction of reconstruction of reconstruction. Although none of Martone's other stories about Indiana celebrities has primary source material such as the Schliemann journal, the process of creative reconstruction in them remains essentially unchanged. In addition to all its other layers of meanings, "Schliemann in Indianapolis" offers an engaging picture of Martone's historical method as a writer.

In "Fidel," a story added to the 1993 edition of *Fort Wayne Is Seventh on Hitler's List,* a woman in the habit of listening to WOWO, her father's favorite radio station, begins mysteriously to hear the interminably long broadcast speeches of Fidel Castro, thanks to atmospheric conditions and the nature of clear-channel stations.

The final three stories in the 1993 edition, all previously uncollected, are the interior monologues of Indiana native Dan Quayle, vice president under President George H. W. Bush. They were republished with nine other stories in *Pensées: The Thoughts of Dan Quayle* (1994). In this ninety-page chapbook, Martone's Quayle thinks about his place in history, the ramifications of his power, and the role of ceremony in the health of the republic. There are also meaningful forays into late-night television and Hoosier basketball. *Pensées* is not a spoof and does not leap at any of the easy jokes about Quayle's spelling, malapropisms, and public awkwardness. Instead, Quayle becomes a Midwestern outsider in various tableaux of American political power. Judged by others as innocuous at best and a knave at worst, Quayle in Martone's hands is more complicated than the figure that one might construct from comedians' jokes and so many front-page headlines. Capable of deviousness, calculation, a somewhat playful, if slightly rambling, self-consciousness, and anger at his enemies, Quayle is the thinker at the heart of *Pensées.*

The book demonstrates Martone's continued interest in stories that take the form of monologues. Quayle thinks about his actions, whether detonating explosives to inaugurate the construction of the Indiana Highway of Vice Presidents (not fictional) or visiting the Tomb of the Unknown Soldier, and the stories about him become portraits of consciousness. What might be termed the action of the stories is almost always internal. Each of the stories in *Pensées* presents a mind caught in the act of thinking. Most catch him waiting to do things. For example, "On Anesthesia," in which Quayle is serving as president while President Bush is having surgery, catches Quayle at an idle moment. His thoughts of power turn to pride, which evolves into his desire to impress an old girlfriend, before the seriousness of the office and its power reassert themselves, bringing his thoughts into a more orderly line at the end of the story.

Pensées was originally published as a chapbook small enough to fit comfortably in a shirt pocket. Martone has said he intended the design to be suggestive of Mao Tse-tung's little red book, that is, a book of advice, thoughts, and musings from the leader to his people. While he was writing much of *Pensées,* Martone and John Crowley taught two graduate seminars at Syracuse University on the production of American literature in the nineteenth and twentieth centuries. Issues of literary production–everything from how a book is published to how it is distributed, sold, and received–figured significantly in Martone's thinking about his writing at this time.

With *Pensées* Martone was considering his work in terms of the fiction he writes and the physical form the book finally takes. In "My Situation," an essay written in response to a series of questions posed by the editors of *American Literary History* and published in summer 1999, he says, "I don't only want to create the written

Dust jacket for Martone's 1988 book, stories unified by the notion that "safety" cannot be understood without reference to "danger"

text but have a hand in the creation of the frame, the context in which it appears. I want to create the delivery vehicle as well."

Several questions related to the frame or context of a book become important for Martone, questions such as how do the ideas of a book circulate, by whom and how are they received, and how is a book finally used? With chapbook publication in general and Broad Ripple Press in particular, Martone was able to gain tight control over how the book was made. This control, as Martone's remark suggests, extends also to the distribution of the book and the context in which it is seen. For example, Martone worked to include copies of his book in the vice president's official archives and museum in Indiana. In addition to being available for purchase at bookstores or at Martone's readings, the book of fictions is now a part of the official record of Quayle's political life.

Similarly, Martone pointed out in a 1997 interview that the *Indianapolis Star,* a newspaper owned by the Quayle family, gave the publication of Quayle's autobiography a great deal of attention. This autobiography, of course, can claim little more authenticity than Martone's book of Quayle's thoughts because the autobiography, like nearly every political memoir, was ghostwritten. Yet, the newspaper covered its publication from every angle, with a book review in its arts pages, an editorial on the op-ed page, and a front-page news story. In the midst of all that coverage, a sidebar on the front page also included information on *Pensées,* Dan Quayle's other book.

Seeing Eye (1995) includes twenty new stories and some stories from earlier collections, including the dozen *Pensées* of Dan Quayle, which have been slightly revised. Read in a new context, the republished stories reveal different sides than in their original publication and make apparent how deep Martone's interest in local cultural history runs.

In *Seeing Eye* much of that history concerns war, specifically the effects of war on the home front. In "Dish Night" the memory of how in the decade immediately preceding World War II movie theaters gave away dishes with the purchase of tickets becomes a meditation on the passage of time and the effects of warfare on domestic life. "The Mayor of the Sister City Talks to the Chamber of Commerce in Klamath Falls, Oregon" concerns post–World War II America. In "Blue Hair" a girl whose hair was used to fashion the crosshairs in gun and bomb sights–an officer suggests it is an honor, a form of voluntary service, and moreover a secret–gets her hair done years later. In the context of these stories, a republished story such as "The Teakwood Deck of the U.S.S. *Indiana*" acquires new meaning, offering a picture of the symbolic and in some way meaningful dismantling of the equipment of the war effort into bits and pieces, scrap really, to be distributed all across the state and made into things that containing memories and a history of the place.

A writer of historical fiction faces a choice between emphasizing the grand historical event or what was relevant day to day. The choice may be posed as one between Abraham Lincoln and Lincoln Logs. Martone's history concentrates on personal history, the kind that owes its roots to the French *Annales* school, that is, history that emphasizes the daily lives of people over the lives of kings and leaders. The stories in *Seeing Eye* form a history of common things and everyday ways. Often the common and daily measure time, as in "The War That Never Ends," in which the narrator remembers: "I had lived through an age of service. Bread trucks delivered then. Men sharpened knives at your door. There were brushes for everything. Milk in bottles appeared on the stoop."

Readers of *Seeing Eye* will encounter other artifacts of the past, including Nehi bottles, drive-in movies, hand-painted clown faces, and a Chatty Cathy doll. In Martone's hands they provide more than setting and nostalgia and more than pop-culture allusions; for him they are golden opportunities for metaphor, chances to open a time up and see how it worked.

These stories piece together the past from what is left and what is remembered, "the whole imagined from a few bits." A farmer in "Outside Peru" stores the wreckage of a plane in his barn: "The wingtip, dented and discolored . . . implies the missing wing." There are also bits of dinner-table stories, about the chalk signs left by tramps during the Depression, for instance. Reading the stories becomes like browsing in antique shops with someone knowledgeable. In Martone's stories objects such as the wing of a model plane, an old wristwatch with the minutes marked by radium paint, or a gravy boat orphaned from its pattern start to fall into place. The woman in "Fidel" listening to her father's favorite station hears: "After midnight scratchy recordings of big bands were introduced by Listo Fisher, who pretended the broadcast still came from the ballrooms of the Hotel Indiana. Alfonse Bott, Tyrone Denig and the Draft Sisters, the brothers Melvin and Merv LeClair. . . ." The list in Martone's story goes on, a broadcast without break, until the narrator punctuates it with this thought: "It was as if I had tuned into my father's era." Readers may find that they tuned into another era in each of Martone's short stories. They can tell what period it is from details in the stories.

Martone is now taking his fiction farther away from traditional literary forms. For the past several years he has been working on "The Blue Book Guide to Indiana," a recently completed collection of stories that comprises a fictional travel guide to the state. The book includes entries detailing all the places to visit, museums, amusement parks, federal facilities, historical landmarks, and some of the culinary high points along the way. Martone's language in these fictions–and all are fictional–is not immediately recognizable as literary language. It is instead the language of travel guides, with their breathless wonder, their adjectives and enthusiasm, their tireless fascination with facts and figures and dates, and their chamber-of-commerce boosterism and Babbittry.

To most readers Martone's "travel guide" may be indistinguishable from any nonfiction travel guide. That is Martone's intention. Much as the first two editions of *Gulliver's Travels* (1726) appeared not as fiction by Jonathan Swift but instead as a travel account by Lemuel Gulliver, Martone's fictional travel writing appeared first as nonfiction accounts of things to do and places to go on weekends. Many of the travel-guide pieces have appeared in several Indiana newspapers, where they are treated not as pieces of fiction but as actual reporting, feature articles, and travel tips. Writing in "My Situation," Martone explains how following questions of the frame or context of fiction to their logical conclusion has fundamentally altered how he considers the place of his writing in the world: "I now think of the work I do more as the making of things, of objects, instead of simply the generation of text. I would like these artifacts to then, more or less, modulate the stream of dreaming which is present in our collective consumption of narrative everywhere."

What is ingenious about Martone's travel writing is that the pieces acquire meaning in their publication, particularly in their placement. In a traditional model of literary publication, most literary magazines separate fiction, poetry, and nonfiction, creating a kind of order and rigidly enforcing distinctions between forms and modes of expression. Bookstores do the same on a much larger scale, Martone's travel pieces will be categorized as fiction, according to this traditional model, but once safely labeled they will lose their ability to play with the reader's expectations. Martone's travel work will appear as fiction *in the form of* travel writing. Readers will look at it in the context of contemporary American fiction. While this approach has validity, Martone realizes that it produces only a certain, limited kind of reading.

By publishing his work outside the traditionally literary venues Martone is looking for a way to get his fiction before unsuspecting eyes. Readers who encounter the travel pieces as fiction go through the usual motions to suspend their disbeliefs. Readers who encounter the same writings with no labels attached approach it in the same way they do other forms of everyday nonfiction writing, such as mail from businesses, instructions for the safe operation of appliances, letters to the editor of the local newspaper, and the fine print on boxes of cereal. Martone's travel pieces exist first and foremost in the world. "More and more," writes Martone in "My Situation," "I think of these fictions as viral. That is, they are designed to infect the memory of the reader, any reader."

The point of the travel pieces, however, is not just to fool the reader, though Martone does want to draw attention to the frames around everything people read. The central question of Martone's recent work is: How does the context alter the object under study? That is, how does the vehicle that delivers the text–be it bookstore or literary journal–alter the meaning and reception of the text?

Nor is Martone's object chiefly satiric. Satiric projects are frequently destructive. Through irony, exaggeration, and elaborate reversals of meaning, they seek to disabuse readers of accepted, but unconsidered values. Martone's travel writing is more constructive than such satires. For Martone, looking closely at the effects of the frame that surrounds a text has led him back to a consideration of stories and local mythology, subjects that have informed his fiction from the beginning. By creating places such as the Tomb of Orville Redenbacher, the Bronze Mortuary at the Cemetery at Naked City, and the National Monument for Those Killed by Tornadoes in Trailer Parks and Mobile Home Courts, Martone is in some sense creating a new Indiana, or at least constructing imaginative additions to the existing one. By publishing his fictions in traditionally factual contexts, he seeks to add his civic memorials to the existing Indiana landscape. By producing nonfictional fictions such as the Federal Research and Testing Center for Coffin and Casket Standards, Eli Lilly Land (an amusement park sponsored by and dedicated to the achievements of the company that gave the world Prozac and other pharmaceutical wonders), and the Trans-Indiana Mayonnaise Pipeline, Martone is adding to the store of Indiana myths. Like Martone's slightly more factual exploration of Indiana mythology and celebrity in *Alive and Dead in Indiana,* the travel writing represents new elements in Martone's ongoing creation of a mythical Indiana. The state is wide open in its geography and its literature. Martone has discovered that there is considerable joy for the writer who fills in the great, empty spaces of Indiana with fiction.

Interview:

Fred Santiago Arroyo, "Adventures on the Cultural Landscape: An Epistolary Interview with Michael Martone," *Sycamore Review,* 9 (Summer/Fall 1997): 93–115; republished in *Delicious Imaginations: Conversations with Contemporary Writers,* edited by Sarah Griffiths and Kevin Kehrwald (West Lafayette, Ind.: Purdue University Press, 1998), pp. 173–193.

Reference:

James Grove, "The Fiction of Michael Martone," *High Plains Literary Review,* 11 (Fall–Winter 1996): 152–171.

Papers:

Michael Martone's papers, including literary correspondence with his agent and editors and various stages of manuscripts and proofs for all his collections of short fiction through *Seeing Eye,* are held at the Museum of Jurassic Technology in Culver City, California.

William Maxwell

(16 August 1908 -)

Dale Hrebik
Delgado College

See also the Maxwell entry in *DLB Yearbook 1980.*

BOOKS: *Bright Center of Heaven* (New York & London: Harper, 1934);

They Came Like Swallows (New York & London: Harper, 1937; London: Joseph, 1937);

The Folded Leaf (New York & London: Harper, 1945; London: Faber & Faber, 1946);

The Heavenly Tenants (New York & London: Harper, 1946);

Time Will Darken It (New York: Harper, 1948; London: Faber & Faber, 1949);

The Chateau (New York: Knopf, 1961);

The Old Man at the Railroad Crossing and Other Tales (New York: Knopf, 1966);

Ancestors: A Family History (New York: Knopf, 1971);

Over By the River and Other Stories (New York: Knopf, 1977);

So Long, See You Tomorrow (New York: Knopf, 1980; London: Secker & Warburg, 1988);

Five Tales (Omaha: Cummington Press, 1988);

The Outermost Dream: Essays and Reviews (New York: Knopf, 1989);

Billie Dyer and Other Stories (New York: Knopf, 1992);

All the Days and Nights: The Collected Stories of William Maxwell (New York: Knopf, 1995);

Mrs. Donald's Dog Bun and His Home Away From Home (New York: Knopf, 1995).

RECORDINGS: *Richard Bausch and William Maxwell Reading Their Short Stories* (Washington, D.C.: Archive of Recorded Poetry and Literature, Library of Congress, 1992);

William Maxwell Reads "So Long, See You Tomorrow" (Columbia, Mo.: American Audio Prose Library, 1997).

OTHER: *Stories,* by Maxwell, Jean Stafford, John Cheever, and Daniel Fuchs (New York: Farrar, Straus & Cudahy, 1956); republished as *A Book of Stories* (London: Gollancz, 1957);

William Maxwell (photograph by James Hamilton; from the dust jacket for Billie Dyer, *1992)*

Charles Pratt, *The Garden and the Wilderness,* edited by Maxwell (New York: Horizon, 1980);

Sylvia Townsend Warner, *Letters,* edited by Maxwell (London: Chatto & Windus, 1982).

Perhaps best known as a fiction editor at *The New Yorker* for more than forty years, William Maxwell has enjoyed an even longer career as a writer. Since the publication of his first book, *Bright Center of Heaven,* in 1934, he has written several novels, essays and reviews, a book-length family history, stories for children, and short stories. His stories fall into two distinct types: realistic traditional short fiction and short, moralistic fables, or "improvisations," as he calls them.

If Maxwell's long service as a fiction editor at *The New Yorker* shaped his writing, or if his aesthetic informed his editorial work, is unclear. It is indisputable, however, that he has established a reputation as a writer whose fiction has the kind of elegance for which the magazine is also known. As Sanford Pinsker wrote in his review of *All the Days and Nights* (1995), "Maxwell's stories ultimately find their way to those quiet places where a nuanced phrase matters greatly, and silence perhaps more. Put another way: the marriage between the traditions associated with *New Yorker* fiction and Maxwell's individual talent is a seamless one" (*Studies in Short Fiction,* Summer 1996).

Given their Midwestern settings, it is not surprising that Maxwell's widely praised stories have been compared to the fiction of Sinclair Lewis and Sherwood Anderson. Much of Maxwell's fiction draws on his boyhood in Lincoln, Illinois, and the distinction between autobiography and fiction is often blurred. In his preface to *All the Days and Nights,* Maxwell said about Lincoln, "three-quarters of the material I would need for the rest of my writing life was already at my disposal. My father and mother. My brothers. The cast of larger-than-life characters. . . . All there, waiting for me to learn my trade and recognize instinctively what would make a story or sustain the complicated cross-weaving of longer fiction."

William Keepers Maxwell Jr. was born in Lincoln, Illinois, on 16 August 1908, the son of William Keepers and Eva Blossom Blinn Maxwell. During Maxwell's youth, his father traveled throughout Illinois selling fire insurance and was gone from home for days at time. His father's absences probably contributed to the particularly close relationship Maxwell had with his mother: "She just shone on me like the sun." This relationship figures directly in much of his writing, including short stories such as "The Front and Back Parts of the House," and "The Value of Money," as well as the novels *They Came Like Swallows* (1937), *The Folded Leaf* (1945), and *So Long, See You Tomorrow* (1980). Of her death in a Spanish influenza epidemic that raged across the country in 1918–1919, when he was ten, Maxwell later wrote:

> it happened too suddenly, with no warning, and we none of us could believe it or bear it. My father's face turned the color of ashes and stayed that way a whole year. The nightmare went on and on. He did all a man can do in those circumstances; he kept the family together. But he could not make what had happened not have happened, and the beautiful, imaginative, protected world of my childhood was swept away.

Maxwell has written of his mother throughout his long career, a testament to the strength of their relationship and the importance she had in his life.

Four years after her death, when Maxwell's father received a promotion, the family moved to Chicago. By this time Maxwell's father had remarried. Maxwell attended Nicholas Senn High School, where he found teachers who encouraged his interest in literature and music. It was a welcomed relief for the unathletic Maxwell, who once confessed to a *New Yorker* colleague that he had committed forty-two errors by "actual count" in a single baseball game during which he played shortstop, a switch from his usual refuge in right field.

One incident at his Chicago high school had a major impact on Maxwell's writing. As a boy in Lincoln, he had played with Cletus Smith, who lived on a nearby farm. One summer, Cletus vanished quite suddenly. Later, Maxwell learned that Cletus's father had found out his wife was having an affair and killed his wife's lover and himself. Years later, Maxwell unexpectedly passed Cletus in the hallway at school. No words or glances of recognition were exchanged. Maxwell's guilt over not acknowledging his friend led him to wonder about the events that led up to the deaths and ultimately to write *So Long, See You Tomorrow,* which he called a "roundabout futile way of making amends." In this book Maxwell moves from clear-cut memoir into an imaginative extrapolation of the events. Writing for the 4 May 1992 issue of *The New Republic,* Pearl K. Bell described the novel as "explicitly set out to demonstrate the various ways a writer can use the intertwining of memory and imagination, and how in the process fact and fantasy are wound into an indissoluble skein." She called it "Maxwell's most persuasive expression of his lifelong belief in the inseparability of autobiography and fiction," a belief that is also demonstrated by his short stories.

Maxwell earned a B.A. from the University of Illinois in 1930 and received a scholarship to pursue graduate work at Harvard University, where he earned his M.A. in 1931. After teaching at the University of Illinois for two years and publishing his first novel, *Bright Center of Heaven* (1934), he headed to New York City with letters of reference from his publisher to three magazines, *The New Republic, The New Yorker,* and *Time. The New Republic* did not take him, and he never made it to *Time* because *The New Yorker* hired him before he could get there. He started in the art department, but

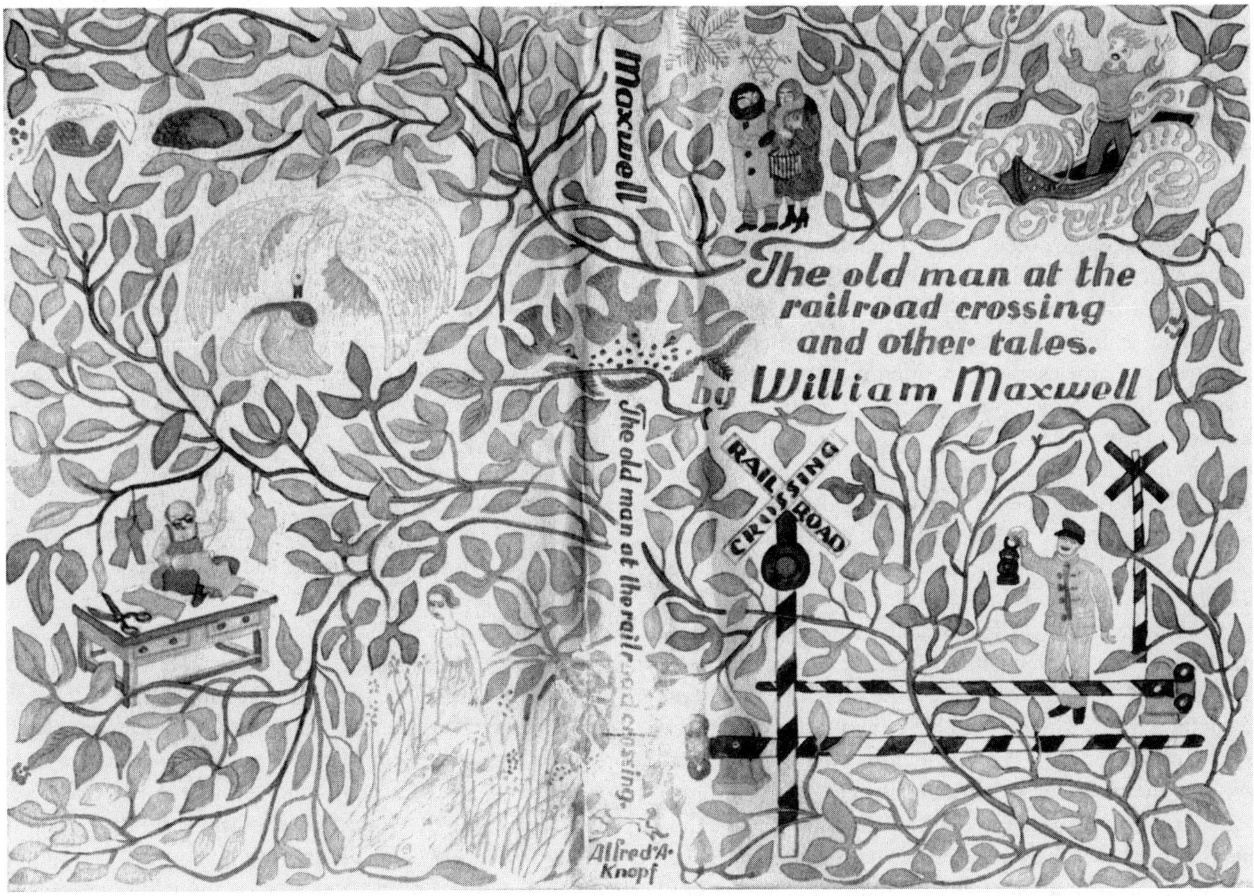

Dust jacket for Maxwell's 1966 book, a collection of short, moralistic fables that he calls "improvisations"

eventually became a fiction editor, where he worked with authors such as Shirley Hazzard, Mary McCarthy, Vladimir Nabokov, J. D. Salinger, and Eudora Welty, plus–as they were called around the office–"the three Johns": Cheever, O'Hara, and Updike. Maxwell also edited the work of Frank O'Connor, which led to a long friendship and the publication of *The Happiness of Getting It Down Right: Letters of Frank O'Connor and William Maxwell, 1945–1961* (1996). He enjoyed his time at the magazine, staying for more that four decades before finally retiring in 1978. Describing his editing philosophy in a 1982 *Paris Review* interview, Maxwell said that "it is not the work of an editor to teach writers how to write. . . . Real editing means changing as little as possible." He later told Harvey Ginsberg in an interview for *The New York Times Book Review* (22 January 1995) that he is "always happiest with what isn't there." Ginsberg did not find this statement surprising because he remembered Maxwell's "refusal to use two words when one will do, or even one word when that word might be superfluous." A similar sentiment was echoed by Josephine Humphreys in her review of *Billie Dyer and Other Stories* (1992): "What he doesn't say, and why he doesn't say it, are the heart of the book" (*The New York Times Book Review,* 16 February 1992).

After retiring from *The New Yorker* Maxwell remained in New York City, where he lives with his wife, Emily Gilman Noyes Maxwell, whom he married on 17 May 1945. Their two children, Katharine Farrington and Emily Brooke, are both grown. Several of Maxwell's stories are set in New York, but, despite his having lived in that city for most of his life, Lincoln, Illinois, remains the imaginative setting for the bulk of his writing.

In 1966 Maxwell published his first collection of short fiction, *The Old Man at the Railroad Crossing and Other Tales.* In his preface Maxwell called these twenty-nine short works "tales" and described the process of writing them:

> I didn't so much write them as do my best to keep out of the way of their writing themselves. I would sit with my head bent over the typewriter waiting to see what was going to come out of it. The first sentence was usu-

> ally a surprise to me. From the first sentence everything else followed. . . . I have sometimes believed that it was all merely the result of the initial waiting with an emptied mind–that this opened a door of some kind, and what emerged was an archaic survival, the professional storyteller who flourished in all the countries of the world before there were any printed books. . . .

Indeed, all the tales seem "old," reminiscent of Aesop's fables or the fairy tales of the Brothers Grimm. Royalty and castles often appear, as do traditional character types such as fishermen, tailors, and woodcutters. They are usually nameless and are identified only by their occupation or some characteristic; for instance, "The half-crazy woman," or "The man who loved to eat," descriptions that also serve as titles. The writing is straightforward and plain, with a tone more of conversation than of polished prose. All the tales offer morals or proverbs of some sort, though they are often more ironic than those traditionally found in fairy tales. The tales often celebrate attributes such as incessant jabbering (as in "The woman with a talent for talking") or creativity and illogic (as in "The kingdom where straightforward, logical thinking was admired over every other kind"). While the form may be almost archaic, the meaning is decidedly current.

In "The fisherman who had no one to go out in his boat with him" an aging fisherman, with no one to talk to on his boat all day, sings to himself. Running out of songs, he starts going to class with children to learn more, and, lacking any particular talent for singing, he is considered rather eccentric. One day during a storm, all the fishing boats are threatened by high waves and fog. The old fisherman starts to sing; the other boats cluster around the sound of his voice, and they all find their way safely home.

Another eccentric is the main character of the title story, an old man who raises and lowers the gate at the railroad crossing. As he does so, he says "Rejoice" to all who pass by him. Materialistic people do not hear him; others are embarrassed for him; and children make fun of him. His daughter cannot stand the way he repeats "Rejoice" over and over. Only one woman listens to him, and she finds meaning and comfort in his message.

Reviewing the book for *The New York Times Book Review* (13 March 1966), Laurence Lafore wrote that Maxwell's stories "are fables not so much for our time, since their meaning is intended to be universal, but certainly they are very much of our time. . . ." He called their style not "so much mannered as simply appropriate." Writing for *The New York Review of Books* (28 April 1966), Bernard Bergonzi agreed that Maxwell was not "unmodern," adding: "many of his seemingly artless pieces effectively turn on the problem of identity and other hot contemporary issues." He continued with a word of criticism, "I found the whole collection odd, charming, repetitious, and with rather too calculated an air of uplift and inspiration."

Maxwell's next collection, *Over By the River and Other Stories* (1977), includes twelve stories written between 1941 and 1976, all of which were previously published, nine of them in *The New Yorker*. These stories fit more easily into the modern short-story form and show the autobiographical influences that also shaped Maxwell's novels. Four of the stories are set in Lincoln (called Draperville) and include incidents from Maxwell's childhood. When asked by Harvey Ginsberg in 1995 about his constant return to his childhood home for a fictional setting, Maxwell replied, "The fact that I had not lived [in Lincoln] since I was 14 years old sealed off my memories of it, and made of it a world I knew no longer existed, that seemed always available for storytelling."

For instance, in "A Final Report" Maxwell's narrator describes a picture hanging in a deceased aunt's house. The young child looking at this picture of horses jumping over a dreaming man's bed fears for the safety of the dreamer, as did Maxwell when he was a boy and saw just such a picture in a neighbor's home. Similarly, in "The Value of Money" a scholarly son returns from New York to Draperville to visit his father for a quiet reconciliation of differences in a relationship hampered by, among other things, the death of the mother. Commenting on these stories in *The New York Times Book Review* (16 October 1977), Nicholas Delbanco wrote, "Strangely, the author's persona seems least at home in . . . his 'hometown' stories; the elegiac mode appears a touch too pat."

Two of the stories concern Americans traveling in France, also the setting for Maxwell's 1961 novel *The Chateau.* Both stories describe the disillusionment the characters experience when the country fails to live up to their expectations. In "The Pilgrimage" a couple vainly pursues a recommended but apparently unattainable meal with hilarious determination, while in "The Gardens of Mont-Saint-Michel" a husband and wife bring their two daughters to a favorite spot in France only to find it overrun by tourists and nearly unrecognizable.

Several of the stories center on New York City. "The Thistles of Sweden," for example, is the story of how a young couple finds temporary refuge from the difficulties of modern life in their New York apartment. Commenting on this story in a review of *All the Days and Nights* (1995) Mary Flanagan wrote that "a roomful of furniture is so sensitively rendered as to become numinous" (*The New York Times Book Review,* 22 January 1995). The title story has a similar theme: members of

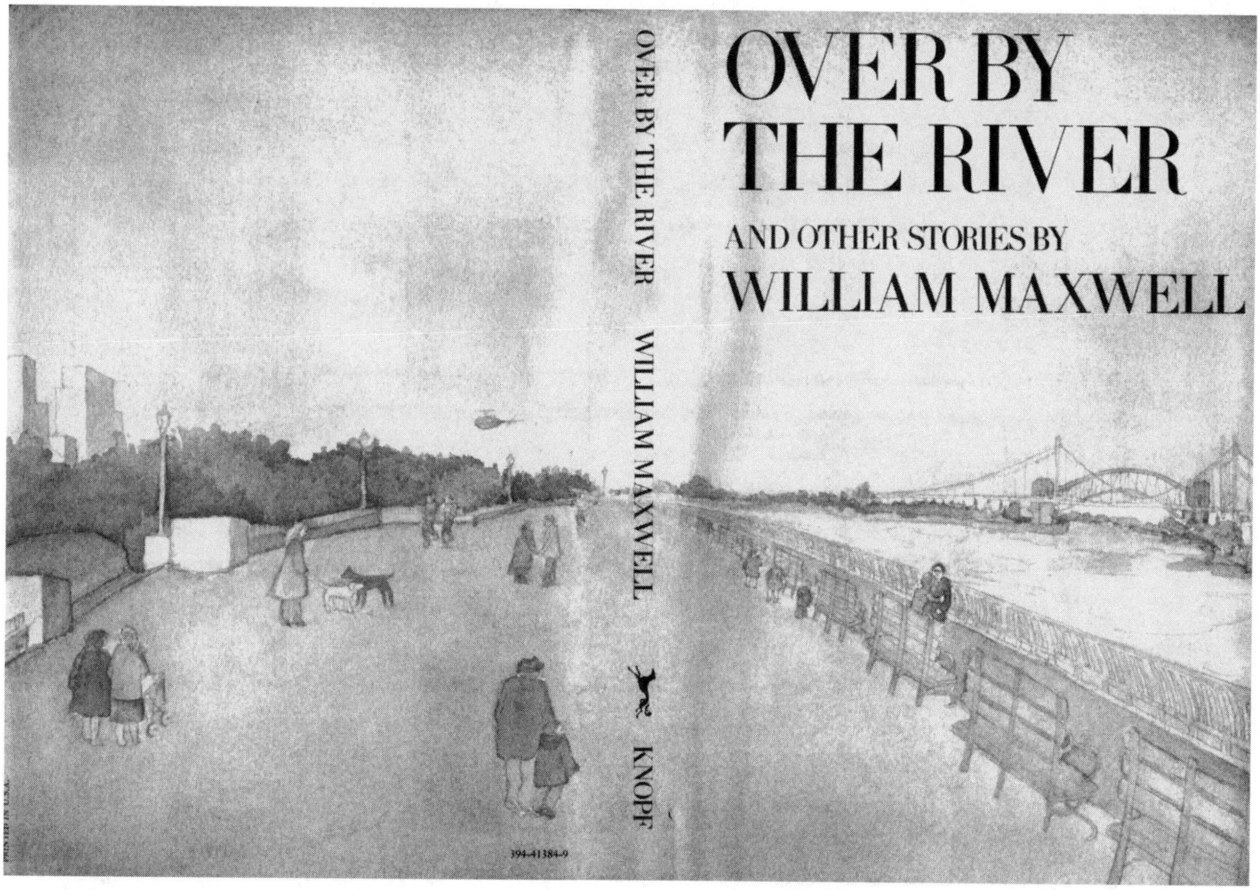

Dust jacket for Maxwell's 1977 book, in which four of the stories include incidents from Maxwell's childhood

a family try to shelter each other from the anonymous threats of the city, as represented by one young daughter's irrational, but accepted, belief that a tiger is stalking her. Reviewing the book for *The New Republic* (10 September 1977), Joyce Carol Oates commented that Maxwell "is not unaware of what might be called evil and he is willing to explore the possibility that, yes, civilization is in decline." Oates also praised Maxwell's ability "to impose upon his material a gentle, rather Chekhovian sense of order: whatever happens is not Fate but the inevitable working-out of character, never melodramatic, never pointedly 'symbolic.'"

In *Billie Dyer and Other Stories* (1992) Maxwell makes use of his past even more directly than in his earlier fiction. All the stories have a first-person narrator who, while not named explicitly, seems to be Maxwell himself, raising the question whether these stories are, in fact, fiction. Draperville returns to its true name of Lincoln, a change Maxwell addressed in a 1995 interview with Harvey Ginsberg: "originally I felt that what I was writing was fiction, that is to say a mixture of things I had experienced or known about with events that I felt free to imagine if the novel or story required it. Gradually over the years I came to have such respect for the storytelling aspects of life that it more and more seemed a good idea to stick closer to what actually happened, and the result was certainly that the fiction became more autobiographical. It seemed simpler when I was writing about actual people as I knew them to use Lincoln. This doesn't mean I had moved over into reminiscence, because reminiscence is largely an accumulation of things remembered, whereas I wanted the material to have the shape and form and effect of fiction."

One motive for Maxwell's new approach may be found in "The Front and Back Parts of the House," in which Maxwell, in his early forties, returns to Lincoln, where Hattie Dyer, his family's old cook, is working for Maxwell's aunt. When Maxwell embraces Hattie, she does not respond, causing Maxwell to wonder what "unforgivable" affront is bothering Hattie and who might have offended her. He brings up all his memories of Hattie in his house and her interactions with his mother and others. Considering them in the light of

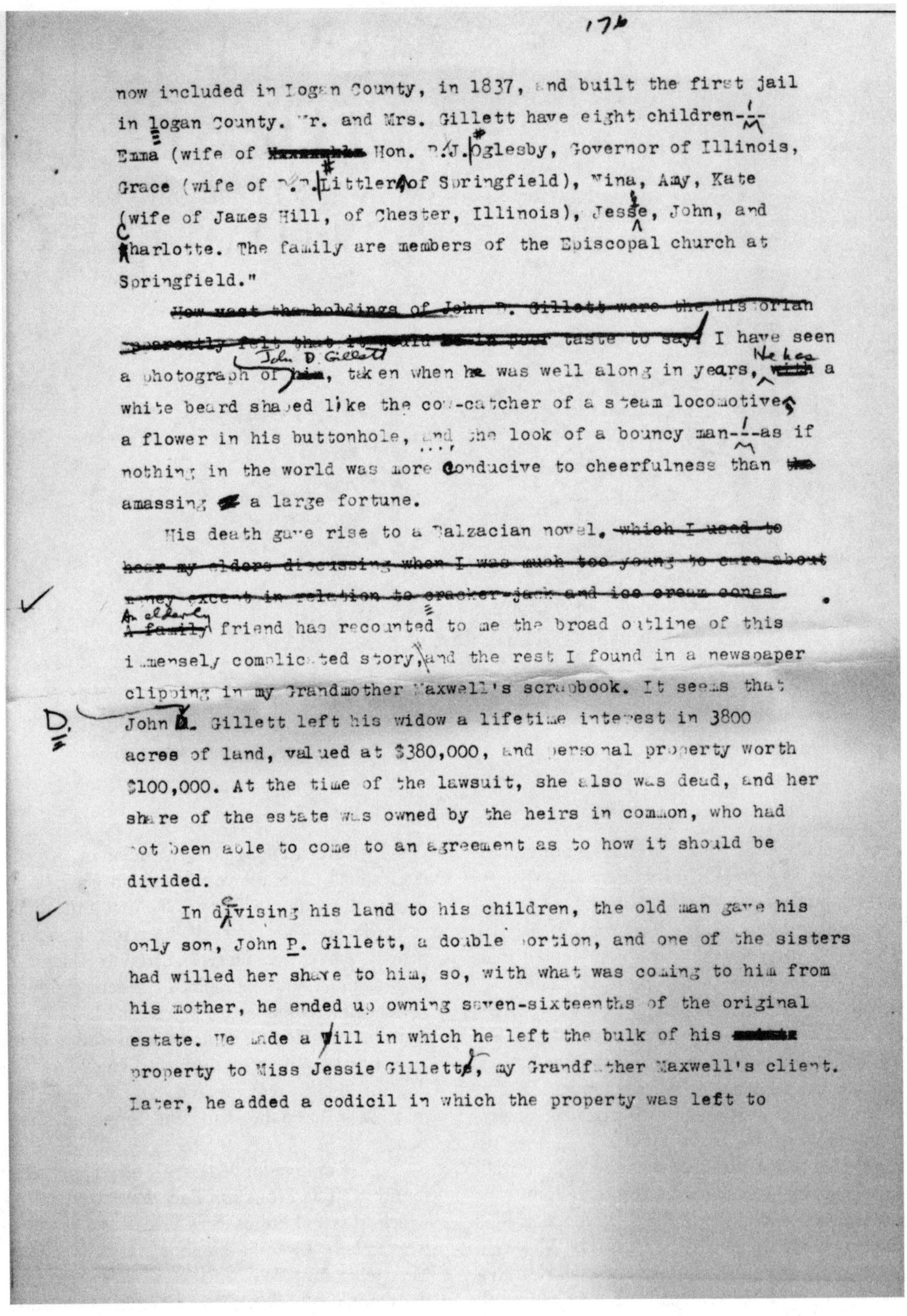

17b

now included in Logan County, in 1837, and built the first jail in Logan County. Mr. and Mrs. Gillett have eight children--Emma (wife of [redacted] Hon. R.J. Oglesby, Governor of Illinois, Grace (wife of R.R. Littler of Springfield), Nina, Amy, Kate (wife of James Hill, of Chester, Illinois), Jessie, John, and Charlotte. The family are members of the Episcopal church at Springfield."

~~How vast the holdings of John D. Gillett were the historian apparently felt that it would [redacted] in poor taste to say.~~ I have seen a photograph of John D. Gillett, taken when he was well along in years. He has a white beard shaped like the cow-catcher of a steam locomotive, a flower in his buttonhole, and the look of a bouncy man--as if nothing in the world was more conducive to cheerfulness than [redacted] amassing [redacted] a large fortune.

His death gave rise to a Balzacian novel. ~~which I used to hear my elders discussing when I was much too young to care about money except in relation to cracker-jack and ice cream cones.~~ ~~A family~~ An elderly friend has recounted to me the broad outline of this immensely complicated story, and the rest I found in a newspaper clipping in my Grandmother Maxwell's scrapbook. It seems that John D. Gillett left his widow a lifetime interest in 3800 acres of land, valued at $380,000, and personal property worth $100,000. At the time of the lawsuit, she also was dead, and her share of the estate was owned by the heirs in common, who had not been able to come to an agreement as to how it should be divided.

In devising his land to his children, the old man gave his only son, John P. Gillett, a double portion, and one of the sisters had willed her share to him, so, with what was coming to him from his mother, he ended up owning seven-sixteenths of the original estate. He made a will in which he left the bulk of his [redacted] property to Miss Jessie Gillett, my Grandfather Maxwell's client. Later, he added a codicil in which the property was left to

Page from the revised typescript for Ancestors, *Maxwell's 1971 family history (Collection of William Maxwell)*

possible racial tensions, he is not satisfied with unstated racial resentment as the explanation. In all his memories his mother and Hattie were "simply easy with one another."

Later, when Maxwell's brother mentions that the man who takes care of his yard is reading one of Maxwell's books, he suddenly realizes what gave affront. Maxwell's novel *Time Will Darken It* (1948) draws on an occasion in his family's history when relatives visited from Mississippi. The characters include a family maid who has had quite a few children out of wedlock and a drunken and dangerous man who has fathered at least one of them. Maxwell did not base them on Hattie or her husband, but because the situation in which he placed his fictional characters corresponded to actual circumstances of his past, her confusion is easy to imagine. "If Hattie did indeed read my book," Maxwell muses, "then what could she think but that I had portrayed her as a loose woman and her husband as a monster of evil." In his later writing, when he uses his imagination to fill in holes in his memories of actual events, Maxwell admits the distortion.

In "My Father's Friends" a man named Dean Hill tells Maxwell, "What the book is about is a matter of indifference to me. I am interested in the writer." Maxwell could be describing his own approach to writing stories. In her review of *Billie Dyer and Other Stories,* Josephine Humphreys remarked, "'What the book is about' is the writer." Perhaps it would be more accurate to say that what the book is about is what Maxwell remembers.

As he explains in the title story, "For things that are not known–at least not anymore–and that there is now no way of finding out about, one has to fall back on imagination. This is not the same thing as the truth, but neither is it necessarily a falsehood." Although Maxwell occasionally undercuts it, the narrative voice speaks with an authoritative air. Billie Dyer is an African American from Lincoln who, through perseverance and determination, manages to attend and graduate from medical school just after the turn of the century. The brother of Hattie Dyer, Billie Dyer joined the army after medical school and was sent to France as a doctor for the black soldiers during World War I. Maxwell's story includes excerpts from the diary Dyer kept while overseas, and a large part of the story is based on fact. Parts, however, are imagined. After relating an incident from Dyer's childhood, Maxwell tells the reader, "There is no record of any of this. It is merely what I think happened. I cannot, in fact, imagine it not happening." The stories are both nonfiction and fiction, and Maxwell seems to question whether any true separation between the two can be made. In "The Man in the Moon" he describes his grandfather's house and one particular room that especially struck him. In the front parlor,

> it was always twilight because the velvet curtains shut out the sun. If I stood looking into the pier glass between the two front windows I saw the same heavy walnut and mahogany furniture in an even dimmer light. Whether this is an actual memory or an attempt on the part of my mind to adjust the past to my feelings about it I am not altogether sure.

For Maxwell, memory is not wholly to be trusted.

"The Holy Terror" is about Maxwell's older brother and the secret about why his leg had to be amputated before he was six years old. In her review for *TLS: The Times Literary Supplement* (1 May 1992) Mary Hawthorne comments, "The story is not only a vivid portrait of his brother but a disconcerting reminder of the limits of our knowledge about anything–even, or perhaps especially, ourselves. Maxwell knows as well as anyone that the mysteries of childhood, while the most alluring, remain the most impermeable."

In one of his meditations on memory, Maxwell claimed that "in talking about the past we lie with every breath we draw." In this instance lying is not a purposeful attempt to deceive but rather the inevitable consequence of human fallibility, particularly as reminiscence becomes fiction, and age begins to diffuse the separation between memory and imagination. In this sense the stories are wholly fictional, despite their grounding in actual events.

Maxwell elaborated on the connection between autobiography and fiction further in his 1982 *Paris Review* interview: "autobiography is very different from anything I've ever written. . . . I don't feel that my stories, though they may appear to be autobiographical, represent an intention to hand over the whole of my life. They're fragments in which I am a character along with all the others. . . . As I get older I put more trust in what happened, which has a profound meaning if you can get at it."

The first part of *All The Days and Nights* (1995) includes all the stories from *Over By the River* and *Billie Dyer* as well as four previously uncollected stories: "A Game of Chess," "The Poor Orphan Girl," "The Lily-White Boys," and "What He Was Like." The second part of the book includes twenty-one "improvisations," many of which appeared in *The Old Man at the Railroad Crossing.* One of the new improvisations is the title story. An old man lies in bed at night, trying not to let go of any part of his day because "he felt that he was about to leave a large part of his life (and therefore a large part of himself) behind, he couldn't accept it as inevitable and a part of growing old. What you do not accept you do

Dust jacket for Maxwell's 1992 book, fictionalized accounts of his early life in Lincoln, Illinois

not allow to happen, even if you have to have recourse to magic." He decides to go in search of all the days and nights of his life, and a year later he returns to his wife, telling her "They're all there." As a parable about the importance of memory, the story demonstrates Maxwell's beliefs and intentions with regard to his writing. Maxwell told Ginsberg, "I write about the past not because I think it is better than the present but because of things that happened that I do not want to be forgotten."

Writing of this past in her *TLS* review of *All the Days and Nights* (6 June 1997), Claire Messud commented, "Maxwell's triumph is to bring brightness, and a seething, submerged emotion, to this past, to an America long dead. Taken together, the stories about the characters of his youth amount to a town portrait as full and irreplaceable as Sherwood Anderson's Winesburg, Ohio. . . . William Maxwell offers us scrupulously executed, moving landscapes of America's twentieth century, and they do not fade."

In a rare uncomplimentary review in *The New York Times Book Review* (22 January 1995), Mary Flanagan complained of Maxwell's treatment of women and minorities, saying "This is an 'us' book, so there are inevitable problems with 'them.'" While she praises "his warm, amiable voice," she accuses him of "sacrificing structure to discursiveness and flirting with the literary equivalent of easy listening" and observes, "The last few stories are so similar that I kept wondering whether I was rereading the same one."

Most other reviewers praised the book. In the *Chicago Tribune* (8 January 1995), for example, Penelope Mesic wrote, "Maxwell, dealing in very ordinary days and nights, makes them luminous by the skillful use of contrasts, as the impressionists made a dull rain-washed street shine–not by using colors of garish brightness but by using one tone to bring another into prominence."

Speaking to Ginsberg about writing his improvisations, Maxwell compared himself to an ancient storyteller. In one of the new improvisations, "A fable begotten of an echo of a line of verse by W. B. Yeats," the main character is "an old man who made his living telling stories." As he admitted to Ginsberg, Maxwell was describing himself. In fact, there may be no better description of Maxwell's writing and its relationship to autobiography and memory than this comment about the old man's storytelling: "if it was a familiar story he was telling, he added new embellishments, new twists, and again it would be something he had never told before and didn't himself know until the words came out of his mouth, so that he was as astonished as his listeners, but didn't show it. He wanted them to believe what was in fact true, that the stories didn't come from him but through him, were not memorized, and would never be told quite the same way again."

Letters:

The Happiness of Getting It Down Right: Letters of Frank O'Connor and William Maxwell, 1945–1961, edited by Michael Steinman (New York: Knopf, 1996).

Interviews:

"Interview with William Maxwell," *Publishers Weekly,* 216 (10 December 1979): 8–9;

George Plimpton and John Seabrook, "William Maxwell: The Art of Fiction LXXI," *Paris Review* (July 1982): 106–139;

Harvey Ginsberg, "A Modest, Scrupulous, Happy Man," *New York Times Book Review,* 22 January 1995, pp. 3, 20–21;

Kay Bonetti, "An Interview with the Author," on *William Maxwell Reads "So Long, See You Tomorrow"* [recording] (Reed Publishing, 1997).

References:

Pearl K. Bell, "Book of Laughter and Remembering," review of *Billy Dyer and Other Stories, New Republic,* 206 (4 May 1992): 38–40;

Matthew J. Bruccoli, *The O'Hara Concern: A Biography of John O'Hara* (New York: Random House, 1975), pp. 261–262;

Bruccoli, ed., *The Selected Letters of John O'Hara* (New York: Random House, 1978);

Brendan Gill, *Here at the New Yorker* (New York: Random House, 1975), pp. 162–163, 278.

Wright Morris

(6 January 1910 – 25 April 1998)

Joseph J. Wydeven
Bellevue University

See also the Morris entries in *DLB 2: American Novelists Since World War II; DLB Yearbook 1981;* and *DLB 206: Twentieth-Century American Western Writers, First Series.*

BOOKS: *My Uncle Dudley* (New York: Harcourt, Brace, 1942);
The Man Who Was There (New York: Scribners, 1945);
The Inhabitants (New York & London: Scribners, 1946);
The Home Place (New York & London: Scribners, 1948);
The World in the Attic (New York: Scribners, 1949);
Man and Boy (New York: Knopf, 1951; London: Gollancz, 1952);
The Works of Love (New York: Knopf, 1952);
The Deep Sleep (New York: Scribners, 1953; London: Eyre & Spottiswoode, 1954);
The Huge Season (New York: Viking, 1954; London: Secker & Warburg, 1955);
The Field of Vision (New York: Harcourt, Brace, 1956; London: Weidenfeld & Nicolson, 1957);
Love Among the Cannibals (New York: Harcourt, Brace, 1957; London: Weidenfeld & Nicolson, 1958);
The Territory Ahead (New York: Harcourt, Brace, 1958);
Ceremony in Lone Tree (New York: Atheneum, 1960; London: Weidenfeld & Nicolson, 1961);
What a Way to Go (New York: Atheneum, 1962);
Cause for Wonder (New York: Atheneum, 1963);
One Day (New York: Atheneum, 1965);
In Orbit (New York: New American Library, 1967);
A Bill of Rites, A Bill of Wrongs, A Bill of Goods (New York: New American Library, 1968);
God's Country and My People (New York: Harper & Row, 1968);
Green Grass, Blue Sky, White House (Los Angeles: Black Sparrow, 1970);
Wright Morris: A Reader, edited by Granville Hicks (New York: Harper & Row, 1970);
Fire Sermon (New York: Harper & Row, 1971);
Love Affair: A Venetian Journal (New York: Harper & Row, 1972);
War Games (Los Angeles: Black Sparrow, 1972);
A Life (New York: Harper & Row, 1973);

Wright Morris (photograph from the dust jacket for A Life, *1973)*

Here Is Einbaum (Los Angeles: Black Sparrow, 1973);
About Fiction: Reverent Reflections on the Nature of Fiction with Irreverent Observations on Writers, Readers, and Other Abuses (New York: Harper & Row, 1975);
The Cat's Meow (Los Angeles: Black Sparrow, 1975);
Structures and Artifacts: Photographs, 1933–1954 (Lincoln: University of Nebraska Press, 1975);
Real Losses, Imaginary Gains (New York: Harper & Row, 1976);

The Fork River Space Project (New York: Harper & Row, 1977);
Earthly Delights, Unearthly Adornments: American Writers as Image-Makers (New York: Harper & Row, 1978);
Plains Song, for Female Voices (New York: Harper & Row, 1980);
Will's Boy: A Memoir (New York: Harper & Row, 1981);
Photographs & Words, edited by James Alinder (Carmel, Cal.: Friends of Photography, 1982);
Picture America, by Morris and Alinder (Boston: New York Graphic Society, 1982);
The Writing of My Uncle Dudley: *Remarks at the Opening of an Exhibition, "First Books by Notable Authors," at the Bancroft Library, February 21, 1982* (Berkeley, Cal.: Friends of the Bancroft Library, 1982);
Solo: An American Dreamer in Europe, 1933–1934 (New York: Harper & Row, 1983; Harmondsworth, U.K. & New York: Penguin, 1984);
Time Pieces: The Photographs and Words of Wright Morris (Washington, D.C.: Corcoran Gallery of Art, 1983);
A Cloak of Light: Writing My Life (New York: Harper & Row, 1985);
Collected Stories 1948–1986 (New York: Harper & Row, 1986);
Time Pieces: Photographs, Writing, and Memory (New York: Aperture, 1989).

Editions: *Writing My Life: An Autobiography* (Santa Rosa, Cal.: Black Sparrow, 1993)–comprises *Will's Boy, Solo: An American Dreamer in Europe, 1933–1934, A Cloak of Light;*
Three Easy Pieces (Santa Rosa, Cal.: Black Sparrow, 1993)–comprises *The Fork River Space Project, Fire Sermon, A Life;*
Two for the Road: Man and Boy and In Orbit (Santa Rosa, Cal.: Black Sparrow, 1994);
The Loneliness of the Long-Distance Writer: The Works of Love and The Huge Season (Santa Rosa, Cal.: Black Sparrow, 1995).

OTHER: "The Inhabitants," in *New Directions in Prose and Poetry 1940,* edited by James Laughlin (Norfolk, Conn.: New Directions, 1940), pp. 147–179;
"Where's Justice?" in *Cross Section 1948,* edited by Edwin Seaver (New York: Simon & Schuster, 1948), pp. 221–230;
The Mississippi River Reader, edited by Morris (Garden City, N.Y.: Doubleday/Anchor, 1962);
Richard Henry Dana, *Two Years Before the Mast,* afterword by Morris (New York: New American Library, 1964), pp. 376–383;
Mark Twain, *The Tragedy of Pudd'nhead Wilson,* foreword by Morris (New York: New American Library, 1964), pp. vii–xvii;
Sherwood Anderson, *Windy McPherson's Son,* introduction by Morris (Chicago: University of Chicago Press, 1965), pp. vii–xix;
"How Things Are," in *Arts and the Public,* edited by James E. Miller and Paul D. Herring (Chicago: University of Chicago Press, 1967), pp. 35–52, 230–253;
"*One Day:* November 22, 1963 – November 22, 1967," in *Afterwords: Novelists on Their Novels,* edited by Thomas McCormack (New York: Harper & Row, 1969), pp. 10–27;
"Being Conscious," in *Voicelust: Eight Contemporary Fiction Writers on Style,* edited by Allen Wier and Don Hendrie Jr. (Lincoln: University of Nebraska Press, 1985), pp. 23-36;
"How I Put in the Time," *Growing Up Western: Recollections,* edited by Clarus Backes (New York: Knopf, 1990), pp. 99–124.

SELECTED PERIODICAL PUBLICATIONS–UNCOLLECTED: "Privacy as a Subject for Photography," *Magazine of Art,* 44 (February 1951): 51–55;
"The Character of the Lover," *American Mercury,* 73 (August 1951): 43–49;
"The Cars in My Life," *Holiday,* 24 (December 1958): 45-53;
"Henry James's *The American Scene,*" *Texas Quarterly,* 1 (Summer–Autumn 1959): 27–42;
"Nature Since Darwin," *Esquire,* 52 (November 1959): 64–70;
"The Open Road," *Esquire,* 52 (June 1960): 98–99;
"Made in U.S.A.," *American Scholar,* 29 (Autumn 1960): 483–494;
"Conversations in a Small Town," *Holiday,* 30 (November 1961): 98–108;
"Man on the Moon," *Partisan Review,* 29 (Spring 1962): 241–249;
"Letter to a Young Critic," *Massachusetts Review,* 6 (Autumn–Winter 1964–1965): 93–100;
"The Lunatic, the Lover, and the Poet," *Kenyon Review,* 27 (Autumn 1965): 727–737;
"The Origin of a Species, 1942–1957," *Massachusetts Review,* 7 (Winter 1966): 121–135;
"How I Met Joseph Mulligan, Jr.," *Harper's* (February 1970): 82–85;
"Babe Ruth's Pocket," *Ford Times* (September 1972): 50–55;
"Trick or Treat," *Quarterly Review of Literature,* 18 (1973): 368–378;
"Uno Más," *New Yorker,* 64 (6 February 1989): 28–31;
"What's New, Love?" *American Short Fiction,* 1 (Fall 1991): 98–105.

Best known as a novelist and photographer, Wright Morris published fewer than forty short stories in his half-century career. Yet, from the start of his artistic life, Morris experimented with short fiction in a variety of ways, and when his strengths as a novelist gave way in the early 1980s, he wrote first-rate stories, some of which were included in *The Best American Short Stories* and *O. Henry Award* anthologies. His work as a photographer had an enormous impact on his fiction, making for an emphatically visual style and a subtle version of literary minimalism. Morris's best short stories require close attention from readers because of their frequent compilation of cumulative effects, narrative elusiveness, and occasional indeterminacy, all supporting Morris's view that human beings are complex and their experiences mysterious. Although there continues to be good criticism written on Morris's novels, photographs, and photo-texts, little commentary has been produced on his short stories.

Wright Marion Morris was born in Central City, Nebraska, on 6 January 1910. That his mother, Ethel Osborn Morris, died within a week of his birth is crucial, for part of the cornerstone of his works is his need to fill the void she left behind, one his father, William Henry Morris, could not occupy because of his frequent leaves of absence from his son's life. Nevertheless, Morris's childhood was richly filled with experiences he later called "raw material," to be mined and shaped by memory and imagination. Morris spent much of his adolescence in Omaha and Chicago before attending Pomona College in Claremont, California, from 1930 to 1933. He left Pomona without graduating in order to travel to Europe in what he called his *Wanderjahr,* spending a long winter in 1933–1934 in an Austrian castle, then cycling in Italy, and finally making his way to Paris.

On his return to the United States in 1934 Morris married Mary Ellen Finfrock–the couple divorced in 1961–and began the experiments with photography and prose that culminated in his photo-texts. His developing interest in photography was expressed both by his haunting images and by his purchase of bigger and more sophisticated cameras. Between 1935 and 1940 Morris also wrote drafts to several autobiographical novels, but he did not publish until 1940. With ambitious plans, in 1940–1941 he traveled solo around the United States on what he called his "photo-safari," intending a series of volumes of photo-texts about American folkways and regional "structures and artifacts."

At the end of the trip Morris completed his first novel, *My Uncle Dudley* (1942). The book was the first of some twenty novels, the best of which are set at least partially in Nebraska: *The Home Place* (1948), *The Works of Love* (1952), *The Field of Vision* (1956), *Ceremony in Lone Tree* (1960), and *Plains Song, for Female Voices* (1980). Other important novels are *The Deep Sleep* (1953), an examination of the 1950s American family; *The Huge Season* (1954), a contrast of the 1920s with the repressiveness of the 1950s, represented by Sen. Joseph McCarthy; and his paired short novels, *Fire Sermon* (1971) and *A Life* (1973), which deal with an octogenarian curmudgeon, Floyd Warner.

Believing his powers had diminished, Morris chose to stop writing in the early 1990s, but not until after he had put his career in order in the preceding decade, writing three volumes of memoirs–*Will's Boy* (1981) is a classic–and collecting his photographs in the superb *Photographs & Words* (1982), his critical essays on photography in the important *Time Pieces: Photographs, Writing, and Memory* (1989), and his short stories. He was eighty-eight years old when he died in Mill Valley, California, on 25 April 1998. He was survived by his wife, Josephine Kantor Morris, whom he had married in 1961. Morris had a long and productive life, one spanning most of the twentieth century. He was awarded Guggenheim Fellowships in 1942, 1946, and 1954, as well as a host of other awards, including the National Book Award for *The Field of Vision* and the American Book Award for *Plains Song, for Female Voices.* He has also been the recipient of a considerable amount of critical inquiry, while winning a following of dedicated readers responsive to his artistic concerns.

Morris published only four collections of short stories in his lifetime: *Green Grass, Blue Sky, White House* (1970), *Here Is Einbaum* (1973), *Real Losses, Imaginary Gains* (1976), and *Collected Stories 1948–1986* (1986). *Collected Stories* reprints all of the stories appearing in the first two volumes and all but one story in the third–the exception is the 1952 "The Rites of Spring." Most important, the final volume includes fourteen stories that had not been collected before, eleven of which had been written and published since 1980. These new stories are among Morris's finest, for many of them deal poignantly with the experience of old age and loneliness from the perspective of long experience; furthermore, as Morris knew his time was limited, he lavished on these stories, with bittersweet humor, all his powers of language. These final works appear to be a carefully orchestrated farewell both to his life and to his craft.

One of the peculiarities of Morris's career as a writer is its beginnings in his apparent indecision over whether to pursue photography or writing as his major effort. During his *Wanderjahr,* as reported in his second memoir, *Solo: An American Dreamer in Europe, 1933–1934* (1983), Morris purchased a camera and began taking pictures. On his return to the United States he began a series of word sketches to accompany some of these

A photo-text from Morris's The Inhabitants *(1946), a collection of experimental works that combine short narratives and photographs taken by the author*

photographs. As Morris described, these sketches are best characterized by "an economy that occasionally defied comprehension" and rely on implication and inference in relation to the accompanying photographs. Some of these photo-text experiments were published, as "The Inhabitants," in *New Directions in Prose and Poetry 1940* and exhibited at the New School for Social Research in New York. Morris's continued interest in this genre is evidenced by his four book-length photo-texts: *The Inhabitants* (1946), *The Home Place, God's Country and My People* (1968), and *Love Affair: A Venetian Journal* (1972).

In *The Inhabitants,* a book responsive to Henry David Thoreau's idea that buildings organically express the lives of those inhabiting them, Morris includes a running commentary to Thoreau and a word text on the page facing each photograph. The texts exist almost palpably on the verge of narrative, in some way similar to the extended expositions Morris often employs later in his novels and short stories. One text, juxtaposed with a photograph of a worn church and house in Virginia City, Nevada, reads as follows:

> I've come to see the land is here for spreadin' me on. Never been in Ox Bow or Wahoo, never been in Wagon Mound or Steamboat Springs, but I can tell you I'm there–there's part of me there right now. Never owned a house or a piece of land, never owned a woman, no kid is mine–but maybe I'd rather make talk like this than a family. Like when I tell you, though I don't own it, the land is mine. And if you ask me what kind of land that is, I'll tell you that too. Mister, the land is that part of me I can't leave behind. When I hear the name Corn Hill I see it, or the name Bowling Green, Tombstone, or Lone Tree–and when I hear it I see myself waitin' there for me. Hellsfire, Mister, there was a time all I thought a man did was unravel–now I see that all he does is wind himself up. Where I've been is somethin' but it's nothin' beside where I've yet to go.

Some twenty years later, in *God's Country and My People,* Morris used the same photograph, with a different text, once more attuned to autobiography–including his creation of characters who seem to have achieved lives beyond the texts:

> Some of these places prove to be real with people in them who answer their mail: some prove to be sur-real and answer only to God. Others, like Scanlon and Boyd, seem to be part of an expanding fiction; they answer only to the man who conjures them up. The landscape they inhabit is a windy ruin of ghosts. . . . Bells clatter in empty belfries, shades stand immaterial at paneless windows, or bulge the screens of unhinged doorways, as if these places, known to be dead, had returned to life. . . . Where Scanlon's wife stands at the window a fly is trapped between the pane and the blind. She can see its shadow crawling. Perhaps she is waiting for it to buzz. The green blind, stitched with seams of light, sucks inward as a train roars past and the dangling cord leaves a chicken-like track in the dust on the sill.

These texts are remarkable both for the images they call up and for the associations they bring with such ease to the reader's mind. The texts are often fiercely visual on their own, and, interestingly, while motion is described in words, the photographs take on the detailed characteristics of still lifes. The preceding narrative employs metafictional awareness, with Morris both inside the experience and clearly commenting on the production of narrative. In "The Inhabitants" Morris writes that these expositional texts and the photographs they accompany are to be understood by the reader-viewer through a mental operation he cryptically–and without further explanation–calls a "third view."

After Morris gave up photography in the early 1950s, his prose continued to have this visual quality, so that sometimes, as in *The Works of Love* and *Plains Song, for Female Voices,* the narrative texts are reminiscent of photographic sequences. Particularly in Morris's later stories, those produced in the 1970s and 1980s when he transferred some of his skills as a novelist to the short-story form, his prose is sometimes remarkably dense, the narrative long on exposition and short on action. Hiram Haydn, in his *Words and Faces* (1974), might have been referring to these stories with his humorous observation that Morris is "a man who is terrified, beyond all else, of the possibility of being obvious." As Morris wrote in *About Fiction: Reverent Reflections on the Nature of Fiction with Irreverent Observations on Writers, Readers, and Other Abuses* (1975), "The reader's pleasure is often in proportion to what is left unsaid, or ambiguously hinted. To read such fiction well is to grasp some of the skills involved in its creation. As in music, the writer calls for this response, playing on the sensibility of the reader." (It may be telling that one of Morris's dedications in *Collected Stories* is "To the music of / ANTONIO VIVALDI / *Late acquaintance / Constant companion.*")

Morris's complex prose sometimes offers expansive accumulations of observed details and actions, most of which are intended to intensify complexity of character and provide depth to human experience ordinarily considered mundane. This detailed practice sometimes serves to showcase his humorous observations of daily life–as in "Fellow Creatures" (1984), a late story involving a comic accumulation of examples showing how Colonel Huggins, "U.S. Army, retired," comes to consider human duplicity toward animals. Huggins observes that people who love their pets are nevertheless capable of nonchalantly eating fryers, chicken-fried rabbit, roast spring lamb–even *filet de cheval américain.* One day Huggins turns away in rejection from the spare ribs he has been cooking and begins to experience kinship with a variety of animals, leading ultimately to a kind of mystical communion with them. He reconstitutes his diet, questions the ubiquitous disappearance of pets, and comes to understand that grackles and pullets have their own languages and that a cow's face "was like a piece of the landscape seen in closeup."

Some of Morris's accumulating details, however, function subtly as narrative clues. Similar to camera shifts that frame fresh perspectives, Morris's descriptive words have an additive effect: the reader's comprehension of situation and character is subtly modified in the process of reading down the page. Readers are encouraged to respond inductively, sometimes to confront sentences so densely packed and juxtaposed they appear to be non sequiturs. This style, based on modification of detailed meaning, makes reading strenuous for readers, who sometimes find Morris's world as difficult to pin down as the less controlled one outside their windows.

This characteristic method is seen, for example, in "Green Grass, Blue Sky, White House" (1969), in which Morris withholds the exact nature of the relationship between the absent Floyd Collins and the narrator until the final page, when it is revealed that the narrator is Floyd's lawyer. Floyd, it turns out, is in jail for writing a letter to the president of the United States threatening the president's life if he does not end the Vietnam War: better one man should die than "tens of thousands of innocent men, women, and children." The story is obviously not plotted in the typical manner, and as readers never meet Floyd, the work is rather a study of the family and neighborhood culture that Morris perhaps means to suggest are constituent parts of Floyd's makeup. Delicately, and without a trace of judgment, the lawyer describes the environment as if in search of hints to the causes of Floyd's hapless and misplaced idealism.

In Ordway, Missouri, the setting of the story, typical American life is carried on: the generations change with time, and classes and races live side by side. Decent social values are found in Floyd's mother's Quakerism and a neighbor's decision to enter the Peace Corps. "Everything," the lawyer says, "is here to make the good life possible." Ultimately, the story provides at once a portrait of a town, motivational support for Floyd's audacious letter, and a picture of the consciousness of the recording lawyer. Readers sense the lawyer's approval that people in Ordway do not lock their doors and that during his stay with the Collins family certain household members continue to use his bedroom as a shortcut. He occasionally compares events and customs in Ordway to those occurring in his own past. His defense of Floyd, based on his observations, will be not only competent but also understandingly compassionate: "What is a little violence," he imagines the town thinking, "in the larger ceremony of innocence" everywhere around them?

The story is shored up symbolically through the lawyer's observation when contemplating the tree roots obstructing the house's sewer system: the sentiment behind "what a root will do in its search for water defies belief" concisely parallels Floyd's audacious political act whereby he finds essential purpose by threatening the president. The Collinses' white house set in its green grass (under blue sky) connects and contrasts with the White House addressed in Floyd's letter. Through these subtle uses of language, Morris engages readers, encouraging them to extract meanings from their own passing experiences, much as the lawyer is observed doing.

"Green Grass, Blue Sky, White House" can hardly be considered a political story. Its message is social, but Morris's purpose is less to persuade others as to appropriate social positions than to suggest the density of experience in which social actions are embedded. He moves his readers through the strength of detailed observations, a method paradoxically encouraging compassion. This quality occurs as well in "Here Is Einbaum" (1971), a story in which Morris employs descriptions of the "openly tainted" Jew, Einbaum, in terms of snapshots taken from his life in World War II Europe. These "snapshots" show Einbaum's conflicting allegiances to his Jewish heritage and his German nationalism; his exploitation by Sophia Horvath, a "secretly tainted" Jewess who is murdered in Spain for her jewelry; and his eventual arrival in New York City, apparently spared almost as a result of his essential innocence.

Morris's frequently extended travels and long stays in Europe and Mexico appear to have given him healthy attitudes toward race and diversity: his work is totally free of negative racial attitudes. Moreover, he is capable of drawing finely wrought portraits of ethnic people, and his work is sprinkled with transplanted and displaced Europeans and Mexicans living in America. On the other hand, when he does incorporate problematic ethnic characters into his work, Morris does not rely on liberal platitudes to soften his material, as indicated by his portraits of "Protest" Jackson in *One Day* and George Blackbird in *A Life*. Morris is decidedly not a social writer, however; his interests and convictions lead him to the hidden interiors of lives.

On the question of race and race relations in the United States, Morris is subtle. An early story, "Where's Justice?" (1948), based on Morris's chance visit in 1940 to a friend of William Faulkner, the lawyer Phil Stone, deals with exchanges among a Northerner, Cape; his Southern host, Carter Hickman; and Hickman's black servants. The story plays on the irony of Hickman's criticism of "you people" (apparently Northern liberals) for supporting Franklin Delano Roosevelt's New Deal instead of dealing with "the true problems of the governing of men"–while it is made clear that Hickman's servants both manage his household and control him. The servants almost openly mock their employer and are barely willing to serve him; a black woman, for example, through years of cleaning Hickman's silver goblets has twisted their stems until they are no longer of practical use. Morris revisited this story thirty-six years later as "Going into Exile" (1984), employing the same central events, although with greater sophistication and the inclusion of Northern annoyance and guilt.

Race is also at the apparent center of "A Fight Between a White Boy and a Black Boy in the Dusk of a Fall Afternoon in Omaha, Nebraska" (1970), but the real focus of the story is the narrator's act of remembering the fight long after the event, while he drives through Omaha with his wife asleep beside him: the point is that memory keeps alive what is long gone and can never be conveyed in detail except through deliberate imaginative acts of remembering. Morris made clear his personal social views regarding race in America in the epilogue to *A Bill of Rites, A Bill of Wrongs, A Bill of Goods* (1968): "It is not the intent of the white American to destroy the black American, but that is what he is doing"–primarily by supplying funds for the purchase of things, not a better life. "We are preparing for the fire next time by preparing for fires. . . . and nothing has changed." Such a social position is never stated so blatantly in his fiction, however.

Many of Morris's stories are really finger exercises for his novels, opportunities for him to practice the themes and ideas from longer works. A series of works, for example, were derived from drafts and versions of

The Works of Love, the laconic and ironically compassionate novel based loosely on his father, over which Morris labored for seven years, from approximately 1945 to 1952. "The Lover" (1949) deals with the young Will Brady's offer of marriage to the prostitute Opal Mason, her mocking rejection of him, and his subsequent rebound offer to a pregnant teenager, Mickey Ahearn. "A Man of Caliber" (1949) concerns Brady's relations with T. P. Luckett, the man who runs the Union Pacific commissary and who gives Brady an exaggerated sense of worth in order to persuade him to become an entrepreneur in the chicken business, a role for which Brady is ill prepared. "Lover, Is That You?," published in 1966 but seemingly written much earlier, details Brady's search for a proper mother to bring up his son, Willy: the story is largely an accumulation of interviews with obviously incompetent, pathetic women. The events in that story are continued, although from a different point of view, in a story called "Magic" (1970), in which "Mr. Brady" appears as a "lover" stricken with amnesia.

The period from 1945 to 1960 was extremely productive in Morris's development, during which he was richly remembering and reinventing his adolescence and making applications to mature experience. The events transpiring in Morris's prolonged visit to his uncle Dwight Osborn in Texas were fictionalized in "The Rites of Spring" (1952) as well as in *Man and Boy* (1951), with Violet Ames Ormsby more or less acting as fictional counterpart for Morris, and *The Field of Vision,* in which Walter McKee is given that role. Some of the events in "The Safe Place" (1954) were carried over into Colonel Foss's odd adventures in *War Games* (written in the early 1950s but unpublished until 1972) and later fragmented in *The Field of Vision* and *Ceremony in Lone Tree.* Similarly, "Wake Before Bomb" (1959) recounts an encounter that the protagonist of *The Field of Vision,* Gordon Boyd, has with the atomic bomb mentality in Las Vegas as he makes his way to Nebraska from Mexico, and "The Scene" (1960) served as the basis for the perfected opening panorama in *Ceremony in Lone Tree.*

The best example of a Morris story later incorporated into a novel is "The Ram in the Thicket" (1948), the first–and longest–of his stories to be published and the best known. It has frequently been anthologized as a set piece about the American family in the years following World War II and is clearly related to Philip Wylie's examination, in his *Generation of Vipers* (1942), of "Momism," a kind of American disease causing gross sentimentality in those it afflicts. The story is basically the first half of *Man and Boy,* Morris's first major exploration of the war between the sexes, a topic he returned to with greater authority in *The Deep Sleep.*

"The Ram in the Thicket" focuses on the relationship between Roger and Violet Ames Ormsby on the morning they are about to leave for New York, where Mother–as Roger calls his wife–is to christen a ship, the *Ormsby,* named after their son, Virgil, who was killed in action. In the story Mother holds Roger accountable for the boy's death, for he bought Virgil a BB gun and thus introduced him to the male violence she associates with hunting and war: Virgil took to the intimacy of hunting birds, which Mother knows only by their Latin names. She is depicted as controlling, reducing her daily life to formulas and slogans and preserving her house by covering the floors and chairs with newspapers while the leftovers she stores in the refrigerator grow mold and threaten to explode.

Morris hints that Mother's desire to control makes her ultimately responsible for Virgil's death, as she had made life inside the house unbearable: Roger escaped into work and the basement, Virgil into the outdoors. Virgil seemed to have some prescient knowledge of his mother's character, for as a baby he had "refused, plain refused, to nurse with Mother."

The title refers to the biblical story of Isaac and Abraham; in the story Virgil is sacrificed on Mother's metaphorical altar. That Ormsby, despite his ineffectuality, loves his son is apparent from the beginning, when he dreams that Virgil has the head of a bird, wears "bright, exotic plumage," and holds his hand, like St. Francis, to other birds hovering in the air. At one point Mother coolly points out to Ormsby that his name is on the ship, and although "the U.S.S. *Ormsby* was a permanent sort of thing," it is made possible only through his loss of their son, which Roger had experienced even while Virgil was still alive.

In her anthology, *Images of Women in Literature* (1973), Ferguson includes "The Ram in the Thicket" as a "dominating wife: the bitch" story, while Robert Benard includes the story in his collection of *war* stories, *A Short Wait Between Trains* (1991), and Knox Burger, in the introduction to that anthology, calls it "a home-front story." The war, that is, appears to have been carried into the American home, its destructions imbedded in debilitating relationships between men and women. The story suggests that the Orsmbys' circumstance is not an isolated instance, that there are more rams in the thickets of American marital and family relationships.

Another theme found frequently in Morris's stories, especially in the 1950s, is that of transformation, based on an imaginative use of Darwinian evolution, as found in *The Field of Vision* and *Love Among the Cannibals* (1957). Perhaps the most memorable of these stories is "Drrdla," based on the sound made by a creature found in the recesses of Walter Fechner's basement. Walter becomes so fascinated with the challenge of bringing

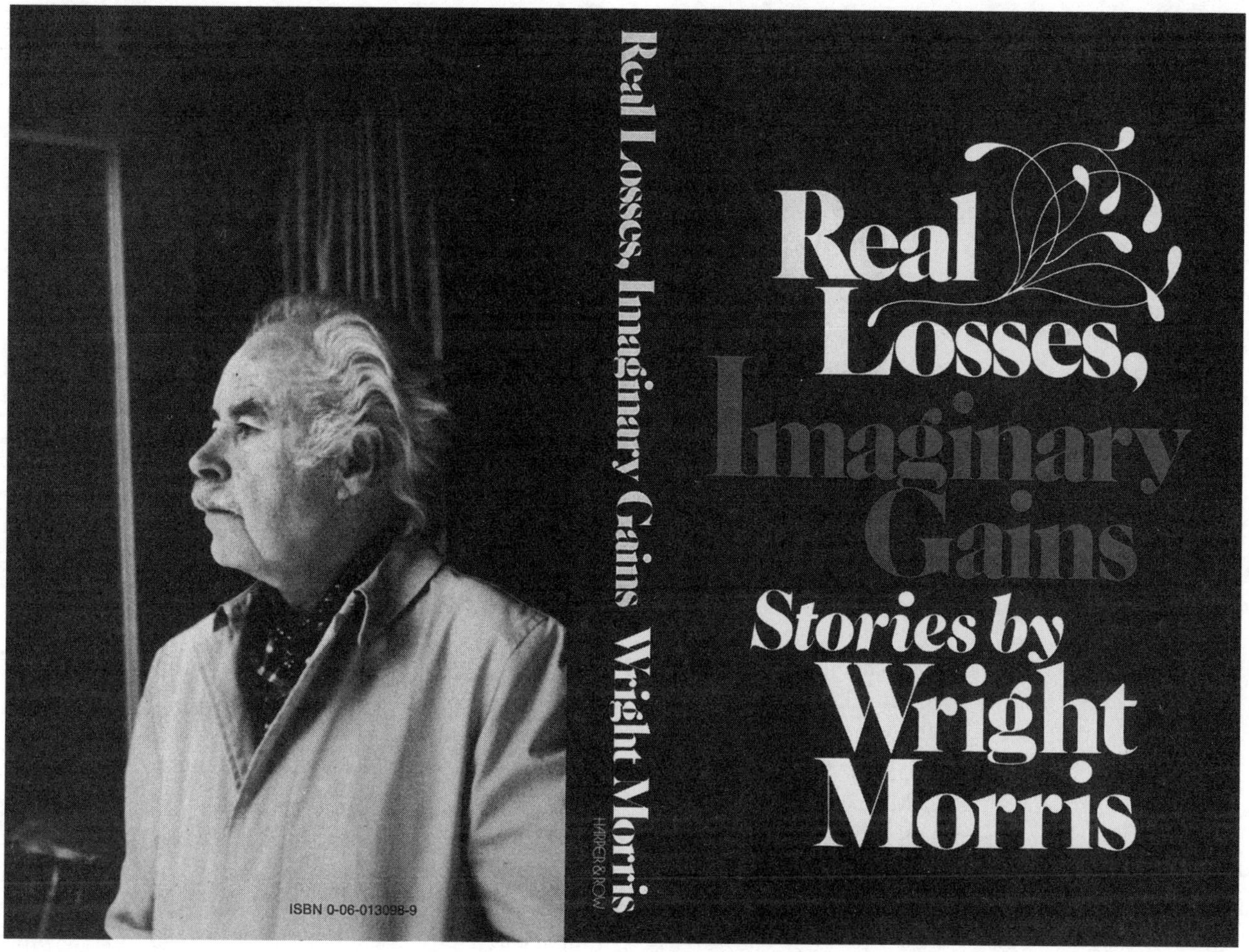

Dust jacket for Morris's 1976 book, a collection of autobiographical short stories

what turns out to be a cat back to health that he begins to spend the majority of his time with her. Walter's wife, Hanna, is understandably ironic about this situation (she frequently inquires about Walter's "rodent"), and both she and Walter's friend Lewin are disturbed by "Walter and Drrdla, against the unknown," strikingly like "lovers otherwise speechless with emotion." In the end, however, Drrdla surprisingly gravitates to Hanna and starts to sleep with her in the bed Walter has abandoned; shortly afterward, Lewin enters Hanna's bed as well. In a deliberately ambiguous ending, the narrator remarks that if Walter had not pursued his reach into the darkness, "neither Walter nor Lewin would have on his hands a female creature awakened to life." (The idea of transformation is intriguingly revisited in "Fiona," where the title character more or less blocks human "development" by relying on homespun cryogenics to keep her husband "alive" until future science finds a means to revive him; meanwhile, she considers any effort to thaw his body a form of attempted murder.)

Cats in Morris are generally, and oddly, connected to the nature of changing affections in marital relationships. In the grotesque "The Cat in the Picture" (1958), perhaps indebted partially to Poe, the pictured animal is a large black cat, and as in "Drrdla," the cat displaces the protagonist, the Captain, in his wife's bed. The Captain, having taken up painting since his retirement, discovers he can keep the cat on edge by throwing tubes of paint on the floor; when the cat finally sinks its teeth into one of the tubes and is poisoned, his wife hurries the cat to a veterinarian, while the Captain moves to a nearby hotel. His wife sends his personal belongings to him–and in the suitcase he finds the cat, leading him to wonder "if the cat had died while eating the paint, or if he had been stuffed into the bag with his shirts while still alive."

In "The Cat's Meow" (1975) the relationships prevailing among Morgan and Charlotte and their respective cats, Bloom and Pussy-baby, are less outrageously explored. The story concludes with renewed "alliances" and Morgan's mild recognition that "in the nature of things he could see no reason why one creature, in union with another, through affliction and affection, in sickness and in health, should not dispense with the obvious." The story seems to suggest that through their cats Morgan and Charlotte renew their understandings of human responsibility. Given certain hints and connections to comments Morris makes in his memoirs, it is difficult to resist the temptation to read these stories as having coded relations to his personal life.

Morris insists that he remembered belatedly and enhanced memory with the aid of imagination; nevertheless, some of his stories are hardly stories but character sketches from Morris's life. In "Real Losses, Imaginary Gains" and "How I Met Joseph Mulligan Jr.," for example, the narrator is identifiably Morris himself, recounting experiences found also in his memoirs as well as transferred into such novels as *The Works of Love* and *One Day*. This problem of genre identification is one of the most intriguing characteristics of Morris's career, for it recurs continually, although it is doubtful Morris was pursuing complexity with the same intentions as his postmodernist contemporaries.

Not surprisingly, given Morris's fragile relationship with his frequently absent father and the importance he always placed on his dead mother, his best stories are those that deal with the tenuous, fragile nature of human relationships, sometimes attempting to bridge the gap between people with extremely subtle gestures or moments of ironic compassion. Morris deals with a variety of themes in his work, but his most memorable and powerful stories may best be described as poignant, stories in which profound emotional experience is at the center. Because Morris was both suspicious of–and subject to–sentimentality, he used irony with a vengeance, so as not, one may sometimes suspect, to be caught with tears in his eyes. (Morris felt later that he had allowed himself too much sentimentality in *The Works of Love*.) It is interesting to see how often, especially in the later stories, Morris recounts situations in which characters disguise their tears, even from themselves.

A key element in many stories is the theme of love and love lost or displaced, ironized, grown stale, turned futile. There is often something in men and women, Morris suggests, that love baffles and confuses. A character in "Country Music" (1985), for example, asks: "What was the matter with people? Offered love, why would they turn away from it?" Morris often pities the lovers in his fiction. In *The Works of Love* Will Brady hears a voice from "out of the sky" tell him there are "no lovers in heaven": "There's no need for great lovers in heaven. Pity is the great lover, and the great lovers are all on earth."

Other stories about the intricacies of love are "The Lover" and "Lover, Is That You?," associated with *The Works of Love;* "The Character of the Lover" (1951), indebted to Morris's fascination with F. Scott Fitzgerald; and "The Lover and the Beloved" (1981), in which Paul, an "older companion" to fourteen-year-old Lois (who is in transformation into adulthood), finds her sneaking a cigarette and concludes, "for the pity he now felt for lovers, especially himself, he was grateful."

As in his novels, Morris's compassion is often disguised, especially when he deals with the connection between mortality and time and the theme of old age. Morris dealt with aged characters throughout his career, and time and memory are major themes in both his novels and his photographs, as well as central to many of the stories found in *Collected Stories 1948–1986*. Eleven of the twenty-six stories in that volume were first published in the 1980s, many in *The New Yorker,* when Morris was putting his career in order and making a bid for posterity–as well as approaching old age. Consequently, many of those stories reflect on time and the processes of memory.

One story in which the effects of time is a major theme is "To Calabria" (1984), in which Morgan is led to remember a half-century before, when he had abandoned his friend Hal on a bicycle tour along the Italian coast in order to "spend April in Paris." The story incorporates his friend's bicycle mileage meter, which Morgan is given after Hal's strange disappearance. When Morgan twists the meter to advance or reverse the mileage on the dial, he imagines the action gives him the physical power to move once again toward Calabria, as if he can erase the intervening years. When in the present he walks past the fire station near his home, a fine mist of spray from the firemen's hoses takes him back to the moment when he had left Hal, ocean spray covering his glasses, making him look as if he were weeping. That poignant moment highlights Morgan's withdrawal from real life into memory, as he belatedly regrets the loss of his friend and mourns the ravages of time.

Another story about time and human sorrow, "The Origin of Sadness" (1984), concludes *Collected Stories;* as it is the only story in the book that departs from chronological arrangement by publication date, it may be seen as anchoring the book thematically, aptly signifying Morris's symbolic means of coming to terms with death. The protagonist is based on Morris's friend Loren Eiseley, who died in 1977. Like Eiseley, Schuler is an anthropologist who has come to doubt Charles Darwin's version of evolution and who accepts as axiomatic that sadness is an inevitable companion to consciousness. When his wife dies unexpectedly and his aged mother fails to recognize him, Schuler decides "to slip time's noose."

What Schuler experiences is a form of homelessness, which Morris expresses symbolically by having Schuler drive in the darkness, coming upon a house being moved along the road. At one of the windows a cat's eyes glitter, making Schuler think of "visitations" from beyond: "A voice speaking from on high would not have surprised him. In the winter sky the stars were dazzling, and on the balls of his eyes he could feel the prickling rain of light"–that is, he feels an oceanic sadness associated with mortality. The story ends with Schuler waiting for death, having "accidentally" fallen into one of the Kansas arroyos near his childhood home; "under the covering of snow, he found the familiar fossil fragments" that connect him to both his own past and the geological record.

Morris's ability to plumb the depths of sadness without collapsing into excessive emotion is found in several stories focused on old age or loneliness. "The Customs of the Country" deals with the case of Hapke, a peace-loving old man who came to America from Switzerland and works as a gardener at a school. He has been happy there over the years, but recently the school has expanded so that it serves older as well as the younger children Hapke enjoys. He now has to learn to deal with older boys whose destructive habits baffle and anger him. When he complains of their behavior, the boys apparently retaliate by destroying one of his carefully tended shrubs. Hapke's contentment in life is shattered.

One day he observes one of the older boys accost a younger child, drowning her in the creek near the playground. He is unable to save her. At the trial Hapke is accused by the "prankish" boy's father of failing to intervene, further destroying the old man's peace of mind and causing him to withdraw. In this frame of mind, one day Hapke leaves the playground accompanied by a small boy; finding himself "part of the boy's deep brooding," he experiences "a tremor of fear." The boy comes up to him, however, and puts "his small, soft hand into Hapke's big rough one. For a moment he held it like an injured bird." In neglecting to identify the antecedent to *he,* Morris ambiguously allows the suggestion that the "injury" is felt by both young and old participant. The story concludes with Hapke's renewed empathy: he forgives it when "the boy's free hand absently plucked the leaves and twigs from the bushes they were passing . . . as if it helped him with his thinking, as Hapke was sure that it did."

The story "Victrola" involves a bond between an old man, Bundy, and his dog, named after the RCA phonograph, the potential for pathos deflected by irony and humor. Man and dog have a "close relationship," but it is in fact begrudged: they are close simply because they have grown old together and have come to rely upon each other. At any rate, Bundy has come to see himself as a "human parallel" to the dog. One day (during Whole Grains Cereal Week, Morris characteristically writes), Bundy walks the dog to the market and ties it to a bicycle rack. While Bundy is in the store, the dog is attacked by other dogs and dies, apparently from fright. When Bundy finds Victrola dead, Morris informs readers that recently Bundy's "eyes had filmed over" during the television broadcast of the royal wedding of Prince Charles and Princess Diana. The story is framed by the command to "Sit!": in the beginning Bundy tells the already sitting dog to sit; in the conclusion someone tells Bundy to sit. Bundy, however, finds that he cannot: his knees will not bend. That he dwells at all on his loss is reflected indirectly in his focus on a revolving police car beacon, then on a chaperone helping "one of those women who buy two frozen dinners and then go off with the shopping cart and leave it somewhere."

Another story in this vein–perhaps Morris's finest story–is "Glimpse into Another Country" (1983), in which "another country" means old age, death, and the vanity of desires for immortality. The protagonist is an old man named Hazlitt, who journeys from San Francisco to New York in quest of "life assurance" from a medical specialist, apparently to get a second opinion on a diagnosis that Morris does not disclose. The story recounts Hazlitt's adventures in New York, many of which occur while his consciousness is altered, suggesting both their unreality and their occurring in "another country" of experience. Throughout much of the story he is deprived of the use of his Visa card, another symbolic device, intended to enhance Hazlitt's "obscure elation" because he now carries "no positive identification."

First on the plane and then several times in the city, Hazlitt encounters an eccentric woman, Mrs. Thayer, who plays a role in helping him come to terms with his new identity. Much of his time in New York, he thinks of his wife: he buys her a purse, then considers buying her a bracelet, and at night he faithfully reports in to her by telephone from the hotel. Hazlitt gets a reprieve from the specialist; when he leaves the doctor's office, he feels "free of a nameless burden." At Bloomingdale's he purchases for his wife a strand of pearls; its cost "astounded but did not shock him." Hazlitt walks to the Metropolitan Museum of Art, recalling his past visits there with his wife, but in the museum lavatory he is accosted by several small boys who rob him of the pearls. Before he leaves the museum, he buys a pin "of

Dust jacket for Morris's 1986 book, which brings together his first three collections of short fiction and fourteen previously uncollected stories

Etruscan design, that he felt his wife would consider a sensible value."

Outside he pauses beside a bus and sees one of the riders inside tapping at the window. It is the woman from the plane yet again, and although Hazlitt can see her face only dimly, he thinks she is signaling him. Although "what appeared to be tears might have been drops of water" on the window, her eyes are "mild, and gave him all the assurance he needed." As he watches, the bus carries her away.

The story of Hazlitt's mythic journey concludes with almost nothing certain, and the reader is left with a cluster of broad and potentially archetypal allusions in which the title plays a significant but indeterminate role. One interpretation suggests that the story details an elaborate rite of passage into new experience and final understanding of the vanity of human wishes for immortality. In this archetypal drama the ubiquitous Mrs. Thayer appears to serve as a symbolic witness-guide, deliberately tinged with erotic attraction to Hazlitt. The teeming crowds inserted several times into the story suggest the vigorous transactions of human life, of which Hazlitt may soon be deprived by death. When confronted by the boys, Hazlitt is "pleased . . . to have their close attention," suggesting the scene has an important ritualistic function. The whole scene is highlighted by water–the lavatory floor is flooded from an overflowing bowl–and sea imagery: the pearls delivered to one boy's "coral palm" look "as if just fished from the deep." The boys who grapple for the pearls are "slippery as eels," and their companions have the appearance of a "writhing, many-limbed monster."

The occurrence of this ritual in water suggests a mythic rebirth, perhaps into another phase of life in which old age and its consequences are palatable. That the costly pearls are so easily replaced by an inexpensive pin suggests their function as a symbol of male vanity, one Hazlitt must surrender if he is to successfully make his way into the next stage. In the end he achieves the ability to relinquish his hold on life, to surrender his place among the flowing human crowds. Stripped of final vanities, Hazlitt gains the assurance that his continued existence ceremonially reaffirms the human condition and allows him to accept the inevitable, now freed of futile desire.

Morris's last two published short stories, "Uno Más" (1989) and "What's New, Love?" (1991), both too late to be included in *Collected Stories,* are together excellent examples of Morris's characteristic method and indirectly compassionate attitude toward ordinary, not particularly gifted human beings caught up by fate. Both stories observe the lives of women, leading readers to draw their own conclusions and make their own ultimate judgments. This attitude, it might be argued, may be drawn from Morris's thinking about photography: as photographs typically picture events without explicit commentary, so also frequently with Morris's prose, which reserves judgment but which is nonetheless capable of pointed suggestion.

"Uno Más" is a finely observed portrait of Maria, born near Oaxaca in Mexico but transplanted to California, where she works as a live-in servant-cook-babysitter for the middle-class Drysdales. The title comes from one of the Drysdale children's love for the phrase "uno más" (one more) in relation to Maria–symbolically indicating that he cannot get enough of what Maria offers him–which bothers the pregnant Mrs. Drysdale because her child's speaking Spanish touches on her latent xenophobia and exacerbates her fear that Maria is insufficiently hygienic. The story works through brief contrasts of Maria's life in the Drysdale house with the life she gladly escaped in Mexico, followed by an accumulation of detailed experiences indicating the qualities–and problems regarding squeamishness–Maria has brought to these California lives.

After a typically lengthy exposition, Mrs. Drysdale's solution is laid out: in order to remove Maria's influence over the children, Maria is sent to work elsewhere. Peanuts, the Drysdales' son, objects, however, and it is already obvious that Maria must be returned if there is to be peace in the household. Mr. Drysdale immediately makes another trip to reclaim Maria, driving her back in guilty silence. With Maria reinstated in the Drysdale household, the phrase "uno más" is once again heard ringing through the house. Through all of this, Maria is passive, her face a "mask" as, seemingly powerless, she plays out her apparent destiny. Yet, Morris plants a subtle clue that Maria is not simply a victim of chance or power, that she had so strongly decided never to return to Mexican poverty that she had made herself indispensable in the only way she knew, by serving well and keeping her own quiet counsel.

Morris's final story, "What's New, Love?," is also one of his most poignant and puzzling, combining distanced compassion and the grotesque. The story takes its title from the customary greeting an unnamed William Holden appears to give to Molly when he comes into the restaurant where she is a late-night waitress–or at least she believes he enters and speaks to her. Molly, "a sunny, friendly, cheerful Irish girl with the face so broad she seemed to have no features," works for Doc, and she has been moved to the graveyard shift because the other daytime waitresses "resent" her. Molly has little education and few prospects, and her sickly mother, who spends most of the time in the bathtub soaking because of arthritic pain, is totally reliant on her; when she sees a movie "about a poor, battered woman . . . her whole life so terrible that Molly couldn't bear to watch it," she sees her own life.

All Molly looks forward to is Holden's entrance from the night and his "What's new, love?" At home she thinks of him in his roles opposite Kim Novak or Gloria Swanson or John Wayne: "She was a sucker for a loser"–those parts Holden played best and most convincingly.

The present action begins when Molly sees Holden's face under the newspaper headlines announcing his death; she feels bereft, saddened that she had not been there when he died, alone, "his poor dear head bleeding, for almost a week." In the following days Molly becomes more and more despondent, and Doc asks a friend, Lennie, to watch out for her. One night when Lennie brings her home, water covers the floor. In the tub, dead, is her mother, in "water so hot it almost cooked her." Her telephone is mysteriously off the hook. The circumstances that caused her death remain unknown, but at the funeral, when Molly looks into the coffin, it is Holden's face she sees.

Morris gives few clues to the meaning of this story, and readers must struggle to draw definitive conclusions. That Molly is unstable is obvious, but is she a murderer? There are potential clues, such as when Morris notes that Molly and her mother would occasionally discuss "what might become of Molly if she wasn't around to keep an eye on her." The story is thick with references to movie stars: not only Holden, but also Novak, Shirley Booth, and above all, Swanson. *Picnic* and *Come Back, Little Sheba* are mentioned, but most important of all is *Sunset Boulevard,* the movie that brought Holden and Swanson together. Readers of "What's New, Love?" may liken Molly's mother's death in the bathtub to the fate of Holden's character in *Sunset Boulevard,* who is shot by Swanson's Norma Desmond and falls dying into her swimming pool. What other similarities Morris may intend are open to conjecture.

As in many of Morris's works, his vexing elusiveness compels readers to return again and again to "What's New, Love?" In Morris's best stories, as in his most memorable novels, readers are encouraged both to keep looking for further meaning and to take pleasure in richly suggestive language. Morris's style is one of textures and shadows, derived from years of remembering and imagining and focusing through camera lenses. Appreciated for these qualities, Morris's work gives intense pleasure, returning readers to the mysterious and detailed facticity of experience while encouraging a measured compassion toward life in all its extraordinary profusion.

Interviews:

Harvey Breit, "Talk with Wright Morris," *New York Times Book Review,* 10 June 1951, p. 19;

Sam Bleufarb, "Point of View: An Interview with Wright Morris," *Accent,* 19 (Winter 1959): 34–46;

Gabor Kovacsi, "An Interview with Wright Morris," *Plum Creek Review* (Spring 1965): 36–40;

Fred Pfeil, "Querencias and a Lot Else: An Interview with Wright Morris," *Place [Neon Rose],* 3 (June 1973): 53–63;

Jim Alinder, "Interview," in Morris's *Structures and Artifacts: Photographs, 1933–1954* (Lincoln: University of Nebraska Press, 1975), pp. 110–120;

Jerry Nemanic and Harry White, "Interview," *Great Lakes Review,* 1 (Winter 1975): 1–29;

Robert Knoll, ed., *Conversations with Wright Morris* (Lincoln: University of Nebraska Press, 1977);

Bill Golightly, "Wright Morris: An Interview," *Society for the Fine Arts Review,* 5 (Fall 1983): 5–7, 20;

"Wright Morris's Field of Vision: A Conversation," *Black Warrior Review,* 10 (Fall 1983): 143–155;

Olga Carlisle and Jodie Ireland, "Wright Morris: The Art of Fiction CXXV," *Paris Review,* 33 (Fall 1991): 52–94.

Bibliography:

Robert L. Boyce, "A Wright Morris Bibliography," in *Conversations with Wright Morris,* edited by Robert Knoll (Lincoln: University of Nebraska Press, 1977), pp. 169–206.

References:

Laura Barrett, "The True Witness of a False Event": Photography and Wright Morris's Fiction of the 1950s," *Western American Literature,* 33 (Spring 1998): 27–57;

Jonathan Baumbach, "Wake Before Bomb: *Ceremony in Lone Tree,*" in his *The Landscape of Nightmare: Studies in the Contemporary American Novel* (New York: New York University Press, 1965), pp. 152–169;

Roy K. Bird, *Wright Morris: Memory and Imagination* (New York: Peter Lang, 1985);

Wayne C. Booth, "The Shaping of Prophecy: Craft and Idea in the Novels of Wright Morris," *American Scholar,* 31 (Autumn 1962): 608–626;

Booth, "The Two Worlds in the Fiction of Wright Morris," *Sewanee Review,* 65 (Summer 1957): 375–399;

A. Carl Bredahl, "Wright Morris: Living in the World," in his *New Ground: Western American Narrative and the Literary Canon* (Chapel Hill: University of North Carolina Press, 1989), pp. 126–134;

Knox Burger, "Introduction," in *A Short Wait Between Trains: An Anthology of War Short Stories by American Writers,* edited by Robert Benard (New York: Delacorte, 1991), pp. 1–11;

Christopher Coates, "Image/Text: Wright Morris and Deconstruction," *Canadian Review of American Studies,* 22 (1991): 567–576;

G. B. Crump, *The Novels of Wright Morris: A Critical Interpretation* (Lincoln: University of Nebraska Press, 1978);

Crump, "Wright Morris: Author in Hiding," *Western American Literature,* 25 (May 1990): 3–14;

Reginald Dyck, "Revisiting and Revising the West: Willa Cather's *My Antonia* and Wright Morris' *Plains Song,*" *Modern Fiction Studies,* 36 (Spring 1990): 25–37;

Chester E. Eisinger, "Wright Morris: The Artist in Search for America," in his *Fiction of the Forties* (Chicago: University of Chicago Press, 1963), pp. 328–341;

Mary Anne Ferguson, ed., *Images of Women in Literature* (Boston: Houghton Mifflin, 1973);

Peter Halter, "Distance and Desire: Wright Morris' *The Home Place* as 'Photo-Text,'" *Etudes Textuelles,* 4 (October–December 1990): 65–89;

Granville Hicks, introduction to *Wright Morris: A Reader,* edited by Hicks (New York: Harper & Row, 1970), pp. ix–xxxiii;

Leon Howard, *Wright Morris,* University of Minnesota Pamphlets on American Writers, no. 69 (Minneapolis: University of Minnesota Press, 1968);

Marcus Klein, "Wright Morris: The American Territory," in his *After Alienation: American Novels in Mid-Century* (Cleveland: World, 1964), pp. 196–246;

Robert Knoll, ed., *Conversations with Wright Morris: Critical Views and Responses* (Lincoln: University of Nebraska Press, 1977);

David Madden, *Wright Morris* (New York: Twayne, 1964);

Madden, "Wright Morris' *In Orbit:* An Unbroken Series of Poetic Gestures," *Critique,* 10 (Fall 1968): 102–119;

Raymond I. Neinstein, "Wright Morris: The Metaphysics of Home," *Prairie Schooner,* 53 (Summer 1979): 121–154;

David Nye, "Negative Capability in Wright Morris' *The Home Place*," *Word and Image*, 4 (January–March 1989): 163–169;

Sandra S. Phillips and John Szarkowski, *Wright Morris: Origin of a Species* (San Francisco: San Francisco Museum of Modern Art, 1992);

Rodney Rice, "Wright Morris and the Poetics of Space: Photographing the Material Imagination," *Texas Review*, 19 (Spring/Summer 1998): 45–62;

Alan Trachtenberg, "The Craft of Vision," *Critique*, 4 (Winter 1961): 41–55;

Trachtenberg, "Wright Morris's 'Photo-Texts,'" *Yale Journal of Criticism*, 9 (Spring 1996): 109–119;

Colin S. Westerbeck Jr., "American Graphic: The Photography and Fiction of Wright Morris," *Views: The Journal of Photography in New England*, 6 (Spring 1985): 5–11;

Joseph J. Wydeven, "Focus and Frame in Wright Morris's *The Works of Love*," *Western American Literature*, 23 (1988): 99–112;

Wydeven, "Myth and Melancholy: Wright Morris's Stories of Old Age," *Weber Studies: An Interdisciplinary Humanities Journal*, 12 (Winter 1995): 36–47;

Wydeven, "Visual Artistry in Wright Morris's *Plains Song for Female Voices*," *MidAmerica*, 19 (1992): 116–126;

Wydeven, *Wright Morris Revisited* (New York: Twayne, 1998).

Papers:

The Bancroft Library at the University of California, Berkeley, has most of Wright Morris's notes and manuscripts, galley and page proofs, and many miscellaneous items. The Harry Ransom Humanities Research Center at the University of Texas at Austin has a typed manuscript and galley and page proofs for *The Field of Vision* and other miscellaneous items.

Bharati Mukherjee

(27 July 1940 –)

Teri Ann Doerksen
Hartwick College

See also the Mukherjee entry in *DLB 60: Canadian Writers Since 1960, Second Series.*

BOOKS: *The Tiger's Daughter* (Boston: Houghton Mifflin, 1972; London: Chatto & Windus, 1973);

Wife (Boston: Houghton Mifflin, 1975);

Kautilya's Concept of Diplomacy: A New Interpretation (Columbia, Mo.: South Asia Books, 1976; Calcutta: Minerva, 1976);

Days and Nights in Calcutta, by Mukherjee and Clark Blaise (Garden City, N.Y.: Doubleday, 1977; revised and enlarged edition, Markham, Ont. & Harmondsworth, U.K.: Penguin, 1986);

Darkness (Markham, Ont. & New York: Penguin, 1985; Harmondsworth, U.K.: Penguin, 1985); selections republished as *Wanting America: Selected Stories* (Stuttgart: Reclam, 1995);

The Sorrow and the Terror: The Haunting Legacy of the Air India Tragedy, by Mukherjee and Blaise (Markham, Ont. & New York: Viking, 1987);

The Middleman and Other Stories (Markham, Ont.: Viking, 1988; New York: Grove, 1988; London: Virago, 1989);

Jasmine (New York: Grove Weidenfeld, 1989; London: Virago, 1990);

Political Culture and Leadership in India: A Study of West Bengal (New Delhi: Mittal, 1991);

Regionalism in Indian Perspective (Calcutta: K. P. Bagchi, 1992);

The Holder of the World (Toronto: HarperCollins, 1993; London: Chatto & Windus, 1993; New York: Knopf, 1993);

Leave It to Me (London: Chatto & Windus, 1996; New York: Knopf, 1997).

SELECTED PERIODICAL PUBLICATIONS–UNCOLLECTED: "Response: American Fiction," *Salmagundi,* 50–51 (Fall 1980–Winter 1981): 151–171;

"An Invisible Woman," *Saturday Night,* 96 (March 1981): 36–40;

Bharati Mukherjee (photograph from the dust jacket for The Holder of the World, *1993)*

"A Conversation with V. S. Naipaul," by Mukherjee and Robert Boyers, *Salmagundi,* 54 (Fall 1981): 4–22.

Bharati Mukherjee has developed a reputation for exploring, through her writings, the meeting of the Third World and the First from the perspective of the immigrant to North America–to Canada and to the United States. Although she is well known for her novels, she has received critical acclaim for her two volumes of short stories, as well; several stories from her first collection, *Darkness* (1985), were singled out for awards, and her second collection, *The Middleman and Other Stories* (1988), earned a National Book Critics Circle Award. Her stories focus on the immigrant experience, but she resists attempts to categorize her as a "hyphenated" writer whose appeal is limited to certain ethnic groups; instead, she characterizes herself as an American writer in an established American tradition. She says in the introduction to *Darkness:*

> I see my "immigrant" story replicated in a dozen American cities, and instead of seeing my Indianness as a fragile identity to be preserved against obliteration (or worse, a "visible" disfigurement to be hidden), I see it now as a set of fluid identities to be celebrated. I see myself as an American writer in the tradition of other American writers whose parents and grandparents had passed through Ellis Island.

Mukherjee is one of a growing number of authors who resist efforts to push to the sidelines literature featuring the richness of immigrant and ethnic communities and who redefine through their works what it means to be American. Along with the Native Americans Paula Gunn Allen and Leslie Marmon Silko and the Chinese American Amy Tan, Mukherjee depicts a United States that can no longer imagine itself in monolithic terms, that "is about diversity, not uniformity," as Allen was quoted as saying in an article in the *Chicago Tribune* (17 March 1991). In the same article Mukherjee said that "The ethnic voices were always there, but there wasn't a recognition of a community of writers until the de-Europeanization of our country became physically evident in the mid-80s." Mukherjee's short stories reflect her growing interest in representing a more and more inclusive view of what it means to be American. While most of the stories in both volumes are set in the United States or Canada, the first collection focuses primarily on Indian immigrants; the second presents a kaleidoscope of perspectives, including those of an Anglo Vietnam veteran, a newly arrived Ugandan American, and a third-generation Italian American introducing her family to her Afghanistani refugee boyfriend.

Mukherjee's renderings of interracial tensions, of the encounters between East and West, and of the experience of expatriation to Canada and immigration to the United States are drawn from her personal history. Mukherjee was born in Calcutta on 27 July 1940 to Sudhir Lal Mukherjee, a wealthy chemist who had traveled and studied in Germany and Britain, and Bina Barrejee Mukherjee. Both parents were Bengali Brahmins, members of the highest Hindu caste. Although Bina Mukherjee had not had an advanced education, she, like her husband, believed that their three daughters should be educated. In a 1987 interview with Geoff Hancock, Mukherjee said that her father "wanted the best for his daughters. And to him, the 'best' meant intellectually fulfilling lives. . . . My mother is one of those exceptional Third World women who 'burned' all her life for an education, which was denied to well-brought-up women of her generation. She made sure that my sisters and I never suffered the same wants."

Although Mukherjee's first language was Bengali, she was taught English at a bilingual Protestant missionary school in British-ruled Calcutta. Soon after India gained its independence in 1947, the Mukherjee sisters left with their parents for their first trip outside the country; Mukherjee attended boarding schools in England and Switzerland for three years before returning to Calcutta and enrolling at Loreto House, an English-speaking school run by Irish nuns. In a 1990 interview with *The Iowa Review* she recalled:

> There was an instilling of value systems, cultural value systems, which now strikes me as so ironic. The nuns were Irish to begin with, but in the outpost, they became more British than the British. And during the schooldays we were taught to devalue . . . Bengali plays, Bengali literature, Bengali music, Bengali anything. And then we went home–I came from a very orthodox, traditional family–so we had to negotiate in both languages. But, as I'm sure happens with minority children who are being channeled into fancy prep schools and all, it created complications within the Hindi community, within the Indian upper-class community of my generation.

Tensions between Third World and First World values became the foundation for much of Mukherjee's writing.

After graduating from Loreto House, Mukherjee attended the University of Calcutta, where she received a B.A. in English, with honors, in 1959. At about that time her father had a dispute with a business partner and moved the family to Baroda in western India, where he worked for a large chemical firm. Mukherjee received an M.A. in English and ancient Indian culture from the University of Baroda in 1961.

After Mukherjee finished her M.A., her father arranged for her to attend the University of Iowa Writer's Workshop. She received an M.F.A. from Iowa in 1963. On 19 September 1963–during their lunch hour–she married Clark Blaise, a Canadian novelist, whom she had met at the university. They have two sons, Bart and Bernard.

Mukherjee became an instructor in the English department at Marquette University in Milwaukee in 1964; in 1965 she took a similar position at the University of Wisconsin at Madison. In 1966 she and Blaise accepted positions as lecturers at McGill University in Montreal. Mukherjee received her Ph.D. in English and comparative literature from the University of Iowa in 1969 and was promoted to assistant professor.

While teaching at McGill, Mukherjee wrote her first novel. In *The Tiger's Daughter* (1972) Tara Banerjee Cartwright returns to India to find that her childhood memories of wealth and Brahmin gentility do not jibe with the dirt, poverty, and political upheavals she encounters. Tara's father, "The Tiger," is closely based on Mukherjee's father. In 1973 Mukherjee became an associate professor and went to India on sabbatical. In her second novel, *Wife* (1975), Dimple Dasgupta, an Indian woman, moves with her Indian husband to New York City. The gap between her husband's expectations of her and those of the culture in which she finds herself are so large, and her mental state is so shaky, that she finds herself torn between killing herself and killing her husband; she chooses the latter alternative, stabbing him in the neck as he eats a bowl of cereal.

Mukherjee and Blaise spent 1976–1977 in India, where Mukherjee was directing the Shastri Indo-Canadian Institute in New Delhi. They had contracted with a publisher to record their experiences independently, Blaise as a Westerner visiting the country for the first time and Mukherjee as a returnee whose perspective had been shifted by ten years in North America. The result was *Days and Nights in Calcutta* (1977). Mukherjee became a full professor at McGill in 1978. She also served as the chair of the writing program and as director of graduate studies in English.

In the 1990 interview with *The Iowa Review* Mukherjee noted that after the Canadian government allowed Ugandan Asians with British passports to enter the country in 1973, "I started to notice on a daily basis little incidents in my corner Woolworth's in Montreal, or in hotel lobbies, on buses, things just not being quite right. Then it ballooned into very vicious physical harassment by 1977, 1978." Soon after *Days and Nights in Calcutta* was published, Mukherjee and Blaise moved to Toronto, a hotbed of racist violence in Canada, and learned of people of color being thrown onto railroad tracks and run over intentionally on the streets. Paralyzed by anger over her encounters with racism in her adopted home, Mukherjee stopped writing for almost ten years, and she and Blaise decided to leave Canada permanently. They resigned their tenured positions and took part-time, temporary teaching jobs at colleges around New York City. When Mukherjee began to write again, she chose a new genre: the short story.

Mukherjee's first book of short stories, *Darkness,* published in 1985, reveals her outrage at the racism she had encountered in Canada and the optimism she associates with living in the United States. Most of the twelve stories in the collection were written while she was writer-in-residence at Emory University in Atlanta in the spring of 1984, although some had been written in Canada. The tone of the stories moves from bitterness about the difficulty of maintaining Indian identity in Canada to a cautious hopefulness about the potential for successful assimilation into the culture of the United States.

The stories in *Darkness* feature characters from Southern Asia and provide a mosaic of perspectives on this kind of immigrant experience. Several stories are either set in Canada or involve characters who live there and depict the overwhelming racism encountered there by people of Indian origin. "The World According to Hsü" is told from the point of view of Ratna Clayton, an Indian woman married to a white Canadian academic in Montreal. The couple is on vacation on an island off the coast of Africa; the uprising and coup that occur during their visit correspond to the internal upheaval Ratna feels at the news that her husband wants to take a position in Toronto: "In Montreal she was merely 'English,' a grim joke on generations of British segregationists. It was thought charming that her French was just slightly short of fluent. In Toronto, she was not Canadian, not even Indian. She was something called, after the imported idiom of London, a Paki. And for Pakis, Toronto was hell."

Other stories extend beyond the middle and upper classes to the experience of poor immigrants–who are almost always assumed by those in authority to be in Canada illegally. In "Tamurlane" a Toronto restaurant is raided by Royal Canadian Mounted Police officers who are looking for illegal immigrants. Gupta, a lame cook who has his papers, at first resists the unjust arrest in the only way he knows how–with his cleaver–then reaches for his passport; but one of the Mounties shoots him through the very document that proves that they should not have tried to arrest him in the first place. In the award-winning "Isolated Incidents" a young white Toronto social worker is made aware of the vast gap between classes when a visit to an old school friend, who is now a famous pop singer, coincides with an incident in which an Indian immigrant is pushed in front of a subway train and an encounter with a plaintive Hispanic client who wants her to save his sister from being deported.

In "Nostalgia" the reader is introduced to Dr. Manny Patel, who is proud of his white wife, Camille;

his young son; and the money he has earned in the United States. At the same time, however, he longs for the familiarity of the culture he left behind in India. Patel's nostalgia takes on substance in his lust for an Indian girl he meets at the market and romances at an expensive restaurant. Patel ignores the waiter's plea for help in getting a visa for his nephew, because "he didn't want this night to fall under the pressure of other immigrants' woes," only to find, in an ironic twist, that the entire experience was engineered: the girl he is romancing is the waiter's niece, and he is blackmailed into helping with the visa and giving them money, as well. Patel, suddenly aware of his disconnectedness from his Indian heritage, reacts in a way that proves that he is also disconnected from his family: as the story ends he is planning to bribe his wife with a cruise to make up for his infidelity and humiliation. A story later in the volume, "Saints," illustrates the long-term repercussions of Patel's detachment. Many years later Camille and Manny have divorced; their son, Shawn, cannot understand his father's coldness or his mother's attraction to men who cheat on her and batter her, and at the end he is walking the midwinter streets "like a Hindu saint," peering through the windows at Indian families and hoping for a glimpse of his own identity.

The most pervasive theme in the volume, appearing in some form in nearly all of the stories, is the tension between the changed cultural and sexual expectations confronting Indian women immigrants to North America and the unchanged values of their traditional Indian parents and husbands. "A Father" is a particularly vivid illustration of this theme. Mr. Bhowmick discovers that his daughter is pregnant and is overjoyed by his visions of a grandson and by the notion that his intelligent but awkward daughter is loved by a man. He is willing to forgive the fact that she is pregnant out of wedlock; after all, he reasons, "Girls like Babli were caught between the rules." He congratulates himself on his progressive ideas; but the brittleness of his position becomes apparent when he discovers that his daughter was impregnated by artificial insemination rather than by a boyfriend. His self-congratulatory acceptance explodes into rage and violence, and he beats his daughter with a rolling pin until his wife calls the police.

"Visitors" also plays on immigrant uncertainty about how much acceptance of Western culture is allowable. Vinita, a young immigrant bride, is receiving visitors on her first afternoon in her new home. She is faced with a difficult decision when a young man she has met comes to the door: in Calcutta it would be inappropriate to be with him unchaperoned, but the rules are different in New Jersey. He, however, judges her by Calcutta rules, taking her invitation to tea as an acknowledgment of her desire for him. She repulses his attack, but the experience has made her long for something more than she has. She finds herself longing to "run off into the alien American night where only shame and disaster can await her."

Dust jacket for Mukherjee's second collection of short stories, all of which were written after her move from Canada to the United States

Darkness received generally favorable reviews. Mahnaz Ispahani commented in *The New Republic* (14 April 1986): "Mukherjee has created some complicated inner lives, and evoked the sensations and the traditions and the combustion of two very different cultures. Unlike many writers about the immigrant experience, Mukherjee does not succumb to guilt or to maudlin memories about the past. Instead her work soberly celebrates resilience. Like most of her characters, she has no thoughts of turning back."

After *Darkness* was sent to the publisher, Mukherjee acquired a National Endowment for the Arts grant and took time off from teaching to begin writing another series of stories about Indian immigrants to the United States. This work was interrupted by an event that led to another nonfiction book: the 23 June 1985 bombing off the Irish coast, apparently by Sikh terrorists, of Air India flight 182, en route from Toronto to New Delhi via London, in which 329 people were killed. In 1987 Mukherjee and Blaise published *The Sorrow and the Terror: The Haunting Legacy of the Air India Tragedy,* in which they argued that ultimate responsibility for the disaster lay with misguided Canadian government policies on immigration and multiculturalism.

After the completion of *The Sorrow and the Terror* Mukherjee returned to the stories she had begun earlier, but in a much different frame of mind. During the intervening years she had settled permanently in the United States, and as she wrote the last of the stories for her second collection she was preparing to become a citizen. She continued to be concerned with the racism facing Indian immigrants to Canada, but she began to approach the issue from a more hopeful perspective. Early in 1988 she took her citizenship oath in New York City; a few months later *The Middleman and Other Stories* was published.

The Middleman and Other Stories reflects an exuberance that contrasts with the uncertainty and sense of betrayal that pervades many of the pieces in *Darkness;* Mukherjee said in the 1990 interview that "by the time I came to write *The Middleman,* I was exhilarated, my vision was more optimistic. I knew that I was finally where I wanted to be." The stories also shift away from her earlier focus on Indian immigrants to include new arrivals from Uganda, the West Indies, and Afghanistan. Except for a few darker stories, the collection celebrates the kaleidoscopic nature of the new American population. Finally, Mukherjee adopts a new narrative perspective in the stories: while *Darkness* explored the immigrant experience from a third-person-omniscient standpoint, *The Middleman and Other Stories* allows many of these new American voices to speak for themselves; some of the narrators are native-born Americans who are learning to live with the changes brought to the country by the recent arrivals. All of the stories address the tensions and hopes produced when "new" Americans meet "old" ones.

As diverse as the stories are, they fall into definable categories. The first is a new one for Mukherjee: stories told from the point of view of white Americans who are seeking, with differing degrees of success, to make sense of the new America emerging around them. In "Loose Ends" the Vietnam veteran Jeb Marshall has become an assassin-for-hire in Florida. Bitter and unable to accept the changes that immigrants have brought to the United States, he sees people of Hispanic and East Indian descent as threats and views himself and his wife as "coolie labor in our own country." In Vietnam, he thinks, he sacrificed to "barricade the front door" and protect his country; now he wonders, "who left the back door open?" Checking into a cheap motel run by an East Indian family, he is enraged when he realizes that to them he is unimportant: "They 've forgotten me. I feel left out, left behind. While we were nailing up that big front door, these guys were sneaking in around back. They got their money, their family networks, and their secretive languages." He rapes and murders the young Indian woman who shows him to his room, believing that by doing so he is taking back "his" America. In "Fathering" another veteran, Jason, faces a power struggle between his common-law wife, Sharon, and his daughter, Eng, whom he fathered in Vietnam and who has just arrived in the United States.

The largest group of stories consists of those that are told from the point of view of first- and second-generation Asian immigrants as they become acculturated in the West. In the title story, "The Middleman," Alfie Judah, an Iraqi who has just become a United States citizen, is employed by an arms-dealing syndicate in a Central American republic; the syndicate is secretly run by an American businessman and the president of the country. Alfie has an affair with the businessman's wife, who is also the president's mistress. When–to his surprise–he survives the discovery of the affair, he decides to see how much money he can make from his inside information about his former bosses. This jaundiced view of entrepreneurship in the Western world is echoed in "Danny's Girls." The unnamed narrator, a teenage Ugandan refugee, admires Danny Sahib, another boy in his building, whose business is "selling docile Indian girls to hard-up Americans for real bucks." But when he becomes infatuated with Rosie, a Nepalese mail-order bride, he realizes "what a strange, pimpish thing I was doing, putting up pictures of Danny's girls, or standing at the top of the subway stairs and passing them out to any lonely-looking American I saw–what kind of joke was this? How dare he do this, I thought, how dare he make me a part of this?"

Two stories explore meetings between new immigrants and families who are well established in the United States. In "Jasmine" an illegal emigrant from Trinidad finds a job in Michigan caring for the daughter of the Moffitts. The feminist Lara Hatch-Moffitt is blithely unaware of the hypocrisy of her exploitation of the teenage immigrant to further her own career; Bill Moffitt also exploits Jasmine by having an affair with her. (The explosive potential of the situation established in "Jasmine" led Mukherjee to expand it into a novel of the same title, which was published in 1989.) In "Orbiting," one of the strongest pieces in the collection, a second-generation Italian American family gathers for that most traditional of American holidays, Thanksgiving, at the home of the eldest daughter, Rindy. The dinner is complicated by the introduction of Rindy's new boyfriend, Ro, an Afghan refugee. Ro's presence changes the way the more-established Americans see the holiday they are celebrating, and the assumptions they have about what it means to be an American. When Ro explains the politics that forced him to leave his country and the torture he suffered in jail, Rindy's father and brother are shocked out of their complacent belief that "only Americans had informed political opinions–other people staged coups out of spite and misery." As Ro's story continues, Rindy observes that her father is beginning to look ill; she notes with acerbity that "The meaning of Thanksgiving should not be so explicit." Victoria Carchidi calls the story "a comedy of manners worthy of Jane Austen, whom Mukherjee has acknowledged as an influence on her work. We see misunderstandings, and correct understandings, where least expected as the characters enact in miniature the ballet of complementary moves that is America."

The last group of stories encompasses a category that is familiar from Mukherjee's previous work: stories of Indian women who have immigrated to the United States or Canada and are struggling with the distance between their cultural background and the new society in which they find themselves. In "A Wife's Story" Panna Bhatt is studying for a doctorate in special education in New York City. When her husband, who manages a cotton mill north of Bombay, arrives for a visit, he asks why she has not worn his mother's gold and ruby ring to the airport. She explains that it is not safe to do so: "He looks disconcerted. He's used to a different role. He's the knowing, suspicious one in the family. . . . I handle the money, buy the tickets. I don't know if this makes me unhappy." By the end of the story she knows that she will not return to India with him. The final image is of a woman discovering a new sense of herself: "I watch my naked body turn, the breasts, the thighs glow. The body's beauty amazes. I stand here shameless, in ways he has never seen me. I am free, afloat, watching somebody else." In "The Tenant" a young professor from India is torn between her desire for a connection with her Indian heritage and her desire for independence. She has dinner with the family of an Indian colleague; afterward, he drives her home and then masturbates at the wheel of the car while she watches, aghast. She turns to personal advertisements for Indian companionship, then to her armless landlord, and, finally, back to the man she had met through the personals. It is a story of searching without finding, but without the bleakness that might have pervaded a similar story in *Darkness.*

The most powerful work in the collection, "The Management of Grief," grew out of Mukherjee's experience researching the Air India crash. Mrs. Bhave's husband and two sons are killed in the disaster, and in the following weeks she becomes a focal point for misunderstandings between the Canadian government and the grieving families. She is disappointed in herself for being unable to show the emotion she should, for not wailing for the dead; others in her community wonder if she really loved her family, since she can take their loss so silently. The Canadian authorities, on the other hand, try to use her to inspire a similar stoicism in the other bereaved Indian families. The authorities also assume that the survivors will be comforted by the identification of the bodies of their loved ones, while Mrs. Bhave and the others take their only solace in the belief that somehow their families might have survived: "*In our culture, it is a parent's duty to hope.*" When Judith Templeton, a social worker, asks for Mrs. Bhave's help with the other families, she reluctantly agrees; but Templeton's ignorance is too much to bear. Not only does Templeton want Mrs. Bhave to talk with a Sikh family–members of the ethnic group responsible for bombing the plane in which Mrs. Bhave's family died–but she also confides that the "stubbornness and ignorance" of two survivors "are driving me crazy." Finding herself more in sympathy with her traditional enemies than with the Canadian social worker, Mrs. Bhave asks to be let out of the car at a subway stop. This strong declaration of self is followed by eventual release from grief: after many months, she hears her family's voices telling her to "*Go, be brave,*" and she begins a new life, a new "voyage."

The Middleman and Other Stories was a commercial and critical success, garnering the National Book Critics Circle Award for Fiction. Eleanor Wachtel noted in *Maclean's* (29 August 1988): "In *The Middleman,* Mukherjee has plunged herself into the throes of American society. In return, she offers acute insights into the clashes that mark a nonwhite's entry into that culture."

At the time of the publication of *Jasmine* Mukherjee was invited to become a distinguished professor at the University of California at Berkeley. Since then she has published two nonfiction books, *Political Culture and Leadership in India: A Study of West Bengal* (1991) and *Regionalism in Indian Perspective* (1992), and two novels, *The Holder of the World* (1993) and *Leave It to Me* (1996). Critics have found Mukherjee's work to be a shaping force in a new American literature that reimagines the United States as a multifaceted rather than a monolithic entity, and her work is beginning to be the focus of scholarly inquiry. She speaks to an America that is culturally rich and diverse; while she acknowledges that such diversity comes with discomfort and sacrifice, she shows that it also provides tremendous rewards.

Interviews:

Geoff Hancock, "An Interview with Bharati Mukherjee," *Canadian Fiction Magazine,* 59 (May 1987): 30–44;

Alison B. Carb, "An Interview with Bharati Mukherjee," *Massachussetts Review,* 29 (1988): 645-654;

Michael Connell and others, "An Interview with Bharati Mukherjee," *Iowa Review,* 20 (Fall 1990): 7–32.

References:

Fakrul Alam, *Bharati Mukherjee* (New York: Twayne, 1996; London: Prentice-Hall International, 1996);

Victoria Carchidi, "'Orbiting': Bharati Mukherjee's Kaleidoscopic Vision," *MELUS,* 20 (Winter 1995): 91–102;

Norman Libman, "Ethnic Voices Producing Literature of Diversity," *Chicago Tribune,* 17 March 1991, section 6, p. 2;

Sherry Morton-Mollo, "Cultural Collisions: Dislocation, Reinvention, and Resolution in Bharati Mukherjee," *Proteus,* 11 (Fall 1994): 35–38;

Emmanuel S. Nelson, ed., *Bharati Mukherjee: Critical Perspectives* (New York: Garland, 1993);

Sudha Pandya, "Bharati Mukherjee's *Darkness:* Exploring the Hyphenated Identity," *Quill,* 2 (1990): 68–73.

Grace Paley

(11 December 1922 –   )

Charlotte Zoë Walker
State University of New York College at Oneonta

See also the Paley entry in *DLB 28: Twentieth-Century American-Jewish Fiction Writers.*

BOOKS: *The Little Disturbances of Man: Stories of Women and Men at Love* (Garden City, N.Y.: Doubleday, 1959; London: Weidenfeld & Nicolson, 1960);
Enormous Changes at the Last Minute (New York: Farrar, Straus, Giroux, 1974; London: Deutsch, 1975);
Later the Same Day (New York: Farrar, Straus, Giroux, 1985; London: Virago, 1985);
Leaning Forward (Penobscot, Me.: Granite Press, 1985);
Long Walks and Intimate Talks, text by Paley, paintings by Vera B. Williams (New York: Feminist Press at the City University of New York, 1991);
New and Collected Poems (Gardiner, Me.: Tilbury House, 1991); republished as *Begin Again: New and Collected Poems* (London: Virago, 1992);
The Collected Stories (New York: Farrar, Straus, Giroux, 1994; London: Virago, 1999);
Just as I Thought (New York: Farrar, Straus & Giroux, 1998);
Begin Again: The Collected Poems of Grace Paley (New York: Farrar, Straus & Giroux, 1999).

RECORDING: *Grace Paley,* Lannan Literary Videos, Lannan Foundation, 1996.

OTHER: "Midrash on Happiness," in *The Writer in Our World,* edited by Reginald Gibbons (Boston: Atlantic Monthly Press, 1986);
New Americas Press, ed., *A Dream Compels Us: Voices of Salvadoran Women,* preface by Paley (Boston: South End Press, 1989);
Rita Falbel, Irene Klepfisz, and Donna Nevel, eds., *Jewish Women's Call for Peace: A Handbook for Jewish Women on the Israeli/Palestinian Conflict,* preface by Paley (Ithaca, N.Y.: Firebrand Press, 1990).

SELECTED PERIODICAL PUBLICATIONS–UNCOLLECTED: "Conversations in Moscow," *WIN,* 23 May 1974, pp. 4–12;

Grace Paley

"A Symposium of Fiction," by Paley, Donald Barthelme, William Gass, and Walker Percy, *Shenandoah,* 27 (Winter 1976): 3–31;
"Living on Karen Silkwood Drive," *Seven Days,* 6 June 1977, pp. 11–12;
"The Seneca Stories: Tales from the Women's Peace Encampment," *Ms.* (December 1983): 54–62, 108.

Few other fiction writers in late twentieth-century American letters have had so great an influence as Grace Paley on the basis of so few books in a lifetime of work. Even fewer fiction writers–one thinks mainly of Raymond Carver–have attained such a reputation on the strength of their work in the short story alone.

There are other ways, as well, in which Carver's and Paley's stories might be compared. Both in their different ways experiment with forms of apparent simplicity, each creating a new type of story distinctively his or her own. Both love the sound of the human voice; both are concerned with people in poverty and distress; and both use humor in their fiction. Paley's work differs from Carver's, however, on issues of politics and gender. Her stories are far more overtly political than Carver's, expressing her feminism as well as her leftist and pacifist political concerns. And while Carver's experiments with form have been characterized as "minimalist" though taking their inspiration from Anton Chekhov and Ernest Hemingway, Paley experiments boldly with self-reflexive narratives that can be viewed in the light of postmodernism or romantic irony.

The youngest of three children, Paley was born Grace Goodside in the Bronx, New York, on 11 December 1922. Her Jewish parents, Isaac and Manya Ridnyik Goodside, had anglicized their last name from Gutseit after immigrating to the United States from the Ukraine in 1906, when both were just twenty-one years old. Her father had worked first as a photographer and then attended medical school. By the time of Paley's birth he was a practicing physician. Paley's life and work have been much influenced by those beginnings. Her biographer Judith Arcana notes that the family's home "was a kind of way-station for people coming to the United States from Russia." Some people stayed for weeks and even months, and "Every Friday or Saturday night, there was company, mostly family; they would all sit at a big round table in the dining room, talking about events in the old country or American politics."

Born sixteen years after her brother, Victor, and fourteen years after her sister, Jeanne, Grace grew up a much-loved youngest child among a virtually all-adult family. She has described herself as a tomboy in her early years: "When I was a little girl I was a boy–like a lot of little girls who like to get into things and want to be where the action is, which is up the corner someplace, where the boys are."

Arcana describes the Goodsides' friends as "immigrant families in the Jewish Bronx neighborhood–no longer 'socialist' but certainly 'social democrats'–[who] were almost always egalitarian in their ideas, but rarely in their daily lives." Paley grew up thinking "that . . . the excitement was with the men . . . with the boys in the street and with the men in their talk, men's talk." She "found the men alluring; where the women's talk was understood to be trivial by definition . . . the men were 'mysterious.'" Ultimately Paley realized, however, that "Sometimes the men would talk politics, and occasionally they would quarrel. But the women's talk was about what actually happened in life."

Paley attended Hunter College in the late 1930s and New York University in the 1940s but did not complete her studies. She married motion-picture cameraman Jess Paley on 20 June 1942. They had two children, Nora and Danny, and were divorced in 1972. Later that year, on 26 November, Paley married poet and playwright Robert Nichols, who shares her lifelong commitment to activism in antiwar, antinuclear, and environmental movements.

Arrested several times while participating in protests, Paley has been a member of the War Resisters' League, Resist, and Women's Pentagon Action. She was also one of the founders of the Greenwich Village Peace Center. In 1969 she was part of a small delegation that traveled to Hanoi in North Vietnam to bring back three prisoners of war, and she has written about this experience in some of her nonfiction. Her political activism is also featured in some of her short stories, such as "Faith in a Tree," "Politics," and "The Immigrant Story" in *Enormous Changes at the Last Minute* (1974) and "Somewhere Else" and "Listening" in *Later the Same Day* (1985). Her intense involvement in social causes also absorbed much of the time that another writer might have put into her fiction.

Despite her small output–three volumes of short stories that were subsequently republished in *The Collected Stories* (1994)–Paley has received recognition for her writing. She won a Guggenheim Fellowship in 1961 and a National Endowment for the Arts award in 1966. In 1980 she was elected to the American Academy of Arts and Letters, and in 1982 *Delta,* a French journal of contemporary literature, published a special issue on her work. In 1986 Paley won the PEN/Faulkner Prize for fiction for her third book, *Later the Same Day.* Also in 1986 she was named the first State Author of New York, receiving the Edith Wharton citation of merit from the New York State Writers Institute. In 1987 Paley became a senior fellow of the Literature Program of the National Endowment for the Arts. She is a member of the Executive Board of PEN and has taught at Columbia and Syracuse Universities, City College of New York, and Sarah Lawrence College, where she taught creative writing and literature for eighteen years, retiring in 1988. As Arcana notes, Paley's retirement has not diminished her commitment to her writing and her causes: "Essentially, Grace has 'retired' to free herself to work."

Paley's three collections of short stories, *The Little Disturbances of Man: Stories of Women and Men at Love* (1959), *Enormous Changes at the Last Minute* (1974), and *Later the Same Day* (1985), are widely separated in time and reflect their period of composition, partly through the ages of the characters and partly through the historical conditions under which the stories were written and in which they are set. Also, Paley's experiments with narrative are considerably more sophisticated in the second and third books than they are in the first. This statement can be a misleading, however, because even her earliest stories speak with the confident and distinctive voice that established Paley as a significant and innovative practitioner of the short story.

Insights regarding women and men are one of the most striking features of Paley's work. The jaunty, warm, honest, and ironic voice of the stories in *The Little Disturbances of Man: Women and Men at Love* speaks truths that women immediately recognized, in a manner that men found amusing rather than threatening. This unusual combination has its roots in her immigrant Jewish background and the neighborhood life of the city. (Paley expressed her distress when a 1973 edition of *The Little Disturbances of Man* changed the politics of the title by switching words in the subtitle, making it *Men and Women in Love.* As Arcana observes, "Not only was her inversion of the genders ignored but her prepositional suggestion of the adversarial quality of emotional relationships between women and men, a central theme in almost every story of that volume, was erased.")

Many of the stories in *The Little Disturbances of Man* have been frequently anthologized. The first story, "Goodbye and Good Luck," was selected by Saul Bellow for inclusion in his anthology *Great Jewish Stories* (1971). The story introduces many of Paley's themes and techniques. At the beginning of the story she immediately establishes a lively, ironic, and humorous narrative voice (Aunt Rosie) and creates a sense of dialogue by placing a listener (Lillie) within the story. She also sets women's concerns in the foreground:

> I was popular in certain circles, says Aunt Rose. I wasn't no thinner then, only more stationary in the flesh. In time to come, Lillie, don't be surprised–change is a fact of God. From this no one is excused. Only a person like your mama stands on one foot, she don't notice how big her behind is getting and sings in the canary's ear for thirty years. Who's listening? . . . So she waits in a spotless kitchen for a kind word and thinks–poor Rosie . . .
>
> Poor Rosie! If there was more life in my little sister, she would know my heart is a regular college of feelings and there is such information between my corset and me that her whole married life is a kindergarten.

The story seems simple: in a reversal of expectations a spinster aunt finally marries the Yiddish actor with whom she had an affair as a young woman. The complexity of the story is carried in Rosie's voice as she describes the compromises she has made, the limited choices that were available to her, her conflict with her married sister (who seems not to have experienced the sensual pleasures Rosie has enjoyed), the triumph of Aunt Rosie's buoyant spirit, and the future hopes of the niece to whom she relates the story. As she leaves, Rosie instructs Lillie to "tell this story to your mama from your young mouth. She don't listen to a word from me. She only screams, 'I'll faint, I'll faint.' Tell her after all I'll have a husband, which, as everybody knows, a woman should have at least one before the end of the story." Her final words are "Hug Mama, tell her from Aunt Rose, goodbye and good luck."

Reviewing the book for *The Saturday Review* (17 April 1968), Granville Hicks said of this story "It is Miss Paley's masterly use of the vernacular that makes us feel Rosie's vitality. In this, as in several other stories, the language is that of persons who have been influenced by Yiddish, and Miss Paley knows how to get the most out of the colorful idioms of that speech; but the voice is always unmistakably her own–alive, eager, fearless, a little tough, a little tender." In 1990 Neal D. Isaacs observed, "Aunt Rose has lived her life her way. Her niece Lillie, the silent audience in the story, must be saying with us, 'More power to her.'" He also points out the "comic irony" that Rosie becomes her own, modern woman "by moving away from her middle-class family and its values into the world of the Yiddish theater."

Arcana mentions two other stories in *The Little Disturbances of Man,* "The Contest" and "An Irrevocable Diameter," as examples of Paley's ability to write convincingly and interestingly from a male point of view, noting the origins of Paley's first two extraordinarily realistic male narrators in her childhood fascination with the "male mystique" and her wondering, "if all they did was grumble or yell at each other over the cardtable, why were they so much more important and powerful?" Isaacs sees "The Contest" as a witty put-down of its male narrator, whose "rationalizations are betrayed by his tone, his language, and his self-satisfied, self-pitying, self-indulgent values. His narcissism, in other words, reflects back on him an image of self-destroying, alienating male ego." Isaacs adds, however, that "Paley's performance is too funny to be mean."

In "The Contest" Frederick P. Sims's voice reveals his complacency right away. The story begins:

Paley at a Wall Street demonstration (photograph by Dorothy Marder)

> Up early or late, it never matters, the day gets away from me. Summer or winter, the shade of trees or their hard shadow, I never get into my Rice Crispies till noon.
>
> I am ambitious, but it's a long-range thing with me. I have my confidential sights on a star, but there's half a lifetime to get to it. Meanwhile I keep my eyes open and am well dressed.

He also reveals his superficial and chauvinistic views of women:

> I told the examining psychiatrist for the army: Yes, I like girls. And I do. Not my sister–a pimp's dream. But girls, slim and tender or really stacked, dark brown at their centers, smeared by time. Not my mother, who should've stayed in Freud. I *have* got a sense of humor.
>
> My last girl was Jewish, which is often a warm kind of girl, concerned about food intake and employability. They don't like you to work too hard, I understand, until you're hooked and then, you bastard, sweat!
>
> A medium girl, size twelve, a clay pot with handles–she could be grasped.

The story introduces Dotty Wasserman, a character who reappears in dialogues in Paley's third collection, *Later the Same Day.* As the story progresses, the reader is led to amused sympathy with the narrator, as he resists Dotty Wasserman's attempts to maneuver him into marriage–but at the end, in an abrupt feminist turn, the story gives Dotty Wasserman her dignity and Freddy Sims his comeuppance.

Paley's Jewish immigrant roots and her discovery of her voice as a writer are apparent in "The Loudest Voice," a charming, humorous story whose lively child narrator, Shirley Abramowitz, is chosen for a speaking part in the school Christmas play because of her loud, strong voice. The family's conflicting responses to Shirley's role in a Christian pageant raise important cultural issues. Shirley's father tells her mother, "You're in America! Clara, you wanted to come here. In Palestine the Arabs would be eating you alive. Europe you had pogroms. Argentina is full of Indians. Here you got Christmas . . . Some joke, ha?" But her mother responds, "If we came to a new country a long time ago to run away from tyrants, and instead we fall into a creeping pogrom, that our children learn a lot of lies, so what is the joke? Ach, Misha, your idealism is going away."

After the humorously described pageant reaches a successful conclusion, the family and their fellow immigrant neighbors discuss it, with her father offering the opinion that "it was certainly a beautiful affair, you have to admit, introducing us to the beliefs of a different culture." A neighbor says it seems unfair that the Christian children got "very small parts or no part at all" because "After all, it's their religion." But Shirley's mother responds, "what could Mr. Hilton do? They got very small voices; after all, why should they holler? The English language they know from the beginning by heart. They're blond like angels. You think it's so important they should get in the play? Christmas . . . the whole piece of goods . . . they own it." Shirley tells the reader that she "listened and listened until I couldn't listen anymore," bringing in the theme of listening, which shows up more and more in Paley's later stories. Yet, the emphasis in this story is on speaking, on having a voice. Shirley concludes her narration by saying, "I was happy. I fell asleep at once. I had prayed for everybody: my talking family, cousins far away, passersby, and all the lonesome Christians. I expected to be heard. My voice was certainly the loudest."

Two stories in *The Little Disturbances of Man,* "The Used-Boy Raisers" and "A Subject of Childhood," are grouped together as "Two Short Sad Stories from a Long and Happy Life," asking the reader to link them more closely to one another than to the other stories in the collection. They introduce the character Faith, who appears in six stories in Paley's second collection and in ten stories in her third. As Isaacs points out, these two stories are also "the first of Paley's diptychs, pairings of stories that stand independently but take on more complete significance, to fuller effect, in conjunction with each other." He adds, "It should hardly be surprising that a writer whose idea of storytelling is to wait until she hears two things–incidents, characters, scenes, and so on–'bumping into each other' before she has a story to tell should use the diptych form," and explains that though only this one pair of stories in Paley's first book are set apart in this way, "Three pairs in *Enormous Changes at the Last Minute* and perhaps one more in *Later the Same Day* can be considered in this way (and, arguably, a threesome in each as well). . . ."

"The Used-Boy Raisers" and "A Subject of Childhood" both show a woman's irritation with, and weariness from, the obtuseness and egotism of the men in her life, doing so with an ironic humor whose warmth counterbalances the irritation. The first story begins with the wry narration of petty complaints over food:

> There were two husbands disappointed by eggs.
>
> I don't like them that way either, I said. Make your own eggs. They sighed in unison. One man was livid, one was pallid.
>
> There isn't a drink around here, is there? Asked Livid.
>
> Never find one here, said Pallid. Don't look; driest damn house. Pallid pushed the eggs away, pain and disgust his escutcheon.

Although many readers have assumed that this story is more or less autobiographical, Paley informed her readers otherwise when she dedicated her *Collected Stories* to her friend Sybil Claiborne thirty-five years later: "I visited her fifth-floor apartment on Barrow Street one day in 1957. There before my very eyes were her two husbands disappointed by eggs."

During the fifteen years that lapsed between *The Little Disturbances of Man* and her second book, *Enormous Changes at the Last Minute,* Paley was busy living her life. According to Arcana, the stories in *Enormous Changes at the Last Minute* "were all written between–or during–meetings, actions, classes, and readings." In the late 1950s Paley and her friends, who were already protesting militarization and nuclear proliferation, began working with the American Friends Service Committee to establish neighborhood peace groups. Through this work Paley got to know her second husband, Robert Nichols. During these years Paley's literary reputation was also growing, and, when *Enormous Changes at the Last Minute* finally appeared, it was eagerly welcomed by her readers.

Paley's friendship with her neighbor and fellow fiction writer Donald Barthelme may have led her to experiment more in her writing. Certainly he was influential in getting her to compile *Enormous Changes at the Last Minute.* In a brief elegiac essay about Barthelme, included in *Just as I Thought* (1998), Paley wrote:

> He was my neighbor and a true friend. *This* kind of friend. One day in 1973 he crossed the street to talk to me on my stoop. "Grace," he said, "you now have enough stories for a book." . . . "Are you sure? I kind of doubt it," I said. "No, you do–go on upstairs and see what you can find in your files–I know I'm right." I spent a week or so extracting stories from folders. He looked at my list at dinner at his house. "You're missing at least two more," he said. "You've got to find them now. I'll wait here."

The kinship of Barthelme's and Paley's writing is also of interest. In the same essay, speaking of their conversations, Paley commented, "He was always worried in the very act of hilarious opposition. There was sadness in our lightest conversations, across that literature of his. We laugh, but the poem in the prose is dark." Though there is "sadness in [the] lightest conversations" in Paley's stories as well as in Barthelme's, her narrative experiments are emotionally quite different from his. Other writers she has spoken of reading with a writer's interest are W. H. Auden, when she was writing primarily poetry, Virginia Woolf, and Gertrude Stein.

Isaacs sees a noticeable difference between Paley's first and second books. In *Enormous Changes at the Last Minute,* he notes, "We recognize the voice, the phrasing is familiar, but we find a speaker more confident in her own speaking persona and thus also more comfortable with stretching her story forms to adopt or hear the voices of other personae." One of the changes he observes is that many of the stories are shorter in length than most of the stories in her first book.

"Wants," the opening story in *Enormous Changes at the Last Minute,* is less than three pages long; yet, in its humorous, ironic way, it covers a lifetime in its account of a woman meeting her former husband when she goes to the library to return two books that are thirty-two years overdue. In a dialogue that is exaggerated and humorous, yet also has the ring of truth, he accuses her of not wanting enough, and she is left musing that:

> Now, it's true I'm short of requests and absolute requirements. But I do want *something.*
>
> I want, for instance, to be a different person. I want to be the woman who brings these two books back in two weeks. I want to be the effective citizen who changes the school system and addresses the Board of Estimate on the troubles of this dear urban center.

> I *had* promised my children to end the war before they grew up.
>
> I wanted to have been married forever to one person, my ex-husband or my present one. . . .
>
> Well! I decided to bring those two books back to the library. Which proves that when a person or an event comes along to jolt or appraise me I *can* take some appropriate action, although I am better known for my hospitable remarks.

The titles of "Faith in the Afternoon" and "Faith in a Tree" convey the connection of the two stories. In their presentation of a woman's contemplation of her life and the world around her, they are key stories in the series about Faith, whose life experience and situation make her strongly aware of feminist and pacifist concerns on the personal and family level, on the local level of community and playground, and on the international level. "Faith in the Afternoon" begins with an invocation: "As for you, fellow independent thinkers of the Western Bloc, if you have anything sensible to say, don't wait. Shout it out loud right this minute. In twenty years, give or take a spring, your grandchildren will be lying in sandboxes all over the world, their ears to the ground, listening for signals from long ago." The story develops in leisurely fashion, presenting Faith's unhappiness as a single mother and her attempts to understand her life by examining her family's European Jewish background and the experience of her parents, who have recently moved to a retirement home. Faith has visited them there only once since she realized that, because of her breakup with her husband, Ricardo, "she would have to be unhappy for awhile. Faith really is an American and she was raised up like everyone else to the true assumption of happiness." Her parents do not share this assumption: "Their minds are on other matters. Severed Jerusalem, the Second World War still occupies their arguments; peaceful uses of atomic energy (is it necessary altogether?); new little waves of anti-Semitism lap the quiet beaches of their accomplishment." Furthermore,

> They are naturally disgusted with Faith and her ridiculous position right in the middle of prosperous times. They are ashamed of her willful unhappiness.
>
> All right! Shame then! Shame on them all!

In the concluding scene Faith's father, Mr. Darwin, confides that he is torn between his liberal political activities and a new desire to write poetry. As the two of them part, he urges her to visit again soon:

> "Oh, Pa," she said, four steps below him, looking up. "I can't come until I'm a little happy."
>
> "Happy!" He leaned over the rail and tried to hold her eyes. But that is hard to do, for eyes are born dodgers and know a whole circumference of ways out of a bad spot. "Don't be selfish, Faithy, bring the boys, come." . . .
>
> "O.K., O.K.," she said, wanting only to go quickly. "I will, Pa, I will."
>
> Mr. Darwin reached for her fingers through the rail. He held them tightly and touched them to her wet cheeks. Then said, "Aaah . . .," an explosion of nausea, absolute digestive disgust. And before she could turn away from the old age of his insulted face and run home down the subway stairs, he had dropped her sweating hand out of his own and turned away from her.

While "Faith in the Afternoon" is told from the third-person viewpoint of Faith, in "Faith in a Tree" Paley employs the first-person narration that she uses in much of her best work. Set in a city playground, the story is as ironic as "Faith in the Afternoon" and at the same time more humorous in tone and more politically charged. As the story opens, Faith muses, "Just when I most needed important conversation, a sniff of the man-wide world, that is, at least one brainy companion who could translate my friendly language into his tone of undying carnal love, I was forced to lounge in our neighborhood park surrounded by children." She invokes the "One God who was King of the Jews, who unravels the stars to this day with little hydrogen explosions." Describing all that this God can see in a vast world centered in New York City, she moves from this expanded vision to the narrowed focus of herself: "But me, the creation of His soft second thought, I am sitting on the twelve-foot-high, strong, long arm of a sycamore, my feet swinging, and I can only see Kitty, a co-worker in the mother trade–a topnotch craftsman. She is below, leaning on my tree, rumpled in a black cotton skirt made of shroud remnants at about fourteen cents a yard. Another colleague, Anne Kraat, is close by on a hard park bench, gloomy, beautiful, waiting for her luck to change." One of the first things to be noted in this description is that the humor with which Paley characterizes the mothers is accompanied by a clear urge to dignify their work as serious work: "the mother trade" practiced by "a topnotch craftsman." Also, by placing Faith in a tree, she suggests the desire for an enlarged perspective–not unlike the early feminist expression of desire in Charlotte Brontë's *Jane Eyre* (1847), when Jane looks out from the roof of Thornfield and declares that women have as great a need to know the world as men do.

Paley also depicts the men in the world of these mothers as being less responsible and having more enjoyment than the women: "here come the whistlers, the young Saturday fathers, open-shirted and ambitious. By and large they are trying to get somewhere and have to go to a lot of parties. They are sleepy but pretend to great energy for the sake of their two-year-old sons (little boys need a recollection of Energy as a male resource). . . . Then the older fathers trot in, just a few minutes slower, their faces scraped to a clean smile, every one of them wearing a fine gray head and eager eyes, his breath caught, his hand held by the baby daughter of a third intelligent marriage."

In further ironic comment on gender, Faith observes an argument between her son Tonto and a little girl, after Tonto tells her that girls may not play his game with him. Through her mother's adoration of her child, she is complicit in his male privilege, but her summary of that privilege is nonetheless drenched in feminist awareness:

> "Are you the boss of the world?" Antonia asked politely.
> "Yes," said Tonto.
> He thinks, he really believes, he is. To which I must say, Righto! You are the boss of the world, Anthony, you are prince of the day-care center for the deprived children of working mothers, you are the Lord of the West Side loading zone whenever it rains on Sundays. I have seen you, creepy chief of the dark forest of four gingko trees. The Boss! If you would only look up, Anthony, and boss me what to do, I would immediately slide down this scabby bark, ripping my new stretch slacks, and do it.

As the story develops, Faith is shown in the process of change. She is depicted not only in her motherly pride, but in her strong and disappointed sexual loneliness. Participating in a conversation in which two other characters move toward a possible affair, she observes that she will soon be excluded from it:

> "Say!" said Philip, getting absolutely red with excitement, blushing from his earlobes down into his shirt, making me think as I watched the blood descend from his brains that I would like to be the one who was holding his balls very gently, to be exactly present so to speak when all the thumping got there.
> Since it was clearly Anna, not I, who would be in that affectionate position, I thought I'd better climb the tree again just for the oxygen or I'd surely suffer the same sudden descent of blood. That's the way nature does things, swishing those quarts and quarts to wherever they're needed for power and action.

Yet, as in other Paley stories, personal desire makes room for social responsibility. A small parade protesting the Vietnam War comes through the park. One marcher carries a poster that asks "WOULD YOU BURN A CHILD"; another carries the reply, "WHEN NECESSARY," and "The third poster carried no words, only a napalmed Vietnamese baby, seared, scarred, with twisted hands." A neighborhood discussion results, mingling liberal ideas with more conservative ones, including those of Doug, "our neighborhood cop," who tries to break up the demonstration. The story ruthlessly makes fun of his idea of order: "Behind his back, the meeting had been neatly dispersed for about three minutes. He ran after them, but they continued on the park's circumference, their posters on the carriage handles, very solemn, making friends and enemies." Faith speaks out: "'They look pretty legal to me,' I hollered after Doug's blue back."

As in other stories, Faith's children are the agents of epiphany. Her older son, Richard, is outraged at the policeman's bullying, and at the end of the story his fierce clarity moves his mother to political awareness and action. Accusing his mother and the other adults of inaction, he asks, "Why didn't they just stand up to that stupid cop and say fuck you," and taking a piece of chalk, "In a fury of tears and disgust, he wrote on the near blacktop in pink flamingo chalk–in letters fifteen feet high, so the entire Saturday walking world could see–WOULD YOU BURN A CHILD? And under it, a little taller, the red reply, WHEN NECESSARY."

The story concludes with Faith's explanation of the change her son's deed brought about in her: "And I think that is exactly when events turned me around, changing my hairdo, my job uptown, my style of living and telling. Then I met women and men in different lines of work, whose minds were made up and directed out of that sexy playground by my children's heartfelt brains. I thought more and more and every day about the world."

All Paley's stories are characterized by humor. Jacqueline Taylor explains "that Paley has borrowed from a rich Jewish tradition of subversive humor in her woman-centered contradictions of male dominance," and she says Paley has created her "distinctively female subversive humor by being earthy and earthbound, by being simultaneously realistic and optimistic, and by drawing on the vision available to her as a doubly muted woman to make light of and in women's oppression." Calling Paley's fiction "the irreverent voice of a survivor," Taylor says that her "narrative strategies . . . challenge the monologic power of the narrator while promoting empathy and identification with the other." In this approach to her narrative voice, Taylor comes close to some of the strategies of romantic irony but does not articulate them. Viewing Paley's work through the lens of romantic irony yields interesting insights about her style.

As Lilian R. Furst points out in *Fictions of Romantic Irony* (1984), Friedrich von Schlegel made an interesting distinction between lower irony, which he dismissed as "cynical and tinged with viciousness," and higher

Dust jacket for Paley's 1994 book, which includes all the stories from her three collections

irony, which is more philosophical and, in Furst's words, "denotes the capacity of irony to confront and, ideally, to transcend the contradictions of the finite world." Beyond the philosophical nature of this higher irony is its aesthetic manifestation: "Schlegel envisages the artist as both involved in and detached from his creation, aware of the contradictions of his endeavour, but able to transcend them. He is simultaneously committed to his work and to himself as creator. The dimension of reflection and self-consciousness is, for Schlegel, intrinsic to creativity." Schlegel associates irony with paradox, stating that "irony is the form that paradox takes," and "Everything that is at once good and great is paradoxical." As Furst points out, Søren Kierkegaard, like Schlegel, envisages irony "as a means of transcendence and self-transcendence." Both philosophers believe that "the intent of the highest kind of irony is to raise the individual above the paradoxes that constitute the dialectic of life. Irony is simultaneously the mode of perceiving and of overcoming those paradoxes."

In discussing Paley as a romantic ironist, it should be noted that her friend Donald Barthelme once wrote "Kierkegaard Unfair to Schlegel," a story in the form of a dialogue, which poses the question, "Do you think your irony could be helpful in changing the government?" The answer begins, "I think the government is very often in an ironic relation to itself. And that's helpful." Paley has also acknowledged the influence on her early poetry of W. H. Auden, a master of irony. Paley's fiction is deceptive. The voices are colloquial, spontaneous, often comically self-deprecating; yet, her artistic vision is far reaching and sophisticated. Arcana refers to her as a "metafictionist."

Unlike many metafictionists, however, Paley uses narrative devices in the service of an honesty combined with passionate caring about other human beings. Often she employs romantic irony to raise questions about the narrator's failings, as well as in an often-humorous attempt to balance the paradoxical elements of her vision. In Paley's third collection, *Later the Same Day,* Isaacs detects "a new emphasis on self-reflexivity," and Taylor refers to Paley's participation in "Women's storytelling styles (and communication styles in general) [that] move away from the monologic styles of the male dominant standard toward a collaborative style that empowers multiple choices." She quotes Paley's remarks that "I can't find my own way of speaking until I have other voices" and that fiction "is a way of trying to get the world to speak to you."

Paley has, in fact, stated that all the stories in *Later the Same Day* are about listening–a quality that is clearly important to all her writing. In an interview with Wendy Lesser for the internet magazine *Salon,* she spoke of her early poetry in which she imitated Auden: "I didn't yet realize that you have two ears. One ear is that literary ear, and it's a good old ear. It's with us when we write in the tradition of English writing, or Western writing that includes Proust and Flaubert, and German writers and so on, and also Joyce. But there was also something else that I had but I didn't know it. I only knew it in my own speech, and that is the ear of the language of home, and the language of your street and your own people. When I started writing stories, I had a kind of a breakthrough. I had enough poetry from this ear, and I suddenly broke into the language that I then continued to write with. . . . I was able to use both ears suddenly."

In "Friends," one of the most moving stories in *Later the Same Day,* Paley manages without sentimentality to convey the pain and warmth of a group of women visiting another friend who is dying of cancer. As is common in her work, the story moves easily between dialogue and narration, spoken voice and descriptive voice, as Faith, the narrator, moves easily back and forth in time, giving the reader just enough cues to follow her. For instance, as Faith, Ann, and Susan ride the train home after their visit to Selena, they discover disagreements among themselves on how to cope with the pain of Selena's dying. Ann tries to deal with it by being critical of Selena's attempt to view her hard life in a positive light: "Selena's main problem, Ann said–you know, she didn't tell the truth." The next line is the simple question "What?" Paley's refusal to use quotation marks often creates an intentional and artful ambiguity. Here, the "What?" (without quotation marks) may be spoken–or may be an unspoken expression of surprise by the narrator, who then presents Ann's point of view, followed by her own: "A few hot human truthful words are powerful enough, Ann thinks, to steam all God's chemical mistakes and society's slimy lies out of her life. We all believe in that power, my friends and I, but sometimes . . . the heat. Anyway, I always thought Selena had told us a lot. . . ."

The narrator then proceeds to intersperse information about Selena's difficult life, which includes the death of her daughter Abby, throughout her dialogue with Ann. As Faith and Ann continue to struggle with grief, their irritability with one another vies with the steadiness of their longstanding friendship. When Ann accuses Faith of being "lucky," Faith responds that her mother is dead while Ann's is still alive. When Ann retorts that her mother is "very sick," Faith tells the reader, "I decided not to describe my mother's death. I could have done so and made Ann even more miserable. But I thought I'd save that for her next attack on me. These constrictions of her spirit were coming closer and closer together. Probably a great enmity was about to be born."

Then Susan, who has been dozing off and on during the trip, opens her eyes and comments, "The death or dying of someone near or dear often makes people irritable. . . ."

This statement prompts Faith to tell the reader parenthetically, "(She's been taking a course in relationships and interrelationships.)" As so often happens in Paley's later stories, a narrative comment like this one draws a riposte from a character–as if the character were listening to the story as it is being told or written. Susan continues, "The real name of my seminar is Skills: Personal, Friendship and Community. It's a very good course despite your snide remarks."

Near the end of the story Faith is at home with her son, Anthony (an older version of Tonto in "Faith in a Tree"), who attempts to comfort her with "one of the herbal teas used by his peer group to calm their overwrought natures." Anthony moves from comforting her to accusing her of always trying to be too optimistic: "Next thing you'll say people are darling and the world is so nice and round that Union Carbide will never blow it up." But Faith tells the reader, "I have never said anything as hopeful as that. And why to all our knowledge of that sad day did Tonto at 3 a.m. have to add the fact of the world?"

At the conclusion of the story, after hearing that Selena has died, Faith recalls the beginning of a friendship: "I remember Ann's eyes and the hat she wore the day we first looked at each other. Our babies had just stepped howling out of the sandbox on their new walking legs. We picked them up. Over their sandy heads we smiled." Illuminating paradox with the light of the romantic ironist, the story concludes:

> Meanwhile, Anthony's world–poor, dense, defenseless thing–rolls round and round. Living and dying are fastened to its surface and stuffed into its softer parts.
>
> He was right to call my attention to its suffering and danger. He was right to harass my responsible nature. But I was right to invent for my friends and our children a report on these private deaths and the condition of our lifelong attachments.

As the narrator steps out of the story she declares it not a story, but "a report," foregrounding the act of witnessing or testimony rather than the aesthetic product.

In "Listening," the final story of *Later the Same Day,* Paley uses her technique of moving in and out of the story in particularly surprising and pleasing ways. The opening pages seem to be a story about two men told by a first-person narrator. Then the time and setting shift. The reader discovers that Faith is telling the story to her husband, Jack, at breakfast, and Jack is one of the characters in her story. Jack tells Faith, "You don't have to tell stories to me in which I'm a character, you know. Besides, all those stories are about men, he said. You know I'm more interested in women. Why don't you tell me stories told by women about women?" Faith responds, "Those are too private."

As the middle-aged Faith and Jack converse about her unexpected desire to have a child with him, her account of her reasons, as well as her social and political concerns, is interrupted by Jack, who, like Susan in "Friends," seems to hear the story Faith is relating to the reader. He makes an amusing reference to the textuality of the story–"You know, I like your paragraphs better than your sentences"–and goes on to suggest making love. When Faith begins to describe their lovemaking for the reader, Jack interrupts her again: "Think think, talk talk, that's you. Stop it! Come on, kid, he said, touching my knee, my thigh, breast, all the outsides of love." Faith tells the reader,

> So we lay down beside one another to make a child, with the modesty of later-in-life, which has so much his-

> tory and erotic knowledge but doesn't always use it.
> How else is one to extract a new person from all-refusing Zeus and jealous Hera?

And she is interrupted again: "My God, said Jack, you've never mentioned Greek gods in bed before. No occasion, I said."

This story takes a completely unexpected turn as it moves from Faith's comfortable heterosexual relationship, to her dialogue with Cassie, a friend who is a lesbian. Suddenly in the midst of other thoughts and observations, Cassie turns on Faith and asks, "Listen, Faith, why don't you tell my story? You've told everybody's story but mine. I don't even mean my whole story, that's my job. . . . But you've just omitted me from the other stories and I was there. . . . Where is Cassie? Where is *my* life?"

As Faith takes in the truth of Cassie's accusation, she stops the car in which they have been driving and sits with Cassie for twenty minutes, absorbing this truth about her own blind spot. Cassie has the last words: "You are my friend, I know that Faith, but I promise you, I won't forgive you, she said. From now on, I'll watch you like a hawk. I do not forgive you." A clear stand-in for Paley in this story, Faith must acknowledge that despite all her concerns about political and social issues and all her desire for inclusiveness and community, she has ignored her lesbian friend's life in her writing. There is a great love in Cassie's determination to watch her like a hawk, and in Faith/Paley's recording of this challenge.

Taylor notes that this "scene is the culmination of a technique Paley has developed throughout her corpus" and identifies Faith as the character who comes the closest to expressing Paley's "values and viewpoint." In the scene with Cassie, says Taylor, "Even the most well-intentioned listener, Paley reminds us, is prone to suppress voices of difference. Only the most demanding politics of inclusion, one unafraid to turn the critique of monologism on the self, can begin to create the sort of open discourse that will allow everyone to find a voice. Even then Paley would not be satisfied, for she recognizes that a truly polyvocal literature depends not only on texts that open up to many voices but on many voices creating the tales. As Cassie recognizes, anyone who wants her whole story told must tell it herself."

Commenting on this same story, Isaacs refers in another way to the link it makes between politics and art: "Self-reflexively referring to several of the earlier stories and their themes, . . . Paley makes a gesture that pulls them all together while looking forward to a continuing process of developing her narrative art."

Arcana concludes her critical biography of Paley by commenting on Paley's belief "that lives may be held, preserved, contained in stories, that literature can change the world–maybe even save it–that one's writing '*can* change things, even if you don't always believe it *will*.' . . . Since Grace Paley knows that we all 'have to remember the world still has to be saved–every day,' there is little chance that she will abandon her task." A close look at Paley's three books of short stories leaves the reader with an expanded vision of political and social urgencies and of her passionate investment in the power of love, intelligence, and, indeed, listening. Paley's experiments with the short story convey an energetic commitment to art and life. She has few imitators because she is nearly inimitable; yet, the greatness of her example and the expanded possibilities her work represents stand ready to inspire many future writers.

Interviews:

Frieda Gardiner, "The Habit of Digression: An Interview with Grace Paley," *Wordworth,* 28 (October 1979): 127;

Maya Friedman, "An Interview with Grace Paley," *Story Quarterly,* 13 (1981): 32–39;

Gerhard Bach and Blaine H. Hall, eds., *Conversations with Grace Paley* (Jackson: University Press of Mississippi, 1997).

Biography:

Judith Arcana, *Grace Paley's Life Stories: A Literary Biography* (Urbana & Chicago: University of Illinois Press, 1993).

References:

Judith Arcana, "Truth in Mothering: Grace Paley's Stories," in *Narrating Mothers,* edited by Brenda O. Daley and Maureen Reddy (Knoxville: University of Tennessee Press, 1991), pp. 195–208;

Minao Baba, "Faith Darwin as Writer-Heroine: A Study of Grace Paley's Short Stories," *Studies in American Jewish Literature,* 7 (Spring 1988): 40–54;

E. M. Broner, "The Dirty Ladies: Earthy Writings of Contemporary American Women–Paley, Jong, Schor and Lerman," *Regionalism and the Female Imagination,* 4, no. 3 (1979): 33–43;

Melissa Bruce, "*Enormous Changes at the Last Minute:* A Subversive Songbook," *Delta,* 14 (May 1982): 97–114;

John Crawford,"Archetypal Patterns in Grace Paley's 'Runner,'" *Notes on Contemporary Literature,* 11 (September 1981): 10–12;

Jeanne Sallade Criswell, "Cynthia Ozick and Grace Paley: Diverse Visions in Jewish and American Literature," in *Since Flannery O'Connor: Essays on the*

Contemporary American Short Story, edited by Loren Logsdon and Charles W. Mayer (Macomb: Western Illinois University Press, 1987), pp. 93–100;

Blanche H. Gelfant, "Grace Paley: A Portrait in Collage," in her *Women Writing in America: Voices in Collage* (Hanover, N.H.: University Press of New England, 1984), pp. 56–71;

Katherine Hulley, "Grace Paley's Resistant Form," *Delta,* 14 (May 1982): 3–18;

Hulley, ed., *Grace Paley,* special issue of *Delta: Revue du Centre d'Etude et de Recherches sur les Ecrivains du Sud aux Etats-Unis,* 14 (May 1982);

Nicholas Peter Humy, "A Different Responsibility: Form and Technique in Grace Paley's 'Conversation With My Father,'" *Delta,* 14 (May 1982): 87–96;

Carol Iannone, "A Dissent on Grace Paley," *Commentary* (August 1985): 54–58;

Neal D. Isaacs, *Grace Paley: A Study of the Short Fiction* (Boston: Twayne, 1990);

Rose Kamel, "To Aggravate the Conscience: Grace Paley's Loud Voice," *Journal of Ethnic Studies,* 11 (Fall 1983): 29–49;

Dena Mandel, "Keeping Up with Faith: Grace Paley's Sturdy American Jewess," *Studies in American Jewish Literature,* 3 (1983): 85–98;

Joyce Meier, "The Subversion of the Father in the Tales of Grace Paley," *Delta,* 14 (1982): 115–128;

Anne Z. Michelsen, *Reaching Out: Sensitivity and Order in Recent American Fiction by Women* (Metuchen, N.J.: Scarecrow Press, 1979);

Hilda Morley, "Some Notes on Grace Paley While Reading Dante: The Voice of Others," *Delta,* 14 (May 1982): 67–72;

Clara Claiborne Park, "Faith, Grace and Love," *Hudson Review,* 38 (Autumn 1985): 481–488;

Ronald Schlieffer, "Grace Paley: Chaste Compactness" and "A Bibliography of Writings by Grace Paley," in *Contemporary Women Writers: Narrative Strategies,* edited by Catherine Rainwater and William J. Scheik (Lexington: University Press of Kentucky, 1985), pp. 31–50;

Helen J. Schwartz, "Grace Paley," in *American Women Writers,* volume 3, edited by Lina Mainiero (New York: Ungar, 1981);

Adam J. Sorkin, "'What Are We, Animals?': Grace Paley's World of Talk and Laughter," *Studies in American Jewish Literature,* 2 (1982): 144–154;

Jacqueline Taylor, *Grace Paley: Illuminating the Dark Lives* (Austin: University of Texas Press, 1990).

Reynolds Price

(1 February 1933 -)

R. Baird Shuman
University of Illinois at Urbana-Champaign

See also the Price entry in *DLB 2: American Novelists Since World War II.*

BOOKS: *A Long and Happy Life* (New York: Atheneum, 1962; London: Chatto & Windus, 1962);

The Names and Faces of Heroes (New York: Atheneum, 1963; London: Chatto & Windus, 1963);

A Generous Man (New York: Atheneum, 1966; London: Chatto & Windus, 1967);

The Thing Itself (Durham, N.C., 1966);

Love and Work (New York: Atheneum, 1968; London: Chatto & Windus, 1968);

Late Warning: Four Poems (New York: Albondocani Press, 1968);

Permanent Errors (New York: Atheneum, 1970; London: Chatto & Windus, 1971);

Things Themselves: Essays & Scenes (New York: Atheneum, 1972);

Presence and Absence: Versions from the Bible (Bloomfield Hills, Michigan & Columbia, S.C.: Bruccoli Clark, 1973);

The Surface of Earth (New York: Atheneum, 1975; London: Arlington Books, 1978);

The Good News According to Mark (Privately printed, 1976);

Early Dark: A Play (New York: Atheneum, 1977);

Oracles: Six Versions from the Bible (Durham, N.C.: Friends of the Duke University Library, 1977);

Lessons Learned: Seven Poems (New York: Albondocani Press, 1977);

A Palpable God: Thirty Stories Translated from the Bible with an Essay on the Origins and Life of Narrative (New York: Atheneum, 1978);

Question and Answer: The Second Archibald Yell Smith IV Lecture (Chattanooga: Baylor School, 1979);

Nine Mysteries (Four Joyful, Four Sorrowful, One Glorious) (Winston-Salem, N.C.: Palaemon Press, 1979);

The Annual Heron (New York: Albondocani Press, 1980);

A Final Letter (Los Angeles: Sylvester & Orphanos, 1980);

Reynolds Price (photograph © 1989 by Caroline Vaughan; from the dust jacket for Clear Pictures: First Loves, First Guides, *1989)*

The Source of Light (New York: Atheneum, 1981);

Country Mouse, City Mouse (Rocky Mount: Friends of the Library, North Carolina Wesleyan College, 1981);

A Start (Early Work) (Winston-Salem, N.C.: Palaemon Press, 1981);

Vital Provisions (New York: Atheneum, 1982);

Private Contentment: A Play (New York: Atheneum, 1984);

Kate Vaiden (New York: Atheneum, 1986; London: Chatto & Windus, 1987);

The Laws of Ice (New York: Atheneum, 1986);

A Common Room: Essays, 1954-1987 (New York: Atheneum, 1987);

House Snake: A Poem (Northridge, Cal.: Lord John Press, 1987);

Real Copies: Will Price, Crichton Davis, Phyllis Peacock, and More (Rocky Mount: North Carolina Wesleyan College Press, 1988);
Good Hearts (New York: Atheneum, 1988);
Back Before Day (Rocky Mount: North Carolina Wesleyan College Press, 1989);
Clear Pictures: First Loves, First Guides (New York: Atheneum, 1989);
Home Made (Rocky Mount: North Carolina Wesleyan College Press, 1990);
New Music: A Trilogy (New York: Theatre Communications Group, 1990)–includes *August Snow, Night Dance,* and *Better Days;*
The Use of Fire (New York: Atheneum, 1990);
The Tongues of Angels (New York: Atheneum, 1990);
The Foreseeable Future (New York: Atheneum, 1991)–includes *The Fare to the Moon, Back Before Day,* and *The Foreseeable Future;*
Blue Calhoun (New York: Atheneum, 1992);
An Early Christmas (Rocky Mount: North Carolina Wesleyan College Press, 1992);
The Collected Stories (New York: Atheneum, 1993);
Full Moon and Other Plays (New York: Theatre Communications Group, 1993)–includes *Early Dark, Private Contentment,* and *Full Moon;*
The Honest Account of a Memorable Life: An Apocryphal Gospel (Rocky Mount: North Carolina Wesleyan College Press, 1994);
A Whole New Life (New York: Atheneum, 1994);
The Promise of Rest (New York: Scribners, 1995);
The Three Gospels (New York: Scribners, 1996)–includes *The Good News According to Mark, The Good News According to John,* and *An Honest Account of a Memorable Life;*
The Collected Poems (New York: Scribners, 1997);
Roxanna Slade (New York: Scribner, 1998);
Learning a Trade: A Craftsman's Notebook, 1955–1997 (Durham, N.C.: Duke University Press, 1998);
Letter to a Man in the Fire: Does God Exist and Does He Care? (New York: Scribner, 1999).

Editions: *Mustian: Two Novels and a Story Complete and Unabridged* (New York: Atheneum, 1983)–includes *A Generous Man,* "A Chain of Love," and *A Long and Happy Life;*
A Singular Family: Rosacoke and Her Kin (New York: Scribner, 1999)–includes *A Generous Man,* "A Chain of Love," *A Long and Happy Life,* and *Good Hearts.*

PLAY PRODUCTIONS: *Early Dark,* WPA Theater, April 1978; Cleveland Playhouse, Fall 1989;
August Snow, Hendrix College (Arkansas), November 1985; Cleveland Playhouse, Fall 1989;
Full Moon, Duke University, November 1988; Cleveland Playhouse, Fall 1989.

PRODUCED SCRIPT: "Private Contentment," television, *American Playhouse,* PBS, April 1982.

OTHER: "The Only News," in *Eudora Welty Photographs* (Jackson: University Press of Mississippi, 1989), pp. vii–xii.

Reynolds Price is most accurately described as a writer whose sharp realism and striking use of the local color of northern North Carolina are tinged with fantasy and, at times, mysticism. Price embraces the area about which he usually writes with understanding, insight, and compassion. By concocting Gothic tales that present with authenticity and honesty a cast of characters who recur in many of his works, Price escapes the sentimentalism that might destroy his objectivity. To classify him as a Southern writer is perhaps too facile; while the South is his usual literary venue, the scope of his writing far exceeds a narrow regionality.

Edward Reynolds Price was born on 1 February 1933 in Macon, North Carolina, a small town near the central northern border. His parents were William Solomon and Elizabeth Rodwell Price; his brother, William, is eight years his junior. He has spent most of his life little more than an hour's drive from his birthplace, living first in Raleigh, the state capital, during his adolescence, then in Durham, where he attended Duke University (earning an A.B. in 1955) and where he has taught since 1958. He was named James B. Duke Professor of English there in 1977.

In 1984 Price entered the Duke University Medical Center to find out why his left foot slapped the pavement in an unaccustomed manner when he walked. Extensive medical testing revealed that a malignant tumor about the length of a pencil had insinuated itself into Price's spine from the top and was affecting vital nerve centers, which accounted for the change in his gait. The condition was viewed as progressive; the prognosis was bleak. After three operations and more than a month of radiation therapy, Price's physicians gave the novelist only weeks to live. His surgeries eventually left him a paraplegic.

Price not only survived his illness but also entered a period of greatly heightened productivity, part of it attributable to the regular hypnosis that he underwent at Duke University Medical Center to relieve the almost unabated pain he was suffering. Hypnosis shook loose from his unconscious mind memories that were buried so deep within it that they had been all but lost. In 1986 he published his novel *Kate Vaiden,* which was in progress when his illness struck; the novel received a National Book Critics Circle Award. Three years later,

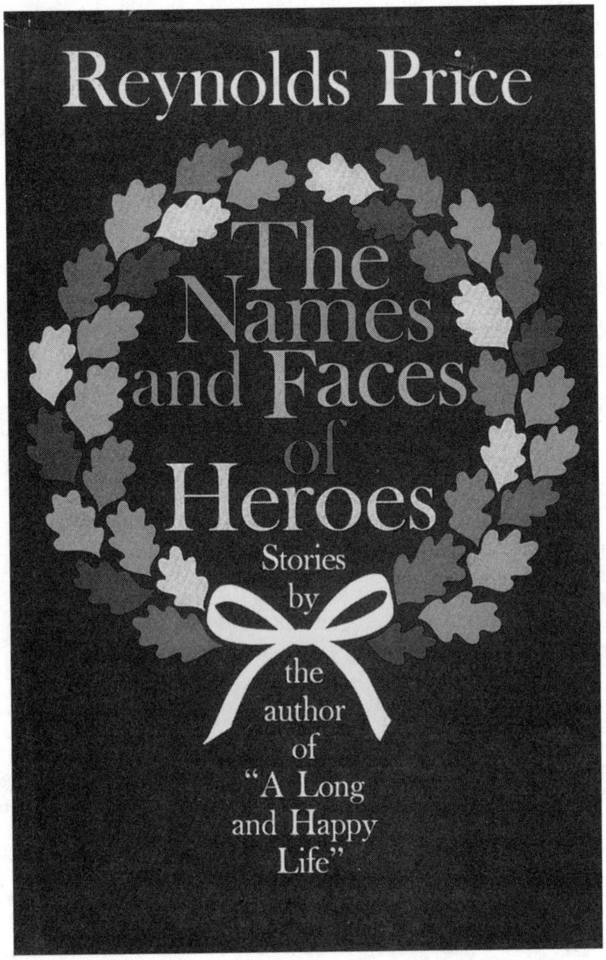

Dust jacket for Price's 1963 book, the title story of which is an exploration of a boy's connection to his father

drawing heavily on the seemingly lost memories his hypnosis had unleashed, he published an autobiography, *Clear Pictures: First Loves, First Guides* (1989).

Throughout his creative career Price has written short stories, the first of which, "Michael Egerton," was completed in 1954 when he was an undergraduate student at Duke University. It commanded the attention of Eudora Welty, who had come to Duke at the invitation of William Blackburn, Price's creative writing teacher and mentor, to work with Blackburn's students. Price published his first collection of short stories, *The Names and Faces of Heroes,* in 1963. It was followed in 1970 by a second collection, *Permanent Errors.* During the fifteen years after the publication of *Permanent Errors,* Price concentrated less on the short story, focusing more on writing plays, poetry, novels, and essays. The publication in 1993 of *The Collected Stories* brought together the fifty stories that Price has chosen to represent his short fiction. About half the stories had been published in the author's earlier collections–seven in *The Names and Faces of Heroes* and nineteen in *Permanent Errors.* They cover a time span of thirty-eight years from "Michael Egerton" to "An Evening Meal," written in 1992. The volume was nominated for the Pulitzer Prize in fiction.

Price's first story to appear in print was "A Chain of Love," published in 1958 in *Encounter,* of which Stephen Spender was editor. Price had grown close to both Spender and W. H. Auden during his three years at Merton College, Oxford, where he earned a B.Litt. as a Rhodes Scholar (1955–1958). "A Chain of Love," which predates the author's first novel, *A Long and Happy Life* (1962) by four years, focuses on the Mustian family–central characters, along with Wesley Beavers, in the novel. The Mustians and Wesley are the least autobiographical of Price's protagonists. In *Clear Pictures* Price acknowledges having known people like them as he grew up, but through abbreviated glimpses of them from the sidelines.

The occasion for "A Chain of Love" is the serious illness of Papa Mustian, whose daughter-in-law, Emma, drives him from his home in Afton to Raleigh, an hour to the south, where he is to be hospitalized. Emma cannot stay in Raleigh with her father-in-law, as she feels duty-bound to do, because she has agreed to coordinate the Children's Day pageant at her church. She is torn between duty to her husband's father and duty to those in the community who are depending upon her.

Emma's daughter, Rosacoke, and son, Rato, go to Raleigh with her, because it is unthinkable that Papa Mustian should be left in the hospital alone. Rosacoke and Rato are able and willing to remain there with their grandfather for the week, even though to do so means that they will have to sleep on chairs in his hospital room. Price carefully builds the feeling of closeness and the concern of Southern families for their members by creating a sharp contrast between Papa Mustian's situation and that of Mr. Ledwell, a recent transplant from Baltimore, who is dying of lung cancer in a room across the hall from Papa Mustian's.

Rosacoke, ever the caregiver, is deeply concerned about Mr. Ledwell, even though she has never met him. She inquires about his health and, after his surgery, she is determined to call on him. According to her Southern code of etiquette, however, one does not go calling empty handed. She writes to her mother in Afton, asking her to bring some blooming altheas with her when she comes to Raleigh the following Sunday so that she can take the flowers to Mr. Ledwell.

By the time Emma arrives with the altheas, Mr. Ledwell is on his deathbed. Rosacoke has viewed him only fleetingly through the half-open door of his semi-dark hospital room, where his wife and son are maintaining a death watch. Price's readers, like Rosacoke, see Mr. Ledwell only through the crack in the door and, like Rosacoke, draw subtle inferences about him and his situation from the scant information they glean through their fleeting impressions and stolen glances.

A statue of Christ outside Mr. Ledwell's room sets a religious tone for the story, which is buttressed by other religious imagery, most notably Mr. Ledwell's receiving the last rites in a semidark room lighted by a flickering votive candle, and the dabbing of Mr. Ledwell's parched lips with a moist ball of cotton, suggestive of Christ's lips being dabbed with vinegar as he hung from the cross. When Rosacoke's mother finally brings Rosacoke the flowers to give to Mr. Ledwell, he is hovering near death. When Rosacoke enters the room, no one pays much attention to her beyond a glance, their concentration riveted on the dying man. She leaves her flowers and departs.

The chain of love that provides the title of the story has to do not only with familial love but also, in Rosacoke's case, with a love that both encompasses and far exceeds the family. Rosacoke is a wholly sensitive person, attuned to the suffering of others and always seeking ways to mediate their pain. She works anonymously, never seeking and seldom gaining recognition for her deeds. She emerges as well meaning but as someone on the outside looking in on a situation that she can never be an integral part of and that she probably does not fully understand.

This first-published Price story is among his best. It captures the essence of the concerned family by contrasting the Mustians and Ledwells as they are each faced with the serious illness of one of their members. Price employs with remarkable success the play of light and dark in the physical and emotional environments of the story. Writing of Price in *The New York Times Book Review* (4 July 1993), fellow novelist George Garrett observed that "nobody I know writes so well about the joys and sorrows of the family. Nobody else can so deftly capture the lyric intensity of simple happiness." In his comments Garrett also touched on Price's ability to maintain a high and consistent artistic level over a long period.

Price's short stories can be categorized in various ways. More than three-fourths of his stories are regional ones set in the part of North Carolina in which Price has lived most of his life. The remainder consists of stories that reflect his three years of living in England, his travels on the Continent, and his visit to Israel. A simple regional classification, however, tends to be overly simplistic and ultimately misleading, just as it is misleading to identify Price as a Southern writer, as often happens. All of Price's North Carolina stories succeed not because they reconstruct and reflect a specific region but because they deal with universal concerns that are acted out in the region that Price knows best. His intimate knowledge of place lends a verisimilitude to the broader ideas with which he is fundamentally interested.

Many of Price's stories focus on the trials and tribulations of love and consider questions of unrequited love such as that hinted at in "A Chain of Love," in which Rosacoke's early devotion to Wesley Beavers is substantial but is not reciprocated. "The Anniversary" relates how Lillian Belle Carraway came within three days of marrying Pretty Billy Williams, who, staying with the Carraways prior to the forthcoming nuptials, goes riding, is thrown from his horse, suffers a broken neck, and dies after being tended by a seventeen-year-old stranger, Nettie Pitchford, who is closer to Pretty Billy in his final moments than his betrothed has been.

Throughout this story, one of relatively few Price short stories told partly from the viewpoint of a female protagonist, Price continually hints that all is not well between Lillian Belle and Pretty Billy, that little harmony exists between the two. Nevertheless, Pretty Billy, leaving no immediate family, is buried in the Carraway family cemetery. Lillian Belle, the grieving near-widow, having lost Billy and eschewing further romance, has regularly decorated his grave on the anniversary of his death. On this forty-fifth anniversary, however, she is three days late in decorating the grave.

This intricate story overwhelmingly suggests that people often act as social custom dictates rather than according to their own inner desires. At age twenty-eight Lillian Belle has reached the point at which society demands that she marry. When her plans to marry are derailed by Pretty Billy's death, she is relieved of that social obligation. Now the object of people's understanding and sympathy, she can live languorously, much as she lived before the energetic Pretty Billy entered her life.

The contrast between Lillian Belle and Nettie Pitchford is striking. Nettie is the caregiver, the person who instinctively ministers to the dying Billy in ways that Lillian Belle cannot, leaving the clear suggestion of the horror that Billy's marriage to Lillian Belle might eventually have become.

Throughout many of the stories, Price presents the multicultural fabric of the South. "The Anniversary" has a strong subplot that shows the relationship of the white community to the black community: blacks remain subservient but are loyal to the white people who help them survive. The black people in "The Anniversary" have a loyalty to Lillian Belle and she to them. She helps them–cooking for Betty, the black cook, when her husband dies, attending their funerals, and seeing to their needs–although she does these things dutifully rather than enthusiastically.

When Papa Mustian enters the hospital in "A Chain of Love," he is wheeled into his ten-dollar-a-day hospital room by Snowball Mason, a black man from Warren County, who not only takes an interest in the Mustians because he and they come from the same place, but who also keeps Rosacoke informed about Mr. Ledwell's condition. Blacks and whites live harmoniously in Price's South, although the lines of racial separation are realistically drawn.

The title character in the autobiographical "Uncle Grant" is a black man who has spent much of his adult life with the Price and Rodwell families. Although they are not affluent and cannot support a hired man, they give Uncle Grant a place to sleep, see to it that he has medical attention when he needs it, arrange for him to be looked after when he is no longer able to take care of himself, and finally buy the casket in which he is buried.

A deep affection exists between Will Price, the author's father, and Uncle Grant, who recurs in "The Names and Faces of Heroes" as Uncle Hawk. Will, however, financially strangled during the Great Depression, faces a struggle for his family's survival that sometimes must preclude Uncle Grant. When Will loses his house in Asheboro to foreclosure, he can no longer provide Uncle Grant with a place to live, so Uncle Grant returns to Macon and fends for himself for a time before moving into a basement room in the Rodwell house.

Uncle Grant has left a wife and son in Chatham, Virginia, not far from Macon, but he never sees them. His loyalty is to the Price and Rodwell families. Theirs is an easy relationship, devoid of the guilt that Uncle Grant feels in his relationship with his wife and son, both of whom he has abandoned. If Uncle Grant has family, he has manufactured it from the Prices and the Rodwells who clearly qualify in his own mind as the people closest to him. Price captures the importance of what scholar Constance Rooke refers to as "undefined relationships, those which transcend the usual categories of attachment."

The most significant body of Price's short stories is concerned with questions of coming of age, often combined with the growing awareness of sexual identity that accompanies maturation. Homosexual overtones exist in many of these stories, although these overtones are usually quite restrained, as in "Michael Egerton," the first-written of Price's published stories.

Michael Egerton has been sent off to summer camp because his parents are estranged and his father, a romantic figure, a newspaperman who travels extensively throughout the world, cannot look after him. Michael and the first-person narrator form a bond and remain somewhat aloof from the other boys who share the cabin.

As Michael's father drops him off at the beginning of the story, Michael unabashedly kisses him in front of the other boys, and Michael's attachment to his father is clear. Later his mother comes to visit, accompanied by a man she introduces to Michael as his "new father." The shock causes Michael to withdraw from all activities and retreat into himself; the other boys, not comprehending, torment him. Finally, on the last night of camp, in a cruel sort of initiatory rite, four boys, not including the narrator, humiliate Michael by tying him like some pathetic animal to two cots in a kind of mock crucifixion. The narrator leaves with the other boys for the evening activities but, conscience-stricken, finally goes back to the cabin to untie Michael, who by this time has untied himself and is locked in the bathroom. The narrator, calling to him, "Mike, it's me," receives no response. Presuming that Michael has not heard him, he returns to the festivities.

In this story and in others, notably "The Names and Faces of Heroes," Price suggests that young boys at given times in their development have a sexual affinity with their fathers. This affinity remains controlled and restrained, but it exists nevertheless.

In "The Names and Faces of Heroes" nine-year-old Preacher is riding home from Raleigh with his father, Jeff McCraw. The two have been to a revival meeting. Preacher is reminded of what a minister told him on the last day of summer camp: "The short cut to being a man is finding your hero, somebody who is what you are not but need to be." The boy is searching for a hero.

The sexual innuendo in "The Names and Faces of Heroes" is strong and unmistakable. Preacher and Jeff are in the front seat of their old Pontiac, Jeff "slumped huge at the wheel, I the thin fork of flesh thrust out of his groin on the seat beside him, my dark head the burden in his lap his only hollow that flushes beneath me with rhythm I predict to force blood against any weight through nodes of tissue, squabs of muscle that made me ten years ago." Preacher traces his name on the skin of his father's wrist, as lovers might carve their initials on tree trunks to memorialize a romantic event.

In this story, the abandonment theme is also strong and unsettling to Preacher, who questions whether he is really the son of the parents who have raised him and why his father leaves him in the car for long periods while he makes his sales pitches. In a dreamlike vision of his father's death, Preacher cups his own undeveloped groin, which now grows into the groin of a mature man. Preacher, dreaming that "our skin has joined maybe past parting," tries to remove his hand from his father's groin, but this action causes his father to stir as though Preacher had "given love not pain." At the end of the story, Preacher knows his father will die someday, but as his father carries him into the house, Preacher thinks, "They did not separate us tonight. We finished alive, together, whole. This one more time."

"Troubled Sleep" in *The Names and Faces of Heroes* is an early Price story that deals with homoeroticism more overtly than "Michael Egerton." Edward loves his cousin Falcon Rodwell but is too withdrawn to make open advances to him. One night, Edward's father sends him to bed early because he has called Falcon a cheat. Edward escapes from the house to the Dark Ring, a nearby clearing that is mysterious and, at night, quite frightening. When Falcon comes to the clearing, Edward hopes for some advance, some touch, some gesture that will encourage him erotically. Falcon, however, does not have anything of the sort in mind, so Edward's hopes are dashed. The two finally end up falling asleep next to each other.

Similar in theme is "Deeds of Light," written years after "Troubled Sleep" and included in *The Collected Stories.* The adolescent protagonist, Marcus Black, lives with his widowed mother in a North Carolina army town at the beginning of World War II. The townspeople offer Southern hospitality to many of the lonely young draftees who soon will be sent to war, encouraging them to come to church on Sundays and sometimes inviting them for Sunday dinner after the service.

One day Marcus meets Deke Patrick, who somehow knows Marcus's name and who inexplicably fascinates him. Marcus's weeks begin to revolve around his fantasies of Deke, whom he knows will soon have to ship out. Finally, on what is to be Deke's last weekend before deployment, the young man comes to Sunday dinner, during the course of which Marcus's mother is summoned unexpectedly to a neighboring town by the serious illness of her mother. As it turns out, she must spend the night there. Marcus realizes the possibilities with which he is confronted. He thinks, "Something crucial to my whole future might happen here, in a minute or never. So I tried to turn loose and take what came, though I braced myself by thinking *He's a lonesome human that'll leave here soon.*"

After spending the rest of the day keeping Marcus company, Deke stays the night, sharing Marcus's room. Marcus wakes up to find Deke examining him-

Dust jacket for Price's second collection of short fiction (1970), with a photograph of his parents, William Solomon and Elizabeth Rodwell Price, in 1926

self in the mirror, and realizes: "*Deke is memorizing his bones in case he's wounded or loses a part or comes back home a frozen corpse or just a free invisible spirit, recalled by maybe his mother and me for our short lives.*" Then Deke climbs into bed with Marcus, though all they do is sleep next to each other. When dawn breaks, Deke has already stolen away without waking Marcus, who, experiencing his first faint stirrings of manhood, is left with his memories and regrets. In these stories and in others, such as "The Enormous Door" in *The Collected Stories,* Price writes delicately about sexual awakening and about the innocence of how unsophisticated boys come to grips with their burgeoning sexual natures as they move themselves gently toward maturity.

A different sort of coming of age faces twelve-year-old Crawford Langley in "His Final Mother."

This story becomes increasingly mystical as it progresses. Crawley's mother, Adele, falls dead suddenly while hanging an ancient quilt on the clothes line. Young Crawford is summoned from school and matter-of-factly kisses his mother's cold forehead. Then the cook "went to fix normal supper." Crawford occupies himself until his father's return by reading *Robinson Crusoe.* When the father returns, Crawford meets him to inform him of Adele's death. In what follows, Crawford assumes an almost parental responsibility for his father. He also gropes for religious guidance that does not come. He feels abandoned by God and wonders why it happened: "Had he someway caused his mother pain in broad daylight alone in the yard?"

Later that night, Adele returns in a vision as the young woman she was when Crawford's father married her, and Crawford watches as she comforts his nearly suicidal father: "He sat at the foot and knew his father had surely prayed her back to life to tame him down and save her son." Finally, he "shucked his clothes (the room was still warm) and then for the first time entered his sheets as naked as he left her lovely body long ago in pain and blood." As are the protagonists in "Deeds of Light" and "The Names and Faces of Heroes," Crawford is on the brink of assuming adult responsibility. Price captures with considerable deftness one of the fundamental commitments of coming of age.

The collection titled *Permanent Errors* is, according to Price's foreword, "the attempt to isolate in a number of lives the central error of act, will, understanding which, once made, has been permanent, incurable, but whose diagnosis and palliation are the hopes of continuance." The first section of this collection, bearing the subtitle "Fool's Education," consists of four stories that can be read independently but that, when read together, form a larger, enhanced story.

The main character in these stories–"The Happiness of Others," "A Dog's Death," "Scars," and "Waiting at Dachau"–is Charles Tamplin, an Oxford scholar whose relationship with his lover, Sara, ends as the first story begins. Tamplin is spending one last day with her before the transatlantic voyage that will take her away from him. This story is in part the explanation of how he drove her away, of how the two have conflicting views of what purpose there is in life, as exemplified by the defining mottoes each has chosen. Tamplin's is from Ben Jonson's lines on the bust of Lucius Cary; Sara's is a somewhat inferior epitaph from a mass grave. Tamplin represents the head, Sara the heart, and herein lies the root of their incompatibility.

In the second story, "A Dog's Death," Sara has departed and Tamplin has closeted himself in his rented room. He craves isolation, although his solitude is constantly violated. In "A Dog's Death" Tamplin's landlady intrudes on him to tell him that her aged dog is "chocked with tumors" and must be put to sleep; Tamplin and the dog have never liked each other. She wants Tamplin to be with the dog at the end, because she cannot bear to be. Tamplin agrees, already having shown in the first story that he is not one to avoid association with death.

Tamplin protests the dog's demise briefly, but then the veterinarian proceeds with it, proclaiming the peaceful death to be beautiful. Once the dog is dead, the rules that Tamplin has set for himself permit him to touch it. He feels the dog's ear and is reminded that now would be the time for him to kill his love for Sara, just as the veterinarian has killed the diseased dog, but he cannot do so.

"Scars" involves another intrusion upon Tamplin's much-desired solitude. The landlady and her friend, Mary, invade Tamplin's room, which he views as a "sufficient fort against all but death." Tamplin, with only a towel around his middle, is teased by the women until he finally strikes Mary and, in so doing, notices a scar that lingers from a blow inflicted by her cuckolded husband. The moment is a revealing one: "He saw of course his mother's face, Sara his love's, in the stranger's, half-hidden but judging, waiting, two feet away." The next morning, the landlady tells Tamplin Mary's history, which inspires him to turn it into a story.

Later Tamplin's privacy is again violated by Mary's coming to his room looking for a place to hide with her newest lover. Rejected, Mary moves on, fleeing with her lover, leaving her husband behind and ignoring the fact that her father is dying. Mary insists on remaining a part of the cruel world that Tamplin, in his isolation, rejects: "All surrendered but him. He envied them all. For this moment, he worshiped their wasteful courage, ruinous choices, contingency."

Certainly the most celebrated story among those in "Fool's Education" is "Waiting at Dachau." Although this story is last in the section, it takes place prior to the other three and helps to explain a great deal that is in them, most significantly, the break-up between Tamplin and Sara. It is told in the first person by Tamplin, addressing Sara: "I need to know several things–my version, your version, then the truth."

The rest of the story is his version. The two are on holiday in Europe during the summer of 1957; Tamplin has planned the details of the trip. He and

Sara have an idyllic time in Scandinavia, then set out through Germany on their way to Salzburg. Tamplin has included a visit to Dachau as a part of their itinerary as they approach the Austrian border. When they arrive, Tamplin offers to stop short of the camp, to revise the itinerary. Sara, however, insists that they press on, but then, without explaining, she refuses to enter the camp.

As he tours Dachau alone, Tamplin struggles less with the realization of what the German captors did to their Jewish internees than with the notion of what some Jewish internees did to each other, in some cases betraying fellow Jews for their own benefit. This lack of trust and integrity is what gnaws at Tamplin, who is involved in a situation with Sara in which betrayal figures prominently.

In this story, it becomes clear that Tamplin cannot sustain normal romantic relationships. In one scene, he and Sara are approached in a restaurant by gypsies who ask if she wants her picture taken with a sleepy, motherless lion cub. The cub bites Sara, but she calms it and bandages her wound while Tamplin eats the chocolate cake that the proprietor brings them as "recompense." Scholar Constance Rooke offers this interpretation of the scene with the lion: "Tamplin's sexual vulnerability, his parasitic relationship to Sara, and his complex and usually hidden concern with his own mother are all contained and associated by this tableau." This story is a complex one both in its function of providing insights into the other three stories in "Fool's Education" and in its broad scope that includes not only an overlay of classical mythology but also fleeting reminiscences that lurk in Tamplin's extremely complicated unconscious mind.

In most of Price's stories, the presence of death is intermixed with a sense of continuance, of recurrence. The Biblical concept that the sins of the parents are visited on their children, so prevalent in Price's novels, also occurs in many of the short stories. Still, as he makes clear in stories such as "The Names and Faces of Heroes" and "Truth and Lies" (from *Permanent Errors*), the chain of being that the generations imply can in itself be a salvation. In both stories the husbands, Jeff McCraw and Nathan Wilson, are destroying themselves with drink. When the survival of Jeff's wife in childbirth is extremely doubtful, Jeff makes a pact with God (as Price's own father did at the time of the author's birth) that if his wife and child survive, he will give up drinking and turn his life around, as he has.

Nathan Wilson, on the other hand, is a drunkard and a philanderer. His wife, Sarah, is unable to give him a child, although she blames their childlessness on Nathan. He continues in his profligate ways, and his paramour, Ella, becomes pregnant and aborts Nathan's child. In the end, in a scene in which a distraught Sarah runs down a rabbit with her car, feeling its "brittle death" in her own fine bones as she grips the steering wheel, Sarah now realizes it is she who made the permanent error, who stopped her life with Nathan through deception and denial.

"An Early Christmas," published separately in 1992 and placed as the last piece in *The Collected Stories,* is distinctive among the stories; it is set in Israel shortly before Christmas. The Israeli-Arab conflict is festering and is apparent at every turn, yet the backdrop for it, ironically, is Bethlehem with its overtones of Christian love, charity, and rebirth. The narrator is an artist, Bridge Boatner, recalling the events of his trip and reflecting on how, now confined to a wheelchair, his "hands and eyes work on above the cooling ruins and make each day an art to match, in one respect, all art I know this side of Athens, Florence, Rome (Jerusalem proves how little art counts, being all but bare of intentional art)." He goes on to speak of his "driving will to show the world its visible likeness," which must be considered a fundamental aim in most of Price's writing.

In his introduction to *The Collected Stories* Price offers his definition of what the genre can accomplish:

> If for me the broad subject of novels has been the action of time–its devastation and curious repair–the story has charted briefer stretches of concentrated feeling, and it always speaks an intimate language. . . . the story shorter than, say, fifty pages is the prose narrator's nearest approach to music–duo, trio, quartet, serenade, dance or the deeper reaches of song: the lean lament or ballad of hunger, delight, revulsion or praise.

He adds an assessment of his own intentions: "From the start my stories were driven by heat . . . and my general aim is the transfer of a spell of keen witness, perceived by the reader as warranted in character and act."

Interviews:

Wallace Kaufmann, ed., "A Conversation with Reynolds Price," *Shenandoah,* 17 (Spring 1966): 3–25;

William E. Ray, *Conversations: Reynolds Price and William Ray* (Memphis: Memphis State University, 1976);

Frederick Busch, "Reynolds Price: The Art of Fiction CXXVII," *Paris Review,* 33 (Winter 1991): 150–179;

Jefferson Humphries, ed., *Conversations with Reynolds Price* (Jackson: University Press of Mississippi, 1991);

Susan Ketchin, "Narrative Hunger and Silent Witness: An Interview with Reynolds Price," *Georgia Review,* 47 (Fall 1993): 522–542.

Bibliography:

Stuart Wright and James L. W. West, III, *Reynolds Price: A Bibliography 1949–1984* (Charlottesville: University Press of Virginia, 1986).

References:

Paul Binding, "Reynolds Price," in his *Separate Country: A Literary Journey through the American South,* second edition (Jackson: University Press of Mississippi, 1988), pp. 157–191;

Gary M. Ciuba, "The Discords and Harmonies of Love: Reynolds Price's *New Music,*" *Southern Quarterly,* 29 (Winter 1991): 115–130;

Ciuba, "Price's *Love and Work:* Discovering the 'Perfect Story,'" *Renascence,* 44 (Fall 1991): 45–60;

Clear Pictures, Direct Cinema, 1994;

Jefferson Humphries, "'A Vast Common Room': Twenty-five Years of Essays and Fiction by Reynolds Price," *Southern Review,* 24 (Summer 1988): 686–695;

Sue Laslie Kimball and Lynn Veach Sadler, eds., *Reynolds Price: From "A Long and Happy Life" to "Good Hearts," with a Bibliography* (Fayetteville, N.C.: Methodist College Press, 1989);

Reynolds Price: A Writer's Inheritance, New York University Journalism Department, 1986;

Constance Rooke, *Reynolds Price* (Boston: Twayne, 1983);

The Roots of Solitude: The Life and Work of Reynolds Price, Carolina Video, 1992;

James A. Schiff, ed., *Critical Essays on Reynolds Price* (Boston: G. K. Hall, 1998);

Schiff, *Understanding Reynolds Price* (Columbia: University of South Carolina Press, 1996);

Allen Shepherd, "Notes on Nature in the Fiction of Reynolds Price," *Critique: Studies in Modern Fiction,* 15, no. 2 (1970): 83–94;

John W. Stevenson, "The Faces of Reynolds Price's Short Fiction," *Studies in Short Fiction,* 3 (1965–1966): 300–306;

Anne Tyler, "Reynolds Price: Duke of Writers," *Vanity Fair,* 49 (July 1986): 82–85.

Papers:

The bulk of Reynolds Price's papers available to the public are housed in the Perkins Library at Duke University.

James Purdy
(14 July 1923 –   )

Brian Evenson
Oklahoma State University

See also the Purdy entry in *DLB 2: American Novelists Since World War II.*

photograph by Thomas Victor

BOOKS: *Don't Call Me By My Right Name* (New York: William-Frederick, 1956); republished as *63: Dream Palace, A Novella and Nine Stories* (London: Gollancz, 1957); enlarged as *Color of Darkness: Eleven Stories and a Novella* (New York: New Directions, 1957; London: Secker & Warburg, 1961);

63: Dream Palace (New York: William-Frederick, 1956); republished in *63: Dream Palace, A Novella and Nine Stories* (London: Gollancz, 1957);

Malcolm (New York: Farrar, Straus & Cudahy, 1959; London: Secker & Warburg, 1960);

The Nephew (New York: Farrar, Straus & Cudahy, 1960; London: Secker & Warburg, 1961);

Children Is All (New York: New Directions, 1962; London: Secker & Warburg, 1963);

Cabot Wright Begins (New York: Farrar, Straus & Giroux, 1964; London: Secker & Warburg, 1965);

An Oyster Is a Wealthy Beast (Los Angeles: Black Sparrow, 1967);

Eustace Chisholm and the Works (New York: Farrar, Straus & Giroux, 1967; London: Cape, 1968);

Mr. Evening: A Story and Nine Poems (Los Angeles: Black Sparrow, 1968);

On the Rebound: A Story and Nine Poems (Los Angeles: Black Sparrow, 1970);

Jeremy's Version (Garden City, N.Y.: Doubleday, 1970; London: Cape, 1971);

The Running Sun (New York: Paul Waner, 1971);

I Am Elijah Thrush (Garden City, N.Y.: Doubleday, 1972; London: Cape, 1972);

Sunshine Is an Only Child (New York: Aloe, 1973);

The House of the Solitary Maggot (Garden City, N.Y.: Doubleday, 1974; London: Owen, 1986);

In a Shallow Grave (New York: Arbor House, 1976; London: W. H. Allen, 1978);

A Day after the Fair: A Collection of Plays and Short Stories (New York: Note of Hand, 1977);

Narrow Rooms (New York: Arbor House, 1978; London: W. H. Allen, 1978);

Lessons and Complaints (New York: Nadja, 1979);

Sleep Tight (New York: Nadja, 1979);

Two Plays (Dallas: New London, 1979);

Proud Flesh: Four Short Plays (Northridge, Cal.: Lord John, 1981);

Scrap of Paper & The Berry-picker: Two Plays (Los Angeles: Sylvester & Orphanos, 1981);

Mourners Below (New York: Viking, 1981; London: Owen, 1984);
Don't Let the Snow Fall; Dawn (Utrecht: Sub Signo Libelli, 1984);
On Glory's Course (New York: Viking, 1984; London: Owen, 1985);
In the Hollow of His Hand (New York: Weidenfeld & Nicolson, 1986; London: Owen, 1988);
The Candles of Your Eyes and Thirteen Other Stories (New York: Weidenfeld & Nicolson, 1987; London: Owen, 1988);
The Garments the Living Wear (San Francisco: City Lights Books, 1989; London: Owen, 1989);
Collected Poems (Amsterdam: Athenaeum, 1990);
63: Dream Palace, Selected Stories 1956–1987 (Santa Rosa, Cal.: Black Sparrow, 1991);
Out with the Stars (London: Owen, 1992; San Francisco: City Lights Books, 1992);
Gertrude of Stony Island Avenue (London: Owen, 1997; New York: Morrow, 1998).
Edition: *Dream Palaces: Three Novels* (New York: Viking, 1980).

One of America's most original and dynamic writers, James Purdy has always been regarded as something of an outsider. He achieved international recognition before being somewhat grudgingly recognized by American critics, and he has continued to attract more critical attention outside his home country than within it. This circumstance is due partially to the attack on middle-class American values that his work undertakes and partially to his willingness to delve deeper into the dark spaces of the human soul than most other American writers.

Purdy's work has been translated into more than two dozen languages. John Cowper Powys declared him "the best kind of original genius of our day. His insight into the diabolical cruelties and horrors that lurk all the time under our conventional skin is as startling as his insight into the angelic tenderness and protectiveness that also exist in the same hiding place." Gore Vidal has declared Purdy "an authentic American genius," and George Steiner dubbed him "a writer of fantastic talent. His books take one by the throat and shake one's bones loose."

Purdy's short fiction of the 1950s and 1960s in particular is well ahead of its time, prefiguring trends in American fiction that did not come into fashion until decades later. Perhaps partly for this reason, Dame Edith Sitwell declared, "I am convinced that long after my death James Purdy will come to be recognized as one of the greatest writers America has ever produced." Purdy remains an innovator, a highly distinctive writer whose influence on contemporary fiction has been consistently underestimated. Indeed, Carole Polsgrove suggests in *It Wasn't Pretty, Folks, but Didn't We Have Fun?* (1995), when *Esquire* editor Gordon Lish dramatically revised the work of a short-story writer who went on to become one of America's most noted–Raymond Carver–he used Purdy's "flat ironic style" as a model.

Purdy's stories frequently investigate themes that middle America tries to avoid: overwhelming authority figures, problematic family relations, and the difficulties in developing and maintaining personal identity while at the same time trying to establish a relationship with others. In Purdy's stories people try to make human connections but have difficulty interacting on more than a superficial level. Whether they seek their human connection in traditional marriage and family ties, in less traditional relations (such as homosexuality), or in transgressive acts such as incest, rape, and violence, the results seem to be the same. When people do connect on a slightly deeper level, the intensity of the relation tends to destroy one of them. Purdy explores relationships of all kinds, through this exploration establishing a larger investigation of the individual's need to be him- or herself and at the same time to share with others.

Purdy has been reticent to speak of his life, as Stephen Adams notes, preferring "not to give a biography since his biography is in his work": "it is apt to think of his work as an alternative form of biography." James Amos Purdy was born close to Fremont, Ohio, on 14 July 1923, the middle child of three boys, a fourth child having died before Purdy's birth. He is the son of William Purdy and Vera Covick Purdy. In his youth his parents were divorced, and he lived alternately with his mother, father, and grandmother. After several moves, Purdy left for Chicago, later attending the University of Chicago and then the University of Puebla in Mexico. He taught English in Havana before returning to take graduate courses at the University of Chicago and, later, at the University of Madrid. In 1949 Purdy began teaching English and Spanish at Lawrence College (now Lawrence University) in Wisconsin. He taught there until 1953, when he quit to devote himself full-time to writing. Around 1960 Purdy moved to New York, where he has lived ever since.

Purdy's writing life began with frustration. Though he began writing in his twenties, he had little success for nearly a decade. His attempts to interest publishers in his fiction were rebuffed, often in caustic terms. Purdy has been outspoken about the weaknesses of New York literary publishers, criticizing them for wanting easy stories and rarefied socialite fiction. "They want recycled recycled," he said in a 1982 interview in *Conjunctions*. "It's all about clothes and fashion." Speaking of fame in literary America in a letter to *Contemporary Authors* (NRS, 19), Purdy declared: "reputations are made in America by political groups backed by money and power brokers who care nothing for original and distinguished writing, but are bent on forwarding the names of writers who are politically respectable."

In 1955 Osborn Andreas arranged to have nine of Purdy's short stories printed privately under the title *Don't Call Me By My Right Name.* In the same year, a chemist friend of Purdy's, J. J. Sjoblom, borrowed money to publish privately Purdy's novella, *63: Dream Palace.* The two books were published by William-Frederick, a subsidy press, in 1956. Purdy sent copies of these works to writers and critics and received many enthusiastic responses. Among them was one from Sitwell, who wrote back praising the stories and later, in a letter to Purdy dated 26 November 1956, declared *63: Dream Palace* "a masterpiece from every point of view." Through her influence she helped convince Victor Gollancz to publish the stories and the novella together in England under the title *63: Dream Palace.* Soon after, New Directions Press, which had previously turned down everything that Purdy had sent them–including the same stories and the novella–for nearly a decade, published both the novella and the stories in America under the title *Color of Darkness,* with two additional stories.

Anthony Bailey in *Commonweal* (17 January 1958) called Purdy's first stories "a novel departure in the craft of the short story" that makes "the work of many highly skilled writers seem extremely dependent on literary convention." Purdy was exploring new ground, using a bare style to attack middle-class sensibilities and literary conventions, exploring the destructive tensions between family members and examining the way in which social norms and the individual often come into conflict.

The title story of *Color of Darkness* concerns a man living in a state of lassitude with his young son after a divorce. He finds himself unable or unwilling to care about his son, frequently pawning him off on his housekeeper despite her warnings about the boy's loneliness. As the story progresses, he forgets the color of his wife's eyes, then his housekeeper's, then finally his son's. Living in his own world, he cannot build relationships with others: he might as well be living in darkness. The son, without any source of relief for his confusion and pain, begins to grow difficult, finally erupting into verbal and physical violence toward his father. As with many of the stories in *Color of Darkness,* the style is spare and exact, the use of language meticulous. Purdy is restrained in his use of metaphors and symbols, opting for few such comparisons, but those he does use, such as a wedding ring the boy chews on as a repressed reaction to the divorce, have genuine resonance. A great deal is left unspoken but is communicated by implication.

"Why Can't They Tell You Why?" is the story of the relationship of a child to his mother. Paul, a sickly and perhaps mentally ill boy, knows nothing of his father until he discovers a box of photographs of him. He regards them constantly. His mother, though at first ignoring his obsession with the photographs, eventually confronts him, claiming that they are the source of his illness. She demands that he choose between the pictures and her. The mother's threats and the child's anxiety are portrayed at a distance until the ending of the story, when "black thick strings of something" spill out of the boy's mouth "as though he had spewed out the heart of his grief."

Two stories, "Eventide" and "Cutting Edge," depict mothers unable to let their sons live their own lives. "Eventide" shows Mahala grief-stricken over the "loss" of her son, Teeboy, who has left home to hang out in jazz parlors. Mahala's love for Teeboy, suggests Stephen Adams, has been frozen in the "first phase of motherhood"; indeed, for Mahala perfect happiness would be for Teeboy to be a helpless baby that she could take care of again. "Cutting Edge" shows Mrs. Zeller's struggles to impose her will on her son, Bobby, when he returns home with a beard then later sunbathes naked in the garden. As is often the case in Purdy's short fiction, the dispute over the beard stands in for more fundamental issues in the relation of mother to child, the beard symbolizing the communication that should occur but does not.

In "You May Safely Gaze," Guy tells Phillip of two bodybuilding coworkers seen at the beach, revealing himself obsessed with them though he claims to be disgusted. Along with the humor of the story, the underlying tension–which involves the bodybuilders' unwillingness to conform to social norms by being embarrassed when their shorts rip–serves to express Philip's repressed wish to be able to step out of conformity as well. The struggle with sexual identity, the ability to express oneself sexually, is linked in this story to Purdy's larger concerns with imposed social authority and the pressure it puts on individual identity.

Sexual identity and its collision with the social conformities of marriage is the subject of "Man and Wife." Here, Peaches learns that her husband, Lafe, has been fired from his job for being suspected of homosexuality. They speak around the issue, never quite willing to say the word *homosexual.* Lafe seems intent on trying to get Peaches to admit that he has satisfied her while still insisting that he is "not a normal man." He wants to break the lockstep of conformity and explore the desires that he has been denying. Yet, the story ends by his vowing to Peaches, "I will always stand by you any-

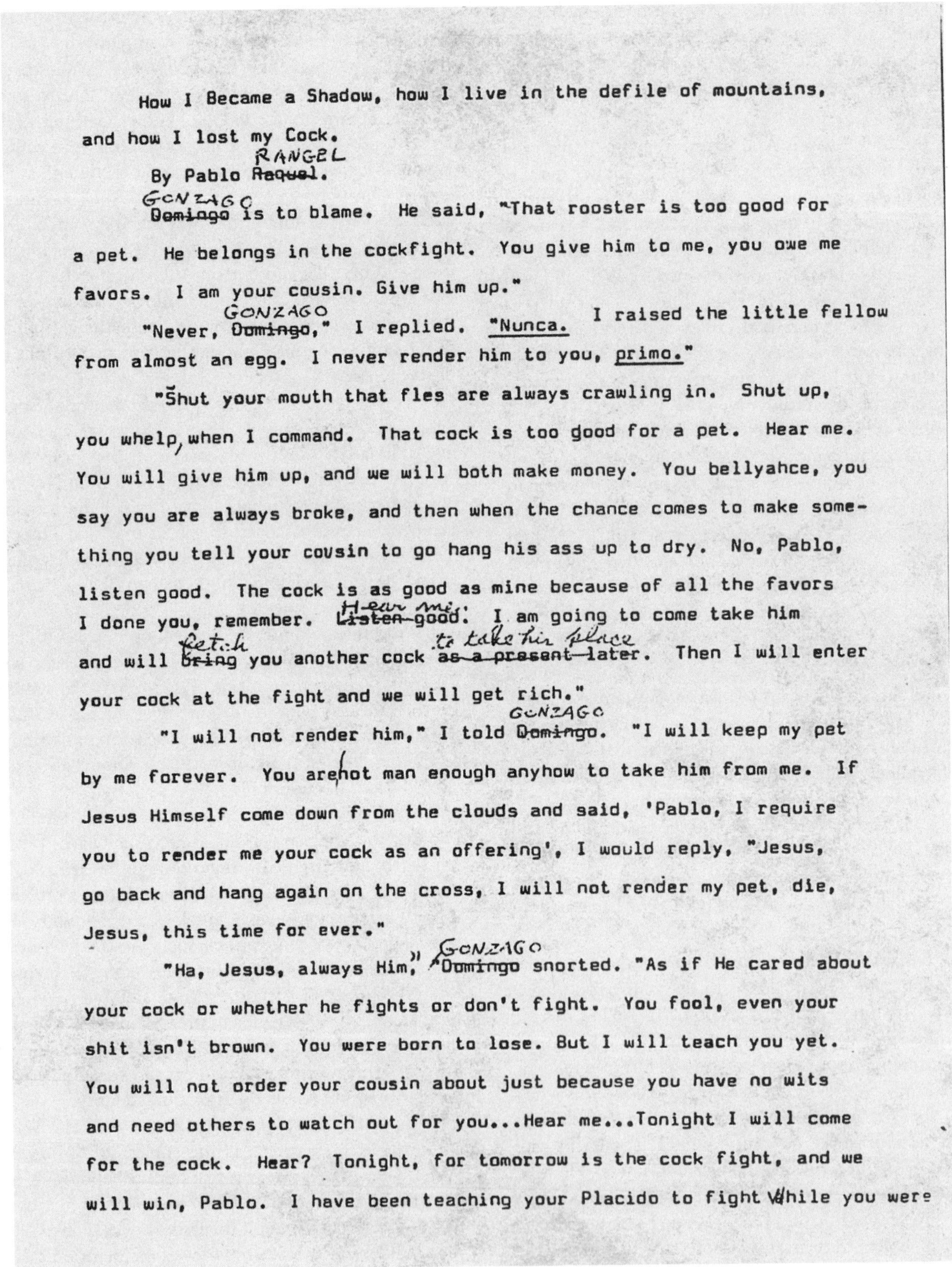

How I Became a Shadow, how I live in the defile of mountains, and how I lost my Cock.

By Pablo ~~Raquel~~ RANGEL.

~~Domingo~~ GONZAGO is to blame. He said, "That rooster is too good for a pet. He belongs in the cockfight. You give him to me, you owe me favors. I am your cousin. Give him up."

"Never, ~~Domingo~~ GONZAGO," I replied. "<u>Nunca.</u> I raised the little fellow from almost an egg. I never render him to you, <u>primo.</u>"

"Shut your mouth that fles are always crawling in. Shut up, you whelp, when I command. That cock is too good for a pet. Hear me. You will give him up, and we will both make money. You bellyahce, you say you are always broke, and then when the chance comes to make something you tell your cousin to go hang his ass up to dry. No, Pablo, listen good. The cock is as good as mine because of all the favors I done you, remember. ~~Listen good~~ Hear me! I am going to come take him and will ~~bring~~ fetch you another cock ~~as a present later~~ to take his place. Then I will enter your cock at the fight and we will get rich."

"I will not render him," I told ~~Domingo~~ GONZAGO. "I will keep my pet by me forever. You are not man enough anyhow to take him from me. If Jesus Himself come down from the clouds and said, 'Pablo, I require you to render me your cock as an offering', I would reply, "Jesus, go back and hang again on the cross, I will not render my pet, die, Jesus, this time for ever."

"Ha, Jesus, always Him," ~~Domingo~~ GONZAGO snorted. "As if He cared about your cock or whether he fights or don't fight. You fool, even your shit isn't brown. You were born to lose. But I will teach you yet. You will not order your cousin about just because you have no wits and need others to watch out for you...Hear me...Tonight I will come for the cock. Hear? Tonight, for tomorrow is the cock fight, and we will win, Pablo. I have been teaching your Placido to fight while you were

Page from the revised typescript for one of the stories collected in Purdy's 1987 book, The Candles of Your Eyes *(Collection of James Purdy)*

how," a promise suggesting that he will continue to repress his sexuality for the sake of social duty. The story typifies the Purdean dilemma: Lafe wants to be close to Peaches, but to do so he must deny a part of himself that he wants to have recognized. To come close to her, he must assume a false face, and thus even when he is close, he is not close. He is transfixed on the horns of an unresolvable dilemma.

It is not just homosexual anxiety that creates such a dilemma of connection versus independence: for Purdy this dilemma is to be found in all kinds of relationships and is indeed part of what it means to be human. "Sound of Talking," like "Man and Wife," is about what cannot be acknowledged in a husband and wife's relationship. Virgil, a paraplegic, is confined to a wheelchair and remains tight-lipped and bitter. His wife talks to him to keep him company and to avoid looking too closely at their life together. The story suggests a dilemma often present in Purdy's fiction, the characters faced with two alternatives, neither of which, because of their own character, is satisfactory. As Bettina Schwarzschild explains, the wife "hurts her husband by not looking at his crippled legs and hurts him when she does. She is reduced to a life of furtive glances, as trapped as her husband in the wheelchair."

Several of the stories dissect the dilemma of marriage. "Don't Call Me By My Right Name" explores a recently married woman's discomfort with her new last name, Klein, which seems alien to her. Drunk at a party, she asks her husband to change his name. As the argument progresses and the husband begins to assault her, all the dissatisfactions of married life and the difficulties of self-identity within marriage get wrapped into the ludicrous fight over the name. Indeed, the discomfort with the name stands in for the challenges to the self that any love relationship, gay or straight, brings about.

"You Reach for Your Hat" centers on a widow's attempt to understand her relationship to her husband as she recounts her story to a friend. "A Good Woman" investigates Maud's relationship to small-town life as she sits sipping sodas, running up a bill that she cannot pay. Intrigued by her friend Mamie's tales of a better life in the city, fascinated with Mamie, and disturbed by her obsession with happiness, Maud slips into the dream enough to run up a large bill and is afraid to tell her husband about it. When the drugstore owner attempts to take a sexual substitute for payment, Maud manages to slip away, his interest nonetheless reviving a sense of herself as desirable that has been lost in her relationship with her traveling-salesman husband.

"Plan Now to Attend" recounts the meeting of two classmates, Fred Parker and Ezra Graitop. After twenty years Graitop has acquired a religious disingenuousness: once an avowed atheist, he is now the head figure in a religious movement. As he gets so drunk he has to be carried out of his room, believing he has brought Fred into the "movement," the superficiality of his religious commitment reveals itself.

63: Dream Palace, the novella that concludes the collection, ranks among Purdy's best works of any length. It recounts the story of Fenton Riddleway and his brother, Claire, who, upon arriving in Chicago from West Virginia, are directed to a rooming house on Sixty-third Street. The house, though, is a ruin, a "not-right kind of place" that "has survived by oversight." They sleep there anyway, taking turns on the single cot. While Fenton manages to find sponsors and begins to move into society, Claire grows ill. Ultimately Fenton, after stumbling home from an orgiastic and drug-ridden night, wakes up to find that he has strangled Claire. Schwarzschild argues that Claire is a part of Fenton and that in killing Claire he is killing himself, which she feels is what gives the story a broader resonance, raising its tattered characters to tragic dimensions. Other critics seem to agree that *63: Dream Palace* is one of Purdy's most trenchant works.

When *63: Dream Palace* was originally published in London, publisher Victor Gollancz, because of fear that he might face an obscenity lawsuit, made changes to Purdy's title novella, omitting some offensive language. Sitwell, in the introduction to *Color of Darkness* (which restores Purdy's original text), defends Purdy's ending, declaring it "utterly appalling, but it is also full of an unutterable tenderness and a deep meaning." In this characterization one might find a map for reading Purdy in general: the appalling and the tender go hand in hand. Whatever sort of flaying the characters and the reader undergo reveals both harsh and delicate aspects of human interaction that can be seen only when the "conventional skin" is destroyed.

In 1962 Purdy published *Children Is All,* a volume of ten stories and two plays. As with *Color of Darkness,* the style seems simple and stripped, nonetheless conveying a genuine intensity and a depth of understanding of the human condition and again foregrounding the dilemma of trying to establish and maintain meaningful relationships. The characters are often suffering and desperate, trying and failing to make contact with one another.

In "Daddy Wolf," Benny is alone and trying to connect with anyone at all. Throughout the story Benny offers an extended explanation to a stranger as to why he has been using the phone booth in the hall of the apartment house for such a long time. His wife, he tells, has left him, taking their son with her. Before leaving, she had been calling Daddy Wolf's crisis line and confessing that she has been turning tricks to make ends meet. She is advised to "go to Sunday School and Church and quit going up to strange men's hotel rooms." Since Daddy Wolf will accept calls only from women, the pathetically solitary Benny is telephoning random numbers, trying to find anyone who will listen to his story.

Like "Sound of Talking," "Home by Dark" is about what cannot be acknowledged between two people. It portrays a conversation between a grandfather and his grandson as they sit on the porch, skirting the issue of the boy's parents' death. When the grandfather suggests to the boy that pure wishes must come true, the little boy makes another wish: that his parents might still be alive. The story evokes a complex mood of grief and hope, engaging the reader in the grandfather's failing attempts to navigate between the two.

"Night and Day," another story of a grandfather and grandson, again strands its main character, Cleo, on the horns of a dilemma. Grandy, not at all interested in his grandson, is sexually attracted to Cleo, the boy's mother. As the story progresses, he declares he wants to marry her but demands that she send her boy to live with his father, threatening to cut off financial support if she does not agree. Cleo must either give up motherhood or lose her support. She chooses to remain with her child, calling Grandy a "whoring old goat!"

While Cleo chooses motherhood and a more natural, genuine attachment, Purdy's other characters deliberately choose to reject their blood relatives. "About Jessie Mae" takes place in a country kitchen as a conversation among women. It concerns inner and outer untidiness, the disparity between outward appearances and internal attitudes, providing a variation on Purdy's view of the connection between social veneer and inner reality. Jessie Mae's cousin Myrtle refuses to visit Jessie Mae "because of her untidiness." Instead Myrtle spends her time in the immaculate kitchen of Mrs. Hemlock, slandering Jessie Mae and indulging her appetite.

Many of Purdy's characters are slaves to their appetites–sometimes a hunger for food, sometimes for the security and comfort of love or money, sometimes a craving for power and control. Stumbling attempts to express love and desire can be found in several stories. In "The Lesson," for example, Purdy traces the appetite for love evolving into an appetite for dominance. Sixteen-year-old Polly has become infatuated with Mr. Diehl, her swimming instructor. Trying to make Mr. Diehl sexually aware of her, she argues that women should be allowed to use the pool during private lessons. As they argue, she puts her hand on his arm, then realizes that she has the power to make him uncomfortable. Concerned with the paths that desire allows itself to take when society demands its repression, "The Lesson" instructs the reader in the dynamics of sexual manipulation.

Polly's sexual initiation occurs early; others of Purdy's child characters come into their own sense of power later in life. "Mrs. Benson" is about the Paris reunion of the divorced Mrs. Benson with her thirty-year-old daughter, Wanda Walters. They discuss an invitation Mrs. Benson received shortly after her first divorce some years ago to stay with a Mrs. Carlin. Many divorces later, Mrs. Benson recounts the story as if it were some indication of her being wanted or needed. She is beginning to reveal, perhaps without realizing it, her doubts to her daughter when Wanda ends the reunion by declaring in a bright, loud, artificial voice that such reunions are a pleasure. Wanda's unmistakable effort to keep their relationship on the superficial level of convention proves the effectiveness of Mrs. Benson's parental tutelage. As Mrs. Benson has always kept husbands and acquaintances securely distanced, so is Wanda now firmly holding Mrs. Benson herself at bay.

The tensions of highly critical parent-child interactions inform many of Purdy's works. This subject receives an uncharacteristically light treatment in the brief piece "Sermon," but even this humorous work echoes with darker reverberations. "Sermon" is a toastmaker speech by God. It criticizes mankind for simply existing instead of becoming something significant but insists as well "there is, in fact, no hope for you and there never was." God goes so far as to admit "I, of course, am a Mistake." "Sermon" presents an intriguing mix of religious fatalism and parody. By presenting the First Parent as flawed, Purdy effectively dooms all future families to dysfunctionality.

In "Encore," a stunningly dysfunctional mother uses authoritarian control as a substitute for love. The story explores the relationship between Merta and her bastard son, Gibbs. Wanting Gibbs to be successful in college and to spend time with the "right set," she objects to his associating with Spyro, the son of a Greek restaurant owner. As do many of Purdy's mother characters, she engulfs and stifles her son. Her pain and desperation in not being able to live vicariously through her son's success, though self-imposed, is nonetheless horrifying.

Purdy's power struggles involve parents and children, lovers, and friends. He explores the power relationships between two boys, their odd interdependence, in "Everything Under the Sun." It is the story of two roommates, Jesse and Cade, sharing a squalid room in a large city. Cade's voluntary unemployment upsets Jesse, who must spend all his earnings to support them. He feels honor-bound to support Cade nonetheless, since Cade's brother lost his life saving Jesse during the war. Complicating matters is the fact that Jesse has recently experienced a religious conversion: he has given up the drinking, smoking, and womanizing that he and Cade had previously enjoyed together. Mocking Jesse's hasty conversion with a quick reversal, Purdy suggests that indulgence in the physical appetites is a less serious vice than the fanaticism of religion.

"Goodnight, Sweetheart" is one of the most unsettling stories of the collection and also one of the finest, clearly delineating the emotional isolation shaded and implied in the other stories. Having been raped in her classroom by the brother of one of her students, Pearl Miranda is left without clothing. Fleeing "stark naked from her classroom," she manages to get to the house of Winston, a student she taught twenty years before. Pearl tries to deny the rape, claiming "I've had a trick played on me is all." As Winston's probing discovers the truth, he becomes physically ill and takes to his bed. When Pearl begins to shiver in delayed shock, Winston encourages her to get into the bed as well. As the story ends they are both in the bed but unable to turn to one another for comfort: "they both lay there close to one another, and they both muttered to themselves in the darkness as if they were separated by different rooms from one another." Not even physical and emotional intimacy can bring them to a true embrace.

The stories in *The Candles of Your Eyes and Thirteen Other Stories* (1987), as a reviewer in *Library Journal* (1 May 1987) noted, "confirm Purdy's true gift for fiction" and serve as "a hearty antidote to the Yuppie boredom of most contemporary short fiction." The formal range of this book is perhaps greater than Purdy's other volumes, from parodies such as "Lily's Party" to strange, short pieces to meditations on being, such as "Some of These Days." Shared themes–the difficulty of building relationships, the problems of families, the slippery nature of identity–lend coherence to the collection, however.

"Some of These Days," which opens the volume, is the story of a man released from prison who wants to see his gay landlord again (whom he begins to call, with religious implications, "My lord"). Yet, because of a prison injury, he cannot recall his landlord's name. Remembering that his landlord would sometimes patronize porn theaters, he stops eating and spends his time giving "favors to the men in the porno," hoping to catch a glimpse of his landlord. He is picked up and delivered to an asylum, where he gives his landlord's name as his own. When asked if there is anyone he would like to get word to, he offers his own name. "Some of These Days" is at once an extremely successful creation of a voice and a powerful investigation of the relation of one's name to one's sense of self. While "Don't Call Me By My Right Name" centers on the rejection of a name, the man in this story is desperate to find a name and attach himself to it. He takes his landlord's name as his own in an attempt to appropriate the landlord's being, to establish a relationship with someone who is not there. In taking the landlord's name, however, he loses himself, as the wife in "Don't Call Me By My Right Name" fears she will lose herself in her husband's name and in marriage.

Some of Purdy's characters become lost outside a relationship, requiring the presence of another to define themselves. "Scrap of Paper" pursues the relationship of Mrs. Baker to her former maid, Naomi, whom she has turned out, supposedly for fading her carpets. Mrs. Baker, after a bit of huffing, offers Naomi her job back, a position Naomi says she will take only if Mrs. Baker will sign a statement of apology. The two jockey back and forth, irritating each other in a way that suggests Mrs. Baker and Naomi's not altogether healthy interdependency.

Lost relations may be replaced in Purdy's works, but rarely in a completely satisfactory way. "Summer Tidings" is set at Rupert Aveline's birthday party when news of his grandmother's death arrives. As with "Home By Dark," the death hovers in the background, present but not quite discussed. Key to the story is Galway, the Jamaican gardener from next door, who seems dizzy with the sight of so many children and who has been promised a piece of birthday cake. A relationship has developed between Galway and the thirteen-year-old Rupert, who "liked to touch Galway as he would perhaps a horse." Galway, for his turn, seems more than a little taken by the boy, even trying when alone with him to break out of the social codes that keep them from interacting. "Summer Tidings" is at once a social critique and the investigation of the restraint imposed on Galway both by others and by himself.

"Mr. Evening" is written in a darker, more dreamlike vein, reminiscent of *63: Dream Palace*. In the story, the elderly but beautiful Mrs. Owens and her sister, Pearl, own a trove of antiques and heirlooms. Mrs. Owens is interested in Mr. Evening, a young collector who desperately covets one of Mrs. Owens's antique cups. Mrs. Owens uses this desire to control him; gradually, he loses more and more of his will, until he has become something to be added to her collection. The portrayal of Mrs. Owens is impeccable, cruel, and sublime, as is the portrayal of Mr. Evening's confusion over what is happening to him, what he is becoming.

The appetites for food, sex, power–which are prominent in *Children Is All*–again figure largely in *The Candles of Your Eyes*. "Lily's Party" is a parody of pornographic writing, featuring pies made for a church picnic, a "preacher," pie-throwing, and movements back and forth between eating and sex. It deals with many of

Dust jacket for Purdy's 1987 book, a collection of stories that one reviewer called "a hearty antidote to the Yuppie boredom of most contemporary fiction"

Purdy's other concerns but does so in a way that replaces the anguish of the characters with parody of a genre. While "Some of These Days" uses the pornography as a background presence, "Lily's Party" is the only story that formally takes pornographic fiction as its organizing principle. A little racy, the story is written with tongue firmly in cheek, an effective send-up.

"On the Rebound" is narrator Rupert Douthwaite's recounting of Georgia Comstock's attempted return to societal success. Willing to do anything to return to public favor, she agrees actually to kiss the ass of black novelist Burleigh Jordan. Jordan manages, however, to use the act to humiliate her severely and condemn her into permanent social exile. Though Erika Munk, in *The New York Times* (6 September 1987), found the implications of the story potentially racist, it can be read as an effective commentary on the mad rush of authors, editors, and other literati as they attempt to ally themselves to political correctness and minority writing for entirely selfish reasons. Like many of Purdy's other social climbers, Georgia needs the superficial benefits of social status to avoid facing her more profound loneliness and isolation. Her public exile is only a more visible ratification of an internal sense of solitude.

While some characters seem born to solitude, others have solitude thrust upon them. In "Ruthanna Elder" a brief moment of incest with her uncle (who is two years younger than she) has damaged Ruthanna's commitment to marry Jess. Unable to commit to Jess though she loves him and not the uncle, unable to escape the sensuality of the affair, Ruthanna remains in a quandary. Appalled at the enormity of her social transgression, she cannot confess her complicity to Jess. Her acceptance of what is socially appropriate places her in a moral bind, without any tolerable options. Her fiancé, guessing at the truth, kills both the uncle and himself, leaving Ruthanna bereft of both of them, without either lover or companion. Paralyzed by her guilt and conflicting desires, she suffers the consequences of her part both in transgressing and perpetuating social convention. Conventions and transgression often seem, in the final lines of a Purdy story, to have been illusory, constructs of subjective perceptions. Even those characters granted a moment of what seems to be objective clarity find that revelation oddly, emptily disappointing.

"Sleep Tight" plays on the discrepancy between a situation and the way in which a child interprets that situation. Little Judd is awakened by a fleeing and injured criminal, whom he thinks must be the Sandman. After the criminal dies, Judd continues in his mistaken belief, glimpsing the truth only when morning arrives. Thinking he is establishing a relationship with a mythical figure, he discovers he has been conversing with a dead man, a characteristically Purdean vacuity.

In "Short Papa," a father who has been in jail returns home briefly for a furtive meal with his son, leaving the boy with a gold watch. Years later, after the watch is misplaced, the boy consults a fortune-teller, who tells him not only where the watch is, but also that his father is dead. Returning home, he finds the watch and learns from his mother that Short Papa had indeed died some time before. Like the loss of the photographs in "Why Can't They Tell You Why?," the loss of the watch fills the boy with anxiety, since it serves as a memento of his father, but the return of the watch only confirms the father's absence.

Purdy's investigations into the mysteries of desire, love, and loss produce a rich variety of situations in *The Candles of Your Eyes*. In addition to the speech in "Sermon" and the parodic pornography of "Lily's Party," several other pieces actively manipulate form. "Mud Toe the Cannibal" is a fable of a retired cannibal's visit to a pianist in Greenwich Village. Highly stylized, it has a playfulness and lightness distinct from the rest of the stories in the collection. "How I Became a Shadow" is the story of how Gonzago steals his cousin Pablo's pet cock, Placido, and takes him to a cockfight, where the bird loses his eyes. Pablo, in revenge, blinds Gonzago and kills him. A parody of revenge ballads, "How I Became a Shadow" mixes tragedy with comic bathos, drawing about all that can be drawn out of a man's love for his chicken.

The last three stories in *The Candles of Your Eyes* are more directly involved with homosexual experience than most of Purdy's stories, though in his *Contemporary Authors* interview Purdy warned against people classifying him as a gay writer: "I'm just a writer. A writer is a writer. And when you say you're a 'gay writer' or a 'straight writer' you're through." Indeed, whether his characters are straight or gay or some combination, Purdy returns to the same themes of profoundly human relationships and problems.

The theme of the parent who substitutes control for love reappears in "Dawn," which explores the relationship of Timmy to his overbearing father. Narrated by Timmy's lover and roommate, the story recounts Timmy's father's sudden arrival in New York. Aggressive and demanding, the father forces his son to his will, taking him away from New York and his modeling career. The roommate, who loves Timmy, is left to weep, while Timmy's father proves to be a worse nightmare than the pseudo-authority figure of the criminal Sandman in "Sleep Tight."

"The Candles of Your Eyes" is a story of love turned wrong. It tells of Soldier, who fell in love with a boy named Beaut and then "protected or perhaps imprisoned Beaut out of his love for the boy." Their love is such that it blocks out all future and past, both of them living solely in the present. One night Soldier fails to come home. When he does return months later, Beaut has taken up with someone else, and both he and his new lover have frozen to death. Shooting the corpses, Soldier convinces himself he has murdered them. His need for human connection is so great he would rather believe that he has killed the couple–thus tying him to them–than that he has deserted Beaut.

"Rapture" is about the struggle between individual selfhood and desire. In the story, a boy's uncle gathers his hair from a comb, establishing a kind of secret devotion to him that the boy's dying mother approves of. After the mother's death and a few false steps, their relationship becomes at once desperate and intensely ecstatic and, at least for the moment, satisfying.

In 1991 Black Sparrow Press published *63: Dream Palace, Selected Stories 1956–1987.* In addition to reprinting *Color of Darkness* and *Children Is All* in full, as well as several stories from *The Candles of Your Eyes,* it includes an additional story, "In This Corner . . . ," which is similar to "Rapture." In "In This Corner . . . ," Hayes, in his forties, after the death of his second wife becomes involved with a youth named Clark Vail. After a single night the boy leaves, and Hayes is distraught, though in the end Clark returns. "Rapture" and "In This Corner . . ." both end at a moment of ecstasy, and both can be read as offering a more positive vision of love. Though there is no telling what will occur once the rapture has passed, the characters seem to be opening themselves up in a way that sets the facades at least partly aside.

Bettina Schwarzschild has suggested that "James Purdy's work is about love. Love between mother and child, brother and brother or sister, husband and wife, aunt and nephew, friends, neighbors, strangers. People stumbling, groping towards each other, and failing. Always failing cruelly, tragically, when the very survival of the beloved depends on love." People fail because "what we call love is often one façade falling for another façade. Yet, in the *inside,* in our central experience, is all human reality. In James Purdy's stories, the need to be recognized and accepted for one's *inside* is so desperate that his characters cannot live without it. Without the recognition of their human reality, they themselves do not know who they are. This puts them at the mercy of everyone's whims and finally destroys them."

Indeed, the nature of love and the substitution of facades for loving experiences are topics dealt with in nearly all of Purdy's stories: from the withdrawal of divine love in "Sermon" to the struggle between mother and son in many other stories, to the battle between husband and wife in "Man and Wife" or "Don't Call Me By My Right Name." Purdy's searching consideration of love in its various forms incorporates the stranger's appeal for someone to hear his story in "Daddy Wolf," the appropriation of Mr. Evening by Mrs. Owens in "Mr. Evening," and the released convict's attempt to find his landlord and redeem himself in "Some of These Days." Throughout his work Purdy is expert both at capturing the facades and at showing how they are stripped away–not to love, but to destroy. His work is unblinking and uncompromising, offering some of the most astute and painfully honest explorations of humanity in contemporary literature.

Interviews:

Bradford Morrow, "Interview with James Purdy," *Conjunctions,* 3 (1982): 97–111;

Patricia Lear, "Interview with James Purdy" *StoryQuarterly,* 26 (1989): 55–76.

Bibliography:

Jay Ladd, "James Purdy: A Bibliographical Checklist," *American Book Collector,* 2 (September–October 1981): 53–60.

References:

Stephen Adams, *James Purdy* (New York: Barnes & Noble, 1976);

Frank Baldanza, "James Purdy on the Corruption of Innocents," *Contemporary Literature,* 15 (Summer 1974): 315–330;

Baldanza, "James Purdy's Half-Orphans," *Centennial Review,* 18 (Summer 1974): 255–272;

Baldanza, "Northern Gothic," *Southern Review,* 10 (1974): 566–582;

Baldanza, "The Paradoxes of Patronage in Purdy," *American Literature,* 46 (1974): 347–356;

Baldanza, "Playing House for Keeps with James Purdy," *Contemporary Literature,* 11 (Autumn 1970): 488–510;

Shirley W. Burris, "The Emergency in Purdy's 'Daddy Wolf,'" *Renascence: Essays on Value in Literature,* 20 (Winter 1968): 94–98;

Henry Chupack, *James Purdy* (New York: Twayne, 1975);

Thomas H. Fick, "Reading a Dummy: James Purdy's 'Plan Now to Attend,'" *Studies in Short Fiction,* 25 (Winter 1988): 13–19;

Warren French, "James Purdy, Will Moses: Against the Wilderness," *Kansas Quarterly,* 14 (Spring 1982): 81–92;

French, "The Quaking World of James Purdy," in *Essays on Modern American Literature,* edited by Richard E. Langford (De Land, Fla.: Stetson University Press, 1963), pp. 112–122;

Paul W. Miller, "James Purdy's Early Years in Ohio and His Early Short Stories," *Midamerica,* 11 (1984): 108–116;

Donald Pease, "James Purdy: Shaman in Nowhere Land," in *The Fifties: Fiction, Poetry, Drama,* edited by French (De Land, Fla.: Everett/Edwards, 1970), pp. 145–154;

Regina Pomeranz, "The Hell of Not Loving: Purdy's Modern Tragedy," *Renascence: Essays on Value in Literature,* 16 (Winter 1964): 149–153;

Stanley Renner, "'Why Can't They Tell You Why?': A Clarifying Echo of *The Turn of the Screw,*" *Studies in American Fiction,* 14 (Autumn 1986): 205–213;

Bettina Schwarzschild, *The Not-Right House: Essays on James Purdy* (Columbia: University of Missouri Press, 1968);

Edith Sitwell, Introduction to *Color of Darkness* (Phildelphia & New York: Lippincott, 1961), pp. 9–14;

Reed Woodhouse, "James Purdy Revisited," *Harvard Gay and Lesbian Review,* 2 (Spring 1995): 16–17.

Papers:

James Purdy's papers are held at the Beinecke Library, Yale University.

Lynne Sharon Schwartz

(19 March 1939 –)

Michael Depp
University of New Orleans

BOOKS: *Rough Strife* (New York: Harper & Row, 1980; London: Gollancz, 1981);

Balancing Acts (New York: Harper & Row, 1982; London: Gollancz, 1981);

Disturbances in the Field (New York: Harper & Row, 1983);

Acquainted with the Night and Other Stories (New York: Harper & Row, 1984);

We Are Talking About Homes: A Great University Against its Neighbors (New York: Harper & Row, 1985);

The Melting Pot and Other Subversive Stories (New York: Harper & Row, 1987);

The Four Questions (New York: Dial Books for Young Readers, 1989);

Leaving Brooklyn (Boston: Houghton Mifflin, 1989; London: Minerva, 1990);

A Lynne Sharon Schwartz Reader (Hanover, N.H.: University Press of New England, 1992);

The Fatigue Artist (New York: Scribners, 1995);

Ruined by Reading: A Life in Books (Boston: Beacon, 1996);

In the Family Way: An Urban Comedy (New York: Morrow, 1999);

Only Connect? (Boston: Beacon, 2000).

TRANSLATION: Liana Millu, *Smoke Over Birkenau* (Philadelphia: Jewish Publication Society, 1991).

SELECTED PERIODICAL PUBLICATION–UNCOLLECTED: "The Trip to Halawa Valley," *Shenandoah,* 45 (Winter 1995): 13–25.

Lynne Sharon Schwartz (photograph by Philippe Cheng; from the dust jacket for Ruined by Reading, *1996)*

A prolific and widely praised novelist and essayist, Lynne Sharon Schwartz has also won considerable acclaim for her short fiction, most of which has been collected in two volumes: *Acquainted with the Night and Other Stories* (1984) and *The Melting Pot and Other Subversive Stories* (1987). As in her novels, the characters in Schwartz's short stories are intelligent, educated, and driven members of the middle class unflinchingly pursuing self-definition, if not necessarily happiness. Along this sometimes profitable, sometimes painful, path, Schwartz vigorously scours away the veneer of her characters' seemingly commonplace lives. Often she exposes raw nerves, long-smothered feelings, and shades of emotional honesty with a comparatively rare psychological explicitness in American fiction. It might be this quality that has hampered her commercial, though not her critical success. As she told Wendy Smith in a 3 August 1984 *Publishers Weekly* interview, "I really try to get at these things that nobody wants to look at, and that's why people don't love to read my work."

Schwartz's narrative style is inextricably bound to this goal, another trait that may fail to endear her to a broader readership. She often explores a territory of domestic unrest, and she does so in a language that is frank and direct while recognizably different from the popular "dirty realism" style. She constructs her stories in a manner that seems deliberately antithetical to the terse, minimal, and often elliptical stories of such contemporaries as Raymond Carver and Richard Ford. As she told Mickey Pearlman, "The trouble with minimalists is that they have anomie, ennui, and despair, which we all have . . . but they refuse to allow [for] the richness of life." While her stories are not laden with overdescriptiveness or excessive action, they are nevertheless relentless in their unearthing of suppressed thoughts and feelings in a language and form that appropriately reflect her methods of exploration.

Lynne Sharon Schwartz was born in Brooklyn, New York, on 19 March 1939, the second of the three children of Jack M. Sharon, a lawyer and accountant, and Sarah Slatus Sharon. Their Brooklyn was a melting pot of immigrants and cultures, and the drama of assimilation was enacted for her in her own household. At age twelve, her father had immigrated to the United States from a small town near Kiev, Russia, to flee persecution.

The presence of Schwartz's father looms large over her fiction and nonfiction works, and throughout her writing she grapples with his steadfast desire to define himself as an independent American, unencumbered by historical or cultural baggage. In an unpublished 1998 interview Schwartz described her father and his family as "angry, rebellious, anarchic, and always discontented"–all traits that motivate many of her feisty characters. Jack Sharon clearly emerges as one of the author's earliest and most powerful formative influences.

Schwartz's mother was a first-generation American born in New York to Russian-Polish Jews. Her family was more steeped in tradition, both religious and cultural, and this markedly different perspective informed a marriage rife with opposing imperatives. Schwartz mines this conflict in her work, in which unquestioning adherents to tradition are apt to meet with challenges from a loving yet persistent opposition.

On 22 December 1957 Lynne Sharon married Harry Schwartz, a city planner, and two years later she received her B.A. from Barnard College, graduating Phi Beta Kappa with honors in English. She earned an M.A. in English from Bryn Mawr College in 1961, winning a Woodrow Wilson Fellowship. After working as associate editor for *The Writer* magazine in Boston (1961–1963) and as a writer for Operation Open City in New York (1965–1967), she undertook further graduate work in comparative literature at New York University (1967–1971), completing all the requirements for her Ph.D. except a dissertation because she found herself unable to settle on a subject. She was a lecturer at Hunter College in 1970–1975 and has since taught fiction workshops at the University of Iowa (1982–1983), Columbia University (1983–1984, 1985), Boston University (1984–1985), Rice University (1987), the University of California at Irvine (1991), the University of Hawaii at Manoa (1994), and Washington University in St. Louis (1996–1998).

Schwartz has two daughters, Rachel Eve, a criminal-defense attorney, and Miranda Ruth, a book reviewer and copyeditor. Although Schwartz began writing at age seven, she did not begin publishing her work until relatively late. She was a mother of two in her early thirties and about to embark on her dissertation before she realized that her graduate studies were circumventing her childhood writing ambition. "I let myself drift and wait and do nothing–I don't know why," she told Smith. In an interview with Christopher Woods for the winter 1987–1988 issue of *The Short Story Review,* she concluded, "All that had gone before was not as intense as it could have been." Her stories frequently portray introspective professional women galvanized by an urgent sense of belated purpose.

Schwartz's first major work began with a series of five short stories written in the 1970s. These stories, set over a period of twenty years, concern the courtship, marriage, infidelities, child rearing, and professional and personal development of Caroline and Ivan, an idealistic couple who vow to create an enduring marriage in a climate of divorce and defeat. Whether or not their marriage is distinguished by anything other than its sheer stamina is a matter of critical contention. One of the stories, "Rough Strife," won Schwartz the first of three recognitions in the *Best American Short Stories* series (1978), as well as placement in the *Pushcart Prize* and the *O. Henry Prize Stories* anthologies of the 1970s. Through this early acclaim, Schwartz met editor Ted Solotaroff, who encouraged her to gather the stories into a longer, unified narrative. The result was her first novel, *Rough Strife* (1980), which was nominated for a National Book Award and a PEN/Hemingway First Novel Award. In *Ms.* (June 1980), reviewer Lore Dickstein likened *Rough Strife* to an American twist on Ingmar Bergman's movie *Scenes from a Marriage* (1973). Katha Pollitt, writing in *The New York Times Book Review* (15 June 1980) said that Schwartz "registers the fluctuations of marital feeling with the fidelity of a Geiger counter" but added that "the emotional dynamics of Caroline's marriage are not interesting enough to bear the close inspection Miss Schwartz bestows." Pollitt blamed an overall imbalance in the novel on Schwartz's relentless focus on the marriage itself and her disinclination to explore other avenues in the couples' lives.

After Schwartz's success with *Rough Strife* she published two more novels, *Balancing Acts* (1982) and *Disturbances in the Field* (1983). Her first short-story collection,

Acquainted with the Night and Other Stories, appeared in 1984. The collection includes "Plaisir d'amour," which was included in the 1979 *Best American Short Stories* anthology. The story combines a vivid fantasy with a visceral sense of physical longing and repression, unleashing a torrent of sublimated fears and passions in its protagonist, a lonely widow named Vera. With her independent adolescent daughter drifting away and her husband in a premature grave, Vera regularly retreats to the pristine fantasy world of Brauer and Elemi, a young couple who come to her in a dream. Bringing the couple into her conscious world, she "follows" them through a series of adventures from one idyllic episode to the next, splendidly attractive and doting on one another yet remarkably chaste. Inevitably, Vera's fantasy veers out of her control. When the couple unexpectedly appear and defiantly make love before her, she faces–and is palpably moved by–their unleashed display. Her body is left limp in its wake, overwhelmed by the jarring, insistent physicality of the lovemaking that she is powerless to stop and unable to ignore.

This sudden loss of control in a carefully structured, detached life also befalls the protagonists of "The Accounting" and "The Sunfish and the Mermaid." In "The Accounting" a middle-aged, workaholic mystery writer is visited by her accountant, who arrives with "his five small children from various marriages." The writer tries to remain patient with the children's various tantrums and outbursts, which impede the progress of her meeting, but when events take a fantastic turn and a crafts fair suddenly begins to gather amid the chaos of her apartment, she is driven to near hysteria. The writer's environment is wrested from her control by crying children, potters, and various craftspeople, and she is momentarily transported to her past as a young mother. In those days, the needs of her small children and then-husband made her long for emptiness and quiet. Yet, then as now, despite her solipsistic pursuit of work as a "private province" and a means to self-assertion, she cannot shield herself successfully from what she perceives to be a world of tirelessly demanding outsiders.

"The Sunfish and the Mermaid" features a male protagonist who finds himself in similar straits as the mystery writer and the widow. The twenty-eight-year-old securities analyst, vacationing on a lakefront with friends, is fond of solitary outings on a Sunfish sailboat. Never one to lose his bearings or take risks, he keeps a watchful eye on wind, water, and land, a life jacket always in reach. But, when an alluring and quicksilver visitor arrives radiating sexuality, he finds himself unnervingly unmoored. Inviting herself for a sail, the woman tosses aside the life jacket, casts off, and, of course, rocks the boat. The story is the weakest in the collection, for where Schwartz imagines peculiar and fanciful scenarios for her two female protagonists' difficult catharses, the use of symbolism and metaphor in "The Sunfish and the Mermaid" clumsily overweights an already repetitive narrative. A similar problem affects the otherwise lucid "Grand Staircases." Its narrator, recounting a difficult romantic friendship with a man earlier in her life, remembers the root of its failure–her friend would not leave his architect/lover who was abroad studying the staircases of the title. While Anne Hulbert commended the "introspective accuracy" of the story in *The New York Times Book Review* (26 August 1984), she criticized the way "the metaphor and the mystery collapse in therapeutic cliche."

Schwartz employs a fable structure in "Sound is Second Sight," an uncharacteristically opaque tale. In this story a reclusive farmer "of austere habits" takes on a devoted dog and later an attractive young wife. Both predecease him–first his wife and later his jealous dog–and return to him in nightly visits as disembodied voices. Schwartz told Woods that the story stemmed from a dream that she endeavored to improve fictively; yet, "I still suspect the story fails because something is not fulfilled." The story highlights the theme of loss, one Schwartz revisits in various abstractions elsewhere in the collection.

In "The Death of Harriet Gross" loss figures on several simultaneous levels. The narrator recounts the life and early death in childbirth, of a peripheral and unremarkable childhood friend. "Mortality in general, like city air, is unacceptable," quips the narrator, and the injustice of her young friend's premature death forces her into the denial that closes the story. The loss, which the narrator extends to Harriet's widowed husband, orphaned child, lonely father, and eventually to the dead woman herself (who was deprived of the inconspicuous, quietly happy life she might have had) is too acute for her to manage.

"Life is an Adventure, With Risks" also contemplates loss on several different planes. The narrator compares her loss of small, yet symbolically significant, objects such as an eyebrow pencil and underwear to more-consequential events such as forfeiting the opportunity to have a lover and the near loss of her daughter by drowning. While these reflections seem to culminate less in a story than a mannered, abstract meditation, "Mrs. Saunders Writes to the World" finds its protagonist actively working to ameliorate her loss. The title character is an elderly woman, widowed with grown children and living in an apartment complex where she is well liked by, but not intimate with, her neighbors. In her entire sphere of friends and acquaintances, no one knows her first name. Rather than resign herself to a partial loss of identity–effectively the loss of her past

Dust jacket for Schwartz's first collection of short fiction; the title story re-creates the mood of Robert Frost's poem "Acquainted with the Night"

life–she undertakes a campaign of vandalism, assertively writing and spray-painting her name all over the complex and her town.

Schwartz's Russian-Jewish heritage and her father's attempts to divorce himself from it provide the grist for "The Opiate of the People." The protagonist, Lucy, is seen at ages six, eleven, fifteen, eighteen, and twenty-six, each time confronting increasingly pressing questions of ethno-religious identity with her father, David, an immigrant fiercely proud of his thorough American assimilation. Schwartz only slightly exaggerates her father's personality in David, who has taught himself English from *The New York Times,* graduated from law school, and done everything in his power to obfuscate his foreign past. Lucy's growing inquisitiveness into this past, however, and her chance meeting of one of her father's childhood friends from Russia at a wedding, make for a moment of cultural reckoning that leaves neither father nor daughter unscathed. James M. Mellard concluded that the story ultimately "presents admirable but conflicting ways of approaching Old World history."

The father figure also appears in "The Wrath-Bearing Tree," which takes its title from T. S. Eliot's poem *Gerontion* (1920). The narrator of Schwartz's story visits her father, who is slowly dying of cancer, and is reminded of her girlhood. She remembers intimate moments of reading together with her older sister and considers her frustration with her father's lifelong avoidance of displays of emotional sentiment. "That he is dying is an evident obscenity that cannot be spoken," laments the narrator, who fears that her father might perceive any outward gesture of feeling, even in his final days, as being in bad taste.

In "The Middle Classes" Schwartz also delves into her past, this time to examine her relationship with an African American piano teacher from her girlhood. While he was welcomed into her household without discrimination and liked by her parents, because of the still-restrictive outlook on race in the late 1940s and early 1950s, the teacher and Schwartz's family remained in different social orbits. Their inability to come together informs the narrator's reflective sense of loss. "It's a story about lack of vision," Schwartz told Woods. The story is one of the best instances of her ability to infuse the personal with the political, using introspection in place of preachiness.

Schwartz also avoids outright condemnation in "The Age of Analysis," which instead employs satire to critique faddish obsessions with psychoanalysis. Centering on Paul, the adolescent son of a psychoanalyst father and psychotherapist mother, the narrative uses his vivid, sometimes violent, outbursts as a counterpoint to the coolly distant jargon employed by his parents in their own conflicts. When Paul's parents separate, his explosions become more alarming. They reflect a greater self-honesty than his parents' deflective, psychoanalytic justifications. While the story achieves its satirical aim, it has not aged as well as it might have, given the receding importance of psychoanalysis in American culture.

An itchy sense of growing intolerance pervades "Over the Hill" and "The Man at the Gate." In "Over the Hill," a moody preteen girl is frustrated with her thirtyish mother's attempts to stay youthful. Worried that her mother might actually be having more fun than she is, the girl mean-spiritedly attempts to thwart a moment of carefree escapism. "The Man at the Gate" marks a slow-growing frustration in the protagonist, whose rakish boyfriend becomes more of an endurable habit than a genuine love. "Epistemology, Sex, and the Shedding of Light," which is peopled with Schwartz's own husband and daughters (referred to by name), might seem at first to be a nod to postmodernism. Given the author's predisposition to think of herself as an "unfashionable" nineteenth-century writer rather than a twentieth-century one, however, such a reading seems unlikely. In an unpublished 1998 interview Schwartz revealed that the story took its initial shape as an essay for the now-defunct "Hers" column in *The New York Times,* to which she was once a contributor. This circumstance accounts for the essay-like feel of the story, though its examination of everyday instances of coincidence in a Paul Auster vein might justifiably lead some readers to view the story as postmodern.

The title story, "Acquainted with the Night," which shares the title and mood of a poem by Robert Frost, effectively uses psychological realism to peel away the layers of its protagonist's anxious consciousness. The middle-aged architect finds his insomnia exacerbated by the unsettling appearance of a spot in his vision. As it persistently remains, it comes to vex him with the intensity of Edgar Allan Poe's "The Tell-Tale Heart" (1843), sending its sufferer into a catalogue of his past losses and transgressions. His increasingly desperate inward search prompted Hulbert to assert that "Schwartz at last sustains the wry tone and the sort of spiritual struggle at which she excels."

In *We Are Talking About Homes: A Great University Against its Neighbors* (1985), Schwartz's first nonfiction book, she chronicles the struggles of her family and neighbors after a small fire displaced them from their building, which was owned by Columbia University–a displacement they feared Columbia meant to make permanent. Schwartz next returned to fiction with her second collection of stories, *The Melting Pot and Other Subversive Stories* (1987). Explaining the title to Woods, Schwartz commented, "I think of them as subversive–that is, challenging and undermining the received wisdom." In *The New York Times Book Review* (11 October 1987), Perri Klass called the volume "extremely varied" with stories that are "successful in a wide variety of modes." The eleven stories do not wander from familiar themes, however, as personal and ethnic history, childhood reflections, sublimated fears, and strained marriages all reappear, though Schwartz shows a hesitancy to revisit the fable form as explicitly as in her earlier volume.

The identity struggle is most vigorously illustrated in "The Melting Pot," which Mellard suggested "offers a powerfully evocative variation on the dominant elements of 'The Opiate of the People.'" At the center of "The Melting Pot" is Rita, who is a first-generation American and an immigration lawyer working in San Francisco. She has spent her entire young life piecing together the shards of her cultural identity. Her father having died at an early age, she has been raised by her paternal, immigrant Jewish grandparents–her grandfather, Sol, a rigid traditionalist (recalling Schwartz's mother) and her grandmother, Sonia, a wry nonconformist (like Schwartz's father). As she matures, Rita hunts for clues about her Mexican-born mother and eventually takes up with a much older Indian lover. At work she eases immigrants' legal assimilation into American society, but privately, according to Mellard, she "suffers an existential unease because she does not know who or what she is." The story is one of Schwartz's best, foregrounding several of Schwartz's habitual themes in Rita's struggles with the Gordian knot of inter-ethnic/religious identities and opposing cultural values.

A darker side of the Jewish cultural past is unearthed in "Killing the Bees," Schwartz's haunting and enigmatic allegory of Holocaust atrocities. Ilse, the middle-aged protagonist, leads a life of quiet complacency until an infestation of bees appears in the walls of her comfortable home. When she later comes on a heaping pile of their freshly exterminated bodies in her garden, the sight transports her to the story of her father, a victim of the Nazi massacres. Schwartz deftly juxtaposes the narrative of Ilse's flight from Europe after her father's death with the unraveling of her middle-aged contentment. Klass remarked that the story "exemplifies Ms. Schwartz's skill at using the small intricacies of daily life to tell stories about big subjects."

Echoes of "Plaisir d'amour" are heard in "The Painters," the story of Della, a woman in her forties whose husband left her for another woman. Installing herself in a new apartment, Della retreats into a fantasy world centered around the painters she has hired to transform her new abode into a brighter place. The title characters are young lovers who work on apartments to supplement their artistic endeavors, and the abandoned Della comfortably takes refuge in the happiness she perceives in their lives. Her idyll is eventually eroded by the intrusion of real circumstances, and the fragility of her self-deceptive interpretations is amplified by a particularly effective recurring image: two toddlers dangling out of a high-rise apartment window across the street.

Marriages of varying degrees of success are featured throughout the volume. "The Subversive Divorce" seems painted in the same hues as *Rough Strife,* albeit with a somewhat different conclusion. The unnamed couple in the story continue to like and even love one another across the tumultuous years of their relationship; yet, "what they loathed was the distortion of identity marriage produced, marriage so public and powerful, marriage imposing its rites, grinding away the personal in the service of an inferred higher good." Their ultimately "subversive" fate is to divorce secretly and abide in a state of unspoken limbo in which such distortions of self are at least temporarily fended off.

"The Sound of Velcro" depicts marital discontent in what seems initially to be a healthier union. Joe and Vanessa are relatively affluent, affectionate, and efficient people living a life that seems to suit both with an acceptable measure of resignation. The arrival of Joe's mildly retarded brother at their home calls into question fundamental differences between husband and wife, and Joe finds himself confronting incompatibilities that thrust him into a self-awareness more alienating than he could have imagined. The story is remarkable as another of Schwartz's rare explorations of a male sensibility, one that succeeds both for its plausibility and for its depth of unflinching introspection.

A happier marriage is found in "What I Did for Love," in which sustaining love and respect exist between Chris, the first-person narrator, and her husband, Carl, who meets an untimely death. Rather than retreat into escapist fantasy or mawkishness, Chris relates episodes of their marriage and the period after, through stories about a succession of her daughter's guinea pigs. Her care for these relatively frail pets acts as a poignant signal of her greater familial love. In shifting her fictive lens to the guinea-pig narratives, Schwartz achieves just the right measure of remove from sentiment while retaining an emotional pulse as steady and delicate as the small animals' heartbeats.

In a longer story, "The Infidel," Schwartz follows Martin Solomon–artist, professor, woman chaser, and husband–through a series of career developments and relationships, most notably his marriage to Alice, a university instructor and translator. In their twenties their coupling begins with intellectual vigor and feverish devotion, but the passage of time leads to disenchantment and alienation driving a wedge between them. Once again traces of the turbulent yet cohesive marriage in *Rough Strife* appear in the story, but here the relationship is truncated by Alice's slow dying from cancer. Unlike *Rough Strife,* however, this story suggests an authorial indictment against the husband's compulsive womanizing, especially when Martin attempts to reconcile it within his artistic philosophy. Despite the occasionally satirical bent, the judgmental title of the story invites such an interpretation.

In "The Last Frontier," a foray into fantasy, Schwartz's African American protagonist, George Madison, a Caribbean islander, finds himself and his recently immigrated family homeless after a New York apartment fire. Leery of the dangers in their temporary accommodations at a low-rent hotel, George moves his tired family into the streets in search of more suitable housing. They end up squatting at night on the set of a television sitcom–possibly *The Jeffersons*–as the story toes the line between irony and fantasy. While it is effective in that respect, the narrative is undermined by Schwartz's uneven attempts to reproduce Caribbean dialect.

In "The Two Portraits of Rembrandt" the paintings of the title are effectively used as bookends around a short reminiscence of Schwartz's father. The result is another effort that seems only nominally a short story. Given the closeness by which the biographical details in *Ruined by Reading* corroborate the events in this "story," one senses that it would be more appropriately classified as an essay or the beginning of a memoir. The story is vividly recounted and serves to emphasize the importance of the author's father in her personal and intellectual development, helping to illuminate the source of her investment in the power of well-chosen words. "The Thousand Islands" also seems somewhat like an essay or memoir, perhaps because of its Brooklyn milieu and its first-person voice, which is quite similar in tone to Schwartz's nonfiction writing. It is generally an unremarkable and meandering recollection of her parents' travels and her own.

The provocatively titled "So You're Going to Have a New Body!" is considerably more sure-footed than "The Thousand Islands," offering wry dispensations of advice to a hysterectomy patient. By again adjusting her fictive lens just to the side of the patient (rendering her the "you" of the title), Schwartz circumvents sentimentality. Instead, she uses an almost ruthlessly honest third-person narrator to recount and advise about the often-overlooked physical and emotional changes that follow such an operation.

Schwartz followed this collection with a children's book, *The Four Questions* (1989), illustrated by Ori Sherman, which explains the significance of the Jewish Passover celebration and the Seder meal. While it might seem odd for a secular Jew to write such a book, Schwartz explained in an unpublished 1998 interview that the quality of the illustrations and the persistence of publishers persuaded her to do it. Her next effort was *Leaving Brooklyn* (1989), a coming-of-age novel that again draws on her childhood memories and a familiar setting. The novel was nominated for the 1989 PEN/Faulkner Award for Fiction and won the *Hadassah Magazine* Harold U. Ribalow Award. This work was followed by *A Lynne Sharon Schwartz Reader* (1992), a collection of her essays, poems, and short stories.

Schwartz's introduction to *A Lynne Sharon Schwartz Reader* is useful for its insight into her creative processes and her disdain for being primarily recognized as a novelist. She writes, "the inner process of writing paid no heed to genres, so why must my notion of what sort of writer I was?" Schwartz also confesses that her writing occasionally combines fictional and nonfictional strategies, explaining her disinclination to categorize herself as a writer of any one kind of narrative.

All but one of the stories in this reader were previously published in *Acquainted with the Night and Other Stories* and *The Melting Pot and Other Subversive Stories.* The one exception is "Francesca," which returns in part to the Italian settings of *Rough Strife.* The author uses the story to contemplate again notions of coincidence, as a cancer researcher meets the daughter he never knew, whom he fathered during a year at a university in Rome. The daughter comes to him years later as a translator, and in their encounters he reflects on his Roman excursion and its significance to him. Meanwhile, he keeps his relationship to his daughter a secret from her (she believes her father is still in Rome) and his wife, whom he suspects mistakes his interest in the young translator as romantic. The story adroitly presents the scientist's study of cancer cells, which are "capable of the most unpredictable, riotous, malign behavior," as a metaphor for his own ability for action in this most unlikely of chance meetings.

Schwartz's next books were *The Fatigue Artist* (1995), a novel inspired by her bout with chronic-fatigue syndrome, and *Ruined by Reading: A Life in Books* (1996), a well-received chronicle of her reading life. Also in 1996 her short story "The Trip to Halawa Valley" was selected for inclusion in *The Best American Short Stories* anthology for that year. Its unusual Hawaiian setting is most likely inspired by her visiting professorship at the University of Hawaii at Manoa in 1994. While the backdrop is a departure, the divorced couple at the center of the story bears familiar traits. Again using the juxtaposition that lent "Killing the Bees" such dramatic strength, Schwartz visits Jim and Lois in the days after their son's tropical wedding. Having only one another's company for sightseeing, the two endeavor to reach the perilous valley of the title, giving occasion for Lois to reflect on the equally arduous path of their marriage. Schwartz skillfully meshes nostalgically remembered domestic peccadilloes and unexpected familial heartbreaks with the exotic flourishes and hidden pitfalls of the valley. She eschews excess sentiment while penetrating the couple's emotional recesses. Jim and Lois never reach Halawa Valley. The story marks a clear success for an author writing at the peak of her craft. "The Trip to Halawa Valley" anticipates future short stories of confident, insistent power. "I like my stories to have an aftershock," Schwartz told Woods. Her body of stories, for all of their prodding and mining, often succeed in reaching an emotional seismic center. Her most recent books are a novel, *In the Family Way: An Urban Comedy* (1999), and a collection of essays, *Only Connect?* (2000).

Interviews:

Wendy Smith, "Lynne Sharon Schwartz," *Publishers Weekly,* 226 (3 August 1984): 68–69;

Christopher Woods, "An Interview with Lynne Sharon Schwartz," *Short Story Review,* 5 (Winter 1987–1988): 2–3, 23;

Mickey Pearlman and Katherine Usher Henderson, *Inter/view: Talks with America's Writing Women* (Lexington: University Press of Kentucky, 1990): 190–194.

Reference:

James M. Mellard, "Resisting the Melting Pot: The Jewish Back-Story in the Fiction of Lynne Sharon Schwartz," in *Daughters of Valor: Contemporary Jewish American Women Writers,* edited by Jay Halio and Ben Siegel (Newark: University of Delaware Press, 1997), pp. 175–193.

Elizabeth Spencer

(19 July 1921 –   )

Terry Roberts
University of North Carolina at Greensboro

See also the Spencer entry in *DLB 6: American Novelists Since World War II, Second Series.*

BOOKS: *Fire in the Morning* (New York: Dodd, Mead, 1948);

This Crooked Way (New York: Dodd, Mead, 1952; London: Gollancz, 1952);

The Voice at the Back Door (New York: McGraw-Hill, 1956; London: Gollancz, 1957);

The Light in the Piazza (New York: McGraw-Hill, 1960; London: Heinemann, 1961);

Knights and Dragons (New York: McGraw-Hill, 1965; London: Heinemann, 1966);

No Place for an Angel (New York: McGraw-Hill, 1967; London: Weidenfeld & Nicolson, 1968);

Ship Island and Other Stories (New York: McGraw-Hill, 1968; London: Weidenfeld & Nicolson, 1969);

The Snare (New York: McGraw-Hill, 1972);

The Stories of Elizabeth Spencer (Garden City, N.Y.: Doubleday, 1981; Harmondsworth, U.K.: Penguin, 1983);

Marilee: Three Tales (Jackson: University Press of Mississippi, 1981);

The Salt Line (Garden City, N.Y.: Doubleday, 1984; Harmondsworth, U.K.: Penguin, 1985);

Jack of Diamonds and Other Stories (New York: Viking, 1988);

The Night Travellers (New York: Viking, 1991);

On the Gulf, text by Spencer, art by Walter Anderson (Jackson: University Press of Mississippi, 1991);

The Light in the Piazza and Other Italian Tales (Jackson: University Press of Mississippi, 1996);

Landscapes of the Heart: A Memoir (New York: Random House, 1998).

photograph by Piroska Mihalka

PLAY PRODUCTION: *For Lease or Sale,* Chapel Hill, N.C., Paul Green Theater, January 1989.

The 1981 publication of *The Stories of Elizabeth Spencer* precipitated a remarkable change in Elizabeth Spencer's literary reputation. Before that time she had published only one collection of stories, *Ship Island and Other Stories* (1968), and the last two of her seven novels, *No Place for an Angel* (1967) and *The Snare* (1972), had received insensitive and often unfavorable reviews. The thirty-three works of short fiction in *The Stories* allowed readers to consider a large and important body of

Spencer in Milan, during her summer 1949 visit to Italy (Collection of Elizabeth Spencer)

work. Because she arranged the stories in the order in which they were written, this book traces Spencer's artistic evolution and captures her major themes. Critics were forced to regard her as an important short-story writer, and reviewers, including poet James Dickey and fiction writer Reynolds Price, lavished praise on the collection. In 1983 Spencer received the Award of Merit Medal for the Short Story from the American Academy and Institute of Arts and Letters. The publication of five more stories in *Jack of Diamonds and Other Stories* in 1988 reaffirmed judgments about her mastery of the form.

In her preface to *The Stories* Spencer described her growth as a writer in terms of the image of herself "walking down a certain path, a personal road." Certainly her personal road has taken her on a fascinating and, at times, exotic journey. She was born and raised in Carrollton, a small Mississippi hill town that is depicted lovingly in many of her stories. Her parents, James Luther and Mary James McCain Spencer, were affluent and conservative members of what in time became a stifling community. After earning a B.A. (1942) at Bellhaven College in Jackson, Mississippi, Spencer received an M.A. (1943) at Vanderbilt University, where, studying under Donald Davidson, she was witness to and part of the later stages of the Southern Renascence. She taught English at Northwest Junior College in Senatobia, Mississippi (1943–1944) and Ward-Belmont in Nashville (1944–1945) before working as a reporter for the *Nashville Tennessean* (1945–1946). She visited New York City often during the 1940s and 1950s, infiltrating the literary scene, and she lived there during the winter of 1955–1956. When her first novel was published in fall 1948, she had just begun teaching English at the University of Mississippi, where she remained until 1951. After her early success as a novelist, she received a Guggenheim Fellowship in 1953 and went to live in Italy, where she met her future husband, Englishman John Rusher, whom she married on 29 September 1956. They settled in Montreal in 1958. In 1986 Spencer and Rusher went to live in Chapel Hill, North Carolina.

Spencer's primary themes have to do with tension between the individual and the group, often with how family or community ties support but also bind the individual in search of identity. As several commentators have pointed out, this interest in community is a characteristically Southern concern, and it defines Spencer's work even when she sets her stories in Europe or Canada. When one reads Spencer's short fiction in the order in which it was written, two patterns emerge. First, as Spencer has continued to explore the relationship between self and community in her work, she has come to focus increasingly on her characters' inner lives, specifically on how they are affected by the surrounding community. Second, her stories display an increasing technical sophistication in her use of structure and point of view to mirror her thematic concerns. In fact, repeated readings of her entire corpus of stories suggest an organic connection between her increasing technical mastery of the form and a growing spiritual acceptance of the complexities of human relations.

Spencer organized the stories in her 1981 collection in four chronological groups that suggest her development. The six stories in the first section, written between 1944 and 1960, are set mostly in rural Mississippi and deal with the demands that closely knit Southern culture places on individuals born there. The six stories of the second group, written in 1961–1964, are set in Italy as well as in the South and suggest a more fragmented worldview, one in which traditional communities have broken down under the stress of modern life. This section culminates in the long story *Knights and Dragons* (1965), one of two Italian novellas that had been previously published separately. The thirteen stories in the third section, written in 1965–1971, suggest first the nihilism of *Knights and Dragons* and then a slowly growing sense of reconciliation with place and community. Many of the stories in this section are set once again in the South. The eight stories of the fourth section, written from 1972 to 1977, plus the five stories in *Jack of Diamonds and Other Stories,* represent Spencer's most mature work, exploring the inner lives of her characters as they plumb the mysteries of close relations. Often the characters of this period face complications internal and psychological as well as external and communal. Finally, then, in these stories artistic experimentation is followed by artistic mastery, and fragmentation and dislocation are followed by what Spencer calls in her preface "something like acceptance, the affirming of what is not an especially perfect world" for her characters.

The stories written between 1944 and 1960 are almost all set in Mississippi and almost all told omnisciently with the events flowing in simple chronological order. They concern the power of family or community to constrain, protagonists who escape from that constraint, and what Peggy Prenshaw calls "the concomitant sense of loss and freedom" they experience as a result. They also deal with the power of the past over the present and the future. A clear example of this stage in Spencer's career is the regularly anthologized "First Dark," which deals directly with how a young woman named Frances Harvey is ensnared by her family and the past. The title refers to that time of day when the town ghost regularly appears in Richton, Mississippi, and as Spencer writes, "the door to the past was always wide open, and what came in through it and went out of it had made people 'different'" in the world of this story. Because Frances is not strong enough to tear free from the twin ties of family and the past on her own, it takes her mother's apparent suicide and a determined and loving man (another tie, of course) to pull her free of Richton.

Another important story in the first section is "A Southern Landscape," the first of Spencer's three stories narrated by a fictional alter ego named Marilee Summerall. In "A Southern Landscape" Marilee recalls her comic high-school romance with Foster Hamilton, an entertaining but alcohol-sodden older beau. Late in the story the mature Marilee admits that she feels "the need of a land, of a sure terrain, of a sort of permanent landscape of the heart," suggesting that she is re-creating her past to suit her present purposes and suggesting as well how Spencer uses her own fiction. Marilee Summerall is an artist prototype through whom Spencer explores the writer's craft, and tracing Marilee's evolution through this and later stories reveals much about how Spencer regards her craft. This story, as well as the later Marilee stories, is about what Marilee the storyteller does with her own past.

The last story in this section, "The White Azalea," marks a transition from Spencer's use of the rural South as her primary landscape to her exploration of a much larger and more complex world. In "The White Azalea" the middle-aged Miss Teresa Stubblefield of Tuxapoka, Alabama, has finally escaped years of servitude "nursing various Stubblefields . . . through their lengthy illnesses" and made her way to Rome. There, she is greeted by two letters from home, one announcing a death in the family and the other subtly demanding that she return to her duties. After a few moments of angry reflection, she tears up the letters and buries them in the pot of a huge white azalea that workmen have set near her in anticipation of a street festival. "It was not the letters but the Stubblefields that she had torn open" and buried, and Theresa is thrilled by her small act of defiance and her resulting sense of freedom.

This story is significant in two ways. First, Miss Theresa is particularly vulnerable to family pressure because she is an unmarried, middle-aged lady whose role is frighteningly clear in the minds of her family. In seizing her freedom she anticipates dozens of Spencer heroines who struggle for liberation and then must face the resulting vertigo. Second, in "The White Azalea" Spencer focuses on Theresa's inner, psychological struggle rather than the beautiful floral festival going on around her. By portraying a fierce confrontation between internalized social forces, the story anticipates Spencer's later fiction.

Even so, "The White Azalea" does not fully prepare the reader for the existential dilemmas that await her characters once they venture into the larger world. The next two important "stories" in the Spencer canon are not really stories at all: *The Light in the Piazza* (1960) and *Knights and Dragons* (1965) are full-length novellas that began as stories and outgrew the form. Both deserve comment however, because they shed light on the stories written between 1961 and 1964. *The Light in the Piazza* first appeared in a single installment in *The New Yorker* (18 June 1960), and Spencer included *Knights and Dragons* in the 1981 *Stories* even though it had previously appeared as a 169-page book.

In *The Light in the Piazza* Margaret Johnson and her daughter Clara are traveling in Italy. As a result of a childhood accident, Clara has the mind of a ten-year-old. As Margaret soon realizes, however, in Italy Clara is capable of becoming a wife and mother, a role that would require nothing more of her than innocence, devotion, and fertility. Margaret Johnson decides to arrange such a marriage for Clara, an act that is profoundly significant. Margaret disregards the anticipated objections of her powerful husband while carrying on a subtle and flirtatious negotiation with the groom's father. This powerful woman does not ignore or escape social convention but rather charts a difficult and dangerous course through it. The book and the M-G-M movie version (1962) remain popular primarily for their romantic setting and glossy surface, but Spencer has consistently pointed out that there is a dark world stirring beneath. Margaret Johnson is the first of the mature Spencer heroines who seizes control of her life by manipulating social custom to her advantage.

The dark forces that she defeats in so doing, however, rise menacingly to the surface in *Knights and Dragons*. Margaret Johnson's counterpart in this novella is an American diplomatic attaché named Martha Ingram, and her story is as full of darkness as Margaret Johnson's is of light. After her divorce from Gordon Ingram, a powerful personality and influential scholar, Martha Ingram has come to Italy to escape his psychological influence as well as his physical presence. Fleeing this figurative dragon, she becomes involved with two potential knights: a traveling American economist, who becomes her lover, and her boss at the embassy, a sympathetic confidant. Neither man can vanquish Ingram, however, and she must rely on her instincts in her fight for independence. Ultimately, however, her freedom comes at the price of her emotional health as she loses the ability to feel anything at all.

Spencer commented in a 1982 interview with Elizabeth Pell Broadwell and Ronald Wesley Hoag that during this period, she "searched for women who could sustain a weight of experience, both intellectual and emotional," and she admitted that "often the women characters I found did not do this." *Knights and Dragons* is a disturbingly dark and difficult narrative that holds the key to understanding the psychic fragmentation and alienation that Spencer's characters face in story after story.

Like Martha Ingram, the protagonists of the key stories of Spencer's second period–"The Visit," "Ship Island," and "The Pincian Gate"–experience a fundamental displacement from their worlds. In "The Visit," the first story in the section, Judy and Bill Owens are invited to visit the enigmatic Thompson, the reigning scholar in Bill's academic field. In Bill's mind the success of his most ambitious book (on Roman portraiture), and his career itself, depend on the success of his visit to Thompson's villa. The day that the young American couple spend at the villa is comically disorganized and inconclusive, and it is significant because they experience it so differently. "Bill was disappointed to the point of despair by his visit," but Judy is erotically and spiritually moved by her encounter with Thompson. At the end of the story readers realize that they have witnessed the disintegration of Judy and Bill's marriage.

Spencer and John Rusher on the day of their wedding, 29 September 1956 (Collection of Elizabeth Spencer)

"Ship Island" is an especially important story because it portrays just how dramatically displaced Spencer's heroines of this period can become. Its subtitle, "The Story of a Mermaid," flows from the imagery Spencer uses to define her protagonist, Nancy Lewis. Nancy is out of place in her own family and her boyfriend's socially affluent group. At a key juncture she abandons her boyfriend in a restaurant to disappear with several mysterious men. This sudden decision, which seems dangerously irrational, has been foreshadowed from early in the story with the sea imagery surrounding Nancy. She is so irrationally drawn to the dark and mysterious ocean that she feels herself to be a creature of a different species from Rob or her family. She can barely breathe in their element and must turn elsewhere for emotional nourishment. The painful surrealism of her displacement suggests the extent to which Spencer is questioning the nature of community.

The last story in this section, "The Pincian Gate," shares the Italian setting of most of these narratives and illustrates Spencer's increasing technical experimentation. This *short* short story of fewer than six pages is a study in controlled irony. An American woman living

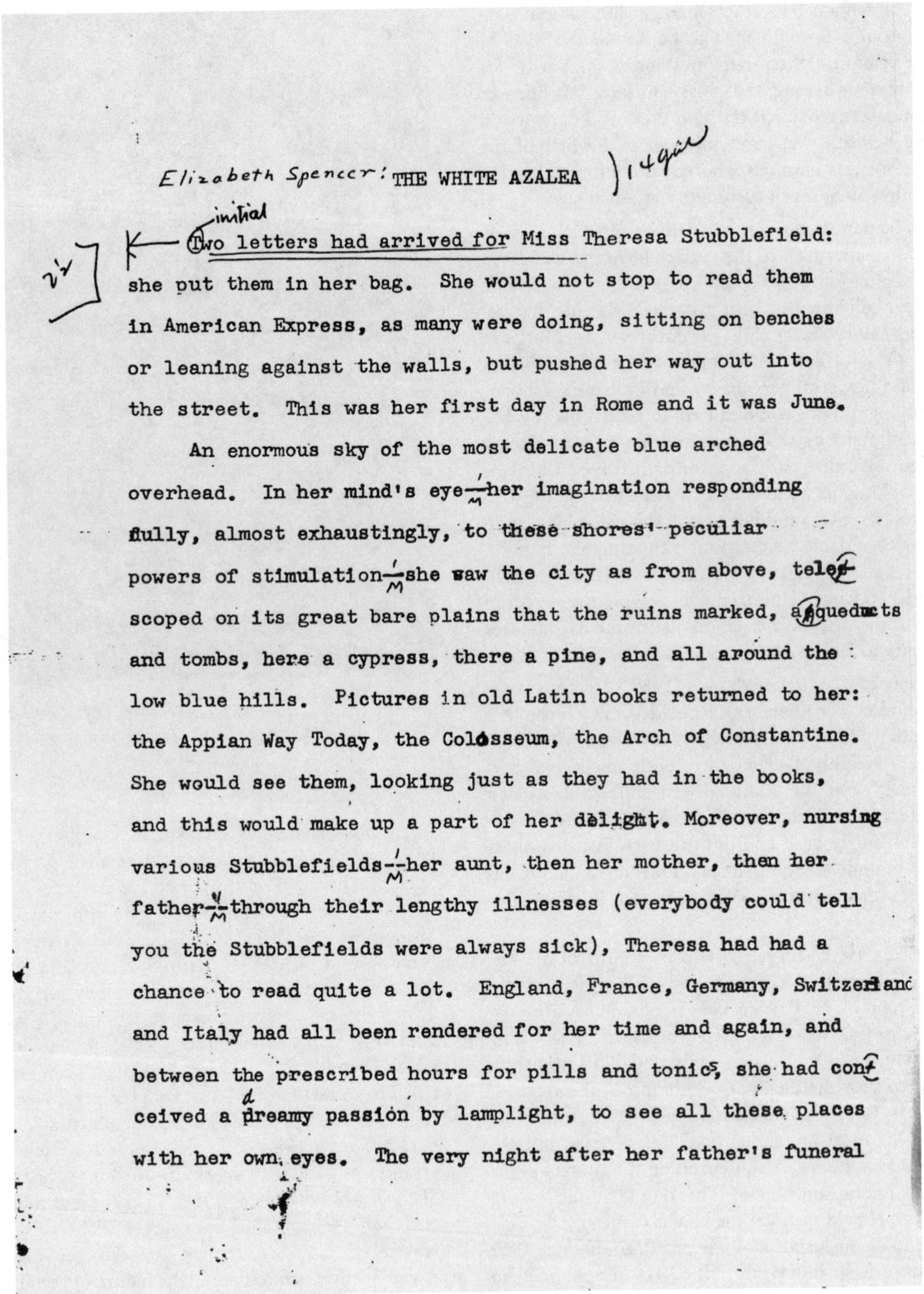
Elizabeth Spencer: THE WHITE AZALEA

Two letters had arrived for Miss Theresa Stubblefield: she put them in her bag. She would not stop to read them in American Express, as many were doing, sitting on benches or leaning against the walls, but pushed her way out into the street. This was her first day in Rome and it was June.

An enormous sky of the most delicate blue arched overhead. In her mind's eye--her imagination responding fully, almost exhaustingly, to these shores' peculiar powers of stimulation--she saw the city as from above, telescoped on its great bare plains that the ruins marked, aqueducts and tombs, here a cypress, there a pine, and all around the low blue hills. Pictures in old Latin books returned to her: the Appian Way Today, the Colosseum, the Arch of Constantine. She would see them, looking just as they had in the books, and this would make up a part of her delight. Moreover, nursing various Stubblefields--her aunt, then her mother, then her father--through their lengthy illnesses (everybody could tell you the Stubblefields were always sick), Theresa had had a chance to read quite a lot. England, France, Germany, Switzerland and Italy had all been rendered for her time and again, and between the prescribed hours for pills and tonics, she had conceived a dreamy passion by lamplight, to see all these places with her own eyes. The very night after her father's funeral

Page from the setting copy for a story first collected in Spencer's 1968 book, Ship Island and Other Stories *(The National Library of Canada)*

in Rome is going to visit Gowan Palmer, an American artist who lives within the Roman wall near the Pincio, to remind him of his social and financial obligations. She believes her motives are generous and for most of the story the reader shares her assumption because Spencer confines the third-person point of view to the woman's perspective. The reader shares her outrage when Palmer playfully ridicules her concerns and is as shocked as she when suddenly, he "turned her face abruptly to his and gave her a long, staggering kiss" that shatters her illusions. Rereading the story confirms that the clues were there from the beginning; she is a condescending meddler, and Spencer has manipulated the point of view to suggest how easily readers can become part of the controlling community surrounding her characters.

Nine of the thirteen stories in the third group, written between 1965 and 1971, are set in the South. During this period Spencer continued her search for characters "who could sustain a weight of experience, both intellectual and emotional." In particular, she was interested in artist prototypes through whom she could explore the way a creative personality responds to an often stifling society. In two important stories from this period–"The Finder" and "Sharon"–Spencer uses creative characters to explore the artistic process and her own relationship to the South.

One reason Spencer may have been interested in the ability of powerful individuals to gain control of their lives is that this period of her creative life is marked by a growing sense of reconciliation. Although the emotional pain and intellectual fragmentation of the earlier period continues in stories such as "Judith Kane," "A Bad Cold," and "Instrument of Destruction," a growing sense of spiritual or creative empowerment is also present, particularly in such stories as "The Day Before," "Presents," "On the Gulf," and "Sharon."

One of Spencer's finest stories, "The Finder," captures both sides of this conflict between acceptance and rejection of the South, and at its core is one of her most fascinating characters. The story opens with the description of a small Southern town reminiscent of the opening of "First Dark":

> Dalton was such a pleasant town–still is. Lots of shade trees on residential streets, lots of shrubs in all the front yards, ferns in tubs put outside in the summer, birdbaths well attended, and screen side porches with familiar voices going on through the twilight. Crepe myrtle lined the uptown streets.

The protagonist of "The Finder," Gavin Anderson, is firmly entrenched in one of the oldest, most influential families in Dalton and is proof that small-town Southern society is as stifling for men as for women. He has developed an extrasensory ability to find lost objects and, as it turns out, lost people. As he matures, marries, and becomes a father, he becomes more and more firmly entangled in family and community life until he meets a young widow named Naomi Beris, for whom he "finds" a lost ruby ring. Attracted by Naomi's cosmopolitan sensuality–an alien presence in the closely knit, traditional society of Dalton–he becomes intimately involved with her for a time, and during that period he loses his gift. Alarmed by the loss of his close connection to wife and family, he ends the affair and rejoins the "long table" of his extended family. The story seems about to end predictably when he is suddenly, wrenchingly transformed into the long-dead lover of Naomi's grandmother. The shocking end of this story does not resolve Gavin's dilemma because the story is less about the nature of the man than it is about the nature of his gift. His ability to see through and within the world is analogous to artistry itself, a curse as well as a blessing. As Gavin Anderson's story shows, the creative gift holds the key to reconciling the needs of the individual to the life of the community, but it takes a wise individual to contain and control the gift.

Spencer continues this exploration into the nature of the artistic gift in other stories in the third section, notably "The Day Before," narrated in the first person by a woman looking back on "the day before" she started first grade. After starting school, the narrator realized, "if I lived to be a thousand I would never do anything but accept" her eccentric neighbors and laconic family. Even so she "was losing them; they were fading before my eyes." This story is about the past and how people lose what they love. Yet, at the end the narrator has an uncanny experience of mysterious recall. "Had they [friends and family] never been lost then at all?" she wondered. "A great hidden world shimmered for a moment, grew almost visible, just beyond the breaking point of knowledge. Had nothing perhaps ever been lost by the great silent guardian within?" Once again, Spencer brings both narrator and her readers face to face with the recuperative power of the imagination.

Spencer's second Marilee story, "Sharon," combines the tension between individual and community in "The Finder" and the mature imagination at work in "The Day Before." In "Sharon" the mature Marilee Summerall remembers a season from her childhood when she was often invited to visit her Uncle Hernan at his farm, named Sharon. Though young Marilee is a favorite of her uncle's, her mother forbids her to visit Sharon uninvited, a temptation that is too much for the young girl. One reason her mother warns Marilee away from Sharon is her evident dislike for Uncle Hernan's

Eudora Welty and Elizabeth Spencer in Baton Rouge, Louisiana, 1985 (Collection of Elizabeth Spencer)

cook and housekeeper, a young black woman named Melissa. One day, when Marilee gives in to her curiosity and crosses over to Sharon unannounced, she looks through the parlor window and sees her Uncle Hernan and Melissa behaving with the relaxed intimacy of a couple long used to one another. Suddenly the young Marilee and the reader reach the conclusion that the older narrator has staged for them: Melissa's children, "perfect little devils" every one, are Marilee's cousins. Her world opens up enormously in terms of family, community, and even sensuality.

By using the mature Marilee to narrate this story about her childhood, Spencer suggests how the artist must come to accept and eventually re-create her world. This story ends with the young Marilee thinking about her newly discovered cousins:

> I felt differently about them now. Their awful racket seemed a part of me–near and powerful, realer than itself, like their living blood. That blood was ours, mingling and twining with the other. Mama could kick like a mule, fight like a wildcat in a sack, but she would never get it out. It was there for good.

The mature Marilee has come to understand and is teaching the reader that the phrase "for good" means both "forever" and "for the benefit of all." For Spencer the adult Marilee is an artistic alter ego, a mature storyteller who knows that one has first to accept the intricate complexity of the human community before she can fully re-create it.

The third and last Marilee story makes an effective introduction to the fourth and last period of the 1981 *Stories.* Told in Marilee Summerall's familiar voice, "Indian Summer" deals with events Marilee experienced as an adult and is technically the most complex of the three stories. Marilee tells the story of her Uncle Rex (Hernan's brother), who is fighting to establish his personal efficacy after having married into a landed family. Confronted by his wife and son over a real-estate decision, he leaves farm and family in disgust, taking only his favorite riding mare in a trailer pulled behind his pickup. Marilee eventually locates him living in the Delta with an informal family:

> There is such a thing as father, daughter, and grandchild–such a thing as family that is not blood family but a chosen family. I was seeing that. . . . Now, . . . I see the problem Rex Wirth must be solving and unsolving every day. If this was the place he belonged and the family that was–though not of blood–in a sense, his, why leave them ever? . . . Wasn't this where he belonged? . . . Should I run out of the woods and tell him that? No, the struggle was his own.

Like Rex, Marilee Summerall is "solving and unsolving" the problem of "blood family" versus "chosen family" in every story she tells. Her newfound distance–leaving Uncle Rex to solve his own problems–suggests Spencer's growing objectivity as she studies how mature individuals learn to govern their own lives, even in the midst of complex family and community life.

The complexity of "Indian Summer" is representative of the fourth group of stories, which tend to focus on what Spencer once termed "mystery in close relationships." The mysteries of intimate relations that concerned Spencer during the 1970s often required all the skills of her technical maturity. The stories from this period are characterized by subtle shifts in point of view and chronology as well as a consistent attention to the inner lives of the characters. As Spencer wrote in the introduction to *Marilee: Three Tales* (1981), "it's the voice you talk about it with that matters" in the telling of these complex stories.

In "I, Maureen" the first-person narrator's voice all but splits into actor and observer, suggesting the same sort of psychological turmoil that haunted *Knights and Dragons.* Spencer suggests this split in the first line of the story, when the narrator introduces herself as "I (Maureen)," emphasizing the subconscious distinction between the two. The text of the story is unsettling in its syntactic displacement, and Spencer uses the first-person voice to dramatize Maureen's deeply disturbed personality. Maureen's failure to reconcile the turbulent forces surrounding her stands in even greater contrast when juxtaposed against Marilee Summerall's confident control–both of her voice and of her life.

The fourth group of Spencer's short fiction extends beyond the 1981 *Stories* into *Jack of Diamonds and Other Stories,* published in 1988. Several of the stories in this collection are characterized by the same concern with the mysteries of intimacy. Furthermore, in stories such as "The Cousins" and "The Business Venture," Spencer exhibits her mastery of the form. Increasingly, her characters from this period have found ways to "sustain a weight of experience, both intellectual and emotional," meeting social and cultural challenges with personal imagination and resourcefulness. It is impossible to say whether Spencer's growing reconciliation of individual with communal forces was the cause or the result of her maturing craft, but it seems certain that the two processes are vitally connected.

The heroine of "Jean-Pierre," the first story in *Jack of Diamonds,* marries a mysterious French Canadian who, a year after their wedding, disappears suddenly and without warning. Having rejected her family to marry this difficult man, Callie is forced to fend for herself by taking a job in a local library, where she reads Emily Dickinson and befriends a lonely young man. For no apparent reason, however, she turns instinctively back to her husband, who returns just as mysteriously as he had left. The mystery in this close relationship has to do with the fact that Callie and Jean-Pierre are mismatched in age, culture, and language and yet know intuitively that they belong together.

Spencer's characters of this period often discover their "chosen family" in the face of considerable odds. In "The Business Venture," for example, Nelle Townshend tries to open a dry-cleaning business in a small Southern town despite social and legal complications. At first her problems seem to stem largely from the fact that her friend and partner is a black man, but a deeper reading reveals a subplot even more threatening than those involving race and gender prejudices. This story is narrated by Eileen Waybridge, a sometime friend of Nelle's. Eileen's philandering husband, Charlie, is particularly insulted by Nelle's "business venture," and at the end of the story Eileen accidentally overhears Charlie threaten Nelle over the phone–not for the reasons the reader and Eileen might have suspected but because Charlie is Nelle's jealous lover. In shock, Eileen realizes that in their web of interconnected relationships, they "are all hanging on a golden thread," ignorant of "who has got the other end." What has seemed a social comedy turns out in the end to be a much more ominous story.

At the center of *Jack of Diamonds* is "The Cousins," which may be Spencer's greatest story. It is a long, entertaining first-person narrative told by fifty-year-old Ella Mason, who recalls for the reader a trip she made to Europe thirty years before with two male cousins and several other friends. During the trip she fell in love with her second cousin Eric. After a brief idyll, however, they were forced apart by the disappointing news that he had not been admitted to law school and by the shock waves this rejection sent through their small, tightly knit group. "The Cousins" includes all Spencer's characteristic themes: individual evolution within a stifling family or community environment, the shock of familiar versus exotic settings, the often-painful mysteries of intimacy, and the powerful influence of the past on the present. In the present time of the story, Ella Mason is on the way to Italy for a long-postponed reunion with Eric, and within her mind and voice the reader is skillfully shifted back and forth between past and present in counterpunctual rhythm. Also within her mind and voice, the reader eventually learns of Ella and Eric's intimacy in the past and of their rediscovery of one another in the present. The story ends in the present with Ella and Eric "sitting holding hands on a terrace in far-off Italy," and though they are talking together in "the pitch black dark," the ending is suffused with a figurative light. By rediscovering Eric and joining with him in re-creating their past, Spencer's Ella Mason heals tremendous wounds of time and distance.

If one studies Spencer's artist figures Gavin Anderson, Marilee Summerall, and Ella Mason, it appears that the role of the artist is to find the lost fragments of communal lives–whether they be objects, stories, or people–and re-unite them in a more powerful whole. Thus, storytelling is a healing process: reconciling past with present, the isolated inner life with the communal outer life, the life of the divided mind with that of the healing spirit. In Elizabeth Spencer's world, it is often "the voice you talk about it with that matters," the voice of the story that knits up the ties that bind.

Spencer's mature voice has both the objectivity praised by Reynolds Price (who described Spencer as a "smiling sibyl, unafraid of her news") and the "power" praised by Eudora Welty (in her foreword to the 1981 *Stories*). Reading Spencer's stories from start to finish suggests that she had to develop both characteristics in order to portray characters capable of solving the mysteries of intimacy and creating community out of chaos. Although Elizabeth Spencer has been writing and publishing short fiction since the mid 1940s, it is only since the publication of the 1981 *Stories* that critics have realized the extensive range and depth of her work.

Interviews:

Peggy Whitman Prenshaw, ed., *Conversations with Elizabeth Spencer* (Jackson: University Press of Mississippi, 1991).

References:

Peggy Whitman Prenshaw, *Elizabeth Spencer* (Boston: Twayne, 1985);

Reynolds Price, "The Art of American Short Stories," *New York Times Book Review,* 1 March 1981, pp. 1, 20;

Terry Roberts, *Self and Community in the Fiction of Elizabeth Spencer* (Baton Rouge: Louisiana State University Press, 1994).

Papers:

Elizabeth Spencer's manuscripts are at the University of Kentucky Library and the National Library of Canada in Ottawa.

Richard Stern

(25 February 1928 –)

Blake Bailey
University of New Orleans

See also the Stern entry in *DLB Yearbook: 1987.*

BOOKS: *Golk* (New York: Criterion, 1960; London: MacGibbon & Kee, 1960);

Europe: Or Up and Down with Schreiber and Baggish (New York: McGraw-Hill, 1961); republished as *Europe: Or Up and Down with Baggish and Schreiber* (London: MacGibbon & Kee, 1962);

In Any Case (New York: McGraw-Hill, 1962; London: MacGibbon & Kee, 1963); republished as *The Chaleur Network* (Sagaponack, N.Y.: Second Chance Press, 1981; London: Sidgwick & Jackson, 1981);

Teeth, Dying and Other Matters (New York: Harper & Row, 1964; London: MacGibbon & Kee, 1964);

Stitch (New York: Harper & Row, 1965; London: Hodder & Stoughton, 1967);

1968: A Short Novel, An Urban Idyll, Five Stories and Two Trade Notes (New York: Holt, Rinehart & Winston, 1970; London: Gollancz, 1971);

The Books in Fred Hampton's Apartment (New York: Dutton, 1973; London: Hamilton, 1974);

Other Men's Daughters (New York: Dutton, 1973; London: Hamilton, 1974);

Natural Shocks (New York: Coward, McCann & Geoghegan, 1978; London: Sidgwick & Jackson, 1978);

Packages (New York: Coward, McCann & Geoghegan, 1980; London: Sidgwick & Jackson, 1980);

The Invention of the Real (Athens: University of Georgia Press, 1982);

The Position of the Body (Evanston, Ill.: Northwestern University Press, 1986);

A Father's Words (New York: Arbor House, 1986);

Noble Rot: Stories, 1949–1988 (New York: Grove, 1989);

Shares and Other Fictions (Harrison, N.Y.: Delphinium, 1992);

One Person and Another (Dallas: Baskerville, 1993);

A Sistermony (New York: Donald I. Fine, 1995).

OTHER: *Honey and Wax: Pleasures and Powers of Narrative,* edited by Stern, illustrated by Joan Fitzgerald (Chicago: University of Chicago Press, 1968).

Richard Stern (photograph by Lloyd DeGrane; from the dust jacket for Shares and Other Fictions, *1992)*

The phrase "writer's writer" is often considered something of a backhanded compliment, implying critical distinction, a difficult but esoterically rewarding literary style, and low sales. These qualities all apply to some degree to Richard Stern, who, despite a highly acclaimed output that includes seven novels, five books of short fiction, and five books of nonfiction, remains virtually unknown among the wider public. Sven Birkets points out in *The New Republic* (20 February 1989) that Stern is "hardly a household name" and wonders that "in an era when writers barely old enough to drive are garnering enormous advances and, worse, enormous reputations, how is it that a writer of Stern's caliber still waits for recognition?" The answer may be found in the fact that Stern writes purely to please himself and pays no heed to topical concerns, sensationalism of any kind, movements, or trends. He is sometimes classified as a Jewish writer, like his good friends and staunch admirers Philip Roth and Saul Bellow, but this characterization is misleading; though Stern addresses the subject of anti-Semitism in his novels and short stories, it is at best an incidental concern, and most of his fiction has little or nothing to do with Jewishness per se. Stern has also been called an academic writer, since much of his fiction is set in an academic milieu (most often the University of Chicago, where Stern has taught for more than forty years) and features academic protagonists–but again, academia is only a single aspect of Stern's almost inexhaustible range.

Much of Stern's relative obscurity may be blamed on what he himself concedes is a "difficult" style for many readers: "Some of my work is not sufficiently articulated," Stern said in a 1988 interview with James Schiffer. "There's not enough explanation. There's a little too much joy in obliquity." Indeed, Stern's style hearkens in some respects to another, perhaps more literate age; he has acknowledged the influence of modernists such as T. S. Eliot and Ezra Pound, with their fragmented images and juxtaposed cultural allusions, which create an elliptical effect that some may find daunting. While Stern's diction tends to be rooted in an easy (if cerebral) colloquial style, with a delight in mundane and ribald details that recalls Bellow among others, it is often fraught with an erudition that is liable to baffle some readers. As Bernard Rodgers Jr. notes in his introduction to *Golk* (1960), Stern mixes "the street and the library, what he has seen and heard and what he has read and thought." Finally, Stern likes to structure his narratives in such a way that may disorient the casual reader even as it delights the more adept: in keeping with his modernist legacy, Stern tends to scramble chronology and alter point of view, allowing an image or a snatch of dialogue to unify a story and resonate with meaning. As Birkets writes, "The stories . . . almost always plunge us in medias res and set our reading antennae to bristling. We have to work to sort out the references, chronologies, and twists. . . . While the exertion is initially great, often slowing our involvement, the payoff is worth it."

The fact remains that Stern is much less difficult than more famous authors whose more determined quirkiness has at least ensured them a devoted coterie of readers who insist on the frankly experimental in their fiction. In his essay "Country Fiddlers, City Slickers: Virtuosi and Realists," collected in *The Position of the Body* (1986), Stern categorizes such better-known writers as John Barth, Robert Coover, and Donald Barthelme as "virtuosi"–that is, the kind of writer who "takes off from other writers' works. His virtuosity strikes the eye immediately: his language is different, the arrangement of it is different. We feel the eloquence, farce, fantasy, and technical mastery of his work." Stern, for all his own technical virtuosity and admiration of these authors, believes that style should be subordinate to the demands of the narrative; and while he admits to "virtuoso impulses" in his own work, he places himself firmly in the "realist" camp, with the kind of writer who "focuses on what's *there* or could be. The realist wants his work to seem real." This self-placement may help to explain why Stern's reputation remains somewhat lost in a limbo between a more popular brand of realism–for example, that of minimalists such as Raymond Carver and Ann Beattie–and a strenuously innovative postmodernism.

Richard Gustave Stern was born in New York City on 25 February 1928, the son of Marion and Henry George Stern, who were the children of German and Austro-Hungarian Jewish immigrants. His father was a successful dentist and a fine storyteller in his own right; one of Stern's earliest memories is of listening in his crib to his father's tales. (When he was seventy-eight years old, Stern's father applied his narrative gift to a brief memoir, *Reminiscences of a Gentle Man,* which Stern and his sister, Ruth Stern Leviton, published privately.) Stern was a bookish child who spent long hours in the Eighty-second Street Library; he developed an astigmatic crossed eye that required many visits to eye doctors until adolescence. The condition recurred in his late fifties and has bothered him since. Stern attended the Hunter Model School in Manhattan, a school for gifted children, and later Stuyvesant High School. Though he was a good student, his applications to Harvard, Yale, and the University of Michigan were rejected, and he went to the University of North Carolina at Chapel Hill instead, where he graduated Phi Beta Kappa in 1947. After receiving his M.A. from Harvard in 1949, Stern went abroad to teach at the Collège Jules Ferry in Versailles, an experience that later provided material for such short stories as "Wissler Remembers" and "Good Morrow, Swine." That fall he met fellow American Gay Clark, and they were married the following spring. Their first child, Christopher, was born in 1951 while Stern was teaching at the University of Heidelberg. Stern found the experience of being an American Jew in postwar Germany "pleasurable," as he recalled to Schiffer, and some of his observations from this time seem to have found their way into his story "The Good European." Stern returned to the United

States in 1952 and enrolled as a Ph.D. candidate in English literature and creative writing at the University of Iowa. His daughter, Kate, was born that summer, and Stern's first published story, "Cooley's Version," appeared two years later in the *Kenyon Review*. Two more stories were published in 1954, "After the Illuminations" and "The Sorrows of Captain Schreiber," the latter of which was included in *Prize Stories of 1954: The O. Henry Collection*. Stern later incorporated both stories into his novel *Europe: Or Up and Down with Baggish and Schreiber* (1961).

Stern began teaching at the University of Chicago in 1955 and has remained there ever since (his younger children, Andrew and Nicholas, were born in Chicago in 1957 and 1961), except for occasional stints at the University of Venice, University of Urbino, University of Nice, State University of New York at Buffalo, University of California at Santa Barbara, and Harvard. An ardent traveler, Stern's fiction has benefited not only from his experiences in Europe–the American abroad is one of his most frequent themes–but also throughout South America, Africa, Asia, and Australia. By far the most common locale of his stories, though, is Chicago, which he described to Schiffer as "the setting for excess, rapidity, confusion, gorgeousness, bitter triumph, overreaching, bitter collapse." In 1991 the University of Chicago rewarded his many years of service by naming him the Helen A. Regenstein Professor of English and General Studies in the Humanities. Stern's marriage to Gay Clark ended in 1972, and in 1985 he married his longtime companion, the poet Alane Rollings, a former student.

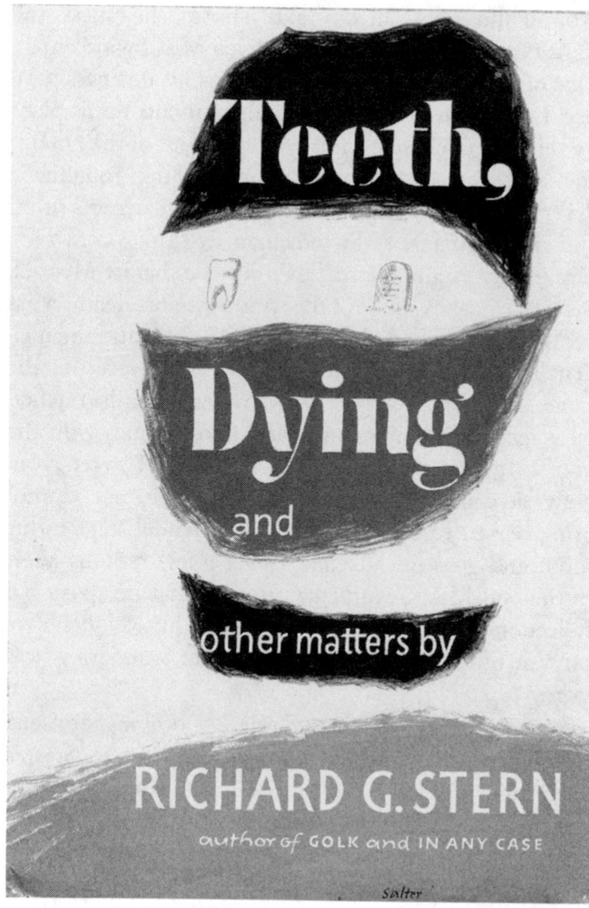

Dust jacket for Stern's first collection of short stories, published in 1964

Teeth, Dying and Other Matters (1964) is Stern's first published book of short stories. "Teeth" is the sadly comic story of Miss Ethel Wilmott, "a low-grade instructor in the History Department" of the University of Chicago, whose lonely life is made more miserable by an abscessed tooth, which brings her to a sympathetic, cut-rate dentist, Dr. Hobbie, with whom she falls in love. The story begins with a lyrical litany of questions that may as well have been posed at the end of the story, when Miss Wilmott's romantic quest results in predictable failure: "Ah, Miss Wilmott, how did you come to think what you did? Is all your interpreting so askew, so deformed by self-interest? . . . To think that you were misled as wisdom itself was being certified in your aching jaws?" The kindly Dr. Hobbie seems oblivious to Miss Wilmott's ardor–as well as her attempts to discuss pertinent literature from his dentist's chair ("Ever read ahhh Poe's 'Ber-ahhh-niece'?" "Nope. Spit out, Miss Wilmott.")–and he maunders on about his own troubles with his estranged wife, Suzanne. The dentist senses her loneliness, however, and goes so far as to arrange a date between Miss Wilmott and an autodidactic house-painter, Mr. Givens, who tries to discuss Marxism with her. By the end of the story her life is brought to the brink of calamity when she learns that her long essay on opium consumption in the nineteenth century is fatally flawed by a miscalculation of the number of pounds in a picul. Finally, she returns to Dr. Hobbie to have her abscess lanced and learns that he has reunited with his wife.

An even more desolate portrait of loneliness and romantic failure is given in "Wanderers." Miss Swindleman, an aging cashier at a Jewish hotel in New York, maintains a collection of "four hundred and fifty post cards which memorialized the wanderings of Hotel Winthrop guests for a quarter of a century." The collection, conspicuously displayed behind the bars of her cage, serves as an example of order to the restive inhabitants of the hotel, a reproach to the "avaricious disorder" that Miss Swindleman believes is the foremost barrier to the proper assimilation of the Jews. She is annoyed, however, by the Jews in her hotel who do not travel–most notably the grouchy, taciturn Harvey Mendel, a designer of men's suits, who seems content to sit around the lobby all day and whose "cheapness and third-rate vanity" galls the fastidious Miss Swindleman. One of Mendel's occasional visitors is his business partner, Lepidus, whom Miss Swindleman puts in his place by refusing to change a fifty: "You a guest of the hotel?" she asks him in a tone "as icy as the roughneck deserved." When Lepidus returns to his partner's room and denounces Miss Swindleman as "a piss-cold anti-semitischer virgin-whore," then starts to berate Mendel, the latter pushes him out the window to his death. Miss Swindleman defends Mendel to the police, and the incident is written up as "accidental." Things are not the same afterward, however: Miss Swindleman is touched by a sense of human connection and wrestles with the urge to go to Mendel's room and say, "I saved you. Now save me. I'm yours. Be mine?" But she cannot bring herself to do so; meanwhile, Mendel stays in his room and goes into decline, dying a few months later. In the end Miss Swindleman notices that her postcard collection is "in wretched shape" and has the bellboys carry it off to the garbage heap. "Her wandering was over."

The protagonist of "Orvieto Dominos, Bolsena Eels," Edward Gunther (who also appears in Stern's 1965 novel *Stitch* and two other stories), is the prototypical Sternian American tourist. A dilettante who combines a modest amount of learning with facts gleaned from a Baedeker travel guide, Edward divides his enthusiasm between the cultural heritage of Europe and an American ingenue named Vicky whom he manages to spirit away from her tour group. Though his first priority is seduction–to which purpose he flaunts his knowledge at every opportunity–Edward is genuinely enchanted by the art and architecture, as well as the copious servings of affordable gourmet cuisine with which he constantly gorges himself. At the cathedral in Orvieto, Italy, he becomes so absorbed in Luca Signorelli's frescoes that he almost forgets his lovely companion: "The damned were twisted, their bones showed, their tendons and muscles were knotted, idolaters, lusters, killers, sloths, gluttons, doubters, whipped, choked, and wrestled by devils." As he marvels over this lurid scene of damnation, the object of his lust is reclaimed by her tour group, and Edward, alone again, consoles himself with yet another enormous meal. Finally he goes for a swim in Lake Bolsena (ignoring a sign that warns not to swim for at least three hours "*dopo pasta*"), gets cramps, and almost drowns, vomiting into the lake and paddling back to shore. Thus Edward almost pays the ultimate price for his thoroughgoing–culinary, cultural, sexual–gluttony. "I ought to pay attention to these damn signs," he muses at the end.

A different kind of cultural experience is depicted in "The Good European," in which the Jewish protagonist, Henry ("Heinz") Pfeiffer, is forced to return to postwar Germany and come to terms with its Nazi past. Stern addresses this other side of the European cultural tradition–the history of anti-Semitism, pogroms, and insidious class-consciousness–in much of his fiction. Pfeiffer, who barely managed to escape Germany fifteen years before, has to go back after his capricious tyrant of an employer has a nervous breakdown and Pfeiffer is asked to manage the company's office in Frankfurt. Confronted by the ruinous consequences of the war, Pfeiffer has mixed feelings: "He was not unpleased by the destruction. On the other hand, he was not displeased by the construction projects going on over most of the city. 'They can begin again too,' was his notion." He observes the signs of renewed material prosperity–the hard-faced prostitutes, the sheepish bravado of Germans telling smutty jokes–and feels a deep sense of identification and forgiveness: "His country's misery was a version of his own; he saw in her looseness and silly posturing the awkward attempts to atone for the misery she had madly inflicted in her fifteen-year exile from European sanity." Such a reconciliation with one's betrayer/tormenter is a common thread in Stern's fiction, intertwined with related themes of anti-Semitism, lapsed friendship, and dysfunctional families.

The latter is addressed in "Arrangements at the Gulf," whose elderly protagonist, Fred Lomax, feels a deep sense of alienation from his children. At a Thanksgiving dinner with his extended family, prior to returning to Florida for the winter, Lomax suddenly announces, "I think I'm going to die in Florida." Consequently his family accompanies him en masse to the train station, taking their leave of him with such remarks as "It's been fun taking care of you, Papa." Lomax is disgusted by the scene, by the whole history of miscommunication and false sentiment between him and his children, and asks his bachelor friend, Granville, to be with him when he dies. "Old friends are true family," he tells Granville. "You meet me in the right way, say the right things, the right way." The two friends understand each other. The story serves as an early, rather caustic treatment of a common theme in Stern's work–the problematic nature of family relations, particularly between parents and children.

Husbands and wives do not fare much better, as may be seen in the story "Gardiner's Legacy." Gardiner, a minor writer in life, is rescued from posthumous obscurity by his wife, who discovers several unpublished masterpieces in the attic. In the course of sifting through her husband's work, however, she discovers that he regarded her as a "Lilith" and "a lump of dung" and that he had affairs with no fewer than eighty-six women during their marriage. The story is written in the form of retrospective essay, the narrator

Stern (right) and novelist Philip Roth (photograph by Ross Miller)

marveling over the complexity of Gardiner's relationship with his wife; he can only conclude that the woman deserves a commensurate amount of credit for her husband's legacy, for serving as a kind of antimuse and adept curator who made Gardiner's genius what it was: "She did not write the books, nor the journals and letters. No, but the universe within which they were written, did she not provide that, shape that? And did he perhaps see her rightly all along?"

Some of the stories in Stern's next collection, *1968: A Short Novel, An Urban Idyll, Five Stories and Two Trade Notes* (1970), bring a more affirmative theme to the fore, perhaps the most abiding concern of Stern's fiction–as Tom Rogers puts it in his review in the *Chicago Sun-Times Book Week* (29 January 1989) of Stern's later collection *Noble Rot: Stories, 1949–1988* (1989), "Vitality and the power to survive seem to be at the very top of Stern's pyramid of values." Such values, Rogers adds, are "never achieved by indifference to others, or by cutting oneself off." Holleb, the protagonist of "Ins and Outs," is an exemplar of these principles. The business manager of a neighborhood weekly newspaper in Hyde Park, Holleb writes a high-minded column on civic concerns while caring for his feckless teenage son, Artie, and enduring the ridicule of an amoral wife. When the latter abandons him with a pithy note of farewell–"I'm taking off for the Coast. See you in the funny papers"–Holleb responds stoically, continuing to send his love through his son ("'You got some to spare?' yukked Artie"). Holleb's ultimate reward for his decency comes in the form of a savage beating from a black man who pretends to collect money for the Biafra relief fund. Even then, Holleb can hardly bring himself to seek revenge: "*Tout comprendre, tout pardonner,*" he tells himself. Just as he struggles to understand–and hence forgive–his ungrateful son and wretched wife, so he tries to pardon his assailant. Like Pfeiffer in "The Good European," Holleb serves as a redemptive illustration of humanity at its best, of a man who responds to betrayal with forgiveness.

A despairing illustration of a similar theme is given in "East, West . . . Midwest." Bidwell, the protagonist, hires Miss Freddy Cameron to type his translation of *The Secret History of the Mongols.* Though her work is competent enough at first, the unstable Miss Cameron begins to form a delusion that Bidwell is Ghengis Khan himself (or "Chinghis Khan," as Bidwell insists on translating it) and harasses him with a series of insane phone calls: "Tell me why you stood at the window," she wails. "Naked you were. Pudgy you are. Yet you had your way. With me." Bidwell, who possesses the "classic hangups of the twentieth-century burgher," nonetheless tries to help Miss Cameron, meeting her for coffee and arranging for her to get treatment at a psychiatric hospital. Four years later she calls again–somewhat recovered but still unwell–and Bidwell lets her back into his life, engaging her in therapeutic, weekly phone calls and meeting her for coffee once a month. One day she fails to call, and Bidwell reads in the next day's *Sun-Times* that Miss Cameron has jumped to her death from a tenth-floor window of the Playboy Building. "What a death the poor narrow thing had constructed for herself," he reflects. "No campaign, no successor, no trip to the cool mountains, only an elevator ride, a smashed window, an untelephoned farewell: 'This is it. I can't ask you anymore. Let alone by phone.'"

The interdependent relationship between an aberrant personality and a more normal, tolerant one is further explored in "Gifts," which also returns to the subject of parents and children. Williams, a man whose only confidant is his sixteen-year-old son, Charley, is a typical Sternian tourist who takes annual excursions to Mexico for "cultural, historic, and scenic accumulation." He also goes out of his way to pick up girls and duly confides the prurient details to his son, who "had overcome uneasiness at his father's confidences. It was odd, but there it was, he was his father's closest friend." Williams's most recent adventure goes badly awry, however, when a playful bit of grappling with an Indian girl guide results in her tumbling to the bottom of a pyramid in Uxmal. Williams panics and abandons her, leaving an envelope of pesos for her at their hotel in the event she survived the fall. Charley persuades Williams to call the hotel and see if the girl is all right–"she'd only broken her arm," Williams reports back–after which the son decides that "he had heard the man's last confession."

Another story that combines the themes of damaged family relations and the rapacious behavior of Americans abroad is "Gaps." William McCoshan is a lonely, cynical man who also has but one confidante in life–his wife, Elsa, who is decapitated in a car accident. Though McCoshan has never been close to his daughter, Winnie ("she was not his type"), he proposes they take a European excursion together, during which she promptly falls in love with a boy in Rome and begs her father to go to France without her. While en route to Saint-Tropez, the bored McCoshan picks up a hitchhiker, a teenage Flemish girl, who is "pretty in a stupid way." At one point he takes her picture "before a wall on which was scrawled in charcoal, '*U.S. Assassins. Viet Cong Vaincra*'"–which serves to point up the implications of what later transpires between the two when McCoshan roughly deflowers her on a beach. Finally, he returns to Rome and is greeted by his flustered daughter, on whose face he "smells an unscheduled knowledge." McCoshan seems to sense an ominous parallel between his relationship with his daughter and his behavior with the Flemish girl.

In a review of *1968* for the *New York Review of Books* (13 August 1970), D. A. N. Jones makes a complaint that is fairly typical of dissenting views toward Stern's work: "Stern's English is Butch Academic, allusive and exclusive, mingling a studied demotic with a little learning, none too lightly worn, so that each sentence seems designed to impress rather than communicate." While Stern may be allusive, he is hardly exclusive; his embroidery of certain erudite details–Mongol history, for example, or the cultural miscellanea of Europe and elsewhere–tend to mesh seamlessly with matters of theme and character, enhancing rather than detracting from the overall effect of his stories.

Stern's next collection, *Packages* (1980), continues to explore the related themes of betrayal and botched relationships. In "Lesson for the Day" protagonist Mervyn Kiest is embittered by his wife's professional success in the academy. Unemployed himself and given to brooding, Kiest begins to cultivate an ineffectual misogyny, referring to women as "slits" (à la the loutish Ty Cobb) and planning to gain some measure of revenge through an adulterous affair with the "frizzily gorgeous" Angela Deschay, an assistant professor in his wife's department. His only moment of relative triumph, however, occurs in the pulpit rather than in bed: he rescues Angela's minister husband from disgrace when the latter becomes panic-stricken at the prospect of delivering his inaugural sermon. Kiest addresses the congregation instead, making excuses for the husband and quoting from the "wicked Earl" of Wilmot (the subject of Kiest's dissertation): "Birds feed on birds, beasts on each other prey, / But savage Man alone does Man betray." Faced with the "nodding, scratching, shaking heads" of the bemused congregation, Kiest adeptly concludes, "So . . . the betrayal in the midst of the celebrating feast is the essential savagery of man which, in hours, Jesus will die to redeem." That night Kiest waits in vain for a visit from the minister's grateful wife, but instead his own wife comes home from her Sunday play-reading group and treats him to an inept recitation of Samuel Taylor Coleridge's "Frost at Midnight."

The theme of sexual betrayal–successfully accomplished in this case–is also treated in "Double Charley." Schmitter and Rangel are a songwriting team known as "Double Charley" because they have the same first name. Moderately prosperous in the 1940s, they begin to founder when Schmitter stops writing lyrics, without which Rangel cannot find the inspiration to compose a tune. "Soon as he had a few bucks salted away," Rangel says of his indolent partner, "he could become what he always was, a spieler, a schmooser. . . . He's the most profoundly self-contented man in the world." Meanwhile, Schmitter spends his days in cheerful philandering, shuttling between his wife, Agnes, and a dim-witted mistress, Olive Baum. When at last he dies, leaving no lyrics for Rangel, Rangel asks Schmitter's widow to allow Olive to come to the cemetery and pay her respects. Agnes, disgusted, responds to this manful request by revealing her husband's long affair with Rangel's own beloved, "off-and-on-again companion," Maggie. Rangel–unlike some of Stern's duped protagonists–is stunned and unforgiving: "Here in New York, Double Charley's last song began, the mean act of betrayal that was Charley Rangel's to set, to live with. 'I'd've punched his goddamn nose for him,' he said. 'I'd've bloodied the big bastard's nose.'"

Dust jacket for Stern's 1992 book, stories that chronicle parents' physical or emotional abandonment of their children

"Dr. Cahn's Visit" and "Packages" are further reflections on the relations between parents and children, a subject that seemed to preoccupy Stern after his own parents died within six months of each other in the late 1970s. The first story is mostly concerned with a reunion between the senile Dr. Cahn and his dying wife, though a related sense of reconciliation is suggested on the part of their son, Will, who has grown closer to his mother during her illness: "For the first time in his adult life, Will found her beautiful. Her flesh was mottled like a Pollock canvas, the facial skin trenched with the awful last ditches of self-defense; but her look melted him. It was human beauty." A more bleak assessment of this relationship is given in "Packages," which begins with the narrator ruminating over the sparsely attended funeral of his mother five days before, as he buries a mysterious "silvery can" in the garbage beneath a "plastic sack of rinds and fishbones." The son reflects on his mother's life with brutal honesty, admitting that there were times when he had wished for her death, that she was "a nagger, a boss, the idle driver of others, an anal neurotic for whom cleanliness was not a simple, commonsensical virtue but a compulsion nourished by her deepest need." While he concedes her "intelligence" and "energy," he deplores the uses to which they were put–in the service of, at best, her "tutelary deity," a banal practicality. She is, however, redeemed somewhat in his eyes by her heroic death–"She died bravely, modestly, with decorum"–and as a last, rather appalling tribute to his mother's lifelong values, he leaves her ashes to be taken away with the rest of the garbage: "it was the *practical* thing to do," he concludes. "*Wasn't it, Mother?*"

Noble Rot was published in 1989 and won the *Chicago Sun-Times* Book of the Year Award. A selection of Stern's best work from the previous volumes, the book also includes a few uncollected stories, such as "Zhoof," perhaps the author's most searching treatment of the anti-Semitism theme. Its protagonist, Arthur Powdermaker, is a photographer's model who fills "a gap in an advertiser's gallery: the faintly Jewish gentleman." As a Model Jew, Powdermaker affects a cheerful cosmopolitanism as he travels about Europe; his fear of exclusion and insult is latent at best. "Son and grandson of assimilated German-Jewish burghers, his slogans were theirs: let sleeping dogs lie; don't cry over spilt milk." His complacency is shattered, however, by an encounter with an anti-Semitic German on a train. The man calls him a "zhoof" (or *jouf,* a French anti-Semitic slur) and insists on moving away from him to the opposite end of the dining car. The episode forces Powdermaker to confront his buried feelings of alienation and self-disgust: "*Zhoof.* Am I so clearly that? The eyes? The big nose? . . . My open mouth–the Whiner's deferential mouth, the Ingratiator's smile . . . Jewiness. *Zhoofheit.*" For a while he considers challenging the man in some way, perhaps colliding with him and demanding an apology. In the end, however, he realizes the anti-Semite–a "twisted fellow," a "hater"–has served a good purpose, and he meets the man's eyes with a look of "amused contempt" as he comes out of the toilet.

A similar instance of self-recognition and compassion is explored in the title story of the book, "La Pourriture Noble," in which protagonist Derek Mottram's life of calm, reclusive bachelorhood is disrupted by the arrival of Denis Sellinbon, the disturbed son of Mottram's former employer. As in the past, Mottram gives the obnoxious young man a place to stay, and Sellinbon returns the favor by disgracing both of them at an elegant party with his lunatic behavior; he also kills Mottram's cherished ficus plant and tapes a hideous painting over a favorite, valuable nude. *La pourriture noble,* or "noble rot," refers to the Semillon and Muscadet cuttings that Sellinbon's father, a vintner, had planted into an Ozark Hill–"They never grew the right mold"–and, of course, extends to the troublesome son as well. More significantly it relates to the "rot" that Mottram himself feels in old age, as his capacity for emotion gives way to an "inner chill," a sterile sense of obligation. There is redemption in this conscious (if rather benumbed) determination to act nobly, however, as is suggested by Mottram's dream at the end of the story: a little child, who is somehow both his daughter, Deirdre, and Denis, runs weeping into his arms. "'I'll never leave you,'" he tells the dream-child. "In his body, he felt her/his sobbing relief."

At least two of the stories in Stern's latest collection, *Shares and Other Fictions* (1992), return to what Joseph Coates, in the *Chicago Tribune Book World* (6 September 1992), calls the "Laius Complex" in his work: "the tendency of fathers to make life as hazardous as possible for sons, to leave them as infants on some psychic or actual hillside." In "The Degradation of Tenderness," the father, Charlie, is a psychiatrist who writes a witheringly "objective" journal article about his children, "The Father as Clinical Observer I, II." His doting daughter, Patricia, who once helped her father with a malpractice suit brought by the unstable daughter of a famous actress, is characterized in the article as having committed an "act of parricide" when she later wrote a book about the case. His son, Alfred, responds with a bitter letter signed "your repellent clown of a son." Unappeased by an apologetic letter from Charlie, Alfred and his punk-activist girlfriend, Porphyria, picket his father's office while dressed in burlesque Nazi costumes. The family goes into a collective tailspin: Charlie loses his practice and dies, as does Alfred, and the daughter is last seen as part of an anti-American mob in Amman, Jordan.

Charlotte Trowbridge of "In a Word, Trowbridge" is left on a psychic hillside by both of her parents. Left for dead after a brutal mugging on the streets of New York, the thirty-seven-year-old Charlotte can only mutter her celebrated last name–thereby invoking the lifelong mugging she has received at the hands of an abusive mother and a neglectful, manic-depressive father, a famous painter. Charlotte's mother, embittered by her husband's fame and womanizing, accused her daughter of "ugliness" and of dragging the family name through the mud. Charlotte, for her part, seems to adhere to the advice implied by her father's dying words: "take it." Like other Sternian stoics, Charlotte attains a kind of heroism through her determination to endure. "Success was less important than resolve," she concludes.

A writer of insight and dazzling technical gifts, the prolific Stern must content himself with a continuing succès d'estime. He has won prestigious awards over the course of his long career–including the National Institute of Arts and Letters Fiction Award in 1968, the Carl Sandburg Award for his novel *Natural Shocks* (1978) in 1979, and the American Academy and Institute of Arts and Letters Medal of Merit for the Novel in 1986–but recognition among the general reading public is nowhere in sight. "Of America's most under-appreciated novelists," wrote Philip Roth in 1970, "probably none is neglected with such thoroughgoing regularity, with such dedication, as Richard Stern. It's appalling."

Interview:

Elliott Anderson and Milton Rosenberg, "A Conversation with Richard Stern," *Chicago Review,* 31 (Winter 1980): 98–108.

References:

Sven Birkets, "Chekhov in Chicago," *New Republic* (20 February 1989): 46–48;

Mark Harris, "The Art of Being Brief," *New Republic* (15 November 1980): 32–34;

James Schiffer, *Richard Stern* (New York: Twayne, 1993).

Peter Taylor

(8 January 1917 - 2 November 1994)

Joe Nordgren
Lamar University

See also the Taylor entries in *DLB Yearbook 1981* and *DLB Yearbook 1994.*

BOOKS: *A Long Fourth and Other Stories* (New York: Harcourt, Brace, 1948; London: Routledge & Kegan Paul, 1949);

A Woman of Means (New York: Harcourt, Brace, 1950; London: Routledge & Kegan Paul, 1950);

The Widows of Thornton (New York: Harcourt, Brace, 1954);

Tennessee Day in St. Louis: A Comedy (New York: Random House, 1957);

Happy Families Are All Alike: A Collection of Stories (New York: McDowell, Obolensky, 1959; London: Macmillan, 1960);

Miss Leonora When Last Seen and Fifteen Other Stories (New York: Obolensky, 1964);

The Collected Stories of Peter Taylor (New York: Farrar, Straus & Giroux, 1969);

Presences: Seven Dramatic Pieces (Boston: Houghton Mifflin, 1973);

In the Miro District and Other Stories (New York: Knopf, 1977; London: Chatto & Windus, 1977);

The Early Guest (a sort of story, a sort of play, a sort of dream) (Winston-Salem, N.C.: Palaemon Press, 1982);

The Old Forest and Other Stories (Garden City, N.Y.: Dial/Doubleday, 1985); republished as *The Old Forest* (London: Chatto & Windus/Hogarth Press, 1985);

A Stand in the Mountains (New York: Frederic C. Beil, 1986);

A Summons to Memphis (New York: Knopf, 1986; London: Chatto & Windus, 1987);

The Oracle at Stoneleigh Court (New York: Knopf, 1993; London: Chatto & Windus, 1993);

In the Tennessee Country (New York: Knopf, 1994; London: Chatto & Windus, 1994).

OTHER: *Randall Jarrell, 1914–1965,* edited by Taylor, Robert Lowell, and Robert Penn Warren (New York: Farrar, Straus & Giroux, 1967).

Peter Taylor (photograph by Bill Sublette)

"A century from now," novelist Anne Tyler suggested in a 26 January 1985 *USA Today* article, "when our descendants look back and marvel at our ignorance, they might very well mention the relative lack of homage we paid to Peter Taylor. He is, after all, the undisputed master of the short story form." Taylor's techniques and themes are neither startling nor sensational, which might account for his lack of popular acclaim. Scholar Albert J. Griffith states, "The voice that speaks in his stories is essentially the voice of a gentleman–cultured but not dilettantish, ironic but not cynical, urbane but not foppish; Taylor preserves what was best in the genteel tradition in American letters, without any of the mawkishness and prudery often associated with it." Although Taylor has been overlooked by the general public, critics regard him as one of the most accomplished American short-story writers of the twentieth century. During a literary career that spanned six decades, Taylor won a Pulitzer Prize; PEN/Faulkner and PEN/Malamud awards; an O. Henry Memorial Award; a Ritz Hemingway Prize for fiction; and Guggenheim, Fulbright, National Institute of Arts and Letters, National Endowment for the Arts, and Ford and Rockefeller fellowships and grants. Taylor's eight short-story collections make known his concerns about history, tradition, family and change.

The youngest of four children, Peter Hillsman Taylor was born on 8 January 1917 in the small country town of Trenton, Tennessee. His parents, Matthew Hillsman and Katherine Baird (Taylor) Taylor, were avid storytellers in the Southern oral tradition, and many of Taylor's narratives are based on things that his mother told him about her ancestors and relatives. Tennessee politics ran deep in Taylor's family. His great-grandfather Nathaniel Green Taylor was a Unionist and Commissioner of Indian Affairs under President Andrew Johnson. Both of Taylor's grandfathers were politicians and lawyers. His maternal grandfather, Robert Love ("Bob") Taylor, served as a United States congressman, United States senator, and three-term Democratic governor of the state. In Bob Taylor's first and most famous campaign for governorship, he ran against his father, Nathaniel Green, and his brother Alf in the Tennessee version of the "War of the Roses." Bob Taylor won the 1886 race, and some thirty-five years later Alf Taylor was elected governor at the age of seventy-three.

Taylor's father also showed an early interest in politics. Three years after he graduated from Vanderbilt Law School, Matthew Hillsman Taylor was speaker of the Tennessee House of Representatives, and he was attorney general for the Thirteenth Judicial Circuit of Tennessee when Peter was born. In a 1987 interview with Barbara Thompson for *The Paris Review,* Taylor admitted: "We grew up, in my generation, with political battles at home that were sometimes bloody between those great-uncles and aunts. But I think it did give me a sense of history, a sense of the past. I began to make up stories about these things, the old houses, Robert E. Lee, Southern things that I was obsessed by even then, at eight or nine." Apart from politics, Taylor's father was a successful attorney and businessman. In 1924 he moved his family from Trenton to Nashville and in 1926 from Nashville to St. Louis, where he became president of the Missouri State Life Insurance Company and was said to have arranged the largest reinsurance deal of his day. Taylor told Thompson about his upbringing: "there are no more loyal Southerners than those who grew up *just* outside the South or in the Border States. We lived in a little South of our own in St. Louis. We had a houseful of servants from my father's farm in the cotton country of West Tennessee, and the adults–black and white–would talk about the South, about the way things used to be there." In 1932, after he was betrayed by a friend and business partner, Taylor's father moved the family back to Tennessee.

Taylor graduated from Memphis Central High School in 1935, and having been awarded a partial scholarship to Columbia University, he intended to go east and study writing. His father, however, wanted him to earn a law degree from Vanderbilt; but rather than follow in his father's footsteps, Taylor decided to forgo college and to work his way to England on a freighter. When he returned from England, he took a job with the Memphis *Commercial-Appeal* and started taking courses at Southwestern (now Rhodes College), where Allen Tate was his freshman English instructor. Taylor recalled to Thompson, "It was his genius as a teacher that he made young people feel the importance of literature, the importance of art. That came just at the right moment for me." Before leaving Memphis in 1936, Tate encouraged Taylor to enroll at Vanderbilt and study under John Crowe Ransom, Tate's former mentor and a leading figure of the Fugitive poets and New Critics. Taylor spent one year at Vanderbilt, but when Ransom left for Kenyon College in Gambier, Ohio, Taylor dropped out of school and turned to selling real estate. Within a year he transferred to Kenyon and became close friends with Randall Jarrell, then a young instructor, and Robert Lowell, with whom he shared a room in the Douglass House residence where Ransom had arranged for his students to live. Taylor recalled during a 1987 conversation with James Curry Robison: "Lowell and I were so completely different, but we both were wild to write. . . . he was a driving, hard-working writer from the beginning, a classicist and all that. And I was always much dreamier and more intuitive." Taylor generated the poetry that was expected of him by his teachers and peers, yet he was also writing short stories on the side–his first published story was "The Party," which appeared in the Oxford, Mississippi literary magazine *River* in March 1937.

By the fall of 1938 Taylor had completed "A Spinster's Tale," the first of many Taylor memoir stories in which a middle-aged or elderly first-person narrator (some are far more reliable than others) recounts a decisive episode from the past. In this case a recluse named Elizabeth tells of her inaugural encounter with evil. The recalled action takes place in Nashville sometime before World War I and a few months after the narrator's mother has died following the delivery of a stillborn baby. One late October afternoon Elizabeth, who is thirteen at the time, spies the neighborhood drunk, Mr. Speed, staggering by her family home on Church Street. Her disgust for the man, whom Griffith identifies as "the dreamlike projection of some unbridled masculine principle that the motherless girl unconsciously fears and resents," so overwhelms her that she begins noting the drunkard's flaws in her own father and brother. She determines several months later that all men are to be despised. The young girl's crisis occurs on a May afternoon when Mr. Speed stumbles into her hallway in order to escape from a rainstorm. Loathing and fear drive her to telephone the police and have the man taken away from her father's property. From that day onward, Elizabeth stays aloof in her imagined superiority to men, and by opting for self-imposed exile, she paradoxically protects and alienates herself from sexual intimacy, change, and maturity.

Taylor explained to Stephen Goodwin in a *Shenandoah* interview (Winter 1973) that when he finished "A Spinster's Tale" he gave the story to Lowell, hoping for praise. When Lowell accused him of being "prim and puritanical," he vowed to prove his friend wrong and wrote the first sentence of a new story–"He wanted no more of her drunken palaver"–without having any clear idea of where he was headed. Within a few weeks he had written "The Fancy Woman," one of his frequently anthologized pieces. Unlike the prim Elizabeth, Josie Carlson in "The Fancy Woman" shamelessly surrenders to her desires for liquor and men. Having lived on the proverbial wrong side of the tracks, she aspires to Memphis upper-class respectability, but to her detriment Josie thinks and acts like a prostitute in the final scene when Buddy, her wealthy lover's youngest teenaged son, invites her to his room so that he can draw a portrait of her. Josie infers that he wants her to "pose" (strip) as a prelude to something else. Put off by her actions, Buddy says: "I didn't know you were that sort of nasty thing here. I didn't believe you were a fancy woman." Josie Carlson is "so corrupt," Taylor noted in an interview with J. William Broadway for the *Chattahoochee Review* (Fall 1985), "that she cannot recognize innocence when she sees it."

After earning his B.A. in English from Kenyon College in 1940, Taylor entered the graduate program at Louisiana State University, adding Robert Penn Warren and Cleanth Brooks to his list of famous instructors. Lacking a scholar's inclination, he stopped attending classes before Thanksgiving and focused on reading his favorite authors and producing fiction. Taylor was influenced by a wide range of modernist writers, most obviously William Faulkner, Henry James, James Joyce, D. H. Lawrence, Thomas Mann and Marcel Proust. Ivan Turgenev and Anton Chekhov were the writers whose examples meant the most to him, however. From Turgenev he drew confidence that he could write about people and events from his own background, and from Chekhov he acquired the artistic determination to look at things from all sides. Before 1940 ended Warren published "A Spinster's Tale," "The Fancy Woman" and "Sky Line" in the *Southern Review,* and "The Fancy Woman" was subsequently chosen for *The Best American Short Stories 1942.*

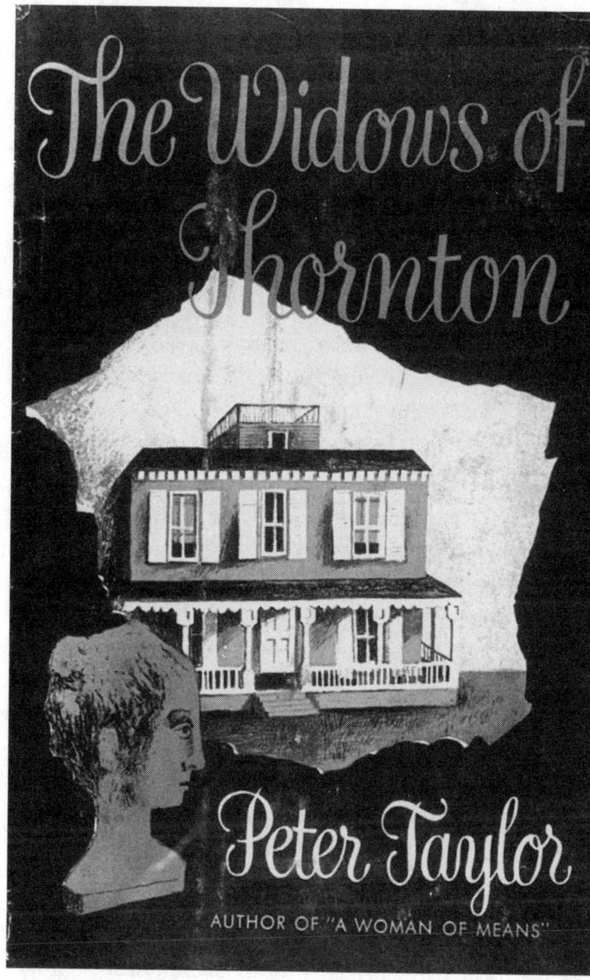

Dust jacket for Taylor's 1954 book, a group of stories about characters from Thornton, Tennessee

World War II interrupted Taylor's professional start. In June 1941 he enlisted in the army and was stationed for two and half years at Fort Oglethorpe, Georgia. While he was there, Allen Tate and Caroline

Gordon introduced him to poet Eleanor Lily Ross of Norwood, North Carolina; six weeks later, on 4 June 1943, he and Ross were married. They had two children: Katherine Baird, named after her grandmother, in 1948, and Peter Ross in 1955. Soon after his marriage, Taylor was sent overseas and spent two years in the Rail Transportation Corps at Tidworth Camp in England. He had advanced to the rank of sergeant when he was honorably discharged in December 1945. After the war Taylor and his wife lived for a brief time in New York, where he worked as a reader for Henry Holt Publishers. In the fall of 1946 he joined the English department faculty at the Women's College of the University of North Carolina at Greensboro and was reunited with Tate and Jarrell.

Two years after moving to Greensboro, Taylor published his first short-story collection, *A Long Fourth and Other Stories* (1948). In his introduction to the volume, Warren was the first to articulate that Taylor's stories are "officially about the middle-class world of the upper South" and its "disintegration of families, attrition of old loyalties and collapse of old values." Among the seven stories in the book, "Sky Line," "The Scoutmaster," and "A Long Fourth" exemplify Taylor's core strategies and themes. From his years at Vanderbilt and Kenyon, Taylor had long sympathized with Agrarian ideals, but he doubted that an industrialized South would ever revert to being an agricultural-based civilization. He illustrates that doubt in "Sky Line," in which his characters are dragged along by modern changes occurring in the unnamed Southern city in which they live.

The plot develops via a chronological sequence of fifteen self-contained units, starting when Jimmy, the protagonist, is a young boy and ending approximately a decade later. At the beginning of those years, Jimmy's father quarrels with his next-door neighbor; but when his rival dies, Jimmy's father invites the man's widow and little girl to move into his home. As the cityscape alters, so does Jimmy's family life: his father loses his job during the Depression and becomes involved with the widow; his mother unexpectedly dies during an operation; the once bashful next-door girl, Susie, grows up to be a high-school slut. Jim's father and Susie's mother disappear one weekend, and after telling Jim that their parents are honeymooning in Chicago, Susie invites him into his former bedroom and offers to be his first. Jim turns away and gazes out from the bedroom window of his childhood. While staring at the disjointed skyline–new churches, new schools, new houses and apartment buildings–he understands that the familiar people and places of his youth have disappeared beyond reclaiming.

Whereas "Sky Line" depicts changes that occur over a period of years, "The Scoutmaster" portrays a minor Thanksgiving Day family event that took place, the narrator says, when he was ten years old. The generational problems in the story are played out against a backdrop of losing loved ones to death and adjustments in marital status. The foremost conflict occurs when the narrator's parents unexpectedly return home early from the traditional holiday football game at the local university and discover their teenage daughter, Virginia Ann, necking with her boyfriend, Bill Evers. The parents banish the boyfriend and send Virginia Ann to her room; the narrator is shuffled along with his Uncle Jake to the weekly Thursday evening Boy Scouts meeting over which his uncle presides. Virginia Ann's indiscretion is heavy on Uncle Jake's mind as he stands, the narrator says in a moment of epiphany, like a "half ridiculous and half frightening gigantic replica of all the little boys" to whom he sermonizes about seeing in one's own family "the effects of our failure to cling to the teachings and ways of our forefathers."

"A Long Fourth" is one of the stories in which Taylor situates events within the context of World War II. Harriet Wilson, the central figure, is a matron of Southern decorum, and for days she has been directing efforts to make sure that Son (Taylor quite often distinguishes characters by their relation or function) and his female guest will enjoy what might be their last Fourth-of-July weekend together, since Son will be entering the army. The seriousness of these few days is defused by several occasions for laughter. Harriet wants romance for her two daughters, but Kate and Helena are gangly, overeducated women in their thirties who are destined to be spinsters given the obvious shortage of available men. Son, the only Wilson male heir, has escaped to New York and writes disturbing articles for which he has gained, at his mother's expense, liberal notoriety. Son's Platonic girlfriend (he does not believe in marriage), Ann Prewitt, edits a birth-control magazine and quotes from Karl Marx and Aldous Huxley. Harriet's servant, Mattie, has a nephew, B.T., whom Harriet wants to get off her property because of his offensive odor. Finally, the North and South clash again at the Wilson dinner table on Saturday evening when Ann debates race relations with Kate and Helena while Mattie serves them chicken necks.

Taylor introduces a key subplot before Son and his girlfriend arrive. On the morning they are to come, Mattie tells Harriet that B.T. has been ordered to report to an aircraft factory to work. When Mattie compares losing B.T. to Mrs. Wilson losing Son, Harriet turns livid. As the weekend progresses, however, Harriet begins empathizing with Mattie's unspeakable loneliness. In the closing scenes Mattie sits in B.T.'s shack for "the sole purpose of inhaling the odor" while Harriet kneels on her bedroom floor and searches for a comforting prayer. Harriet Wilson faces two losses, claims Robison: "One is the natural loss of her children to time and growing up, and the other is an unnatural loss, the discovery that she has never had any real closeness to them anyway."

Reviews of *A Long Fourth* were few, but favorable. One reviewer for the *New Republic* (8 March 1948) cited the stories for their "variety of character and incident." A critic for the *New York Herald Tribune Books* (14 March 1948) described the collection as "a little island of excellence" amidst the "stream of books flowing from the South." And reviewers for *Commonweal* (25 July 1948) and *The New York Times Book Review* (21 March 1948) praised Taylor for distancing himself from the grotesqueries of his regional predecessors William Faulkner and Erskine Caldwell.

Taylor was directing the creative-writing program at Indiana University when he began his thirty-year association with *The New Yorker* magazine, which published "Middle Age" (later retitled and collected as "Cookie") in its 6 November 1948 issue. In "Middle Age," Taylor's briefest story, readers eavesdrop on an evening meal discussion involving a philandering doctor, his wife, and their black servant. After dispensing with family pleasantries and small talk, the husband asks Cookie about her gossipy friend Hattie. When Cookie reports that her friend says the husband has been seen sneaking in and out of Doc Palmer's "meeting house" for men and women, the husband and wife brush aside her remarks as a sign of "old-nigger uppitiness." Even though the couple sidestep the truth, harsh rules of their world stand out: a black female servant must know and keep her place; a subservient wife must silently endure her spouse's infidelity; and a wealthy cad of a husband can do whatever he wishes.

Taylor left Indiana University in 1949 and returned to his former teaching position in Greensboro. In 1950 he completed *A Woman of Means,* a short novel that reviewers faulted for its lack of ambition and limited effect. In that same period he was awarded a Guggenheim Fellowship for 1950–1951, and his story "A Wife of Nashville" (published in *The New Yorker,* 3 December 1949) was selected for *The Best American Short Stories 1950.* In 1952 Taylor moved from Greensboro for a second time, going first to the University of Chicago before joining the faculty at Kenyon College, where he taught from 1952 to 1957. Taylor received a National Institute of Arts and Letters award in 1952, and some months later the *Western Review* printed the first lengthy critical study of his work as part of its series on "New Writers," placing him alongside Theodore Roethke and Saul Bellow.

While he was at Kenyon, Taylor published his second book of short fiction. *The Widows of Thornton* (1954) ranks as Taylor's most unified collection, calling to mind James Joyce's *Dubliners* (1914) and Sherwood Anderson's *Winesburg, Ohio* (1919). In an article for the *Kenyon Alumni Bulletin* (Winter 1954), quoted on the dust jacket for the book, Taylor explained his intention to link his characters to the particular locale of Thornton, Tennessee: "My idea was to write a group of stories dealing with the histories of four or five families from a country town who had migrated, during a period of twenty-five years, to various cities of the South and Midwest. . . . I wanted to give the reader the impression that every character carried in his head a map of that simple country town while going about his life in the complex city." To make this point he sets two of the stories in Nashville, two in St. Louis, one in Chicago, and one in a Pullman car making its way to Memphis.

Sylvia Harrison of "The Dark Walk" is the only literal widow in the book. After her husband, Nate, suddenly dies in his office in 1939, she reflects on the past two decades of moving from city to city for the sake of Nate's business career. Now an attractive forty-four-year-old woman who is being courted by two suitors, Sylvia contemplates taking her children back to her hometown. In the end she sends her "old and inherited" furniture back to Tennessee and determines to stay in Chicago and look for an apartment that she can decorate with "new and useful" things. Exchanging the old for the new connects to the title of the story, which alludes to the riverside walk in Thornton where Nate had proposed to Sylvia. She believes that many young women of her generation became widows when they "pledged their love" on the Dark Walk. When she agreed to become Mrs. Nate Harrison, she began a twenty-year sojourn of acquiescing to her husband's demands, thereby becoming one of the widows of Thornton. Other such widows include Mrs. Cornelia Weatherby in "Their Losses," the unnamed wife in "Cookie," and Helen Ruth Lovell in "A Wife of Nashville."

Taylor explained to Thompson how growing up in a traditional Southern family, surrounded by siblings, cousins, uncles, aunts, and servants, led to some of the concerns he explores in this collection:

> I didn't begin with any conscious philosophy, but I had a store of stories that I knew, that I had been told, and I felt I had to write them. And I discovered in writing them that certain people were always getting the short end. I found the Blacks being exploited by white women, and the white women being exploited by white men. In my stories that always came through to me and from the stories themselves I began to understand what I really thought.

Dust jacket for Taylor's 1959 book, stories that focus on family relationships

In *The Widows of Thornton* Taylor shows not only the dangers that women encounter when they pledge their love to ambitious men but also the perils that black servants encounter when they pledge their loyalty to white families. In "What You Hear from 'Em?," for instance, the narrator tells of an old black woman named Aunt Munsie, who at one time had been a focus of concern to the people in Thornton. Aunt Munsie had been a servant in the Tolliver household, and when Dr. Tolliver's wife died, he charged her with bringing up his children. Although Aunt Munsie slighted her own daughter in the process, she succeeded in raising "the whole pack of towheaded Tollivers," and for that accomplishment the townspeople tolerated her idiosyncrasies. By the 1920s, however, the Tolliver children have grown up and moved away, and kindness deteriorates into subterfuge. Keeping to her daily routine, Aunt Munsie drags her slop wagon down the center of the main street, impervious to the fact that she brings traffic to a grinding halt. The townspeople want her off the streets, and they enlist Thad Tolliver, an upscale car dealer in Memphis, in their cause. Thad suggests that the town pass a law banning swine within the city limits, and when Aunt Munsie discovers that one of her favorites has schemed against her, she bashes down her pen and drives away her pigs. Aunt Munsie lives for another twenty years, telling of the old days in Thornton and in the Tolliver family. To those who listen to her rambling tales, she seems a leftover token of racial and social consanguinity in the fading life of a country town.

Taylor published only five stories between April 1954 and June 1959, likely a result of shifting professional interests. Supported by a Fulbright grant, he brought his family to Paris in 1956 and did research about Southern expatriates who had settled in the French capital after the Civil War. Following his year in Paris, he returned to Gambier, Ohio, and brought out *Tennessee Day in St. Louis* (1957), his first full-length play. Taylor left Kenyon College in the fall of 1957 and joined the faculty at Ohio State University, where he taught for six years. Of the few stories he completed during these years, "1939," originally titled "A Sentimental Journey" (published in *The New Yorker,* 12 March 1955), and "Venus, Cupid, Folly and Time" (published in the *Kenyon Review,* Spring 1958) stand out because they differ significantly from his previous work. "1939" is as close as Taylor ever came to writing a strictly autobiographical story; it is a thinly veiled memoir of a Thanksgiving holiday trip that he and Robert Lowell once made. The narrator, a successful writer and teacher, recounts when he and his friend Jim Prewitt, an apprentice poet, were once inspired to escape from Kenyon and spend a long weekend in New York. After being disappointed by their love interests and their commonplace encounters, on a train back to Ohio they attempt to shape their thoughts into literature: the narrator writes a poor imitation of Jamesian fiction, and Jim writes a vacuous imitation of Yeatsian poetry. After each criticizes what the other has written, the two get into a shoving match in an empty smoking car but eventually make their peace by the time they reach their destination at one o'clock in the morning. In pursuit of raw material for his artistic temperament, the narrator concedes that he is too inexperienced to know what he is about.

Scholar Walter Shear points out that in "Venus, Cupid, Folly and Time" Taylor creates a story that "exudes decadence from beginning to end." The action is set in Chatham, a fictional composite of the urban areas in which Taylor had lived, and involves a bizarre coming-of-age ritual. Mr. Alfred Dorset and his old-maid sister, Louisa, emerge from their strangely dilapidated house to sell artificial flowers, to peddle withered figs (an obvious sexual allusion), and once a year to gather up the thirteen- and fourteen-year-old sons and daughters of the prominent local families and bring them to their home for an evening of dancing. Although the reasons are never expressly stated, the Dorsets' party remains a rite of passage that has been safeguarded by tradition. Once they are inside the Dorset home, the young teens' attention is directed to a plaster replica of Auguste Rodin's *The Kiss,* an antique plaque of Leda and the Swan, and a color print of Il Bronzino's *Venus, Cupid, Folly and Time.* In addition to showing their guests these sexually explicit works of art, the Dorsets tell of their personal family history and advocate "living with your own kind" and remembering that "love can make us all young forever." Everything about this elderly pair hints at incest. Unknown to the Dorsets, a mischievous brother and sister, Ned and Emily Meriwether, have smuggled a lower-class friend, Tom Bascomb, into the party. When the Dorsets finish offering their dating advice, Tom, who has been introduced as Ned, leans forward and kisses Emily. All except the Dorsets recognize that a cruel prank has been played. Ned, meanwhile, feels a tinge of jealousy when he sees Tom kissing his sister, and perhaps wonders if he could become like the grotesque Alfred. During the course of the evening, one charade gives way to another, and in the end, the Dorsets have hosted their final party. In the years that follow, Ned and Emily are sent away to school and become "indifferent to each other's existence." Although the narrator identifies Alfred and Louisa as perverse "social arbiters" of a particular place and time, readers question what set of values the new generation will subscribe to, given that generation's indifference to family and home. Taylor said to Thompson about the story:

> I really had in mind almost an allegory. One of the things that it was is a story about incest–not just the brother and sister, but all the young people. It's a form of incest to want to marry only in your own class, your own background exactly. That was the world I had grown up in. I had seen my brothers and sisters in it. And some of those young people–it was very sad–*couldn't* marry anyone but that way, and never married because there was nobody in that set for them. They had other choices to marry, but nobody that would fit; it had to be "in the family" so to speak.

"Venus, Cupid, Folly and Time" was chosen for *The Best American Short Stories 1959* and was also the winner of the 1959 O. Henry Award.

Taylor published his third collection of stories, *Happy Families Are All Alike,* in 1959; one critic for *The New York Times* (12 January 1960) heralded the volume as "a literary event of first importance." The ten stories in *Happy Families* are divided into two parts. Part I is titled "Chatham" and comprises three stories (including "Venus, Cupid, Folly and Time") in which Taylor pries into connections between family and community. Part II is titled "Other Places" and includes seven stories in which he explores relationships within specific family units. In the semipersonal *"Je Suis Perdu"* of Part II, a middle-aged father discovers on his last day in Paris that the glimmer in his daughter's eyes can dispel the pensive melancholy that has had a mysterious hold over him in the past. In "A Friend and a Protector" the narrator recounts being a young man in Memphis and learning that for some people the "pale unruin of their own lives" will compel them to destroy others. Set at a vacation cottage near Chattanooga, "Heads of Houses" debunks aristocratic pretentiousness, and Taylor wins empathy for a "fond old bachelor son" who quietly plays out the role others assign to him. And a fifty-year-old father in "Promise of Rain" recounts an afternoon when he shared a vision with his teenaged son and learned that seeing the world through the eyes of another "will begin to tell you things about yourself." Taylor placed tremendous importance on being a husband and father, and he used his considerable artistic talent to promote family values; as he told Broadway, "any society that doesn't have the family as a basic cultural and economic unit is a barbarian dunghill. I think that we don't have it; it's going fast."

Within a few years Taylor published his fourth collection, *Miss Leonora When Last Seen and Fifteen Other Stories* (1964), which is a retrospective collection that brings together six new stories with four stories from *A Long Fourth* and five stories plus the one-act play *Death of a Kinsman* from *The Widows of Thornton.* Of the six new pieces, the one that most reveals Taylor's playful side is "Reservations: A Love Story." He disclosed to Goodwin that he had purposely invented "all sorts of Freudian and phallic symbols" just to "make the story as sexy as I could," which apparently went unnoticed by the editors of *The New Yorker,* who selected it for their 25 February 1961 issue. The narrative begins as Franny and Miles Crowell are escaping from their evening wedding reception at a fancy Memphis country club. Culturally speaking, the young wife and husband are from different worlds. Franny is a spoiled, attractive debutante draped in old Tennessee money, and Miles is a handsome, upwardly mobile orphan from the West Coast. Their reception takes place during a snowstorm in the dead of January, and even though Miles and Franny had intended to honeymoon in Biloxi, they end up reserving a room in the downtown convention-filled hotel in which Miles has been living for the past eighteen months. When Franny accidentally locks herself in the bathroom, she and Miles begin haranguing one another about their respective backgrounds and previous relationships. Things get so out of hand that Franny threatens to drown herself in the bathtub while Miles ineptly works away at taking apart the door hinges. Conveniently, their bathroom connects to a second room, which is occupied by a gentleman and a prostitute. The gentleman, apparently knowing a thing or two about locked doors, rescues Franny, and when she and Miles reunite, they embrace as if all is happiness and bliss. The newlyweds promise never again to deceive or mistrust one another; however, deception and mistrust have been occupying the adjoining room. As a couple Franny and Miles have failed to extricate themselves from their first predicament, and readers surely have reservations about where the Crowells are headed.

Taylor explained to Broadway that he meticulously worked out the title story, "Miss Leonora When Last Seen," as an allegory about "those old ladies who had lived in a secure life but in a world that was going to pieces in a way." Miss Leonora Logan is Taylor's last great spinster. She is a retired schoolteacher and small-town eccentric who occasionally sneaks away on obscure automobile trips during which she dresses up in different costumes and "orbits" her native state of Tennessee. The narrator, one of Miss Leonora's former students, is concerned for her welfare because two weeks ago she packed up and drove away after he had been sent to notify her that her house was being condemned in order to make way for a new consolidated high school. Her disappearance "is making it look very bad for Thomasville." Throughout the history of the town, generations of wealthy Logans have opposed all types of economic development, wanting to keep Thomasville unspoiled for themselves. Although he is respectful of Miss Leonora as a symbol of tradition, the narrator concedes: "times do change, and the interests of one individual cannot be allowed to hinder the progress of a whole community." When he recalls going to tell her of the court's ruling, he says he noticed that Miss Leonora had lost her stylish eccentricity and looked much like every other ordinary, blue-haired old lady he had known. Figuratively speaking, the woman he expected to see had already disappeared. At the present moment he wonders if his former teacher will find any satisfaction in her present "escape into a reality that is scattered in bits and pieces along the highways and back roads" that she travels. Miss Leonora is a missing person, and perhaps there is no use in looking for her.

Taylor had made the short story his primary genre, but under a Ford Foundation Fellowship for the 1960–1961 school year he went to London and studied practical theater techniques at the Royal Court Theatre. After a year in London he returned to his post at Ohio State but began to feel that he was staying there only for the money. He contacted Jarrell, and in 1963 he returned to Greensboro for a third time. Both Jarrell and Taylor's father died within a few months of one another in 1965. In that same year Taylor was awarded a Rockefeller Foundation grant and was able to devote the 1966–1967 school year to his writing. Then in 1967 Taylor joined the English department at the University of Virginia, where he stayed until he retired from teaching. Three days after his mother passed away in Memphis in May 1969 Taylor was inducted into the National Institute of Arts and Letters.

Before the decade closed Taylor published a second retrospective collection. *The Collected Stories of Peter Taylor* (1969) combines five new tales with sixteen previously collected stories. The first two stories, "Dean of Men" and "First Heat," place in the foreground the theme of betrayal. Set in the turbulent 1960s, "Dean of Men" is a lengthy dramatic monologue in which a college president and divorced father recounts for his son, Jack, who is soon to be married, how his grandfather, his father, and he were respectively betrayed in politics, business, and academe. Throughout, the narrator stresses that it is quintessential for a man to go on living among men, regardless of the sacrifices he inevitably will make. Taylor mentioned in an interview with Hubert H. McAlexander that despite the narrator's rhetorical eloquence, Jack will not profit from what he hears because he knows that his father has sold out.

While "Dean of Men" is from the point of view of one who has been betrayed, "First Heat" is from the point of view of a betrayer. Set in a cramped Washington, D.C., hotel room where the air-conditioning is broken, the story centers on an anonymous state senator who earlier in the day had undermined a friend and colleague by pulling his support from a crucial vote. The senator now sweats out his guilt while waiting for his spouse to arrive, as he will be escorting her to a scheduled reception. In facing his wife he will be facing his conscience, and the heat is unbearable.

None of the five new tales in the collection differs significantly in tone, style, or theme from Taylor's earlier pieces. In the Winter 1971 *Southern Review* Joyce Carol Oates referred to *The Collected Stories* as a gathering of Taylor's best work, "one of the major books of our literature," a book of "stories that move us deeply, refusing as they do to imitate the formlessness around us."

By the time *Collected Stories* appeared, Taylor had spent the better part of thirty years writing short fiction. He admitted to Goodwin that by 1970 he had tired of the constraints the form had imposed upon him, so he broke from its genre barriers and turned more frequently to playwriting. Taylor did not bring out a single short story between 1970 and 1973; he did, however, publish *Presences: Seven Dramatic Pieces* (1973), a series of one-act ghost plays that deal with subjects atypical for him such as homosexuality, student protest, and abortion. Taylor believed that the ghosts people see and the inner voices people hear have the power to teach them things about themselves that they otherwise would not know. *Presences* received mixed reviews and failed to garner critical attention. Paul Theroux volunteered a lone dissenting voice in the *Washington Post Book World* (25 February 1973), calling Taylor "a playwright of the first rank."

In the summer of 1974 Taylor suffered a heart attack while at his eighteenth-century Clover Hill home outside of Charlottesville. Despite this setback Harvard University offered him a four-year appointment, which he accepted. Taylor enjoyed the academic community in Cambridge, but the cold winter months forced him to stay in bed for days at a time. He resigned after his first full term and resumed his duties at the University of Virginia. Coinciding with those changes, he returned from playwriting to short fiction, but he did so with an experimental intent. From 1974 to 1985 he initially wrote all of his stories in "broken-line prose" or "stoem" form. When a stoem (Taylor's term) became either too long or too difficult to sustain, he would rewrite it in traditional prose. As a consequence of his hybrid experiments, Taylor's first all-new story volume to appear in eighteen years, *In the Miro District and Other Stories* (1977), includes four conventional prose tales and four stories in verse.

The collection opens with a traditional prose story about an exchange that has been going on for generations between the cities of Nashville and Memphis. As background for his personal recollection, the narrator begins "The Captain's Son" by explaining that a disgraced young man in one city will pull up stakes and move to the other, planning to make a fresh start. As a general pattern, when the immigrant arrives in either Nashville or Memphis, he falls in love with some "distant connection," gets married and bears children. Following this explanation, the narrator returns to his high school days and tells of his sister, Lila, falling in love with a new man in town, Tolliver Bryant Campbell. As fate would have it, Tolliver Bryant Campell is the handsome son of the Captain Campbell who had once ruined their grandfather's senatorial aspirations. That is not the only strike that Tolliver has against him, however. He is also the only son of a "mixed marriage": his opportunistic father wed the daughter of the most prosperous land owner in all of Mississippi, and everyone knows that Mississippi is "beneath" Tennessee. The Captain and Mrs. Campbell are hopeless alcoholics, which partially accounts for Tolliver's move to Nashville. When Lila falls in love with him in 1935, Tolliver is thirty years old and "rich as Croesus." After the couple marry, Lila's father invites the newlyweds to live at home until Tolliver can settle into some notable career, which, of course, never happens. Months pass and Tolliver and Lila slip into "a sort of joint boozing," prompting the narrator's parents to rid themselves of their son-in-law and daughter and refuse every opportunity to visit them once they have moved to Memphis.

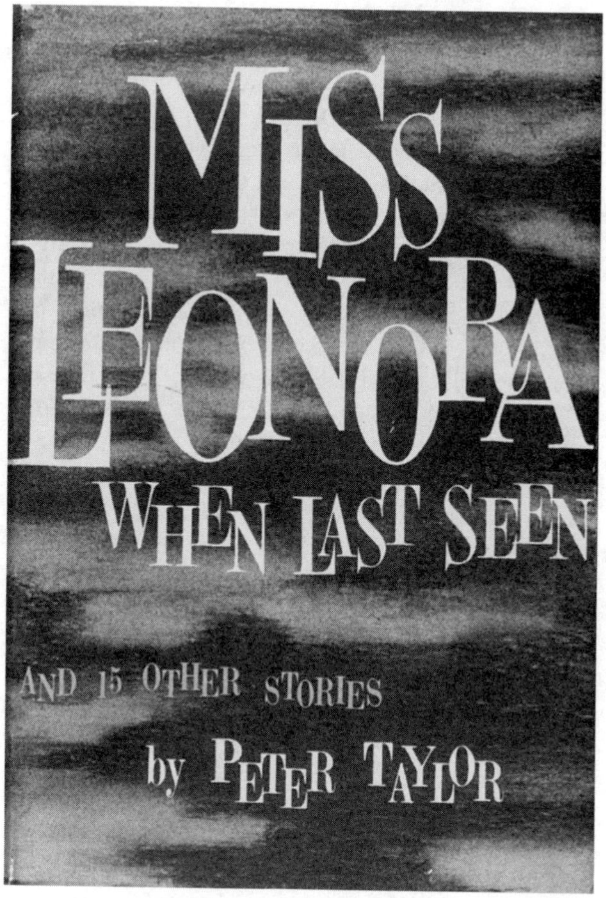

Dust jacket for Taylor's 1964 book. He called the title story an allegory about "those old ladies who had lived in a secure life but in a world that was going to pieces in a way."

Taylor stressed to Thompson that writing fiction depends upon knowing the right moment for a story to be told. In "The Captain's Son" approximately twenty years have elapsed since Tolliver and Lila were married. The narrator has chosen to remain a bachelor, and over the years he has pitied his brother-in-law and sister, thinking they might have "the bad luck to live forever–the two of them, together in that expensive house they bought, perched among other houses just like it, out there on some godforsaken street in the flat and sun-baked and endlessly sprawling purlieus of Memphis."

Other traditional stories in *In the Miro District* are variations of basic plots that Taylor had addressed earlier in his career. "The Throughway," for example, sets up a situation similar to that of "Miss Leonora When Last Seen"; however, in this story Taylor steps away from the upper-class gentry and writes about a middle-aged couple, Harry and Isabel, who must leave the house they have rented for thirty years. The entire block on which the house is located is being demolished in order to make way for one leg of the new city throughway. On the day that they evacuate, Harry and Isabel painfully discover that at any given moment the world can step in and estrange one person from another, even a husband from a wife.

In the title story the narrator recalls the summer during which he was "paired off" with his seventy-nine-year-old grandfather, Major Basil Manley, a cantankerous Civil War veteran whose beliefs are distinctly archaic in the milieu of the 1920s. The narrator is eighteen when he and his grandfather are thrown together, and the two are able to tolerate their generational differences until the afternoon that his grandfather discovers the boy's naked girlfriend hiding in his bedroom closet. On two previous occasions, the Major has allowed for his grandson's indiscretions, but this time he is outraged at the young man for involving a girl of his own social rank in a sexual liaison. Taylor told Robison that he plotted out "In the Miro District" to show a "man who is defeated by his culture," since the Major's "ideal of a love that he would have in a society based on family just does not exist anymore." After his unsettling discovery the Major surrenders his independence, moves into his daughter's home, and becomes a doddering exhibit of the once valiant Confederacy. It is an unhappy ending for a grandfather who is inflexible about social mores and for a grandson who knows he has destroyed an old man's sentimental vision of class decorum.

Taylor wrote fiction and poetry during his student days at Kenyon College, and his story-poems indicate a mature extension of that experience. In each piece he sets out to achieve the same depth and intensity that he would pursue in a longer story, and knowing of that intention, critics discuss "The Instruction of a Mistress" and "The Hand of Emmagene" as two of Taylor's best broken-line prose stories. "The Instruction of a Mistress" is divided into three parts and concerns the relationship between a famous New York poet and his former mistress of five years. Part 1 is a journal entry by the poet, Part 2 a letter found posthumously among his former mistress's belongings, and Part 3 a second journal entry by the poet, written sometime after the mistress has committed suicide.

In Taylor's version of the Pygmalion-Galatea myth, readers learn of the poet's obsession with transforming unattractive and uneducated young women into beautiful objects for public admiration. When the poet/artificer grows bored with a creation, he discards the finished product and seeks another young girl whom he can shape and refine. His former mistress knew of this obsession, and five years earlier, she and her lesbian lover devised a scheme wherein the young woman would put herself forward to attract the poet's attention. Ultimately, the two expected to profit by writing a new psychobiography about the poet's early life, guessing that his most powerful poems had been inspired by a homosexual relationship during his youth. That plan goes awry when the mistress becomes emotionally attached to her place of privilege, and in her letter in Part 2 she is writing to inform Maud, her lover, that she will not be coming back. The mistress learns, however, that she lacks the power to be an unending source of creative vitality for the poet. After he turns her out she kills herself in a car wreck. Expressing neither responsibility nor remorse for her death, the poet admits in Part 3 that years ago a young man had likewise committed suicide after being rejected by him. These experiences from the past have not altered the way the poet interacts with others. He has taken on a new mistress, insisting, "We must create creatures whom we can love." "The Instruction of a Mistress" is the only piece in Taylor's canon in which he presents characters who have no redeeming traits. As the price for their callousness, Taylor excludes the poet and the mistress from the joys of abiding love.

"The Hand of Emmagene" is Taylor's most violent piece. What begins as a gesture of family courtesy ends in self-mutilation and death. The speaker and his wife, Nancy, were born in Hortonsburg, Tennessee, yet they have risen from their country roots and have settled into Nashville sophistication. Still loyal to the past, the couple open their home to relatives from Hortonsburg, and thus Nancy's twenty-one-year-old cousin, Emmagene, comes to stay with them and look for a job. Having been raised in a strict fundamentalist family, Emmagene is devoted to hard work, cleanliness, and decency. Her hands are her most attractive feature, yet they symbolize both her strength and degeneracy. The narrator and his wife encourage Emmagene to go out with young men who express an interest in her, and therein lies a problem. Emmagene lacks the social upbringing to cut a figure among the Nashville country club set, so she dates young men from Hortonsburg who likewise have come to the city.

A crisis occurs one night while Emmagene is getting ready to go out with George, one of the Hortonsburg boys whom she has been seeing. Nancy is curious about Emmagene's private life, and she wants to be assured that these young men do not misbehave with her cousin. Emmagene has guarded her virginity, but when she is pushed to answer, she blurts out: "It's my hands they like / It's what they all like if they can't have it any other way." Overcome by shame, Emmagene dashes into the kitchen, picks up an ax, chops off one of her hands and then runs from the house to George's car; she dies before George can get her to the nearest hospital. According to Robison, Emmagene's death is "not the pathetic end of a religious fanatic but the tragic loss of a moral person who finds herself under pressures too great to endure."

In 1978 the American Academy and Institute of Arts and Letters gave Taylor its Gold Medal Award for the short story. Five years later he was inducted into the American Academy of Arts and Letters, the highest recognition of artistic merit in the country. In that same year, 1983, he retired from the University of Virginia as emeritus professor in English. In 1984 he received a $25,000 Senior Fellowship from the National Endowment for the Arts. Taylor published only two new stories between 1977 and 1985, and both–"The Gift of the Prodigal" and "The Old Forest"–are included in his final retrospective collection, *The Old Forest and Other Stories* (1985). In addition, *The Old Forest* includes eleven of Taylor's best stories that were not in his previous *Collected Stories,* and one short play. "By comparison with *The Old Forest,*" a critic for the *Washington Post Book World* (27 January 1985) insisted, "almost everything else published by American writers is recent years seems small, cramped, brittle, inconsequential."

Taylor develops vicarious experience as the central theme in "The Gift of the Prodigal." The story has no literal plot, for the action takes place in the narrator's mind as he gazes from a second-story window at his wayward twenty-nine-year-old son Ricky sauntering up the driveway that leads to the side door of his house. As his son approaches, the father recounts some of the unsavory incidents–shady business dealings, gambling operations, extramarital affairs–in which Ricky had called upon him once matters had gotten out of hand. The details of Ricky's current predicament are irrelevant, because the story concerns the father's need to be bailed out from the uneventful circumstances of old age. About to live through another of his youngest son's escapades, the father says: "I am listening gratefully to all he will tell me about himself, about any life that is not my own."

Written late in his career, "The Old Forest" is the story for which Taylor is best known. Nat Ramsey, the narrator, recounts an experience from forty years ago that nearly abraded his future. The critical action begins on the snowy Saturday afternoon of 4 December 1937 when Nat and a lower-class Memphis working girl named Lee Ann Deehart are involved in a minor car accident on an icy road. When the car spins to a halt, Lee Ann runs from the scene of the collision and disappears into the primeval forest beyond nearby Overton Park. Nat's immediate predicament is compounded by the fact that he is to marry Caroline Braxley, a young woman of his own social standing, the following week. After fleeing from the wreck, Lee Ann stays in hiding for four days. When the men fail to find the missing girl, Nat's fiancée takes charge and eventually figures out Lee Ann's secret. Caroline explains to Nat why she had to help him find Lee Ann: "Even if it had been *I* that broke our engagement, Nat, or even if you and I had been married before some second scandal broke, still I would have been a jilted, a rejected girl. And some part of my power to protect myself would be gone forever." Taylor makes Caroline Braxley the heroine of the story in order to articulate his views about prescribed codes of behavior and female power. To a greater and more complex extent than in any of his other stories, Taylor exemplifies "the binding and molding effect upon people of the circumstances in which they are born."

Taylor accepted a position as Visiting Professor at the University of Georgia for the spring term of 1985; it was his last such teaching post. In May 1986 he received the PEN/Faulkner Award for fiction for *The Old Forest and Other Stories,* and on 24 July he suffered a stroke that temporarily deprived him of his ability to speak and write. While recovering his health, he published *A Summons to Memphis.* Critics had been waiting decades for Taylor to produce a novel, and in the interview with Broadway he half-jokingly described *A Summons to Memphis,* which is slightly longer than 200 pages, as "a short story that got out of hand." Although the novel generated a short list of formidable detractors, Walter Sullivan and John Updike among them, most critics embraced it for what it was called on the dust jacket: "The crowning achievement in a distinguished career."

Taylor rarely involved himself in professional controversy; nonetheless, in late 1986 when *A Summons to Memphis* and *World's Fair* by E. L. Doctorow were nominated for the American Book Award, he denounced the nominating process and refused to attend the awards ceremony. Taylor argued that the award committee was misguiding people into thinking that writers were in the business of competing with one another. In his estimation the process and ceremony lacked good taste and good judgment. *A Summons to Memphis* was not to be denied, however. In 1987 it was selected for both the Ritz Hemingway Prize and the Pulitzer Prize for fiction.

Taylor struggled against deteriorating health for the next eight years, and in 1993 he published his final collection, *The Oracle at Stoneleigh Court.* Although the eleven stories in this volume turn on strange coincidences and ghostly visitations, Gail Godwin observed in *The New York Times Book Review* (21 February 1993) that Taylor raises the same questions he had pursued for over fifty years: "How much of our destiny is decided for us before we are ever born? How do we learn to recognize the voice that will save us? Do we really *want* to be saved, if it means having to risk ourselves in love?" These questions figure prominently in the novella-length "The Oracle of Stoneleigh Court." In the first part of the story Roger, the narrator, is a young soldier on temporary duty in Washington D. C. While there, he and his dream girl, the strikingly beautiful Lila Montgomery, become entangled with Roger's great-aunt Augusta St. John-Jones, a seventy-five-year-old widow who reads fortunes and communes with the dead in her apartment at Stoneleigh Court. After Roger introduces Lila to Aunt Gussie, their lives interconnect on issues of thwarted love and guided ambition. Aunt Gussie wants Roger to distinguish himself in some profound way so that he will carry forward the torch lighted by his renowned ancestors. Inspired by the family apparitions his great-aunt has summoned for him, Roger anxiously proposes to Lila, but Lila turns him down because his Aunt Gussie has convinced her that she will be happy only if she marries a Washington power broker.

After this awkward jilting, the story jumps forward in time. World War II has ended, and after spending two years in a military hospital, Roger returns to Memphis as a decorated war hero. Because he fainted during his heroic exploit and cracked his head against a stone, Roger has no recall of single-handedly capturing two dozen German soldiers during the D-day invasion at Normandy. Moreover, he is embarrassed by his fame since before going to war he had sought to be classified as a conscientious objector. As a further problem, Lila arrives in Memphis with Aunt Gussie, who is dying. Acting as if she is still under Aunt Gussie's spell, Lila aggressively pursues Roger, whose hero status now qualifies him for her attention. Frightened of Lila's power, Roger decides to marry a quiet, less intimidating local woman who reads the classics to her mother and raises tomatoes. When Lila hears that Roger plans to marry someone other than her, she faints, and at precisely the same moment that Lila faints, Aunt Gussie dies in a hospital on the other side of town.

There are other eerie occurrences throughout the collection. In "The Witch of Owl Mountain Springs" a spurned young woman takes refuge in a decaying mountain resort and waits for decades to use her "remarkable powers" to take her revenge on the couple who betrayed her. In "The Decline and Fall of the Episcopal Church" a marble baptismal font is reduced to a birdbath during a sacrilegious comedy of errors. Mysteries abound at the ends of these stories because Taylor was not so much interested in readers having a clear understanding of events, he told an interviewer in 1993, as he was interested in having them fascinated by what has occurred.

Peter Taylor died on 2 November 1994 at his home in Charlottesville, Virginia. Taylor was a writer in the purest sense of the word, seeking always to discover himself through the work he was doing.

Interviews:

Hubert H. McAlexander, ed., *Conversations with Peter Taylor* (Jackson: University Press of Mississippi, 1987).

Bibliographies:

Victor A. Kramer, Patricia A. Bailey, Carol G. Dana, and Carl H. Griffin, *Andrew Lytle, Walker Percy, and Peter Taylor: A Reference Guide* (Boston: G. K. Hall, 1983);

Stuart Wright, *Peter Taylor: A Descriptive Bibliography, 1934–87* (Charlottesville: University Press of Virginia, 1988).

References:

Albert J. Griffith, *Peter Taylor,* revised edition (Boston: Twayne, 1990);

Hubert H. McAlexander, ed., *Critical Essays on Peter Taylor* (New York: G. K. Hall, 1993);

David M. Robinson, *World of Relations: The Achievement of Peter Taylor* (Lexington: University of Kentucky Press, 1998);

James Curry Robison, *Peter Taylor: A Study of the Short Fiction* (Boston: Twayne, 1988);

Walter Shear, "Peter Taylor's Fiction: The Encounter with the Other," *Southern Literary Journal,* 21, no. 2 (1989): 50–63;

C. Ralph Stephens and Lynda B. Salamon, eds., *The Craft of Peter Taylor* (Tuscaloosa: University of Alabama Press, 1995).

Paul Theroux

(10 April 1941 –)

Julia B. Boken
State University of New York at Oneonta

See also the Theroux entry in *DLB 2: American Novelists Since World War II.*

Paul Theroux (photograph by Jerry Bauer; from the dust jacket for The Collected Stories, *1997)*

BOOKS: *Waldo* (Boston: Houghton Mifflin, 1967; London: Bodley Head, 1968);

Fong and the Indians (Boston: Houghton Mifflin, 1968; London: Hamilton, 1976);

Girls at Play (Boston: Houghton Mifflin, 1969; London: Bodley Head, 1969);

Murder in Mount Holly (London: Alan Ross, 1969);

Jungle Lovers (Boston: Houghton Mifflin, 1971; London: Bodley Head, 1971);

Sinning with Annie and Other Stories (Boston: Houghton Mifflin, 1972; London: Hamilton, 1975);

V. S. Naipaul: An Introduction to His Works (London: Deutsch, 1972; New York: Africana Publishing, 1972);

Saint Jack (Boston: Houghton Mifflin, 1973; London: Bodley Head, 1973);

The Black House (Boston: Houghton Mifflin, 1974; London: Hamilton, 1974);

The Great Railway Bazaar: By Train through Asia (Boston: Houghton Mifflin, 1975; London: Hamilton, 1975);

The Family Arsenal (Boston: Houghton Mifflin, 1976; London: Hamilton, 1976);

The Consul's File (Boston: Houghton Mifflin, 1977; London: Hamilton, 1977);

A Christmas Card (Boston: Houghton Mifflin, 1978; London: Hamilton, 1978);

Picture Palace (Boston: Houghton Mifflin, 1978; London: Hamilton, 1978);

The Old Patagonian Express: By Train through the Americas (Boston: Houghton Mifflin, 1979; London: Hamilton, 1979);

London Snow: A Christmas Story (Wilton, Salisbury & Wiltshire: Michael Russell, 1979; Boston: Houghton Mifflin, 1980);

World's End and Other Stories (Boston: Houghton Mifflin, 1980; London: Hamilton, 1980);

The Mosquito Coast (London: Hamilton, 1981; Boston: Houghton Mifflin, 1982);

The London Embassy (London: Hamilton, 1982; Boston: Houghton Mifflin, 1983);

The Kingdom by the Sea: A Journey around Great Britain (Boston: Houghton Mifflin, 1983); republished as *The Kingdom by the Sea: A Journey around the Coast of Great Britain* (London: Hamilton, 1983);

Sailing through China (Wilton, Salisbury & Wiltshire: Michael Russell, 1983; Boston: Houghton Mifflin, 1984);

Doctor Slaughter (London: Hamilton, 1984);

Half Moon Street: Two Short Novels (Boston: Houghton Mifflin, 1984)–includes *Doctor Slaughter* and *Doctor DeMarr;*

The Imperial Way: Making Tracks from Peshawar to Chittagong, by Theroux and Steve McCurry (Boston: Houghton Mifflin, 1985; London: Hamilton, 1985);

Patagonia Revisited, by Theroux and Bruce Chatwin (Wilton, Salisbury & Wiltshire: Michael Russell, 1985; Boston: Houghton Mifflin, 1986); republished as *Nowhere is a Place: Travels in Patagonia* (San Francisco: Sierra Club Books, 1992);

Sunrise with Seamonsters: Travels and Discoveries, 1964–1984 (Boston: Houghton Mifflin, 1985; London: Hamilton, 1985);

O-Zone (Franklin Center, Pa.: Franklin Library / New York: Putnam, 1986; London: Hamilton, 1986);

The Shortest Day of the Year: A Christmas Fantasy (Leamington Spa, U.K.: Sixth Chamber, 1986);

The White Man's Burden: A Play in Two Acts (London: Hamilton, 1987);

Riding the Iron Rooster: By Train through China (New York: Putnam, 1988; London: Hamilton, 1988);

My Secret History (New York: Putnam, 1989; London: Hamilton, 1989);

Doctor DeMarr (London: Hutchinson, 1990);

To the Ends of the Earth: The Selected Travels of Paul Theroux (New York: Random House, 1990); published in different form as *Travelling the World: The Illustrated Travels of Paul Theroux* (London: Sinclair-Stevenson, 1990);

Chicago Loop (London: Hamilton, 1990; New York: Random House, 1991);

The Happy Isles of Oceania: Paddling the Pacific (New York: Putnam, 1992; London: Hamilton, 1992);

Millroy the Magician (London: Hamilton, 1993; New York: Random House, 1994);

The Pillars of Hercules: A Grand Tour of the Mediterranean (New York: Putnam, 1995; London: Hamilton, 1995);

My Other Life (Boston: Houghton Mifflin, 1996; London: Hamilton, 1996);

Kowloon Tong (Boston: Houghton Mifflin, 1997; London: Hamilton, 1997);

Sir Vidia's Shadow: A Friendship across Five Continents (Boston: Houghton Mifflin, 1998; London: Hamilton, 1998).

Editions and Collections: *On the Edge of the Great Rift: Three Novels of Africa* (London & New York: Penguin, 1996)–includes *Fong and the Indians, Girls at Play,* and *Jungle Lovers;*

The Collected Stories (New York: Viking, 1997; London: Hamilton, 1997);

The Collected Short Novels (London: Hamilton, 1998).

PRODUCED SCRIPTS: *Saint Jack,* by Theroux, Peter Bogdanovich, and Howard Sackler, motion picture, New World Pictures, 1979;

London Embassy, by Theroux, T. R. Bowen, and Ian Kennedy Martin, London Television, 1987;

Chinese Box, by Theroux, Wayne Wang, Jean-Claude Carrière, and Larry Gross, motion picture, Trimark, 1998.

OTHER: "Reminiscence: Malawi," in *Making a Difference: The Peace Corps at Twenty-Five,* edited by Milton Viorst (New York: Weidenfeld & Nicolson, 1986), pp. 81–86.

Paul Theroux has achieved international fame and literary accolades for his travel writings, novels, short stories, poetry, and critical essays. Just as his literary interests shape his travel writings, so do his global travel experiences inform his fictional narratives, which frequently center on characters who find themselves displaced in foreign climes. Some few of Theroux's characters learn about others and themselves in alien lands; most, however, find only confirmation of long-established preconceptions. Many of Theroux's themes are somber, but his treatment of even the most serious subjects displays a full range of comedy, from black humor to the lightly acerbic. In fact, Theroux once said that one of his primary aims in writing is to entertain the reader. He most often laughs at preening, postcolonial racists, those with education and power but without humility, compassion, or any real understanding of other cultures.

For Theroux, travel is an integral part of the writing process. "Travel is everything," he has said, and "My way of travel . . . is more like a way of life." In his travel writings Theroux has described himself as an unrepentant eavesdropper, a self-description also used by one of his most important fictional characters, the diplomat who narrates the stories in *The Consul's File* (1977) and *The London Embassy* (1982). Whether he is working in the fictional or nonfictional genres, Theroux's vividly rendered international settings are both motivation and telling backdrop for his characters.

Paul Edward Theroux was born on 10 April 1941 in Medford, Massachusetts, a town he subsequently scorned. His father, Albert Eugene Theroux, worked as a salesman for the American Oak Leather Company; his mother, Anne Dittami Theroux, taught at the Hancock School, a grammar school. Both of Theroux's parents came from large families (each had five siblings), and together they produced another full household. In *Sunrise with Seamonsters: Travels and Discoveries, 1964–1984* (1985), a pastiche of reminiscences, travel pieces, and literary criticism, Theroux writes, "It was part of my luck to be born into a populous family of nine unexampled wits." The Therouxs remain a closely knit family, with many of them living at least part of each year near each other on Cape Cod, Massachusetts.

Theroux describes his high-school teachers as "willfully uninspiring" and the education they offered as "mediocre–non-intellectual rather than anti-intellectual." Unstimulated by his classes, Theroux avoided the school library; instead, he chose to spend his time thinking about "guns, bombs and fires." He graduated in 1959 and enrolled at the University of Maine, then transferred to the University of Massachusetts in 1960 and earned a B.A. in 1963. After further study at Syracuse University in 1963 Theroux lectured briefly at the University of Urbino in Italy and joined the Peace Corps later that year. Remembering his Peace Corps training, Theroux recalls only selfish motivations: "I had thought of responsibilities I did not want–marriage seemed too permanent, grad school too hard, and the army too brutal." He describes the Peace Corps as a kind of "Howard Johnson's on the main drag to maturity."

The Peace Corps assigned him to Malawi, East Africa, to teach at Soche Hill College. During this time, he began writing articles and poems for magazines in the United States, Great Britain, and Africa. While in Malawi, Theroux caught the American ambassador's unfavorable attention by publishing a critique of the Vietnam War and by writing essays for a magazine later revealed to be associated with the German secret police. He was also unwittingly involved in a failed coup d'état, for which he was summarily expelled from Malawi and from the Peace Corps in 1965 and fined for six months' unsatisfactory service. Despite this conclusion, which soured his opinion of American bureaucrats, Theroux wrote in "Reminiscence: Malawi" (1986) that his Peace Corps experience had many positive aspects. He felt happy and committed while teaching English and planting trees. He says "the Peace Corps allowed me to be myself," and he learned that one makes one's own life.

Because Theroux found working in Central Africa challenging, he quickly returned to teach English at Makerere University in Kampala, Uganda. There he met and married Anne Castle, an Oxford graduate from London. Their first son, Marcel Raymond, was born in 1968. Shortly thereafter, Theroux and his family moved to Singapore, where for the next three years he taught Jacobean drama at the University of Singapore and Anne taught at Nanyang University. In 1970 their second son, Louis Sebastian, was born. Theroux was also establishing himself as a novelist; after his first novel, *Waldo,* was published in 1967, he wrote three novels about postcolonial Africa: *Fong and the Indians* (1968), *Girls at Play* (1969), and *Jungle Lovers* (1971). By the time the Therouxs decided in 1971 to leave for England, where Anne had a job as a radio producer for the BBC, Theroux was determined never to have another job except being a writer. Employment, he felt, was an "oppression and an intrusion on my work."

In 1973, when he published his fifth novel, *Saint Jack,* Theroux began to receive greater critical notice. In 1975 he published the first of his acclaimed travel books, *The Great Railway Bazaar: By Train through Asia,* which became a bestseller. Theroux seemed to have found his niche in the publishing world when his next travel book, *The Old Patagonian Express: By Train through the Americas* (1979), sold 35,000 copies. His fame as a travel writer, however, did not preclude his success in other genres. Theroux published four books of short stories before his *Collected Stories* appeared in 1997: *Sinning with Annie and Other Stories* (1972), *The Consul's File, World's End and Other Stories* (1980), and *The London Embassy.* All deal primarily with culture clashes experienced by outsiders and drifters in foreign countries. Theroux draws upon his global travels to impart a keen sense of place, and particularly upon his traveler's "eavesdropping" skills to reproduce the subtly nuanced language of his varied characters.

Theroux and his first wife divorced in 1993, and he remarried two years later. For many years Theroux has divided his time between England and Cape Cod, where he has a house near the homes of his siblings. Since 1990 he has lived part of each year on the island of Oahu in Hawaii.

In the introduction to *Collected Stories* Theroux writes, "I inhabit every sentence I write! I tear them out of my heart!" In a 1985 interview with Charles Ruas, Theroux said that the "short story is often a piece of mimicry, or like ventriloquism, it's assuming another voice, another posture; that's the fun of it, actually. You can just project or extend your mind and say 'I'm this other person.'" In Theroux's stories the reader can hear him assuming the voices of a variety of natives and wanderers in East Asia, Africa, England, and the Caribbean. Several critics have noted that the short story seems an ideal genre for Theroux.

Sinning with Annie and Other Stories transports the reader from Russia, Malaysia, Singapore, and Tanganyika to Theroux's native New England. This collection features an array of hypocrites, lechers, miscellaneous eccentrics, and deceptive traitors. "What Have You Done to Our Leo?," set in Dar es Salaam, Tanganyika, presents a series of public and private betrayals. To obtain a divorce, Ernie Grigson solicits Leo Mockler's false testimony: Mockler swears under oath that he has had a liaison with Grigson's wife, Amy. Grigson assures Leo that the divorce notice in the paper

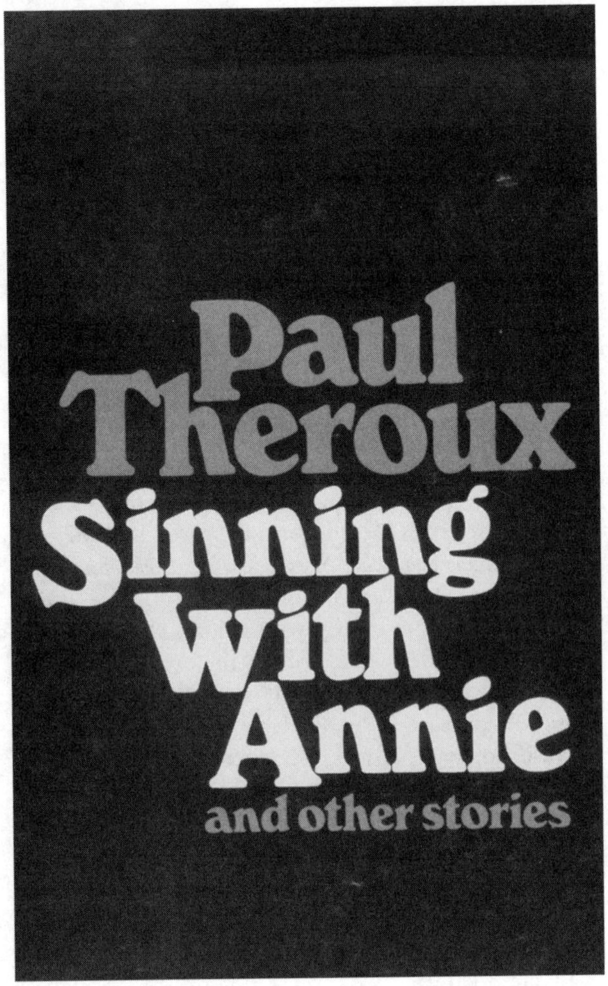

Dust jacket for Theroux's 1972 book, which includes stories set in Africa, East Asia, Russia, and New England

will not bear Leo's name; it does, however, and costs Leo his reputation and his job. En route home to London, Leo stops in India to visit Amy, to whom he has been writing; they have a lackluster one-night encounter, and Leo learns that same night that Amy is already remarried, to an Indian. Both Grigsons, he sees, have used him. The title of the story is explained by Leo's dream of his mother snarling at Ernie, "What have you done to our Leo?" In the dream, "Ernie had replied by sticking his tongue out at the old lady." Oaths and promises mean nothing in this story: friends betray friends, husbands betray wives, wives betray lovers. Traditional values and loyalties have been discarded, and the very fabric of society seems to be unraveling.

Another story of a stranger abroad is "A Love Knot," narrated by Daneeda "Danny" Schum, an Indian from Calcutta, who comes to Boston as an exchange student. When his mother dies, she leaves him a gold love knot, which he gives to an Indo-American girl he admires. His dream of friendship and marriage evaporates, however, when she tells him that her father would never permit her to marry an Indian–and that she is leaving for India.

Throughout the story, Danny dwells in the realm of fantasy. His view of Boston as "the city of quaintness and crime" is shaped by the novels he has read. His very sense of self is constructed by the imaginations of other people: he agrees to be "what other people take me for; I never challenge their assumptions." All of Danny's fantasies explode, however, when his love token fails.

Clashing cultures and misunderstandings again take the foreground in "A Real Russian Ikon," in which a souvenir-hunting American in Russia relentlessly pursues the purchase of a traditional religious icon. Like many of Theroux's travel books, this story condemns tourists as a species. Fred Hagberg, an insensitive American lout, covets an icon owned by an elderly, apple-faced woman who treasures the crumbling portrait of the Virgin and Child, praying before it with simple religious fervor. Fred unfeelingly presses some low-life black-marketeers to tell her that "she'll get into trouble if she keeps on praying, because it's against the rule of law [Communism]. And you know what *that* means! Siberia, right? Right. Go ahead, tell her." In possession of the icon, but worried about getting it through customs, Fred finds himself attending the elderly woman's funeral, and is cravenly inspired by this religious ceremony: he leaves the church shamelessly planning to smuggle the icon through customs in a casket. While all of these characters are specifically drawn, the unmistakable likeness between the Russian thugs and the Mafia bullies of Fred's homeland delineates a pattern of predation–young preying on old, powerful preying on weak–that transcends national boundaries.

The vagaries of national and personal character are again a motif as eighty-three-year-old Arthur Viswalingam, the narrator of the title story, relates his retrospective tale. He ironically dubs his painful story a "jolly memoir," as he relives his arranged marriage at age thirteen to eleven-year-old Annie. The two Hindu children are sexually ignorant, but eventually, "a little animal, a nasty little beast like the sort we worshiped," appears: the beast of lust. "I burned," Arthur says, "I married *and* burned." Arthur's revision of the Pauline Gospels limns his predicament. St. Paul, after praising celibacy as the best choice, reluctantly admits that for those Christians who cannot remain celibate, it is better to marry than to burn in hell for unsanctioned sexual concourse (1 Cor. 7:9). For Arthur, however, to marry is to burn with lust and shame, and ultimately to burn in hell. Arthur cannot forgive his own lust, even within marriage. Because lust "involves other people," Arthur believes it must be the greatest of all the sins. His remembered, unredeemable shame overwhelms him, even in his Christian, celibate old age. He has spent his whole life moving toward that final, late conversion, gradually assimilating the British colonizers' contempt for himself and his fellow Indians: "I was at the Delhi Gate when the British returned; I led them to the flea pots and flesh pits, the drink shops and temples, and, in a bloody crusade, we crushed the life out of the verminous population."

Arthur's reminiscences chronicle the process of Western imperialism choking an indigenous culture, focusing specifically on the way Christian colonization smothers the natural joys of sexual revelry, even within marriage. In his dotage, Arthur has become one of T. S. Eliot's "hollow men"; he paraphrases Eliot's "Gerontion" (1920) when he describes himself as "an old man in a wet month." Indeed, Eliot's description in "Gerontion" of an old man as "a dull head among windy spaces" aptly describes Arthur in the final lines of Theroux's story.

In this first collection of short stories, Theroux does not break any new ground in style or technique. Within his chosen traditional forms, he is in firm control of theme and characterization, and his portrayal of cultures at odds with each other is filled with irony. One reviewer for *The New York Times* (5 November 1972) called this collection "very fine" and compared Theroux to Joseph Conrad, Joyce Cary, Evelyn Waugh, and even to Franz Kafka. Another critic for *The National Review* (10 November 1972) found some of the stories strained, but praised the title piece. Reviewers generally appreciated the bittersweet humor that permeates virtually every story, palliating, if not quite softening, Theroux's scathing satire.

The second and fourth collections of Theroux's short stories, *The Consul's File* and *The London Embassy,* both feature the consul Spencer Savage, unnamed throughout the first volume and identified only on the last page of the companion collection. Both books offer a series of character studies as the consul relates tales of eccentric, polyglot figures, focusing in the earlier collection on the British in Malaysia. The British, who came to Malaysia after World War II to capitalize on the rubber tree trade (now moribund since olive palm trees yield more profit), live in isolated cocoons of cultural solipsism, outcasts from their own society in England, alienated from the Malays and other Asian natives, and mostly divorced or separated from their spouses. They are condescending, boorish racists who continue to live as if colonial rule had never ended. These interconnected tales also depict the bizarre and exotic Malaysians, Chinese, Japanese, Tamils, and Laruts. The stories in *The Consul's File* are set in Ayer Hitam (meaning "Black Water") in Malaysia and are narrated by the American consul, the "unrepentant eavesdropper," who is closing the consulate.

The consul is often the butt of British wit, and although politely accepted into the exclusive British Ayer Hitam Club, he remains an outsider, like the Malays, Chinese, Japanese, and Tamils. One of the consul's tales, "The Tennis Court," concerns another alienated club character. Shimura is a Japanese man whose people "lost the war and gained the world; they were unreadable . . . it was a total absence of trust in anyone who was not Japanese." Shimura is "one of these new men, a postwar instrument, the perfectly calibrated Japanese."

Shimura, automatically granted privileges at the club only because of his membership at the Selangor Club in Kuala Lumpur, draws the racist wrath of the British club members. The consul likes him, but maintains a diplomatic distance: "I was ashamed of myself for not actively defending him, but I was sure he didn't need my help." An accomplished tennis player, Shimura beats the best players in the club. The British use every ruse to rid themselves of this intruder. The consul says of the British, "The war did not destroy the English–it fixed them in fatal attitudes."

Shimura wins a match with a Malay ball-boy carefully trained by Evans, a virulent Japanese-hater; but Evans accuses Shimura of breaking the rules by not registering the ball boy as a guest. Shimura accepts Evans's humiliating chastisement politely enough, but in due time arranges to turn Evans's xenophobia against him and the other club members in an inspired and subtle countermove: he puts the ball boy up for membership in the Selangor Club, knowing that will give the Malay equal privileges at the British Club, something the club members would never have allowed. The consul remarks, "even those who hated Shimura and criticized his lob were forced to admire the cleverness of his oriental revenge."

Americans do not escape critical scrutiny in this collection, which includes two unflattering portraits of the consul's problematic compatriots: Miss Harbottle in "Pretend I'm Not Here" and Dr. Smith in "The Butterfly of the Laruts." Miss Harbottle is a middle-aged freeloader who trumpets her success at never having to buy her own food. She imposes on the consul for bed and board, promising that she would be an invisible guest (hence the title of the story) and offering to sleep in the garden of the consul's residence, counting on his insistence that she take one of the bedrooms. She soon becomes a catalyst for discord to everyone around, an international nuisance: "The Malays wanted to humiliate her; the Chinese suggested turning the matter over to a secret society; the Indians had pressed for some

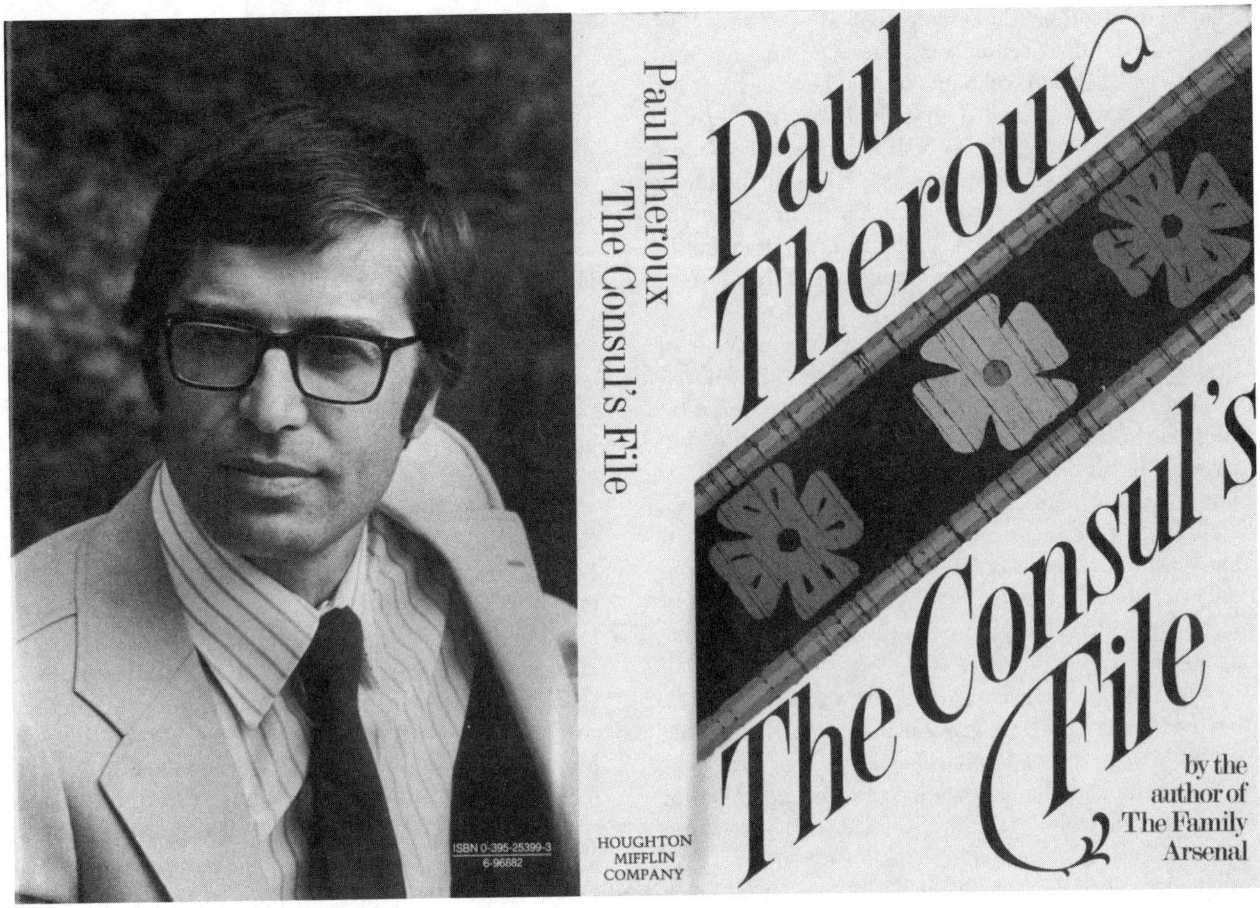

Dust jacket for Theroux's 1977 book, the first of two collections of short stories that chronicle the experiences of American consul Spencer Savage

expensive litigation." She finally sneaks out of town on the Singapore bus; but the consul observes that the common annoyance she provided led to the first time the town was united. While less condescending than the British, Miss Harbottle stands as an indictment of the thoroughly American tourist's brashly oblivious presumptions.

Dr. Smith, an American anthropologist, causes even more consternation than Miss Harbottle in this Asian corner of the world. Dr. Smith arrives in Ayer Hitam, armed with her camera, to study the Laruts, "true natives, small people with compressed negroid features, clumsy innocent faces and long arms, who had been driven into the interior as the Malays and Chinese crowded the peninsula." All of the Laruts are shy and nonviolent. The few who come to town attend schools, visit the medical clinics and sell merchandise along the road–colorful parrots, orchids, and butterflies.

Dr. Smith, not content merely to observe these natives, tries to become a Larut herself, adopting their dress and their habits; she even appropriates their elderly chief, becoming his ninth wife. But several months of her disruptive presence moves the chief to leave the safety of the forest: he visits the consul personally to request assistance in Dr. Smith's removal. The consul solves the chief's problem by introducing him to the concept of divorce. Freed of Dr. Smith, the whole Larut tribe retreats even farther into the green Malaysian interior. Theroux spares neither gender nor nationality in portraying these two arrogantly narcissistic Americans who, thoughtlessly imposing their own agendas on others, remain blind to the very cultures they have traveled so far to observe.

Other stories in this collection trace a parade of multi-ethnic characters wandering through each other's lives and territories. In "Coconut Gatherer," Sundrum, a Chinese-Indian writer, political activist, teacher, and village leader, increasingly distressed by the foreign occupation of Malaysia, withdraws from contented clarity into bitter and haunted mania. Nina, a Hokkien girl who has been exposed to her parents' leprosy, is the victim of an attempted kidnapping by a Chinese secret society obsessed with physical purity in "Triad." In "The Tiger's Suit," one of Theroux's Gothic tales, a *bomoh* (medicine man) sues a group of farmers for breach of contract when they refuse to pay him for making it rain; they in turn find him guilty of the murder of a little girl killed by a tiger, the event that brought the rain. In "Reggie Woo," a Westernized Chinese passes up a Fulbright scholarship and a local teaching position, gambling unsuccessfully on an acting career as his ticket to London. The consul's tales are of murder, infidelity, snobbery, and racism, and all are colored by the hypocrisies of vestigial colonialism.

In the title story, which opens *The Consul's File,* the consul begins the task of closing the consulate; in the concluding story, "Dear William," he has completed his work (all but the writing of his final report to the State Department). This epistolary conclusion is addressed to William Ladysmith, a character who appeared earlier in the collection in "Dengué Fever." The consul's letter offers a rather disheartened review of his two years in Ayer Hitam: "I never made a friend here. If I had I think I would have seen much less of this place. I am old enough now to see friendship as a constraint." He feels he has disappointed many people in the district, that he was "pretty ordinary, in a place that saw little of the ordinary." The reader will probably disagree with this assessment. The consul has revealed himself as a complex personality whose sophisticated sensitivity stands in sharp contrast to the obtusely parochial colonialism he has documented in his "files." The consul has seen through the romantic delusions of most Westerners in Southeast Asia, a romanticism he blames on W. Somerset Maugham's novels: "What tedious eccentricity Maugham was responsible for! He made heroes of these time-servers; he glorified them by being selective and leaving out their essential flaws."

Theroux continued exploring people's essential flaws in subsequent stories. *World's End and Other Stories,* Theroux's third collection, further demonstrates his versatility and his almost tactile feeling for place, extending from Africa, Corsica, and Puerto Rico to Germany, Paris, and London. The stories range from the Gothic tale to the comedy of manners to the domestic melodrama. A reviewer for the *Library Journal* (August 1980) wrote of these stories that "There is a love of farce and eccentricity in these character sketches, of witty talk and odd predicaments, but there are moments of poignancies and insight, too." The recognition and deflation of egotism recurs as a unifying theme.

In "Algebra," Theroux presents the denizens and domiciles of the London literary scene. Michael Insole, abandoned by his male lover, recoups some self-esteem by insinuating himself into the literary crowd, first as an ingratiating guest and then as a successful dinner-party host; his sole but quite sufficient strategy is shameless flattery of writerly egos. In "Words are Deeds," narcissism is again punctured. The shabbily dressed, affected American professor Sheldrick, abandoned by his wife in the south of France, imagines that a beautiful waitress will allow him to whisk her away to a new marriage and new future. He does convince her to leave with him, but soon discovers that she is a nagging, insensitive virago.

Narcissistic overconfidence again lies at the heart of "The Imperial Icehouse," set in the West Indies. Mr. Hand, a newly arrived plantation owner, idiotically attempts to transport a wagonload of ice across a steamy island in the midday heat. A quintessential bully, Hand threatens his black workers as the ice melts: "If you don't pull hard, . . . I'll free the horses and hitch you to the wagon." While attacking one of the men, Hand is killed with an ice pick. The workers ride into town in triumph on the wagon, "which rumbled like a broken catafalque," the melted ice replaced by the body of the hubristic newcomer.

The title piece of this collection is set in the World's End pub at the end of King's Road in London. Robarge, an American, comes to a new job in England with his wife and six-year-old son, Richard, in tow, feeling he "had not merely moved his family but rescued them." England, he believes, upholds the "domestic reverencies" more than America does. He is happy. Returning from a trip, he brings back a kite for his son; when they go to fly it, the boy innocently remarks that he has been to the same place to fly a kite with "Mummy's friend." Robarge's kite, ominously, disintegrates. After Robarge lies, while attempting to recruit his son as a domestic spy, Richard begins to deny that his mother has a friend. Robarge then realizes that he has spun a web of distrust, and that he has lost his son. In the interview with Ruas, Theroux declared this story a bleak one that offers no way out for Robarge: "What people find horrible, and yet it happens all the time, is that there's a child being privy to the domestic secret of infidelity. . . . [the child] is treated as a love object, as a possession, as a kind of mainstay, as the proof of [Robarge's] right decision." Theroux believes that children are "rather fragile creatures who can't live with many contradictions, and certainly want to know who they belong to." Richard, however, is bewilderingly shuttled between two dishonest parents as the disintegration of the family runs its course. Life abroad has become nightmarish for Robarge. British valorization of the "domestic reverencies" has not "rescued" his family, and for Robarge, the end of his family is the end of his world.

The longest story in this collection, "The Greenest Island," begins in 1961, when out-of-wedlock pregnancy still seemed shamefully scandalous to middle-class America. To avoid their parents' disapproval, twenty-one-year-old Paula and her nineteen-year-old boyfriend, Duval, have impulsively fled the country and are living on meager and rapidly diminishing funds in San Juan, Puerto Rico. They no longer love each other. Duval had planned to become a writer, "but that was before Paula had shrunk this future he imagined." Paula worries that Duval, "an unreliable boy," will abandon her. When Duval gets a job in a hotel restaurant, their new financial security only frightens them with the prospect of permanence: a claustrophobic future of quarrelsome parenthood in airless rented rooms on a small green raft of an island, "an intolerable trap." Duval finds a metaphor for this imagined marriage while he is observing roosters in their cages just prior to a bloody cockfight. After examining the blinded, mangled corpse of the defeated bird, he makes a resolution: "*I will never get married.*" At the end of the story, Duval leaves his hotel job, and readers understand that he will leave Paula as well: "It was so simple to go. . . . You walked away without a sound and kept walking."

The elliptical last lines of the story offer a lingering image of tumult: "The wind was on the sea, and the waves tumbled like lost cargoes of silver smashing to pieces on the beach." Theroux has commented that Duval, "being an American, is hopeful about his destiny." In that closing scene, readers can see Duval losing all that one destiny had to offer him as he gambles on a different future; ironically, the imminent birth of his child is coinciding with the death of Duval's old self and his rebirth into a new life. The wind is on the sea, and Duval is embarking on a new life, unencumbered by wife or child.

Theroux's placement of "World's End" at the beginning and "The Greenest Island" at the end of this collection was deliberate: "Perhaps this collection would have a different slant if it began with a story which is about hope and ended with one about horrible disclosure, but I did not choose that because I wanted to end on a somewhat hopeful note of someone marching into the world." Both of these stories begin with the arrival of deluded Americans in foreign countries, where their expectations will be dashed, their confidence in themselves and each other shattered. Each story depicts the disintegration of a family's future. Only the young aspiring writer Duval senses a dark glimmer of possibility for himself, a future that remains unwritten.

Theroux's fourth collection of stories, *The London Embassy,* begins with the consul's move to "the center of the civilized world, the best place in Europe, the last habitable city." In London, the consul, Savage, now a political officer, is assigned to track influential figures and curry their favor for American interests. Linking the stories in this collection are Savage's acutely observant sensibility and the setting of London, characterized as a city of ambiguities, a city of secrets, where political language is opaque and vague and the very houses conceal "plots" (in the gardens behind the buildings). Despite their shared cultural roots, the British are disdainful of American colonials–the nations are indeed "separated by a common language," as Winston Churchill observed. In "The Exile," British intellectuals regard the American embassy as "a stronghold of corrosive philistines, reactionaries, anti-Communists, and America Firsters–a nest of spies." Within the embassy as well as without, Savage is embroiled in political power plays. In "Reception," at a party celebrating his arrival, Savage gets a clear preview of his new duties, as he is required to navigate diplomatically through a room full of political pitfalls. The British regard embassy personnel as "high-living and rather unserious." Savage's American honesty breaks through his diplomatic mask when he frankly rejects a London peer's invitation to join a club that bars women.

The characters introduced in "Reception" reappear throughout the collection, including the black economist Errol Jeeps, an American who returns in "Namesake" to tell a story comparing American and British forms of snobbery and racism. In "Children," another embassy staffer from the reception guest list, the Italian-American Vincent Scaduto, introduces Savage to his wife and children, who embarrassingly parrot the elitism and racism of their condescending British acquaintances and teachers. While not immune to British snobbery himself, Scaduto recognizes the ill effects of prolonged exposure to British public-school values, which his impressionable children have quickly absorbed. Scaduto yearns for a transfer to Rome, not only to please his immigrant Italian father, but also to enroll his children in the American school there.

Americans bring their own stereotyped perceptions to England, however. "Charlie Hogle's Earring" examines the constricted, intolerant, and impoverished perceptions common among American embassy staffers. A "dogsbody" (British slang for "drudge"), Charlie is a dedicated telex operator who begins wearing an earring "too small to be a pirate's, too simple for a transvestite." Unreasonably discomfitted by the unutterable implications of this development, Everett Horton, the "number two" man at the embassy, gives Savage the unenviable task of persuading Charlie to remove his earring, which Savage actually admires. At first demurring, despite the possible loss of his job, Charlie finally acquiesces in response to Savage's ploy of arranging to meet him in a gay bar and implying that people think the earring means Charlie is gay. Theroux's humor centers on the triviality, the inanity, even the absurdity, of an issue that becomes a serious test of Savage's future in embassy politics. In the end, Savage is ashamed of his role as Horton's mediary and more concerned about Horton's sexual orientation than about Charlie's.

Savage fields another difficult assignment in the critically lauded story "The Exile." This time, his job is to find Walter Van Bellamy, a character Theroux loosely based on the American poet Robert Lowell. Savage is to convince Van Bellamy to join an international culture seminar that will enhance the American image. Savage finally locates the elusive poet in a mental hospital, where Van

Dust jacket for Theroux's 1980 book, stories that explore how character flaws are often exposed in foreign settings

Bellamy, with "eyes as blue as gas flames, [and] a stern bony Pilgrim Father's face," is rewriting his already-published poetry. Savage, who in his youth admired Van Bellamy's work, is nauseated to see that the poet, a viciously demented anti-Semite, has titled one of his poems "The Jewnighted States": "It was poisonous–Bellamy's . . . babbling about the beauties of Auschwitz." One of Van Bellamy's doctors quotes a Jewish writer: "'All men are Jews', meaning all men are victims"; but the doctor continues, "It's not true, you know. The opposite is closer to the truth. All men are Nazis, really. I mean, if all men are anything, which of course they're not." Theroux's poetic madman must remind readers not only of Lowell but also of Ezra Pound, the poet who during World War II collaborated with the Nazis and Fascists in radio broadcasts against the Allies and who, returned to the United States after the war, was confined to a mental institution.

Savage's skills as a detective–seen in his solving of two murders in *The Consul's File* and in his ability as a locator of missing persons in "The Exile"–are again exercised in the Gothic tale "Tomb with a View." Although no crime has been reported, the Muslim Abdul Wahab Bin Baz has been accused of stealing by his landlady, who has found rare and expensive artifacts under his bed. Concealed in a graveyard, Savage learns that Abdul has been plundering the tomb of Sir Richard F. Burton, the British explorer who so thoroughly plundered Islam. When Savage locks Abdul in Burton's tomb for the night, the reader may be reminded of Fortunato, the character permanently, vengefully walled up in the catacombs of Edgar Allan Poe's "The Cask of Amontillado" (1846). Unlike Poe's unforgiving Montresor, Savage relents, releasing Abdul in the morning. Savage is satisfied, however: "I had announced myself as the avenging Christian." Theroux's delight in the Gothic and the macabre, most traditionally indulged in "Tomb With a View," is also evident in *The Consul's File:* in "Lies," the story of a supposed curse; in the ghoulish and hallucinatory atmosphere of "Dengué Fever"; and in his horribly comic ghost story, "The Flower of Malaya."

In *The Consul's File* there is a conspicuous absence of any sexual or romantic attachment involving Savage. In *The London Embassy,* however, several tales richly embroider Savage's relations with women, which range from anticipated sex to mechanical sex to, finally, an affair combining the ideal trinity of sex, romantic love, and friendship.

Sophie Graveney, in "An English Unofficial Rose," clearly flirts with Savage, who quickly becomes obsessed with her but who never successfully demonstrates his sexual prowess. Eventually she attempts to exact a realtor's finder's fee for having suggested a flat for Savage. Savage, never aware of any agreement and reluctant to pay such a fee, is astonished by Sophie's sudden transformation: "with a few blunt swears, she lost her nationality and became any loud, crude, bad-tempered bitch spitting thorns at me." Chivalrously, he sends her the case of champagne he had already planned to give her, but no commission. Sophie's sexual attractions have quickly faded.

Another distraction from Savage's lonely bachelorhood is Miss Margaret Duboys, in "Sex and Its Substitutes," who is obsessed with her six cats. Because Savage shows some sympathy with her pets, Margaret permits him to have empty, "animal" sex with her–the only kind of union possible in the midst of her menagerie. Because it is meaningless, the affair is soon over.

In the last three stories of *The London Embassy,* however, Savage is involved with a lovely Mexican-American literature professor from Bryn Mawr, Flora Christine Domingo-Duncan, a biographer of Mary Shelley. Savage meets her in "The Winfield Wallpaper" and is dazzled. The story ends with a promise of a future liaison. The courtship evolves in "Dancing on the Radio," in which Savage becomes more deeply attached to this smart, beautiful, witty feminist: "I had had lovers, but I had never had such a good friend and for this friendship I loved her." He discovers that his is a transformed personality, which now admits a "kinder, dependent, appreciative side" inspired by Flora, who says that love is an "extreme paranoid condition" but who is nonetheless deeply in love with Savage. "Memo," the short concluding piece in this collection, provides a satisfying coda: it ends with their visit to the Chelsea Registry Office, where Savage finally reveals his name as he marries Flora.

Theroux's embattled embassy, home to a discordant crew charged with the projection of the American vision onto the international landscape, provides an appropriate setting for his mordantly witty lampoons of human foibles, particularly for his perceptions of the "essential flaws" of the British national character. In all of his short fiction Theroux scrutinizes his flawed characters with acuity and a temper both sympathetic and indignant. Like Savage, Theroux has been a worker and resident both in Asia and in England, and he knows his subjects well.

In 1997 *The Collected Stories* was published, a volume of sixty-eight tales that includes nearly all of the stories in the four earlier collections. Theroux arranged the volume, beginning with "World's End," in which the title story is given prominence. His first collection, "Sinning with Annie," is next, followed by four previously uncollected stories in Part III, designated as "Jungle Bells." Parts IV and V are labeled "Diplomatic Relations (i): The Consul's File," set in the East, and "Diplomatic Relations (ii): The London Embassy," set in the West. The four stories in "Jungle Bells" begin with "Polvo," resembling a short travel piece set in Patagonia, a settlement of dour, unwelcoming Welsh. The other three are tales of corruption and exploitation. In "Low Tide" a white captain lures two black boys into a rowboat and proceeds to lecture them interminably about life and the sea. In "Jungle Bells" a drunk Caucasian in Lusaka, Zambia, at Christmas time, permits two Africans to lure him into the hinterlands, where they virtually hold him captive for days. He then craftily eludes them, returns to Lusaka, and eventually reaches Rhodesia (now Zimbabwe). The title is a corruption of "Jingle Bells," the Africans' mispronunciation. In "Warm Dogs" a sterile couple attempting an adoption are caught in a tangle of street waifs who turn on the couple and at the end of the story are about to maim or kill them. These stories, focusing on racial and class attitudes, display Theroux's imaginative irony and the wide diversity of character, theme, and place that is apparent in all his short fiction, supporting his general view of people and their unconscious behavioral attitudes. A reviewer for *The New York Times Book Review* (20 July 1997) commented, "Read one after another, the stories accumulate weight and presence, making up a sort of novel." A significant unifying element throughout the collection is Theroux's often teasing and impatient wit, which suffers tourist fools not at all.

In the *Saturday Review* (2 February 1982) Jonathan Raban, a writer of many genres, including travel books, called Theroux "the most gifted, most prodigal writer of his generation," who should be read "for his unsparingly witty eviscerations of human vanity and pretence." While Theroux is perhaps most often recognized for his travel writing and his best-known novel, *The Mosquito Coast* (1981), his short fiction is an equally significant part of his contribution to American literature.

Interview:

Charles Ruas, "Paul Theroux," in his *Conversations with American Writers* (New York: Knopf, 1985), pp. 244–264.

References:

James Atlas, "The Theroux Family Arsenal," *New York Times Magazine,* 30 April 1978, pp. 22–24, 49, 52, 54, 58, 60, 62, 64;

Samuel Coale, *Paul Theroux* (Boston: Twayne, 1987).

John Updike

(18 March 1932 -)

Robert M. Luscher
University of Nebraska at Kearney

See also the Updike entries in *DLB 2: American Novelists Since World War II; DLB 5: American Poets Since World War II; DLB 143: American Novelists Since World War II, Third Series; DLB Yearbook 1980; DLB Yearbook 1982; and DLB Documentary Series 3: Saul Bellow, Jack Kerouac, Norman Mailer, Vladimir Nabokov, John Updike, Kurt Vonnegut.*

John Updike (photograph by Martha Updike)

BOOKS: *The Carpentered Hen and Other Tame Creatures* (New York: Harper, 1958); republished as *Hoping for a Hoopoe* (London: Gollancz, 1959);

The Poorhouse Fair (New York: Knopf, 1959; London: Gollancz, 1959); republished, with a new introduction by Updike (New York: Knopf, 1977; London: Penguin, 1978);

The Same Door: Short Stories (New York: Knopf, 1959; London: Deutsch, 1962);

Rabbit, Run (New York: Knopf, 1960; London: Deutsch, 1961);

Pigeon Feathers and Other Stories (New York: Knopf, 1962; London: Deutsch, 1962);

The Centaur (New York: Knopf, 1963; London: Deutsch, 1963);

Telephone Poles and Other Poems (New York: Knopf, 1963; London: Deutsch, 1964);

Olinger Stories: A Selection (New York: Vintage, 1964);

The Ring (New York: Knopf, 1964);

Assorted Prose (New York: Knopf, 1965; London: Deutsch, 1965);

A Child's Calendar (New York: Knopf, 1965);

Of the Farm (New York: Knopf, 1965; London: Deutsch, 1966);

Verse (Greenwich, Conn.: Fawcett, 1965);

The Music School: Short Stories (New York: Knopf, 1966; London: Deutsch, 1967);

Couples (New York: Knopf, 1968; London: Deutsch, 1968);

Midpoint and Other Poems (New York: Knopf, 1969; London: Deutsch, 1969);

Bech: A Book (New York: Knopf, 1970; London: Deutsch, 1970);

Rabbit Redux (New York: Knopf, 1971; London: Deutsch, 1972);

Seventy Poems (Harmondsworth, U.K.: Penguin, 1972);

Museums and Women and Other Stories (New York: Knopf, 1972; London: Deutsch, 1973);

A Good Place: Being a Personal Account of Ipswich, Massachusetts Written on the Occasion of Its Seventeenth-Century Day, 1972, by a Resident (New York: Aloe Editions, 1973);

Buchanan Dying: A Play (New York: Knopf, 1974; London: Deutsch, 1974);

A Month of Sundays (New York: Knopf, 1975; London: Deutsch, 1975);

Picked-Up Pieces (New York: Knopf, 1975; London: Deutsch, 1976);

Marry Me: A Romance (New York: Knopf, 1976; London: Deutsch, 1977);
Couples: A Short Story (Cambridge, Mass.: Halty Ferguson, 1976);
Tossing and Turning: Poems (New York: Knopf, 1977; London: Deutsch, 1977);
The Coup (New York: Knopf, 1978; London: Deutsch, 1979);
Sixteen Sonnets (Cambridge, Mass.: Halty Ferguson, 1979);
Too Far to Go: The Maples Stories (New York: Fawcett Crest, 1979); republished as *Your Lover Just Called* (Harmondsworth, U.K.: Penguin, 1980);
Problems and Other Stories (New York: Knopf, 1979; London: Deutsch, 1980);
Rabbit Is Rich (New York: Knopf, 1981; London: Deutsch, 1982);
Bech Is Back (New York: Knopf, 1982; London: Deutsch, 1983);
The Beloved (Northridge, Cal.: Lord John Press, 1982);
Hugging the Shore: Essays and Criticism (New York: Knopf, 1983; London: Deutsch, 1984);
The Witches of Eastwick (New York: Knopf, 1984; London: Deutsch, 1984);
Facing Nature: Poems (New York: Knopf, 1985; London: Deutsch, 1986);
Roger's Version (New York: Knopf, 1986; London: Deutsch, 1986);
Trust Me: Short Stories (New York: Knopf, 1987); republished as *Trust Me: Stories* (London: Deutsch, 1987);
S. (New York: Knopf, 1988); republished as *S.: A Novel* (London: Deutsch, 1988);
Self-Consciousness: Memoirs (New York: Knopf, 1989; London: Deutsch, 1989);
Just Looking: Essays on Art (New York, Knopf, 1989; London: Deutsch, 1989);
Rabbit at Rest (New York: Knopf, 1990; London: Deutsch, 1990);
Odd Jobs: Essays and Criticism (New York: Knopf, 1991; London: Deutsch, 1992);
Memories of the Ford Administration (New York: Knopf, 1992; London: Hamilton, 1992);
Collected Poems, 1953–1993 (New York: Knopf, 1993; London: Hamilton, 1993);
Brazil (New York: Knopf, 1994; London: Hamilton, 1994);
The Afterlife and Other Stories (New York: Knopf, 1994; London: Hamilton, 1995);
A Helpful Alphabet of Friendly Objects (New York: Knopf, 1995);
In the Beauty of the Lilies (New York: Knopf, 1996; London: Hamilton, 1996);
Golf Dreams: Writings on Golf (New York: Knopf, 1996; London: Hamilton, 1997);
Toward the End of Time (New York: Knopf, 1997; London: Hamilton, 1998);
Bech at Bay: A Quasi-Novel (New York: Knopf, 1998; London: Hamilton, 1999);
More Matter: Essays and Criticism (New York: Knopf, 1999);
Gertrude and Claudius (New York: Knopf, forthcoming, 2000).

Collection: *Rabbit Angstrom: A Tetralogy* (New York: Knopf, 1995; London: Random House, 1995).

PLAY PRODUCTION: *Buchanan Dying,* Lancaster, Pa., Green Room Theater, 29 April 1976.

RECORDINGS: *John Updike Reads John Updike,* CMS Records, CMS 523, 1967;
Prose and Poetry of John Updike, read by Updike, Guilford, Conn.: Jeffrey Norton, 1967;
John Updike Reads from Couples *and* Pigeon Feathers, Caedmon, TC 1276, 1969;
Selected Stories: John Updike, read by Updike, New York: Random House Audiobooks, 1985;
Trust Me, read by Updike, New York: Random House, 1987;
S., read by Updike, New York: Random House, 1989;
Rabbit at Rest, read by Updike, New York: Random House, 1990;
The Afterlife and Other Stories, read by Updike, New York: Random House, 1994;
Brazil, read by Updike, New York: Random House, 1994;
Golf Dreams, read by Updike, New York: Random House, 1996;
Bech at Bay and Before, read by Updike, New York: Random House, 1998.

OTHER: *The Magic Flute,* music by Wolfgang Amadeus Mozart, adapted and illustrated by Updike and Warren Chappell (New York: Knopf, 1962; London: Deutsch & Ward, 1964);
Bottom's Dream: Adapted from William Shakespeare's A Midsummer Night's Dream, music by Felix Mendelssohn (New York: Knopf, 1969);
Vladimir Nabokov, *Lectures on Literature,* 2 volumes, edited by Fredson Bowers, introduction by Updike (New York: Harcourt Brace Jovanovich; Columbia, S.C.: Bruccoli Clark, 1980, 1981);
Franz Kafka, *Complete Stories,* edited by Nahum N. Glatzer, foreword by Updike (New York: Schocken Books, 1983);
The Best American Short Stories 1984: Selected from U.S. and Canadian Magazines, edited by Updike and Shan-

non Ravenel, introduction by Updike (Boston: Houghton Mifflin, 1984);

Kathleen G. Hjerter, *Doubly Gifted: The Author as Visual Artist,* foreword by Updike (New York: Abrams, 1986);

George Plimpton, ed., *Writers at Work: The Paris Review Interviews, Seventh Series,* introduction by Updike (New York: Viking, 1986);

Arnold Haultain, *The Mystery of Golf,* afterword by Updike (Bedford, Mass.: Applewood, 1988);

John O'Hara, *Appointment in Samarra,* introduction by Updike (Boston: Boston Book, 1988);

The Complete Book of Covers from the New Yorker, 1925–1989, foreword by Updike (New York: Knopf, 1989);

Magnum Photos, Inc., *Magnum Images: Heroes and Anti-Heroes,* introduction by Updike (New York: Random House, 1991);

Mary Steichen Calderone, *The First Picture Book: Everyday Things for Babies,* afterword by Updike (New York: Library Fellows of the Whitney Museum of American Art, 1991);

Craig Yoe and Janet Morra-Yoe, eds., *The Art of Mickey Mouse,* introduction by Updike (New York: Hyperion, 1991);

Henry Green, *Loving; Living; Party Going,* introduction by Updike (Harmondsworth, U.K. & New York: Penguin, 1993);

Herbert A. Kenny and Damon Reed, *New England in Focus: The Arthur Griffin Story,* introduction by Updike (Winchester, Mass.: Arthur Griffin Center for Photographic Art, 1995);

Samuel Shem, *The House of God,* introduction by Updike (New York: Dell, 1995);

Graham Tarrant, ed., *Writers on Writers,* introduction by Updike (London: Aurum, 1995);

Jill Krementz, *The Writer's Desk,* introduction by Updike (New York: Random House, 1996);

Søren Kierkegaard, *The Seducer's Diary,* edited and translated by Howard V. Hong and Edna H. Hong, foreword by Updike (Princeton: Princeton University Press, 1997);

Herman Melville, *The Complete Shorter Fiction,* introduction by Updike (New York: Knopf, 1997);

Frederic Tuten, *The Adventures of Mao on the Long March,* introduction by Updike (New York: Marion Boyars, 1997);

The Complete Lyrics of Cole Porter, edited by Robert Kimball, foreword by Updike (New York: Da Capo Press, 1998);

Louis Auchincloss and others, *A Century of Arts & Letters: The History of the National Institute of Arts & Letters and the American Academy of Arts & Letters as Told, Decade by Decade, by Eleven Members,* edited by Updike (New York: Columbia University Press, 1998);

Lee Lorenz, *The World of William Steig,* introduction by Updike (New York: Artisan, 1998);

Arnold Roth, *Poor Arnold's Almanac,* introduction by Updike (Seattle: Fantagraphics, 1998);

Lawrence Boadt, ed., *Song of Solomon: Love Poetry of the Spirit,* foreword by Updike (New York: St. Martin's Press, 1999);

Robert Marshall, *The Haunted Major,* introduction by Updike (Hopewell, N.J.: Ecco Press, 1999);

The Best American Short Stories of the Century, edited by Updike and Katrina Kenison, introduction by Updike (Boston: Houghton Mifflin, 1999).

SELECTED PERIODICAL PUBLICATIONS–UNCOLLECTED: "Homage to Paul Klee: or A Game of Botticelli," *Liberal Context,* 12 (Fall 1964): 8–12;

"Morocco," *Atlantic Monthly,* 244 (November 1979): 45–48;

"The Burglar Alarm," *New Yorker,* 63 (14 December 1987): 30–31;

"Spat (An Architectural Fiction)," *Architectural Digest,* 46 (March 1989): 26–29;

"The Lens Factory," *Granta,* no. 28 (Fall 1989): 263–269;

"The Women Who Got Away," *New Yorker,* 71 (9 October 1995): 78–81;

"Lunch Hour," *New Yorker,* 71 (18 December 1995): 96–99;

"New York Girl," *New Yorker,* 72 (1 April 1996): 82–87;

"The Cats," *New Yorker,* 72 (9 December 1996): 92–102;

"My Father on the Verge of Disgrace," *New Yorker,* 73 (10 March 1997): 80–85;

"Natural Color," *New Yorker,* 74 (23 March 1998): 82–85;

"Oliver's Evolution," *Esquire,* 129 (April 1998): 148;

"Licks of Love in the Heart of the Cold War," *Atlantic Monthly,* 281 (May 1998): 80–90;

"His Oeuvre," *New Yorker,* 75 (25 January 1999): 74–81;

"Questions of Character: There's No Ego as Wounded as a Wounded Alter Ego," as Henry Bech, *New York Times,* 1 March 1999, p. E1;

"How Was It Really? Theirs Was the Last Divorce of All," *New Yorker,* 75 (17 May 1999): 78–83.

While his stature as a short-story writer may be perpetually overshadowed by the novelistic achievements of the Rabbit tetralogy–*Rabbit, Run* (1960), *Rabbit Redux* (1971), *Rabbit Is Rich* (1981), and *Rabbit at Rest* (1990)–John Updike has exhibited a sustained mastery of the short story throughout his career. With a canon of more than two hundred stories–as well as some

Dust jacket for Updike's first collection of short fiction, published in 1959

prose sketches that he no longer includes in his volumes of short fiction–Updike has devoted a significant portion of his career to the genre that perhaps best suits his style and narrative talents. Rachel C. Burchard contends that "Updike reaches his highest range of achievement in this medium," presenting "all of his major themes with intensity and artistic discipline more refined than that of his novels." In his *Self-Consciousness: Memoirs* (1989) Updike cites his "cartoonist's ability to compose within a prescribed space" as one of his assets as a novelist; yet, that ability may be of greater value in the confines of the short story, where his linguistic precision, his gift for metaphor, and his talent for capturing the significance of everyday incidents come together on a canvas limited in scope but rich in depth.

John Hoyer Updike was born on 18 March 1932 in Reading, Pennsylvania, the only child of Wesley R. Updike, a high-school mathematics teacher, and Linda Grace Hoyer Updike, an aspiring writer who finally realized her literary ambitions with the publication of the novel *Enchantment* (1971); her short-story collection *The Predator* appeared posthumously in 1990. The first thirteen years of Updike's life were spent in Shillington, Pennsylvania. In 1945 he moved with his parents and maternal grandparents to the Hoyers' eighty-acre farm near Plowville, Pennsylvania; this dislocation to a more rural area and to the sandstone farmhouse in which his mother was born provided him with the subject for his early–and some later–short fiction. Updike's early ambitions included becoming an artist for Walt Disney Studios and writing for *The New Yorker*.

After graduating in 1950 from Shillington High School, where he wrote for the school paper, Updike attended Harvard University on a scholarship. There he drew cartoons for, contributed fiction to, and eventually edited the *Harvard Lampoon*. He married Mary Pennington, a Radcliffe fine-arts major, in the summer of 1953. The following year he graduated summa cum laude with a B.A. in English and sold his first short story, "Friends from Philadelphia," to *The New Yorker*. He and his wife spent the next year in England after Updike was awarded a Knox Fellowship to attend the Ruskin School of Drawing and Fine Art at Oxford; only one story, "Still-Life," in *Pigeon Feathers, and Other Stories* (1962), uses this experience as a subject. While he was in England–where his first child, Elizabeth, was born in 1955–Updike was offered a job with *The New Yorker*. He was a roving reporter for the "Talk of the Town" section until 1957, the year his son David was born; he is still a frequent contributor of fiction, poetry, essays, and reviews to the magazine (more than six hundred of his pieces have appeared in it).

Moving from New York to Ipswich, Massachusetts, in 1957, Updike began selling short fiction and launched the career that has produced at least one book almost every year since his first such publication, a poetry volume titled *The Carpentered Hen and Other Tame Creatures* (1958). His first published novel, *The Poorhouse Fair* (1959), received the Rosenthal Foundation Award and was a finalist for the National Book Award. Also in 1959 Updike received a Guggenheim Fellowship and had his story "A Gift from the City" included in *Best American Short Stories 1959*. That same year his third child, Michael, was born, and his first collection of short fiction, *The Same Door,* was published. Throughout his prolific career Updike has continued to alternate the publication of novels with collections of short fiction and work in other genres. While his first novel concerned elderly characters, his fictional protagonists have generally aged along with their creator, providing a chronicle of modern American social history.

The Same Door includes sixteen stories from *The New Yorker* that exhibit a great deal of self-assurance and demonstrate Updike's promise as a writer. From the

New Yorker school of fiction Updike derived a commitment to realism and to the search for significance in the quotidian, though his stories rise above urbane social satire to sympathetic insights into contemporary life's compromises, yearnings, and regrets. The characters in the collection look back at the receding past while moving through an uncertain present that holds surprising and often ambiguous rewards. Epigraphs from Henri Bergson and T. S. Eliot draw attention to the difficulty of recapturing past pleasures.

The first three stories in the collection are set in Olinger, the fictional version of Updike's hometown, Shillington. In "Friends from Philadelphia" John Nordholm, sent into the city on an errand by his parents, endures not only the sarcasm of his schoolmate Thelma Lutz but also her father's barbed comments about the failure of his educated parents to achieve economic success. John becomes the unwitting bearer of Mr. Lutz's message when he returns home with an expensive bottle of wine that Mr. Lutz has purchased for him. Ace Anderson, the title character in "Ace in the Hole," a former high-school basketball star who has just lost his job as a car salesman, foreshadows Rabbit Angstrom, the more fully developed protagonist of Updike's tetralogy. Ace's propensity to alternate rather than reconcile his adolescent tendencies with his mature ones is illustrated by his remarks in the opening scene, which shift from a youthful idiom to more standard diction. Plagued in his domestic skirmishes by the "tight feeling" he was once able to vanquish on the court by scoring baskets, Ace is mature enough to realize the inevitability of compromise even as he tries to postpone it by using his charm to deflect the tension of an argument with his wife about losing his job. Confronted with her pragmatism–she throws the newspaper chronicling his basketball record in the trash–Ace turns on the radio and spins her in a dance, briefly recapturing the freedom he once felt on the basketball court in a momentary respite that moves him no closer to resolving his problems or crossing the threshold into maturity. Mark Prosser, the high-school English teacher in "Tomorrow and Tomorrow and So Forth," is a younger version of George Caldwell in Updike's novel *The Centaur* (1963): he is similarly compassionate but more aloof from his students and less deeply wounded by his work. Like Ace, he is caught in routine, feeling his life creep along at the "petty pace" of the Macbeth soliloquy whose implications his students seem unwilling or unable to grapple with as they maintain their "quality of glide" through life. Describing how William Shakespeare "pierced through the ugly facts and reached a realm where facts are again beautiful," Prosser could be describing his own efforts–as well as those of the other characters in the volume–to transcend the mundane. His belief that a flattering note intercepted from a female student is not simply a prank flies in the face of the facts he later discovers, but his male pride clings to this redeeming construction.

Most of the other stories in the volume concern young married couples living in New York. They vary in technique and focus, but all depict the early waning of marital bliss that results from the compromises of domestic life and the receding of youth. "Toward Evening" shows Updike consciously beginning to experiment with a looser short-story form, creating an imagistic counterpoint within a stream-of-consciousness chronicle. Rafe, carrying a mobile of rubber birds for his children, journeys home through an urban realm dominated by demolished buildings and advertising and afflicted with a paralysis reminiscent of James Joyce's Dublin. Intimations of flight produced by recurrent bird imagery suggest the escape he seeks from the ennui that overwhelms him. Surprisingly, his epiphany is achieved through contemplation of an emblem from the spiritually empty world of advertising. "Snowing in Greenwich Village" uses a more traditional narrative to present the nascent marital problems of the Maples, a couple who recur in later stories and are finally given a book of their own. The dialogue is rich with implications as the Maples communicate on a plane of familiarity inaccessible to their guest, Rebecca Cune; her remarks and actions after Richard walks her home are full of sexual innuendo, inviting him to stray from his sick wife. If Rebecca is his "unexpected gift," Richard draws back from pursuing the opportunity, although the story reveals his vulnerability and the marital fault lines that later stories will explore. "A Gift from the City," one of the more developed and ironic stories in the collection, concerns Liz and James, transplants to New York whose isolation cuts them off from the city's unexpected gifts when they banish the perceived threat of a persistent African American beggar with guilt money.

"Who Made the Yellow Roses Yellow?" is close in spirit to the work of J. D. Salinger; the main character, an imaginative extrapolation from Updike's days as editor of the *Harvard Lampoon,* is a blue-blooded version of Ace Anderson who is striving to keep his youthful glory alive. In "Sunday Teasing" Arthur finally realizes that the petty cruelties he inflicts on his wife, as well as his shortsighted intellectualism, yield nothing but loneliness. Religious themes, which figure strongly in *Pigeon Feathers and Other Stories* and subsequent works, first appear in "Dentistry and Doubt," in which a student's crisis of faith is unexpectedly resolved by a visit to the dentist. "Intercession" depicts a dissatisfied comic-strip writer's encounter on the golf course with a brash teenager who becomes the embodiment of his youthful self.

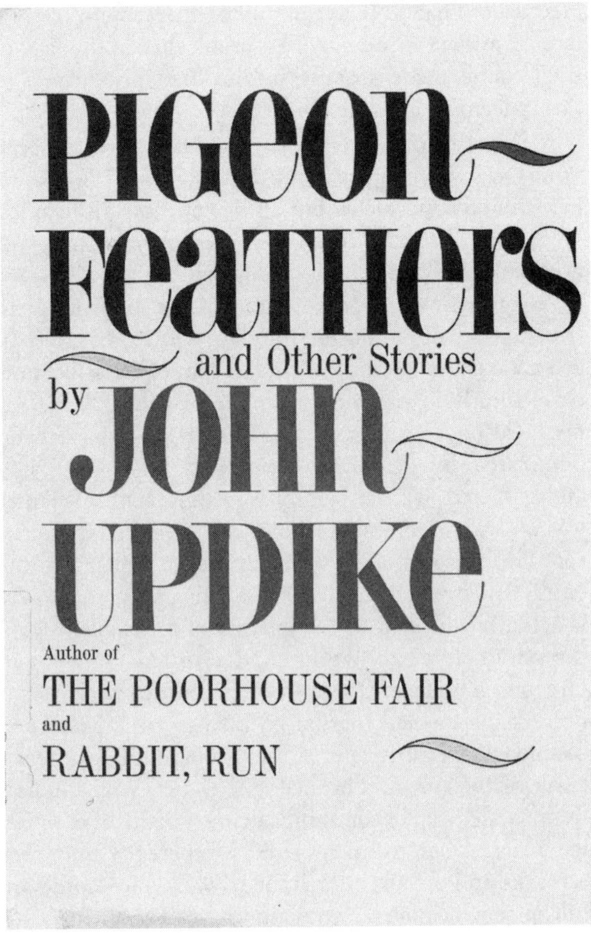

Dust jacket for Updike's 1962 collection of stories, in which he experiments with narrative techniques

His epiphany occurs with a slice that he accepts as divine intercession, interrupting the progress toward the next green that he has envisioned as paradisaical. In a modern reenactment of the Fall, he heads home across a barren field being graded for construction, wiser but sadder as he reconciles himself to an acceptance of maturity and an understanding that real life–not lawless, unencumbered youth–contains its own intrinsic satisfactions.

Updike returns to Olinger for the last two stories in the volume. "The Alligators" is the tale of a young boy "driven and derided by vanity," frustrated in his attempt to realize his vision of love. Although the revelation of his folly and blindness hardly approaches the more tragic consciousness of Updike's older characters, the story demonstrates youth's lack of immunity to incipient alienation. "The Happiest I've Been" rounds out the volume with the return of John Nordholm from "Friends from Philadelphia" in a retrospective and meditative first-person narration of the experience of lingering on the threshold between youth and maturity. The stories in *The Same Door* explore the sense of loss, the redemptive nature of memory, and the discovery of ordinary life's spiritual essence–issues that have preoccupied Updike throughout his career.

Published in 1960, the year in which his daughter Miranda was born, the novel *Rabbit, Run* solidified Updike's reputation as a compelling and articulate voice in contemporary fiction. His second short-story collection, *Pigeon Feathers and Other Stories,* appeared two years later. It exhibits Updike's versatility as he employs a variety of narrative strategies, including first-person experiments that include epistolary, lyric, and montage stories. In the lyric story Updike discovered a form suited to his stylistic gifts and to his talent for capturing the detailed texture of domestic life: this richly imagistic version of the dramatic monologue allows him to depict the mind's search through the darkening past for some spark that might illuminate the present and guide his characters through maturity's increasing complexities. The montage stories that conclude the volume juxtapose seemingly disparate lyric segments whose loose coherence comments thematically on the possibility of creating coherence from the reimagined past. The protagonists in the collection range from ten years old to the late twenties. While the younger characters appear to be fleeing from the past, those who have crossed the threshold from adolescence to maturity flee toward the past, yearning to recapture its mystery and vitality. In general, the characters in *Pigeon Feathers, and Other Stories* grapple more with doubt than those in Updike's first collection as they ponder the increasing narrowness of their lives. As the past recedes and concerns about mortality arise, their struggle against loss assumes greater urgency; but their backward glances only stir more discontent with the present. Most successful are Updike's artist figures, who discover that the redemptive possibilities of art can lead beyond regret and mere nostalgia.

In the opening story, "Walter Briggs," Jack and Clare, spending "enforced time together" while driving home from a party, recall the early days of their marriage. Clare's superior skill in this memory game irritates her husband, though their shared excursion into the past helps them temporarily to transcend their marital difficulties. In "The Persistence of Desire" Clyde Behn returns to Olinger seeking a cure for an eye problem; amid reminders of time slipping away, he latches onto an old flame as an emblem of past joy. His epiphany, however, like those of many characters in the volume, is tinged with ambiguity: he receives a note from her that presumably contains her phone number, but with his blurred vision he is unable to read it. Hoping to recapture an idealized past, he remains in "a tainted world where things evaded his focus." "You'll Never Know Dear, How Much I Love You," a variant of

Joyce's "Araby" (1914), depicts young Ben's frustrated attempt to lose his money at a carnival whose commercial facade quickly disgusts him. While Joyce's idealistic protagonist retrospectively depicts his lost innocence, this third-person story culminates in Ben's confused retreat when Olinger's inherent protectiveness manifests itself in a midway-game operator's refund. The narrator of "Flight," Allen Dow, reviews his flight from Olinger, an escape that shattered his mother's dreams for him. As he relates his tale of leaving his mother, he comes to a recognition of her suffering and her sacrifice. In contrast, "A Sense of Shelter" features a protagonist who, lacking Allen's ambition to soar, prefers the insular environment of Olinger High School.

Jack and Clare recur in the well-crafted frame tale "Should Wizard Hit Mommy?" in which a simple bedtime story manifests the tensions that exist in the marriage. Jack's attempt to escape into fantasy through his story goes awry when his identification with the character he creates leads him into a narrative corner: allowing the wizard's magic to triumph, as his daughter wishes, would condone resentment of the mother–and, by extension, his own resentment of Clare; but the more realistic ending denies the transforming power of art and his own narrative wizardry. The story ends with his reluctant descent to the world of marital responsibility, with his final words–"Poor kid"–a self-pitying lament for the vanishing child within himself.

Exploring similar territory, "Wife-Wooing"–Updike's first story to be included in *Prize Stories: The O. Henry Awards*–is a linguistic tour de force that begins with the narrator celebrating his wife's attractiveness, then adopting a wounded posture when his attempt to seduce her fails. In a self-satiric dramatic monologue the narrator portrays the anxious, striving male psyche as it is rebuffed and baffled. When he encounters his wife's indifference, his meditations on her "smackwarm" garters swiftly give way to observations of her aging. Her brief impromptu wooing of him the next day, however, leads to the consummation that eluded him previously.

In "Archangel," another lyric story that showcases Updike's linguistic prowess, a heavenly narrator strives to capture the past's fleeting treasures and uncover the beauty inherent in memory or in everyday detail; his gifts, however, are not readily accepted in the world outside Olinger, where change and loss predominate. Another narrator, the divinity-school student and title character in "Lifeguard," celebrates his own virtue as he perches above his charges on the beach. He likens himself to Christ, a savior atop a tower with a red cross, yet his reflections reveal him as aloof and lost in abstraction. Musing on the problems of faith in the modern world, he waits in vain to be called by his "congregation" of indifferent sun worshipers.

In "The Astronomer" Walter, the narrator, recalls a visit from an astronomer in which his uncertain religious beliefs were challenged. Surveying this incident from his past, which he likens to the night sky in which stars appear to shine randomly, Walter proves to himself that his faith is superior to the atheism of the astronomer, who fears the desert's open spaces. "Pigeon Feathers" couples David Kern's religious doubts with the physical separation from his parents that their move to a farm outside Olinger brings. After reading an H. G. Wells work denying Christ's divinity, he experiences a vivid premonition of extinction that sends him searching for some solid foundation of faith to allay his fears. Neither his mother's diffuse pantheism, his father's perfunctory Protestantism, nor the minister's vague analogies can provide him with solace. Yet, when he kills some pigeons that have been soiling the furniture his parents brought from Olinger and stored in the barn, he finds an unlikely source of religious affirmation: in observing their intricate beauty he finds assurance of God's hand and care.

"The Doctor's Wife," about the prejudice that corrupts a young husband's Caribbean vacation, was included in the *O. Henry Prize Stories 1962.* "A&P," however, has become Updike's most frequently anthologized story. While it is atypical in its fast-moving plot and brash teenage narrator, it features Updike's trademark attention to detail and focuses on thematic concerns that are similar to those in the other stories in the volume. Relating his impulsive attempt to be a hero to three girls in bathing suits who are confronted by the store manager for being inappropriately attired, Sammy depicts his quitting of his cashier job as a principled act. While his celebration of the girls' physical virtues is marked by sexism, his perception of the butcher's ogling provides him with a glimpse of his own attitude. His attraction to the girl he nicknames "Queenie," however, consists of lust mingled with the allure of her socioeconomic status–signified by the herring snacks that she is there to purchase–and his own yearning to be a free spirit who is not corralled in the checkout lane of the A&P. Like other characters in the collection, Sammy is caught between the pulls of romance and realism.

The collection concludes with two stories that Updike characterizes in *Hugging the Shore* (1983) as "farraginous narratives": they are assembled from independent segments artfully linked via metaphor as the narrators revisit old memories in search of connectedness. The long titles of the pieces signal their composite nature. "The Blessed Man of Boston, My Grandmother's Thimble, and Fanning Island" ostensibly records three successive artistic failures; but readers should be wary of accepting the narrator's pronounce-

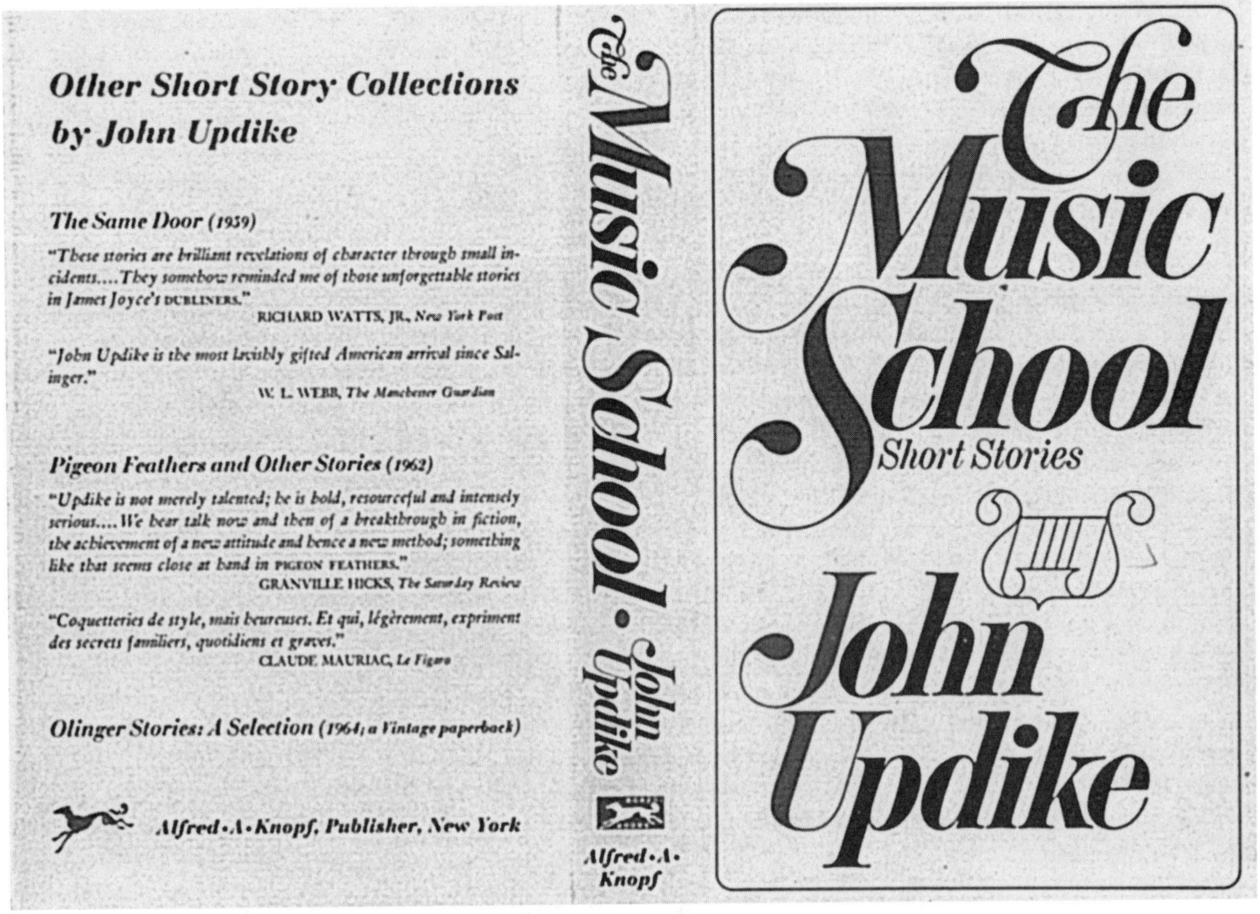

Dust jacket for Updike's 1966 collection of stories, some of which are set in the suburb of Tarbox

ment at face value, as each section moves toward an understanding of how recovery of the past's minutiae can put one in touch with a larger body of memory. More explicitly connected are the segments of "Packed Dirt, Churchgoing, A Dying Cat, A Traded Car," in which John Nordholm, returning from *The Same Door,* wears a new path through the rubble of adult life through forays into his past, each centered on a single image or incident. As Updike notes in *Hugging the Shore,* the story interweaves themes that "had long been present to me: paternity and death, earth and faith and cars" and makes the past resonate with a "bigger, better kind of music."

After the publication of his first children's book, an adaptation of Wolfgang Amadeus Mozart's opera *The Magic Flute* (1962); his novel *The Centaur,* for which he received his first National Book Award as well as the Prix du meilleur livre étranger; and his second book of poetry, *Telephone Poles and Other Poems* (1963), Updike brought his early career to a close with *Olinger Stories: A Selection* (1964), which arranges the tales featuring Updike's younger protagonists in rural Olinger into a loose bildungsroman of a composite character Updike calls a "local boy" in his foreword. Olinger appears as a realm of grace where, as Updike remarks in the foreword, "the muddled and inconsequent surface of things now and then parts to yield us a gift." The same year *Olinger Stories* was published, Updike became, at age thirty-two, the youngest person ever elected to the National Institute of Arts and Letters. *Assorted Prose,* his first volume of collected essays, reviews, and other occasional pieces; *A Child's Calender,* a book of poems for children; and the novel *Of the Farm* all appeared in 1965.

Updike's third collection of short fiction, *The Music School* (1966), transposes the themes of memory and its redemptive power, the tension between spiritual yearnings and their physical realizations, and the ambiguous blessings of domestic life into a new key suited to characters who can no longer linger in memories of young adulthood. Updike's middle-aged protagonists have moved from idyllic Olinger to suburban Tarbox, where romantic discord, infidelity, and perplexity arise from their attempts to realize some mature version of the romantic pastoral. Separation is the dominant experience chronicled in the stories, which exhibit an impressive variety of techniques ranging from traditional linear narrative to the meditative lyric mode, the Hawthornesque sketch, and an epistolary experiment. As Updike departs from Olinger and youth's unexpected gifts, he seeks new modes of narrative to capture the different texture of experience. What Updike calls the "abstract-personal" mode of a story such as "Leaves" is especially suited to many of his characters' conditions: at this crux in their lives they are more disposed to reflect than to act.

The opening story, "In Football Season," is a lyric meditation highlighting the joys and fears of the local boy who grows to transcend his milieu. Evoking the realm of relative innocence with sensory immediacy, the narrator memorializes its ephemeral beauty while portraying its imminent dissolution. Images of autumn and darkness are interwoven with memories of young girls, communal identity, and paternal protectiveness, like the complex fragrance of perfume that he recalls. Ultimately, the adult "winds of worry" are held at bay in his memory's vivid resurrection of the past–a past to which access will become more problematic, as subsequent stories in the volume show.

Four other stories are rendered in this abstract-personal mode, whose plotless meditative form accentuates the protagonist's self-enclosed condition and poignantly depicts the pain aroused when memory and desire mingle. Among these, "Leaves" is a tour de force of poetic language that grows organically, like the grapevines that prompt the musings it contains. In nine artful paragraphs Updike's narrator self-consciously lays bare the pain of separation; his reflections on his infidelity result in a "sharpening of the edge" between himself and nature, but his efforts enact a healing ritual akin to the weavings of the spider he watches, as his words embody a kind of "subjective photosynthesis" that incorporates and transmutes his surroundings. While Updike rarely responds to criticism of his work, concerning this story he has retorted, in a piece collected in *Hugging the Shore:* "if 'Leaves' is lace, it is taut and symmetrical lace, with scarce a loose thread. . . . The way the leaves become the pages, the way the bird becomes his description, the way the multiform world of nature is felt rubbing against the dark world of the trapped ego–all strike me as beautiful, and of the order of 'happiness' that is given rather than attained."

The power of verbal art to create continuity among diverse elements becomes a dominant theme in "The Music School" and "Harv Is Plowing Now," which showcase Updike's talents with language and metaphor. Dramatic monologues, these stories depend on startling juxtapositions of metaphorically rich fragments to create a complex synthesis of memories whose coalescence embodies a fleeting victory over time. "Harv Is Plowing Now" links art and archaeology as it depicts the narrator's meditative descent through the layers of his past. Although the man he remembers plowing those fields has sold the farm and moved to Florida, the actual continuation of Harv's plowing is less important than its enduring memory, which serves as a metaphor for plowing up the ground of the recent past that has been left fallow by the narrator's separation from his wife. Similarly, in the title story the novelist Schweigen's meditations on a computer programmer's random death, the church's changing interpretation of the Eucharist, his infidelity, and his daughter's music lesson blend into a richly metaphoric reflection on existence in time and the "paradox of being a thinking animal."

In "The Rescue" Updike explores the familiar territory of infidelity through a rare excursion into the female consciousness. "Giving Blood" marks the return of the Maples, whose troubles flare up in a verbal bloodletting as they argue, while they drive to Boston to donate blood for a relative, about Richard's flirting at a party. The experience of lying perpendicular to his wife as they simultaneously give blood provides an epiphany for Richard, restoring peace and promising invigoration of their anemic marriage. The story ends with a masterful scene at a pancake restaurant, where Richard's lack of cash leads to a self-pitying lament about the sacrifices that marriage has forced him to make. While Joan's ostensible comment about the bill–"We'll both pay"–exhibits an understanding of marriage's dynamic, Richard misses the point that mutual sacrifice might replenish rather than diminish their union. "Twin Beds in Rome"–another Maples story–and "Avec la Bébé-sitter" depict husbands who harbor an inner wound that defeats their attempts to revive their marriages by travel abroad with their wives; both remain mired in their "immense ambiguous mass of guilty, impatient, fond, and forlorn feelings" for their spouses.

The epistolary "Four Sides of One Story" explores a love triangle by juxtaposing the reflections of four isolated characters who act out a modern version of the Tristan and Iseult legend–a recurrent interest of Updike's that becomes the central fable of his novel *Brazil* (1994). "The Christian Roommates," Updike's only story set at Harvard, is not about marriage but explores a relationship filled with similar conflicts. As Orson, a self-assured premed student from South Dakota, clashes with his roommate, Hub, a vegetarian pacifist who weaves and practices yoga, his certitude begins to waver. The 1984 television-movie version of the story, *The Roommate,* is set at Northwestern University rather than at Harvard and, oddly, leaves out any reference to the only commonality that bonds this odd couple–their Christianity–even though their nicknames indicate how markedly their practices of faith differ. Hub is the ascetic "Saint" who goes on to divinity school, while Orson is the self-righteous "Parson" who loses his desire to pray after he and Hub fight about a stolen parking meter and decide to go their separate ways.

The penultimate story, "The Family Meadow," is a plotless sketch that presents a still life of an epoch that will soon fall prey to progress. Updike almost photographically captures the moment before the transformation of rural country into suburban neighborhood. The voices of progress persistently whisper in the background, but the implicit response of the story is "at what cost?" Concluding the volume, "The Hermit" examines the fragility of the pastoral idea in the modern world and provides a balance to the opening story's hymn to the idyllic past.

The novel *Couples* (1968) earned Updike his first magazine-cover feature in the 26 April 1968 issue of *Time,* an article titled "The Adulterous Society." This chronicle of infidelity and partner swapping marks Updike's shift in focus to the suburban realm with which he and the other "Johns"–Cheever and O'Hara–with whom he playfully links himself in *Bech at Bay: A Quasi-Novel* (1998) have become synonymous. In 1969 Updike published *Bottom's Dream* (1969), a children's-book adaptation of Shakespeare's *A Midsummer Night's Dream* (circa 1595–1596), and *Midpoint and Other Poems* (1969), perhaps his most refined single volume of poetry, providing a self-assessment of his life and work. In 1970 *Rabbit, Run* was made into a movie starring James Caan, and the inclusion of "Bech Takes Pot Luck" in *Prize Stories 1970* accompanied the publication of *Bech: A Book,* the first of three linked collections featuring Updike's literary alter ego, the fictional Jewish writer Henry Bech.

While Updike's Rabbit novels appeared regularly, once per decade, the generically hybrid books featuring his other repeated character, Henry Bech, have appeared at less regular intervals, with twelve years between the first two and sixteen between the second and the latest. Some critics persist in treating the Bech volumes as novels, even though Updike lists them under the heading "Short Stories" in the publications list included in his books. In an interview with Charlie Reilly included in *Conversations with John Updike* (1994), edited by James Plath, Updike observed that the first Bech book was "conceived piecemeal" and that "the whole texture of the book was that of short stories, and I couldn't bring myself to call it a novel." Bech serves as the vehicle for Updike to chronicle various incidents and impressions–often gleaned from foreign travels, such as his visit to Eastern Europe as part of the U.S.-U.S.S.R. Cultural Exchange Program in 1964–that comprise an extended reflection on the American writer's condition.

Even some of Updike's harsher critics have given his Bech books a favorable reception, praising these attempts in the satiric mode that shun the belletristic style of his earlier writings. The Bech books have a picaresque quality, with Bech–who characterizes himself as a "monotonous hero"–generally powerless to end his drift or shape his identity. While Bech by no means shares his writer's block with his creator, he embodies Updike's fears about the diminishment that would result without art to preserve memory, as well as the tribulations of an author's public life and the panic of continually asking "what next?" after each work. Bech is the artist whose celebrity blocks his creativity, and his travels in that role are experiences that he, unlike Updike, is unable to translate into literature.

Unmarried, Jewish, nine years older than Updike, and a denizen of Manhattan rather than of Massachusetts, Bech purposely diverges from his creator. From behind this mask Updike can rebuke the literary industry for the writer's current condition, while simultaneously satirizing those authors who eagerly accede to the industry's lures by becoming cultural emissaries and celebrities and forsaking their role as artists. For Bech, travel and love are quick fixes for a sagging ego and further diversions from his art. Despite his romantic disappointments, missed opportunities, artistic failings, and existential panic, however, Bech is curiously insulated from real harm.

These "quasi-novels"–as Updike subtitles the latest, though a more accurate term would be short-story sequences–follow a similar pattern, using foreign travels for framing purposes or juxtaposing them with a series of adventures closer to home. As the first in the series, *Bech: A Book* opens with a preface attributed to Bech: a belabored and self-conscious benediction that questions his creator's accuracy but grudgingly admits the capture of his essential qualities. Bech recognizes in his portrait allusions to many Jewish writers, as well as "something Waspish, theological, scared, and insulatingly ironical that derives, my wild surmise is, from you." Updike complements his ruse of verisimilitude with a bibliography of Bech's works that humorously settles a few scores with critics. In the Bech books Updike seems liberated by the comic veneer; yet, the themes he treats are serious and related to those examined in previous and subsequent work: imminent mortality; vocation as self-definition; the ambivalence of attained rewards; the conflict between self-realization and love; and the tension between art and ardor.

Bech is introduced in "Rich in Russia" as an "artistically blocked but socially fluent" cultural emis-

Dust jacket for Updike's first collection of stories about his fictional alter ego, the Jewish novelist Henry Bech, published in 1970

sary suddenly wealthy from unexpected royalties that he vows to spend before leaving the country. Plagued with feelings of inferiority, nostalgia for his Jewish past, and his obsession with spending his rubles, he fails to realize that he has not reaped the full value of Russia's potential gifts until he receives a farewell kiss from the female translator whom he has treated merely as a guide. "Bech in Rumania" continues the motif of missed connections with Bech's inability to engage in meaningful dialogue with the country's literary underground. Although he manages to gain from his translator some insight into the motivations that inspired his career, the conclusion of the story is typical: Bech looks down from the plane only to see clouds blotting out the country that has never been clear to him–an ironic epiphany about his own lack of perceptivity.

"The Bulgarian Poetess," the first Bech story Updike wrote and winner of the first prize in the *O. Henry Prize Stories* competition in 1966, was first collected in *The Music School.* Its theme of unfulfilled longing links it with the other stories in that volume, but in the context of the sequence of stories in *Bech: A Book* it represents a temporary revival of Bech's dormant ardor and reverence for art. Vera Glavanakova, the poet he meets at a state dinner, has a profound effect on Bech: while he sees himself sinking "deeper and deeper into eclectic sexuality and bravura narcissism," Vera awakens him to a "romantic vertigo." Nonetheless, in his brief encounters with her he discovers that "actuality is a running impoverishment of possibility" and that the love growing from separation and longing is the purest form–themes that are echoed in stories throughout Updike's career.

"Bech Takes Pot Luck" comically depicts an experiment with marijuana that goes awry. Bech experiences a temporary clarity of vision but becomes ill and succumbs to a momentary panic about his inadequacies as an artist, which leads him to begin an affair with his girlfriend's sister. "Bech Panics," which Updike has said that he composed specifically as a bridge between "Bech Takes Pot Luck" and the following story, "Bech Swings," is the most serious of the comic escapades in the volume. A severe panic arises in Bech during a visit to a Southern women's college to judge a poetry contest: the fecundity of nature and the students' "massed fertility" topples his tenuous mental balance and sets him to thinking about "the shifting sands of absurdity, nullity, death." Bech tries to maintain his authorial facade, though at the nadir of his panic he lies prostrate on the forest floor. His final respite is achieved through a sexual liaison with a Jewish literature professor, whose effect on his fragile psyche is illustrated by his ability the next morning to praise the contest winner's unpolished poems for an attitude that he can only hope to emulate: "gracious toward the world, and in their acceptance of our perishing frailty, downright brave."

"Bech Swings," the penultimate story, takes Bech across the Atlantic to lampoon the parasitic nature of the interview process, which stifles the dormant artistic impulse revived by his fling with a gossip columnist who will become the central character in his new novel. While she tries to teach him that he must "learn to replace ardor with art," Bech insists that "art *is* ardor." The volume concludes with "Bech Enters Heaven," in which Bech is admitted into a society that resembles the American Academy of Arts and Letters (to which Updike was elected in 1977). What should be a triumph turns out to provide the same ambivalent satisfaction that love and travel have yielded as he sees that this "haven of lasting accomplishment," idealized in his youth, looks quite hollow when viewed from the inside: it is a "cardboard tableau lent substance only by the credulous." The volume concludes with Bech's anticlimactic question, "Now what?"

Updike's sixth volume of short fiction, *Museums and Women and Other Stories* (1972), published in the year his father died, is a collection of pieces written during the previous dozen years and organized into three sections: fourteen miscellaneous tales; ten sketches titled "Other Modes" that range from a meditation on language to illustrated comic fables; and five stories featuring the Maples. Critical reception of the collection might have been more favorable had Updike omitted the "Other Modes"; perhaps in response to this criticism, Updike subsequently included such prose experiments only in his collections of criticism and other prose. While some reviewers criticized this collection for lacking the vigor and originality of his earlier fiction, it is Updike's characters who have lost their energy. His middle-aged suburbanites are frequently fatigued; their emotional peaks are leveled out. The characters have become, as the narrator of "When Everyone Was Pregnant" reflects, "survival conscious" and less intent on gripping the past as "the decades slide seaward."

Whatever criticisms might be leveled at the collection, the title story is on a par with Updike's finest short fiction. Using the montage technique, he strings together a series of lyrical meditations that recapitulates the arc of the narrator, William Young, from adolescence to maturity, marital discontent, and beyond. The structure of the story resembles the archways that figure so prominently in its museums' architecture, with a marble nude discovered in a faraway museum as the "thin keystone" in a parabola constructed of museum visits with his mother and his first wife on the ascending side and later erotic attractions and disappointments on the descending side. William's concluding epiphany, the realization that "nothing about museums is as splendid as their entrances–the sudden vault, the shapely cornices," aptly characterizes his relationships and represents his reconciliation to a cycle of disenchantment.

In "The Day of the Dying Rabbit" the narrator, a photographer, reconstructs the "dying light" of the day his son's innocence ended with the death of their pet rabbit. He recalls the moment that day when the single star he located on an evening canoe trip winked out; this intimation of mortality gave way to his perception of new light generated by the phosphorescence of a pond. The reprieve was only momentary, however, ending when he steered the kayak into the bank and then returned to the chaos of family life.

"When Everyone Was Pregnant" is narrated by a securities broker who recalls the 1950s as a fertile and guiltless era when comfort and paternity replaced poverty and chastity. He fears that ripeness lies behind him and that his accumulated memories amount to nothing. Updike's talent as a social historian is evident in "The Witnesses," another story that steps back to "high noon of the Eisenhower era," and in "The Hillies," a sketch set in the 1960s that depicts the Tarbox community's response to a "less exotic" breed of hippies who occupy an undeveloped slope near the town green. The latter story and "The Carol Sing"–about the absence of a leading Tarbox citizen, who committed suicide, from the annual event that constitutes the title–use a first-person narrator who speaks with the voice of the community.

Updike returns to the abstract-personal mode in "Solitaire," which treats marital infidelity through the protagonist's reflections during a game of solitaire. Each card he turns over yields some metaphoric link with his adulterous situation, seemingly steering him toward breaking up his marriage and committing himself to a new life with his mistress. In the end, however, he rejects this course in the realization that no ultimate relief from life's essential solitariness is possible. The same issue is treated more conventionally in "I Will Not Let Thee Go, Lest Thou Bless Me," in which a computer-software expert seeks the blessing of his former mistress before moving away with his family to a new job in another locale. For him, "departure rehearses death," and his difficulty in departing from this phase of his life leaves him enervated.

The aftermath of marital separation is the subject of "The Orphaned Swimming Pool," which traces the dissolution of a marriage through the objective correlate of the couple's swimming pool. Abandoned with their separation, the pool becomes "desolate and haunted, like a stagnant jungle spring: it looked poisonous and ashamed." It springs back to life as a communal neighborhood watering hole for summer revels; once, this "public carnival" traps the husband and his mistress within the house during a weekend tryst. After the divorce the pool becomes an emblem of loss for the former wife–"one huge blue tear." Finally, it is drained and sealed by the new owners of the house, who are concerned for their child's safety. "Plumbing," an ingenious metaphoric meditation, likens the problems that accrue in a long marital history with the deposits that build up in the subterranean plumbing of a house that the unnamed characters are leaving.

The most significant piece in the "Other Modes" section is "The Sea's Green Sameness," in which Updike adopts a pose of authorial self-consciousness. While one of Updike's purposes is to offer a defense of his highly adjectival style, the more central issue is the nature of human attempts to penetrate reality and capture its meaning. Most of the other pieces in this section are cameo portraits, whimsical sketches, and satires; some include illustrations that draw on Updike's artistic training. Familiar serious themes are not absent, however: "The Slump," for example, is narrated by a baseball player who seeks a cure for his spiritual torpor in the writings of the philosopher Søren Kierkegaard, as well as in the batting cage.

The Maples stories that conclude the volume add furthur nuances to Updike's depiction of the emotional and spiritual crises that accompany maturity and marriage. Updike later incorporated these stories, along with his earlier ones about the couple, into *Too Far to Go: The Maples Stories* (1979).

In addition to publishing his second novel in the Rabbit trilogy and traveling to Africa as a Fulbright lecturer in the early 1970s, Updike engaged in extensive research on Pennsylvania-born President James Buchanan; the result was the closet drama *Buchanan Dying* (1974) rather than the novel he had started out to write. *A Month of Sundays* (1975), a novel, was followed by Updike's second volume of prose, *Picked-Up Pieces* (1975). *Marry Me: A Romance* (1976) was published the same year Updike was elected to the Academy of the National Institute of Arts and Letters.

Updike had separated from his wife in 1974; in 1976 they were granted one of the first no-fault divorces in Massachusetts. The next year Updike married Martha Bernhard. A volume of poems, *Tossing and Turning* (1977), was followed by one of Updike's most daring

Dust jacket for the 1972 collection of Updike pieces that includes the experimental "Other Modes" section

narrative experiments, *The Coup* (1978), in which he assumes the voice of a raving African dictator.

Updike's experiences during his first marriage, transmuted into fiction through Joan and Richard Maple in much the same fashion that his travels became the Bech stories, formed the basis of *Too Far to Go,* the manuscripts for which were reviewed by his former wife. This definitive gathering of Maples stories might not have been part of Updike's canon had the producer Robert Geller not decided to adapt the stories for a television drama starring Michael Moriarty and Blythe Danner, which led Updike's publisher to request a tie-in edition and spurred Updike to create a work that diverged significantly from the movie. It includes seven previously uncollected stories and two that, Updike says in the foreword, "from internal evidence appear to take place in Richard Maple's mind." More closely autobiographical than the Bech books that it resembles in form, *Too Far to Go* is a poignant study of the cycles of attachment and detachment that occur with the stresses of contemporary marriage. Although Updike may originally have had no plans to gather the stories together, the resulting volume is symmetrical and tightly crafted, balancing the first four stories, which conclude with the Maples' reluctant decision to separate in "Twin Beds in Rome," with the final quartet, in which the resolve is finally acted on. Revisions–such as those in the opening story that depict Richard's behavior as less innocent and juvenile–adjust readers' perceptions of the characters; story juxtapositions and repeated motifs, such as Richard's illnesses, the focus on homes, and allusions to Hansel and Gretel, provide contrast and coherence. As marriage tends to subsume them into a single entity, Joan and Richard struggle to maintain their identities: the narrator of "Sublimating" observes how their eyes "had married and merged to three." Most of the stories are related through Richard's consciousness, revealing how the marriage binds him, though his viewpoint is open to scrutiny and is not the definitive perspective.

Although the couple seems to be on the verge of splitting up in the early stories from previous collections, Richard's pronouncement in "Twin Beds in Rome" that they have "come too far" in their marriage and "have only a little way more to go" turns out to be mistaken by ten years and thirteen stories. Neither of the Maples seems able to go physically or emotionally far enough away from the other to separate, despite their adulteries; neither can they make the concessions that would move them toward reconciliation. In his foreword to the book Updike characterizes the couple as possessing "an arboreal innocence," like the trees evocative of suburban life for which they are named. As the volume progresses, he remarks, their behavior is like "a duet . . . repeated over and over, ever more harshly transposed." Early doubts, temptations, and overtures toward separation give way to frustration, demystification, and adultery; after bogging down in a series of arguments and stalemates, their relationship ends in a legal separation. But focusing on the marriage's decline and fall, Updike observes, ignores the way in which the stories "illumine a history in many ways happy. That a marriage ends is less than ideal; but all things end under heaven, and if temporality is held to be invalidating, then nothing real succeeds."

"Marching Through Boston," the first story from the Maples section in *Museums and Women and Other Stories* and a selection for *Prize Stories 1967,* picks up where "Twin Beds in Rome" leaves off: with the motif of walking–one of the many subtle echoes that lends the book coherence. Ill, Richard revels in his pain during a civil-rights march and–although the story is told from his viewpoint–his behavior comes across as a self-centered cry for attention. Their experiences in subsequent stories, such as "Eros Rampant," "The Red Herring Theory," "Sublimating," and "Nakedness" move them no closer to renewal. The conclusion of "Sublimating" is typical of their predicament: lying in bed, they pronounce their experiment in celibacy a success and continue to hold out, though neither believes that sublimating has solved their problems any more than their adulterous experiments have.

Included in *Prize Stories 1976,* "Separating" provides the inevitable but continually deferred climax toward which the Maples have been moving. Each time the couple has resolved to separate, Richard's attraction to Joan has paradoxically grown stronger; in "Separating," which poignantly sketches their final day together, their resolve to end the marriage becomes a painful actuality. Richard's last-minute repairs to the house he is leaving are part of a futile attempt to orchestrate an orderly departure from this marriage before he embarks on another with his current mistress. Similarly, the couples' plan to reveal the news of their separation to their children at a reunion dinner goes awry when Richard is unable to control his emotions and begins crying, forcing Joan to make the announcement. The task of breaking the news to their eldest son, Dickie, who is away at a concert, remains Richard's, and he initially appears to have accomplished the task smoothly during their drive home, despite the ironic location of the revelation: halfway between the church and Richard's mistress's house. But Dickie's desperate good-night kiss and his simple whispered question–"Why?"–ultimately undo Richard's artfully constructed defenses. "Separating" is told from Richard's point of view, eliciting sympathy for a character who, while selfishly engaged in the breakup of his family, nonetheless feels a profound affection for them and suffers intensely for the pain he is inflicting.

"Gesturing," selected by Updike's co-editor, Katrina Kenison, for inclusion in *The Best American Short Stories of the Century* (1999), moves the Maples to their trial separation, during which they discover that the lovers for whom they are ostensibly sacrificing their marriage are less real than their shared history. More sympathetic in this story, Richard progressively becomes aware that the memory of enduring gestures will transcend any legal decree of separation. Though on the surface the story is a haphazard assembly of memories, Updike skillfully weaves together a series of vignettes with common motifs. The central symbol, Boston's Hancock Building, is subtly likened to the Maples' marriage: though it attempts to realize an ideal form that harmonizes contradictory elements, unstable pieces keep slipping off, revealing the ugly substructures beneath the facade. Up close, its "tangled mucky roots"–like the clogged pipes in "Plumbing"–are evident, just as the Maples have become all too aware of the mundane elements of domestic life. Only as they recede from daily contact does their marriage assume greater luster.

Concluding the volume, "Here Come the Maples" plays off the irony of the language required by the affidavit of the Maples' no-fault divorce. Designed to expedite the process and reduce the tangle of allegations, the no-fault concept is particularly appropriate to the Maples, suggesting, as it does, the impossibility of blaming the demise of their marriage on either party. Richard's journeys in preparation for the divorce become excursions into memory, punctuated by his reading of a scientific article on nature's forces that provides oblique commentary on the forces holding couples together and pushing them apart: while time and boredom work to destroy relationships, love and habit continue to exert their pull even as the Maples legally undo their marriage, ending it in an ironic symmetry with a kiss and the words "I do."

Updike's other 1979 collection, *Problems and Other Stories,* concentrates on the adversities of middle age. During this "idling time," as he characterizes it, "when things are cooking but nothing comes to a boil," relationships collapse and troubles increasingly obscure youth's more acute perception of mystery and of the past. Like Ferguson in "The Egg Race," the characters are more oriented toward present sorrows than past bliss; former ties no longer bind, but they complicate any attempt at a fresh start. Divorce carries a profound burden of guilt for these troubled protagonists, and the emotional wreckage strewn in the wake of separations fills the landscape with what the title of one story calls "Guilt-Gems." The dedication to Updike's four children highlights the number of stories featuring children, whose suppressed anguish erupts as the gulf between them and their separating parents widens. Further experiments with the sketch, the abstract-personal mode, a journal form, and the montage story all appear, along with stories featuring excursions into memory and two of the stronger Maples stories, "Separating" and "Gesturing." Updike's figurative language still unexpectedly transforms the texture of everyday objects and events; but sustained lyric flights of prose become less frequent, and the style becomes less heavily adjectival–in line, perhaps, with the characters' inability to transcend the traumas of separation and mortality that accompany their progress into middle age.

"Commercial," a rare metafictional experiment using a narrator who adopts the first-person plural, opens the volume with a camera's-eye narrative that juxtaposes two parallel scenes: one from a television commercial for natural gas and the other from the life of the male viewer, whose wife is sleeping nearby. The narrator is fascinated with the commercial's artistic con-

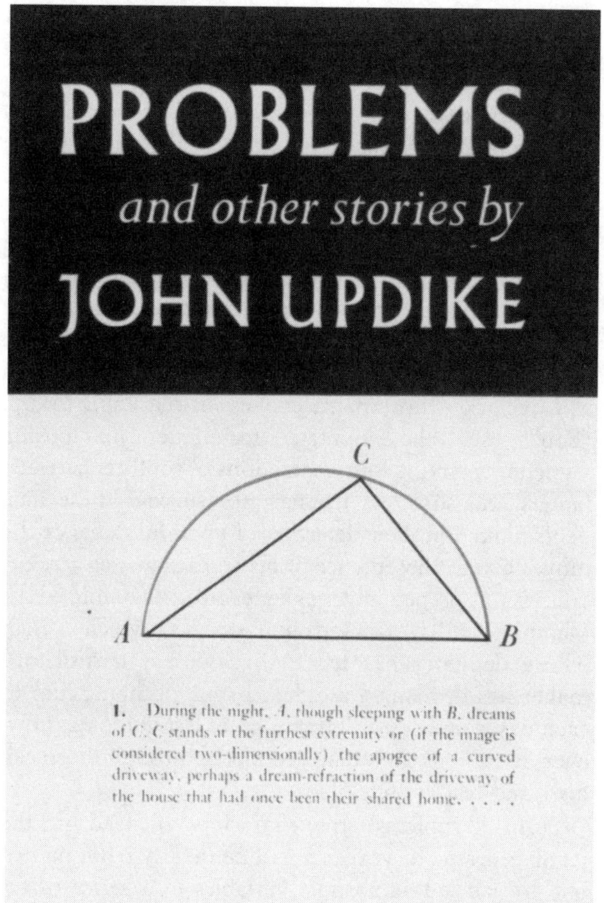

Dust jacket for Updike's 1979 collection of stories, about the vicissitudes of middle age

trivance, which yields a neater message than the problematic domestic scene, where the character's unfulfilled lust and longing for ideal beauty are less easily resolved. Vignettes are spliced together using a cinematic quick-cut method in "Believers," in which the ironically named protagonist, Credo, employs his reading of St. Augustine to fuel his ardor for seduction. Unable to grapple with the spiritual turbulence of Augustine, he becomes aware of his distance both from the past "giants of faith" and from the present inferior refabrications, symbolized by the construction flaws of the new church building.

In "The Gun Shop," a more conventional narrative, Ben, a Boston lawyer, tries to bring his city-bred son Murray closer to the rural world of his own boyhood; but the attempt fails when his old gun, in which his son has shown an interest, misfires. When they visit the gun shop, run by Dutch, a gruff gunsmith who serves as a surrogate father figure for Ben, both father and son enter an unfamiliar realm. Dutch embodies the virtues of artistic craftsmanship, as well as an ability to "descend into the hard heart of things," as he shapes metal for a new firing pin. The experience provides the basis for a temporary alliance between three generations, although it also brings out the latent tensions between both sets of fathers and sons. The action culminates in Ben's realization that his displacement by his son is part of the natural order of continuity and succession.

Other stories concerning parents and children include "Nevada," which depicts the aftermath of a divorce: the protagonist hopes to "extract some scenic benefit from domestic ruin" as he drives through the desert with his daughter; they pass through towns such as Lovelock, whose name evokes his marital breakup. "Son" uses the montage technique, juxtaposing vignettes spanning four generations of conflicts between fathers and sons. As the narrator surveys these incidents, linked in their depiction of youthful defiance, he moves toward acceptance of his son's status as a reluctant visitor, perpetually seeking escape. "Daughter, Last Glimpses Of" is a companion story in which a man whose daughter has left to live with a harpsichord maker has developed a callused soul, numbing him to each day's newness. This collage of last glimpses, however, represents an attempt to pierce through those calluses and recover bits of lost joy.

In "Problems" the characters engaged in the familiar drama of yearning and betrayal are not named but are labeled as abstract variables in a series of six interrelated mathematical teasers. Together, they form a clever composite portrait of the difficulties of separation and its ensuing guilt. Updike adapts the mathematical genre of the word problem but undercuts its form, as there are no simple correct answers to be reached. No traditional math problem would ask one to calculate which woman was "more profoundly" betrayed, for example, and even though the final section provides solutions to the preceding problems, there is no final resolution to the problems of guilt and discontent.

"Domestic Life in America" is almost a concrete illustration of the principles more abstractly outlined in "Problems," illustrating the principle of "Tristan's Law" in that story: that attraction exists in inverse proportion to psychic distance. As Fraser's crumbling first marriage fails to provide the stability he once hoped for, he feels out of place both at his old home and at his mistress's apartment–mirror-image domestic spheres between which he is currently suspended. "Guilt-Gems," which begins at a similar stage in its protagonist Ferris's life, is another collagelike story that is less concerned with forwarding a narrative line than with exploring the paradoxical nature of guilt-gems: shimmering, piercing moments that have "volunteered for compression" from the "gaseous clouds of being awaiting a condensation and preservation–faces, lights that glimmer out, somehow not seized, save in this gesture of remorse." As presented in this story, guilt is a way to hang onto people and memories from which the past threatens to sever one, especially as it is exacerbated by divorce and by the inability to live up to one's self-expectations.

"From the Journal of a Leper" transmutes Updike's struggle with psoriasis–chronicled in the "At War with My Skin" chapter of *Self-Consciousness*–into an examination of the relationship between art and alienation. The story follows a leprous potter's periodic remissions and ultimate cure. The potter's disease spurs him to create smooth, delicate pottery; after his cure, however, his designs become marked by granulation and stains, and his former artistic intensity is lost. Updike says in *Self-Consciousness* that only when he was cured of his own skin condition did he realize how much "my sly strength, my insistent specialness" was linked to it. The potter discovers himself to be in the same situation.

Archaeology and paleontology, among Updike's favorite metaphors because of their preoccupation with digging into the past, are involved in three stories. Sapers, the protagonist of "The Man Who Loved Extinct Mammals," retreats from the complications of his domestic life into the study of prehistoric mammals, whose lives provide him with an archetype of his own failure to move in the "essential directions" that would lead to a more thriving existence rather than toward extinction. "The Egg Race" features an archaeologist, Ferguson, who is all too aware that he is limited to bringing the hidden past to light; unlike the archaeologist narrator of "Harv Is Plowing Now" in *The Music School,* he cannot use the past as a buffer against encroaching time. Ferguson's story is a series of layered journeys that explores the "stratum of middle age," where "the middle distance blurs, and the floor appears to tilt, as if in unsteady takeoff toward some hopelessly remote point." This time of life, he reflects, is one when "the mail, once so pregnant with mysteries and stipulations, can now be read without opening the envelopes" and sent "into the wastebasket . . . unopened, cleanly posted to the void."

The collection concludes with "Atlantises," in which the narrator, Farnham, and his wife, a displaced couple who purportedly came from the fabled lost island, seek news from the inundated past. Atlantis, with its marshy landscape and perpetual parties, resembles Updike's suburban Tarbox. By conflating snippets about the legendary island from Plato's *Critias* with his own reflections, the narrator creates a lost past of mythic dimensions as he depicts himself and his wife living in exile, consigned to eke out an existence in a new land while remaining in touch with the old. As they drive toward the coast for a reunion, the memory of an acquaintance who taught Atlantis frogmen how to surface serves as a metaphor for how to make a smooth passage from the submerged depths of memory to the surface of the present.

Following the publication of his third Rabbit novel, the receipt of the Edward MacDowell Medal for literature, and a BBC documentary on his roots–all in 1981–Updike further mined his own literary travels in *Bech Is Back* (1982); its publication was accompanied by another *Time* cover feature, "Going Great at 50," on 18 October 1982. The second Bech book more broadly examines the perils of success as Updike's literary alter ego breaks through his writer's block with the dubiously successful potboiler, *Think Big*. Married and living in the suburbs, Bech overcomes the stasis that garnered him the Melville Medal for the most meaningful silence, only to become further entwined in the publishing industry's "silken mechanism." *Bech is Back* consists of seven stories–four previously published and three written to complete the book–loosely strung together to form a sequence. "Bech Wed," the penultimate novella-length work, occupies nearly a third of the book. Like the volume itself, several of the stories are composites, made up of self-contained vignettes related by theme or locale.

"Three Illuminations of an American Author" focuses on Bech's striving to attain financial and ego enrichment by seizing on opportunities for remunerative travel. These attempts lead only to further diminishment, highlighting corners of his life that might best have been left in the shadows. "Bech Third Worlds It" juxtaposes his African travels with journeys to Venezuela and Korea. In every locale Bech is challenged by the emerging country's concern with the writer's political role and its contrast with America's (and Updike's) definition of the artist as one who is concerned with a more personal vision. "Australia and Canada" is broken into a dozen alternating episodes, each of which dovetails neatly into the next, making the point that Bech's experiences in different hemispheres are marked by a blurry sameness. These safer lands only heighten his yearning for the conflict of New York.

Travels as a husband rather than as a media creature follow in a symmetrical pair of stories, "The Holy Land" and "Macbech," that take Bech to the Middle East and Scotland. For Bech, marriage is a way to "escape his famous former self"; for his wife, Bea, it is an exercise in improving him. She finally succeeds in doing so in "Bech Wed" when she forces him upstairs into his study at their home in Ossining, New York–the locale of the infamous Sing Sing penitentiary–and pressures him into writing his long-deferred next novel. Despite favorable reviews, Bech knows that he has abandoned whatever sense of artistry he once cherished

Dust jacket designed by Updike for his 1987 collection of stories

in churning out the work, which his publisher turns into a marketing success with a campaign whose slogan provides the title for Updike's volume. Bech cannot dismiss his suspicion that his new work consists of "idle dreams, hatched while captive in Sing Sing," and his marriage begins to unravel when he takes up with his former mistress, Bea's sister Norma.

Bech's misgivings about his new status as a literary lion are confirmed in the final story, "White on White," where he perceives the contrast between his sullied achievements and the purity of those by other artists. Yet, the pretentious avant-garde world of whiteness at the book premier has, he suspects, its murky underside, which he pronounces "Treyf"–Yiddish for "unclean." As the book closes, Bech awaits his rescue from the party by a female mud wrestler named Lorna, a celebrity who symbolizes the muddying of his ambitions and talents. Bech's return to print is an ambiguous triumph, difficult for him to savor and leaving him, once again, dissatisfied and manipulated by the publishing industry. While Updike himself seems adept at fulfilling the author's public role without compromising his art or integrity, through Bech he offers a wry appraisal of the literary world's potentially deleterious effect on its own.

Updike's contribution to literary criticism was recognized with a National Book Critics Circle Award for *Hugging the Shore* in 1983. The title is taken from Updike's remark in the foreword that "Writing criticism is to writing fiction and poetry as hugging the shore is to sailing in the open sea," but he also observes there that his criticism–"the fruit of eight years' purposeful reading"–reveals "a fervent relation with the world." The next year he made a significant contribution to short-story criticism with his introduction to *Best American Short Stories 1984,* of which he was co-editor. His next novel, *The Witches of Eastwick* (1984), was made into a movie starring Jack Nicholson, Cher, Susan Sarandon, and Michele Pfeiffer three years later. Another volume of poetry, *Facing Nature* (1985), was followed by the novel *Roger's Version* (1986).

Updike's tenth short-fiction collection, *Trust Me* (1987), reasserts his place as Joyce's successor in refining the epiphanic short story. This volume, for which Updike was awarded Italy's Premio Scanno Prize in 1991, may be his most consistent effort, full of poignant and expertly crafted tales that mark a renewed interest in dramatic action and a leaner style that accentuates the poetic precision of his language. The stylistic flights of his earlier lyric fiction are muted, and the meditative mode has been supplanted by narrative experiments that span a significant stretch of time–even an entire marriage–within the compass of the short story.

Updike's familiar concerns–suburban life, marriage, sex, and mortality–dominate the volume; the characters are generally older than in his previous works, having passed through divorce and middle-aged restlessness and assumed an increasing consciousness of death. Many have established new relationships, but the foundations of trust in themselves, in others, in social structures, and in religion are often shaken, even in their seemingly placid suburban lives. The theme of trust is indicated by the illustration on the dust jacket, designed by Updike: poised in midair and about to fall, Icarus foreshadows the breaches of trust, the fragility of promises, the familial betrayals, and the inevitable shattering of faith in human nature that Updike's characters confront.

The lead story, "Trust Me," weaves together four vignettes of incidents involving trust and betrayal that cover the territory from childhood to beyond divorce: young Harold jumping toward the outstretched arms of his father, who is treading water in a pool and unable to catch him; a near accident on a flight during Harold's first marriage that undermines the "falsely assuring . . . elaborate order" of the rivets on the plane's wing; Harold's false reassurance to his new girlfriend that she is ready for an advanced ski trail; and his son's casual indifference to the effect that marijuana-laced brownies might have on Harold's emotional state during a rocky period in this new relationship. Updike deftly ties these vignettes together through his protagonist's recognition of the patterns within his past and with an epiphany involving a common object–a dollar bill–that embodies a reminder that trust, despite its problematic nature, remains the prevalent currency of human affairs. "More Stately Mansions" has a structure that resembles the spiral chambers of its central symbol, the nautilus shell about which the narrator lectures to his class. He reveals a personal history of guilt, infidelity, and tragedy yet rises above his "low-vaulted past" to reach a tenuous reconciliation characteristic of Updike's protagonists. "Made in Heaven" is a sweeping chronicle that traces the history of a marriage against a backdrop of changing presidents. The story depicts a husband's progressive sapping of his wife's religious faith as she struggles to preserve it against his masculine control and intrusion. In choosing this story for *New American Short Stories: The Writers Select Their Own Favorites* (1987) Updike cited its subject matter–"the mystery of church-going"–as well as the development of a long-term marriage's "secret and final revenge, its redressing of a long-sustained imbalance."

Older protagonists dominate the collection as Updike explores the pressure mortality exerts on his characters' fragile structures of belief. In "The City," selected for *Prize Stories 1983,* a sixty-year-old salesman becomes vulnerable to middle-aged restlessness when he is hospitalized while on business in a new city. "Slippage" features a history professor of about the same age who loses his "heart for history" and his grip on certainty after an earthquake illustrates for him the insecurity of the foundation of his daily life, as well as the chasm between his present routine and his unrealized ambitions. "The Wallet," which includes a scene of existential panic reminiscent of David Kerns's in "Pigeon Feathers," depicts a retired investment broker's erosion of confidence in his memory and in the psychological props that keep the void at bay after he misplaces his wallet.

Trust Me also includes trademark Updike stories that explore domestic life's shadowy corners by centering on the epiphanic moments that simultaneously reveal its beauty and its fragility. "Still of Some Use," included in *Best American Short Stories 1981,* exhibits Updike's talent for realism as its protagonist mines the texture of the ordinary–in this case, the discarded games of an earlier era–to discover some redemption in his provisionally remade life. As he clears out the attic of his former wife's house with his youngest son, his memories crack open like the game boxes that land in the truck they will drive to the dump; in discarding the outworn remnants of an old life, father and son forge new bonds that transcend this loss. "Learn a Trade" links an artist's past rebellious relationship with his father to his current conflict with his own son. Aware of the unhappiness that has accompanied his own success, the artist passes along the advice he ignored from his father–to "learn a trade" rather than follow the artistic muse to frustration and insecurity. Swayed by the beauty of his son's fragile mobiles, however, he realizes that he must allow the boy to pursue this uncertain path.

"A Constellation of Events" and "Killing" make rare ventures into the female consciousness. In the former a bored wife finds that four key images help to assuage her guilt as she embarks on an affair. In "Killing" a woman's painful decision to forego life support for her terminally ill father and to oversee his protracted death lends her life some needed purpose after her recent divorce. Although she is absent when her father dies, she finds unexpected consolation in a failed sexual encounter with her former husband.

Another story focused on mortality, "Poker Night" features an atypical for Updike blue-collar narrator attempting to control his dread after learning that he has cancer. Attending his regular poker game, he exhibits a courageous refusal to succumb to despair, refusing to fold when the cards seem to be against him. Nonetheless, the cards, described with typical Updike precision–"silver foil beaten to just enough thickness to hide the numb reality that was under everything"–present a vision of his own fragility. Although his wife is uncertain how to "play her cards" after he reveals the news to her, it appears that their marriage will provide a solid foundation of support for him during his trial. "The Lovely Troubled Daughters of Our Old Crowd" seems on the surface to be a bemused study of a contemporary type: single women in their late twenties whose withdrawal from the traditional pattern of marriage that failed their divorced parents has left them on the fringes of the community. The narrator's mildly ironic and somewhat condescending treatment of their plight fails to take into account his generation's role in causing their wariness and arises, in part, from his wistful memories of former wives and lovers whom these daughters resemble.

"Unstuck" is about a young couple whose marital problems are metaphorically portrayed through their attempts to get their car moving in the snow. Their success heralds future cooperation on other aspects of their relationship. Five families–older versions of the young suburban couples in Updike's earlier fiction–form an ensemble cast in "Leaf Season," an experiment in using the short form to explore a group dynamic that earned inclusion in *Prize Stories 1988;* in both style and substance the story has the flavor of an Updike version of the movie *The Big Chill* (1983), although its mood is more autumnal. Another story lacking a central protagonist is "The Ideal Village," set in Latin America and treating the theme of the perpetual unrest and dissatisfaction of the human spirit, even in a seemingly idyllic setting.

Updike returns to his more typical milieu, suburban New England, and exhibits his talent for social satire in "Getting into the Set," which turns a critical eye on the social pretensions of a young couple who undergo a destructive initiation rite to be included among the "beautiful people" in a class-conscious town. "Beautiful Husbands" focuses on the psychology of sexual attraction in its depiction of a husband who is drawn to another woman through his admiration of her husband. Updike also explores the vagaries of attraction in "The Other" and "The Other Woman." The former sketches the course of a twenty-five-year relationship in which a man maintains a fixation upon his wife's twin sister. Living a parallel marriage on the opposite coast, she represents an unreachable ideal, while his wife is an all-too-familiar reality. After both couples divorce, however, the twin becomes simply another woman when he finally initiates a relationship with her. In "The Other Woman" a husband's discovery of his wife's affair leads him to concoct an elaborate scheme to extricate himself from his marriage by pairing her off frequently with her lover, in the process betraying the trust of the lover's unknowing wife.

During the 1980s Updike received many awards, among them the National Arts Club Medal of Honor, a Life Achievement Award from Brandeis University, the Bobst Award for Fiction, and the PEN/Malamud award for excellence in short fiction. His novel *S.* was published in 1988, followed in 1989, the year his mother died, by *Just Looking: Essays on Art* and *Self-Consciousness.* The early 1990s brought the appearance of the final Rabbit novel, as well as *Odd Jobs: Essays and Criticism* (1991), *Collected Poems* (1993), and the novels *Memories of the Ford Administration* (1992) and *Brazil.*

The Afterlife and Other Stories (1994), Updike's eleventh collection, features protagonists who are, as he says of Fanshawe in the story "Playing with Dynamite," more comfortably familiar with "death's immediate neighborhood" than were his earlier characters. They share Fanshawe's lament that "Things used to be more substantial" and the feeling that there are too many mysteries to pursue as they enter the "afterlife" when their children are grown, their marriages have failed, and they have settled into new relationships. A winding

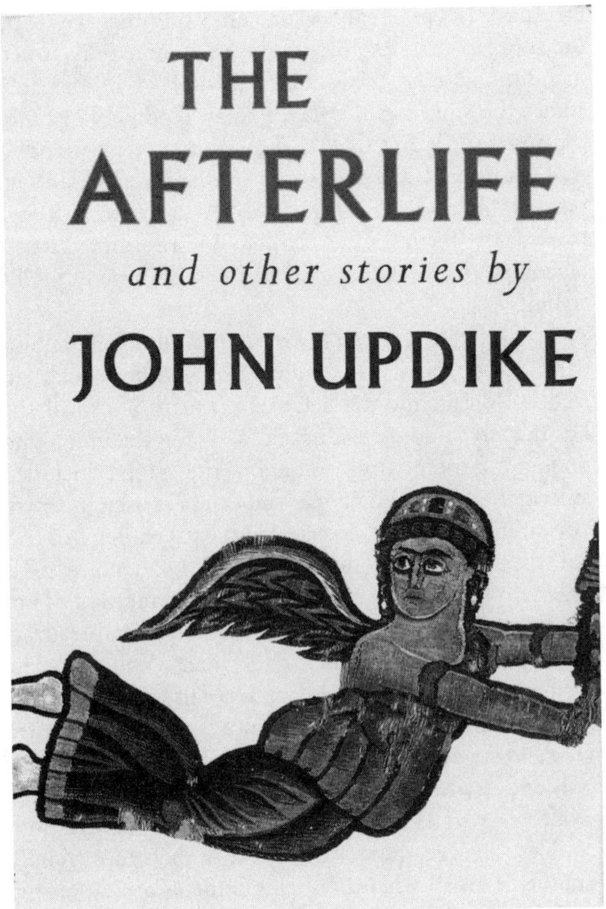

Dust jacket for Updike's 1994 collection, featuring older protagonists who are becoming familiar with "death's immediate neighborhood"

down of aspiration pervades this phase, when even the moments that rise above the quotidian have less impact. With death occurring around them, these exclusively male protagonists have developed a layer of insulation from experience that evens out the disappointments and the satisfactions, so that neither upsets the equilibrium. Characters may be "Playing with Dynamite," but the risk of an explosion seems curiously defused as the ache of memory becomes less immediate and profound.

In the title story (included in *Best American Short Stories 1987*) Carter Billings and his wife are visiting England in emulation of friends who are doing "sudden surprising things" while their own lives have drifted on uneventfully. For Carter, who has trouble generating excitement for adventures beyond his accustomed sphere, there are "vast areas of the world he no longer cared about." As the Billingses and their hostess drive around the countryside, Carter sees, in the rearview mirror, a heron that resembles an angel. His elevated mood leads to a risky drive through a storm, followed by an uncharacteristic purchase of an antique elm chest. In Carter's newly sensitized state, "A miraculous lacquer lay upon everything, beading each roadside twig, each reed in the thatch on the cottage roofs, each tiny daisy trembling in the grass by the lichen-stained field walls."

"Wildlife" provides an AIDS-era analogy in the Lyme disease that threatens the town to which Ferris–from "Guilt-Gems" in *Problems and Other Stories*–returns periodically to visit his children. Although his visits always provide him with an uplift to a "sexier, more buoyant self," he is not nostalgic; the area's natural beauty, he observes, verges on wildness and threatens to erupt into violence. A tick bite to his grown son, discovered before the symptoms become severe, leads Ferris to conclude that he has made a timely escape from his former life, despite its retrospective appeal.

In "Brother Grasshopper" Fred Emmett reviews his relationship with his deceased brother-in-law, Carlyle, before scattering the latter's ashes at sea and comes to understand that their shared "conglomerate times" were "priceless–treasure, stored up against the winter that had arrived." Memories of the deceased also comprise "His Mother Inside Him," in which Allen Dow, from "Flight" in *Pigeon Feathers, and Other Stories,* is spurred by a friend's remark about his physical resemblance to his mother to discover how he also embodies her character traits. In "Journey to the Dead" the protagonist unwittingly uses a sick friend to help him relive parts of his past with his former wife.

"A Sandstone Farmhouse," featured both in *Best American Short Stories 1991* and as the First Prize winner in *Prize Stories: The O. Henry Awards* the same year, chronicles the protagonist's return to his parents' farmhouse after his mother's death. When he finishes his self-appointed task of cleaning out the house and readying it for sale, he believes that he has "reduced the house to its essence" and removed all traces of his family's life there. In reality, as he sifts through memorabilia and handles the artifacts of their past, he internalizes that essence and rediscovers the vibrancy of his mother's life and of the rural existence that he had so passionately yearned to escape. Other stories also involve returns to hometowns. While family mementos in "The Brown Chest" produce memories of the past with a surprising freshness and immediacy, the protagonist in "The Other Side of the Street" is content to experience the wash of nostalgia from a house across from the one in which he used to live. A return visit by a mother and son in "The Black Room" produces a more unsettling effect for the mother when she is confronted by the enigma of the title room.

In "Conjunction" Parrish buys a telescope and focuses it on the conjunction of Mars and Jupiter, an image that evokes memories of earlier conjunctions with his wife; in a characteristically apt Updike metaphor, Parrish's ineffectuality in recapturing their lost ardor through these memories is concurrent with his losing his fix on the area of the sky where he spotted the planetary conjunction.

As always, Updike astutely depicts the pressures within relationships, adapting his focus to the new landscape that age creates. A two-part story, "George and Vivian," chronicles the husband's admission that his third wife is "no comfort" as they grate on each other during their European travels, while "Farrell's Caddy" treats the discord in the twilight of a second marriage in a delightfully comic fashion via an astute caddie's reading of the protagonist's golf game. Other protagonists in their sixties, such as Fogel in "Short Easter," are bothered by the sense that "Everything seemed still in place, yet something was immensely missing"; a daylight-savings-time-shortened Easter holiday–with its disorientation and "unnatural ache of resurrection"–acutely brings home this insight to him. In the only first-person narration in the volume, "Falling Asleep Up North," however, fatigue becomes an advantage of age, facilitating a loss of the angst that once rose so intently.

Updike brings Joan and Richard Maple into the "afterlife" phase in "Grandparenting," the final story in the book. Both remarried, they amicably attend the birth of their daughter's first child, although certain tensions endure beneath the surface. Richard's conclusion, as he holds his new grandchild, that "Nobody belongs to us, except in memory," typifies the reflective and somewhat resigned insight that Updike's characters derive from their accumulated experience. Although his stories of this phase are not as achingly lyrical or as highly experimental as some of his earlier work, they nonetheless exhibit his continued craftsmanship, as well as his rare ability to capture the latent significance of the mundane and to use his gift for realistic detail to evoke vividly the pleasures and sorrows of memory.

Updike was awarded the Howells Medal for *Rabbit at Rest* in 1995, the same year that the gathering of his four Rabbit novels was published as *Rabbit Angstrom: A Tetralogy.* To his previous four children's books (one for each of his children), he added that same year *A Helpful Alphabet of Friendly Objects* (presumably with his grandchildren in mind), with photographs by his son David, who has published children's books as well as two short-story collections. Updike's next novel, *In The Beauty of the Lilies* (1996), won the Ambassador Book Award, presented to books that have made an exceptional contribution to the interpretation of American life and culture. That same year Updike published *Golf Dreams* (1996), a collection of his prose works on the sport that has been a consistent avocation as well as a topic of literary reflection. He was honored with the Campion Award as a "distinguished Christian person of letters" the next year, concurrent with the publication of *Toward the End of Time* (1997), a futuristic novel.

Published in 1998, *Bech at Bay: A Quasi-Novel* takes Updike's traveling celebrity from Kafka's grave to the Nobel platform, with meetings of literary intelligentsia, a courtroom appearance, and a literary murder in between. Once again, Updike takes aim in comic fashion at such serious issues as governmental suppression of writers, the diminishment of American writing, the wounds critics inflict on authors, and the dubious honors bestowed on writers by the media culture. Even though Bech calls himself "a vain, limp leech on the leg of literature as it waded through swampy times" and refers to himself as "past my 'sell-by' date," such deprecating remarks arouse reader sympathy for Bech as he frets about mortality, sexual attractiveness and prowess, literary relevance, and his paucity of worthwhile opinions.

In "Bech in Czech," first published in 1987, Bech has fallen into obscurity at home but is admired abroad by writers for whom expression of ideas can mean persecution and imprisonment. Bech's jaded Western definition of the writer as one who is "to amuse himself, to indulge himself, to get his books into print with as little editorial smudging as he can, to slide through his society with minimal friction" is clearly at odds with that of the Czech dissidents. Moved by the craft and commitment it takes to print and circulate their underground books, Bech nonetheless cares more about the attentions of one of the female dissidents than about a translation of his book by an admiring Czech scholar. Yet, his visit to Kafka's grave becomes a further step in confronting his Jewish identity. At the end of the story Bech's existential panic recurs; as he grapples with issues of mortality, it becomes clear that a more serious conception of the writer's role than he holds is the route to the literary immortality he desires.

Duped by his literary rival into becoming president of an elite guild of writers and artists that resembles the Academy within the National Institute of Arts and Letters, Bech unwittingly ends up overseeing its dissolution in "Bech Presides." After shifting roles and defending the establishment that he once castigated as an effete and insulated body, Bech finds himself unable to stop the scheme of one of its members to disband the society so that a relative can profit from the sale of its building. Though Bech makes a good case for preserving the institution, Updike still manages to satirize a Manhattan intelligentsia that is "saturated in poisonous envy and reflexive intolerance and basic impotence."

"Bech Pleads Guilty" examines the repercussions of Bech's negative depiction in print of a Hollywood agent. Bech wins the libel suit the agent brings against him but feels so guilty about his actions because of the

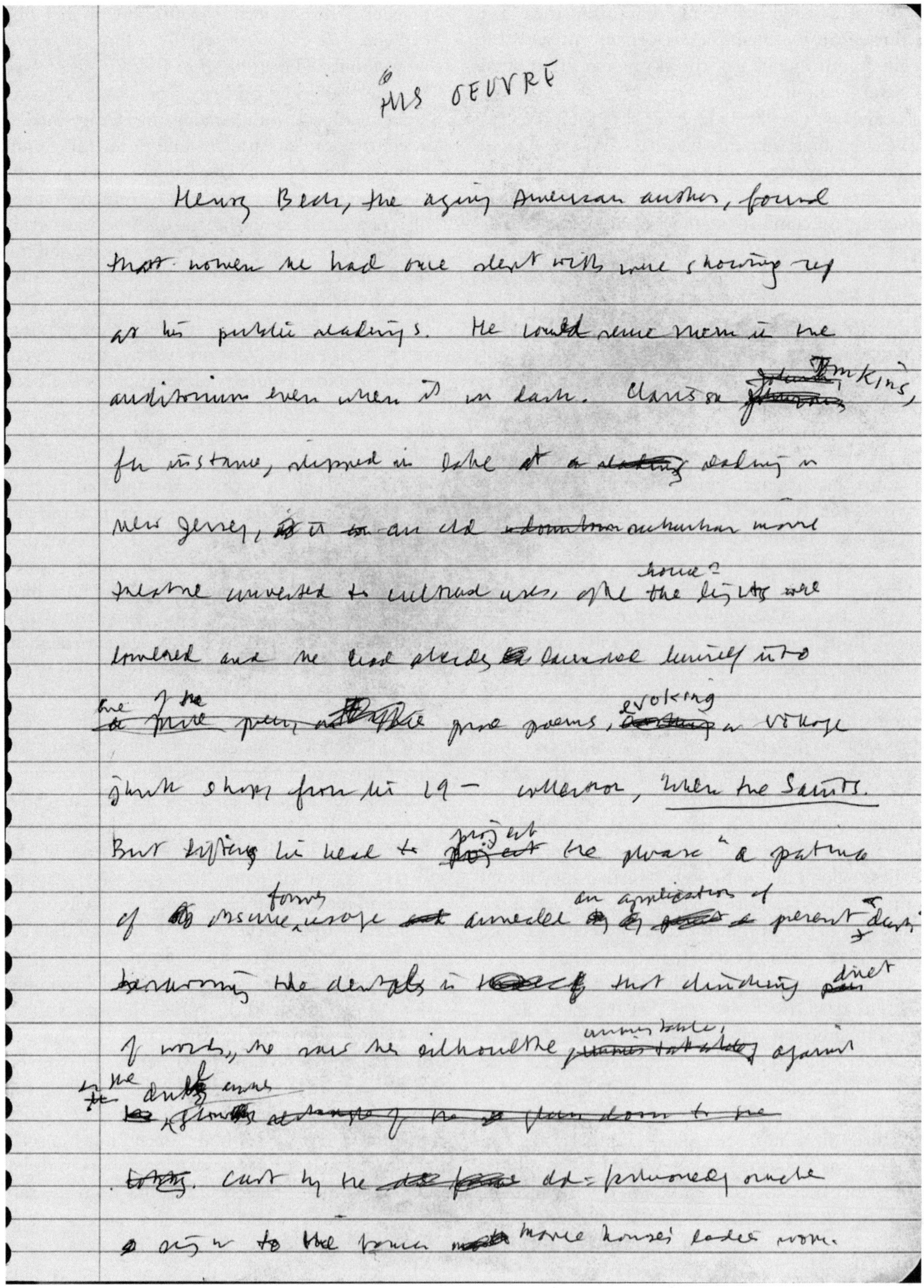
His Oeuvre

Henry Bech, the aging American author, found
that women he had once slept with were showing up
at his public readings. He could sense them in the
auditorium even when it was dark. Clarissa Tompkins,
for instance, slipped in late at a reading in
New Jersey, in an old suburban movie
theatre converted to cultural uses, after the house lights were
lowered and he had already launched himself into
one of the prose poems, evoking Village
junk shops from his 19— collection, When the Saints.
But lifting his head to project the phrase "a patina
of obscure forms, usage annealed an application of [illegible] present day"
[illegible] the details in [illegible] that climbing diet
of words, he saw her silhouette, unmistakable, against
the dusky [illegible]
[illegible] Cast by the [illegible] old-fashionedly ornate
[illegible] to the former movie house's ladies' room.

Pages from the manuscript, written by Updike in an airplane, for a Bech story that appeared in The New Yorker *on 25 January 1999 (Collection of John Updike)*

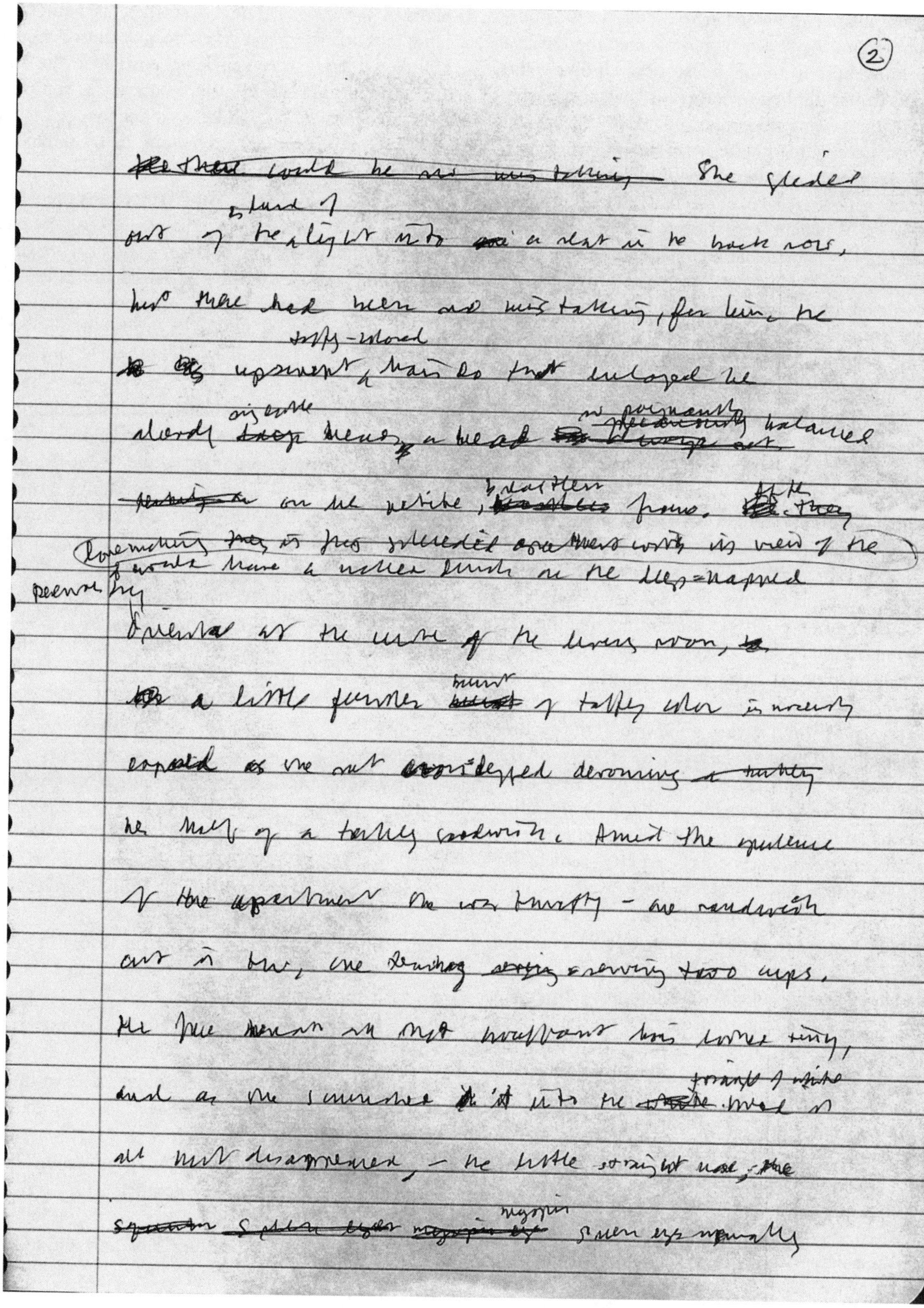

agent's resemblance to his father that he refuses to pursue a countersuit. In "Bech Noir," at once the darkest and the most humorous of the stories, Updike–who early in his career dubbed reviewers as "pigs at a pastry cart"–has the seventy-four-year-old Bech become a serial literary avenger. After he seizes the opportunity to cause the seemingly accidental death of a hostile critic, he concocts a poisoned envelope that kills another of his reviewers. When he confesses to his mistress, she joins him in devising subliminal computer messages that cause another critic who has attacked his work to commit suicide. In their final caper they become "Bechman and Robin," complete with costumes, with Bech pulling the oxygen tubes from a terminally ill critic who remains vituperative to the end as he berates Bech's failure to confront his Jewishness in his art.

The baby that his mistress blackmails him into fathering in "Bech Noir" becomes central to "Bech and the Bounty of Sweden," where Bech wins the Nobel Prize that has thus far eluded his creator. His famous writer's block recurs as he attempts to compose his acceptance speech, a task that is made more difficult by his discovery that his winning was the result of a deadlock and committee politics. Concluding that he has nothing important to say, Bech turns the Nobel platform over to his infant daughter–perhaps his most significant work–who concludes the story and the volume with the word "Hi" and a wave good-bye. If the gesture was intended as Updike's farewell to readers of the Bech stories, it was quickly overridden by a new Bech story, "His Oeuvre," published in *The New Yorker* only a few months later, on 25 January 1999. It appears that Bech will continue to serve as Updike's vehicle for reflections on the profession of writing, as well as on the familiar concerns of aging, mortality, and desire.

Updike's most recent awards include the Harvard Arts First Medal and the 1998 National Book Foundation Medal for Distinguished Contribution to American Arts and Letters. His importance as a writer and critic of short fiction has recently been recognized with the assignment to co-edit *The Best American Short Stories of the Century,* for which he and Kension selected fifty-five stories from the past eighty-five volumes of the *Best American Short Stories* series. In his introduction he expresses concern about the health of the genre, noting that "in my lifetime the importance of short fiction as a news bearing medium–bringing Americans news of how they live, and why–has diminished." His fifth collection of assorted prose, *More Matter* (1999), is his most voluminous such work to date. In a surprising nod to new technology Updike took part in a 1997 contest sponsored by the Internet bookstore Amazon.com, providing the first and last paragraphs of a story that grew progressively via contributions from selected participants. A Web page, "The Centaurian," is maintained by Updike scholar James Yerkes, so that those who follow Updike's busy career can keep posted on his appearances, publications, and other matters. To complement the bibliography of Updike's works that appeared in 1994, a *John Updike Encyclopedia* is to be published in 2000.

Updike's efforts to bring Americans their "news" in short fiction continue unabated. Recent speculation is that Updike will soon work on a gathering of or selection from his more than two hundred stories to create a volume that will stand as a companion to his Rabbit tetralogy and his *Collected Poems,* although he has expressed some ambivalence about such a project. As his list of uncollected short fiction grows, however, other collections are likely, further augmenting Updike's centrality in refining and forwarding the renaissance of the short story in the twentieth century. The qualities that William Abrahams singled out in his 1976 citation for Updike's Special O. Henry Award for Continuing Achievement are still relevant: "the majority of short-story writers continue to conduct their explorations within the visible confines of the tradition itself. Few have done so as consistently, or with such rewarding results, as John Updike. . . . His unflagging mastery is at once an example and a consolation for addicts of the short story, readers and writers alike."

Interviews:

Frank Gado, "A Conversation with John Updike," in *First Person: Conversations on Writers and Writing with Glenway Wescott, John Dos Passos, Robert Penn Warren, John Updike, John Barth, Robert Coover,* edited by Gado (Schenectady, N.Y.: Union College Press, 1973), pp. 80–109;

Josh Rubins, "Industrious Drifter in Room 2," *Harvard Magazine,* 76 (May 1974): 42–45, 51;

Richard Burgin, "A Conversation with John Updike," *John Updike Newsletter,* 10–11 (Spring–Summer 1979): 111;

Philip Seib, "A Lovely Way through Life: An Interview with John Updike," *Southwest Review,* 66 (1981): 34–150;

Kurt Suplee, "Women, God, Sorrow & John Updike," *Washington Post,* 27 September 1981, pp. F1–F3, F8–F9;

Michiko Kakutani, "Turning Sex and Guilt into an American Epic," *Saturday Review* (October 1981): 14–15, 20–22;

Robert Boyers and others, "An Evening with John Updike," *Salmagundi,* 57 (1982): 42–56;

William Findlay, "Interview with John Updike," *Cencrastus,* 15 (1984): 30–36;

Donald J. Greiner, "Updike on Hawthorne," *Nathaniel Hawthorne Review,* 13, no.1 (1987): 1–4;

James Plath, ed., *Conversations with John Updike* (Jackson: University Press of Mississippi, 1994);

Sanford Pinsker, "A Conversation with John Updike," *Sewanee Review,* 104, no. 3 (1996): 423–433;

Philip Yancy, "A Conversation with John Updike," *Image: A Journal of the Arts and Religion,* 21 (Fall 1998): 43-57;

Michael Rogers, "The Gospel of the Book: *LJ* Talks to John Updike," *Library Journal,* 15 (February 1999): 114–116.

Bibliographies:

C. Clarke Taylor, *John Updike: A Bibliography* (Kent, Ohio: Kent State University Press, 1968);

B. A. Sokoloff and David E. Arnason, *John Updike: A Comprehensive Bibliography* (Norwood, Pa.: Norwood Editions, 1972);

Arlin G. Meyer and Michael A. Olivas, "Criticism of John Updike: A Selected Checklist," *Modern Fiction Studies,* 20 (1974): 121–133;

Michael A. Olivas, *An Annotated Bibliography of John Updike Criticism 1967–1973, and A Checklist of His Works* (New York: Garland, 1975);

Elizabeth Gearhart, *John Updike: A Comprehensive Bibliography with Selected Annotations* (Norwood, Pa.: Norwood Editions, 1978);

Ray A. Roberts, "John Updike: A Bibliographical Checklist," *American Book Collector,* new series 1 (January–February 1980): 5–12, 40–44; (March–April 1980): 39–47;

Jack De Bellis, *John Updike: A Bibliography, 1967–1993,* foreword by Updike (Westport, Conn.: Greenwood Press, 1994).

References:

Nicholson Baker, *U & I: A True Story* (New York: Random House, 1991);

Harold Bloom, ed., *John Updike: Modern Critical Views* (New York: Chelsea House, 1987);

Rachel C. Burchard, *John Updike: Yea Sayings* (Carbondale: Southern Illinois University Press, 1971);

Robert Detweiler, *John Updike,* revised edition (New York: Twayne, 1984);

Elizabeth A. Falsey, *The Art of Adding and the Art of Taking Away: Selections from John Updike's Manuscripts. An Exhibition at the Houghton Library* (Cambridge, Mass.: Harvard College Library, 1987);

David Galloway, *The Absurd Hero in American Fiction: Updike, Styron, Bellow, Salinger,* revised edition (Austin: University of Texas Press, 1981);

Donald J. Greiner, *The Other John Updike: Poems/Short Stories/Prose/Play* (Athens: Ohio University Press, 1981);

Alice and Kenneth Hamilton, *The Elements of John Updike* (Grand Rapids, Mich.: Eerdmans, 1970);

George Hunt, *John Updike and the Three Great Secret Things: Sex, Religion, and Art* (Grand Rapids, Mich.: Eerdmans, 1980);

Robert M. Luscher, *John Updike: A Study of the Short Fiction* (New York: Twayne, 1993);

William R. Macnaughton, ed., *Critical Essays on John Updike* (Boston: G. K. Hall, 1982);

Modern Fiction Studies, special Updike issue, 20 (Spring 1974);

Modern Fiction Studies, special Updike issue, 37 (Spring 1991);

John Neary, *Something and Nothingness: The Fiction of John Updike and John Fowles* (Carbondale: Southern Illinois University Press, 1992);

Judie Newman, *John Updike* (New York: St. Martin's Press, 1988);

Charles Thomas Samuels, *John Updike* (Minneapolis: University of Minnesota Press, 1969);

James A. Schiff, *John Updike Revisited* (New York: Twayne, 1998);

Schiff, "Updike Ignored: The Contemporary Independent Critic," *American Literature,* 67 (1995): 532–552;

George J. Searles, *The Fiction of Philip Roth and John Updike* (Carbondale: Southern Illinois University Press, 1985);

Elizabeth Tallent, *Married Men and Magic Tricks: John Updike's Erotic Heroes* (Berkeley: Creative Arts, 1981);

Larry E. Taylor, *Pastoral and Anti-Pastoral in John Updike's Fiction* (Carbondale: Southern Illinois University Press, 1971);

David Thorburn and Howard Eiland, eds., *John Updike: A Collection of Critical Essays* (Boston: G. K. Hall, 1979);

Suzanne Henning Uphaus, *John Updike* (New York: Ungar, 1980);

Philip H. Vaughn, *John Updike's Images of America* (Reseda, Cal.: Mojave, 1981);

James Yerkes, *The Centaurian,* http://www.users.fast.net/~joyerkes.

Papers:

John Updike's manuscripts and letters are at the Houghton Library, Harvard University.

Robley Wilson

(15 June 1930 –)

Jerome Klinkowitz
University of Northern Iowa

Robley Wilson (photograph by Carolyn Hardesty; from the dust jacket for Terrible Kisses, *1989)*

BOOKS: *Returning to the Body: Poems* (LaCrosse, Wis.: Juniper Press, 1977);
The Pleasures of Manhood: Stories (Urbana: University of Illinois Press, 1977);
Living Alone: Fictions (Canton, N.Y.: Fiction International, 1978);
Family Matters: Poems (Cedar Falls, Iowa: Blind Cat Press, 1980);
Dancing for Men: Stories (Pittsburgh: University of Pittsburgh Press, 1983; London: Feffer & Simon, 1983);
Kingdoms of the Ordinary: Poems (Pittsburgh: University of Pittsburgh Press, 1987);
Terrible Kisses: Stories (New York: Simon & Schuster, 1989; London: Hamilton, 1989);
A Pleasure Tree: Poems (Pittsburgh: University of Pittsburgh Press, 1990);
The Victim's Daughter: A Novel (New York: Simon & Schuster, 1991; London: Hamilton, 1992);
A Walk Through the Human Heart: Poems (Kansas City, Mo.: Helicon Nine Editions, 1995);
Everything Paid For: Poems (Gainesville: University Press of Florida, 1999).

OTHER: *Three Stances of Modern Fiction: A Critical Anthology of the Short Story,* edited with introductory commentaries by Wilson and Stephen Minot (Cambridge, Mass.: Winthrop, 1972);
Four-Minute Fictions: 50 Short-Short Stories from The North American Review, edited by Wilson (Flagstaff, Ariz.: Word Beat Press, 1987);
The Place That Holds Our History: The 1990 Missouri Writers' Biennial Anthology, edited by Wilson (Springfield: Southwest Missouri State University, 1990);
100% Pure Florida Fiction: An Anthology, edited by Wilson and Susan Hubbard (Gainesville: University Press of Florida, 2000).

SELECTED PERIODICAL PUBLICATIONS–UNCOLLECTED: Review of *14 Stories,* by Stephen Dixon, *American Book Review,* 4 (November–December 1981): 15;
"Dorothy and Her Friends," *Santa Monica Review,* 2 (Spring 1990): 79–145;
"A Day of Splendid Omens," *Triquarterly,* 103 (Fall 1998): 104–119.

Mimesis, premise, or dream: these are "the three stances of modern fiction" Robley Wilson and his fellow writer Stephen Minot proposed for understanding the range of work by themselves and others in their *Three Stances of Modern Fiction: A Critical Anthology of the Short Story* (1972). Both Wilson and Minot placed their own short stories in the second category, in the company of fiction by John Barth, Donald Barthelme, and Kurt Vonnegut that critics were just beginning to call "postmodern" in the early 1970s. No such rupture with earlier twentieth-century writing interested Wilson: no radical disruptions of conventional practice seemed pertinent to his work. Instead, he would–with eminent politeness–invite readers to consider a preliminary postulate and then, with their consent, proceed to work out all (and perhaps a little bit more) than this premise implied.

Robley Conant Wilson Jr., who dropped the "Junior" from his name on publications in 1990 (by which time his father had died), was born in Brunswick, Maine, on 15 June 1930 to Robley Conant Wilson, a teacher and basketball coach at the Holderness School in nearby New Hampshire, and Dorothy Stimpson Wilson, a PBX switchboard operator at the Pejepscot Paper Company in Topsham, across the Androscoggin River from their home, an inspiration for the fictive town of "Scoggin" in Wilson's later fiction. An only child, Wilson moved at age three with his parents to Sanford, Maine, where his father eventually found work as a public high-school teacher and his mother took occasional employment as a telephone operator and sales clerk. Wilson attended Bowdoin College, dropping out twice to work as a newspaper reporter (in Maine and in Texas). In January of 1951 Wilson received his draft notice, which prompted him to enlist in the U.S. Air Force. In the air force Wilson was first enrolled in a Russian language course at Syracuse University and then stationed in Bremerhaven, West Germany, as a radio operator monitoring Russian military air traffic. Discharged at the rank of staff sergeant in 1955, on 20 August of that year he married Charlotte Lehon, with whom he had two sons, Stephen (born 21 April 1958) and Philip (born 1 April 1960), and returned to Bowdoin College, from which he graduated in 1957. Graduate study in English at the University of Iowa followed; leaving without his master of arts degree, Wilson taught English and Russian as an instructor at Valparaiso University in Indiana from 1958 to 1963, at which point he began a more distinguished career at the State College of Iowa, soon renamed the University of Northern Iowa. The university supported its new faculty member's ambitions with release time for work at the University of Iowa Writers' Workshop (leading to a master of fine arts degree in 1968) and by purchasing the oldest literary magazine in the United States, *The North American Review,* for Wilson to edit, beginning in 1969. Wilson repaid the university by winning the National Magazine Award from the American Society of Magazine Editors for fiction he accepted and published in *The North American Review* and a Guggenheim Fellowship for himself. Having divorced his first wife, Charlotte, in 1991, Wilson married the writer Susan Hubbard in 1995 and retired from the university to join her in Winter Park, Florida, in 1998. He continues as the editor of the journal.

Wilson's career as a writer has been anything but meteoric; his first short stories did not appear until 1961 (when he was thirty-one years old) and not in any great numbers until the 1970s; his first short-story collection, *The Pleasures of Manhood: Stories,* was not published until 1977. Self-promotion is not a trait noteworthy among Bowdoin graduates from old Maine families, and despite the modest circumstances of his upbringing Wilson has always comported himself with the probity and dignity that distinguish the upper classes of the American Northeast. Unsurprisingly, therefore, the innovations within *The Pleasures of Manhood* are subtle and discreet. The title story, appearing second in the volume, establishes the tone for what some critics have called his experimental realism and others his sly manipulation of manners. After "A Stay at the Ocean," which opens the collection with the spectacle of an eerily receding seascape that remains only temporarily under the control of its domesticating characters, in "The Pleasures of Manhood" Wilson exploits commonly shared domestic matters in order to articulate sexual themes that would otherwise remain elusively vague. The occasion is a simple one: a protagonist enjoys a shave with his new electric razor but is uncomfortable with his wife's predictably uncivil behavior whenever his old friend, who was once upon a time her lover, visits. "It must be nice to be a man," she complains to both of them and is rewarded with a hint of one of manhood's presumed pleasures: being lathered up for a straight-edged barber treatment with the friend's top-of-the-line, immaculately maintained razor. Without this event, for which Wilson carefully establishes the premise, the story would be little more than soap opera. With it, the author is able to look past the frustrations of a love triangle to the imaginative qualities of gender. What would otherwise be a matter of simple realism is made problematic (and therefore fictively much more interesting) by letting an exceptional event transpire within the most mundane of circumstances. A visit to the ocean that turns into an all-encompassing disaster, a visit from an old friend who shares a different part in each of his hosts' pasts–these are devices Wilson uses to express what is otherwise too complicated to measure and too subtle to express in the grammar customarily accorded to domestic relations.

"It isn't what you think": this concluding disclaimer from a young woman who has literally (and physically) fallen in love with a piece of rotting fruit in "The Apple" signals the effectiveness of Wilson's techniques. Unlike Richard Brautigan, he does not wish to outrage his readers with extremes of metaphor that stretch the gap between tenor and vehicle so far as to risk incomprehensibility. Nor does he use either the

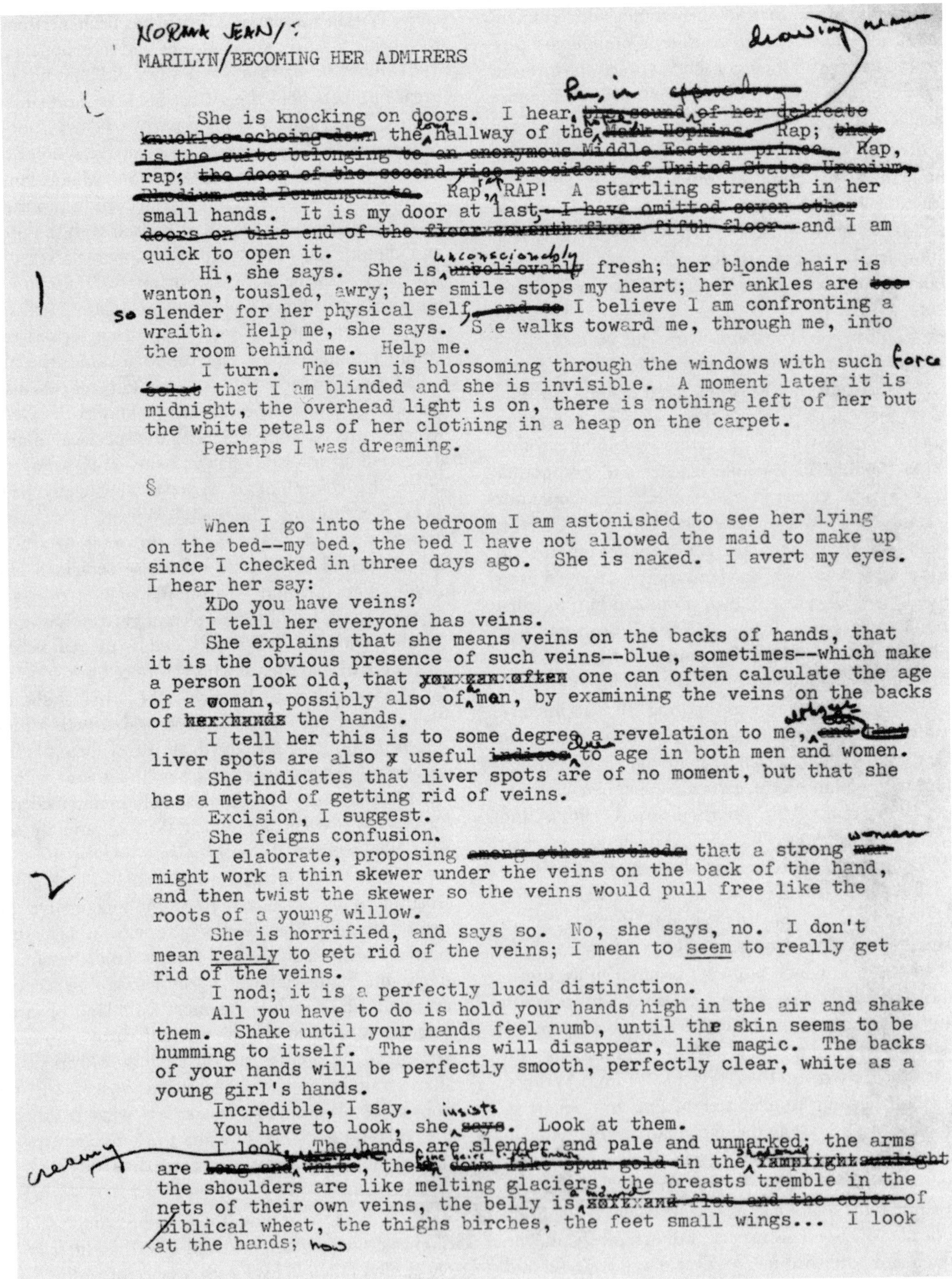

NORMA JEAN/:
MARILYN/BECOMING HER ADMIRERS

She is knocking on doors. I hear, ~~the sound of her delicate knuckles echoing down~~ the long hallway of the ~~Mark Hopkins~~. Rap; ~~that is the suite belonging to an anonymous Middle Eastern prince.~~ Rap, rap; ~~the door of the second vice president of United States Uranium, Rhodium and Permanganate.~~ Rap, rap, RAP! A startling strength in her small hands. It is my door at last, ~~I have omitted seven other doors on this end of the floor seventh floor fifth floor~~ and I am quick to open it.

Hi, she says. She is unconscionably ~~unbelievably~~ fresh; her blonde hair is wanton, tousled, awry; her smile stops my heart; her ankles are ~~too~~ so slender for her physical self, ~~and so~~ I believe I am confronting a wraith. Help me, she says. S e walks toward me, through me, into the room behind me. Help me.

I turn. The sun is blossoming through the windows with such force ~~eclat~~ that I am blinded and she is invisible. A moment later it is midnight, the overhead light is on, there is nothing left of her but the white petals of her clothing in a heap on the carpet.

Perhaps I was dreaming.

§

When I go into the bedroom I am astonished to see her lying on the bed--my bed, the bed I have not allowed the maid to make up since I checked in three days ago. She is naked. I avert my eyes. I hear her say:

XDo you have veins?

I tell her everyone has veins.

She explains that she means veins on the backs of hands, that it is the obvious presence of such veins--blue, sometimes--which make a person look old, that ~~you can often~~ one can often calculate the age of a woman, possibly also of a man, by examining the veins on the backs of ~~her hands~~ the hands.

I tell her this is to some degree a revelation to me, ~~and that~~ liver spots are also x useful ~~indices~~ clues to age in both men and women.

She indicates that liver spots are of no moment, but that she has a method of getting rid of veins.

Excision, I suggest.

She feigns confusion.

I elaborate, proposing ~~among other methods~~ that a strong woman ~~man~~ might work a thin skewer under the veins on the back of the hand, and then twist the skewer so the veins would pull free like the roots of a young willow.

She is horrified, and says so. No, she says, no. I don't mean really to get rid of the veins; I mean to seem to really get rid of the veins.

I nod; it is a perfectly lucid distinction.

All you have to do is hold your hands high in the air and shake them. Shake until your hands feel numb, until thre skin seems to be humming to itself. The veins will disappear, like magic. The backs of your hands will be perfectly smooth, perfectly clear, white as a young girl's hands.

Incredible, I say.

You have to look, she insists ~~says~~. Look at them.

I look. The hands are slender and pale and unmarked; the arms are ~~long and~~ creamy ~~white~~, the fine hairs ~~down like spun gold~~ in the shadowed ~~lamplight sunlight~~ the shoulders are like melting glaciers, the breasts tremble in the nets of their own veins, the belly is a mound ~~soft and flat and the color~~ of Biblical wheat, the thighs birches, the feet small wings... I look at the hands; now

Page from the revised typescript for a story collected in Wilson's 1977 book, The Pleasures of Manhood *(Collection of Robley Wilson)*

commonly disarming speech of Vonnegut's familiar characters or the clipped diction so successful in Barthelme's short fiction. Instead, Wilson narrates with the unmannered voice of realism that dominated twentieth-century American fiction following F. Scott Fitzgerald's rejection of the fussiness of Henry James's writing. His genius is to use this reliable voice, this voice that reserves judgment in favor of letting readers decide the issue, in order to infiltrate his stories with seriously improbable if not utterly impossible events. In "Addison," an airman in basic training fakes an injury to escape K.P. duty, and the event allows Wilson the chance of showing how the quiet persistence of such behavior could in time create an entire U.S. Air Force of walking dysfunctions. "The Demonstration" is equally patient with its spectacle of rest-home residents demonstrating in front of a mortuary. Their grievances are understandable, yet startling in the straight-faced way they are expressed: on placards announcing such sentiments as *The Wages of Death is Sin* and *We're People, Not Prospects.* Outrage in this story remains a matter of reaction, a chance for onlookers to complain that "you can't picket Death" and issue the challenge, "Is nothing sacred?"

"The Demonstration" was first published in 1970, at the peak of an era when social and political protests were filling city streets and university campuses, and so there is a hint of mockery in the author's subject and way of dealing with it, each of which suggests an unappreciative attitude toward contemporary currents. Socially, Wilson is not writing like Charles A. Reich, the author of *The Greening of America* (1970)–a book that had the subtitle *How the Youth Revolution Is Trying to Make America Livable;* artistically he is not using the disruptive style of Brautigan, Barthelme, or other fellow travelers of the youth movement. However, his story is patently disruptive for these very reasons, for going against the grain of prevailing thought and writing. A similar contrariness underlies "Saying Goodbye to the President," first published in *Esquire* in February of 1974 when the ongoing Watergate scandal gave Americans a startling premise to consider: that Richard M. Nixon might well be the first United States president to be forcibly removed from office. Other fiction writers had played with Nixon as a character, notably Philip Roth in *Our Gang* (1971) and Robert Coover in the works-in-progress sections of *The Public Burning* (1977), sections first published in 1973. But unlike the cartoonish portrayals of Roth and Coover, Wilson's depiction of Nixon uses a much different technique that Coover had employed elsewhere, in metafictive rather than satirical work. The model here is Coover's "The Babysitter" (from his 1969 collection, *Pricksongs & Descants*), wherein the author follows a central event by means of discrete paragraphs that in their occasional repetitions and more frequent contradictions track the action in cubist rather than representational fashion. First the narrator and the president stroll in the Rose Garden; then they vacation in Key Biscayne; next comes a meeting on the presidential yacht *Sequoia,* followed by one at Camp David, and so forth through the scenery so familiar to a nation that had spent the last year following the Watergate saga in the news media. Wilson's purpose, of course, is to transcend any references to subject matters by overshadowing them with a fictive treatise on the act of saying goodbye itself, a compulsion that in terms of presidential politics seemed to dominate current history. The action of the story is the story itself, Wilson implies, cleverly adopting a metafictive technique for a topic that would seem the most realistic of all.

"Happy Marriages Are All Alike" is the signature piece that concludes Wilson's first collection. The title alludes to the famous opening line from Leo Tolstoy's novel *Anna Karenina* (seven parts; 1875–1877): "All happy families resemble each other; each unhappy family is unhappy in its own way." This story is Wilson's tribute to nineteenth-century Russian realism, a genre presumably unwritable in the last quarter of the twentieth century. In terms of human nature, however, challenges remain the same, for what happens between husband and wife can escape conventional measurements of both character and action. Therefore Wilson visualizes the couple's relationship in a dramatically overt yet subtly psychological way, having a crop-dusting husband thrill his wife by buzzing their home, pleasing himself by imagining her cut down in machine-gun fire. As with "Saying Goodbye to the President," this offbeat but revealing situation reminds readers that even within the limits of realism the imagination is the prime mover of events, at least in terms of how they are humanly received.

The Pleasures of Manhood was not properly understood; in a typical commentary, the reviewer for *Choice* (July–August 1978) dismissed Wilson's stories such as "The Apple" as too incredible and "Saying Goodbye to the President" as simply whimsical, preferring the richness and detail of the author's presumably "more mature" pieces–a misapprehension in both taste and chronology. Critics were able to better appreciate Wilson's art when the short-story collection *Living Alone: Fictions* appeared less than a year later, in 1978. Coming from a more-venturesome publisher–Fiction International, based in Canton, New York–and free of the restrictive editorial practices of a distinguished university press series, this book let Wilson show readers how his innovations were something more than mere whimsy. In "Girl Gangs" and "Loving a Fat Girl," for example, the narrative premise is deliberately less credi-

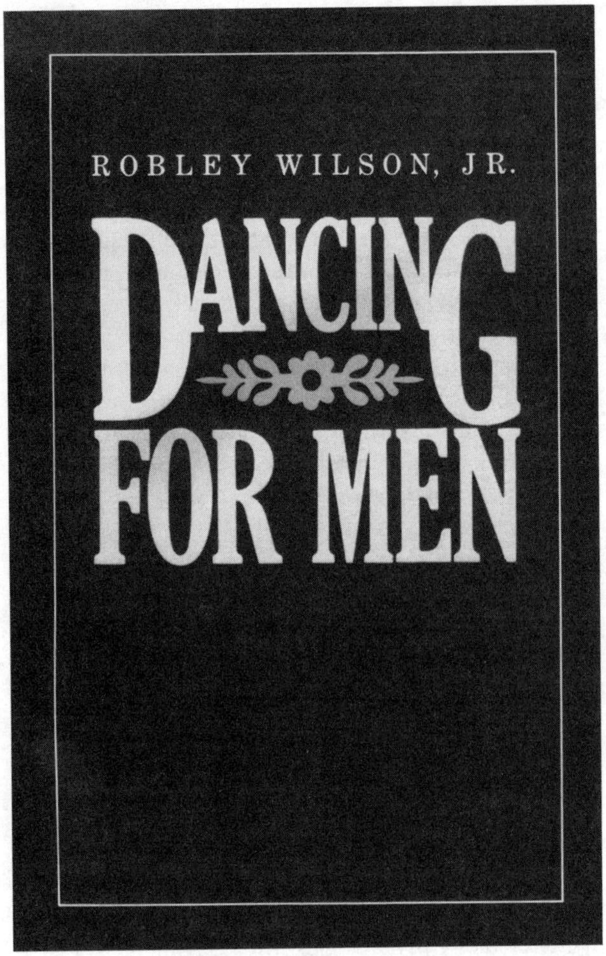

Dust jacket for Wilson's third collection of short stories, which won the 1982 Drue Heinz Literature Prize

ble than in "A Stay at the Ocean" or "The Apple." Hence when the deadpan monologue continues at the same steady pace, readers are given a more exciting ride, thanks to the disparity between manner and subject. "Not much is said these days about the girl gangs of the forties and fifties," the narrator confides, signaling at once his equivocation: not much is said because there were none. Yet, he speaks about them as if they did exist, and his confiding tone is sufficient to carry the action forward, action that turns out to be very much an interior event, for "The girl gangs were not a threat to men, but an inspiration. We daydreamed, we fantasized, we desired, we were raised up." In "Loving a Fat Girl," the narrator is able to generate his story by the simple challenge to his title: "Love a fat girl? Why not?" From such examples Grove Koger, reviewing this second collection in *Library Journal* (15 June 1978), was able to praise Wilson's talent for remaining calmly anecdotal while faithfully recording "the irruption of the absurd and irrational into ordinary life." Critic and fiction writer Welch D. Everman considered Wilson's first two short-story collections in a piece for *American Book Review* (July–August 1981) and appreciated the task Wilson had set for himself. Not just incredible events demanded a premise, Everman argued, for even in his conventionally written character sketches the author was confronting "closed subjects," people "whose selves are sealed off from the selves of others." Decoding them is like figuring out a mystery, something Wilson invites the reader to do. A young girl who falls in love with an apple is therefore no more or less remarkable than a man who imagines his crop-dusting airplane to be a P-51 Mustang, even when the target for his fantasy strafing is his loving wife. True, the story as enacted is pure artifice, but "Artifice becomes a means of trying to reach beyond the isolated self," an attempt at which Everman gives Wilson much credit for success.

Dancing for Men: Stories (1983) is Wilson's third story collection and the first to bring him major honors, including the Drue Heinz Literature Prize and a Guggenheim Fellowship. The short fiction in *Dancing for Men* is distinct from that in Wilson's first two volumes of short stories in several respects. Most of these pieces are mature work, written since his first two volumes were published and with the confidence of an award-winning editor of a major literary journal. The small press boom of the late 1970s and early 1980s brought support for and national attention to what had previously been almost a cottage industry. Now, with grants from the National Endowment for the Arts and the Coordinating Council of Literary Magazines, a writer such as Wilson could become a cosmopolitan figure, meeting regularly with counterparts across the country and becoming almost a regular on the New York literary scene. This sophistication shows both in the new stories and in their larger impact as a collection. The most specific differences are that the stories themselves rarely demand a premise, other than the most natural ones for initiating an action, and that the volume seems less a grab bag of randomly published stories than a selection and arrangement dedicated to achieving an effect.

The effect is a profound one, that of experiencing the social commerce of signs in a way that displays their function as a language. For a writer who stood so nobly apart from the ragtag revolution of American postmodernism, Wilson's adoption of the most salient practice of postmodernism, that of viewing culture semiotically (as a grammar of significations), is a refreshing development. "Signs are signs," says a character in Donald Barthelme's story "Me and Miss Mandible," "and some of them are lies," suggesting how innovators could run riot, if they wished, with the emblems of cultural transmissions. As might be expected, Wilson's approach is subtler and more sophisticated. In his previous collections the author had been drawn to stories of frustrated spouses and lovers, characters who manipulate their own and others' lives as their only outlet for artistic expression. In *Dancing for Men* he not only de-emphasizes premise but takes narrative control of the same processes his protagonists would like to master. As a result, the stories themselves and the collection as a whole replicate the manner of Wilson's own interest in the human condition and his artistic way of dealing with it.

Before one can understand one's life, one must learn how to read the materials out of which it is made. *Dancing for Men* teaches this lesson at almost every turn. In the first story, "Despair," Wilson confronts an impossible situation, that of a husband explaining to himself just why his life, and perhaps his marriage, have failed to live up to their initial promise. Although the situation is realistic, it does not give the author much with which to work; however, instead of turning to a wildly improbable premise, Wilson instead turns to contemporary issues. While his wife has worn herself out campaigning for passage of the Equal Rights Amendment, the husband in "Despair" votes against it, resenting her distraction from household duties and expressing it with the simple complaint of "How much trouble is it to make a casserole?" It is not the casserole itself that matters; it is what the casserole signifies, the absence of which articulates his otherwise vague dissatisfaction. That his wife cannot comprehend it amounts to her own inability (until the end of the story) to read these signs of dismay.

The title story of *Dancing for Men* is also an exercise in reading, prompted by a young woman's wish to see what a carnival stag show provides, both for the men who see it and for the dancer who serves as the entertainment. To gain entry Sarah disguises herself as a boy, which is itself an act of semiosis: changing the language of one's dress in order to signify a different gender (and hence assume a different identity). As with the unhappy husband looking for a casserole in "Despair," Sarah is as much concerned with the sign as with what it signifies, for the dancer is advertised by neon lights spelling out her stage name, "M-E-L-I-T-A."

With his readers thus alerted by these initial cautionary tales, which warn against reading signs as anything other than signs, the author proceeds to develop his themes and techniques in further stories about the pitfalls of misreading and the advantages of undertaking experiments in prose. "Thief" finds an otherwise self-confident man victimized by his own mistaken projections, as a supposed sex object uses him, instead of his using her, in what turns out to be an educational demonstration. "A Fear of Children" runs through all the familiar signs of a schoolgirl's romance, signs that are radically defamiliarized by their new context: the romance takes place in an asylum for the insane. Most impressively, Wilson draws on the experience of friends in a periodically flooded area near his home at the time in Cedar Falls, Iowa, to craft "Land Fishers." His script based on that story won him a $25,000 Nicholl Fellowship in Screenwriting from the Academy of Motion Picture Arts and Sciences in 1995. With eminently visual clues for his readers, the author shows how an otherwise unexceptional woman gains stature and complexity when her world is transformed by an inundation of high waters and some troublesome characters borne on the crest of the wave. The premise here is simple and natural, that everything is changed by a flood. But as he had done with more radical challenges, Wilson draws great subtleties from the occasion, this time made all the more readable by the disruption of visible features.

With a woman's point of view so prominent in these stories, *Dancing for Men* put Wilson at the center of contemporary feminist controversies. Writing in *The Village Voice Literary Supplement* (14 December 1984) Susan Osborn observed that "Wilson excels at depicting emotionally frail or costive men who are terrified or otherwise thwarted by real or imagined female power," but she also suspected that "this exposé of the masculine psyche is not fully intentional." At issue for her is the author's talent at depicting power and control, forces that eventually humiliate every woman character in the book. A different view was taken by Anatole Broyard in *The New York Times* (4 February 1983) where the same narratives are praised for their facility at taking characters out of their familiar worlds and allowing them to analyze their own behavior. A thorough understanding of Wilson's achievement was expressed by William P. Keen in *Studies in Short Fiction* (Fall 1984); by varying his perspective, Keen explained, Wilson "moves artfully between suggestive externality and critical phases of subjective experience," in the process managing to "create a unity similar to that of volumes by such masters as Joyce and Hemingway." "Insight, clarity, and thematic wholeness" were the qualities in *Dancing for Men* that impressed Mary Soete, reviewing for *Library Journal* (15 December 1982), while an unsigned notice in *Publishers Weekly* (15 October 1982) attested that "Wilson has a way of exploring contrary pulls in lives that is both moving and unsettling, as he probes beneath everyday surfaces to the feelings that lurk there."

At this point in his career, Wilson himself provided a critical clue to his development. At the end of 1981, when (according to his contributor's note) the typescript of *Dancing for Men* had just been prepared for

Dust jacket for Wilson's 1989 book, stories that one reviewer called maps of the "notoriously treacherous terrain" of the "heart's geography"

submission, Wilson commented for *American Book Review* on Stephen Dixon's collection *14 Stories* (1980). Dixon is a writer frequently published by *The North American Review,* and Wilson was eager to promote his work; however, he also felt bound to observe, "I wonder if Dixon hasn't been too prolific in more or less the same formula. The formula is: begin with a situation–which puts an urban protagonist into conflict with a person or an institution, and pursue that conflict, usually by means of a dialogue whether direct or indirect, to its absolute end no matter how absurd." For Wilson, this method fails when the subject is trivial, providing just entertainment; but it works with important subjects, namely death, violent crime, and serious love. An example of the first subject is Dixon's "The Signing," where a narrator tries to leave the hospital where his wife has just died, only to be pursued relentlessly and hilariously by various staff members who insist he sign for the disposal of the body. The point for Wilson's own work is clear: that while the type of premise fiction he himself once championed and practiced so well runs the risk of being reductively silly, the idea can still be productive when applied to something as weighty (and as otherwise inexpressible) as grief.

Wilson's fourth collection, *Terrible Kisses: Stories* (1989), is distinguished by just such achievement. Its most typical story, "Favorites," is a virtual response to Dixon's "The Signing," in that a correlative device, unexceptional in itself, is used to speak volumes about what is otherwise so hard to put into words: coming to terms with the death of a deeply loved spouse. The story begins with a sentence that, just as in Dixon's tale, might more comfortably serve as an ending: "On a Saturday afternoon in September his wife was killed in a car accident." There seems to be nothing more for the writer to say. Wilson supplies all the details of notification and other business within the first two pages of the story, solving the problem of what to say by involving the reader in the four remaining pages. Trying to reestablish his routine, the widowed husband cleans the kitchen and is surprised to find that on the morning of her death his wife had prepared dessert, a vanilla pudding cake. Only she could make it; unduplicatable, it was her specialty and his all-time favorite. He, like the reader, has to ask, what should he do with it now? There will never be another. And so he follows dinner that night with one piece, and continues to do so for the rest of the week. The experience brings fond memories and helps him come to terms not just with the loss of his wife but with how wonderful their life together had been, as good a strategy as any for coping with grief. Yet, when a single piece remains, readers can still see there is more to the story. One piece left–what does he do? Simple: he cuts it in half and saves the rest for tomorrow. The next night he cuts the half in half, and so on until there is so little left that it scarcely fills his fork–at which point he eats it up, and the story ends.

This version of Zeno's Paradox shows what great effects Wilson can achieve with the simplest of devices. There is a subversion to his best work, a commitment to the belief that there exists a world beyond spoken language that is fiction's challenge to capture and convey. "Nam" deals with what is now called post-traumatic stress syndrome; "The Eventual Nuclear Destruction of Cheyenne, Wyoming" gives voice to the ponderings of arms workers about an Armageddon they can scarcely comprehend; "Praises" shows how an artist discovers his old lover's radical double mastectomy, an act that makes him "young" even as she is "made whole." Are their comments untrue? Not really, because "A beautiful lie makes beautiful the thing lied about."

Terrible Kisses established Wilson as a major commercial writer and led the same publisher, Simon and

Schuster, to acquire *The Victim's Daughter: A Novel* (1991), a highly sensitive tale of detection that centers less on a solving of crime than on an emotional investigation of the principal character's life. This book covers the same "heart's geography" that a reviewer for *Publishers Weekly* (14 April 1989) described in a review of *Terrible Kisses,* as a "notoriously treacherous terrain" that the author is able to chart "with mastery and subtlety." In his review of this collection (*The New York Times Book Review,* 16 July 1989) Devon Jerslid praised Wilson's "knack for dramatizing states of mind, for taking psychic conditions and, with quirky wit, giving them an external life." Not all readers wish to be taken into such realms; in her *Village Voice* review of *Dancing for Men* Osborn had praised Wilson's talent for keen images and "great psychological acuity" but then warned that "Wilson's sheer technical brilliance is all the more reason to beware of him." Preparing to publish "Saying Goodbye to the President" even as President Nixon clung to his office, the editors of *Esquire* worried that the story might be construed as rallying sentiments for assassination–a law against which had been passed after President John F. Kennedy's murder in 1963; the editors' solution was to print the piece as Wilson wrote it, but with the disclaiming subtitle, "In dreams, anything is possible."

There are no Robley Wilson stories in which characters dream his carefully premised events; everything actually happens, in ways that test but never contradict the realism that keeps matters tense. Wilson is instead "a dream stealer," as he confessed to interviewer Ann Struthers in 1985. His most famous piece of premise fiction, "The Apple," was borrowed from something dreamed by a student and interpreted by Wilson as her teacher: having a sexual encounter with a piece of fruit does not represent a psychological aberration in which the apple is actually a real person–the object really is an apple and has to be treated that way for the story to work. This talent for actualizing the ineffable is what makes Robley Wilson's fiction succeed. "Face the audience of strangers," Vonnegut told Wilson and his classmates at the University of Iowa Writers' Workshop; in his four volumes of short stories Wilson has complied with an engaging civility that marks him as the classiest and most dignified of current innovators.

Interview:

Ann Struthers, "An Interview with Robley Wilson, Jr.," *Groton Review,* 8 (Summer 1985): 20–24.

References:

Welch D. Everman, "*The Pleasures of Manhood* and *Living Alone,*" *American Book Review,* 3 (July–August 1981): 4;

William P. Keen, "*Dancing for Men,*" *Studies in Short Fiction,* 21 (Fall 1984): 408;

Jerome Klinkowitz, "Robley Wilson's Experimental Realism," in his *Literary Subversions: New American Fiction and the Practice of Criticism* (Carbondale: Southern Illinois University Press, 1985), pp. 77–93.

Books for Further Reading

Allen, Frederick Lewis. *The Big Change: America Transforms Itself, 1900–1950.* New York: Harper, 1952.

Allen, Walter. *The Short Story in English.* Oxford: Clarendon Press / New York: Oxford University Press, 1981.

Aycock, Wendell M., ed. *The Teller and the Tale: Aspects of the Short Story.* Lubbock: Texas Tech University Press, 1982.

Barthes, Roland. *S/Z,* translated by Richard Miller. New York: Hill & Wang, 1974.

Bates, H. E. *The Modern Short Story: A Critical Survey.* Boston: The Writer, 1972.

Bayley, John. *The Short Story: Henry James to Elizabeth Bowen.* New York: St. Martin's Press, 1988.

Beachcroft, T. O. *The Modest Art: A Survey of the Short Story in English.* London & New York: Oxford University Press, 1968.

Boland, John. *Short Story Technique.* Crowborough, U.K.: Forest House Books, 1973.

Bonheim, Helmut. *The Narrative Modes: Techniques of the Short Story.* Cambridge, U.K.: D. S. Brewer, 1982.

Bruck, Peter, ed. *The Black American Short Story in the 20th Century: A Collection of Critical Essays.* Amsterdam: Grüner, 1977.

Chatman, Seymour. *Story and Discourse: Narrative Structure in Fiction and Film.* Ithaca, N.Y.: Cornell University Press, 1978.

Current-Garcia, Eugene, and Walton R. Patrick, eds. *What Is the Short Story?* Glenview, Ill.: Scott, Foresman, 1974.

Dijk, Teun A. van. *Macrostructures: An Interdisciplinary Study of Global Structures in Discourse, Interaction, and Cognition.* Hillsdale, N.J.: L. Erlbaum Associates, 1980.

Eikhenbaum, B. M. *O. Henry and the Theory of the Short Story,* translated by I. R. Titunik. Ann Arbor: University of Michigan Department of Slavic Languages and Literatures, 1968.

Friedman, Norman. *Form and Meaning in Fiction.* Athens: University of Georgia Press, 1975.

Gerlach, John. *Toward the End: Closure and Structure in the American Short Story.* University: University of Alabama Press, 1985.

Hanson, Clare. *Short Stories and Short Fictions, 1880–1980.* New York: St. Martin's Press, 1985.

Hendin, Josephine. *Vulnerable People: A View of American Fiction Since 1945.* New York & London: Oxford University Press, 1978.

Hooper, Brad. *Short-Story Writers and Their Work: A Guide to the Best.* Chicago: American Library Association, 1988.

Ingram, Forrest L. *Representative Short-Story Cycles of the Twentieth Century: Studies in a Literary Genre.* The Hague: Mouton, 1971.

Jameson, Frederic. *The Prison-House of Language: A Critical Account of Structuralism and Russian Formalism.* Princeton: Princeton University Press, 1972.

Kenner, Hugh. *A Homemade World: The American Modernist Writers.* New York: Knopf, 1974.

Klinkowitz, Jerome. *The Practice of Fiction in America: Writers from Hawthorne to the Present.* Ames: Iowa State University Press, 1980.

Klinkowitz. *The Self-Apparent Word: Fiction as Language/Language as Fiction.* Carbondale: Southern Illinois University Press, 1984.

Klinkowitz. *Structuring the Void: The Struggle for Subject in Contemporary American Fiction.* Durham, N.C.: Duke University Press, 1992.

Leitch, Thomas M. *What Stories Are: Narrative Theory and Interpretation.* University Park: Pennsylvania State University Press, 1986.

Levin, Gerald, ed. *The Short Story: An Inductive Approach.* New York: Harcourt, Brace & World, 1967.

Lohafer, Susan. *Coming to Terms with the Short Story.* Baton Rouge: Louisiana State University Press, 1983.

Lohafer and Jo Ellyn Clarey, eds. *Short Story Theory at a Crossroads.* Baton Rouge: Louisiana State University Press, 1989.

Magill, Frank N., ed. *Critical Survey of Short Fiction,* 7 volumes. Pasadena: Salem, 1993.

Mann, Susan Garland. *The Short-Story Cycle: A Genre Companion and Reference Guide.* New York: Greenwood Press, 1989.

May, Charles E. *The Short Story: The Reality of Artifice.* New York: Twayne, 1995.

May, ed. *Fiction's Many Worlds.* Lexington, Mass.: D. C. Heath, 1993.

May, ed. *The New Short Story Theories.* Athens: Ohio University Press, 1994.

May, ed. *Short Story Theories.* Athens: Ohio University Press, 1976.

O'Connor, Frank. *The Lonely Voice: A Study of the Short Story.* Cleveland: World, 1963.

O'Faolain, Sean. *The Short Story.* New York: Devin-Adair, 1951.

Peden, William. *The American Short Story: Continuity and Change, 1940–1975.* Boston: Houghton Mifflin, 1975.

Prince, Gerald. *A Grammar of Stories: An Introduction.* The Hague: Mouton, 1973.

Prince. *Narratology: The Form and Functioning of Narrative.* New York: Mouton, 1982.

Reid, Ian. *The Short Story.* New York: Routledge, 1991.

Rohrberger, Mary. *Hawthorne and the Modern Short Story: A Study in Genre.* The Hague: Mouton, 1966.

Rohrberger. *Story to Anti-Story.* Boston: Houghton Mifflin, 1979.

Ross, Danforth. *The American Short Story.* Minneapolis: University of Minnesota Press, 1961.

Scholes, Robert. *Structuralism in Literature: An Introduction.* New Haven: Yale University Press, 1974.

Shaw, Valerie. *The Short Story: A Critical Introduction.* New York & London: Longman, 1983.

Stephens, Michael. *The Dramaturgy of Style: Voice in Short Fiction.* Carbondale: Southern Illinois University Press, 1986.

Stummer, Peter O., ed. *The Story Must Be Told: Short Narrative Prose in the New English Literatures.* Würzburg: Königshausen & Neumann, 1986.

Summers, Hollis, ed. *Discussions of the Short Story.* Boston: D. C. Heath, 1963.

Todorov, Tzvetan. *The Poetics of Prose,* translated by Richard Howard. Ithaca, N.Y.: Cornell University Press, 1977.

Voss, Arthur. *The American Short Story: A Critical Survey.* Norman: University of Oklahoma Press, 1973.

Walker, Warren S. *Twentieth-Century Short-Story Explication, New Series.* Hamden, Conn.: Shoe String Press, 1993.

Weaver, Gordon, ed. *The American Short Story, 1945–1980: A Critical History.* Boston: Twayne, 1983.

Weixlmann, Joe. *American Short-Fiction Criticism and Scholarship, 1959–1977: A Checklist.* Chicago: Swallow Press, 1982.

West, Ray. *The Short Story in America, 1900–1950.* Chicago: Regnery, 1952.

Williams, Williams Carlos. *A Beginning on the Short Story: Notes.* Yonkers, N.Y.: Alicat Bookshop Press, 1950.

Contributors

Blake Bailey . . . . *University of New Orleans*
Stephen Balmer . . . . *Spring Hill Waldorf School*
Deborah E. Barker . . . . *University of Mississippi*
Julia B. Boken . . . . *State University of New York College at Oneonta*
Muriel A. Charpentier . . . . *Université de la Sorbonne-Nouvelle, Paris*
Gwen Crane . . . . *State University of New York College at Oneonta*
Michael Depp . . . . *University of New Orleans*
Teri Ann Doerksen . . . . *Hartwick College*
David Dougherty . . . . *Loyola College in Maryland*
Brian Evenson . . . . *Oklahoma State University*
Reginald Gibbons . . . . *Northwestern University*
Mitchell Goldwater . . . . *State University of New York College at Oneonta*
Ellen Burton Harrington . . . . *Tulane University*
Denis Hennessy . . . . *State University of New York College at Oneonta*
Allen Hibbard . . . . *Middle Tennessee State University*
Dale Hrebik . . . . *Delgado College*
Jerome Klinkowitz . . . . *University of Northern Iowa*
Richard E. Lee . . . . *State University of New York College at Oneonta*
Robert M. Luscher . . . . *University of Nebraska at Kearney*
Paul Maliszewski . . . .
Patrick Meanor . . . . *State University of New York College at Oneonta*
Joe Nordgren . . . . *Lamar University*
Terry Roberts . . . . *University of North Carolina at Greensboro*
Thomas H. Schmid . . . . *University of Texas at El Paso*
R. Baird Shuman . . . . *University of Illinois at Urbana-Champaign*
Kathleen Snodgrass . . . .
Charlotte Zoë Walker . . . . *State University of New York College at Oneonta*
Joseph J. Wydeven . . . . *Bellevue University*

Cumulative Index

Dictionary of Literary Biography, Volumes 1-218
Dictionary of Literary Biography Yearbook, 1980-1998
Dictionary of Literary Biography Documentary Series, Volumes 1-19

Cumulative Index

DLB before number: *Dictionary of Literary Biography,* Volumes 1-218
Y before number: *Dictionary of Literary Biography Yearbook,* 1980-1998
DS before number: *Dictionary of Literary Biography Documentary Series,* Volumes 1-19

A

B

C

D

E

G

H

K

L

M

Meyer, E. Y. 1946- DLB-75
Meyer, Eugene 1875-1959 . . . . DLB-29
Meyer, Michael 1921- DLB-155
Meyers, Jeffrey 1939- DLB-111
Meynell, Alice 1847-1922 . . . . DLB-19, 98
Meynell, Viola 1885-1956 . . . . DLB-153
Meyrink, Gustav 1868-1932 . . . . DLB-81
Mézières, Philipe de circa 1327-1405 . . . . . DLB-208
Michael, Ib 1945- DLB-214
Michael M. Rea and the Rea Award for the Short Story Y-97
Michaëlis, Karen 1872-1950 . . . . DLB-214
Michaels, Leonard 1933- DLB-130
Micheaux, Oscar 1884-1951 . . . . DLB-50
Michel of Northgate, Dan circa 1265-circa 1340 . . . . DLB-146
Micheline, Jack 1929- DLB-16
Michener, James A. 1907?- DLB-6
Micklejohn, George circa 1717-1818 . . . . DLB-31
Middle English Literature: An Introduction DLB-146
The Middle English Lyric DLB-146
Middle Hill Press DLB-106
Middleton, Christopher 1926- DLB-40
Middleton, Richard 1882-1911 . . . . DLB-156
Middleton, Stanley 1919- DLB-14
Middleton, Thomas 1580-1627 . . . . DLB-58
Miegel, Agnes 1879-1964 . . . . DLB-56
Mihailović, Dragoslav 1930- DLB-181
Mihalić, Slavko 1928- DLB-181
Miles, Josephine 1911-1985 . . . . DLB-48
Miliković, Branko 1934-1961 . . . . DLB-181
Milius, John 1944- DLB-44
Mill, James 1773-1836 . . . . DLB-107, 158
Mill, John Stuart 1806-1873 . . . . DLB-55, 190
Millar, Kenneth 1915-1983 . . . . DLB-2; Y-83; DS-6
Millar, Andrew [publishing house] DLB-154
Millay, Edna St. Vincent 1892-1950 . . . . . . DLB-45
Miller, Arthur 1915- DLB-7
Miller, Caroline 1903-1992 . . . . DLB-9
Miller, Eugene Ethelbert 1950- DLB-41
Miller, Heather Ross 1939- DLB-120
Miller, Henry 1891-1980 . . . . DLB-4, 9; Y-80
Miller, Hugh 1802-1856 . . . . DLB-190
Miller, J. Hillis 1928- DLB-67
Miller, James [publishing house] DLB-49
Miller, Jason 1939- DLB-7
Miller, Joaquin 1839-1913 . . . . DLB-186
Miller, May 1899- DLB-41
Miller, Paul 1906-1991 . . . . DLB-127
Miller, Perry 1905-1963 . . . . DLB-17, 63
Miller, Sue 1943- DLB-143
Miller, Vassar 1924- DLB-105
Miller, Walter M., Jr. 1923- DLB-8
Miller, Webb 1892-1940 . . . . DLB-29
Millhauser, Steven 1943- DLB-2
Millican, Arthenia J. Bates 1920- DLB-38
Mills and Boon DLB-112
Milman, Henry Hart 1796-1868 . . . . DLB-96
Milne, A. A. 1882-1956 . . . . . DLB-10, 77, 100, 160
Milner, Ron 1938- DLB-38
Milner, William [publishing house] DLB-106
Milnes, Richard Monckton (Lord Houghton) 1809-1885 . . . . DLB-32, 184
Milton, John 1608-1674 . . . . DLB-131, 151
Miłosz, Czesław 1911- DLB-215
Minakami Tsutomu 1919- DLB-182
Minamoto no Sanetomo 1192-1219 . . . . . . DLB-203
The Minerva Press DLB-154
Minnesang circa 1150-1280 . . . . DLB-138
Minns, Susan 1839-1938 . . . . DLB-140
Minor Illustrators, 1880-1914 . . . . DLB-141
Minor Poets of the Earlier Seventeenth Century DLB-121
Minton, Balch and Company DLB-46
Mirbeau, Octave 1848-1917 . . . . DLB-123, 192
Mirk, John died after 1414? DLB-146
Miron, Gaston 1928- DLB-60
A Mirror for Magistrates DLB-167
Mishima Yukio 1925-1970 . . . . DLB-182
Mitchel, Jonathan 1624-1668 . . . . DLB-24
Mitchell, Adrian 1932- DLB-40
Mitchell, Donald Grant 1822-1908 . . . . DLB-1; DS-13
Mitchell, Gladys 1901-1983 . . . . DLB-77
Mitchell, James Leslie 1901-1935 . . . . DLB-15
Mitchell, John (see Slater, Patrick)
Mitchell, John Ames 1845-1918 . . . . DLB-79
Mitchell, Joseph 1908-1996 . . . . DLB-185; Y-96
Mitchell, Julian 1935- DLB-14
Mitchell, Ken 1940- DLB-60
Mitchell, Langdon 1862-1935 . . . . DLB-7
Mitchell, Loften 1919- DLB-38
Mitchell, Margaret 1900-1949 . . . . DLB-9
Mitchell, S. Weir 1829-1914 . . . . DLB-202
Mitchell, W. O. 1914- DLB-88
Mitchison, Naomi Margaret (Haldane) 1897- DLB-160, 191
Mitford, Mary Russell 1787-1855 . . . . DLB-110, 116
Mitford, Nancy 1904-1973 . . . . DLB-191
Mittelholzer, Edgar 1909-1965 . . . . DLB-117
Mitterer, Erika 1906- DLB-85
Mitterer, Felix 1948- DLB-124
Mitternacht, Johann Sebastian 1613-1679 . . . . DLB-168
Miyamoto, Yuriko 1899-1951 . . . . DLB-180
Mizener, Arthur 1907-1988 . . . . DLB-103
Mo, Timothy 1950- DLB-194
Modern Age Books DLB-46
"Modern English Prose" (1876), by George Saintsbury DLB-57
The Modern Language Association of America Celebrates Its Centennial Y-84
The Modern Library DLB-46
"Modern Novelists – Great and Small" (1855), by Margaret Oliphant DLB-21
"Modern Style" (1857), by Cockburn Thomson [excerpt] DLB-57
The Modernists (1932), by Joseph Warren Beach DLB-36
Modiano, Patrick 1945- DLB-83
Moffat, Yard and Company DLB-46
Moffet, Thomas 1553-1604 . . . . DLB-136
Mohr, Nicholasa 1938- DLB-145
Moix, Ana María 1947- DLB-134
Molesworth, Louisa 1839-1921 . . . . DLB-135
Möllhausen, Balduin 1825-1905 . . . . DLB-129
Molnár, Ferenc 1878-1952 . . . . DLB-215
Momaday, N. Scott 1934- DLB-143, 175
Monkhouse, Allan 1858-1936 . . . . DLB-10
Monro, Harold 1879-1932 . . . . DLB-19
Monroe, Harriet 1860-1936 . . . . DLB-54, 91
Monsarrat, Nicholas 1910-1979 . . . . DLB-15
Montagu, Lady Mary Wortley 1689-1762 . . . . DLB-95, 101
Montague, C. E. 1867-1928 . . . . DLB-197
Montague, John 1929- DLB-40
Montale, Eugenio 1896-1981 . . . . DLB-114
Montalvo, José 1946-1994 . . . . DLB-209
Monterroso, Augusto 1921- DLB-145
Montesquiou, Robert de 1855-1921 . . . . . DLB-217
Montgomerie, Alexander circa 1550?-1598 . . . . DLB-167
Montgomery, James 1771-1854 . . . . . . DLB-93, 158
Montgomery, John 1919- DLB-16
Montgomery, Lucy Maud 1874-1942 . . . . DLB-92; DS-14
Montgomery, Marion 1925- DLB-6
Montgomery, Robert Bruce (see Crispin, Edmund)
Montherlant, Henry de 1896-1972 . . . . DLB-72
The Monthly Review 1749-1844 . . . . DLB-110
Montigny, Louvigny de 1876-1955 . . . . DLB-92
Montoya, José 1932- DLB-122
Moodie, John Wedderburn Dunbar 1797-1869 . . . . DLB-99
Moodie, Susanna 1803-1885 . . . . DLB-99
Moody, Joshua circa 1633-1697 . . . . DLB-24
Moody, William Vaughn 1869-1910 . . . . DLB-7, 54
Moorcock, Michael 1939- DLB-14
Moore, Catherine L. 1911- DLB-8
Moore, Clement Clarke 1779-1863 . . . . DLB-42
Moore, Dora Mavor 1888-1979 . . . . DLB-92
Moore, George 1852-1933 . . . . DLB-10, 18, 57, 135
Moore, Marianne 1887-1972 . . . . DLB-45; DS-7
Moore, Mavor 1919- DLB-88
Moore, Richard 1927- DLB-105

O

Q

R

S

T

U

V

X

Y

Z

ISBN 0-7876-3127-2
90000
9 780787 631277